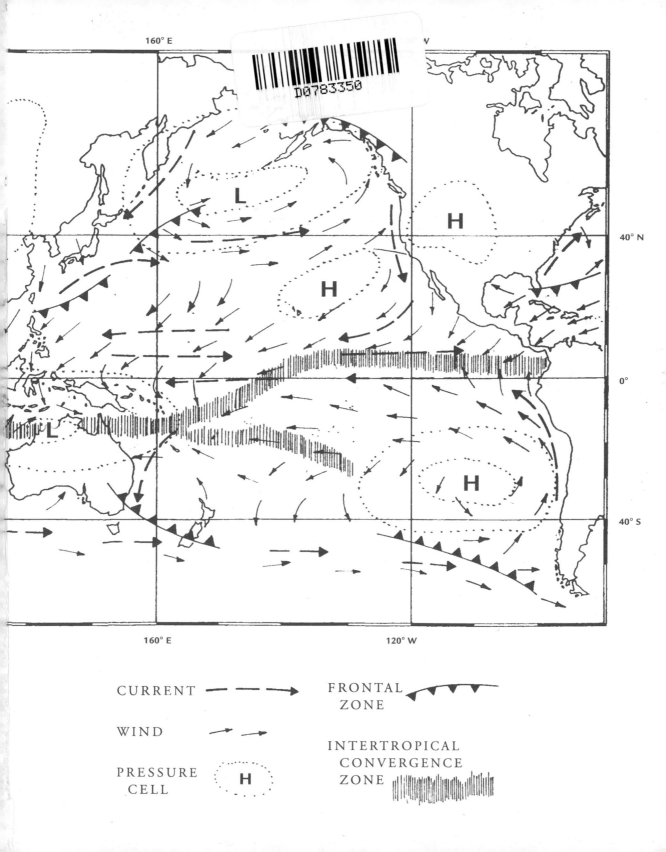

D0783350

CURRENT — — →   FRONTAL
                   ZONE ▼▼▼▼▼

WIND   → →

PRESSURE   (H)   INTERTROPICAL
CELL   CONVERGENCE
                     ZONE

TROPICAL CRUISING HANDBOOK

Mark Smaalders and Kim des Rochers

INTERNATIONAL MARINE / McGRAW-HILL

Camden, Maine • New York • Chicago • San Francisco • Lisbon • London • Madrid • Mexico City •
Milan • New Delhi • San Juan • Seoul • Singapore • Sydney • Toronto

2 4 6 8 10 9 7 5 3

Copyright © 2002 Mark Smaalders and Kim des Rochers
All rights reserved. The publisher takes no responsibility for the use of any of the
materials or methods described in this book, nor for the products thereof. The name
"International Marine" and the International Marine logo are trademarks of
The McGraw-Hill Companies.
Printed in the United States of America.

Library of Congress Cataloging-in-Publication Data
Smaalders, Mark.
  Tropical cruising handbook / Mark Smaalders and Kim des Rochers.
       p.   cm.
  Includes bibliographical references (p.   ) and index.
    ISBN 0-07-137228-8
  1. Yachting—Tropics. 2. Boats and boating—Tropics.
  3. Coral reefs and islands—Tropics.
    I. des Rochers, Kim. II. Title.
  GV817.T73 S62 2002
  797.1′246′0913—dc21   2001005030

Questions regarding the content of this book should be addressed to
International Marine
P.O. Box 220
Camden, ME 04843
www.internationalmarine.com

Questions regarding the ordering of this book should be addressed to
The McGraw-Hill Companies
Customer Service Department
P.O. Box 547
Blacklick, OH 43004
Retail customers: 1-800-262-4729
Bookstores: 1-800-722-4726

This book is printed on 70-lb. Citation by Quebecor Printing, Fairfield, PA.
Design by Blue Mammoth Design.
Photographs by the authors, except those on pages 275 (Don Tremain/alamy.com);
287 (Frank Miesnikowicz/alamy.com); and 294 and 338 (both Corbis Images).
Part-opening photo courtesy Nigel Calder.
Illustrations and maps by Mark Smaalders.
Production by Blue Mammoth Design, Dan Kirchoff and Matt Watier.
Edited by Alex Barnett, Jonathan Eaton, and Jane M. Curran.

NOTICE: The authors and publisher do not guarantee or warrant that the information in this book is complete, correct, or current. In using this book, the reader
releases the authors, publisher, and distributor from liability for any loss or
injury, including death, allegedly caused, in whole or in part, by relying on
information contained in this book.
The maps contained in this book are not for navigational purposes. None of the
material in this book is intended to replace any government-issued navigational
charts or other government publications, including *Notices to Mariners*.
All cruisers should have up-to-date navigational charts on board.

Contents

Part 3
LIFE IN THE TROPICS

Part 4
CRUISING LIGHTLY

Part 5
TROPICAL CRUISING DESTINATIONS

APPENDICES

INDEX

Acknowledgments

We've benefited greatly from the assistance and input of many people. We thank our contributors, whose differing perspectives have helped round out the book: Steve and Marja Vance for their refreshing outlook on the cruising life; Hugh Marriott for his humorous and insightful cruising stories; and Laura Durbin-Hacker and Randy Durbin for their contributions to and comments on the chapter on port life. Thanks also to Nim Marsh for his perspective on riding the Gulf Stream.

Our reviewers have helped to ensure the accuracy of our information (though any remaining errors are our own). Thanks to Dr. Steven Bjorge for reviewing the sections on malaria and dengue fever; Dr. Paul Auerbach for reviewing chapter 13, Dangerous Tropical Marine Organisms; John Roberts for his technical review; Dr. Richard Lee for reviewing chapter 12, Staying Healthy in the Tropics, and Scott Davis for his suggestions on that chapter; and Jerry Powlas and Bart Smaalders for their comments on metal corrosion.

We'd also like to acknowledge the editors at *Cruising World*, *Cruising Helmsman*, *Practical Boatowner*, *Good Old Boat*, and especially *Ocean Navigator* for publishing our articles over the years, thus helping to keep us afloat financially.

Mahalo nui loa to Doug Lamerson and Marjorie Ziegler for their unfailing support, encouragement, and friendship through good times and bad. From help in the boatyard to their many care packages waiting for us at different ports, they've always been there for us. Thanks also to Dr. Matt McGranaghan for slaving in the bilge at Keehi, for his assistance in acquiring communications equipment for our boat, and for oceanographic data for the book. We look forward to another Coach's Platter with Moto and the ChairMatt at our next meeting.

Mahalo to Peter Rappa for his efforts in keeping us in touch with family and friends while at sea; thanks to Dr. Chris McMurray for assistance with mapping software.

Special thanks to Oscar and Alie Smaalders, who have supported our adventures on the water, at the drawing board and the keyboard for many years. They've had confidence in our efforts even when we had doubts, and their continued support has made all the difference. Special thanks also to Aap at Bouget Northwest for handling our affairs, including mail, finances, and boat plans.

We'd also like to acknowledge other cruising sailors we've learned from and exchanged ideas with. This is one of the interesting and fun parts of cruising, and we continue to learn from every sailor we meet.

Thanks to Jon Eaton for his confidence in the original idea for this book and for his thoughtful comments.

Although most of them probably won't ever read this, thanks to the many residents of the tropics we've met for giving us a unique opportunity to share in different cultures and lifestyles.

Finally, no thanks are enough for our lovely boat *Nomad*. She's tirelessly taken us thousands of miles and has never given us reason to be concerned for our safety while at sea.

PART I

TROPICAL ENVIRONMENTS

Chapter 1

Introduction

The tropics are an ideal place to sail. The weather's warm, severe storms are pretty rare, and the winds are the most consistent on earth. The tropics are also a fascinating place to travel. For the adventurous there are countless islands waiting to be explored, many cloaked in rainforest and ringed by coral reefs. The cultures found here are rich and varied, with language and customs often changing completely from one island group to the next. In combination, these qualities are what make the tropics such a popular cruising destination, visited by thousands of boats each year.

The aim of this book is to help sailors prepare for and enjoy tropical cruising. As you read, and as you cruise, you'll find that the tropics are very different from the temperate climates and hectic urban environments in which most of us live. That's part of what makes cruising in this area interesting. We can guarantee that even experienced sailors will find themselves learning and experiencing much that's new and different, and for us that's a big part of the attraction of cruising in these waters.

OUR APPROACH

Although cruising under sail is in some respects simpler than it once was, it still presents a host of challenges and draws on many different skills. This book reflects that, and in the pages that follow we address a wide range of issues, from how reefs grow to how to deal with corrupt customs officials. But there are two themes—beyond the obvious tropical focus—that help to bind this material together. These themes are very much a part of our approach to cruising.

Our cruising philosophy is quite simple: be as self-reliant as you can, and have as little impact on the places you visit as possible. Our focus on self-

reliance comes in part because we've spent a lot of time in some pretty remote tropical areas, where there were no facilities or assistance for hundreds of miles. But it's an approach we recommend to everyone, even if you never plan to cross an ocean. Self-reliance involves informing yourself about where you're going and what challenges you'll face, developing skills so you can meet those challenges, and ensuring your boat's up to the task. The first three parts of this book (Tropical Environments, Tropical Seamanship, and Life in the Tropics) revolve around this theme.

Minimizing one's impact while cruising is not a new idea, and it's becoming increasingly important as more and more cruisers set sail. As individuals, our actions don't have much effect, but when tens, hundreds, or even thousands of boats visit an area each season, impacts are inevitable. We believe all cruisers have a shared responsibility to "leave a clean wake," and this underlies our discussion in part 4 (Cruising Lightly).

TROPICAL ENVIRONMENTS

The tropical environment—the sum of the land, water, and air—is different from that in temperate latitudes. The air feels and smells different, typically warm and humid and smelling of tropical blossoms. The water's warm as well, and that allows for coral growth, resulting in coral reefs, those remarkable living structures that provide playgrounds for snorklers and divers, and graveyards for boats. When the air and water interact—forming clouds, storms, and other weather conditions—the results are unique to the tropics as well. Tropical weather systems move from east to west, in opposition to most temperate weather features. Tropical cyclones, which are among the most destructive storms on earth, develop in warm, largely benign conditions, and still defy accurate prediction. An understanding of this foreign environment forms the foundation on which seamanship skills can be developed; part 1 (Tropical Environments) includes chapter 2 (Tropical Environments) and chapter 3 (Weather in the Tropics).

TROPICAL SEAMANSHIP

Once you know something about the tropics you can set about preparing yourself. Though it comes all too often as an afterthought (squeezed in between work on the boat and seemingly endless equipment upgrades), seamanship is much more important. Because the tropics are such a comfortable place to sail, many sailors are lulled into thinking that the cruising is always easy. This is not the case. Beautiful reef anchorages can become dangerous traps with the passing of a fairly minor cold front, due simply to the change in wind direction. Reefs present problems when underway as well. There may be thousands of reefs in just one island group, so it's not surprising that most aren't marked in any way. The solution is to sail by eye, which is simpler in the tropics than anywhere else, because of the unmistakable color differences that outline reefs. But those color markers can vanish in an instant if a squall moves through or the sun goes behind a cloud.

Modern equipment can help you cope with the various complications of tropical sailing, but there's no substitute for an informed and well-prepared crew. Trouble doesn't normally arise because your boat is too small or lacks a piece of fancy electronic gear. Instead, cruisers typically run into trouble because they and their crews aren't ready for what they encounter. The best equipment in the world won't keep you safe if you don't know how to use it or don't have a backup plan in case it fails. It's become cliché to say *when* electronics failures occur rather than *if*, but, in fact, the cliché has proven more dependable than the equipment it describes. The answer, in our view, lies not in endlessly redundant backup systems, but instead in preparing yourself for your tropical adventure just as diligently as you prepare your boat. Do so, and you'll find yourself far more confident, relaxed, and capable of handling the challenges that come your way. We assume in the chapters that follow that you've learned at least the basics about sailing and navigation. We start from this point and address the special skills that you'll need in the tropics, including visual and intuitive navigation, anchoring among reefs, tropical passagemaking, planning and making passages, and dealing with heavy weather. Together these make up part 2 (Tropical Seamanship).

LIFE IN THE TROPICS

As important as seamanship is, most of one's time will, in fact, be spent in port. One of the joys of cruising is having a flexible schedule, one that allows time for exploring and experiencing the exotic places you visit. But even though cruising can be wonderfully escapist, you'll succeed only if you also take care of the details. The little details are what make life onboard comfortable, and attention to detail is also what's needed when dealing with the bureaucratic side of cruising. Cruising may also expose you to a tropical disease or a dangerous marine organism, which tend not to be found in temperate climates. Finally, due to the intense heat and humidity of the tropics, it's inevitable that you'll be spending more time on maintenance than you're used to. In part 3 (Life in the Tropics) we look at all of these issues in detail, with a view to making the cruising life more comfortable and enjoyable.

FINDING YOUR OWN WAY

There are different ways to cruise the tropics. Although a circumnavigation is many people's dream cruise, in reality it may be far more realistic to charter a boat for a few weeks every year in different parts of the tropics. Others may find equal reward in truly getting to know just a few island groups, or one region. We've written this book for *all* tropical cruisers and hope that it will be as useful a reference for gunkholers in the Bahamas as it will be for those planning to circumnavigate the globe.

We've included no proposed circumnavigations or three-year plans. Instead, we've pointed the way to good references for route planning (in chapter 7, Route Planning) and have included a review of the most popular tropical cruising areas worldwide in part 5 (Tropical Cruising Destinations). We encourage you to use these resources to plan your own voyages, based on what *you* want to see and do.

THE PERFECT BOAT

We don't devote space in the pages that follow to discussing what boat is right for tropical sailing. That may seem odd, as many sailors spend a lot of time, effort, and money in their quest for "the perfect boat." Regrettably, it's a quest doomed to failure, for the perfect cruising boat doesn't exist. Every design is a compromise, and despite many claims to the contrary, no boat can do everything well. Boats of all sizes, shapes, and types are successfully cruising the tropics—from 20-foot (6 m) production sailboats to mega-yachts—and the only fundamental requirement is that the boat be sufficiently seaworthy to undertake the voyages you plan. Obviously, if you're cruising in local waters, you can get by with less boat than if you're headed across an ocean or two. But even for extended voyaging, ensuring that the boat is well built and properly equipped, and that the crew knows what they're up to, are more important than having a big, new one.

If you're on a tight budget, the least expensive option is to buy an older production boat. It will probably need work and upgrading, but most refits can be done by any handy person, and there's plenty of information available to help guide you through the process (see appendix 3, Resources). Building a boat is also an option, but this will almost always cost more than buying secondhand and will likely take years.

Just as there's no perfect design, there's also no ideal construction material. All have advantages and disadvantages, and even boats built of materials with a deservedly poor reputation—such as ferrocement—have sailed long distances successfully. Fiberglass, wood, steel, and aluminum are better bets, but all can develop problems. A boat of any material must be properly designed and built, and all will require extra maintenance in the tropics (as discussed in chapter 14).

Our own boat, *Nomad*, serves as a good example of the inevitable compromises that most cruisers make when selecting a boat. It's a 35-foot (10 m) wood sloop, built in 1964, and though a fine performer and a good sea boat, its narrow beam and low freeboard mean it has less space below than most modern 30-foot (9 m) boats. Its varnished cabin sides look lovely but require a lot of maintenance, and although its 6-foot (1.8 m) draft gives it excellent stability, it's deeper than ideal for some anchorages. In short, *Nomad*'s a compromise, a combination of desirable and not-so-desirable features.

We were aware of these shortcomings when we bought the boat, but the fact is, it was available in the right place and at the right price. By buying *Nomad* rather than a larger, more comfortable (and more expensive) boat, we were able to set sail much sooner than would have otherwise been possible. *Nomad* has given us years of pleasure and taken us safely to many lovely and remote parts of the tropics.

DESIRABLE FEATURES OF A TROPICAL CRUISING BOAT

The fact that you can cruise successfully in many different types of boats doesn't rule out some features that are universally desirable for tropical cruising. For example, the importance of good ventilation quickly becomes apparent: we've been on boats that were perfect for cruising in northern latitudes, but they were the nautical equivalent of a pizza oven near the equator. Desirable features for a tropical cruising boat include

▶ *GOOD SAILING ABILITY.* Many beginning cruisers ignore this point and are then frustrated when their boat won't perform decently. Most boats will move along reasonably well downwind, but upwind ability is also important.

▶ *MODERATE DRAFT.* Our boat draws 6 feet, and though we manage, it's not ideal. If you want to spend time in really shallow areas such as the Bahamas, you'll want a centerboard boat, or perhaps a multihull, with a draft of less than 3 feet (1 m). If you don't have a boat already, give some careful thought to where you'll be sailing before you buy anything with a draft over 5 feet (1.5 m).

▶ *AN EASILY HANDLED RIG.* Opinions on what that is vary widely, but what's important is that *you* find the boat easy to sail and reef. We discuss rigs and sail handling at length in chapter 6 (Sailing in the Tropics).

▶ *GOOD VENTILATION AND SHADE.* We discuss keeping cool in chapter 10 (Life Aboard).

▶ *A COMFORTABLE COCKPIT.* You'll be spending lots of time outside in the tropics, so comfort in the cockpit is as important as it is down below.

▶ *A BOAT THAT'S EASILY HAULED OUT.* Centerboard boats or multihulls can usually dry out almost anywhere, but otherwise life will be simpler if you have a boat with either a long fin or a full keel. We include a brief review of what's available in the way of haul-out and maintenance facilities in our coverage of cruising areas in part 5 (Tropical Cruising Destinations).

Even this brief list of features is subjective, and our own boat doesn't meet all these requirements (sit in our cockpit, and you'll know what we mean). In the end, defining what constitutes an ideal boat is very personal, and what many sailors end up with often has more to do with finances than anything else.

WHAT WILL IT COST?

How much tropical cruising costs will depend to a degree on where you cruise. There's no doubt that cruising is cheaper in Mexico than on many Caribbean islands, and less costly in the Philippines or Indonesia than in Singapore. A much more important factor, though, is your lifestyle. If you live simply, then you can afford to cruise just about anywhere; after all, the residents of most tropical countries are much poorer than even a tight-fisted cruiser, and they routinely manage to feed, clothe, and house their families. If your lifestyle is more extravagant, and you require access to a variety of imported goods, you'll be spending a lot almost anywhere.

Much has been written about the relationship between boat size and cost. It's wise to keep in mind that larger boats don't just cost more to buy; they're also more expensive to equip and maintain, and more difficult for small crews to handle. There are couples out there cruising on 60- and even 80-foot (18 and 24 m) boats, but we shudder to think of the work and money needed to keep those boats in sailing trim, or of the fun of docking without help in any kind of a breeze. Even if we had unlimited finances, we wouldn't want a boat larger than about 40 feet—and that's for permanent living aboard. If you're on a cruise lasting a season or a few years, even that is really more than you need. But larger boats will provide greater comfort and space, and you may find them well worth the extra expense and complication.

How you outfit a boat for tropical cruising is very dependent on preferences and finances. It's possible to have a boat that's more luxurious than most homes, or to cruise with no more amenities than you'd have in a pup tent. If you need air conditioning, a microwave, and a washer-dryer to be comfortable, your boat will be much more costly and harder to maintain than if you can get by without these. But there is certain basic equipment that belongs on every boat headed for the tropics:

▶ *A DEPENDABLE MEANS OF RECEIVING WEATHER FORECASTS.* You can rely on simple voice forecasts or install the latest in satellite receiving equipment, but it's foolish not to stay on top of what the weather is doing. We explain the how and why of tropical weather in chapter 3 (Weather in the Tropics) and look at weather forecasts in appendix 2 (Weather Forecasts).

▶ *GOOD NAVIGATIONAL EQUIPMENT AND REFERENCES.* You never want to be caught without a means of finding your position, and having the proper route-planning materials on board will greatly enhance your freedom as you cruise. We discuss these in part 2 (Tropical Seamanship).

▶ *PROPER ANCHORING GEAR AND THE SKILLS TO USE IT.* We discuss this in chapter 5 (Tropical Anchoring).

▶ *RATLINES OR MAST STEPS.* Tropical navigation demands that you be able to get aloft easily and quickly. We provide instructions for making ratlines in appendix 1 (Ropework and Sewing).

▶ *THINGS TO KEEP YOU COOL.* Awnings, biminis, ventilators, and wind scoops are all-important in the tropics. We discuss these in chapter 10 (Life Aboard), while appendix 1 (Ropework and Sewing) contains step-by-step instructions for making an awning.

▶ *A GOOD MEANS FOR CATCHING, STORING, AND TREATING WATER.* Drinking quality water can be hard (or costly) to come by, and it's important to be as self-sufficient as you can. See chapter 10 (Life Aboard).

CRUISING LIGHTLY

Change is constant and inevitable. It also leads to inevitable comparisons between the present and the past. We'll bet that as you're excitedly preparing for a trip, planning your route, and reading guidebooks, you'll meet some insensitive soul who blurts out: "Oh yeah, the XXXX islands. They were good—about twenty years ago. Ruined now—I wouldn't go there."

Naturally it would have been fascinating to have cruised the tropics years ago, before so many elements of Western culture became as widespread as they are. But you can't turn back the clock. And although some areas may indeed become truly unpleasant as a result of being overrun by tourists, or despoiled by industrial development, some changes may make travel easier and more enjoyable. For example, an increase in the number of visiting yachts may result in a country establishing a new clearance port, which might mean you no longer have to sail several days out of your way just to comply with bureaucratic requirements. With development comes improved communications, better health care, and perhaps a few yachting facilities. Changes such as these may reduce the sense of adventure, but they can also make your cruising simpler and safer.

Whether or not you like the results, there's not a lot you can do to slow the rate of change in most places you visit. What all cruisers can do, though, is to be aware of and sensitive to the impacts that we have on the people and places we visit. Some may be beneficial, such as providing a livelihood for someone who provides services to yachts. But anchoring on coral reefs or collecting endangered species as souvenirs are destructive practices that can have severe impacts if done repeatedly over the years by a succession of cruisers. Impacts are not just environmental: cruisers may also give offense to the people they visit, by flouting customs or being insensitive to cultural differences. We look at some of these cultural and environmental issues in part 4 (Cruising Lightly).

Chapter 2

Tropical Environments

Coral reefs are one of the tropics' most fascinating and beautiful natural features. The riot of bright colors, array of fanciful fish that dart and weave between outcrops of coral, and vague menace from unseen creatures that lurk in the depths provide all the elements of a children's story. Perhaps that's why reefs evoke almost universal delight among swimmers, snorkelers, and divers. That one can enter this vivid fairytale world simply by donning a mask and putting your face in the water is hard for most people to believe. Once they've tried it, most can't get enough of what really is a marvelous experience.

But if coral reefs are considered one of the best aspects of the tropics, then mangrove forests are seen by many tropical visitors as a feature they'd rather do without. Mangroves are highly salt-tolerant trees that grow on the edges of many bays and estuaries, below the high-water mark. Mangroves lack the visual splendor and whimsical feel that make coral reefs so attractive. Not only that, mangroves are often in areas with muddy bottoms; even if the water is clear, such places aren't nearly as attractive for swimming as sandy-bottomed reef environments. The trees tend to cut down on the breeze, so anchorages in mangroves are often warmer than those around reefs.

But despite these seeming drawbacks, we're betting that you'll end up liking mangroves nearly as much as reefs. These two environments complement each other in many ways. As beautiful as they are, reef environments can be treacherous places to sail and anchor, and countless boats and ships have come to grief on them. In contrast, mangroves generally provide excellent holding and often very good shelter, and they can provide the cruiser with a welcome respite from the eternal vigilance that reefs require. And although reef environments are wonderfully alive underwater, above the surface there's often not much happening, except for the odd seabird searching for a meal. Mangroves, on the other hand, are havens for a host of species, and we've spent hours paddling and walking through these flooded forests observing birds, bats, and giant lizards. You may choose not to swim among the roots, but there's plenty happening there as well, as mangrove forests provide shelter and protection for many tropical fish species when they're young and not ready for the rough-and-tumble world of the reef.

Our focus in the pages that follow is on these two environments that make up almost all tropical coastlines. About one-third of the world's coastlines are covered by mangrove forests, whereas one-sixth are made up of coral reefs. We'll discuss them

An underwater scene from the Red Sea.
Mohammed Al Momany, courtesy of NOAA

Mangrove forests are havens for many aquatic and terrestrial species. This mangrove channel is in Jobos Bay, Puerto Rico.
National Estuarine Research Reserve Collection, NOAA

separately, but they're not so exclusive: at times you'll be in both. This is especially true in the Pacific, where it's common to find mangroves growing within a coral lagoon, or coral fringing the edge of a mangrove-lined inlet. We've also tried to give an accurate picture of what's happening to these environments across much of the tropics as human populations expand and economic development proceeds at an ever-increasing pace. By understanding how and where tropical environments are

threatened, you can seek out some of the better remaining examples as you cruise, and do your part to help conserve them.

There's a bit of science in what follows, but bear with us, because what you learn will be useful throughout the tropics. An understanding of reefs and mangroves will not only make your visit more interesting but will also be of practical use as you sail, navigate, and anchor in these different environments.

CORAL REEFS

It often surprises people to learn that coral reefs—and not just the fish and other creatures that live near them—are alive. Reefs are complexes of millions of tiny, soft-bodied animals called coral polyps, which belong to the same family as sea anemones, jellyfish, and sea fans. The notion of corals being soft-bodied might seem strange, especially considering how many vessels have come to grief on reefs, but corals, in fact, are very similar to sea anemones. What makes corals different is that they extract calcium from the surrounding water. Corals use the calcium to form external skeletons, and it is these skeletons that make up the massive limestone structures we try so hard to avoid hitting. Although reefs can be huge, the individual coral polyps are tiny: some single polyps are only 0.04 inch (1 mm) in diameter. Corals that build

reefs are known as "hard" corals; there are "soft" corals as well, which don't build reefs.

Not only are reefs alive, but they are also the product of a remarkable symbiotic relationship. Within the tissues of each hard coral polyp are single-celled algae, which not only help give the various coral species their many vibrant colors, but also help to feed the polyps. The corals provide the algae with shelter as well as carbon dioxide, which the polyps release as a waste product. In return, the algae use sunlight and carbon dioxide to synthesize organic compounds, such as sugars and amino acids, which feed the polyps during the daytime. At night, the coral polyps also feed on tiny animals, called zooplankton, that stray within range of their stinging tentacles.

When coral cover is high, underwater visibility is usually spectacular.

Requirements of Corals

As sailors from temperate waters are well aware, corals don't grow everywhere. For starters, they need warm, but not hot, water. Corals do best in seawater temperatures of the sort most of us like when swimming: 64 to 86°F (18–30°C) is the preferred temperature range, with 77 to 84°F (25–29°C) the ideal. These temperatures are, in general, restricted to the tropics, and corals are rarely found beyond 30° N and S latitude. Corals that grow outside these waters (such as those at Australia's Lord Howe Island, Japan's Kyushu Islands, or around Bermuda) do so because of warm currents. Cold currents and upwelling along the western coasts of the Americas and Africa help explain the relative lack of corals within the tropical East Pacific and South Atlantic.

Corals are large colonies of small animals called polyps. These polyps reside within a cuplike calcium carbonate skeleton. They have a central opening surrounded by tentacles that can be extended to feed on plankton in the water column.
Brent Deuel, Florida Keys National Marine Sanctuary, NOAA

Corals—or more precisely the algae that they depend on—also need light to survive. The amount of light decreases rapidly as depth below the surface increases; water temperature generally falls as well. The result is that corals are rarely found in water deeper than about 150 feet (45 m) and grow best in depths between a few feet and 100 feet (33 m). There are exceptions: black corals, for example, can live at much greater depths because their tissues don't contain the light-dependent algae.

Finally, corals don't like freshwater and so don't tend to grow near river mouths. This is convenient for sailors, because it keeps rivers and estuaries pretty well free of coral growth. Corals also need clear water, because murky water blocks the light and interferes with photosynthesis in the algae that the coral hosts. Water clarity is greatly affected by erosion of nearby land. Both erosion and sediment deposition are natural processes, but they've been greatly accelerated by humans in recent years, with serious negative impacts on corals, as we discuss below.

This elkhorn coral is just one example of the many forms corals take. National Undersea Research Program, NOAA

How Reefs Are Built

When they're young, coral polyps are free swimming. They may be carried hundreds or even thousands of miles by ocean currents before they settle and attach themselves to something. And not just anything: the ocean bottom on which they grow must be hard, so sand and mud won't do. Once it has started, a coral colony grows steadily upward toward the surface, with each new polyp cementing itself to the limestone skeletons of older polyps. Other animals that live around the reef and that also have calcium carbonate shells—including clams, crabs, lobsters, and sea urchins—add to the mix, and a reef structure is slowly built.

The many different species of corals grow in wildly different forms. They often have telltale names: brain, staghorn, mushroom, and table corals all clearly resemble their namesakes. Fairly fragile coral (elkhorn and staghorn, for instance) are more likely to be found in protected areas, away from vigorous wave impacts, than the sturdier types such as brain corals.

Reefs won't grow higher than about the low-tide mark, as they can't handle exposure to the air for long periods of time. Coral colonies grow best on the ocean side of islands where the water is clearer and there are more nutrients in the water. This means you usually won't find the best living corals within a lagoon; instead, they're on the seaward edge or near passes where flushing action is good. Corals grow slowly under the best of circumstances, topping out at about 1.5 to 2 inches (4 to 5 cm) a year.

Coral Reef Ecosystems

So far we've discussed corals without mentioning the many plants and animals that coexist with them. Coral reefs form the backbone of coral reef ecosystems, which are some of the most productive on earth. Reefs serve as nursery grounds for many species of juvenile fish and provide lifelong habitat for thousands of others; collectively, reefs

A large brain coral (right) next to a delicate sea fan.
Stephen Cook, Florida Keys National Marine Sanctuary, NOAA

are home to some 4,000 fish species, or about one-third of the world's total. Reefs also attract large animals such as turtles, sharks, and dugong (a relative of the manatee), which feed on the many organisms found on and around the reef. The different forms of coral provide shelter for many stationary animals as well, including clams, sponges, sea fans, and anemones. The variety within each of these groups is enormous: Australia's reefs alone are home to 5,000 types of sponges, while New Caledonia harbors 6,500 kinds of marine mollusks. The corals themselves are undeniably beautiful, but the fact they are home to such a profusion of underwater life is what makes them so interesting to swim around and such an important part of the tropical world.

Types of Reefs

Although no two reefs are the same, there are some similarities in how they grow. Grouping them into a few different reef types makes it easier to predict what sort of reef you're likely to encounter in different places.

Fringing and Barrier Reefs

As we've seen, corals grow best in warm, clear, clean, fairly shallow water. Given such conditions, they'll proliferate, eventually forming a fringing reef along a coastline or around an island. Many Caribbean reefs are of this type. Some are very narrow because the islands lack a true shelf (including the islands of the Eastern Antilles, Jamaica, Haiti, and the Dominican Republic), while others are more extensive, having developed on much broader coastal shelves (including reefs in the Bahamas, Turks and Caicos Islands, and Cuba).

No matter the width of the shelf, if land and sea level don't change, fringing reefs can grow only so far, because eventually the water will become too deep for a reef to continue growing outward. But if either land or sea level change—and they often do—then a fringing reef can become a barrier reef.

Sinking of the land will cause the reef to slowly grow upward, while at the same time creating a lagoon between the land and the reef. That's how the lagoon at Bora Bora (French Polynesia) formed.

Rising sea levels can produce the same result, and this is what created Australia's Great Barrier Reef (see illustration). The name is a bit of a misnomer in that it is not one continuous reef, but rather comprised of over 2,800 individual reefs, which together form a barrier reef 1,250 miles (2,000 km) long.

Volcanic Islands and Coral Atolls

A coral atoll is typically created through a combination of sinking land and rising sea level, with the birth and death of a volcanic island playing the key role. Charles Darwin figured it out some 150 years ago in what's come to be known as his theory of atoll development.

All midoceanic volcanic islands form on top of "hotspots": cracks in the earth's upper surface where hot, molten magma escapes upward. At first, the magma forms a submarine volcano, but as more magma is released, the volcano slowly builds upward until the lava breaks the surface and a new

This island is surrounded by a narrow fringing reef.

island is created. If eruptions continue, the island will grow upward and outward. The island of Hawaii has reached an elevation of more than 14,000 feet (4,240 m) above sea level.

The earth's surface is composed of a number of distinct pieces, called tectonic plates, which are moving all the time. The hot spots, however, do not move. Over many millions of years, an island moves away from the hotspot that caused it to form. As a result, its volcano becomes extinct, while another

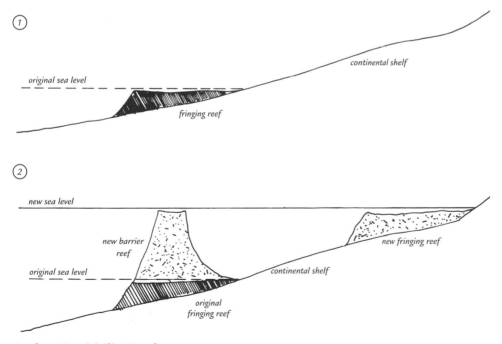

Formation of a continental shelf barrier reef.

new volcano forms above the hotspot. (As you read this, the latest addition to the Hawaiian islands, called Loihi, is struggling to make its way up from the sea floor southeast of the Big Island.) Once this process has repeated itself many times over, a chain of islands is formed, and the chain is aligned with the direction of tectonic plate movement.

The island of Hawaii is still growing; here clouds of steam billow up as molten lava flows into the sea.
U.S. Department of the Interior, U.S. Geological Survey

Corals begin growing while a volcanic island is still young. The polyps attach themselves to a new island's shoreline and over time form a fringing reef. The island of Hawaii, for instance, is at an early stage in this process, with very limited reef development. Other islands in the Hawaiian chain are considerably older and have developed much more extensive fringing reefs.

This alone is not enough to form an atoll, however. Before an atoll can develop, the volcanic island on which the corals grow has to subside, or sink.

A raised coral island with almost no soil development.

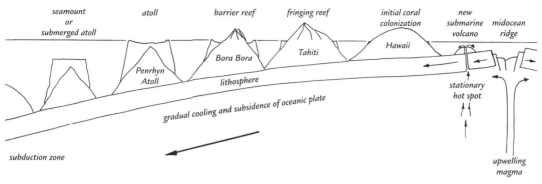

Formation of a midocean island, with examples of successive stages of reef development..

As shown in the accompanying figure, tectonic plate movement works a bit like an escalator: new plate material emerges at one side; on the opposite side, the edge of the plate slips under the edge of its neighbor. The Pacific escalator is headed down: it emerges along the East Pacific Rise, which stretches north and south near Easter Island, and sinks and disappears (is subducted) along much of its western edge, including the very deep Mariana Trench. Any islands that are sitting on the plate slowly sink as this oceanic escalator moves west and descends. This slow sinking causes the corals that encircle the islands to grow upward in order to stay within the shallow, warm, well-lit waters they prefer. As the distance between the fringing reef and sinking island increases, the fringing reef becomes a barrier reef, with a lagoon between the reef and the island. Bora Bora, whose volcanic core is sinking at a rate of ½ inch (1 cm) each century, is at just this stage in a volcanic island's life.

Eventually, due to subsidence and erosion, the last volcanic material disappears below the sea, leaving behind a roughly circular rim of reef, often dotted with motus, or small, sandy islets composed of coral and rubble. This necklace of islets is what we call an atoll. Although not visible anywhere on the reef or the islets, beneath every atoll lies the core of the former volcanic island. The oldest reefs can measure more than 4,000 feet (1,200 m) from the surface down to the base of volcanic rock. The entire process by which a volcanic island is born, becomes a home for reef-building corals, and then slowly sinks and dies while the corals join to form an atoll is one that takes millions of years. There are 425 atolls spread across the world's oceans today, most of them in the Pacific.

The process of reef building acts with uplift and sea-level changes to create other types of islands as well. One that's found here and there throughout the tropics is the raised coral (or limestone) island. They are typically craggy with poor soil development but may have fantastic sinkholes if they're low-lying.

MANGROVES

About one-third of the world's coastlines are covered with mangroves. Sometimes called "forests of the sea," mangroves grow where the land and sea meet. These salt-tolerant trees are among the few land plants that live in intertidal areas, growing between mean sea level and mean high-water spring.

Although mangroves are readily recognizable, they're not all the same; there are some 60 or 70 distinct species throughout the world. Unlike corals, mangroves need a soft substrate or bottom on which to get started, and they're found in areas where silt easily accumulates, such as sheltered estuaries, along

A young mangrove tree at low tide. This mangrove is growing in sand, rather than in the more common mangrove mud.

the banks of rivers, and on shorelines protected from wave and surf either by an outlying reef or by islands. Like corals, mangroves form the basis of an entire ecosystem rich in plant and animal life.

Mangroves employ remarkable adaptations to survive at the edge of the sea. At high tide, mangrove roots are fully immersed in salt water; at low tide, and when rivers and heavy rains bring water from the land, mangroves come into contact with water that is nearly fresh. An additional challenge is posed by the clayey mud that mangroves grow in, and that wants to suck you under. This mud keeps oxygen from the air out, which means that much of the breakdown of mangrove litter is done by organisms that can live without oxygen. This is what leads to the production of hydrogen sulfide, which we recognize as the rotten egg smell so typical of mangrove areas.

To help cope with these lousy conditions some types of mangroves have roots that breathe. These rise from the underground roots and pass through

the surface of the mud into the air. These aerial roots release gas into the air and maintain a store of oxygen in large, internal air spaces. Their roots have also developed a special means of filtering out excess salt.

Mangrove Ecosystems

Mangrove forests are especially rich in food and nutrients, because of the organic matter and detritus the trees produce. Mangroves are essential to the life cycle of many fish and other marine animals, providing nursery grounds for fish, shrimp and prawns, shellfish, and crustaceans. Many species like it so well they never leave, living out their entire life cycle in the marine portion of the mangrove forest.

Mangroves and coral reefs are linked together by the animals that move between the two habitats and by water flow. A number of species of fish and crustaceans that are usually found in offshore waters spend part of their life cycle in the mangroves, including prawns, snapper, and mackerel. The reverse is true as well. For example, mud crabs (delicious tropical alternatives to temperate water crabs), which spend most of their lives in the mangroves, move to the open sea at times in order to spawn. Tides and currents transport nutrients from around mangroves out to the coral reefs.

Because they straddle two worlds, mangroves end up supporting plenty of land animals as well. Most of the terrestrial animals live in the trees, seldom moving down to the mud. These include bandicoots, rodents, lizards, snakes, spiders, and insects. Many birds also make use of mangroves: honeyeaters and colorful lorikeets visit mangroves for nectar during the flowering season, while herons, egrets, and other wading birds roost in mangroves during high tide when the mud banks on which they search for food are covered with water. Mangroves provide refuges for many birds during periods of drought, as well as provide temporary shelter for migratory species.

Saltwater crocodiles—and their close relatives, alligators and caimans—spend time in mangroves, too, usually coming in on a rising tide as they search for food. Juvenile crocs eat crabs, prawns, and small fish while their larger relations dine on large mud crabs, birds, and mammals. Large colonies of fruit bats are often seen hanging from mangroves during the day.

Mangroves serve as a last refuge to a number of plants and animals that are either threatened or endangered. These include several species of orchids from Singapore and Malaysia; the American alligator and the American crocodile (caiman) from Florida; various species of herons, ducks, parrots, and other birds from the Caribbean; the Sumatran and Bengal tigers from Asia; the manatee from Florida and northern South America; and the Florida panther.

Mangrove forests don't just provide habitat for all kinds of animal life, they provide some very tangible benefits to people as well. For starters, they trap and stabilize sediments and so protect coastlines and estuaries from coastal erosion. They also may yield cures for some serious diseases. Western scientists are actively studying mangroves for their medicinal properties. In this they be somewhat behind traditional healers in tropical countries. We were told by a Solomon Islander who practices traditional medicine that a tea made from mangroves is an effective treatment for malaria.

Pelicans are frequent visitors to mangrove forests throughout the tropics.

THREATS TO TROPICAL ECOSYSTEMS

Coral Reefs

Reefs can seem incredibly tough and unforgiving if you graze against some coral when snorkeling, and even your boat's hull won't fare well if you go aground on a reef. Despite their seeming toughness, though, corals are very vulnerable to both natural and human disturbances. Most obviously, corals can be damaged by direct physical impact. This occurs naturally throughout the tropics as a result of storms. Heavy wave action from strong trade winds is enough to limit coral growth in some areas, or to discourage more fragile forms of coral from growing in exposed spots. More destructive by far are tropical cyclones, which can cause large areas of reef to literally be torn apart. As you cruise the

tropics, note which reefs have large coral "boulders" atop the reef flat. You'll find these only in cyclone-prone areas, as the force needed to get these hunks of coral on top of the reef is enormous.

Another naturally occurring impact—one that has devastated many reefs across the tropics in recent years—is coral bleaching, which is caused by seawater that is warmer than normal. Water that is too warm affects the algae within the coral polyps and causes the polyps to expel the algae. Corals turn white when this happens, hence the name coral bleaching. Corals can often recover after relatively minor bleaching, but a serious episode can kill large coral colonies. Cyclic changes in weather and current patterns, such as those known as El Niño and La Niña (see chapter 3,

Weather in the Tropics) have been linked to several major bleaching episodes, and it's thought that global warming is playing a role as well.

Events such as severe storms and warmer than normal water temperatures aren't anything new, although there is good evidence that they are occurring with increasing frequency. What's really changed is the ability of coral reefs to survive such events. In the past, natural stresses were all that corals had to cope with, and this allowed corals to grow over time, despite temporary setbacks caused by storms or El Niño. But today, many reefs are continually under stress as a result of human activities. Even if the human impacts alone don't kill the

---

POLLUTANTS AND CORALS

Different pollutants cause different problems. Sewage and agricultural fertilizers release too many nutrients into the water, causing blooms of algae, which often settle on and smother corals. Industrial pollution and agricultural and urban runoff introduce a mix of pesticides, heavy metals, and hydrocarbons, all of which can act to damage and kill corals. Even soil eroding off the land is a problem, as it can reduce water clarity enough to interfere with photosynthesis and will directly smother corals.

This means that reefs are threatened from almost any kind of development. Industrialized nations that don't adequately treat sewage, control pollution, or limit runoff may be damaging their reefs just as surely as poor nations that allow severe soil erosion to take place. Hawaii has had serious problems in the past caused by inadequately treated sewage, while urban and agricultural runoff is seen as the biggest threat to Australia's Great Barrier Reef. Around the Caribbean, in areas such as Mexico, Costa Rica, Venezuela, and Haiti, soil runoff is the major problem. There, runoff often comes from logging operations or severe slash-and-burn farming that lays bare great areas of soil, which is later washed into the sea by rain. In other places gold mining is to blame. On the south side of the island of Misima in southeastern Papua New Guinea, a gold mine has been operating for the last ten years, 24 hours a day. The locals there told us that their once-productive fishing reefs and rivers are now choked with sediment that has washed off the island from the mining activities. In such instances, it's almost always the nearshore reefs that are most affected.

---

reef, recovery from a periodic natural event is either impossible or extremely slow.

Poor seawater quality is a serious problem that has increased along with population growth throughout the tropics, be it in large densely populated Southeast Asia or tiny, remote "urban" centers such as Majuro in the Marshall Islands. Corals respond differently to different types of pollution, but any deterioration in water quality—from siltation to sewage and on through industrial pollutants such as heavy metals—is bad for reefs.

Corals also suffer from direct physical damage by human activities. Anchor damage from fishermen, recreational boaters, and ships is a major impact in high-use areas. Some reefs in the Caribbean have been virtually destroyed by cruise ships repeatedly anchoring on them. Moorings are an excellent solution to the problem of anchor damage, whether caused by ships or cruising yachts, and they're being installed in many heavily used areas throughout the tropics. Use moorings whenever they're available: you'll avoid any problems with jammed or dragging anchors, as well as avoiding reef damage.

Also very destructive to reefs is the practice of dynamite fishing, in which fishermen toss a stick of dynamite into a school of fish and then collect the fish that float to the surface. Not surprisingly, organisms other than fish are killed, including corals. As strange as it may seem, this has been a problem in some areas for years, with dynamite used in Micronesia's Chuuk Lagoon (formerly called Truk) since World War II. It's now widespread in Southeast Asia and becoming more prevalent in the Pacific. We've heard detonations within the boundaries of Komodo National Park in Indonesia and within Chuuk Lagoon in Micronesia. The practice is outlawed in both areas, but enforcement is lax to nonexistent.

Other physical impacts on reefs include the trade in ornamental coral, which has damaged a number of reefs in the Philippines and Indonesia; the mining of coral for fill and building materials, which is common throughout the tropics; and the extraction of phosphate from raised coral islands, such as Nauru, Banaba, and Makatea.

Finally, although people don't eat reefs, other organisms do, including fish, starfish, and urchins. Populations of the aggressive crown-of-thorns starfish have risen dramatically in some places and have devastated vast reef areas. The sea triton, a huge snail with a beautiful shell, is one of the few known predators of the crown-of-thorns. Research on the Great Barrier Reef has indicated that removal of tritons by enthusiastic shell collectors may have reduced their populations to the point that crown-of-thorns numbers have been able to explode. So even the seemingly natural phenomenon of coral predation by starfish has apparently been influenced by human activity.

How bad are the impacts? Serious and worsening quickly. The accompanying table provides a summary of the present status and future outlook for reefs around the world, based on data from the Global Coral Reef Monitoring Network. As it shows, 16 percent of the world's reefs were effectively destroyed by the 1998 coral bleaching episode alone. Some of these reefs may recover (and prospects are best for remote reefs) but many will not, because of the multitude of pressures they face.

DESTRUCTION OF THE WORLD'S CORAL REEFS

Regions of the World	Reef Destroyed Before 1998, %	Reef Destroyed in 1998, %	Reef in Critical Stage (may be lost in 2001–2010), %	Reef Threatened (may be lost in 2010–2030), %
		(figures in brackets are cumulative totals for each region)		
Arabian region	2	33 (35% dead)	6 (41% dead)	7 (48% dead)
Wider Indian Ocean	13	46 (59% dead)	12 (71% dead)	11 (82% dead)
Australia, Papua New Guinea	1	3 (4% dead)	3 (7% dead)	6 (13% dead)
Southeast and East Asia	16	18 (34% dead)	24 (58% dead)	30 (88% dead)
Wider Pacific Ocean	4	5 (9% dead)	9 (18% dead)	14 (32% dead)
Caribbean Atlantic	21	1 (22% dead)	11 (33% dead)	22 (55% dead)
Figures as a percentage of world's reefs	11	16	14	18
Total proportion of world's reefs that were or will be lost or severely damaged	11 (before 1998)	27 (after 1998 bleaching)	41 (estimate by 2010)	59 (estimate by 2030)

Data source: *Status of Coral Reefs of the World 2000.*

Looking into the future, estimates suggest that 41 percent of the world's reefs will be dead by 2010, and almost 60 percent by 2030. Impacts are lowest in the Pacific, especially in the Southwest, around Australia and Papua New Guinea. Areas that are hardest hit include Southeast Asia and the Indian Ocean. In the Caribbean, fully one-third of the reefs are expected to be dead by 2010.

Threats to Mangroves

Just as reef fisheries have supported tropical residents for generations, coastal communities throughout the tropics have long depended on mangrove forests to supply many requirements of daily life.

DESTRUCTIVE FISHING

Not only are corals impacted or sought after, but so are some of the organisms that live in or use reef ecosystems. In many heavily populated areas, fish and other reef organisms are under threat. In parts of the Caribbean, spiny lobsters, queen conch, and various reef fish and invertebrates have been heavily exploited, particularly where they are in demand by local hotels and restaurants.

The situation is much worse in Southeast Asia, where fish such as Napoleon wrasse, coral trout, and groupers are the primary targets for the live fish trade in Hong Kong and Singapore. In such places, a 90-pound (40 kg) Napoleon wrasse may sell for as much as $5,000 U.S.! Diners there are able to select their choice of fish from a restaurant aquarium mere minutes before eating, thus ensuring the ultimate in freshness. Not only are too many fish being taken, but the fishing methods themselves are very destructive.

The fish trade begins with local fishermen in Indonesia, the Philippines, and more recently in remote islands in the Indian and Pacific Oceans. They typically use a solution of sodium cyanide to capture the fish, which are then picked up and transferred by ship to Hong Kong. Cyanide is known to be lethal to most coral reef organisms, including small fish and invertebrates. Fish stocks in the Philippines and Indonesia are expected to collapse within a few years, after which time the trade will move completely to Pacific and Indian Ocean islands. In fact, it has already begun: as we write this, fishing for the live fish trade is well underway in the island nations of Kiribati and Papua New Guinea.

Mangroves have been used as firewood, burned to make charcoal, and for timber, while the rich mangrove ecosystem has supplied fish, shellfish, and crustaceans. As human populations have increased, so has the use of mangrove ecosystems, and today mangroves are also being used for industrial purposes. For example, there is widespread clear-cutting of mangroves in Southeast Asia for the production of wood chips that are in turn used in the manufacture of rayon.

Mangroves are also cleared simply to make the land available for what are considered "higher uses." In many tropical countries the pressure to increase food production is enormous, and intertidal land is being cleared for both agriculture and aquaculture. In the Indo-Pacific region, Thailand has lost over 25 percent of its mangroves, and Malaysia has lost 20 percent. Large areas of mangrove have been cleared in Australia and the United States as well, making room for marinas, ports, resorts, and housing and residential developments; this takes place in spite of the fact that both countries have laws protecting mangrove ecosystems. In Australia, canal housing development is widespread and has destroyed significant areas of mangroves in southeastern Queensland. Worldwide, an estimated 50 percent of mangrove ecosystems have been altered or destroyed.

When mangroves are cleared, the impacts are often felt far beyond the mangrove forest itself. Typically, large amounts of sediments are washed out to sea, engulfing reefs, blocking sunlight, and smothering corals. Problems with mosquitoes and biting sand flies often increase after mangrove clearing; although these insects do inhabit mangroves, they are most prolific in areas where mangroves have been removed or otherwise disturbed.

The Bottom Line

Although the picture we've painted regarding the condition of many tropical ecosystems may be a depressing one, it's not true to say there is no hope, either for you as a visitor or for the environment itself. The reefs and mangroves in many areas are still in excellent condition, particularly in remote locations. Even in heavily impacted areas such as Indonesia, we've encountered reefs of amazing beauty and mangrove ecosystems that abound with wildlife. In addition, awareness of the fragility of these ecosystems is increasing, as are efforts to protect them. We urge you to assist these efforts whenever you can. There are many organizations working to protect reefs, and you can help out through donations or by getting directly involved in reef protection and management programs in the area where you live or cruise.

All cruisers should do all they can to ensure their actions don't cause further damage to these beautiful but fragile environments; we say more about this in chapters 5 (Tropical Anchoring) and 15 (Green Cruising). To help you find areas of reef and wildlife habitat that are still in good shape, and avoid those that aren't, we've included a more specific review of reef environments throughout the tropics in part 5 (Tropical Cruising Destinations).

Chapter 3

Weather in the Tropics

Mariners have tried to understand weather patterns since they first took to the water thousands of years ago. Historically, most sailors were strictly bound by the dictates of the wind, as it's only recently that sailing craft have been able to make significant progress to windward. But the fact that we can sail to windward doesn't mean that we want to, especially offshore, where seas and swell often make such courses slow and uncomfortable. The result is that most cruisers setting out on a passage seek "fair winds and following seas" just as eagerly as sailors of old, and most long passages follow well-established sailing routes that have been in use for centuries.

The tropics are a great place for passagemaking, thanks to the trade winds. Trade winds got their name because of the role they played in transporting cargo around the world during the age of sail. These winds are the most predictable and consistent on earth and predominate over most of the tropical Pacific, Indian, and Atlantic Oceans. Trade wind patterns are modified in the western Pacific and in the central and northern Indian Oceans, where the wind alternates seasonally in a cycle called the monsoon. These wind regimes are depicted in the global maps on the inside front and back covers.

Persistent and reliable though they are, the trade winds aren't static. They vary in strength from one day to the next, and their geographic range expands and contracts seasonally. Trade winds are affected by long-term cycles, such as El Niño, named after a warm-water current off the coast of South America. And sometimes the low- and high-pressure cells that produce the trades move away from their normal positions, interrupting normal wind and weather patterns for days and even weeks.

Tropical cruisers have a better chance than many temperate-water sailors of avoiding the nastiest weather, as the incidence of gales (other than tropical cyclones) is much lower in tropical waters than it is in mid or high latitudes. But that doesn't mean tropical weather is always benign. Depressions are a fact of life, and even the faithful trades can prove too much at times, blowing for days on end at 25 to 30 knots, keeping most sailors in port. Although we haven't yet figured out how to change the weather, we're getting better at understanding it. Your best defense against bad weather at sea is to avoid it in the first place. To do that reliably requires an understanding of weather patterns and features. This knowledge also makes it possible to take advantage of unusual weather patterns.

Some weather-related decisions—such as determining when to begin a passage and how to vary a route to take advantage of developing conditions—can be made only when you're either about to leave port or actually en route. In those circumstances you need accurate information about local conditions, backed up by good analysis of what the future holds. But other decisions, such as what season to cruise a certain area and your general route across an ocean, must be made well in advance. For that you need an understanding of the "big picture": weather processes and patterns on an ocean and on a global scale.

In this chapter, we familiarize you with the basic processes that cause weather, and we show why tropical weather patterns vary both seasonally and geographically. We then focus on understanding adverse or unusual weather and provide pointers for avoiding it, or for using it to your advantage. The discussion of weather processes and features is supplemented by the discussion of forecasts in appendix 2.

TROPICAL WEATHER BASICS

Although weather can seem impossible to understand at times, it's good to know everything that happens does so for a reason. All winds, no matter what they're called or how hard they blow, are caused by differences in atmospheric pressure. Air moves from areas of high pressure to areas of low pressure. It can help to think of the high-pressure zones as hills, and the lows as valleys. Wind always moves "downhill," and its speed depends on the steepness of the slope. If a high is strong and an adjoining low is deep, then the slope will be steep, and the winds strong. During storms, both pressure differences and winds are much greater than they are during periods of fine weather.

Pressure differences that exist only briefly create winds of brief duration, such as sea breezes that blow just for an afternoon. Other pressure differences are present on an almost permanent basis, and these include the pressure systems that power the trade winds. But both have the same cause: unequal heating of the earth's surface by the sun.

Atmospheric Circulation

Just as warmth from the sun makes life on earth possible, the sun's heat is what powers our weather. It's no mystery that the sun's heat isn't distributed evenly over the earth's surface; after all, that's why most of us set a course for the tropics, rather than the poles. The area that gets the most heat annually is the equator, where the sun's rays are rarely far from overhead. As a result, equatorial latitudes are warm year-round.

Everything heats up there: land, water, air—even your beer. Land, water, and beer don't do much other than change temperature, but air reacts differently: it expands and rises. The result is a drop in the atmospheric pressure at the surface at the equator.

The warm, rising equatorial air climbs until it's high in the atmosphere, then is displaced poleward by the ongoing rise of heated air. In each hemisphere, the air that's moving toward the poles is deflected to the east by the rotation of the earth due to a phenomenon called the Coriolis force (which we discuss below). The result is upper-level southwest and northwest air flows. As the air moves poleward, it cools and a portion of it sinks, at about 30° N and S latitude. The cool, descending air forms large areas of high pressure at the surface in these subtropical latitudes (such as the Bermuda–Azores High and the Pacific High) and spreads north and south as it nears the surface. The air that moves back toward the equator near the surface in each hemisphere (now deflected to the west by the Coriolis force) becomes the northeast and southeast trade winds in the Northern and Southern Hemispheres, respectively, while the air that flows toward the poles is deflected eastward, forming each hemisphere's midlatitude prevailing westerlies. The large-scale circulation of air between the equator and about 30° N and S is known to meteorologists as a Hadley cell, and it's the engine that powers the trade winds.

Although they're of less concern to tropical sailors, there are additional circulation cells farther

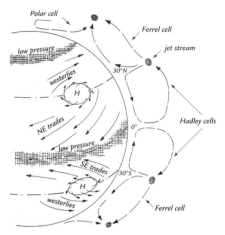

The global atmospheric circulation system.

north and south (the Ferrel and Polar cells) that produce an additional band of surface low pressure in the high latitudes, at about 60° N and S. These low-pressure areas, including the Aleutian Low and the Icelandic Low, matter most to us because they play a role in creating storms. The storms of temperate latitudes can make passages to and from the tropics less than relaxing and, as we'll see, even have a way of sneaking into the tropics now and again, as if to remind us of what we've left behind.

Atmospheric Pressure

Given that differences in atmospheric pressure power the wind, it follows that knowing what the pressure is at any given time plays an important part in predicting wind strength. Fortunately pressure is easily monitored aboard even the smallest boat with a barometer, which simply measures the weight of the air above a given location. The best tool for the job is still a simple aneroid barometer. They're inexpensive and basically foolproof—there are no batteries, liquids, or complicated instructions. Calibrate yours once a year (consult with a weather bureau or airport weather service to get an accurate local reading) and you're ready to go, armed with a reliable and valuable forecasting tool.

Pressure is measured internationally in hecto-Pascals (hPa), which are equal in value to the older unit of millibars.

A change in pressure at any spot on the earth's surface tells you that the amount of air above has changed:

▶ *DECREASING PRESSURE* (a surface low) indicates that air at the earth's surface is rising. Wind at the surface generally streams in toward lower pressure, replacing air that is rising, while in the upper atmosphere air disperses above a zone of lower surface pressure (making room for more rising air).

▶ *INCREASING PRESSURE* (a surface high) indicates sinking air at the surface. Wind at the surface streams out of a zone of higher pressure.

This introduces a concept that's fundamental to understanding weather and is especially important to have in mind when you begin to interpret the weather and do basic forecasting. What happens at the surface is connected to what happens aloft. We commonly talk about weather as if it were a two-dimensional event, with highs, lows, and other features moving about as if on a chess board, but in fact weather takes place in three dimensions, and any understanding of weather processes must take this into account.

Seasons

The picture we've drawn so far of a surface low-pressure zone at the equator and higher-pressure areas at 30° N and S latitude is appealingly simple, but a bit too perfect to be real. For a start, both temperature and pressure change seasonally over most of the earth. Seasonal changes take place because the earth's axis is tilted at 23.5 degrees to the plane of its orbit around the sun. This tilt results in the Northern Hemisphere getting the greatest solar input about 21 June (the Northern Hemisphere's summer solstice), whereas the Southern Hemisphere receives its maximum six months later, on about 22 December. The heat input at low latitudes is fairly constant, with the two peak periods at the equator, occurring when the sun at local noon is directly overhead,

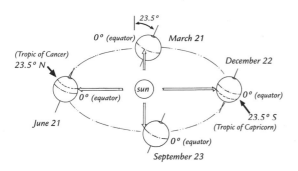

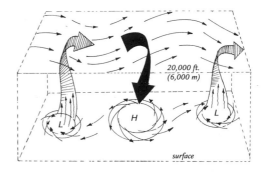

Variations in where the sun is overhead during the course of the year create our seasons.

The presence of high or low pressure at the earth's surface requires that there be a corresponding area of converging or diverging air in the upper atmosphere. Here the surface air streams in toward the two low-pressure cells. Low pressure implies heating at the surface and thus warm, less dense air, which rises above the lows. This sends air into the upper atmosphere, where it diverges. Where the upper-atmosphere air converges (as it does at 30° N and S), the air becomes denser and then sinks. This is happening above the high-pressure cell. When the sinking air (black arrow) reaches the surface, the air streams out of the high center, toward areas of lower pressure. Note that this view is in the Southern Hemisphere, as the circulation of air into the lows is clockwise, while that out of the high is counterclockwise.

about 21 March (the vernal equinox) and again at 23 September (the autumnal equinox).

The area that we call the tropics is defined by the seasonal variation in the sun's altitude in the sky, traditionally called the sun's declination. The tropical zone includes only that area over which the sun is directly overhead at local noon at some time during the year. The farthest point north where the sun is found directly overhead at local noon is at 23.5° N latitude on 21 June (the Tropic of Cancer). As the year progresses, the point of maximum declination moves south, and the sun reaches an altitude of 90 degrees at the equator on 23 September. Continuing southward, the sun climbs to 90 degrees in the sky at local noon at 23.5° S latitude on 22 December (the Tropic of Capricorn). Then the process reverses, with the sun overhead at the equator once again on 21 March.

The changes in the sun's altitude above the earth's surface throughout the year, and the resulting differences in the amount of heat that's received, are what cause seasonal variations in temperature and weather. These differences are greatest in temperate latitudes but exist in the tropics as well. The belts of high pressure at 30° N and S move some 4° of latitude poleward during that hemisphere's summer, causing a related shift in the trade winds, as we'll see.

Trade Winds

The trade winds are the direct result of the pressure differences that we've just described. Air near the earth's surface moves from the higher-pressure zones at 30° N and S to the lower-pressure equatorial zone, producing fairly steady and consistent winds both north and south of the equator. If no other complications were present, those winds would blow fairly consistently from the north and south. But the earth's rotation causes a deflection in the direction of all winds (and currents), due to a phenomenon that's referred to as the Coriolis force (see sidebar). The net result is that the trade winds are deflected toward the west as they blow toward the equator in both the Northern and Southern Hemispheres, producing the northeast and southeast trade winds. Looking at the illustration on page 24, we can see how the trade winds emanating from the high-pressure cells at 30° N and S blow off to the west in both hemispheres.

CORIOLIS FORCE

The Coriolis force isn't really a force at all, but rather a phenomenon caused by the spinning of the earth about its axis. At the heart of the Coriolis force is the principle of the conservation of angular momentum, which says that once in motion (either spinning about an axis, or in orbit around another body) an object will stay in motion unless acted upon by another force.

Although the earth rotates about its axis at a constant rate of one revolution per day, the actual speed at the earth's surface varies, decreasing from a high of about 870 knots at the equator to around 435 knots at 60° N and S latitude and down to nothing at the poles. Fortunately we don't notice this variation in speed on the surface, but it does affect the apparent movement of anything traveling above the earth's surface.

What the conservation of angular momentum means in practical terms is that the eastward speed of all objects moving independently of the earth's surface (including water and air) tends to remain the same as it was before the object was set in motion. For example, if we fired a rocket on a northerly trajectory from a launch pad on the equator, in addition to moving north at whatever speed it's going, the rocket will also be moving eastward at a rate of 870 knots. An observer on the ground watching the rocket's progress will see it flying north, but to an observer hanging motionless in space, the rocket would be moving east as well, at the same speed as the earth below.

As the rocket moves north, away from the equator, it maintains its eastward movement at 870 knots, but the speed of rotation of the ground below steadily decreases. As a result, the rocket moves to the east more rapidly than the surface below and is apparently deflected to the right (or the east). This is shown in the accompanying illustration.

The direction in which an object is deflected varies depending on whether it is moving away from or toward the equator. If our rocket were fired south from the North Pole (where the eastward velocity is 0), it would be traveling east more slowly than the ground below, and would once again be seemingly deflected to the right (but now to the west). A rocket fired in the Southern Hemisphere

The Coriolis force affects anything moving independently of the earth's surface, including wind and water, but it's simpler to understand by thinking of a distinct object. Imagine a rocket is fired due north from A, at the equator, toward B. As it travels north the rocket's easterly movement remains the same as it was at the equator, but the ground over which it is flying is moving eastward at a slower and slower rate, due to the earth's reduced circumference at higher latitudes. As a result, the rocket's trajectory will seem to be deflected, apparently following a course from A to C.

will be deflected to the left, turning westward if traveling toward the equator, and turning to the east if traveling toward the South Pole.

The strength of the Coriolis force varies with distance from the equator, where the force is zero, to the poles, where it's at its maximum. The absence of Coriolis force at the equator explains why tropical cyclones don't occur within the zone from about 6° N to 6° S latitude. Without an appreciable Coriolis force, depressions lack the rotational energy they have at higher latitudes and can't develop into tropical cyclones.

The thought that the easterly trade winds are being deflected westward can be confusing until you remember that winds are referred to by the direction from which they blow, while currents are referred to by the direction in which they flow. So we refer to the trade winds that blow from the SE as "southeast trades," but a current from the same direction as a "northwest," or more clearly a "northwest setting" current.

On average, trade winds cover an area of about 1,200 miles, or 20° in latitude (more or less between latitudes 5° and 25° N), in both hemispheres. Trade

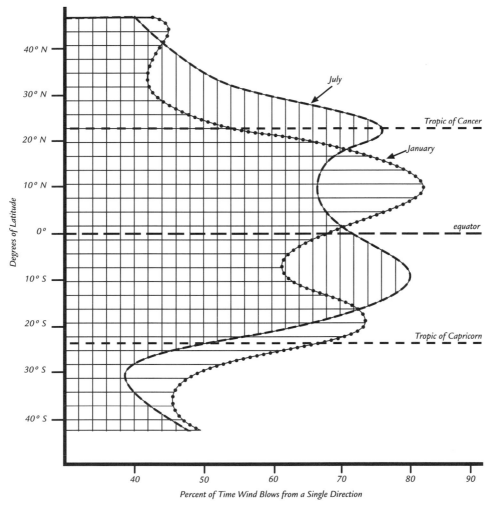

Wind direction is most constant in the tropics: north of the Tropic of Cancer and south of the Tropic of Capricorn, wind direction changes more frequently.

winds generally blow from the E to NE quadrant in the Northern Hemisphere (the northeast trades) and the E to SE quadrant in the Southern Hemisphere (the southeast trades). These wind systems are so consistent that they create their own accompanying currents: the north and south equatorial currents, found in the Pacific, Atlantic, and southern Indian Oceans.

The trades average between 12 and 20 knots, but both their strength and direction can vary considerably between seasons and from one side of an ocean to another. We look at this in detail when we discuss the characteristics of the high-pressure cells that power the trades.

Monsoon Winds

Seasonal variations and the Coriolis force aren't the only complicating factors in our idealized picture of global pressure systems. Large land areas also foul things up. In particular the monsoon winds replace

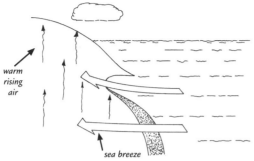

Sea breeze, caused by a low-pressure zone over the warm land.

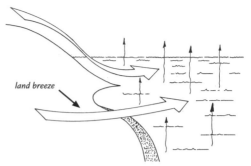

Land breeze, caused by cooling of the land at night, which creates higher pressure than over the adjacent comparatively warm ocean.

the trades in some areas, most notably in the southwest Pacific and Indian Oceans.

Monsoon wind systems are caused by seasonal heating and cooling of large land areas. Land changes temperature more readily than water, and we can see this effect on a small scale in many places. Land heats up quickly during the day, creating an area of relatively lower pressure than the adjacent ocean. Air rushing from the area of higher pressure (the water) to the land results in an afternoon sea breeze. San Francisco is well known for its strong afternoon sea breezes in the summer; these are caused by the contrast between cold offshore air and the very warm air of California's central valley.

Land breezes usually come up at night, especially in areas where the water is warm. In the evening the land cools down quickly, while the water stays at a relatively constant temperature. If the land cools down enough, an area of higher pressure is formed and the air streams off the land toward the water.

These same principles are what power the vastly larger monsoon wind systems. With monsoon winds the pressure differences last for a season, rather than just an afternoon or a night, and are strong enough to interrupt the typical trade wind air flow for some months.

Consider what happens in the Indian and western Pacific Oceans. The Asian landmass is warmed during the Northern Hemisphere's summer months, resulting in a low-pressure system over land, with relatively higher pressure over adjacent

waters. The southwest monsoon's winds begin in the Southern Hemisphere, as an extension of the southeast trades. As the winds cross the equator the effect of the Coriolis force is to bend the winds in the opposite direction, or in this instance to the right. What was a southeast trade wind in the Southern Hemisphere becomes the southwest monsoon, affecting all of the north Indian Ocean as well as the western Pacific and China Sea as far as 40° N, between the months of May and October. See the map on the inside back cover, which depicts wind and pressure systems for July.

The pattern reverses in the Northern Hemisphere's winter, with the Asian landmass cooling and creating a high-pressure cell. Air circulates around and out of this high-pressure cell, toward the lower-pressure trough at the equator. The winds are deflected to the right by the Coriolis force and become the northeast monsoon in the China Sea, North Pacific, and northern Indian Oceans. This monsoon merges with the northeast trades of the western Pacific, so that at the monsoon's height in the northern midwinter, northeast winds predominate across the entire North Pacific Ocean. The monsoon winds ease toward the equator but can be drawn south as far as about 10° S. The Coriolis force deflection is reversed south of the equator, so that in the Southern Hemisphere the northeast monsoon becomes the northwest monsoon. It can be felt in the region north of about 10° S, between about 60° and 180° E, or in both the Indian and western Pacific Oceans. Both the northeast and northwest monsoon winds can be seen on the map on the inside front cover, which depicts winds and pressure systems for January.

The trade and monsoon wind systems are the dominant features of tropical weather—and define to a large extent what tropical sailing is all about. With an understanding of them, you can predict in a very general way what sorts of winds to expect in various parts of the tropics. But these marvelous wind systems are modified and interrupted in a variety of ways, ranging from small-scale, everyday disturbances such as squalls to massive disruptions in the normal circulation pattern, such as El Niño. Taken together, these changes in the trade wind pattern are responsible for determining the weather in a given area during a day or a season. Below, we'll consider the large-scale high- and low-pressure systems with which the tropical sailor must contend. Then we'll look at other tropical disturbances such as convergence zones, squalls, and tropical cyclones.

HIGHS AND LOWS

We've already discussed high- and low-pressure areas in a general way to help explain global circulation patterns. But concentrations of high and low pressure—in what are often called *cells*—are also major determinants of day-to-day wind and weather.

High- and low-pressure cells can vary greatly in size, from hundreds to thousands of miles in diameter. High- and low-pressure cells in each hemisphere have their own characteristic circulation, determined by the Coriolis force, which modifies the flow of air as it moves out of high-pressure cells and into lows. In the Northern Hemisphere, flows are diverted to the right, causing a clockwise flow out of a high and a counterclockwise flow into a low. In the Southern Hemisphere, flows are diverted to the left, meaning that the flow out of a high is counterclockwise and the flow into a low is clockwise.

Air Temperature, Moisture, and Clouds

A few additional concepts will help us understand the behavior of highs and lows. As air moves up and down in the atmosphere, its temperature changes. When that happens, the air's ability to hold moisture changes as well. When moisture condenses (as it must whenever a cloud forms), heat is released into the atmosphere. These three facts influence the formation of clouds and storms.

Horizontal pressure differences across the earth's surface are nothing compared to the pressure differences that exist vertically in the atmosphere: as a parcel of air rises, the surrounding pressure drops dramatically. This drop in pressure causes the rising air to expand accordingly and to drop in temperature. By contrast, air that is sinking contracts and warms as it does so. Meteorologists call this *adiabatic* cooling and heating, but what's most important to remember is what happens to the air's temperature:

▶ air that is sinking is warmed

▶ air that is rising is cooled

Water can be found throughout the atmosphere as a vapor in varying amounts. Relative humidity is the familiar measure of how much water vapor is present at any time; it simply measures the ratio (in percent) of the actual amount of water vapor in the air to the amount the air can hold. When relative humidity is low (say 20 percent, as in the desert) the air feels dry. When it's high (perhaps 80 percent, as it often is in the tropics) it feels humid. When relative humidity reaches 100 percent, we say the air is saturated, and this is typically the point at which condensation occurs. What form the condensed moisture takes depends on many factors but can include dew, fog, clouds, rain, and so on.

The total amount of water vapor the air can hold at any time depends directly on the air temperature: warm air can hold more water vapor than cool air. Air that is being warmed is less likely to become saturated (and produce precipitation) than air that is

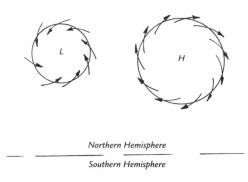

Northern Hemisphere

Southern Hemisphere

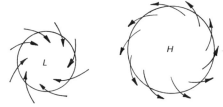

Winds in and out of high- and low-pressure systems in the Northern and Southern Hemispheres.

being cooled. So, the descending (warming) air associated with high pressure is less likely to produce clouds and precipitation than the ascending (cooling) air associated with low pressure.

Low pressure itself doesn't create clouds, but by lifting the air, which then cools, it provides the right conditions for moisture to condense. When this happens heat is released into the atmosphere (this is known as *latent heat*), forcing the air to rise even farther and encouraging additional cooling and condensation. Under the right conditions, in which the rising air is consistently warmer than its surroundings, towering cumulonimbus clouds (or thunderheads) develop, which are many thousands of feet high. Given the right conditions, these can develop into the most extreme tropical low, the tropical cyclone.

High-Pressure Cells

Highs, or anticyclones, are usually classified as being either cold or warm. Cold highs are those that are composed of air that is colder (and therefore denser) than the surrounding air at the surface. Such highs are found, more or less permanently, over Siberia and the Canadian Shield and are among the features that we sail to the tropics to escape. We'll say no more about them. Warm highs (they sound better already) are those in which temperatures at the surface within the high vary little from the surrounding air. In warm highs, the higher pressure is due to a greater density of air in the upper atmosphere, caused by convergence. The subtropical highs that power the trade winds—and which form part of the Hadley cells we discussed earlier—are warm highs.

Warm highs typically contain subsiding air that is warmed adiabatically as it descends, increasing the air's ability to hold water vapor and decreasing the relative humidity. Condensation and precipitation are therefore unlikely. So it's not surprising that within these high-pressure systems you usually find fine, settled weather.

Highs can vary widely in size from just a few hundred miles across to several thousand. The Atlantic has two subtropical highs, one in the north (the Bermuda–Azores High) and the other in the south (the St. Helena High). They're usually positioned at about 25° to 30° N and S, respectively. Neither high is truly stationary, and both change shape almost daily as low-pressure systems and frontal zones impact the western and southern borders of the high-pressure area.

The Pacific is home to four subtropical high-pressure areas, two in each hemisphere. The eastern Pacific high-pressure areas are the most stable of all the world's midlatitude oceanic highs. They're generally situated at about 25° to 30° N and S latitude, with the North Pacific high at about 130° to 150° W longitude, and its South Pacific counterpart well to the east at 95° to 125° W. The western Pacific highs are less persistent, being impacted by frequent strong low-pressure systems from the west; they are normally situated at about 30° N and S, with the northern high at 150° to 165° E, while the western South Pacific high sits near just east of

New Zealand (and 180°). The western Pacific highs are not unlike the Atlantic highs, in that they are always moving and changing shape, with new highs following cold fronts off the continents and merging with the existing oceanic highs. Ocean currents have a significant impact on the stability of these high-pressure systems (see ocean currents below).

The southern Indian Ocean has high-pressure areas not unlike those in the Pacific. A western high is normally situated east of Madagascar, with an eastern high a few hundred miles west of Australia; these occasionally merge. The northern Indian Ocean does not extend to 25° N, so in winter the high-pressure cell develops over land (on the Indian subcontinent). That winter high powers the northern Indian Ocean trade winds, but during summer the high dissipates, allowing the southwest monsoon to develop.

High-Pressure Zones and the Sailor

Highs have a major effect on tropical weather. For a start, the strength and direction of the trade winds are directly related to the pressure and location of the midoceanic high-pressure cells. In the tropics, we're usually on the equatorial side of a subtropical high, between the high and the lower-pressure zone at the equator. The higher the pressure within the high, the stronger the wind it generates. When a high is strong, winds will tend to be from the NE or even NNE in the Northern Hemisphere, from the SE or SSE in the Southern Hemisphere, and will be strongest in the area between about 10° and 25° latitude. Large highs may generate trade winds of 30 knots and more, and these can generally be predicted by keeping an eye on your barometer and following a simple rule:

> The higher the pressure reading, the stronger the wind is likely to be.

Note that this rule applies only in the absence of any low-pressure systems, whether such lows are tropical or extratropical in origin. Such strong trades are often referred to as "reinforced trade winds" and are usually not accompanied by a frontal disturbance. They may bring an increase in the number of squalls and can make conditions uncomfortable, especially if beating to windward or anchored in an area with marginal protection.

Weak highs, or highs positioned farther from the equator, will produce light trades. Such winds will be more likely to blow from the east in both hemispheres.

So far we've discussed the impact of highs on the wind in the tropics. Highs also impact wind strength in the subtropics, or horse latitudes, which stretch from the tropics to about 35° N and S. These regions are known for their calms and variable winds, caused by the presence of vertically moving (sinking) air in the vicinity of the high. In general, the higher the pressure, the less wind you'll find inside the high. If you have lots of fuel, a large, well-placed high can allow you to make an easy trip to and from the tropics, as the weather will typically be fine and settled, due to the dry descending air. If you have limited motoring range, be sure to skirt the edges of subtropical highs.

Although most of the world's high-pressure cells are not stationary, highs do sometimes temporarily stall—simply stop moving—and these are termed *blocking highs*. Blocking highs are a particular hazard in areas with active frontal systems and rapidly moving lows. Lows that run into a stalled high can create an area of steep pressure change and resulting strong winds. Some sailors call these *squash zones*, and although they're more frequent in temperate waters, they are a feature to be reckoned with, especially if making a passage to or from the tropics. You can recognize squash zones easily if you have a weather fax, but if you don't here's a simple clue: if the wind strength increases significantly without a change in barometric pressure, then you're in a squash zone and should keep a careful ear to the weather forecasts to determine the relative movements of the high- and low-pressure cells that are involved. The illustration on page 32 shows what happens in a squash zone.

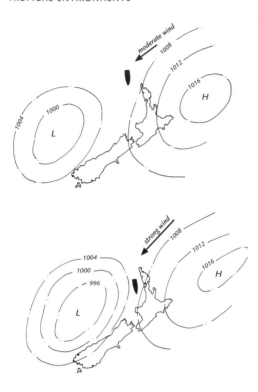

Formation of a squash zone. The barometric pressure measured aboard this boat headed for New Zealand's Cook Strait won't change, but the squeezing of the isobars as the low deepens and piles up against the almost stationary high will make for high winds and nasty seas.

Low-Pressure Cells

Low-pressure cells (also called *cyclones* or *depressions*) are composed of rotating, upward moving air. Because air cools as it ascends, the air within a low can hold less water in the form of vapor than surrounding air. Once the relative humidity reaches 100 percent, condensation often occurs, leading to the formation of clouds and rain. This is one reason lows are associated with bad weather.

As with highs, lows can also be warm or cold. Cold lows, with the coldest air at their center, are found mainly in temperate latitudes and result in extratropical cyclones, or midlatitude lows. Cold lows dominate weather patterns in temperate latitudes, and though they're often too far north or south to be a major factor in tropical weather, they do make an appearance on occasion. Of even greater concern to the tropical sailor are warm lows, which include monsoon depressions and tropical cyclones (discussed in detail below).

Lows vary enormously in both pressure and size. Pressure typically ranges from 960 to 1,000 hPa (but can drop to below 900 hPa), and lows may be a few hundred to 2,000 or more miles in diameter. Cold lows often form along weather fronts, which are the transition zones between different air masses. When air masses of differing densities and temperatures collide, warmer air is forced to rise. This can create a hump or wave along the weather front. Given the right conditions, the wave intensifies, and the rising air creates a low at the surface, which may then develop into a storm. Fronts tend to be most active outside the tropics, in high and midlatitudes, and their passage is usually marked by abrupt wind shifts and changes in temperature. Refer to the maps on the inside covers to see where major fronts are located.

OCEAN CURRENTS

Ocean surface currents are driven primarily by the wind, and their direction generally corresponds quite closely to the prevailing winds. Steady, consistent winds have the greatest influence on surface waters, and the northeast and southeast trade winds are the forces behind the major tropical current systems in the Pacific, Atlantic, and Indian Oceans. The trade winds serve to drive water to the west in a large zone extending between about 25° N and S, except for a narrow band just north of the equator, where the equatorial countercurrent moves in an easterly direction. Currents along the margins of the oceans tend to flow either north or south. In general, warm currents (that bring warm water into colder regions) flow toward the poles along the eastern coasts of continents, while cold currents (bringing cold water into warmer regions) flow toward the equator along the western coasts. This pattern holds true for both hemispheres. In regions with monsoon wind patterns, ocean currents change direction with the seasons.

The cold currents that flow along western coasts in tropical and subtropical latitudes have a definite effect on the climate in these areas. Average temperatures are generally low, with small daily and annual ranges. There is often fog, but generally the areas (southern California and northern Mexico, Peru, and western Australia) are very dry; this is in part because they are on the eastern side of large high-pressure areas, which bring cool, dry air. Conditions are generally stable and not conducive to the development of low-pressure systems.

The warm currents (Kuro Shio off Japan, the East Australian current, and the North Atlantic's Gulf Stream) that parallel east coasts in tropical and temperate latitudes result in warm and rainy climates. These areas (Florida, the Philippines, Southeast Asia, and eastern Australia) are on the western side of the subtropical highs, with relatively unstable conditions. These currents create significant temperature contrasts with the cool air found over the continents in winter and provide energy for the development of low-pressure systems, which helps account for the quickly changing nature of the weather on the oceans' western margins.

For example, the East Coast of the United States in winter is the site of two major frontal zones. Two factors encourage frontal development: abruptly changing sea surface temperatures along the border of the Gulf Stream and the large amount of tropical water that's transported into middle latitudes. Warm ocean currents make large amounts of energy available to storms, and in fact two of the main hurricane tracks in the Atlantic are associated with warm currents. One track follows the warm waters through the Caribbean, while the other follows the warm waters off the northern and eastern coasts of Florida and the Greater Antilles. We take a detailed look at the major currents in each tropical region in part 5, Tropical Cruising Destinations.

TROPICAL DISTURBANCES

Low-pressure cells are the cause of most weather disturbances, and disturbances of one sort or another are more common than one might wish in the tropics, where they account for over 90 percent of rainfall. Knowing how and when the generally pleasant weather patterns may be affected by a disturbance is an important part of understanding tropical weather.

Convergence Zones

Convergence zones are low-pressure areas where wind systems converge. The major convergence zone is called the Intertropical Convergence Zone (ITCZ): the zone of low pressure centered about the equator where trade winds from the Northern and Southern Hemispheres converge. In the age of sail this area went by the much more evocative term of "the doldrums," and that pretty well describes the frequent state of the wind in the ITCZ. The ITCZ typically migrates north across the equator during the northern summer and south across the equator during the southern summer; it is farthest north in August and farthest south in February.

Look at the maps on the inside front and back covers. These show that the ITCZ can move as far as 25° N and 20° S, and the most extreme movement tends to take place over heated land masses, where the ITCZ merges with heat lows. Africa, Asia, and Australia all cause significant shifts in the position of the ITCZ, and these shifts are directly related to the development of monsoon wind systems.

Winds in the ITCZ tend to be light, though squalls and thunderstorms are not uncommon and can be severe. Conditions in the ITCZ tend to be at their worst when trade winds are strong and the zone is narrow (it can shrink to a width of 20 miles); when trades are light and the zone is wide (perhaps 150 miles), conditions are usually favorable. ITCZ conditions are also likely to be

Storm clouds caused by a depression within the South Pacific Convergence Zone.

unfavorable when trade winds meet at a large angle (as when southeast and northeast trades meet); conditions will be more benign if winds on both sides of the zone are more easterly.

The South Pacific Convergence Zone (SPCZ) is a secondary area of convergence that is most noticeable in the southern summer, when the northeast trades (and the related northwest monsoonal winds) penetrate the farthest south. The SPCZ is formed by moist, equatorial air carried south by the northeast trades that meets up with cooler, drier air from the southeast trades. When the SPCZ is active, squalls, rain, wind shifts, and generally bad weather are common in its immediate vicinity.

Convergence zones are not only notable for squally weather and a lack of wind, but are also the prime spawning ground for tropical cyclones.

Troughs

Troughs are elongated areas of low pressure existing both at the surface and aloft. On the surface, they're often associated with temperate-zone lows and fronts, but they can also form in a moist unstable airflow within the trade wind belt. Weak troughs may generate only light squalls and little change in wind direction, whereas an active trough extending out of a temperate-zone low will likely bring a more dramatic wind shift and precipitation.

Temperate-Zone Cold Fronts

Temperate-zone cold fronts will occasionally extend into tropical waters, bringing wind shifts, rain, and squally conditions. They can catch cruisers new to the tropics by surprise, because they come from the opposite direction from the prevailing trades. Extratropical cold fronts and their associated troughs of low pressure typically move against the trade wind flow (i.e., toward the east), in both hemispheres.

Typical wind shifts are different depending on whether one is north or south of the equator. Assuming you're between the depression and the equator, the following usually holds true:

▶ **IN THE NORTHERN HEMISPHERE**, winds veer with the passing of a front. The wind will veer from its normal direction of NE to E around to the S and then shift to between SW and NW. After passage of a trough, winds may remain in the N or NW for some time before returning to the NE.

▶ **IN THE SOUTHERN HEMISPHERE**, winds back as a front approaches and then passes. Here the dominant wind direction is SE to E, and this backs to the NE, shifting to the N and then NW as the front passes. Winds behind the front are usually from the W and SW.

Note that *backing* is a counterclockwise change in wind direction; *veering* is a clockwise change in direction. This is true in both the Northern and Southern Hemispheres.

Temperate-zone fronts that intrude into tropical regions are not usually associated with extremely strong winds, but they can be hazardous nonetheless, as such dramatic shifts in wind direction are otherwise fairly rare in the tropics. The dominant wind direction may shift over the course of a season, especially in areas affected by monsoon winds, but winds are otherwise reasonably consistent on a day-to-day basis. This situation can lull unwary sailors into giving less thought to the security of their anchorage than they should. It's not uncommon for anchorages that are very sheltered from the prevailing trade winds to be

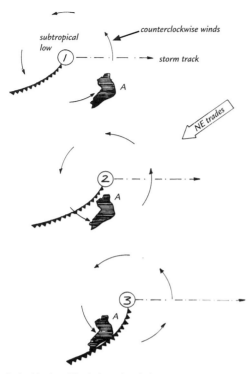

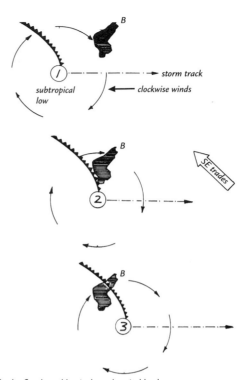

In the Northern Hemisphere the wind veers as a temperate-zone low passes to the north of tropical island A.

In the Southern Hemisphere the wind backs as a temperate-zone low passes to the south of tropical island B.

completely exposed to winds that accompany a front. In seasons with few fronts passing through, it's easy to become complacent about where and how one is anchored, with potentially disastrous results.

Tropical Lows

Strictly speaking, even many weak tropical lows are "tropical cyclones." That's because tropical cyclones are simply warm lows that have a definite, organized circulation. Fortunately, not all of them pose the same threat: the weaker stages of tropical cyclones include tropical disturbances (with no strong winds) and tropical depressions (with winds of less than 34 knots). Tropical lows can form in any season, but winter season tropical lows rarely develop into destructive storms; even most of those that form in the summer season don't mature into really dangerous storms, with hurricane strength winds. Most tropical lows originate within a convergence zone and are characterized by rotating winds around the center of the low (clockwise for those in the Southern Hemisphere, counterclockwise in the Northern Hemisphere), heavy clouds, and rain. In a winter low, winds can typically reach 35 knots; such lows may have a life span of a few days.

Remember that tropical lows usually move *with* the trade wind flow, and the pattern of wind shifts resulting from a tropical low will vary depending on your position with respect to the low. With a tropical low moving from east to west, the wind will veer north of the low and back to the south; the same rule applies in either hemisphere. Under some conditions (which are far more common in the summer months), tropical lows can develop into

Clouds building over an island, associated with a temperate-zone low.

destructive storms, referred to variously as hurricanes, typhoons, and tropical cyclones.

Easterly Waves

Easterly waves are troughs of low pressure embedded within the trade wind airflow over the Atlantic (although some persist across the Caribbean and on into the Pacific). They occur primarily during the summer season, have a wavelength of about 900 miles, and can extend vertically into the atmosphere to some 25,000 feet. Easterly waves are caused by extremely warm temperatures over the Sahara contrasting with substantially cooler temperatures along the northwestern African coast. The waves move generally toward the west in the lower trade wind flow across the Atlantic Ocean. Usual speeds are 10 to 15 knots, but some hum along at 20 to 30. On average, about 60 easterly waves are generated over North Africa each year, or about two per week during the hurricane season.

The weather usually exhibits a gradual but definite change (for the worse) as an easterly wave moves through. Winds increase and back from east-southeast to northeast, gusting to 45 knots in a fairly strong wave. Rain, line squalls, and thunderstorms can all be associated with the wave. As the wave passes the wind will revert to east or southeast but may remain strong for a day or more before easing. The zone of bad weather associated with an easterly wave may extend for 500 or more miles and may take several days to pass through an area. In addition to being associated with wind shifts and squally, rainy weather, easterly waves play a significant role in tropical cyclone development. We discuss this in greater detail below under Tropical Cyclones.

Squalls

As used by most sailors, the term *squall* is imprecise and describes a relatively short-lived disturbance that typically brings an increase in wind, clouds, and rain. But weather forecasters have a more precise definition: a sudden increase in wind speed by at least 16 knots, resulting in the speed rising to at least 22 knots and lasting for at least one minute. In some areas squalls are most frequently associated with landforms, whereas in others they may occur frequently in open waters. The majority of tropical squalls can be described as moderate (winds of no more than 30

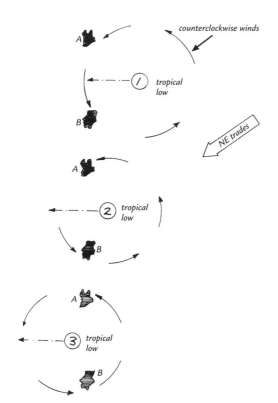

With the passing of a tropical low, winds veer over the northern island (A) and back over the southern island (B), shown here in the Northern Hemisphere.

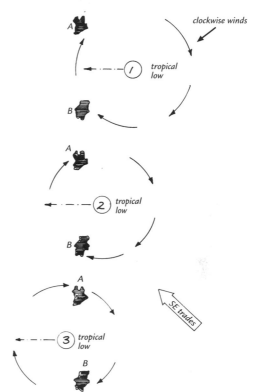

With the passing of a tropical low, winds veer over the northern island (A) and back over the southern island (B), shown here in the Southern Hemisphere.

to 35 knots) and rarely pose a problem for boats sailing offshore. But more violent and dangerous squalls do occur. These are found in conjunction with lightning storms (which at least provide a very obvious warning to sailors). Violent squalls with 50-knot winds *not* accompanied by lightning and thunder can occur and pose the greatest threat, as they may appear in the distance to be no different from a relatively benign 30-knot squall.

There is no hard-and-fast rule regarding how to cope with squalls. We've experienced few violent squalls and in general have had good warning that they were about to hit. Our strategy is usually to run off before the squall and drop the headsail. We'll put a reef or two in the main as well if conditions look a bit nastier than usual. The best

defense against violent squalls is to keep informed about the types that can occur in the area you're sailing and to prepare accordingly.

Thunderstorms

Thunderstorms are composed of rain-producing clouds formed by rising air. Thunderstorms feature squally, gusty winds, heavy cold showers or hail, and lightning and thunder. Thunderstorms form in various ways, but the vital ingredient is lifting of air in an unstable environment, so that the air being lifted is warmer than the surrounding air. The initial lifting force can be localized heating, hills or mountains, or a cool air mass (such as a front). Given the right conditions, air keeps right on rising until it's high in the atmosphere (some

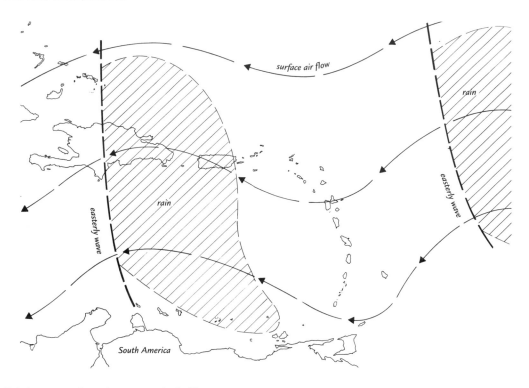

Typical movement of easterly waves over the Caribbean.

45,000 feet), forming a thundercloud. Rain dropping out of the top of the thunderhead gets caught up in the air rising from below, and the rain drops go up and down, get split apart, and generally are tossed around. All of that creates differences in electrical charges within the cloud (which is what causes lightning bolts). The wind that comes out of a thunderstorm is cold, because it's been cooled in the upper atmosphere.

Thunderstorms can and do occur throughout the tropics, but they're least prevalent in very dry areas. As a typical thunderstorm approaches, you'll notice the barometric pressure slowly falling, and the prevailing wind easing, while temperature begins to drop. This is followed by the approach of a dark line of very low clouds, accompanied by winds that may gust as high as 40–80 knots from the direction of the storm. Temperature will drop

suddenly, and as soon as the main thundercloud is overhead, there's a deluge of rain.

The direction in which a thunderstorm moves depends on the weather system with which it's associated. If it's part of a convergence zone or other tropical air flow, then it will move with the prevailing trades, or generally to the west. If it's associated with a frontal system, or extratropical low, it will move eastward. The latter type may be well known to sailors from the East Coast of the United States, where thunderstorms may form an eastward-moving line stretching several hundred miles. This is called a *squall line* and can bring wind gusts of 100 knots (though this is rare). Such a line may precede a cold front, with an accompanying shift in wind direction.

Strong gusty winds are not the only hazard associated with thunderstorms. Lightning can wreak havoc with electronics aboard, and a direct hit from

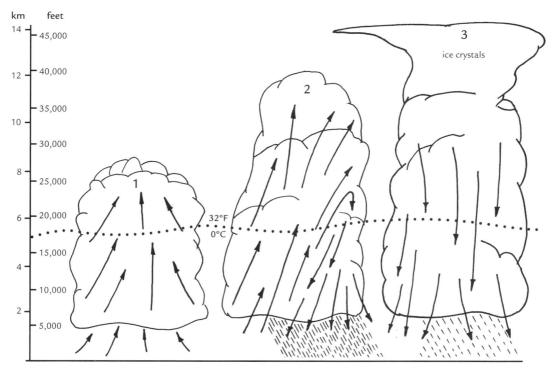

Cross section of a thunderstorm, showing three stages of development.

lightning can disable or sink a boat and severely injure or kill the crew. The best defense against lightning damage to your boat is to ground the mast and rigging properly (to a grounding plate or to an external ballast keel) in order to provide a direct path to the water should lightning strike. In the absence of such a direct connection, the current may find its own path, possibly traveling through bonding wires or other routes. Through-hull fittings have served as the ground on boats struck by lightning, and have been blown out of the hull by the electrical current.

In addition to grounding the rig, it's possible to reduce the chance of a direct hit. Lightning dissipaters are available that serve to reduce the concentration of positive ions around your masthead, theoretically reducing the likelihood of being struck. Electronics (such as a radio and GPS) can be at risk even if your boat is not hit directly. You can protect these to a degree by disconnecting any power and antenna wires. Some sailors go a step further and place their electronics in an onboard Faraday cage—usually, a large cooking pot with the lid on.

EL NIÑO, LA NIÑA, AND THE SOUTHERN OSCILLATION

Disturbances such as thunderstorms are fairly short-lived, but tropical weather patterns are also disrupted over the longer term, chiefly by the phenomenon known generally as El Niño. El Niño has long been used to describe a warm current that replaces the normally cold waters off the west coast of South America. Written records relating to the periodic event go back almost 500 years, and there is geologic

39

HOW FAR AWAY IS THAT THUNDERSTORM?

It's sometimes nice to know how far you are from a thunderstorm. You might be able to deduce that the storm is moving away or parallel to your course. Failing that, at least you'll have an idea how much time you still have to get things shipshape before the action begins.

You can easily calculate your distance from a thunderstorm by timing the interval between the lightning flash (which reaches you almost instantly) and the associated thunderclap. Simply divide the interval in seconds by 5 to determine the distance in miles; dividing the interval by 3 gives the distance in kilometers. For instance, an interval of 10 seconds means the storm is two miles away. If the interval increases, the storm is moving away. If it remains constant, the storm is on a parallel course. If it decreases, get ready.

evidence of past El Niños going back thousands of years. Today we know that the El Niño current is just one part of a much larger weather cycle that's linked to weather changes across the globe.

During "normal years" the trade winds in the Pacific blow with sufficient force to push the surface water layer westward, causing a buildup of warm water in the western Pacific around Indonesia (where sea level is typically some 18 in./46 cm higher than in the eastern Pacific). Cold deep-ocean water wells up along the South American coast to replace the water that is pushed westward, bringing with it nutrients and thus a prolific fishery.

During El Niño years the Pacific Ocean's easterly trade winds are lighter than normal. There is insufficient wind to properly power the "normal" west setting currents, which decline in strength, and water in the eastern Pacific becomes hotter than usual. This causes a reduction in the cold upwelling currents, and abnormally high rainfall along the west coast of the Americas. Countries in the western Pacific and Indian Ocean tend to experience droughts.

La Niña describes a pattern that is the reverse of El Niño, in which "normal" patterns are reinforced: trade winds are stronger than usual, moving warm water even farther west. The result is drought and cool temperatures in much of the Americas and heavy rainfall in northern Australia and Southeast Asia.

The El Niño–La Niña phenomenon has been linked by meteorologists to an oscillation in the air-pressure relationship between the Pacific and Indian Oceans. This has been measured and termed the southern oscillation index (SOI); it's a daunting term but easy to interpret, and it serves as another clue regarding the status of El Niño and La Niña. During El Niño events air pressure is higher than normal in the Indian Ocean and lower than normal in the Pacific. This results in a negative value for the SOI. During La Niñas, the SOI is positive, because pressure in the Pacific is high, and that in the Indian Ocean low. You may see these phenomena referred to as ENSO, for El Niño Southern Oscillation, a shorthand for the cyclic change in pressure, wind, and weather patterns associated with these conditions.

TROPICAL CYCLONES

Tropical cyclones are known by many names and ranked in lots of ways, but whether they're called *typhoons*, *hurricanes*, or *cyclones*, they all amount to the same destructive phenomenon. Tropical cyclones always form over water. There are several conditions that must exist for a tropical cyclone to develop:

▶ *WARM WATER*, above 80°F (26.5°C) at the surface

▶ *AN EXISTING SURFACE-LEVEL DISTURBANCE*, usually with pressure below 1004 hPa; the disturbance could begin as a heat low, an easterly wave, or as a low within a convergence zone

▶ *SIGNIFICANT CORIOLIS FORCE* (found only at latitudes greater than about 6° N or S)

The fact that they depend on warm water and surface-level disturbances helps to explain why

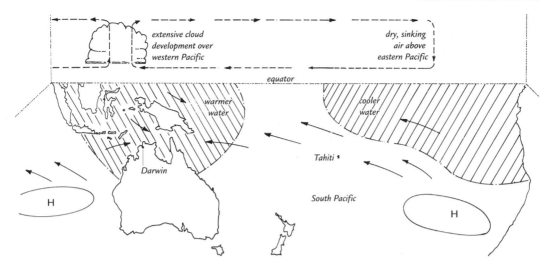

Typical atmospheric circulation and ocean temperatures across the tropical Pacific. The large high-pressure cell in the South Pacific produces strong easterly trade winds and west flowing currents across the Pacific. Temperatures in the eastern Pacific are cool, due to upwelling of cool water that replaces the westward moving surface water. The pool of warm water in the western Pacific promotes cloud and thunderstorm development in that region; air over the eastern Pacific is cooler and drier. The southern oscillation index (SOI), which describes pressure differences between Darwin and Tahiti, will be neutral, or zero.

tropical cyclones generally develop during the summer months. There are significant exceptions to this rule in the western Pacific and North Indian Oceans, caused in part by the alternating monsoon wind systems found in these areas. We take a close look at cyclone seasons in different parts of the world (and at how cyclone frequency is affected by the ENSO cycle) in chapter 7, Route Planning.

The illustrations on page 43 show a cyclone developing from a disturbance into a tropical storm.

Powering a Tropical Cyclone

Tropical cyclones are "fed" by heat released when water vapor condenses (see Air Temperature, Moisture, and Clouds, pages 29–30). As long as they stay over warm water, cyclones have an almost unlimited energy source. Moist air spirals in toward the low-pressure center to replace the rising air. Moisture condenses as the air rises, releasing heat and enhancing the rate at which air is ascending. This, in turn, speeds the rate of condensation. Wind velocity increases, and the entire process ac-

celerates. The cross section on page 43 shows the complex nature of a mature cyclone.

A tropical cyclone is classified as *severe* when wind speeds exceed 64 knots. They occur in all oceans except the South Atlantic. Less than 10 percent of all tropical depressions reach hurricane strength, and the number affecting any island group or region varies from season to season.

Tropical Cyclone Rules of Thumb

Tropical cyclones are anything but predictable, but their behavior does follow some general rules.

▶ **CYCLONES USUALLY MOVE FASTER** than the general surface air flow.

▶ **THEY TEND TO MOVE IN A WESTERLY DIRECTION** at 10 to 15 knots until reaching about 20 to 25° latitude, at which point they may re-curve to the east and toward the pole, often accelerating to 20 to 30 knots.

▶ **CYCLONES THAT DRIFT TOWARD THE EQUATOR** usually don't develop into severe storms.

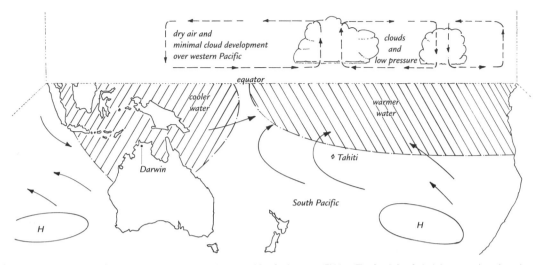

Atmospheric circulation and ocean temperatures across the tropical Pacific during an El Niño. The South Pacific high has moved south, and the trade winds are much weaker, and may often be replaced by westerly winds. The normally strong west setting currents are weaker as a result, and this allows warm water to collect in the eastern Pacific. Because less warm water is being transported westward, ocean temperatures in the western Pacific are lower. The normal atmospheric circulation pattern is altered, with greatly increased cloud and storm development over the eastern Pacific and droughts in the western Pacific. Atmospheric pressure will be higher than normal in Darwin, and low in Tahiti, resulting in a negative SOI.

▶ **CYCLONES DEEPEN MORE RAPIDLY** when a clear eye is present.

▶ **INTENSIFYING CYCLONES EXPAND** their radius of gale force winds at an average rate of 22 miles/day (42 km).

▶ **MATURE CYCLONES** may have an area of 150 miles or more in diameter in which the winds are 120 knots.

The speed with which a mature tropical cyclone can move makes it imperative that you not be caught unaware. We discuss strategies for coping with tropical cyclones (both in port and at sea) in chapter 9, Heavy Weather in the Tropics.

When Cyclones Are Likely to Develop

Some meteorological conditions are more likely to produce a cyclone than others. If an easterly wave pairs up with a bulge in the ITCZ to the north of the equator, then the resulting wind pattern can effectively "jump-start" a cyclone. About 60 percent of Atlantic tropical storms and minor hurricanes have their beginnings in easterly waves, whereas almost 85 percent of the intense (or major) hurricanes start in this way. Many of the tropical cyclones that occur in the eastern Pacific Ocean are also thought to have their origins in easterly waves that cross Central America and continue into the Pacific. Easterly waves that are slow moving are more likely to be the cause of an Atlantic hurricane than those that move through the Caribbean at higher speeds.

Even in the absence of an easterly wave, an active convergence zone can spur on cyclone formation, especially when these convergence zones migrate more than 6 or 7 degrees away from the equator. At these greater latitudes there is enough Coriolis force to start a tropical disturbance spinning, forming a tropical depression, which is the first stage in tropical cyclone formation. The accompanying photo shows the vast area that is affected by a mature cyclone, in this case Hurricane Floyd.

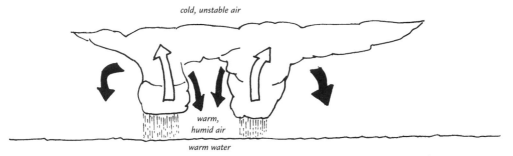

First stage of tropical cyclone development. White arrows indicate warm, rising air; dark arrows indicate cooler air. Comparatively cool air above a mass of tropical thunderstorms encourages air to continue to rise and large towering clouds to develop. This type of system is classed as a tropical disturbance if it remains active for 24 hours or more.

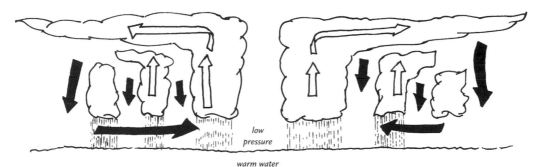

Second stage of tropical cyclone development. A low-pressure area forms at the center, which draws air in toward it. Air spreads out across the tops of the clouds. Moisture in the rising air condenses, releasing latent heat and contributing to intensification of the system. If a distinct eye forms and winds reach 34 knots or more, then the system is classified as a tropical storm.

A satellite view of Hurricane Floyd passing through the Bahamas.

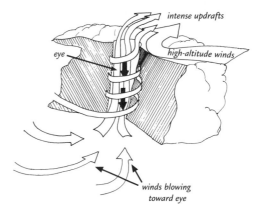

In this cross section of a Northern Hemisphere cyclone, winds spiral counterclockwise into the eye, producing hurricane force winds at the surface and intense updrafts. The eye is kept clear of clouds by cool air that sinks into the storm's core (black arrows).

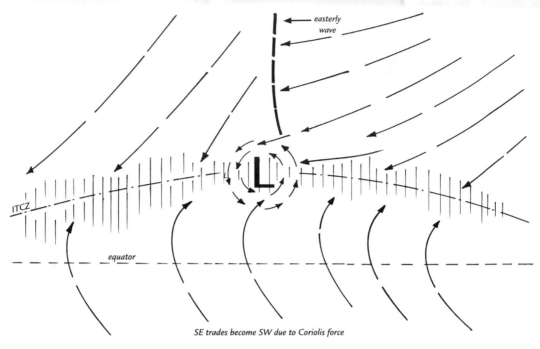

How the convergence zone and an easterly wave can help set a cyclone in motion.

STAGES IN THE DEVELOPMENT OF A TROPICAL CYCLONE

Storm Category	Maximum Sustained Winds (knots)	Wind Gusts (knots)	Barometric Pressure (hPa)	Storm Surge (feet)	(meters)
Tropical depression	25–33	46	980+		
Tropical storm	34–63	88	980+		
Tropical cyclone (also called *hurricanes* and *typhoons*)	64+	90+	980+ to less than 920	4–18+	1.2–5.5+
Cyclone Category					
1	64–82	115	over 980	4–5	1.2–1.5
2	83–95	133	980–965	6–8	1.8–2.4
3	96–112	157	965–945	9–12	2.7–3.6
4	113–134	187	945–920	13–18	4–5.5
5	134+	187+	less than 920	over 18	5.5+

PART 2

TROPICAL SEAMANSHIP

Chapter 4

Navigating in Tropical Waters

Navigation in tropical waters presents some unique challenges, and even skilled sailors from temperate waters will find themselves working harder, taking extra precautions, and acquiring new skills. Reefs are the tropics' principle navigational hazard. For sailors making their way among mud flats and sand bars, groundings are a fact of life and typically of little consequence, particularly on a rising tide. That's not true around reefs: stray onto one, and it's almost certain you'll sustain some damage. Reefs can be hard to see, and the vertical drop offs that make for wonderful "wall" dives using scuba gear won't register on your depth sounder until after you've run aground.

All these factors take on greater importance in those parts of the tropics where charts are old, and where islands and reefs aren't properly positioned with respect to latitude and longitude. This can render your GPS all but useless when navigating in relatively confined quarters. If you're sailing in a remote area, you can add to this mix a general lack of navigational aids, be it lighthouses, beacons, or buoys.

Dangerous reefs, uncertain fixes, and no markers—do these add up to a navigational recipe for disaster? Not at all, if you prepare ahead. Detailed charts are critical. Pilots are also very valuable. These publications supplement nautical charts with additional information on things like reefs, currents, and ports. But more informal information sources may be of equal worth. We've benefited greatly from discussions with local residents and other sailors, and from "mud maps" made on the basis of such talks. You'll need to outfit your boat and crew with some simple equipment that not all boats in temperate waters have: ratlines or mast steps are a must, for example. But most importantly, you'll have to be aware of the environment in which you're sailing and learn to navigate intuitively (if you don't do it already). Intuitive navigation involves using the natural signposts present in all coastal waters and doing so as a matter of course, almost unconsciously.

USE YOUR JUDGMENT

There are two basic elements involved in navigation: determining where you are and deciding how to go from there to where you want to be. If you know the waters in which you're sailing, then both of these elements are dead simple, and you needn't make use of any charts, markers, bearings, or other aids. Sailors have navigated this way for ages, and it's still the norm in many tropical areas. We've encountered many skilled navigators in the tropics who've never used a chart or compass or seen the need for them. They know the waters in which they sail, but they're also constantly aware of environmental clues that help confirm their location. We cruisers must carry along a battery of charts and pilots to make up for our lack of local knowledge. As useful and important as these references and our modern electronics are, they'll never substitute for our awareness. At times that awareness and our judgment—which constitute our intuitive navigation skills—will be all that's between us and the reef.

The best computer on board is the one in your head. Learn to use it and to trust it. If faced with a discrepancy between what your senses tell you and what the electronics indicate, stop to think. Time and again we've met sailors who failed to do this; in addition to causing them embarrassment, it often put them at risk as well.

We were anchored one day in the lagoon of a small isolated island in Tonga. Another sailboat came into view offshore, and we switched on our VHF, figuring they might put out a call to inquire about entering the narrow, somewhat tricky pass. Indeed, the call came, but their initial concern had to do with the fact that their GPS fix, when plotted on their chart,

Many local island navigators have never used a chart or compass, much less a GPS.

placed them on the opposite side of the island. We replied that our GPS fix did the same, and that the island was obviously incorrectly charted. That comment did little to reassure them, and they repeated their concern that the GPS said they were on the "wrong" side of the island. What could we say? We observed that they had indeed found the island and were on the leeward side, and that we were anchored in the island's only lagoon; those were the facts that mattered, not what their GPS said. Only then did they begin to make sense of what they saw before them and inquire about the route into the lagoon.

CHARTS AND PILOTS

The nautical chart is your most important information source. You should aim to get the largest scale charts (which cover the smallest geographic area) possible for any tropical areas in which you plan to do a lot of gunkholing. In addition, cruisers spending much time in an area will benefit from carrying a pilot for those waters, as these will often supply information your chart lacks, such as details about currents and tidal streams. We discuss pilots and cruising guides in greater detail in chapter 7, Route Planning.

When buying paper charts, originals are preferred because of their improved legibility and durability over even the best copies. Charts are costly, however; an inventory of new, original charts for a lengthy voyage can easily run to thousands of dollars. For that reason we and many other cruisers rely heavily on copies (see sidebar).

Most nautical charts are produced by government agencies, although a number of independent publishers offer charts as well (including, for example, the Imray-Iolaire series for the Caribbean).

Two sources offer worldwide coverage: the U.S. National Imagery and Mapping Agency (NIMA), and the British Admiralty. Many other governments offer charts for a region, or for their own waters; a number of small countries don't produce any charts at all. It can be difficult to determine which source offers the best charts for a particular area, unless you're already familiar with those waters. Before you buy a large number of charts for a region, do a bit of research on what charts are available, and check any cruising guides you have for the area, as many include chart recommendations.

Whether you're buying or copying a chart, make sure to check the date—not the date the chart was printed, but the date of the latest survey and update. For localized navigation a chart based on an old survey may work fine, and indeed some old charts contain a wealth of useful detail that has been omitted from modern editions. This is not surprising, as the concern of most ship captains today lies in avoiding reefs, rather than navigating through them. But the older charts may place islands far from their proper position; we've used charts with major islands plotted as much as 7 miles from their actual location. Even where the errors are not as large, there may be significant discrepancy between chart and GPS datum. These discrepancies may amount to hundreds of meters, which is insignificant in midocean, but can be critical when navigating reef-strewn inshore waters.

The problem stems from the fact that many different chart datums have been used over the years, but most are not compatible with the datum used by a GPS. Cartographers have faced many challenges over the years in representing the earth—an imperfect, elliptical shape—on a two-dimensional sheet of paper. To do so they've devised hundreds of geodetic datums, which define the size and shape of the earth and the orientation of the coordinate system by which we determine positions on the earth's surface. (The chart datums we're referring to are typically called "horizontal" or "geodetic" datums, to distinguish them from vertical datums, which refer to the tidal level to which drying and sounding depths on a chart are referenced.) The Global Positioning System uses its own datum, the World Geodetic System 84 ellipsoid (which thankfully is referred to simply as WGS84). Other countries are developing datums based on, and compatible with, WGS84, such as Australia's GDA94 and New Zealand's NZGD2000. But older charts will be based on other datums, and that's when discrepancies between the GPS readout and the chart arise. The chart may be an accurate representation of the waters in which you're navigating, but the coordinates for a geographic feature, as measured off the chart, may not match the coordinates as defined by WGS84.

Corrections can be applied to GPS-derived positions to make them compatible with datums other than WGS84. Most GPS receivers will make some corrections automatically, if you set the datum on the receiver to match that on your chart. Familiarize yourself with the various chart datum settings on your GPS and check the datum of your various charts. If your chart is based on WGS84, agreement

CHART COPIES

The cruiser on a budget, or almost anyone venturing far afield, and needing a large collection of charts, will want to consider chart copies. These are typically black-and-white photocopies, at either two-thirds or full size, and will cost a fraction of the price of originals. They are available commercially, or you can borrow a pile of charts and have copies made. If you order through a firm, make sure to ask first for a sample and to check how recent their originals are; the best use up-to-date, fully corrected originals. Be aware that although U.S. charts can be freely copied, most foreign charts are copyrighted and cannot be legally copied for navigational use. That doesn't mean you won't find someone willing to do it, but they're not likely to advertise their services.

When buying or making copies, we generally prefer full-size ones to reductions, as the latter are invariably more difficult to read. Print fills in, reefs and passes become less distinct, and what should be a simple matter of reading the chart becomes an exercise in frustration. We met one intrepid older couple from Europe who had navigated halfway around the world (including a passage around Cape Horn) using strictly two-thirds-size chart copies. The quality was so poor that a magnifying glass had become standard equipment for them, and even then there was considerable guesswork. Such charts may work fine in the open ocean, or along deep-water coastlines with few rocks or coral. But when we met this couple, they were sailing in New Caledonia's south lagoon, an area strewn with coral. We find that the slight premium one pays to obtain full-size copies is more than worth it.

DETERMINING GPS CORRECTIONS

It is possible to establish your own correction for charts that are not in agreement with your GPS datum. To do this, position your boat at a location that you can very accurately identify on the chart. This may be easiest at anchor and may require use of multiple bearings. Note the position as indicated by your GPS and compare this with the latitude and longitude of your location as indicated on the chart. The difference between the two is the correction that should be applied to any GPS readings before they are plotted on the chart. Note that corrections are reversed if entering waypoints in your GPS whose latitude and longitude were derived from the chart. With some GPS receivers it may be possible to enter this correction and let the black box do the calculating. Check your manual.

Be very careful when you make use of such a correction factor. The corrections you calculate will not necessarily be constant across a chart. There's no hard-and-fast rule for how far out a correction can be applied, as it depends on the accuracy of the surveys used to make the chart and the differences in the datums. The most frustrating—and po-

tentially most dangerous—situation occurs when a correction is accurate only for a small area of the chart. You're most likely to encounter this on very old charts or on small-scale charts (which cover a large geographic area).

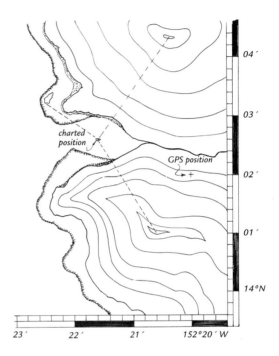

Determining a GPS correction. First, position your boat so that you can pinpoint your position; use multiple bearings if necessary. Here the charted position of the boat is 14°02′36″ N, 152°21′36″ W. Then record the position indicated by your GPS (in this case 14°02′ N, 152°20′ W). The difference between these positions is the correction; in this example it works out to 36″ of latitude, and 1′36″ of longitude. In this case both corrections should be added to the GPS reading, because the real position is farther north and west than the GPS indicates.

between the chart and the GPS should be excellent. If a different datum has been used, but that setting is available on your GPS, chances are the "fit" between GPS and chart will still be good. If no datum is listed, or your GPS does not include the needed datum, then GPS plots may be well off. In either of the latter cases, check the agreement between chart and GPS before assuming that all is well.

Electronic Charts

An increasing number of charts are available in electronic form, accessible with a laptop computer,

GPS receiver, or dedicated chart display. Electronic charts can generally be grouped in two categories. Raster charts are in most cases scanned copies of paper charts. They typically look like (and contain the same information) as the paper charts they're based on. Vector charts are made by separating the information typically shown on a chart into different databases. This approach allows greater flexibility in choosing what to display, and simplifies integrating different types of information. With some vector charts, it is possible to overlay other information (such as weather data) over the chart data. Vector charts are probably the way of the future, but are still in their early stages, and there currently is no standardization in format or accuracy. Do some thorough checking on the availability of electronic charts for remote areas and on the accuracy of those charts before deciding to invest in a particular type.

In our opinion, relying solely on electronic charts of any type is a dangerous practice. Electronics fail, and they fail with disturbing regularity in the tropics. Even the muddiest chart copy is better than a blank screen! We would advise all cruisers to always carry paper charts of the areas they cruise, in addition to any electronic versions. Unfortunately, doing so negates any possible cost savings that might come from using electronic charts, but we see no other alternative that will protect you from electronics failure.

AIDS TO NAVIGATION

The charts you obtain may or may not show many aids to navigation. Although most nations do a good job of maintaining their markers, these markers are often missing in the remote tropics, even when shown on the chart. Many tropical countries are poor and lack the funds and resources to install and maintain aids to navigation; we've found this to be true in much of the tropical Pacific. You may be lucky enough to find markers near major passes, especially if they're used by shipping, but more often than not, you're on your own.

Even when markers do exist, you can't assume they'll be lit, or that their placement will be accurate. Markers are often placed atop reefs, a practice that simplifies their installation. It also means you should not approach too closely, as there may not be deep, clear water up to the marker (see the accompanying illustration and photo showing the reef extending beyond the marker).

We've come across "informal" markers in use in many areas. They usually consist of sticks, put in place by fishermen to help guide them through channels when visibility is poor. These can be very helpful in situations where you'll be transiting the same passage a number of times, but they should never be relied on unless you have already made your way through a passage using your own reconnaissance. Keep in mind also that local boats may be of shallow draft.

VISUAL PILOTING

Tropical waters provide some unique visual clues that can help in determining your position, or in simply making sure you don't pile up on the reef. We've all seen photos of tropical anchorages with beautiful aquamarine water, and water color is certainly a primary

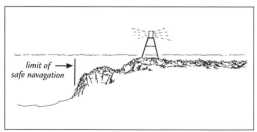

Beware of approaching reef markers too closely, as they often do not mark the actual reef edge.

indicator of water depth and the presence of reefs. Other less obvious clues can also be found, however; for example, the water surface may show ripples or wavelets in a pass, while none are present above the adjacent reef. Reefs exposed to breaking waves can usually be seen if there is any swell in the vicinity of a reef, and rough weather will often send a mist into the air, which may be visible long before the reef break.

You'll quickly become attuned to using water color as a visual depth sounder, but keep in mind that it works only in clear, sunny weather. With the sun overhead, a deep blue indicates deep water that is reef free. As the water becomes shallow the color will gradually lighten, becoming a greenish blue in sandy-bottomed water of 10 meters or thereabouts.

limit of safe navagation →

Isolated coral heads that are well below the surface, and therefore posing no threat, will be brown, but without distinct form. Coral heads that lie near the surface will also be brown but can be seen much more clearly. Large, shallow patch or fringe reefs will also appear brown in color but will often have a light green area adjacent to them, indicating a sandy bottom and a water depth of less than 2 meters—perfect for swimming but too shallow for most boats. These color differences become less distinct in overcast weather, and it's easy to mistake the shadows of passing clouds for patch reefs.

Regrettably, not all reefs are easy to spot. Reefs with a sudden vertical wall can be very hard to see, as the gradual color change that a slowly shoaling sandy bottom produces is not present. Be especially wary sailing in such areas when the visibility is poor. We've made our way through a pass off the Fijian island of Kandavu—guided by a friend who had negotiated it previously—unable to see even a hint of the shallow reefs on either side. Coral can also be very hard to see in areas with muddy bottoms, such as those found near mangroves.

The opposite problem—that of exceptionally good visibility—can occasionally prove a problem as well. We were once sailing through the pass of a small reef south of New Caledonia's Isle of Pines when we became convinced that we were about to run aground, solely because the water was so clear that the corals that lay some 15 feet below us looked to be all but breaking the surface! We reasoned this out and pushed ahead, but not without real trepidation.

Normally, you'll want to do everything you can to maximize visibility. The sun can either be your ally or enemy, depending on its position in the sky and the bearing to the reef. The best time for navigating reef-strewn waters is when the sun is high; be sure to time tricky passages for the hours between 10 A.M. and 2 P.M. Even then, it helps to have the sun either at your back or to one side, but not between you and the reef. The sun's position with respect to the reef becomes increasingly important in the early morning and late afternoon hours.

A reef marker and the nearby reef with the sun blocked by a cloud. The reef near and to the right of the marker is barely visible as indistinct darker patches, although the presence of very shoal water with a sand bottom is clearly indicated by the pale area near the horizon on the left side of the photo. Reef break is typically one of the best reef indicators, as shown on the horizon to the right of the marker.

You can improve your ability to make out the reef at any time of day by increasing your height above the water. Ratlines are the time-honored way to do this and still get our vote for the simplest and cheapest method of getting aloft (see photo page 55). Mast steps are a modern alternative but may not allow you to see easily around a headsail, depending on the point of sail and position of the reef. For this reason, you may want to fit ratlines on both port and starboard sides (see appendix 1 for a step-by-step approach to making rope ratlines). Fitting ratlines or mast steps should

Here there are no clouds or shadows, and the reef to the right of the marker and the pass behind it are clearly visible. Note that the reef extends well beyond (to the left) of the marker.

The three distinct colors indicate a deep pass (the dark foreground) that shoals abruptly to a sandy shallow (here the light gray) surrounding the sandbar (which shows as white, due to wavelets breaking atop the sandbar).

The dark patches in the otherwise pale water in the foreground are typical indicators of sea grass beds.

An abrupt change to a much lighter color usually indicates shoaling water; here the lighter band just below the horizon marks the transition between navigable water of 8 to 10 feet (2.5–3 m) depth and water about 5 feet (1.5 m) deep.

be a "must-do" item for your list of projects before heading into coral waters. Don't plan to stand on the bow pulpit or perch on halyard winches or atop the boom; these are poor substitutes. Boats have gone aground for lack of a lookout aloft.

Glare can be a major hindrance to good visibility, and we consider polarized sunglasses to be a worthwhile investment for anyone navigating by eye. We buy inexpensive "fishermen" versions, as they provide protection from the side as well as directly ahead. The price is such that you can keep a few pairs on board and won't cry if they're lost overboard or sat on. Beware of getting the cheap versions wet, though, as a good dousing causes delamination of the thin polarized film that is sandwiched within the plastic lens.

At times, despite your best efforts, you'll get caught having to navigate in coral waters when the visibility is poor. There are many possible reasons, but two common ones are sudden changes in the weather and trips taking longer than expected. How serious this will be depends on the circumstances. Always keep such possibilities in mind and have some sort of plan, or at least an idea of your options. Choices will include staying at sea (if you're offshore and need to enter a pass); anchoring and not moving on until visibility improves (if you're among reefs and can find a reasonable anchorage); and pressing on regardless (the least desirable option). Radar can help in some circumstances, if there's a large reef break, but it's of no aid in finding reefs when no waves are present.

EPs AND FIXES

The basis of navigation is the estimated position (EP). In most navigation texts, an EP is something quite specific, based on the course you've steered from your last known position and the distance covered. It's plotted on the chart with corrections applied for leeway and for the drift and set of any current.

Although such EPs are important and useful, focusing just on them gives short shrift to the EPs that we should all calculate in our heads as we sail. Good sailors constantly estimate their position, doing a little mental calculation to determine if they've sailed far enough to clear the reef or rocks shown on the chart, or if they'll be run down by the ship that's steaming toward them at 20 knots. Having a running estimated position in one's head at all times frees you from a lot of unnecessary chart work and means you'll always be able to subject a fix (discussed below) to the all-important "commonsense" test.

Modern electronics have allowed sailors in well-charted, temperate waters to become lazy. Who needs an EP when the GPS always gives a fix, shows a position on an electronic chart, and tells what course to steer? There are several reasons why everyone should maintain an EP at all times, even if it's just a rough one kept strictly in your head. That EP is the cornerstone of navigating intuitively; without it you become a driver on the highway, carrying on until a sign—or waypoint—tells you it's time to turn off. That EP is your insurance against electronics failure; black boxes do fail (it's happened to us more than once) and always at inopportune times. Most importantly from the standpoint of navigating in the tropics, by maintaining an EP as a matter of course, you'll be ready for navigation in remote areas, where chart and GPS may not agree and reliance on electronics becomes unsafe.

The slightly darker patches between the boat and the island indicate either sea grass or reef or rocks that are on the bottom.

Imagine you're sailing into reef-strewn waters. You keep a visual lookout to avoid plowing into coral heads and maintain a general heading, but you don't really keep track of where you are. All it takes is a few cul-de-sacs and some doubling back to lose a clear picture of the path you've followed and your boat's position. At that point, any course—whether ahead or back the way you've come—becomes true guesswork. You may be forced to resort to this in areas that lack good charts, but there's nothing to be

Searching for a reef pass in a rainstorm with dusk rapidly approaching. Not recommended!

Climbing a peak is another good way to get a handle on what's out there. This vantage point was sought out by Captain James Cook on one of his voyages of exploration in the 18th century.

gained from doing it when you don't have to.

In summary, the practice we advocate is to maintain an EP at all times in coastal waters. At first, you may want to make a habit of always plotting this position on the chart, though as you gain confidence you'll probably choose to make a plot less frequently. Use basic information, such as distance traveled and course steered, to establish your EP, and then refine it using any of the various information sources available in coastal waters.

Refining Your Estimated Position

You can use any available inputs to refine your estimated position, making it more accurate and useful. Once again, this can be done either in your head or on the chart, depending on the accuracy needed. Water depth can provide an easy check. We usually keep the depth sounder on whenever sailing in shallow tropical waters, and often a quick glance at the depth sounder and chart are all we need to tell us just how far on a particular course line we've come. Of course, there are times this doesn't work, such as when the depth is constant or where there are insufficient depths shown on the chart. So keep a lookout for other clues.

Bearings to an island or geographic feature are an obvious choice, and taking bearings is a basic skill that all sailors should be comfortable with long before they reach the tropics. We routinely make use of a hand-bearing compass, an item that should be carried on any boat voyaging in the tropics. Depending on where your steering compass is mounted, it may be possible to make use of it for taking bearings as well. The biggest problem you'll face in some areas is the lack of clearly defined (or clearly identifiable) features from which to take a bearing. If in doubt about the identity of the feature that you're sighting, go ahead and take the bearing, but don't rely on it unless you can confirm the result with a bearing on another physical feature.

A special type of bearing that can help in getting around the identification problem, and that's dead simple to use as well, is the range or transit. These work in the same way as the formal range markers that are used to assist in entering harbors and channels: by lining up two well-separated features. The only requirement for informal ranges is that both features are easily distinguished and both are charted. We often make use of islands for this purpose. When one island becomes visible or is hidden from view behind another, or when an island's edge aligns with another distant feature, then you can be certain that you're located somewhere on the position line that extends from the two features. No compass is required when making use of a range, but if you're in doubt about the islands or other features you're sighting, check the bearing. If it checks out, and the range lines up, then you know what you're looking at.

You can often use a reef sighting to help refine your position. If sailing in a large lagoon with isolated patch reefs, choose your course so that it takes you near, but still clear of, the reefs. The reefs then become your markers; keep track of them as you move along, and you'll know approximately where you are at any given time. Keep in mind that this strategy works only if visibility is good.

Beware of using buildings or settlements for position checking. Many tropical charts are based on old surveys that haven't been updated; a new edition may have been issued, with features such as markers added, but updates don't always extend to buildings or land features.

Fixes

At some point your EP becomes so refined it can be called a *fix*. When? When you're sure you know where you are. In saying this we need to clarify a few points: that all fixes aren't created equal in terms of accuracy, and that a fix needn't come from any particular source, or be recorded on the chart, to be of use. In fact, if you can pinpoint your position by simply looking around at the water, reef, and land, then you have a fix. Such visual fixes may not seem as accurate as those numbers the black box spits out, but as we saw from our Tongan island example, they are often far more useful. There is no hard-and-fast rule for determining how accurate a position fix should be, other than to say it should leave you feeling comfortable that you know where you are, and should be sufficiently accurate to allow you to keep out of danger. A rough approximation may be all that's needed when you're sailing in open waters with well-separated and easily visible islands and reefs. In contrast, a constantly updated and very accurate visual fix is vital if you're tacking up a narrow, treacherous pass. The latter fix won't be plotted on the chart, any more than the former needs to be, but you'll know where you are as you make your way along. Knowing how much work to put into your fix will come naturally as you develop your intuitive navigation skills.

Any fix should be subjected to a simple test: does it make sense? You should do this with fixes from a GPS just as well as those determined by your proximity to a marker or islet. Even if the GPS and chart

Climbing the ratlines is a smart strategy whenever you're navigating in unfamiliar or unmarked waters or are just uncertain about what's ahead (see text page 51). Here the abrupt color change near the island on the left is visible even from deck level.

datum agree precisely, it's easy to transpose figures when plotting, or for a parallel rule to slip. Having a reasonably accurate EP makes checking easy: you know more or less where you should be, and if your fix doesn't agree, it's time to double-check and to bring in other information if any is available. Ask this question about every fix, whether it's mental or charted, and you'll prevent a lot of potentially serious mistakes.

PUTTING IT ALL TOGETHER

Making a Tropical Landfall

If you're approaching an island or pass from offshore, you'll want a good fix well before making landfall. If you don't have a GPS, or if yours has packed up, then you should endeavor to take a star sight on the evening before and morning of your arrival. In either case, make sure to take into account any potential disagreement between the charted and actual position of the land you're approaching. This is fairly straightforward if such disagreement is noted on the chart, but keep in mind that it may not be. If you have doubts about the accuracy of the charted position of any hazards, navigate conservatively, staying well off any land or reefs. This is particularly important if you're approaching during the night and wish to heave to safely.

If it's an atoll you're headed for, bear in mind that they're rarely visible more than 10 miles out. Midocean reefs will typically be picked up only 2 or 3 miles away, when the breakers or the mist they throw up become visible. That distance will be further reduced in calm weather with no appreciable swell. Your ratlines or mast steps come into play here, as increasing your height above the water pays real dividends in visibility, as the figures in the following table show.

We're all eager to make landfall after spending time at sea, but don't push it. Night landfalls are potentially hazardous in the best of circumstances, and particularly so in the tropics, with a crew that may not be well rested. If it's rough, conditions near islands may worsen instead of improving. Islands disturb, and often enhance, the prevailing swell. Likewise, both wind and current commonly increase in the vicinity of an archipelago. This phenomenon is well known to sailors in Hawaii, where moderate northeast trades of 15 to 20 knots are often accelerated to become 20 to 30 knots between the islands. When such a wind is blowing contrary to the current, steep seas typically result. A tired crew in these conditions is prone to make mistakes, especially at night. Our advice is to play it safe and slow down or heave to rather than making landfall at dusk or in the dark.

HOW VISIBILITY INCREASES WITH HEIGHT ABOVE THE WATER

Height of Eye above the Water		Distance to Horizon
ft.	m	nm
3	0.9	2.0
5	1.5	2.5
7	2.1	3.0
9	2.7	3.5
12	3.6	4.0
19	5.8	5.0

Entering an Unmarked Reef Pass

Unmarked reef passes have struck fear in the hearts of sailors for generations. Consider the comments of the English navigator Matthew Flinders, who wrote in "A Voyage to Terra Australis" about sailing through passes in Australia's Great Barrier Reef:

> The commander who proposes to make the experiment, must not, however, be one who throws his ship's head round in a hurry, so soon as breakers are announced from aloft; if he do not feel his nerves strong enough to thread the needle, as it is called, amongst the reefs, whilst he directs steerage from the masthead, I would strongly recommend him not to approach this part of [the coast].

"Threading the needle" is an apt description of what it's like to negotiate some passes, but it's Flinders's reference to directing steerage from the masthead that is particularly important. Safe negotiation of reef passes relies more on good visibility than any other factor; as we've discussed, visibility in coral waters improves dramatically with height. It may be possible to safely transit some passes with only limited visibility, but these tend to be the exception.

Just how dangerous coral passes can be was brought home to us during a visit to Palmyra Atoll, located in the central Pacific just north of the equator. We negotiated the long pass in midday, with good visibility. We experienced no troubles and found ample depth and width through the pass. In the next few weeks, however, a sailboat, a small cruise ship, and a large coast guard inflatable all went aground. The coast guard and the cruise ship managed to get themselves off, but it took six of us working for a full day to extricate the sailboat from the maze of coral heads into which it had strayed.

The specifics of how a pass should be transited will of course vary, but there are some common features. Never commit to entering the pass unless you are absolutely sure you've correctly identified the entrance. Some passes are wide and distinct, whereas others may be narrow and broken up by patches and coral heads. Such indistinct passes can be hard to spot, particularly if conditions are calm or the pass is on the island's leeward side, as then there is no surf break to help alert you to the presence of reef. Passes on the windward side of islands may be navigable only in moderate weather, when the wave break is not excessive, but are generally easier to locate than passes that lack a break. What is the leeward side of an island with an easterly trade wind will become the windward side during a westerly wind, which can simplify or complicate negotiating passes, depending on the situation.

The best strategy is to proceed slowly. We've often been forced to probe slowly and carefully at the edge of a reef, staying in safe, deep water but close enough to the reef to be able to make out gaps and breaks. When you think you've found the pass, check the bearing with what is shown on the chart. If they agree, proceed cautiously, while maintaining a lookout aloft and an eye on the compass.

The slow and careful strategy needs to be modified in a rough windward pass with a large swell. In such situations you'll want your reconnaissance to be done slowly, but from a greater distance than you would use in a calm, swell-free area. Your lookout should not only try to ascertain the safe route but should also judge the hazards posed by the swell. When—and if—everything checks out, head into the pass and do so at speed, as you won't want to be a sitting duck for the waves.

Negotiating passes under power alone is a common but dangerous strategy. Many sailors seem to think they'll be better off with sails lowered, as they've got enough to do without worrying about the sails in the bargain. What they may not have

considered is how quickly they can be driven onto the reef should their engine die. By all means drop the jib if your course is to windward or if it is impeding visibility, but keep the mainsail up. It'll give you steerage if the engine quits, will steady the boat, and can give you welcome extra drive if a good breeze is blowing.

Pilotage in Reef-Strewn Waters

Pilotage is the art of taking your vessel safely through confined waters. Large ships take on specialists with local knowledge for this task, but for cruisers that's rarely an option. Instead we must become the specialists. Pilotage brings together all the skills we've discussed so far and focuses them on one primary goal: finding a safe passage through a given stretch of water.

Pilotage is easiest when you can determine a safe route using written information (from the chart, pilot, and so forth) and can follow that route without having to rely on visual sightings of coral. Pilotage is most difficult when you can't determine a safe route ahead of time and are thus entirely dependent on the skill and success of your lookout to see you through.

Let's take a closer look at how advance chart work can simplify pilotage, using an actual example: entering the lagoon of Papua New Guinea's remote Hermit Islands, which we did a few years ago.

The islands are mischarted, and although the GPS can help in finding the islands, it's of no use within the lagoon. To enter the lagoon we made use of a range, lining up the northern edge of Jalun Island with a distinctive peak on Luf Island (see illustration next page). Here's an illustration of the fact that ranges are only as good as your identification of the features you're sighting. Had we sighted the wrong peak—using the northern peak on Akib Island—we could have easily missed the pass and gone on the reef. To ensure this doesn't happen, take a bearing; in this case the false range, using Akib, bears 120 degrees, while the proper range, using Luf, lines up at 109 degrees. If we are sailing on the

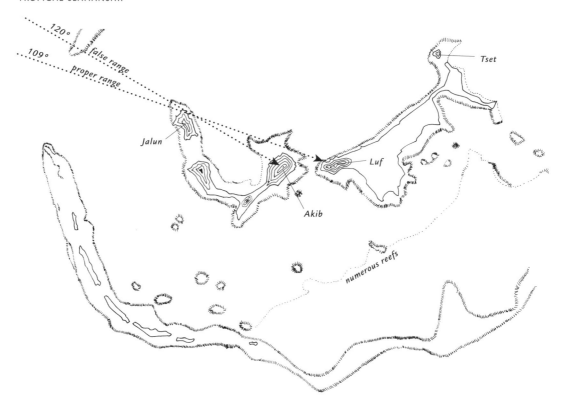

Navigating the lagoon entrance at Hermit Islands. When lining up two features in a range, take a bearing if there is any doubt about what you're looking at. Mistaking the peak on Akib for the one on Luf would be easy to do and potentially disastrous.

latter course and have the island and peak lined up, we know we're heading for the pass.

Once through the pass—which we can determine from the depth and by looking for any wave break—it's time to turn and head south. We want to set a course that avoids the small patch reefs in the lagoon, but keeps us clear of the reefs that fringe the central islands as well. If the visibility is good, we could sail close to the west coast of Jalun, making our turn to the south when we see the reef. But all it takes is a squall to make one wish for a better strategy. Here's where the use of bearings and steering marks comes into play.

On the chart we can easily determine courses that will keep us clear of both patch and fringing reefs; the difficulty lies in ensuring that we stay on those course lines, particularly if there is a current setting us in one direction or another. All it would take is a weak west setting current to have us heading directly for the patch reefs (see illustration opposite). We could take bearings to various islands to fix our position as we go along, thus checking for current set, but in reality there is rarely time for that when maneuvering in confined waters.

A better solution is to make use of a steering mark: something fixed, toward which we can steer, while on a safe course. In this instance, Leabon Islet is ideally placed to guide us safely south; what's more, because it's the last of a number of islets, it is simple to pick out (see illustration page 60). (It's easy to lose one's reference or become confused when steering for an islet that lies in the midst of a group.) If we re-

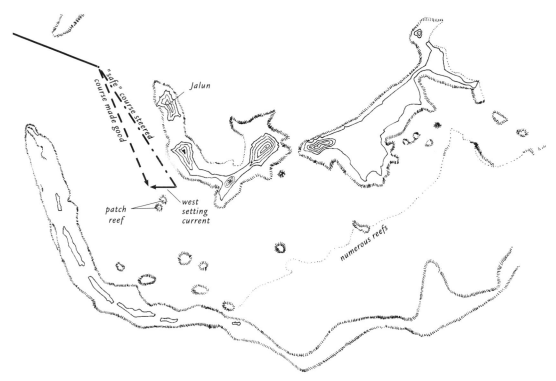

Atolls and island groups such as the Hermits often have strong currents. Reliance on just a compass course isn't wise, as currents and your boat's leeway can easily affect your actual heading, without your realizing it.

main on our initial course of 109 degrees until Leabon Islet bears 154 degrees, we'll be in the midst of a safe route south. If we now steer for Leabon, any change in our compass heading indicates we're being set by current. If the course increases, we're being set east; a decrease in the course indicates a westerly set. If we establish the outer edges of our safe route (151 and 157 degrees), we'll know just from a glance at the boat's compass if we're approaching the edge of the safe area. To correct, simply alter your heading slightly to place Leabon on the port or starboard bow; when it is once again possible to head for Leabon on a course of 154 degrees, then you're back in the midst of the safe zone.

Because they make use of your steering compass and boat's heading, steering marks and safe routes are very simple to use, and the chart work can be done before you enter a lagoon or other tricky area. If you set up safe routes that overlap, you'll always know if you're in deep water. Look at the last chart (opposite) of Hermit Islands. As we head south toward Leabon, there's no guess work about when it's time to turn east: it's safe as long our heading to Luf's southern tip is between 78 and 64 degrees. Once on that course, we can make use of a range (between Luf and Tset) to make our turn toward the anchorage.

Navigating through the lagoon at the Hermit Islands is vastly simplified by the presence of a number of islands and islets, many with distinctive hilltops. In many places, though, there are no islets, and the coast is low and rather featureless, offering few opportunities to establish convenient ranges. In those instances you may have to rely, at least in part, on reef sightings, though you shouldn't pass up any chances to establish a safe route, take a bearing, or grab a fix.

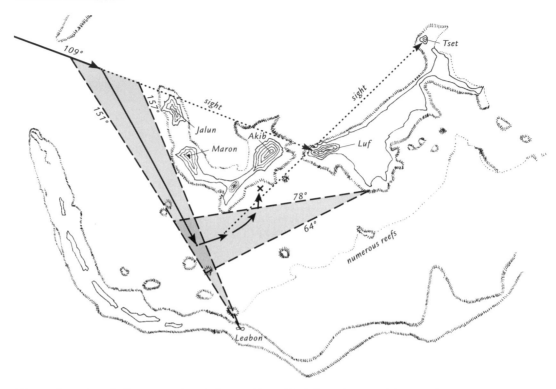

Using steering marks and safe zones to navigate the lagoon at Hermit Islands. This technique can help ensure that your course stays within safe limits, but doesn't require that you take bearings as you sail.

Navigating at Night in Coral Waters

In a word: don't. That's not to say we never do, but in general, we can't recommend it. The only reasonably safe exception is well-charted waters where navigational aids are in place and are lit. Even then, beware of putting yourself in a position where you are entirely dependent on your GPS, radar, or any other electronic aid. For example, the Australian coast is well charted. The "fit" between chart and GPS is good, and it's possible to negotiate even unmarked passes at night with the aid of a GPS. One would be in a pickle, however, should the black box fail in the midst of the exercise. As a result, we always choose passes that are marked and lit.

Even then, be wary! We entered Bali's marked and supposedly lit pass at night under sail, after our engine choked on the high-sulfur Indonesian diesel

(the problem proved to be a clogged injector). We'd transited the pass several times during daylight, so we knew the route, and were initially impressed by the fact that the lights on the markers were working. We made short tacks as we headed up the narrow pass, wanting to stay well clear of the reef to either side, one of which had claimed several fishing boats, a tug, and a barge in the preceding weeks. All seemed fine until a dark shape appeared just to leeward; we shone the spotlight and were confronted by a coral outcrop not more than 10 feet away. We tacked immediately, just missing the reef. We carefully scanned the channel with the light and found the problem: a marker whose light was not working, and that we had not seen as we sailed by. Another 10 feet, and we would have joined the fleet already on the reef.

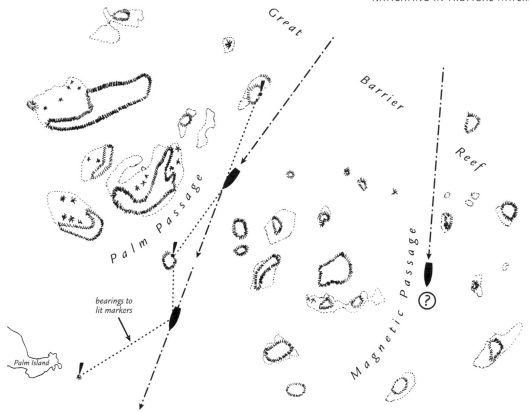

Transiting reef passes at night. Always choose a pass that has lit markers, even when sailing in well-charted waters with good GPS position fixes. A GPS failure in the midst of Magnetic Passage could result in real problems, while Palm Passage can be safely transited by relying solely on the markers.

Planning Ahead

It's easy to think of passage planning strictly as what one does before setting off on a lengthy voyage (as discussed in chapter 7, Route Planning), but the exercise is just as relevant for a single day's sail. The importance of planning increases in areas with unpredictable weather, tricky navigation, and limited shelter.

Begin by examining the charts for the upcoming trip and searching out hazards, potential anchorages, and areas that may have significant currents. It will pay to plot some safe courses in particularly dicey areas, as we just saw in the exercise above, and to plot and enter some GPS waypoints if possible. Check tide and current times and strength, as these may

dictate when you have to depart. Review any pilot books and cruising guides that cover your trip; the latter can be especially valuable when you're navigating with small-scale charts, which may be adequate while you're offshore but next to useless for evaluating potential anchorages.

Check the weather forecast, or the barometer and clouds, to get a sense for the weather you'll have en route and to see what conditions you're likely to encounter when it comes time to anchor. Keep in mind that an anchorage providing superb protection in one set of conditions may quickly become uncomfortable or dangerous if conditions change.

Given the importance of visual navigation in tropical waters, the amount of daylight and the orientation of any reefs with respect to your boat and the sun are quite important. Early mornings and late afternoons are not a good time to have to rely on visual navigation, and this can considerably shorten the distance you're able to cover in the course of a day.

Navigational Hazards

Tropical waters are home to some unique navigational hazards apart from corals. "Deadheads," or all but submerged logs, are common in many temperate waters where logging takes place, but we've never encountered so many logs—and often entire trees— as we have sailing in the waters off Indonesia and Papua New Guinea. Commercial logging activity in tropical countries is widespread, and enough logs

and trees end up in the rivers and ultimately the ocean to constitute a significant navigational hazard. We hit one at night off the coast of West Papua, putting a deep gouge in the planking near the bow. After that we tried to keep a "log watch" during the day, but there was nothing we could do at night, other than slow down so as to minimize damage should a collision occur.

Fishing craft and platforms can be a significant hazard, both close inshore and well away from land. The danger is greatest at night, because many small traditional vessels use no navigation lights. In addition, some moored platforms are unlit, and even during the day nets may be unmarked. Caution and an awareness of the habits of the local fishermen are your best defense.

Chapter 5

Tropical Anchoring

The image of the idyllic tropical anchorage is a powerful one. Peruse most charter company ads, and you'll be wooed by images of perfect anchorages where the water is warm, the sun always shines, and your major concern is keeping the beer cold.

Regrettably, there's usually more to it than that. Anchoring in tropical waters differs in several important ways from anchoring in temperate areas, and failing to heed these differences and prepare for them has caused many sailors and their boats to come to grief.

The most obvious and important difference is the presence of coral reefs. Reefs provide both beautiful and wonderfully sheltered anchorages, but coral will quickly abrade nylon anchor rodes, and can prove treacherous and unforgiving if the anchor drags. Remote tropical areas where marinas and most services are few and far between, call for a high degree of self-reliance. In such places the cruising sailor should be ready to cope with just about anything in the way of weather and anchorages.

That's not to say that anchoring in the tropics is horribly complex, or that it requires radically different ground tackle, though some additions to the temperate water equipment may be in order. What's most important is an understanding of the tropical environment; given that, you can plan ahead, making informed decisions on where to anchor and what gear to utilize.

ANCHORS AND GROUND TACKLE

Many tropical cruisers seem to think the answer to good holding is a heavy anchor. Although there is no doubt that choosing an anchor of suitable weight is important, it's not true that extra weight ensures good holding. What's often overlooked is the importance of matching the anchor to the bottom type. Despite what some manufacturers might claim, no anchor is ideal in all conditions. An anchor that holds your boat securely in gale force winds on a sand bottom may be all but useless if you're anchoring in broken coral or in the soft mud common to mangrove-lined inlets.

Selecting Anchors

Bottom types in the tropics include coral, rock, sand, and mud, and combinations of these. Solid sand and mud provide the best holding and should be chosen whenever possible. If you're using the proper gear and the anchor is properly dug in, you're unlikely to drag unless conditions take a truly

The C.Q.R. has long been the most popular anchor among long-distance cruisers.

dramatic turn for the worse. Loose or very soft sand and mud can offer problematic holding, with the boat apparently well secured but liable to drag if the wind builds to some 30 knots or more. Anchoring in rock and coral is the least certain. Your boat may seem to be securely anchored, only to begin dragging with a slight shift in wind direction. What's more, your anchor is much more likely to become hopelessly stuck in a rock or coral bottom, and if the anchorage is deep, retrieval may be difficult or impossible. Finally, anchoring in live coral can be extremely destructive: hundreds of years of coral growth can be wiped out in a single night by the action of your anchor and chain.

What anchors should you carry in the tropics? Plow anchors (including the venerable C.Q.R., the Bruce, and the Delta) are deservedly popular among cruisers in all latitudes, as they're effective all-around anchors, good in mud and sand. We've found the C.Q.R. to be poor at holding in rocky and dead coral bottoms; our Bruce wedges itself into crevices more easily, and so we tend to favor it in tropical areas. One-piece plows stow well on bow rollers but otherwise present some serious stowage challenges. Any plow is likely to have trouble getting to the bottom if there's a lot of weed or sea grass.

Though rarely seen on boats these days, the fisherman anchor is probably the best at penetrating weed and is also a good choice for rocky and dead coral bottoms. Fisherman anchors present an even bigger stowage problem than plows, and for that reason alone few boats are likely to choose a fisherman as a main anchor. They're excellent as a backup anchor, however, and can be deployed if conditions are such that one's main anchor refuses to hold. Stowage can be eased by choosing a three-piece version; our Luke anchor stows handily in the bilge, out of the way, with its weight contributing to the boat's stability.

Pivoting fluke anchors such as the Danforth and Fortress are very effective in clean sand and hard mud bottoms, but they may drag easily in very fine mud, and they're even worse than plows in coping with weed and sea grass. We've found them to be essentially useless in rock and reef. Many cruisers use them as stern anchors, and they stow easily on the stern rail.

A "pick" or grapnel is a good choice for very rocky or coral bottoms for two main reasons: their low cost makes jettisoning the anchor more acceptable should it become hopelessly stuck, and they do less damage to the bottom than other types of anchors. A pick, however, belongs in the class of "lunch hooks": good for a brief stop, with crew staying on board, but not suitable for an overnight stay.

Carry More than One

The best way to ensure that you can anchor securely in a variety of bottom types is to carry more than one anchor. Small coastal cruising boats—those around 20 to 25 feet (6–7.6 m)—will require a minimum of one working anchor and a "kedge." The kedge is usually a bit smaller than the working anchor, and is what you'll use whenever you need to set an anchor from the dinghy (as you would if you ran aground). The kedge will preferably be of a different type than the main anchor. A good choice for the tropics would be a plow for the main anchor and a smaller plow of a different type for the kedge. Long-distance cruising boats, or small boats that venture far afield, should carry two different types of working anchors and a kedge. This ensures a remaining working anchor in the event that one is lost, gives a choice of anchors to use on different bottoms, and increases anchoring options in bad weather or tricky anchorages.

We carry three working anchors and a kedge. The anchors are all of different types: a fisherman, Bruce, C.Q.R., and a Mason plow, allowing us to select an anchor for almost any bottom type. Being of similar size and strength, the rodes and shackles for each are interchangeable. All the anchors are between 35 and 45 pounds (16–20 kg), so they're easily handled, be it in the water, on deck, or in the dinghy. We don't carry a storm anchor due to the stowage and handling problems that come with a 70- or 80-pound (30–36 kg) hunk of metal. Instead, we rely on using our four anchors in combination. Set properly, they'll deliver incredible holding power and can be used to hold our boat securely even with wind that clocks around quickly from different directions (as can happen during a hurricane). Finally, by placing reliance on separate anchors and rodes, we have invested in considerable "chafe insurance," chafing of anchor rodes being a major cause of problems during tropical cyclones and other severe storms.

Sizing the Anchor

Sizing the working anchor begins with a simple "rule of thumb." Plow-type anchors (such as the C.Q.R., Delta, and Bruce) should generally weigh about 1 pound/foot (1.5 kg/m) of boat length. Pivoting-fluke anchors (such as the Danforth) can be slightly lighter, say 1 pound/foot (1.5 kg/m) of waterline length. Fisherman or yachtsman anchors should be heavier, about 2 pounds/foot (3 kg/m) of waterline length. Select grapnel or pick anchors on the basis of overall size rather than weight. An inch of anchor length for every foot of waterline length (or 10 cm of anchor for each meter of waterline length) is about right. This simple approach to anchor selection is surprisingly effective,

What we're all after. Nomad at anchor in a sheltered lagoon that makes a perfect swimming pool. The depth is less than 10 feet (2.5 m).

The Bruce is our favorite for most tropical anchorages.

65

Fisherman and Delta anchors. It's wise to always have more than one type of anchor aboard.

but whenever possible, check the results against wind loadings and actual anchor holding figures.

The loads placed on anchor and rode are a function of current, waves, and wind. All loads vary with the type and size of your boat. If you're using enough scope and an anchor snubber (we discuss both below), wind loadings become the most significant factor in most situations. Many anchor manufacturers and some independent sources have conducted anchor-holding tests, and their figures can be compared to the loadings. Beware that anchor-holding ability—and the holding figures manufacturers and others come up with—can vary dramatically with the bottom characteristics.

Wind Loading

The loads placed on the anchor due to wind vary with a boat's windage: boats with low freeboard and cabin and a single mast will have lower wind loadings than boxy ketches or schooners. Wind pressure varies as the square of the wind speed, which is why the estimated wind loads for our 35-foot (10.6 m) sloop jump so alarmingly with higher wind speeds: 225 pounds (100 kg) in a 15-knot breeze becomes 900 pounds (405 kg) in 30 knots of wind and 1,800 pounds (810 kg) when it pipes up to 42 knots.

The accompanying table is based on estimates of wind drag developed by the American Boat and Yacht Council. If your boat deviates considerably from the average, you may wish to adjust the figures slightly, up or down.

Day boats and small trailer sailors may wish to base loads on 30-knot winds, but cruising boats should use the 42-knot wind loadings for their working anchor. Some long distance cruisers use the 60-knot wind figures, but we suggest using those figures only for a storm anchor and keeping the working anchor and rode to a more manageable size.

Selecting Ground Tackle

Once you've selected the anchor or anchors suitable for your boat, be sure to match them with appropriate ground tackle. The table of projected loads is quite useful when selecting the line, chain, and shackles to use with your chosen anchor. There's not much point in carrying an anchor that will provide 2,000 pounds (900 kg) of holding power if your rode can't take the strain. The table lists actual loads, incorporating no safety factors. Make sure to select equipment based on the safe working load, not the breaking strength. Never buy shackles, swivels, or any other anchor gear if breaking strength or safe working load figures are not available. You might save a few dollars, but buying inferior gear places your boat and perhaps your life at risk.

Using our own boat as an example, we'd select the anchor and rode as follows. Boat length is 35 feet (10.6 m), so according to the rule of thumb, the weight of the working anchor (plow) should be $35 \times 1 = 35$ pounds ($10.6 \times 1.5 = 16$ kg). The table shows a loading, in winds of 42 knots, of 1,800 pounds (818 kg). The safe working load (SWL) of your rode should equal or exceed this. This calls for 5⁄16-inch (8 mm) chain, with an SWL of 1,900 pounds (864 kg) or 5⁄8-inch (16 mm) line, whose SWL is 2,440 pounds (1,109 kg). Shackles can be the weak link: a 5⁄16-inch shackle has an SWL of only 1,500 pounds (682 kg), so a size

ANCHOR LOADINGS FOR VARIOUS
BOAT LENGTHS AND WIND STRENGTHS

Boat Length		15 knots		30 knots		42 knots		60 knots	
ft.	m	lb.	kg	lb.	kg	lb.	kg	lb.	kg
10	3	40	18	160	72	320	145	640	290
15	4.5	60	27	250	113	500	227	1,000	454
20	6	90	41	360	163	720	327	1,440	654
25	7.5	125	57	490	223	980	446	1,960	890
30	9	175	80	700	318	1400	636	2,800	1,273
35	10.6	225	102	900	409	1800	818	3,600	1,636
40	12	300	136	1,200	545	2,400	1,090	4,800	2,180
50	15	400	182	1,600	727	3,200	1,455	6,400	2,910

larger (⅜ in., SWL 2,000 pounds /10 mm, 900 kg) should be used. (The pin of an anchor shackle will typically fit chain one size smaller.) It's good practice to fit a swivel between the anchor and rode; this should also be one size larger than the chain.

Is it prudent to use the wind loading at 42 knots? What happens in a severe tropical storm, where winds may equal or exceed 60 knots? Decide first if you may ever have to anchor in such conditions. Most coastal cruisers need not worry about these extremes, but ocean voyagers should be prepared to cope with such conditions. Now base your decision on your anchoring strategy. If you intend to place primary reliance in storm conditions on one large anchor, the rode should definitely be sized to cope with 60-knot winds. If you'll be relying on two or more anchors used in combination on separate rodes, then the rode for those anchors can be based on the lower 42-knot figures.

Most tropical sailors select chain for the rode on their primary anchor, and many carry enough chain for a second and third anchor as well. Chain is a wise choice due to the high risk of abrading line on coral. In addition, by using chain you cut the amount of rode needed by half, as you can anchor on chain using only half of the 7:1 scope needed when anchoring on line. The down side of chain is the weight; some tropical anchorages are deep—75 feet (23 m) and more—and this can mean carrying and using 250 or 300 feet (75–90 m) of chain for just one rode. The 5/16-inch (8 mm) chain we use weighs about 1.2 pound/foot (0.55 kg/m). Two rodes of 300 feet (90 m) weigh in at over 700 pounds (318 kg), not to mention the anchors themselves. How do you keep your boat from sinking under all the weight?

The only way is by reducing the amount of chain you carry. We've come up with a compromise solution, based on the conflicting needs of good abrasion resistance, reasonable weight, and the ability to anchor in deep water. The primary rode consists of 160 feet (50 m) of chain spliced to 330 feet (100 m) of line (see appendix 1 for splicing instructions). In anchorages that are 45 feet (14 m) deep or less (and that's most of them), we anchor using all chain. If really bad weather threatens, or the water is deeper, we

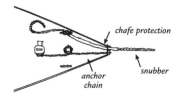

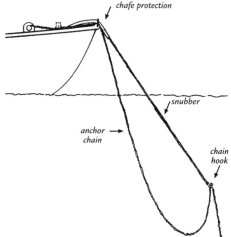

An anchor snubber eases shock loads and is a must when anchoring on all chain.

pay out all of the chain as well as some line. How much line? In light conditions, we limit the length of line to the depth of water, thereby keeping the line clear of the bottom. When the wind pipes up, we pay out additional scope, to equal about 5:1.

For example, if the winds are light, and the anchorage is 70 feet (21 m) deep, we'll pay out all our chain and some 70 feet (21 m) of line as well. If the wind gusts up, we might pay out another 120 feet (37 m) of line, for a combined length of line and chain of 350 feet (107 m), and a scope of 5:1. This still leaves 140 feet (43 m) of line in the anchor locker in case things get really nasty; with all 490 (150 m) feet of chain and line out, the scope would be 7:1. Having a splice between chain and line makes paying out or taking up rode a very simple operation.

Whether you decide to rely on all chain or a chain and line combination for your primary rode, don't stop there; make sure you have a second anchor rode that's ready to go with little or no preparation. If you can carry the weight, all chain is fine; alternatively you can set up the rode for the second working anchor as we described above. We've opted for further weight savings and use a short length of chain (about 30 ft./9 m) spliced to 250 feet (75 m) of line. We carry several additional short lengths of chain that can be shackled to this or used in conjunction with yet more line for our other anchors. Using a second anchor rode of almost all line hasn't proven a problem after years in the tropics, and the weight (and cost) savings are considerable.

Additional Gear

Although anchors and rode constitute the essence of your anchoring gear, there are some additional elements that are also vital. First among these are the cleats or bitts to which your rode will be secured. Always use one of the above, and never rely on your windlass to secure your anchor line or chain. Ensure the attachment point is as strong as you can make it. If you rely on deck cleats, they should be large and bolted through the deck, with large backing plates below. The bitter end of the rode should be equally well secured, somewhere in the chain locker, preferably by a 10- or 20-foot (3–6 m) length of three-strand nylon rode. This can be cut in an emergency but will also act as a built-in snubber.

An anchor snubber is a must for those who anchor on all chain. The function of the snubber is to ease shock loads on your rode, which can be very high when anchored in rough conditions, especially if your chain has accidentally wrapped itself around a coral head, which then reduces scope. The snubber is simple, consisting of a nylon line (equal in size to your rode) that is secured to the chain by means of a rolling hitch or chain hook. The line should be at least 20 feet (6 m) long. Ours is now 40 feet (12 m), after a shorter snubber broke while anchored off Minerva Reef—a midocean reef south of Tonga—with waves breaking over the bow. We

PREPARE FOR THE WORST

Cruising is unpredictable. That's one of its attractions, but also one of the dangers, and a vital part of good seamanship is being able to handle the unexpected. This is as true in anchoring as in any other aspect of seamanship. If you fail to anticipate what *can* happen—as opposed to what you think *will* happen—you can lose your boat. One couple lost theirs in the South Pacific not long ago as a result of not preparing for the unexpected.

Like many tropical anchorages, this one was reasonably sheltered from the prevailing (southeast) trade winds but was very exposed to the west. One of the anchorage's attractions was the many reefs in and around the bay, which offered fine snorkeling, but these also served to make it a very dangerous lee shore.

As we saw in chapter 3, depressions of midlatitude origin are not regular occurrences in the tropical South Pacific, but they do come through a number of times in the course of a winter cruising season, usually accompanied by westerly quadrant winds up to 35 knots. Such a front came through unexpectedly in the middle of the night and caught this couple off-guard. The formerly sheltered anchorage turned rough. As a consequence, their nylon anchor snubber broke. The chain was made fast—not on a samson post, but on the windlass. The shock loads broke the chain brake, and as a result the chain paid out. The bitter end of the chain wasn't properly made fast in the locker, and so it went overboard. All of this happened quickly, so they weren't able to deploy another anchor before hitting the reef—not surprisingly, given the tight anchorage, their boat went aground and was a total loss. They were lucky to escape serious injury.

The incident suggests a number of lessons. Just because the local weather bureau hasn't forecast a depression, don't assume there isn't one on its way. Inspect your gear, such as anchor snubbers, and replace it early. Never forget to secure the chain independently of the windlass, on a very strong cleat or samson post. And always secure the bitter end of the chain.

But there's a bigger lesson as well, one that applies to any facet of cruising: prepare for the worst. This doesn't mean you should never make use of a less-than-perfect anchorage; cruising would be pretty dull if you did that. But always consider what could happen if things go wrong, and prepare yourself accordingly. How you do this depends on the situation, your boat, and your crew. It demands that you carry along sufficient gear to allow you to anchor safely and securely in a wide range of conditions. But more than anything, it requires that you think things through and consider the "what ifs." Make a habit of doing that, and you'll vastly reduce the odds of having your boat end up on the reef.

---

typically pay out only 8 or 10 feet (3 m) of line, but in rough conditions easing out another 20 feet (6 m) does wonders. Make sure you secure the chain to your bitts or cleats independently of the snubber, in case the latter should break. The crew of a yacht failed to do this in Fiji when we were there, and the boat ended up as kindling on the reef.

The rough conditions that call for use of a snubber can also have your rode jumping off the anchor roller or out of the bow chocks. This can result in damage to deck, bowsprit, and gear, as well as greatly accelerated chafe. The remedy is simple: rollers should be fitted with bails, and chocks should be closed to ensure that the rode stays where it should. Don't forget to add some chafe protection—leather or heavy hose—at the point your line or snubber passes over the chock or through the roller.

A small buoy and about 70 feet (21 m) of ¼-inch (6 mm) polypropylene line is your final piece of essential gear. This is a trip line that can be attached to the crown of the anchor and used to help free it should the anchor become jammed in rocks or coral. It can be left in the locker if you're sure the bottom is good mud or sand, but if there's a chance it's foul, rig the trip line.

TROPICAL ANCHORAGES

There's an infinite variety of tropical anchorages, but we'll focus on the three major types: reef anchorages, mangrove anchorages, and river anchorages.

Reef Anchorages

Anchorages in reef environments are the ones you dream about during those long northern winters;

The anchorage at Lizard Island on Australia's Cape York Peninsula. Boats have anchored over the largely sand bottom, leaving enough space to swing without hitting either each other or the large coral patch on the right side of the bay. The dark patches near the beach are shadows caused by clouds. A 180-degree change in wind direction (as would accompany a temperate-zone front) would place these boats on a lee shore with no protection from wind and swell.

they've got the great sandy beaches, swaying palm trees, and beautiful corals and fish. They're also potentially the most treacherous.

In chapter 2 (Tropical Environments) we discussed the various forms of coral reefs, and each presents its own anchoring challenges. Lagoons are typically found within atolls or behind a barrier reef. Lagoons can form ideal anchorages in reasonable weather, but the quality of the anchorage depends on how much protection they afford from sea and swell. If a lagoon is large, or its reef is poorly developed, you'll need to find shelter from wind waves by anchoring behind an islet or patch reef, or by anchoring near the reef in the upwind end of the lagoon. Small lagoons whose reefs provide ample protection enable you to anchor in any area where depths and reef growth allow. Lagoons require special care when dropping the hook, as even seemingly open and clear lagoons often contain patch reefs and isolated coral heads. The bottom within a lagoon can vary from coral rubble to sand and occasionally mud; sand is naturally preferred, with mud a second best.

Patch reefs that lack a lagoon often provide a suitable anchorage in their lee, but the same concern with coral heads and small patches applies. In many respects, patch reef anchorages can be judged by the same criteria you would use for anchoring behind a small island: Is the reef oriented properly to block the prevailing swell? Is there an area of moderate depth in which to anchor? The quality of a patch reef anchorage depends also on how extensive coral growth is, with poorly developed reefs often providing marginal protection at high tide.

Fringing reefs can provide a suitable anchorage, but only if they have a relatively gentle slope; steeply sloping reefs will usually require the use of two anchors, or an anchor and a line ashore, two techniques we'll discuss below. You'll also often find yourself anchored in a bay that has fringing or patch reefs within it.

Anchoring in lagoons or off patch or fringing reefs differs from anchoring in other environments in several ways. First, if there is a narrow pass or numerous coral heads between the anchorage and open water, leaving the anchorage may be feasible only in good visibility (we say more about this below). In addition, the treacherous nature of coral means that a wind shift can place you on a very dangerous lee shore. Keep a careful eye (and ear) on the weather whenever anchoring in a reef environment.

Mangrove Anchorages

The threat of bad weather normally has tropical sailors seeking more sheltered anchorages than what most reef environments are able to provide. More

A secure mangrove anchorage.

Rivers can provide secure and sheltered anchorage, but beware of flooding during periods of heavy rain. The alternating current direction in tidal rivers can lead to a fouled anchor, so consider using two anchors, set 180 degrees apart, both off the bow.

often than not, this means a bay or inlet that's lined by mangroves. The mud bottom typical of mangrove areas is often a welcome change for the sailor who has been coping with coral-strewn lagoons. Care is needed, however, as coral is sometimes found at the edge of a mangrove-lined inlet, and the mud bottom can make this coral very difficult to see. Occasionally, one will also encounter coral patches within a mangrove anchorage. Be careful when approaching the edge of mangrove inlets; use all the clues we discussed in chapter 4 (Navigating

in Tropical Waters) to determine if a fringing reef is present, and keep a close eye on the depth sounder.

River Anchorages

Tropical rivers can often provide good anchorage, and even tidal rivers will be free of coral, due to the presence of freshwater. Slow-moving rivers should present little challenge when anchoring, but when currents in tidal rivers reach several knots or more, special care should be taken. The direction of the current flow in tidal rivers typically changes several times per day, and the anchor can easily foul as a result. The solution is to use two anchors, with both rodes led to the bow, a technique we discuss below. Don't make the mistake of using a bow and stern anchor in a fast-flowing river. If one anchor drags, the resultant force on the anchor rode escalates rapidly as the boat moves sideways to the current. We

lost an anchor, and almost suffered serious injury, while anchored like this. Rivers and creeks can offer shelter in a cyclone or really severe storm conditions, though flooding can be a problem, so inlets without streams or rivers at their head are preferred. We discuss cyclone holes further in chapter 7 (Route Planning).

ANCHORING

Evaluating an Anchorage

Our first reconnaissance of an anchorage usually takes place long before we arrive, and often before we set sail. A detailed chart is the best aid, and safety the primary concern. Consider if the potential anchorage is exposed from a particular direction, and check the forecast, the sky, and the barometer to determine if adverse weather is likely. With a lagoon or other reef anchorage, check to see if you'll be able to leave the anchorage at night should a storm hit. We've anchored in many reef situations where a night departure was impossible, but we did so only when the weather forecast was favorable, the anchorage very sheltered, and the holding good.

If you decide to anchor in an area that you can't leave in the dark, consider putting out a second anchor; be sure to do this if you are uncertain about the weather. A second anchor won't prevent an anchorage from turning roily and uncomfortable, but it can keep your boat from swinging onto the reef if the wind shifts, and affords you peace of mind.

You may also want to take GPS coordinates at various points as you enter the anchorage—for instance, in a pass or at a critical turning point as you avoid patch reefs. If the chart is of an appropriate scale, and the datum is WGS84, you can take the waypoint coordinates from the chart, but we find it more reliable to establish waypoints from the GPS when entering an anchorage. You'll need to weigh many factors before attempting to leave a tricky anchorage at night—and a strong argument can often be made for staying put. But taking

waypoints as you enter may give you an extra option if things turn foul.

As you approach or enter the anchorage, check to see if there's room for your boat to swing without hitting rocks, coral, or other boats. You may need to make some circles with your boat, while keeping an eye on the depth sounder. If you don't have room to swing, either choose a different anchorage or use multiple anchors to reduce your boat's movement.

Choosing Your Spot

Once an anchorage passes the safety test, it's time to search out a reasonable depth and drop the hook. In river anchorages you may want to select an area of least current, while in mangrove inlets the main concern is to ensure the boat will be free of any fringing coral. In coral lagoons and other reef anchorages you should endeavor to drop the hook in sand, away from coral, whenever possible. To zero in on the clearing, make sure the boat has come to a complete stop before you let the hook go. There may be times when you want to send a crew member over the side with mask and snorkel to check the condition of the bottom. On deck, it's quite easy to mistake a dark patch of sea grass for coral, and by doing so you may pass up what would have been a superb anchorage.

What's usually a simple exercise in an empty anchorage can be truly frustrating in a crowded one. We make a practice of visualizing each anchored boat as a large circle whose diameter is determined by the amount of scope they're likely to have out. When choosing your spot, try not to intrude on the circles of other boats. Anchorages fill up quickly this way, but one also sleeps well knowing there's no chance of hitting another boat. Using a buoy and trip line helps in this regard, as they point out to other boats who threaten to intrude on "your" circle just where your anchor is.

Some anchorages can be so crowded that this technique becomes impractical. In that case you're best off anchoring near boats similar to yours— deep-keeled sailboats swing differently than multi-hulls or power launches—as this increases the likelihood that you'll swing in the same fashion to wind or current. If this isn't possible, consider limiting your swing by using two anchors, either rigged bow and stern or both off the bow (see Anchoring Variations below).

Dropping the Hook

How you set the hook can be as important as its size and weight. If your anchor and rode are fouled, the anchor won't dig in properly, and then it represents just a lump of metal on the sea bed that'll easily drag when the wind comes up. Far too often we watch sailors bring their boats to a halt, heave the anchor and rode over the side, all in a pile, and then jump in their dinghy to go ashore.

Instead, once you've found what looks to be a good spot, head into the wind or current and slow or stop the boat. Drop the anchor, letting out enough scope to take the anchor to the bottom, but no more, until the boat begins moving astern. In light winds or current, this may require slowly backing down with the engine. Pay out the rode as you move astern, making fast when sufficient rode is paid out for the water depth. Now set the anchor. In light to moderate winds we do this by backing down with the engine at about half throttle, using more if in doubt about holding; in strong winds the windage of the boat is normally sufficient. Quickly pay out the last few fathoms of rode and make fast, and the boat will drift back and set the anchor. Use a few landmarks ashore, or other anchored boats, to judge if you are holding properly.

Setting the Anchor under Sail

If you have no engine or choose not to use it, anchor setting in light winds requires a different approach (see drawing page 75). Enter your chosen anchorage under sail at a fairly slow speed on a downwind course. Drop the hook while still sailing, paying out rode at a rate that keeps some tension on the rode. This ensures the anchor is oriented properly. When sufficient scope is out, make fast and begin a slow turn upwind. With practice your rode will be taut with the boat part way through the turn, which prevents the rode from scraping on the hull, while the momentum sets the anchor. Lower the sail(s) when the boat comes fully into the wind, and it will then drop back onto the already-set anchor.

Avoiding Coral Wraps

It's not uncommon, especially when anchoring in lagoons, for the anchor chain to become wrapped around coral heads and outcrops. This is destructive to the reef, hard on the chain and its galvanizing, and potentially dangerous as it may prevent you from retrieving the anchor quickly should that become necessary. The simplest way to avoid coral wraps is to find a coral-free area large enough to allow you to swing freely without the chain hitting any coral. In good weather you can minimize the area you need by using less rode. We've often anchored (using our Bruce anchor and chain) with a scope of 2:1, in areas where the anchorage is protected and the winds light. Use this technique only if you'll be staying on board, or if you'll be in the anchorage where you can monitor the conditions. If the wind comes up and you're ashore for the day, you could easily lose your boat.

For situations when you need both security and a limited swing, the best option is to use a weight that is lowered down the rode. Such weights go by various names—"sentinel" and "angel" are two—and come in different shapes and sizes. Whatever the arrangement, they serve the same function: improving holding power without increasing scope by decreasing the angle of the rode relative to the bottom. Typically, they're attached to the rode by means of a large shackle. A retrieving line should be used, so that the sentinel can be retrieved before weighing anchor. Sentinels are commercially available, but any convenient weight of some 20 or 25 pounds (9–11 kg) will do. A few dive weights strapped together would do a fine job, or you could make use of a small stern anchor.

RETRIEVING THE ANCHOR

So far anchoring has required little physical effort, just some thought in selecting ground tackle and anchorage. We'll make up for that now as we wrestle the anchor back on board. Windlasses are increasingly common on boats, with many larger boats and long-distance cruisers using electric windlasses. Yet they are by no means a necessity, unless your boat is large or you are anchoring in deep water on chain. We have a simple hand windlass that's used only when anchored in very deep water, where the combined weight of anchor and chain may be 140 pounds (64 kg), rather more than is comfortable to lift! Windlasses are *not* designed to break the anchor loose from the bottom; this should be accomplished by getting some way on with engine or sails, or with the aid of the boat's motion in a choppy anchorage.

Whether you have an electric windlass or you're pulling in rode hand over hand, be kind to your gear and yourself, and slowly motor or sail (typically with the mainsail only) up to your anchor as you retrieve the rode. When you're above the anchor, break it out by making the rode fast and giving a short burst with the engine, or by trimming your sail or sails. At times—such as in rocky or coral bottoms—the anchor may be jammed. This is when a trip line comes into its own, so do have the foresight to rig one. Slack off the rode a bit, haul away on the trip line, and the anchor should come free. If this fails, or if you don't have the trip line, then some vigorous maneuvering with the engine—forward, astern, and to port and starboard—should work the anchor loose. If it doesn't, it's probably time to get in the water.

Put on your snorkel gear and head down to have a look at how the anchor is jammed. This is often all you need to do. Having seen the crevice or rock that has your anchor captive, you can return to the boat knowing the direction in which to move to free the anchor. At times, though, you'll find the anchor wedged so securely that you have to free it by hand. Unless you're anchored in shallow water—less than 20 feet (6 m)—this is likely to be a challenging operation. How well you fare depends a lot on the water depth and your diving abilities; if you have problems free diving, you might want to consider packing along a small scuba tank for this kind of situation. Don't give up too quickly, and if necessary, try to get some help. There may be other cruisers nearby with diving gear, and some of the islanders we've met are fantastic free divers, capable of diving down to depths of 45 feet (14 m) or more.

But the best solution to this problem is to avoid deep anchorages with rocky or coral bottoms. If you must anchor in such a situation, use a coral pick. Failing that, drop the anchor you're least fond of, and consider using a short length of chain with line attached, so as to avoid losing a long length of costly chain.

ANCHORING VARIATIONS

Although rarely needed, it's good seamanship to have a few anchoring variations ready if conditions demand something different from the standard "one anchor off the bow" technique.

Using a Stern Anchor

A stern anchor is perhaps the most common variation. It can be used in combination with a bow anchor, either to limit swing in a crowded anchorage

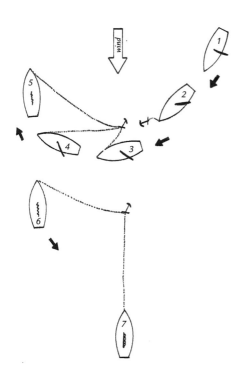

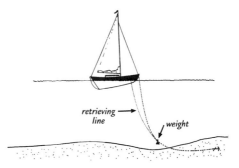

Weighting the anchor. With a weight or "sentinel" in place, boat swing will be reduced to a minimum while security is actually increased, as the pull on the anchor will be more nearly parallel to the bottom.

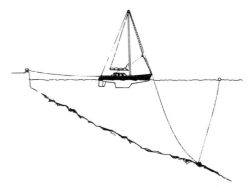

Anchoring on a steep-sloping fringing reef. Anchoring in this manner should be done only during settled conditions and with a close eye and ear to the weather.

Setting the anchor under sail. **1.** Approach your preferred anchorage under sail on a downwind course. **2.** Drop the anchor while paying out rode. **3.** Begin turning upwind and continue paying out rode. **4.** When midway through your turn, snub the rode up tight. **5.** Turn fully into the wind and come to a stop. **6.** Pay out rode. **7.** Settle back onto the anchor.

or to align a boat perpendicular to swell to reduce rolling. Stern anchors are also frequently used with a Mediterranean-type berth, where warps hold the bow to the quay; the same approach works in areas with steep fringing reefs.

The simplest approach to setting a stern anchor is to take it out in your dinghy after the bow anchor is set. If wind or current makes it difficult to set out the stern anchor with adequate scope, try easing out additional scope on the bow anchor first and then setting the stern anchor. You can then let out additional scope on the stern as you take in the excess at the bow. For a Mediterranean-type berth it's most common and practical to drop the stern anchor on your

approach to the quay. It's important not to misjudge the distance and to keep a very close eye on the anchor line in case things go wrong and you're forced to abort the procedure by turning or backing up.

Sitting to a bow and stern anchor, or to an anchor and a mooring line, works well if cross winds or currents are not excessive, but either procedure can become downright dangerous in some conditions. We used a bow anchor and a long stern line tied to shore when at Indonesia's Bandaneira Island, where a very steep fringing reef precluded sitting just to an anchor (see illustration). We sat comfortably for several days until we were hit by a powerful squall, which came at right angles to the boat.

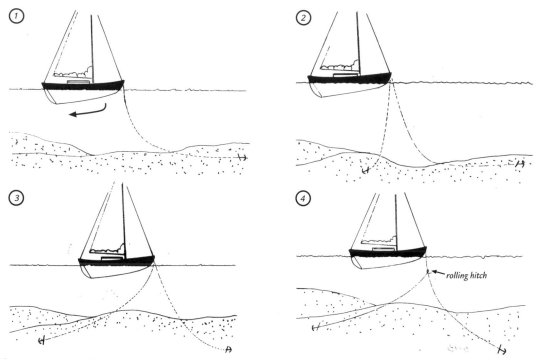

Setting two anchors 180 degrees apart. **I.** Drop the first anchor and pay out twice the normal scope. **2.** Drop the second anchor. **3.** Take up rode from the first anchor and pay out the second until lying between the two. **4.** Secure the second rode to the first with a rolling hitch. Pay out the first rode so that the hitch is below the keel.

Our bow anchor quickly dragged; only by releasing the stern line did we avoid be driven into a nearby jetty. We could easily have lost the boat had we not been nearby at the time.

Setting Two Anchors from the Bow

When there's a likelihood of strong winds or currents, it's usually better to use two anchors, set 180 degrees apart but with the rodes joined below the keel and then both secured to the bow. Drop the main anchor first, letting out twice the required scope. Then drop the second anchor and take up on the primary rode while paying out the second rode. Position the boat midway between the two anchors, securing the second rode to the main one by means of a rolling hitch. Let out enough additional scope so that the rolling hitch is below the keel, and then secure both rodes on deck, making sure to take the strain only on the main

rode. This technique works well either to limit swing or to ensure you don't foul your anchor if moored in a river or passage with strong alternating currents.

You can use a variation on this approach when mooring Mediterranean style, but only in areas with sufficient room to swing. Drop either a bow or stern anchor and then take a line ashore, but allow enough slack that you'll be free to swing freely should the wind blow parallel to the shore. This will place much less load on the anchor and mooring line and will decrease the loading, as your boat will be bow (or stern) into the wind, instead of lying at right angles to it.

You can also use two anchors to increase your holding power. If the wind or current is steady, the simplest approach is to lay two anchors about 45 degrees apart. Start by dropping one in the normal fashion. Once it's set, motor forward at an angle of

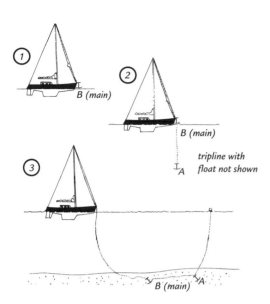

Setting two anchors on one rode. **1.** *Let go enough rode so that the main anchor (B) is just clear of the bow roller or chocks.* **2.** *Secure the second anchor (A) to the main anchor with 20 or 30 feet (6 to 9 m) of chain. Connect them with a shackle placed at the main anchor's swivel or primary shackle. Attach a buoy with a light line to the second anchor, and then ease both anchor and buoy over the bow.* **3.** *Pay out the main rode while backing down.*

Setting two anchors 45 degrees apart. **1.** *Drop the first anchor (A).* **2.** *Pay out the required scope.* **3.** *Motor forward at 45 degrees to the first anchor.* **4.** *Stop when even with the first anchor, and drop the second (B).* **5.** *Pay out scope on the second anchor.*

about 45 degrees to the first rode, and when even with the anchor, drop the second hook. Pay out scope until you are sitting evenly on both anchors. The biggest disadvantage with this technique is that you must reset both anchors if wind or current alters direction appreciably.

In changeable conditions it may be better to set two anchors on the same rode. Connect a second working anchor to your main anchor with a 20- to 30-foot (6–9 m) length of chain. Shackle the second anchor's chain to the main anchor rode at the swivel or shackle if these are strong enough to handle the extra load. Otherwise, shackle the second anchor directly to the main rode just before the anchor. Make sure to attach a trip line to the second anchor.

Begin by easing the main anchor off the bow roller, but secure the rode so that the anchor is above

the water. Then ease the second anchor over the bow, paying out all the chain so that it places tension on the main rode and ensuring that the trip line and buoy are not tangled with the chain. Now pay out the main rode and set the anchor as you normally would.

The two anchors will provide greatly increased holding power and should realign themselves to a wind or current from a new direction, if the strain proves great enough. You may, however, be placing a considerably greater load on your rode than normal. Make sure there are no weak points, and ensure that the rode is protected from chafe. To retrieve the two anchors, take in on the rode until the main anchor hangs just below the bow, and then use the trip line to retrieve the second anchor before bringing the main anchor back on board.

Chapter 6

Sailing in the Tropics

A 20-knot trade wind is blowing on the quarter, a smooth swell rolls up from astern, and your boat is slipping along almost effortlessly. The weather's warm, a moon lights up the night sky, and you've little to do other than check for ships now and again and wonder why you didn't set out to cruise the tropics 10 years ago. This is the sailing life!

You'll have days—and at times even weeks—just like that. But what makes them possible is preparation. This needn't involve spending heaps of money, but it does mean trying out gear and thinking hard about how everything will work when put to the test day after day, mile after mile. Preparation also means being ready for conditions different from those ideal downwind breezes. Headwinds, light winds, and storms are also part of tropical sailing, and you need to ensure that your boat and crew are ready for almost anything that comes your way.

Over years of sailing in the tropics we've learned that the ability to control boat speed easily is paramount to comfort and safety. In light winds you'll want to add sail and keep speed up in order to avoid wallowing and rolling in the trade wind swell. In heavy winds you need to be able to slow to avoid sailing too fast and getting out of control. At the same time, you don't want to end up under-canvassed and be a sitting duck for a nasty wave. Things are complicated by the fact that sails which will carry you comfortably downwind in a given breeze are almost certain to be too much if you're beating to windward. Good speed control depends on two things: having the right selection of sails and setting up your rig and deck gear so that your sails can easily and safely be set, reefed, and changed.

This chapter is organized in the same way that you might prepare your boat for tropical sailing. We begin by discussing the sails you'll need, how they should be constructed, and whether or not you need a pole or poles to keep headsails under control. From there we get into the fun stuff: sailing your boat in the trades.

SAILS

Some years ago, while living in Hawaii, we took some sails in to a local sailmaker for minor repairs, and at the same time we asked for his opinion regarding their condition. He roundly condemned the lot, saying he wouldn't trust our sails for a weekend trip, much less extended voyaging. Granted,

DO DIFFERENT RIGS WORK?

It's easy, when looking at the cruising fleet in most major ports, to forget there are other ways to rig a boat than by using one tall aluminum mast. Bermudan sloops and cutters are by far the most common rig, with some ketches thrown in for variety among the larger boats. These can work well, if properly set up, but they're not the only options. Gaff schooners, three-masted junks, catboats, catamarans with crab claw sails, and who knows what else is out there sailing the trades. So don't be deterred from setting sail if your boat is different than most. It's very possible that it will work better and be more comfortable than a conventionally rigged boat. What's important is that you think about how your boat will respond to the sea and weather conditions you'll find in the tropics, and that you set up the gear and sails so that they're easily handled.

With seven sails set, there's no lack of driving power aboard the gaff schooner Old Glory.

those sails weren't new, but that judgment seemed harsh. We ended up buying a new main shortly thereafter (though not from him), but waited years before retiring two headsails that he'd dismissed as shot. Those sails saw us through an extra six years and many thousands of miles of ocean sailing, and we're still carrying cloth from one as emergency patching material.

Our message is not that old sails are great, but that they can be tougher than you (or your sailmaker) think. If the budget allows, by all means invest in new sails, especially if you plan on sailing long distances. But don't be deterred from heading for the tropics with sails that aren't new. This is especially true if you're new to offshore cruising. After a season or two of sailing offshore, you'll know

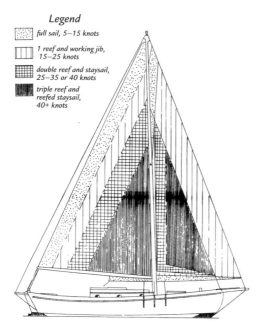

Legend

full sail, 5–15 knots

1 reef and working jib,
15–25 knots

double reef and staysail,
25–35 or 40 knots

triple reef and
reefed staysail,
40+ knots

Your sail wardrobe needs to be able to handle winds from 5 to 60 knots. Note how the sail plan of this cutter remains balanced as the sail area is reduced.

a lot more about how your boat balances and handles, and you'll have a much better idea of how you want a set of cruising sails made.

What Sails Do You Need?

For a start, all boats need a good set of working sails: sails to use in winds averaging 15 to 30 knots, but that can also handle stronger winds when reefed or furled, or when sailing off the wind. Working sails include the main and jib on sloops, plus a staysail on cutters and a mizzen on ketches and yawls. Working sails must be versatile, giving good performance on all courses, and should be easy for your normal crew to handle. Perhaps most importantly, working sails must allow you to sail effectively to windward. Yes, to windward! You'll spend much less time beating to windward in the trades than reaching or running, but you need to be able to do it well, and in foul weather to boot. Even with all the changes in boats and gear over the past few decades,

it's still true to say that your boat's ability to claw to weather may be the only thing that keeps you off a lee shore on some windy night.

In addition to good working sails, you'll need sails that can handle heavy air (winds in the range of 30 to 40 or 45 knots). A well-constructed mainsail should be up to the job, given sufficiently deep reefs. You'll also need a bullet-proof jib, and again it should be able to get you to weather. Your storm sails round out the heavy-weather part of the spectrum and should be designed to handle winds from 45 to 60 knots.

Most cruisers opt for some light-air sails as well, and we highly recommend them. The working sail area of many cruising boats isn't enough to keep them moving to weather when the wind drops below 8 or 10 knots, and will likely prove too small heading downwind in winds under 15. If you're prepared to do a lot of motoring, then you may be able to forgo an investment in light-air sails. Otherwise, larger, light-air sails are the answer when the wind eases.

A large, lightweight sail is especially helpful when sailing on a downwind course, because of the effect of boat speed on "apparent" wind. The idea of apparent wind will be familiar to those who race, but many cruising sailors don't give it much thought. Apparent wind is the wind actually experienced on deck, which varies with the boat's course and speed. Apparent wind will be greater than the actual wind when sailing to windward, as the boat's speed to windward is added to the wind speed. Apparent wind drops when sailing downwind, because the boat's speed is subtracted from the actual wind speed. This is one reason why sailors typically carry more sail when sailing downwind than to windward: a 20-knot breeze is closer to 25 if you're making 5 knots to weather, but it's only 15 if you're headed downwind at 5 knots.

Sloops and cutters, of course, are limited to hoisting larger headsails. They go by a bewildering range of names, but you can easily divide them into two groups: those where the luff is controlled (by hanking to a stay or fitting into a furler) and those that are set "flying" (such as a spinnaker). Boats with two (or more) masts have more options and can hang all manner of sails from the after mast in addition to flying large headsails from the forward mast. No matter what type of light-air sail you choose, these are most effective when constructed from lightweight fabric, which we discuss below.

Jibs

The working jib was once a basic item found on all boats, but that's no longer true now that most are fitted with roller furling. Many cruising boats make do with one fairly large headsail, which is often partially furled if sailing on the wind in even modest 20-knot winds. This solution is not a great one, though. Remember our requirement that the working jib be able to take you to windward effectively in winds up to 30 knots. This rules out a 140 percent genoa furled down to 70 or 80 percent, as the shape of the reefed sail will be poor. (Headsails are commonly referred to by a percentage figure, which gives their area as a percentage of the area of the boat's foretriangle. See figure.)

Sails with a less than ideal shape will work well enough downwind but are a real impediment to effective progress to windward. For that reason some cruisers carry both a good-sized genoa and a smaller yankee for their roller furler, and fit the latter in place if they anticipate working to windward in a breeze. Changing sails on a furler at sea can be a hassle, though, so the smaller sail may not be used if it hasn't been put on in port. If you want to have one roller-furling jib that works effectively on all courses up to about 30 knots, consider a sail no larger than about 110 percent, which will remain reasonably effective even when furled to about 85 percent.

Cutters should be able to get around the problem by using the staysail to get them to windward when the wind builds. Check how well your boat points under staysail, though, as many staysails aren't cut properly for sailing to windward. A good solution for boats that lack space for a permanent staysail is to fit a detachable inner stay a few feet

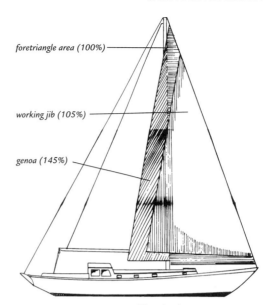

foretriangle area (100%)

working jib (105%)

genoa (145%)

Headsail size as a percentage of foretriangle area.

behind the stem and to carry a small working jib that can be hanked onto this stay if need be. This allows you to enjoy the convenience of carrying a larger genoa on the furler, but will also let you sail efficiently to windward when the wind builds. You won't want to leave such a stay attached permanently (with a narrow slot, tacking a large overlapping genoa becomes a proper pain), but by using either a quick-release lever or a strong tackle the stay can be set up easily at any time. This system also provides a good backup in case the furler develops problems.

Heavy-Weather and Storm Sails

Heavy-weather jibs are intended for use when the wind blows between 30 and 45 knots, and are particularly important when sailing to windward, as beating into winds of this strength puts too much strain on standard working sails. A heavy-weather jib is best hanked onto its own stay. A staysail with reef points can fill this function on a cutter, while a sloop can fit an inner stay as already discussed, hanking the heavy-weather jib to this. Another

SIZING HEAVY-WEATHER SAILS

The Ocean Racing Council (ORC) rules base heavy-weather sail sizes on foretriangle luff length. ORC states heavy-weather jibs should have an area no greater than 13.5 percent of the luff length squared. We would reduce this figure to 9–10 percent. Storm jibs are limited by ORC to an area equal to 5 percent of the luff length squared; 3.5 percent is a better figure. Working this out for our own boat, we get the following:

length of the luff = 38.85 ft. (11.85 m)

heavy-weather jib to be 9–10% of the luff length squared =

$(38.85)^2 \times 0.10 = 150$ sq. ft.; or

$(11.85)^2 \times 0.10 = 14$ m^2

storm jib to be 3.5% of the luff length squared =

$(38.85)^2 \times 0.035 = 53$ sq. ft.; or

$(11.85)^2 \times 0.035 = 4.9$ m^2

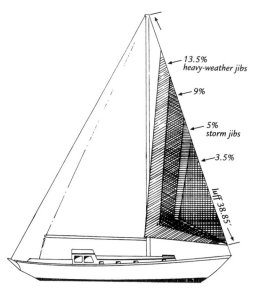

13.5% heavy-weather jibs

9%

5% storm jibs

3.5%

luff 38.85'

Determining the size of heavy-weather sails as a percentage of the luff length squared.

option is to use a well-furled (and strongly made) yankee, but this won't work as well on windward courses. It's also possible to fit a heavy-weather jib with a luff sleeve and attach it around a roller-furled headsail.

Storm jibs can use the same inner headstays as heavy-weather jibs and should be sized for truly severe conditions. Trysails replace the mainsail, and are attached to the mast and sheeted to either the boom or deck. Although you'll rarely, if ever, use storm sails in the tropics, be sure to carry them. Storm sails are indispensable and are a must for every boat that ventures offshore. Many cruising boats carry heavy-weather jibs and storm sails that are larger than they need to be, because many sailmakers base storm sail sizes on the maximum sizes allowed for racing, using a rule formulated by the Ocean Racing Council (ORC). See the Sizing Heavy-Weather Sails sidebar for guidelines on how these rules should be modified for cruisers.

Sail Balance

All sailors are familiar with sailboat balance, if only in terms of how the helm feels. Most boats carry some weather helm, and a small amount is good, as it helps the boat sail more efficiently to windward. Boats that aren't well balanced (and most boats that are overpressed) have lots of it. That's when sailing becomes a struggle between the person at the helm and the wheel or tiller. There are a lot of factors that go into producing weather helm, but there's one easy way of dealing with it: move the center of the sail area forward. That can be easily accomplished by reefing the mainsail (or dropping or reefing the mizzen), a move that normally cures the temporary weather helm that results from carrying too much sail.

In addition to impacting the feel of the helm, the position of the sails fore and aft can affect how well a boat sails. When sail balance gets too far out of whack, you'll notice your boat may be reluctant to maneuver properly. Fly just a jib, and the boat will probably carry lee helm and refuse to point very high. It'll be happy and stable, though, on a downwind course. Fly just the main, and the reverse is true. The boat will point high (though probably sail slowly), may need to be coaxed around to a downwind course, and may easily deviate from it.

These tendencies will be heightened in high winds. This is one reason why we recommend an inner stay for use in heavy weather, as it keeps the center of the sail area closer to the center of the boat and allows the boat to head upwind (or even simply luff upwind) more readily. This is especially important when flying a storm jib by itself, without main or trysail.

Light-Air Sails

Light-air sails probably spend more time in the locker than any other type (other than storm sails), so before investing, consider whether or not you're likely to use them. Many cruisers find free-flying light-air sails a hassle, because they require setting up special gear. Some people are also intimidated by really big sails, whereas other folks would prefer to motor when the wind drops, rather than sail at a slower speed. Keep these points in mind when you consider what sails to get, and make sure the sails you choose will suit you and your boat.

Sails with a controlled luff (that are attached to the forestay in some way, by being either hanked on or fed into the furler) are easier to control than those that are set flying. In general, a sail controlled at the luff will also be usable upwind, which isn't true for spinnakers. But free-flying sails will draw you along off the wind better than anything else. And you'll probably find yourself wanting that extra push on a downwind course much more often, because of the drop in apparent wind speed when sailing off the wind. In addition, sailing upwind in really light airs at sea can be frustrating, because there's often a swell running that works to slow your progress. Many cruisers resort to motor sailing upwind in light conditions for this reason.

It can be hard to judge how big your light-air sails should be. Many coastal cruisers may not have much

experience sailing for long periods in light airs, because the practicalities of local and coastal sailing, with schedules to keep and tides to catch, mean that more often than not the engine is turned on when the wind drops. It may be difficult to assess how much sail you'll need to keep the boat moving in light airs.

The guidelines that exist (see sidebar) compare working sail area and are at most a useful guide to how well your boat will do in light airs under normal (as opposed to light-air) sails. In addition, the light-air sailing ability of different boats varies, which is something these figures don't take into account. Experience in sailing your own boat is invaluable, and you should try to keep track of your speed on different courses and with various wind strengths and sea states. With that information in hand, a good sailmaker can then advise you on what performance you'll achieve with larger sails.

Many cruisers whose boats are fitted with furlers simply set a good-sized genoa (say, 135 percent) on the furler and use this for sailing to windward in

---

SAIL AREA FOR LIGHT AIRS

The biggest determinant of light-air speed is the size of the sail area compared to a boat's wetted surface area. Designers compare these two to determine if a design is going to perform reasonably well in light conditions. You can do it yourself quite easily. Add up your total sail area, using the mainsail and 100 percent of the foretriangle area. Add in one-half the area of the mizzen if you have a ketch or yawl. Then divide the sail area by the wetted surface. If you know the actual wetted surface, use that. Otherwise, make an estimate using the following formula:

$$(LWL \times beam \times 0.78)$$
$$+ \text{(area of keel and rudder, including both sides)}$$
$$= \text{wetted surface}$$

Here's what kind of light-air performance you can expect for various ratios:

$$< 2.0 = \text{sluggish}$$
$$2.0–2.2 = \text{good}$$
$$2.2–2.4 = \text{excellent}$$

The lower the figure, the more your boat will need light-air sails to help move it along when the breeze drops.

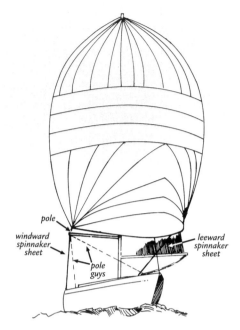

A symmetrical spinnaker is normally used with a pole.

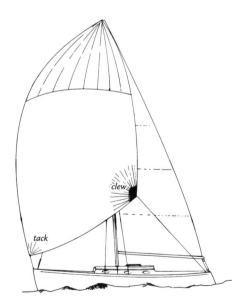

The tack of an asymmetrical spinnaker is attached at the bow. A pole isn't needed on a reaching course.

light air. For most people, a sail of this size will prove adequate and can work pretty well poled out downwind as well. Of course, when sailing downwind you'll need more sail area for a given wind strength than you will upwind, due to the reduction in apparent wind. If your 135 percent genoa moves the boat well to windward in 8 knots of wind, chances are that it'll be about right for sailing downwind in 12 to 15 knots. This is why a number of cruisers carry large, free-flying downwind sails as well.

If the primary sail on your furler is closer to 100 percent, or if you don't have a furler and have relied just on a working jib, then your light-air performance will definitely suffer unless you add a larger headsail to the inventory. If the budget (or space in the locker) is limited, we'd advise investing in a good genoa first; if you have the genoa but still want a light-air sail, then spring for a free-flying sail such an asymmetrical spinnaker.

What's the difference between symmetrical and asymmetrical spinnakers? Symmetrical spinnakers are designed to be used with a pole, which is set up on the windward side of the boat and holds one clew, while the other clew is sheeted to leeward. Asymmetrical spinnakers are cut flatter. They have a distinct tack and clew, so no pole is needed, although a pole may often improve performance when well off the wind.

Mainsails

You get plenty of choice with mainsails. They come with full battens or no battens, fitted to furl into the mast or into the boom, and can be tamed with the help of an array of nifty gadgets. All of these have their place, but don't forget: your main is the one irreplaceable sail on the boat. You can always substitute one jib for another and still make some progress, but the main is hard to do without, especially to windward. So make sure that what you choose will work and keep on working.

Some cruising sailors opt for an extra-heavy main, and although the "nothing too strong ever broke" philosophy usually makes good sense, here it seems a mistake to us, unless you're planning a trip to extreme latitudes with consistently high winds. Most tropical sailing involves light to moderate winds, and an overly heavy mainsail won't perform as well as a lighter sail. A better solution is to fit a main of average weight and then supplement it with a proper trysail for storm conditions.

Many cruising boats now sport fully battened mainsails, although plenty of partially battened sails are still to be seen. We've gone to the opposite extreme, with a battenless main. We've cruised with it for six years now, and have been quite pleased. We opted for no battens for several reasons.

▶ **THE BATTEN POCKETS** on partially battened sails are notorious weak spots, especially at their inboard ends.

▶ **BOTH FULL AND PARTIAL BATTENS** frequently jam behind shrouds when a sail is being lowered or reefed while sailing downwind, something that's never a problem with a battenless sail.

▶ **BATTENS THAT RUB AGAINST** the shrouds greatly speed abrasion of sailcloth.

▶ **OUR BOAT CARRIED** considerable weather helm in moderate conditions, and the battenless main's slightly smaller area and altered shape has cured this.

SAIL CONSTRUCTION

Trade wind sailing is hard on sails, in large part because of the amount of time they're likely to be in use. A 10-day passage in the trades amounts to 240 hours of sailing. That's equal to 24 10-hour days of actual sailing, or probably the equivalent of several seasons of local cruising for most boaters. And that's just one 10-day passage. Sail 5,000 miles in a season (say, 40 to 50 days), and you'll have put more wear and tear on your sails than most coastal sailors do in a decade. If you do this for five years, chances are your sails may be worn out.

Construction Details

What's the solution? Have your sails made from the best cloth (or other material) you can, and pay attention to the construction details, as these largely determine how long sails last. There are a number of critical spots:

▶ **REINFORCING AT CLEW, TACK, AND HEAD.** Reinforcing patches should be large and properly oriented to take the strain that will be imposed on them. Webbing sewn through the eyes at the tack, clew, and head will help keep these from pulling out under high loads and is a good idea if you're beefing up an older sail.

▶ **MAINSAIL BATTEN POCKETS** are notorious

for wearing out. Have them built extra strong, especially at the ends of the pockets.

▶ **MAINSAILS SHOULD HAVE** chafe patches at the spreaders.

▶ **JIBS SHOULD NOT RUB OR TOUCH** the lifelines at the bow. Use a pendant to raise the sail if necessary.

Sailcloth

Sails are made from all sorts of materials these days, but woven polyester (usually known by the trade names Dacron or Terylene) is still the favorite for most cruising sailors. If you're thinking about using laminated sails, we'd suggest you talk to a cruising sailmaker about the various options and then find cruisers who have used such sails for at least a few seasons.

Cruisers and racers define performance differently. Racing boats have to keep pace with technical developments in sails if they're to stay competitive, and they'll spend heaps for incremental improvements in pointing ability or boat speed. To cruisers, that sort of performance may be important, but it must be balanced with ease of handling, longevity, and economy. For most cruisers the speed and pointing edge given by laminates don't outweigh their drawbacks, which include limited life, sensitivity to flogging, and high cost. That's why we and most other cruising sailors persist in using old-fashioned Dacron, which still manages to get us where we're headed. No matter what fabric you chose for your working sails, all heavy-weather and storm sails should be made from woven polyester rather than laminated materials, because of the latter's poor resistance to flogging and tearing.

THINK BEFORE YOU BUY

We're hardly on the cutting edge when it comes to sails. Our headsails hank on, our main has no battens and ordinary slab reefs, and our spinnaker is a simple downwind model left over from the days when that's all that one could buy. Why such simplicity? The answer is primarily cost: furlers, full-batten systems, and snazzy reaching headsails all cost money, and we run our boat on a tight budget.

But there's an added benefit, and that's reliability. Take hanked-on headsails. They're nowhere near as convenient as a roller-furled sail, and there have been plenty of times—usually on a squally night, when making yet another headsail change—that we've questioned our dedication to such old technology. But they do work, and keep on working, no matter what. Maintenance is simple: carry along a few extra hanks, and check over each sail now and then, replacing or lubing hanks as needed. Other than mending any tears (which roller-furled sails may get as well), that's it. They'll never refuse to furl, get stuck halfway in, or jam. You'll never be sitting in a remote port looking for replacements for the "sealed lifetime bearings" or for a bent foil section.

We don't know of anyone who has reverted to hank-on sails after installing a furler, and we're not about to advise you to remove yours. We've mentioned this just to make the point that simple (and even older) gear can work reliably and effectively. New gear can as well, but not all of it may be well proven or designed for easy repair. So before you refit and replace existing equipment, ask yourself three questions:

▷ Does the old equipment really need replacing?

▷ Will the new gear work as (or more) reliably?

▷ Will you be able to fix it if something does break?

If you can answer yes to these, then chances are you're truly improving your boat, rather than just spending money.

Sailcloth is ranked by weight, with heavier cloth being stronger. Comparing different types of woven polyester cloth can be confusing, in part because different units are used in the United States, United Kingdom, and Europe. In the United States, weight is measured in ounces per "sailmaker's yard," which is 36 inches long by 28.5 inches wide (91.4 by 73 cm). In the United Kingdom, ounces per square yard are used, whereas the rest of Europe calculates sailcloth weight in grams per square meter. If you're converting, here are the equivalents:

$$1 \text{ U.S. oz.} = 1.26 \text{ U.K. oz.} = 42.8 \text{ g/m}^2$$

For example, an 8-ounce sail in the United States is equal to a 10-ounce sail in the United Kingdom and a 342 g/m² sail in France.

Further confusion results from the fact that various styles of woven polyester cloth are named by weight—such as 6.1-ounce Dacron—but may not in fact weigh that much. If you're in doubt about how much a cloth really weighs, ask for clarification from your sailmaker.

Impact of Ultraviolet Light

The intense tropical sun will degrade sail fabric and stitching far more quickly than most temperate-zone sailors are used to. When sailcloth is exposed to the sun it loses strength, which makes it more likely to tear. Woven polyester will lose about half of its strength after six months of continuous exposure, while nylon loses that much strength in three to four months.

To counteract such deterioration, keep your sails covered whenever you're not using them. Acrylic canvas (such as Sunbrella) is the best fabric for the job, as it breathes and holds up reasonably well in the tropical sun. Be sure to have a canvas strip put on the leech of each headsail you'll be using in a furler. UV-resistant sailcloth may look nice but won't provide the protection you need. Furl the sail carefully and ensure that the sail is completely covered by the canvas.

HOW HEAVY SHOULD A SAIL BE?

Waterline Length		Cloth Weight in U.S. oz./Sailmaker's Yard			
feet	meters	Main and Jib (100–110%)	Genoa (to 135%)	Light-Air Genoa or Reacher	Staysail or Heavy-Weather Jib
25–30	7.5–9	7–8	5–7	3–4	8–9
31–35	9.5–10.6	7.5–8.5	6–8	3–5	8.5–9.5
36–40	11–12	8.5–9.5	7–9	3–5	9.5–10.5
41–45	12.5–13.7	9.5–10.5	8–10	4–6	10.5–11

Sail Repair

We've had more experience than we'd like to admit with repairing sails, probably because of those old headsails we used for years (perhaps that sailmaker wasn't so far off the mark after all). There are proper ways to fix a sail, and then there are some quick and dirty approaches. We'll leave the discussion of how to do things the right way to the sailmakers out there (see appendix 3, Resources), and we'll focus on the quick fixes: something to keep you going until a better repair can be made (see the Sail Repair sidebar).

DOWNWIND SAILING

There's no better way to rack up the miles than catching a good trade wind breeze. But sailing in the trades is not always the most comfortable and can be quite hard on gear. It's not uncommon for swells and seas to hit from different directions. The Southern Indian Ocean, for example, is well known for its often large southerly swell, in a region where the prevailing trades are from the southeast or east. The Coral Sea off Australia's east coast is often plagued by large southern swells from storms in the Tasman Sea, while cruisers in the North Atlantic must contend with northerly swells from North Atlantic storms. Each boat reacts differently, but sudden sharp lurches and rolls are typical. When things really get cooking, the result can be a free roller-coaster ride, but with the drawback that you can't get off. Soon it seems as though everything on the boat is in motion. A towel can quiet the odd cup or bowl in the dish locker, but what really needs immobilizing is the gear on deck, because movement causes chafe, and chafe will soon destroy the best of sails and gear.

Unfortunately, most coastal cruising boats are not that well set up for long-term downwind sailing. Gear that works fine for the occasional downwind run—such as a standard boom vang led from boom to the base of the mast—is inadequate for tradewind passagemaking. The modifications are easy to make, though, and fortunately much of what you'll want for sailing in boisterous trades will be just what you need when the wind drops. Let's begin by looking at various ways of setting up your headsails, and then we'll move on to the mainsail.

Setting Headsails

With a sloop or cutter rig, downwind options are limited. The most common choice is to sail "wing and wing" by setting the mainsail to leeward, with

Sail repair at the Darwin Sailing Club, Australia, before heading to Indonesia.

a genoa or working jib poled out to windward. This is a convenient and forgiving setup that requires no special sails and allows some course flexibility. You can sail as high as 150 degrees into the wind—and possibly more with a small jib—and sail perhaps 10 degrees by the lee before a jibe threatens. In lighter winds a drifter or spinnaker may replace the jib or genoa, but the basic setup remains the same. Spinnakers are usually more finicky about being properly trimmed, and you'll need to steer a pretty straight course to prevent them from collapsing. We discuss spinnaker and whisker poles below.

The second choice for a single-masted boat is to drop the main and run under two headsails. This has several advantages: it moves the driving force forward, making the boat less likely to round up; it eliminates any concern over jibing the mainsail, saving it from wear and tear in the bargain; and it expands the course that can be steered to about 30 degrees on either side of the wind. You don't need special twin running sails to use this technique; in fact, owners of most boats with such sails have found them too small. Flying a working jib to windward with a pole and a genoa to leeward using either a second pole or the main boom works well in average trade wind conditions; the genoa can be dropped and replaced by a heavy-weather jib if conditions really pipe up.

Those who have two luff grooves in their roller furlers may choose to feed both in and then partially furl the sails if the wind builds. If your furler has just one luff groove, or if you're sailing with just a single stay, then one sail can be flown free, attached only at head, tack, and clew. Free-flying a jib can lead to lots of excitement when you go to drop the sail in a strong breeze, though, and so a better solution is to fit a removable wire stay. It need not be set up as tightly as it would need to be for windward work, as its only job is to keep the sail under control, particularly when it's being dropped.

SAIL REPAIR

Although we carry a hand-crank sewing machine on board, we've never used it at sea. Damage to sails often happens when conditions are rough, and trying to secure our cast-iron sewing machine and then operate the hand crank, while feeding the sail through, and also keeping oneself from flying across the cabin, are beyond the realm of possibility. So, for us, any sewing that's to be done must be done by hand, which is slow and laborious. As a result, we reserve sewing for those spots that absolutely must have it, and we rely on adhesives for the rest.

Small holes or tears in the middle of a sail, be it a main or jib, can be fixed with some sticky-back Dacron tape. For nylon sails (such as a spinnaker), use sticky-back ripstop tape. First, clean and dry the sail, as nothing seems to stick to wet, salty sailcloth. Next, carefully line up the edges of the tear. The simplest way is to work on a flat surface such as the cabin table, the sole, or a bunk board. If the tear is ragged and ugly, you may need some help in keeping the edges of the sail lined up. If necessary, use small pieces of sticky-back tape at right angles to hold the tear closed (much like you would suture a wound with a butterfly bandage) and then cover the tear lengthwise with sticky-back tape. Patch both sides of the sail, and the repair should hold until you get to port.

Things get more interesting if the tear is extensive (say, at least a few feet), or if several seams have blown. If you have sticky-back cloth on board, it can be used to mend large tears, but we've chosen to use standard sailcloth in combination with other adhesives. We've used contact cement, which works great, but be warned that it will always be visible as a somewhat darker area—your sails will never look new again. Spray adhesive may be a viable alternative to contact cement, but we haven't tried it yet.

Go through the same routine as you would for a small rip: cleaning and drying the sail, and aligning the edges of the tear or seam. Then cut two pieces of fabric that extend well beyond the damaged area. Mark these with a few lines from patch to sail, on each edge, to simplify alignment. Next, apply a thin layer of contact cement to the sail and to one patch. A flat spreader works best for this. Let the glue dry completely, and then line things up carefully. You only get once chance! You'll find that it's simpler to work out any ripples if you begin from the middle of the patch and move outward in all directions. Burnish the patch well, and then turn the sail over and repeat for the other side. Once again, no stitching is needed.

Adhesives also work well for repairing ripped seams. The same procedure applies, and the only stitching that may be needed is at the ends of the seam to ensure that the stitching doesn't tear farther past the area you've glued.

The biggest problems come if the damage is in a highly loaded area, such as the foot, leech, or clew. In general, patch as you would elsewhere, but it may be necessary to add extra pieces or strips of fabric to help absorb the loads. Stagger the edges of patches of multiple thickness to avoid a stress concentration (which makes a new tear at the edge of the patch more likely). Once again, sewing is largely unnecessary. The shear strength of the adhesive over the area of a large patch is much greater than the tearing resistance of Dacron fabric at the stitch holes, especially if the fabric is a bit tired.

If a clew ring pulls out, use nylon webbing to replace it. If the old ring is still partially in place, then thread the webbing through it. Otherwise, webbing alone will do the job. The ends of the webbing will be oriented upward toward the middle of the luff (one on each side of the sail), while the midpoint will be led through the clew ring (or placed where the ring was). This repair will have to be stitched. Stagger the webbing so that you're not sewing through both layers at once, and make sure to punch holes through webbing and sail using an awl or sharp ice pick before you start. Some double-stick tape will keep the webbing in place as you work.

Poles

Tropical cruising boats commonly carry poles to control large headsails and to improve their performance while sailing downwind. The two primary types are spinnaker poles and whisker poles. Spinnaker poles are the stronger of the two, as they're designed to handle the considerable loads caused by sailing on a reach with a conventional symmetrical spinnaker. Spinnaker poles are usually equal in length to the distance between the forestay and the mast (think of that as a 100 percent pole). That's not because a longer pole wouldn't come in handy, but because racing rating rules penalize the use of longer poles. Whisker poles are generally lighter for a given length than spinnaker poles, as they're designed only to pole out conventional jibs and genoas. Whisker poles can be had in both fixed- and adjustable-length models.

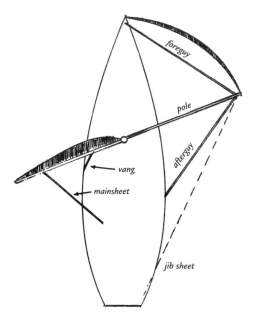

Sailing wing and wing.

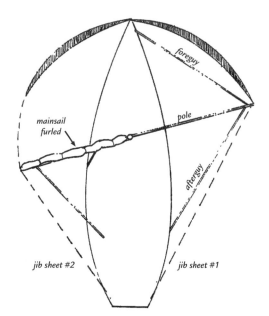

Running with two headsails.

Pole Options

There really aren't any limits to the type of pole you can use. We've seen all sorts, including the familiar aluminum pole, increasingly rare wooden poles, costly carbon fiber poles, and an assortment of off-beat poles made of bamboo and other local materials. What matters most is that the pole be easy to use (so not too heavy) and strong and long enough for the job. We'll focus on aluminum poles, as that's what most cruisers use.

How long should a pole be? It depends on the jib you're using, and the point of sail. When sailing downwind, a 100 percent spinnaker pole that is brought well aft toward the shrouds will be adequate for poling out a genoa of 130 to 140 percent. Come into the wind, however, and the genoa will tend to collapse, unless held out by a longer pole. The optimum then is to have a pole that matches the foot length of your jib or genoa. The fact that the ideal pole length varies depending on your course and the size of the jib being used (or the amount unfurled)

helps to explain the popularity of telescoping poles. With these the length can be adjusted to suit whatever headsail is in use. Not surprisingly, they are considerably more costly than fixed-length poles. If you opt for a fixed-length pole, then a length of about 110 percent of the forestay to mast distance is about right. If you carry two poles, one might be 100 percent and the other close to the foot length of your largest genoa.

Various end fittings are available to fit spinnaker or whisker poles, from piston jaws to articulated toggle systems. End fittings are usually cast aluminum (with stainless steel pistons), and electrolysis between the castings and aluminum poles is common. Make sure that the fittings (especially at the mast) are strong, and keep an eye on these and isolate them (see chapter 14, Boat Maintenance) if corrosion is evident. You'll also need bales or other fittings that can accept the lifts and guys you'll want on your pole (see Setting Up Poles, opposite).

Do you need two poles? It simplifies jibing if you're using one headsail, and makes running under two headsails straightforward. But a second pole is not essential, and if you don't have one you can use the main boom to pole out a second jib. The idea is simple: with the boom sheeted as if on a run, the jib sheet is led to a snatch block on the end of the main boom and from there to a turning block and on to the winch. We'll cover how to set this up in more detail below.

Setting Up Poles

Jib poles should be rigged so that they're always under control. We use two ¼-inch (6 mm) lines leading fore and aft from the end of the pole. One line (usually called a *foreguy*) leads from the outboard end of the pole to the bow, and the other (here called an *afterguy*) leads from the pole end to the rail somewhat aft of amidships. We also use a *lift*, rigged through a block about one-third of the way up the mast. The foreguy, afterguy, and lift need not be led to a winch—a two- or three-part purchase and cam cleat is ample.

The foreguy, afterguy, and lift should be led so that all can be controlled from one location. Our lift is cleated on the mast, near the pole's track; the foreguy is led aft along the pole and cleated on the pole's inboard end; and the afterguy is cleated using a block and cam cleat on the rail abaft the shrouds. This makes it possible for one person to control the pole, with no chance of it running wild.

If we anticipate needing the pole, we'll often rig the lines in advance. The pole itself is readied by clipping the inboard end to the mast ring, while the outboard end is cradled on the pulpit. With the foreguy tight (pulling down on the pole's outboard end), the pole is securely held in place; the pole doesn't interfere with tacking the jib and actually provides a welcome additional handhold on the foredeck. It often spends most of a passage in this position, ready for use.

To raise the pole into position, the foreguy is

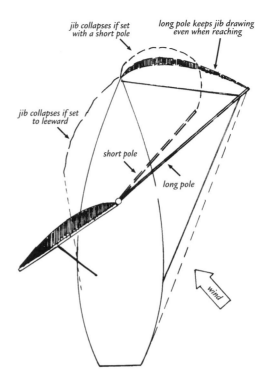

This view from the masthead shows how a long pole enables you to carry a large jib even while reaching.

eased a few feet and then cleated off. Next we hoist the pole using the lift, taking up slightly on the afterguy if needed to keep the pole off the forestay. The lift is cleated when the pole is at the correct height, and the pole is then swung aft by simultaneously easing the foreguy and tightening the afterguy. Simply cleating both afterguys tightly will freeze the pole securely in position, and we've often left the pole up (but unused) for hours—even in 30-knot winds—if we anticipated a wind shift that would allow us to use it again.

This system is ideal with two poles, as you'll never have to handle a pole to jibe the sail. Even with a single pole, jibes are quite safe, as the pole is lowered before one sheet is removed from the outboard end and the other is clipped in. With a single pole it helps to have two sets of guys, which are clipped to the pole

Foreguy, afterguy, and lift keep the pole securely in place.

with snap shackles. This eliminates the hassle of releading the guys when jibing the pole.

Setting Up the Mainsail

Controlling the main boom's movement is as important as keeping a spinnaker or whisker pole under control. Coastal cruisers typically have two means of taming a boom: sheet and boom vang. The mainsheet does a fair job of controlling the boom when close-hauled; on boats with travelers this may also be true when close-reaching. Off the wind, the sheet acts only to limit boom travel but does nothing to prevent lift or swing. The typical vang—a tackle rigged between boom and the base of the mast at an angle of 45 degrees or so—does a reasonable job of keeping the boom from lifting, but is of no help in preventing it from swinging inboard as the boat rolls to a swell. Our solution is a vang in the form of a three-part tackle that leads from the boom to the rail.

This vang does two jobs: keeps the boom pulled down, eliminating sail twist, and (on a close through a broad reach) serves as a preventer by pulling the boom forward. This exerts force in opposition to the mainsheet and keeps the boom from swinging; it also prevents an accidental jibe.

We use two vangs, one on each side, and leave them permanently rigged. They are both slacked off when sailing upwind; as we move off the wind the upwind vang remains slack, while the leeward one is tightened. The only disadvantage is the need to slack off whichever vang is in use before tacking or jibing.

Make sure the rail or other fitting to which such a vang is attached is very strong, as considerable force will be placed on it, especially if your main is accidentally caught aback in a gusty wind. Our vangs used to be attached to our bronze jib tracks, but after these started to bend, we moved the attachment point forward, and the vang is now made fast to the chainplate for the aft lower shroud. You may wish to include a heavy rubber snubber as part of your vang, or use three-strand nylon in place of lower-stretch Dacron; either one will introduce some elasticity into the system and reduce shock loadings.

Vangs can be attached to the boom in various ways. If your boom is fitted with a bail, use it if the placement is fine and the bail is strong. Otherwise, consider using nylon straps. Make loops from 1-inch (25 mm) tubular nylon webbing (also ideal for jacklines), using one for each vang. These can be sewn into loops, or you can tie the ends together, using a rock climbers' water knot (see instructions in appendix 1). They are inexpensive, very strong, and easily moved if necessary. We protect the webbing from chafing on the sail track with a piece of leather, but a bit of plastic hose would do job as well. Nylon is susceptible to weakening from UV, so keep an eye on these straps and replace them if sun damage is evident.

When running with the wind a rail-mounted vang may not be enough to control the boom's swing. In this case, the remedy is to add a true preventer. This is a line that normally lies along the boom, running from a cleat near the boom's inboard end through a block at the outboard end and back to the cleat. To rig the preventer we uncleat one end and, taking it around the shrouds, make it fast on the foredeck. With the preventer tight and pulling in opposition to the mainsheet, and the vang secured to the rail to prevent lift, the boom is effectively immobilized.

The preventer can also be pressed into service to help in sheeting a jib to the end of the main boom. Attach a snatch block to one end of the preventer

Boom vangs led to the rail are essential on a voyaging yacht.

line, rather than making it fast to the foredeck, and pass the genoa sheet through the block. Then take up on the preventer until the block is positioned near the end of the main boom. The snatch block could be fastened directly to the boom, but then rigging and unrigging it would require sheeting the main in, which may be awkward in strong winds. When the preventer is used in this way the boom isn't held as securely as it would be with the preventer secured on the foredeck, but the jib sheet generally does a fine job of keeping the main boom out where it should be.

REDUCING SAIL

At some point you'll find you need to reduce sail. If the wind picks up temporarily, as in a squall, dropping or furling a headsail is the quick way of reducing boat speed. If you're sailing downwind, having the pole securely held in place by guys and lifts pays off, as you won't need to touch it to reduce sail. Simply roll up or drop the jib and carry on. This works whether you're sailing wing and wing with main and jib, or have two jibs set forward. Dropping a hank-on jib that's poled out is

Nylon webbing is an easy and secure way to attach your vangs to the boom.

Jib sheeted to the end of the main boom.

A FEW TWISTS IN SLAB REEFS

Slab reefing is wonderfully simple, and there's little that can go wrong if the gear is well positioned and strong. But there are a few potential trouble spots:

▷ If your reefing lines are led through sheaves at the end of the boom, rather than through cheek blocks positioned slightly aft of each clew cringle, then the pull on the sail will be primarily aft, rather than aft and down. This problem is accentuated with really deep reefs that bring the clew cringle well forward. The result is a sail that isn't held down to the boom as it should be, and a poor sail shape. The solution is either to fit cheek blocks, so that the reefing line pulls in the proper direction, or to reeve a line through the clew cringle after you've taken up on the reefing line, thereby snugging the clew down to the boom (see illustration).

▷ When tying in reef points, always roll up the sail and then fasten the ties around the rolled sail, but not around the boom, as there is insufficient reinforcing around the reef points to take much strain.

▷ Because reef points don't take load, the clew ends up with more stress on a reefed sail than it does on an unreefed main, and of course the winds are stronger as well. Use really beefy cheek blocks for the reefing lines, with hefty fasteners into the boom. Secure the bitter end of the reefing line around the boom, rather than just to an eye strap.

▷ Depending on the tack you're on, the wind can easily blow the sail into the cheek block as you winch in the reefing line, leading to torn and even mangled sails. That's one argument in favor of those boom-end sheaves, but there's another solution. In a typical slab reef setup the reefing line is led from one side of the boom up to and through the clew cringle, down to the cheek block, and then on to the winch. Leave all the hardware where it is, but introduce a twist in the reefing line by leading it from where it is secured around the boom, under the foot of the sail, to the cheek block side. Then lead it around the sail's leech, through the reefing cringle as usual, and down to the cheek block. It sounds complicated but is in fact quite simple, as the accompanying illustration shows. It doesn't chafe the leech, and works like a charm.

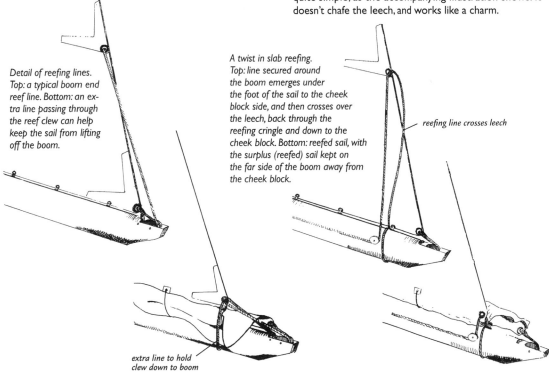

Detail of reefing lines. Top: a typical boom end reef line. Bottom: an extra line passing through the reef clew can help keep the sail from lifting off the boom.

A twist in slab reefing. Top: line secured around the boom emerges under the foot of the sail to the cheek block side, and then crosses over the leech, back through the reefing cringle and down to the cheek block. Bottom: reefed sail, with the surplus (reefed) sail kept on the far side of the boom away from the cheek block.

reefing line crosses leech

extra line to hold clew down to boom

simpler than dealing with one that's not. This is because the pole will keep the clew out of the water. In fact, all that's needed for a quick furl is to wrap a sail tie or two around the sail toward the bow and leave the sheets in place, with the clew still held by the pole.

If the wind increase is there to stay, though, you'll probably want to do things differently. If you're carrying the main, you should reef it in order to maintain good boat balance. Likewise, if you're flying two jibs, you'll probably want to take down the larger one and set a smaller jib in its place, thus reducing sail area but still maintaining good boat balance.

Reefing the Main

Unless your boat is unusually large, one person should be able to handle reefing the main alone and within a few minutes. What's more, you should be able to do so without changing course, particularly if you're reaching or running. Why? If you're reaching or running in boisterous trades and have your boat set up as we've described (with the jib poled out to windward, the main vanged to the rail, and a preventer leading to the bow), changing course more than a slight amount becomes quite a chore. What's more, if the wind is a gusty 25 knots, seas and swell may well be running at 15 feet (4.5 m) or more. The last thing that you'll want to do under these circumstances is turn the boat into the wind; even coming up just 30 degrees will considerably increase the effect of both wind and seas and further overpower your boat. It

is far better to set things up so that you can reef without changing course.

To illustrate how simple reefing should be, we'll describe the system we use on *Nomad*. Our boat is set up with basic slab reefing. Halyards and tack downhaul lines are controlled at the mast, and the reefing lines leading through the clew cringles are led to a winch on the boom.

To reef, one of us goes to the mast and eases the main halyard. We then take up on the appropriate tack downhaul line, using a winch to help out if we're sailing in a stiff breeze. The main is lowered until it's possible to secure the luff cringle on the reefing horn, just above the gooseneck.

Next, the reefing line is winched in, using a dedicated winch on the boom. When the reef's clew is near the boom, and the foot of the main is flat, the line is made fast and the halyard is re-tensioned. The last step involves tying in the reef points, a step that should not be ignored. Leaving the sail loose (a common practice for many racers) allows it to flog; in addition, it can interfere with vision and catch dangerous amounts of water in rough weather.

The specifics of how you reef will depend on your boat and gear; just ensure that your system allows one person to reef the boat quickly, without changing course. A real advantage of this approach is that your wind vane (or autopilot) can steer the boat throughout the maneuver. This is a boon on short-handed boats and means the off-watch can either rest undisturbed or help out if there's a problem somewhere during the procedure.

LIGHT-AIR SAILING

Now that you've heard our thoughts on reefing and heavy weather sails, we can tell you that in the tropics we've experienced light winds of less than 10 knots much more often than winds over 25 knots. Light airs are particularly common in equatorial waters and in the tropics during the cyclone or hurricane season, but even winter season trades can turn light for prolonged periods.

It's easy to overlook the importance of preparing for such conditions. After all, they simply result in a longer passage. What many people don't realize is how light-air conditions can damage your rig and sails, toy with your sanity, and genuinely make life miserable. Luckily, the preparations that you'll have made to cope with boisterous trades will also help with light airs.

Sail Trim

Some light-air offshore tactics are no different from what one would do when sailing in protected waters. Most readers—especially those who race—will be familiar with the basics of light-air sail trim. Surprisingly, many ocean cruisers don't take the time to make these simple but important adjustments. In light airs, sails should have more draft, or camber, than in heavy winds. To do this, keep halyards much looser than normal and loosen the outhaul on main and mizzen. If sailing on the wind, don't sheet the genoa in as hard as you would in stronger winds, and try altering the position of the sheet leads forward, to give the sail more belly. Keep the main traveler a bit farther off-center as well. Simple stuff, but it helps keep you moving.

Sailing Upwind

The biggest problem when sailing upwind in light air is being stopped by opposing swells and waves. If this happens, try easing off the wind a bit. Pinching is never good for speed, and it really undermines your progress in very light wind, when you already lack power to drive through the seas. Easing your course by 10 to 15 degrees can make quite a difference, but don't forget to trim your sails accordingly.

It's also important to keep the bow and stern of the boat light. The more weight that's in the ends, the more your boat will pitch, or hobbyhorse. The time to re-stow gear in order to keep the boat's ends light is before leaving port, and this is worth doing even if you don't anticipate encountering light conditions. The easiest way to lighten the ends is by moving extra gear. For example, many boats carry a second anchor on a bow roller and a stern anchor on the pushpit. That's fine along the coast, but move them toward the middle of the boat before going to sea. They're best placed down below but can be lashed on deck as well.

Sailing Downwind with Free-Flying Sails

The simplest way to add speed downwind is by using a bigger jib. That's all many cruisers ever do, and if you control your pole with guys and a lift as we've discussed, then it's very simple and safe. But there will be times when that's not enough. At that point, you either have to start the engine or switch to a much bigger sail, one that's free-flying.

Many cruisers shy away from using a spinnaker on a passage, but even traditional symmetrical spinnakers are effective and safe if you use them carefully. We've flown ours without interruption for three days and nights on a passage to Australia. Our Aries wind vane steered a fine course the entire time with no jibes or other problems.

A spinnaker sock makes flying a spinnaker much safer. These are essentially fabric tubes that encase the spinnaker, keeping it under control until you're ready to set or douse the monster. Setting the sail becomes a simple matter: hoist the sock (with the spinnaker inside) and then raise the sock by pulling on one of the control lines. To douse the spinnaker, the sheet and guy are eased and the sock pulled down over the sail. This makes it possible for one person to set and take down a spinnaker safely.

Using a Spinnaker Sock

Spinnaker socks are fitted with two control lines. Pull on one, and the sock lifts, allowing the sail to balloon out below. Pull on the other, and the sock comes back down over the sail. These lines should ideally be routed so that the force of the pull is directly below the sock. That's a tall order, though, especially if you'll be jibing the sail. The situation is further complicated because you'll want the sail to be in the lee of the main when you go to douse it. The best solution seems to be to run the sock control lines through a block that is secured to a line. Run this line through another block at the bow, forward of the headstay. By slacking off or tightening up on this line, you can vary the block's position and ensure that the pull on the sock from the control lines is in the right direction.

To set an asymmetrical spinnaker, fasten the sail at the tack (either directly to the stem head or on a line that allows you to adjust the position of the tack).

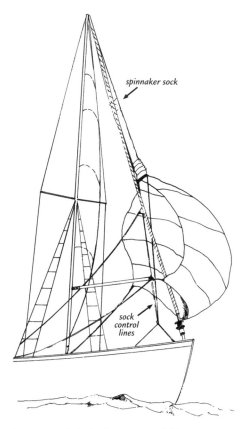

spinnaker sock

sock control lines

Dousing a symmetrical spinnaker using a sock. Note how the sock control lines are led.

Attach the sheets to the clew and lead it aft. Hoist the sock and cleat off the halyard. Ease off the control line block a bit (but not the sock control lines themselves), and then raise the sock, releasing the sail. It pays to mark the sheets so that you can pre-tension them before setting the spinnaker, thus avoiding flapping and fluttering. To douse the sail, the process is reversed. You'll find the maneuver simplest if the sail is in the lee of the main. To get it there, either change course to a run or ease the tack line, allowing the sail to move aft. Slack off the line attached to the control lines block at the same time, and then pull the sock down when the sail is blanketed.

Symmetrical spinnakers are a bit more complicated. First get the spinnaker onto the foredeck, rig the sock control lines, and attach the sheets to the sail. Next set up the pole with its guys and lifts and put it in position, choosing an angle to the boat's centerline that complements the angle of the main boom (the two should form a straight line, with the mast in the middle). Don't forget to pass the spinnaker's windward sheet through the end of the pole before it gets out of reach. With the pole in place, take up on the spinnaker sheet so that the windward clew is at or close to the pole. You'll probably have to slack off the line leading to the control line block to do this. Also, put some tension on the leeward sheet, taking the leeward clew aft about the same distance as the windward clew. Now hoist the sock into position, and if all looks good, pull it up and allow the sail to fill. With any luck the sail will do just that without collapsing.

Dousing a symmetrical spinnaker is best done behind the mainsail, except in very light winds, when all that's needed is to ease both sheets and lower the sock. In stronger winds you should first move the pole forward as much as possible (taking up on the sheet as needed to keep the sail under control) and then ease out the control line block. When that's done, ease the sheet and only then bring the sock down over the sail.

Spinnaker Sailing

Neither type of spinnaker is fun to jibe if you're sailing shorthanded. Most cruisers choose to douse their asymmetrical spinnakers and then reset them on the opposite side after jibing the main. Symmetrical spinnakers can be jibed sailing dead downwind, by unclipping the spinnaker guy from the pole, dipping the pole beneath the forestay, and resetting it on the opposite side. Most symmetrical spinnakers are well behaved on a downwind course; in fact, we've sailed for hours without a pole. The jibe is complicated if you're using separate guys on the pole (as we recommend), but the basic maneuver is not much different from a standard spinnaker jibe. You can simplify spinnaker jibing by using two poles.

Asymmetrical spinnakers tend to collapse on downwind courses (sailing at more than about 140 degrees to the true wind), because they get blanketed by the mainsail. How much of a problem this is depends on your boat speed. On fast boats (say, 10 knots and more) the boat speed will combine with the wind direction to move the apparent wind well forward and keep the sail drawing well. Slower boats won't notice this great a change in apparent wind direction, though, and will need to either tack (or jibe) downwind or resort to using a pole, as one would with a symmetrical spinnaker. Doing the latter negates one of the asymmetrical's biggest advantages, of course.

Symmetrical spinnakers are more likely to oscillate and collapse than asymmetrical sails, due to their fuller shape. You can counter this tendency by positioning the pole a bit farther forward than normal and by running the sheet block farther forward as well.

Alternatives to Spinnakers

If conditions are too squally or changeable for setting a spinnaker—or if you just can't be bothered—set a second jib instead, flying it in addition to your main. If you're headed well off the wind, set your genoa or largest jib to windward using a pole; otherwise, choose a working jib or other smaller sail that you can easily carry on a higher course. Then raise a second jib to leeward, sheeting it to the end of the main boom as discussed above (see Setting Up the Mainsail). Sailing with two jibs and a main is quite effective, particularly on a broad reach when the windward jib acts to force air onto the leeward one; it can also serve to improve airflow over the main. A drifter is another alternative to a spinnaker and in terms of efficiency falls somewhere between a genoa and an asymmetrical spinnaker. Typically made from lightweight Dacron, drifters are cut to be effective on courses ranging from a close reach to a broad reach. Drifters are usually not set free-flying but inserted in a furler or hanked-on to a stay.

Flying two jibs and a mainsail.

They've probably declined in popularity with the advent of roller furling but remain a very practical and efficient sail.

Motor Sailing

There comes a time when, despite all one's efforts, the wind is simply too light to make reasonable progress. For us, this means the boat's speed has dropped to less than 2 to 3 knots, and the wind vane is no longer able to steer the boat. If the sea is calm and we're not rolling, we may be content to simply wait it out. In lumpy conditions we usually start up the engine, motor sailing whenever possible. Most cruisers keep the main up when motoring, sheeting it in hard amidships to prevent rolling. It'll steady the boat but do little to push you along. If there is any air movement at all, try keeping both main and jib up and drawing. This is usually possible if the wind is somewhere on the beam. The anti-roll effect will still be there, and by trimming the sails properly you can often add a knot or two to your speed; alternatively, you can throttle back, thereby saving fuel and extending your range.

Chapter 7

Route Planning

Think of route planning as a game. A chart of your cruising ground is the playing field, while pilots, pilot charts, and cruising guides indicate what you'll find there, and how the weather will be on the way. The goal is for your boat to wend its way across the ocean, deftly avoiding foul weather and reefs, stopping for a time in beautiful anchorages, and once more setting sail. If the pilot charts say you'll meet excessive headwinds, storms, or big seas, a cruising guide has some discouraging remarks about piracy, or a pilot says you've no hope of anchoring off that deserted island, simply turn back the clock and revise your schedule, or choose a different route.

Any clever tricks you can think of to beat the odds are fair game. You can log on the Internet and have a look at the ENSO predictions to get a sense of how El Niño or La Niña may affect trade wind strength or cyclone frequency. Or perhaps you'll dig out a copy of an old pilot to see if there are some remarks about small boat anchorages that have been deleted from the latest edition. And it never hurts to have a chat with some sailors who've recently been where you're going, to get their take on the risks of sailing there. If you win, your real passage will be a good one, and you'll have a great time; if you lose, you pay, be it in bad weather, islands or people that

aren't what you thought they'd be, or a host of other problems or disappointments.

Keep in mind there's an element of chance at work here. The information you consider beforehand isn't necessarily an accurate reflection of what you'll find when you're out there. Some information is pretty reliable: reefs and shoals don't move, and protected anchorages generally stay that way. But the winds and currents forecast by pilot charts are simply averages of past conditions and may not predict the conditions you'll encounter, especially in years of abnormal weather. And some risks—such as those from disease, political unrest, or piracy—can change very quickly. This makes getting hold of up-to-date information especially important: the better your information, the better your chance of beating the odds.

You should always play this "game" before setting out on a major passage or a season's cruising, but it can pay off even for short inter-island cruises. Doing so can make the difference between having consistently good passages or getting hammered (or disappointed) on a regular basis.

Part of the importance of route planning is that it alerts you to what your options are. One secret to cruising happily and safely is having the ability to change your plans easily at almost any time. We always allow plenty of leeway when setting dates that are hard to change, such as airline reservations or rendezvous with family or friends, who may be flying out to meet us. But even with a "loose" schedule, weather, gear problems, and a host of other complications can mess up plans. Our rule is always to have a few alternative plans in mind and not to compromise when it comes to safety.

By carefully evaluating your options while still in port you may also find that you can go places or use routes other than those that you've read or heard about. We've enjoyed ourselves the least when following heavily traveled sailing routes in the company of lots of other cruising yachts. We've had the best time when sailing in regions not often visited or when exploring areas in the off-season. By doing your own route-planning homework, you can determine what will work for you, rather than following a prescribed cruise, be it around the Caribbean, the Pacific, or the world.

To plan your tropical cruising effectively, there are some essentials in the way of information and resources that you'll need:

▶ **AN UNDERSTANDING OF THE SEASONAL PATTERNS** characteristic of tropical weather and of how to use trade winds, depressions, and currents to your advantage. It is also important to know where and how frequently cyclones occur and to develop strategies for avoiding or weathering them.

▶ **ADDITIONAL DETAILS REGARDING THE WINDS, WEATHER, AND CURRENTS** in the region where you'll be cruising. Important reference works include pilot charts, pilots, and cruising guides, as well as the regional section (part 5, Tropical Cruising Destinations) of this book. You'll also want to supplement these resources (which present average conditions) with specific updates of how conditions in the season or even month in which you're sailing may differ.

Planning the next leg of a passage.

▶ **INFORMATION ABOUT THE GEOGRAPHY, CULTURE, AND POLITICS** of your cruising destination. Few things are more frustrating than sailing through a fascinating region but having no references on board to help you understand what you're seeing and experiencing. Cruising guides, travel guides, and more general reference works are all valuable in this regard. Cruisers should also obtain up-to-date information on the risk of piracy and political unrest, if heading for areas where there is the potential for trouble.

▶ **AN ACCURATE IDEA OF YOUR BOAT'S CA-PABILITIES** in terms of speed, ability to handle foul weather, and range under power, and a realistic assessment of your crew's skills. Others might easily and safely undertake a voyage that would be foolhardy for some boats or crews.

CRUISING SEASONS

Winter is the prime time for sailing in the tropics. The tropical cruising season stretches from midfall to midspring: generally November to May in the Northern Hemisphere and May to November in the Southern Hemisphere. As we saw in chapter 3 (Weather in the Tropics), in most tropical areas trade winds blow most consistently during the winter months. The winter season also generally brings cooler, drier weather and a much lower risk of encountering tropical cyclones than the summer. Although it is possible to safely spend the summer months in the tropics, most cruisers choose to stay out of the tropics during this time. As a result, the timing of a tropical cruise—whether it is limited to a few island groups or takes you across an ocean—will largely be determined by the seasons.

Routes through the tropics typically follow the trade winds. The major long-distance cruising routes all take advantage of the predominantly easterly trade winds, and are either downwind routes or will at most place the wind on the beam. This is true for the route from the Mediterranean to the Caribbean via the Canary Islands; from the Panama Canal to French Polynesia and on through the Pacific; and westward passages through the Indian and South Atlantic Oceans. These routes date from the age of sail and still are followed by the majority of ocean voyagers.

Although the seasons and the trade winds generally set the parameters for tropical cruising, there are many variations in these patterns across the globe and many options that can be exercised. Often it's not until you're sailing a classic "downwind route" (but experiencing winds that don't conform to expectations) that the considerable variations in the trade winds become apparent. These variations can often be predicted to a degree, and by sailing when winds are more favorable, it's possible to considerably speed or ease your passage. This tactic is also valuable for sailors searching for alternatives to the tested (but sometimes crowded) downwind routes. We provide detail on variations in trade wind patterns for each ocean basin in part 5 (Tropical Cruising Destinations); here we discuss how these can be used to advantage.

VARIATIONS IN THE TRADE WINDS

Few sailors will choose to make lengthy passages to windward against the trade winds, especially if these are strong, so it is important to plan your route carefully to avoid a bash to windward if possible. This can be done in part by anticipating shifts in the trades that typically occur during the course of a season. For example, in the Caribbean's Lesser Antilles, the trade winds are more easterly or northeasterly in the winter months, turning southeasterly late in the season and during the summer. While such shifts are not large, they may be sufficient to mean the difference between a passage to windward and a close or beam reach.

In addition to seasonal shifts, trade winds in many areas (especially those influenced by nonstationary highs) will shift in a predictable way with the passing of high-pressure cells. In the southwest Pacific the trades are caused by a series of high-pressure cells that move eastward from the Australian continent into the Tasman Sea and then east past New Zealand. Winds in the Coral Sea—in the vicinity of New Caledonia, Vanuatu, and the Solomon Islands—will be southerly when a high is to the west, still in the Great Australian Bight. These winds will shift to the southeast as the high moves eastward across the Tasman, becoming easterly and at times even northeasterly, as the high moves past New Zealand.

Wind strength can be as important as the direction. Sailors embarking on a downwind passage will welcome much stronger winds than they would if their course placed the wind on the beam, or the nose. Trade winds are generally at their strongest during the winter months but will invariably gain strength as high-pressure systems build, and they'll lose strength as the pressure decreases or a high moves away. As a result, although the consistency of the trades would seemingly suggest that a passage can be undertaken at almost any time during the favorable season, it is, in fact, important to time your departure so that the winds are more likely to be of the strength you want for the passage you're making.

USING LOWS TO YOUR ADVANTAGE

Although trade winds dominate the weather picture in the tropical winter, other winds also occur. Most are associated with disturbances, or lows, of various sorts. You can take advantage of these weather features to make passages that would be difficult in typical trade wind conditions. As we saw in chapter 3, temperate-zone lows bring westerly quadrant winds in both the Northern and Southern Hemispheres. These are a primary means by which to make a short passage against the trades. They are not helpful for long passages, as these systems are generally fast moving and will quickly leave your boat behind. The strategy is simple: wait for such a system to come through and then use those winds to sail east. The winds associated with such a low rarely exceed about 35 knots within the tropics and will more often be lower. Be sure to obtain a good forecast before committing to a passage with a low in the vicinity.

Tropical lows (though not tropical cyclones) provide another alternative to trade wind sailing. Although tropical lows generally move with the trade wind flow, they'll alter the wind patterns in their vicinity, at times enough to make an otherwise difficult passage possible. Be sure to do this only during the winter months, when the potential for cyclone development is at a minimum.

THE GULF STREAM

To illustrate how important currents can be in route planning, we'll take a closer look at passage options from the U.S. East Coast to the Caribbean. This can be a difficult passage for two reasons: the Gulf Stream's warm water provides a ready source of energy that can act to kick-start weather systems, while the current itself has the potential to set up large, steep waves if the winds from such a system blow counter to it. Sailors heading south from the East Coast will want to minimize the possibility that they'll get caught in the Gulf Stream at the wrong time.

The Gulf Stream flows in a northeasterly direction, roughly paralleling the U.S. East Coast. Its width and distance from shore vary. The center of the stream averages some 30 miles offshore at Cape Hatteras (at 35° N, in North Carolina), where it's fairly narrow as well. The distance from shore increases to 120 miles at Chesapeake Bay (37° N) and 240 miles at New York (41° N) and points north; the width north of Cape Hatteras increases as well to some 100 miles.

To maximize your chance of crossing the stream with favorable conditions, it makes sense to depart south of Cape Hatteras. The stream is then narrow and close to the coast, and the cruiser will be working on the basis of a 24-hour weather forecast, rather than a 48- or 72-hour forecast, as would be the case farther north.

Other considerations also apply to this passage, of course. Cruisers bound for the Caribbean Leeward Islands will need to make considerable easting. The coast south of Cape Hatteras tends southwest, and cruisers departing from South Carolina or Georgia are likely to have trou-

ble holding their course because of head winds. One option is to head for the Virgin Islands, which lie farther west and won't be as much of a beat. Another alternative is to first sail north along the coast to North Carolina, heading offshore on a southeasterly course at about 34.5° N. Boats sailing from Florida will almost invariably face headwinds. Their options include using the westerly winds associated with a low to the north to get easting, or to use their engines to do the same through the horse latitudes.

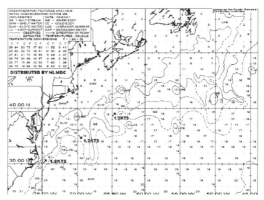

This chart of the North Atlantic includes temperature readings and clearly outlines the boundaries and velocity of the Gulf Stream, as well the presence of warm and cold eddies. Color plots are also available. These images are available at no charge over the Internet (for URLs see Gulf Stream Observations section in appendix 3, Resources), and should be studied in the days and weeks preceding a planned crossing.

TROPICAL CYCLONES AROUND THE WORLD

Ocean Basin	Extent	Name	Season Length	Greatest Danger	Average Number*
North Atlantic	North Atlantic, Caribbean, and Gulf of Mexico	hurricane	June–Dec.	Aug.–Oct.	9.7
Eastern North Pacific	North America to 180° E	hurricane	May–Nov.	June–Oct.	16.5
Western North Pacific					
eastern part	180° E–140° E	typhoon	all year	June–Dec.	25.7
western part	South China Sea, 130° E–110° E	typhoon	all year	June–Dec.	25.7
North Indian Ocean	Bay of Bengal and Arabian Sea	tropical cyclone	April–June; Sept.–Dec.	same	5.4
Southwest Indian Ocean	west of 100° E	tropical cyclone	Oct.–May	Dec.–April	10.4
Southeast Indian Ocean	100°E–142° E	tropical cyclone	Oct.–May	Dec.–March	6
South and Central Pacific	east of 142° E, including Australian East Coast	tropical cyclone	Oct.–May	Nov.–April	9

*Average number is the historical frequency of tropical cyclones with winds over 34 knots. Approximately half of these storms will generate hurricane force winds of 64 knots or more.

COPING WITH OCEAN CURRENTS

Ocean currents can serve to speed or slow a passage, and it makes sense to plan your route with currents in mind for that reason alone. Fortunately the currents along the major (westbound) trade wind sailing routes are generally favorable. The boundaries of the major tropical currents (the North and South Equatorial Current and the Equatorial Counter Current, present in both the Atlantic and Pacific Oceans) are not fixed. These currents shift north and south seasonally, and a small change in your route (north or south) may make a considerable difference in the current that you experience. Currents in areas subject to monsoon wind systems alter with the monsoons.

Currents can turn what would otherwise be an average passage into a potentially treacherous one, if fast-flowing currents encounter strong winds blowing in opposition. Large, steep waves develop very quickly under such circumstances. This situation arises at times in many parts of the world; well-known examples of this phenomenon are associated with the Gulf Stream, which flows along the U.S. East Coast, and the Agulhas Current, flowing along the coast of South Africa. Although both of these currents lie outside the tropics, they routinely affect passages to and from the tropics. See The Gulf Stream sidebar for a more detailed look at planning a passage across the stream.

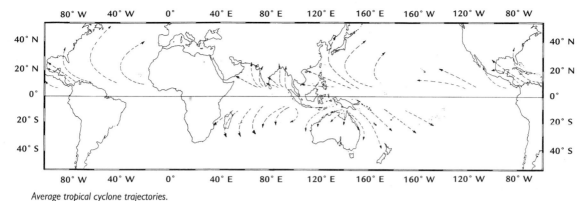

Average tropical cyclone trajectories.

CYCLONE SEASONS AND THE SAILOR

As we explained above, deciding to cruise the tropics during winter is easy; what's difficult is determining what to do during the less desirable and more dangerous summer months. Tropical cyclones place more constraints on cruisers than any other single factor. During cyclone season most cruisers choose to sail in low-risk areas or to avoid cyclone-prone waters altogether. If you do the same, then cyclones will dictate when and where you'll be cruising.

Generally speaking, cyclone season spans six months in both hemispheres. The season stretches from May or June through November or December in the Northern Hemisphere, and mid-October through early May in the Southern Hemisphere. These seasonal limits are approximate and, in fact, don't work at all in the North Indian Ocean, where there are two cyclone seasons, one between each of the monsoons. The designations fail in the northwestern Pacific as well, where there is no season that can be considered free of danger. Even in more typical areas, it's not wise to assume that any month is completely free of cyclone danger. Cyclones have occurred in many places months past the end (or before the start) of the "official season." The best defense is to monitor local forecasts on a regular—preferably daily—basis. The accompanying table shows the typical seasons for cyclones in various parts of the world, along with the various names used for these phenomena.

Tropical cyclones don't occur at or near the equator, because of the absence of Coriolis force (which imparts the "spin" on the winds in a cyclone), so you won't encounter one if you're within 6 to 8 degrees north or south of the equator. That makes equatorial waters a potential cyclone haven during the dangerous summer months, as we'll discuss below.

Tropical cyclones don't develop outside the tropics, but given the right conditions they can end up in the temperate zone, where some have done enormous damage. This means that leaving the tropics for nearby temperate waters does not guarantee safety from cyclones. Not many temperate areas are cyclone prone; using the tracks of past cyclones as a guide, an effort has been made to estimate the statistical probability of suffering a cyclone strike in various tropical and temperate areas. The maps that have been produced as a result of such studies (see opposite) probably provide the best guide to the relative risk of cyclones in different areas.

Sailors moving from one hemisphere to another should be mindful of the need to avoid (or otherwise be prepared for) cyclone season in both hemispheres. For example, sailors heading south from Hawaii will want to leave port and cross to the "safe zone" south of about 8° S before the North Pacific

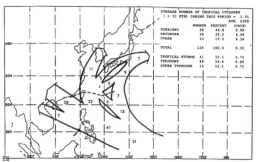

Mean paths for tropical cyclones for 24 June to 8 July. The U.S. Navy's Typhoon Havens Handbook series includes very detailed maps showing mean tropical cyclone paths, based on historical data. This map is from the handbook for the Western Pacific and Indian Oceans (see Navigation and Seamanship section in appendix 3 for URLs).

cyclone season becomes active. This will also allow them maximum cruising time in the Southern Hemisphere before the onset of the cyclone season there (in late November). Cruisers who depart Hawaii later—in late June or July—will still have a number of months in which to cruise safely in the South Pacific but run an increasing risk of encountering hurricanes as they cross the zone between 18° and 10° N, especially in an active cyclone year.

Avoiding Cyclone-Prone Waters

Many cruisers leave the tropics during the summer months, congregating in nearby temperate-zone ports. This reduces the cyclone risk (although as sailors from the southeast United States are aware, it does not necessarily eliminate it). Depending on where you're cruising, however, it may entail a rough or unpleasant passage. For example, many cruisers escaping the South Pacific cyclone season do so by voyaging to New Zealand, but the weather on this route is very changeable and can deteriorate quickly. A significant number of boats have experienced serious problems on this passage in years past. In addition, leaving the tropics for six months out of the year places limits on what one can see and on the number of miles that can be covered within the tropics in the course of a year. This may be a

particular problem for sailors who are on a cruise of limited duration. It also makes an early fall passage from the U.S. East Coast to the Caribbean (prior to November) impossible. But there's no better way to avoid getting hit than to sail in an area where cyclones don't occur.

It's also possible to avoid cyclones by moving to equatorial waters during the summer. Many Caribbean cruisers choose to spend cyclone season in Venezuela, for example. We have spent a couple of southwest Pacific cyclone seasons in Papua New Guinea, the Solomon Islands, and Indonesia. The advantage of using equatorial waters as your cyclone refuge is that you're free to continue your tropical cruising (though only within the safe equatorial zone). Equatorial cruisers should still pay close attention to the weather, as tropical depressions may develop within this area. These storms don't develop into cyclones until they're farther north or south, but they may bring strong (35-knot) winds and very heavy rain.

The downside of seeking refuge near the equator is the heat. Trade winds are generally weak and the temperature and humidity high. Make sure you're prepared to cope with such conditions. The awnings, hatches, and windscoops we discuss in chapter 10 will become more important than ever!

Staying in Cyclone-Prone Waters

We generally stay out of cyclone-prone regions during the danger season and have done so by sailing to higher latitudes or by staying in equatorial waters. But we've broken our own rule by living in two cyclone-prone areas (Hawaii and New Caledonia). Many other sailors also routinely stay in dangerous areas year-round, including such hot spots as Guam and the Northern Marianas, in the Northwest Pacific. A reasonable argument can be made for taking the risk of cruising or passagemaking in cyclone areas during the summer months, but only if you take the appropriate precautions. Even then, the risk will be higher for some boats than others. For example, fast, large boats—which can count on making 250 miles per day and more—can undertake passages through cyclone-prone waters with less chance of being hit than can a boat that is lucky to average 125 miles a day. Be realistic in evaluating the capabilities of both your boat and crew, and err on the side of caution.

In the end, the decision regarding where to cruise during cyclone season is a personal one. Be sure to do your homework early on, and don't be lulled into complacency by a few years without a cyclone. We discuss what to do if you're forced to weather a cyclone—either in port or at sea—in chapter 9 (Heavy Weather in the Tropics).

PASSAGES TO AND FROM THE TROPICS

Careful attention to route planning and the timing of a passage are especially important when embarking on a passage into or out of the tropics, as conditions are often somewhat nastier than you're likely to experience within tropical latitudes. Sailing into the tropics is generally a bit easier than heading out, because with a good forecast you can usually count on at least several days of pleasant conditions. If you make good time during that period, then you'll be that much farther away from any extratropical low-pressure systems that crop up. When sailing out of the tropics toward higher latitudes, it's hard to anticipate what the weather may be a week or more in the future.

Sailors heading to the tropics generally do so in late fall or early winter, at the beginning of the tropical cruising season. It's important not to sail too early, and so risk a late cyclone, but you should also be mindful of the fact that the risk of encountering a severe winter extratropical gale increases as the season progresses. If you're planning such a trip, carefully monitor the weather and conditions at both your port of departure and your destination. There are many routes in and out of the tropics, and each will have its own pitfalls. You'll do well to consult a number of sources—including other sailors and local forecasters—before setting out.

PLANNING YOUR ROUTE

If we're planning a specific cruise, we generally begin by consulting two reference works: *Ocean Passages for the World* and Jimmy Cornell's *World Cruising Routes*. Together these two books cover the basics of sailing routes throughout the world, including the tropics. We recommend these invaluable guides to all serious cruisers; if space or money are limited, the latter alone will suffice. Once we've gotten the general picture from these, it's then time to consult other sources to refine what we can expect in terms of weather, currents, and waves. Chief among these sources are pilot charts.

Of course there's a lot more to tropical cruising than just weather and currents. A strong desire to visit a particular place, or experience a certain culture, may prepare you to fight a headwind or a contrary current. For us, the most exciting part of route planning begins when we leave the winds and currents behind and investigate the places we'll be visiting, choosing what we think will be the gems among the countless tropical islands and coastlines.

Although there is a wealth of information available to help you evaluate potential cruising destinations, much of it isn't written with the cruiser in mind and may provide far more detail than you want on some subjects while not addressing issues important to a cruiser, such as immigration and customs requirements in various places. Part 5 of this book, Tropical Cruising Destinations, can help you make some early decisions about where you'd like to cruise, and includes information that can be hard to pin down, such as where you're likely to find the best reefs and what sort of yachting facilities are available. Once you've made some basic choices, you'll probably want to invest in resources such as cruising guides that provide more detailed information. The Internet is also a valuable resource, especially for information that may change quickly, such as visa requirements (see suggested Web sites in the Tropical Cruising Destinations section in appendix 3, Resources).

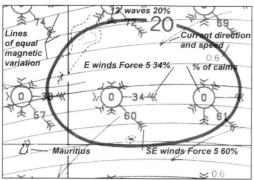

A small portion of a pilot chart for the Indian Ocean for the month of July.

Pilot Charts

Pilot charts provide an overview of the average conditions you'll experience in a region, in the way of wind, current, swell, and storms. The two primary sources of pilot charts are the U.S. National Imagery and Mapping Agency (NIMA) and the U.K. Hydrographic Office. U.S. pilot charts are available in atlases, with each atlas consisting of twelve monthly charts. NIMA atlases cover the following: North Atlantic, Mediterranean, and Caribbean; South Atlantic; Indian Ocean; North Pacific; South Pacific.

We've used U.S. pilot charts exclusively and found them to be generally quite accurate. Keep in mind that pilot charts can do no more than provide an average of past conditions; they won't give you a heads-up regarding unusual weather features or timing during the month or season when you choose to sail. But some sailors seem to expect that and don't use pilot charts because "they're always wrong." Don't ignore these very valuable sources of information just because the conditions you experienced on a passage differed from what the pilot

charts predicted. Instead, try to analyze why conditions varied from the average. If you can figure that out, you'll be in a much better position to predict what might happen on your next passage.

The figure at left shows a small section of a pilot chart for the Indian Ocean for July. The wind information includes the percentage of time the wind blows from various directions, the average strength from each direction, and the percentage of calms. The wind rose in the center shows that easterly winds blow 34 percent of the time and southeasterly winds 60 percent of the time; the frequency of winds from other directions is very low but can be measured using a scale on the chart. Wind strengths from both the east and southeast are force 5, and there are no recorded calms (0 percent). The heavy contour shows that waves of 12 feet (3.7 m) or more occur 20 percent of the time in the area. Currents set southwestly, at a speed of 0.6 knots. There are also small insets (not shown here) with average tropical storm tracks, surface pressure and temperature, air temperature, and the percentage of gales.

Compare the information on the chart for the various months that you're considering sailing in an area, and you'll often see significant differences in terms of wind strengths, directions, and frequencies, as well as in wave heights.

Pilots

The U.S. NIMA and the U.K. Hydrographic Office both publish a series of pilots that cover all oceans of the world. The U.K. versions are known as "Admiralty Sailing Directions," but the individual volumes are called "Pilots" (as in "Pacific Islands Pilot"). There are over 70 separate Admiralty pilots, about a third of which cover tropical areas.

Their U.S. counterparts are also known as "Sailing Directions," but the U.S. versions are published in two parts, one for passage planning (these are "Planning Guides") and the other for use en route (designated "Enroute"). Planning Guides generally cover a large area, while Enroute Sailing Directions are country- or region-specific. For example, there is one Planning Guide for the North Atlantic, but seven different Enroute publications for the same area, including two volumes for the Caribbean. There are a total of 16 Enroute volumes covering tropical waters.

We always carry a pilot (either the U.S. or U.K. version) with us for the areas in which we're cruising. These volumes are targeted at large ships, and for us knowing that good anchorage is available in 20 fathoms (35 m) isn't really that useful. But there is a wealth of other detail about weather patterns, passes, reefs, currents, islands, and ports. Some cruisers don't bother carrying pilots, assuming that this information will be covered in a cruising guide of the area. It may be, but cruising guides are very often selective in what they cover, and not surprisingly, they lack detail about areas that few yachts visit. Pilots generally include information about all navigable waters within the geographic area they address. We see them as standard references that belong aboard every cruising boat.

Cruising Guides

We haven't counted, but there are probably hundreds of cruising guides available to sailors, covering many parts of the world. In heavily cruised areas, such as the Caribbean, there will be a choice of guides for the same waters. Cruising guides can be very useful. If well researched, they can make cruising much easier, not only helping you find anchorages and navigate complicated passes, but also assisting you in finding what you're looking for on land, and advising what precautions to take regarding tropical diseases. Their quality varies enormously, however, and it's especially hard to evaluate a guide if you're buying it via mail order, sight unseen.

A more general reservation we have about these works is that they can change the way that people cruise. Sailors often avoid visits to anchorages and islands that are either not mentioned (or poorly rated) and tend to congregate in those regions that were the author's favorite, which become more crowded as a result. Many cruisers hesitate to deviate from the scripted route, and it reminds us of traveling to popular tourist destinations on land, where one can meet the same travelers in a sequence of attractions, all clutching the same trusty guidebook. You may know where to go, what to do, and what to expect tomorrow, but in the process, much of the adventure of traveling or cruising is lost.

Our advice is to shop carefully for cruising guides and to use them carefully as well. Treat a guide as just one more information source, and don't hesitate to venture to places that are either unfavorably reviewed or not mentioned at all. They might just end up being your favorites.

Tourist Guides and Other Information Sources

Most sailors like to have more information about the culture, history, and environment of the places they're headed than will be included in a cruising guide for the area. This can be hard to get in a concise form, especially if you're out in the sticks already. Travel guides can be helpful, and many cruisers we know have a stock of guidebooks for the areas they're visiting. Of course, such books focus on shore attractions, and much of the information (about where to stay and where to eat) isn't of much use, unless you're planning an extended foray ashore. We're sometimes amazed at how selective guidebook authors are in describing a place. It's a bit like the photos of quaint village scenes that appear in tourist brochures: when you go there, they turn out to have been carefully cropped to hide the tacky hotels that line the beach. Now that photos can be scanned and doctored by anyone with a computer, be on the lookout for shots of beaches that don't even exist!

The books that have given us the most insight into the places we're visiting are not travel guides at all, but simply books that focus on the environment, culture, or history of the area. Such works will give you a much broader appreciation for a place than a travel guide and may help in giving a focus to your travels, something we find very worthwhile.

PASSAGE TIMES

An important consideration when planning and preparing for an offshore passage is how long you're likely to be at sea. Sailors' attitudes toward passage times vary enormously, from the racer's "I got here in 243 hours, 34 minutes. How about you?" to the laid-back cruiser's approach of "Once you leave land, who cares how long it takes?" Of course, you need to have some notion of how long a passage might last, if only to ensure that you're taking along enough food and water. But the need for some reasonable estimates of sailing time goes further: in reality, few cruisers lead lives so unstructured that they don't need to have some estimate of where they'll be in 6 weeks or 3 months. What's more, those setting out on a lengthy season's cruising—say from the Caribbean through the South Pacific to New Zealand—need to know how much time to allow for each leg. Accurate estimates can make the layovers much more relaxed and avoid a time crunch toward the end. Finally, as we've discussed above, boat speed can be an important factor in your ability to dodge cyclones and other nasty weather systems (see Cyclone Seasons and the Sailor on pages 105–7).

Your passage times will vary according to the speed of your boat, the distance traveled, and the wind and weather conditions you experience en route; the latter is often the most important variable, because rough conditions will generally force all boats to slow down, as their crews try to minimize discomfort. Distance is the factor over which the sailor has the least control: a passage from the Galápagos to the Marquesas can't be shortened. But by getting the best out of your boat and choosing a good weather window, you can shorten the time spent underway, giving yourself more time to enjoy the islands you've worked so hard to reach.

Boat Speed on Ocean Passages

It's possible to increase your average boat speed (and not just by buying a faster boat). Two boats of the same design can deliver quite different average passage times, depending on how they're loaded, equipped, and sailed. The simplest ways of getting more out of your boat are not overloading it and trimming the sails properly. But even if you're getting the most out of your craft, if it's a small, heavy-displacement boat, you just won't achieve the same speeds as a long, lightweight design. Reducing weight and increasing waterline length are two sure ways to increase boat speed, and sailing records fall with regularity as boats get lighter and longer.

Length is largely what determines boat speed. Although multihulls are in general faster than heavy-displacement monohulls, a long sailboat of any given type will typically outpace a shorter one.

Medium- and heavy-displacement monohulls—a category that includes most cruising monohulls—will top out at a speed roughly equal to that of a wave as long as the boat's waterline length. This may be exceeded for very brief periods, particularly when sailing downwind in large seas, but average speeds will almost always be lower.

Light-displacement boats generally sail within the same limits but can exceed these speeds (for more than the few seconds achieved by a heavier boat) by planing. This usually happens when reaching or running in medium or strong winds. They may also approach the upper limits of these speed ranges more frequently and thus achieve higher averages.

Multihulls are not limited by the speed of a wave train equal to their length, due to a combination of their light weight, narrow waterline beam, and high stability (which lets them carry lots of sail). Theoretical maximum speeds for multihulls are very high, but in safe, practical terms cruising multihulls will deliver speeds in the ranges shown in the accompanying table. Multihulls are not dependent on surfing and will likely record their best passage times in moderate conditions on a reaching course.

VARIATIONS IN BOAT SPEED FOR DIFFERENT BOAT TYPES AND LENGTHS

Boat Waterline Length		Medium—Heavy Displacement Monohull Maximum, S/L = 1.35*		Light Displacement Monohull, S/L = 1.35–2.0		Fast Cruising Multihull, S/L = 2.0+	
feet	meters	Top Speed, knots	24 hr. Distance, miles	Top Speed, knots	24 hr. Distance, miles	Cruising Speed, knots	24 hr. Distance, miles
25	7.6	6.5–7	150	7–10	150–75	7.5–10	180–240
36	11	8	190	8–12	180–225	9–12	215–75
49	15	9.5	225	9.5–14	225–75	10.5–14	250–330

* S/L = Speed-to-Length Ratio. S/L x $\sqrt{\text{waterline length}}$ = boat speed

Surprisingly, though, many potentially fast-cruising boats tend to achieve speed averages not that much higher than the smaller, slower boats. That's because comfort at sea has a lot to do with how fast most cruisers sail, and pushing one's boat at sea is rarely very comfortable. We discuss the importance of comfort at sea and how to achieve it in more detail in chapter 8, Passagemaking.

Passage Times: Our Experience

We've generally had plenty of wind—and often more than enough—while sailing in the tropics during the winter season. Our average daily run over many thousands of miles in these conditions has rarely dropped below 120 miles and has often been higher. Our boat's waterline length is a short 25 feet (7.6 m); though seemingly slow, 125 to 135 miles in 24 hours corresponds to a speed–length ratio of 1.0 to 1.125, which is in fact a respectable pace when passagemaking. Longer boats, sailed at a comparable pace, would achieve higher speeds and daily runs, as shown in the table above. In sailing at these speeds we've often deliberately slowed

down, both to be kind to our 37-year-old boat and to make the passage more comfortable for us. This figure has pretty well matched averages reported by other boats of similar overall length making similar passages.

Our average speeds have been lower when we've sailed in equatorial areas during cyclone season, when winds are often very light. Boats that carry ample fuel and can motor extensively may be able to maintain higher averages. (Heavy weather can lead to slow passages as well, as heaving-to, sitting to a sea anchor, or dragging drogues all reduce your average speed.) We've clocked higher averages, including one passage with four consecutive days of over 150 miles. This was with the wind on the quarter, in following seas of 8 to 12 feet (2.5–3.5 m). Interestingly, the course was from Brisbane, Australia, to Noumea, New Caledonia, normally considered a difficult passage due to the need to beat into the typically strong southeastly trade winds. Instead, we had strong southwesterly winds and a great sail. The passage was a comfortable one, even though we were sailing fast, as we had no contrary waves or

Although no slouch, the speed of this deep-bodied traditional boat (Iorangi) is limited by the boat's waterline length. The waves at bow and stern and the trough amidships are clearly visible.

swells. If we'd been sailing on a different course, say with the wind and swell on the beam, or if we had an additional swell that caused us to roll, we would've undoubtedly slowed down considerably. This points once again to what is for any sailor the biggest variable in determining the speed and comfort of a passage: the conditions experienced en route.

Range under Power

It's quite feasible, even in this modern age, to sail without an engine, as a few dedicated cruisers have demonstrated. But most of us do have engines, despite the expense and hassle they entail. Why? Because they're another way of expanding your options. Engines are certainly handy when coastal sailing: they make it easier to get in and out of crowded anchorages and harbors, keep to schedules, and make progress against currents and headwinds. But cruisers are also using them increasingly—and deliberately—when on passages. Knowing you have a reliable engine and can motor a certain distance makes it possible to deliberately set off on a passage when winds are light, rather than waiting for that elusive moment when the winds are just right. This can be very handy when making passages to and from the tropics. You should, of course, maintain a healthy reserve, in case fuel is needed later in the passage. But motoring early on may allow you to anticipate and take advantage of favorable weather patterns that are just developing. A reliable engine and reasonable range under power are also a real plus if you're exploring equatorial latitudes where winds are generally quite light.

The simplest way of extending your range under power is not by fitting extra tankage, but by sim-

This 63-foot (19 m) catamaran, Spirit of Gaia, *can cruise easily at 12–14 knots, making 300-mile days a real possibility.*

ply slowing down. If your boat motors at a top speed of 7 knots, by slowing to 5 knots you'll probably double your range. Get a feel for how much fuel you use when motoring at different speeds and then adjust your motoring speed on passages as re-quired to extend your range. Throttling back will also reduce the strain on your engine, which is never a bad idea when you're the only mechanic for hundreds of miles.

REFINING YOUR PLANS: MOVING BEYOND THE AVERAGES

The information sources we mention above, and the basic seasonal patterns we discussed earlier, serve as the foundation of your route planning. Twenty years ago, planning would have ended there, as other supplementary information wasn't readily available. But modern information-gathering tools such as satellites and almost instant communications make it possible to assess conditions as they develop. Of course, the updates you get may vary dramatically in accuracy, and you should always be wary of assuming that a single incident signifies a trend. (That's the beauty of the classic references we mentioned earlier: they're complied from data collected over many years and so give a reasonable picture of the probability of an event.) Predictions relating to climatic phenomena are well worth heeding, and you'll also want to stay current with political and social developments in the area you're sailing (see Piracy and Political Unrest, below).

Although long-range weather forecasting is still difficult, forecasters and climatologists are able to predict the likelihood of some conditions or features

IMPACT OF EL NIÑO AND LA NIÑA
ON TROPICAL CYCLONE FREQUENCY

Ocean Basin		El Niño		La Niña	
		Frequency	Intensity	Frequency	Intensity
North Atlantic		- - -	-	+	+
Eastern North Pacific		+	+ +	-	- -
Western North Pacific	eastern	- -	=	- -	=
	western	+ +	=	+ +	=
North Indian Ocean		=	=	=	=
South Indian Ocean		=	=	=	=
Australia (West Coast)		-	=	+	=
Australia (Central and East Coast)		- -	-	+ +	+
South and Central Pacific west of 160° E		+ +	+ +	- -	-

KEY

slight decrease -	no change =	slight increase +
moderate decrease - -		moderate increase + +
large decrease - - -		

months in advance. Although they may not be able to tell you what the weather will be doing next week, they can provide a guide to an upcoming season, in the way of relative trade wind strength or cyclone probability. That's in part because these are closely linked to the El Niño and La Niña phenomena, which affect weather across much of the globe.

El Niño and La Niña (ENSO) Predictions

As we saw in chapter 3, the El Niño and La Niña phenomena are linked to an oscillation in air pressure between the Pacific and Indian Oceans. During El Niño years, pressure is higher than normal in the Indian Ocean and lower than normal in the Pacific. As a result, the Pacific trade winds and their associated ocean currents are weak; water temperatures in the Eastern Pacific rise as a result. During La Niña years, atmospheric pressure in the Pacific is high, trade winds and currents are strong, and warm water pools up in the western Pacific. These periodic deviations from the "norm" in terms of pressure, wind and currents are often collectively termed El Niño Southern Oscillation, or ENSO.

Because ENSO cycles are long, lasting months and sometimes years, you don't need frequent updates. The simplest way to keep tabs on what's happening is to log on the Internet every few months and check an ENSO forecast. A wealth of information is available, from simple predictions in plain English to highly technical reviews of the latest data. Sea surface temperatures are also available, updated on a daily basis. These sources can be accessed from anywhere, at no cost (other than any Internet service provider fees you may have). See Seasonal Updates on ENSO, Tropical Cyclones and Monsoons, in appendix 3, Resources, for Internet addresses.

Both El Niño and La Niña seem to be occurring more frequently. The 20th century saw some 23 El Niños and 16 La Niñas. The four most powerful El

Niños have occurred in the last twenty years. If this trend continues, then "typical" weather patterns will occur less often, and conditions will be more variable. This can be frustrating if you're counting on having "typical" weather but can be a boon if you can take advantage of relatively unusual winds.

For example, El Niño years may allow one to more easily make a passage against the prevailing trade winds in the South Pacific, because trade winds are replaced by westerly winds more often than normal. Trade winds are also lighter than average. In the Caribbean, an El Niño is associated with a much lower incidence of hurricanes and may make a summer passage safer than it would typically be. During La Niña, the South Pacific convergence zone tends to move south and west, while the ITCZ moves north. The doldrum belt moves west and north as well, and a strong South Pacific high results in stronger than normal trade winds. Voyages in the Atlantic and Caribbean during a La Niña may be riskier, thanks to the higher incidence of cyclones.

ENSO and Tropical Cyclones

One of ENSO's most important impacts, from the perspective of tropical cruising, is on cyclone frequency. Take a look at the table on page 104, which lists cyclone seasons and frequency around the world. The neat precise figures and seasons in this table may be statistically accurate, but the actual incidence often varies dramatically from one year to the next. That's borne out in part by cyclone tracks, which show considerable variation from year to year. It's also been borne out by research that's compared cyclone frequency and tracks with ENSO conditions. The table here summarizes the impact of ENSO on cyclone frequency in various tropical cruising areas, and we provide additional detail below.

Atlantic

▶ **NORTH ATLANTIC.** Contrary to what you might expect, El Niño's biggest impact on tropical cyclone activity is in the North Atlantic, where hurricane frequency decreases by as much as 60 percent. The biggest drop is in low latitudes. Intensity is also reduced. During a La Niña, hurricane frequency and intensity both increase. The alteration in Atlantic hurricane frequency is due primarily to changes in upper-level westerly winds and wind sheer, and not to temperature changes at the surface.

▶ **SOUTH ATLANTIC.** Tropical cyclones are essentially unknown in the South Atlantic.

Pacific

▶ **EASTERN NORTH PACIFIC.** El Niño brings an increase in both hurricane frequency and intensity, whereas both decrease during La Niña.

▶ **WESTERN NORTH PACIFIC.** This region has the greatest number of tropical cyclones worldwide. The impact of El Niño and La Niña are opposite in the eastern and western parts of the region. In the eastern part of the Western North Pacific, the frequency and intensity of typhoons between 140 and 160° E (an area that includes the Caroline and Mariana Islands) increase markedly during an El Niño and decrease in a La Niña. In the western part (the South China Sea), typhoons are less likely during an El Niño and more likely during a La Niña.

▶ **SOUTH PACIFIC.** The total number and intensity of tropical cyclones vary little overall during ENSO cycles, but the distribution of tropical cyclones does change. During El Niño events, there are more cyclones in the eastern Pacific than usual, impacting French Polynesia and the Cook Islands with greater than normal frequency. El Niño means fewer cyclones in the Coral Sea and east coast of Australia. Following an El Niño, the South Pacific cyclone season may be delayed somewhat. The impacts on South Pacific frequency appear to be caused by changes in surface temperature and pressure.

Indian Ocean

The ENSO cycle does not seem to have a significant impact on the overall pattern of Indian Ocean tropical cyclones.

PIRACY AND POLITICAL UNREST

The issue of safety is unfortunately becoming an increasing concern in many areas. Problems include piracy (attacks in coastal waters), political unrest, and more typical crimes such as theft and muggings. Fortunately, most tropical areas remain free of serious problems, and the odds of running into trouble are low. But the risk can be significant in some places. For example, recent data suggests that about 1 percent of cruisers making a passage through the Red Sea in the last few years have been the victims of piracy. Your best defense is to be aware of the relative risk in the area you choose to cruise, and to prepare yourself ahead of time for problems that might develop.

A Worldwide Overview

Piracy against yachts and ships is on the rise; fortunately, most pirates target large ships, and attacks against yachts remain uncommon. According to the International Maritime Bureau (IMB), piracy against ships increased by 450 percent over the last decade. The IMB's Piracy Reporting Centre, based in Kuala Lumpur, Malaysia, issues weekly piracy bulletins. In 2000 they reported a total of 469 attacks against shipping. Although their figures don't count attacks on yachts separately, they do provide an overall picture of the situation in various areas.

Some sophisticated gangs operate by seizing entire ships. Of greater concerns to yachts are pirates who are on the lookout for money and saleable items such as radios. These attacks have been termed "maritime muggings." Yachts probably face the largest risk of attack in very poor areas where government authority is weak or nonexistent.

Cruisers face risks when ashore as well as at sea. Unrest occurs periodically across the tropics and can range from demonstrations to full-scale civil war, and includes cultural or religious clashes. We were sailing in the Mollucca Islands of Indonesia when widespread religious fighting broke out, with hundreds of villagers killed. Typically, such violence is not directed at outsiders, but cruisers shouldn't count on this; in a climate of violence, people may behave very differently than you might normally expect. It's also not inconceivable that yacht crews could be subject to politically or financially motivated attacks or kidnappings. The country with the worst record so far is Colombia, where the kidnappings are so commonplace as to make travel there very dangerous. There have also been widely publicized incidents in the Philippines.

Finally, when cruisers are ashore in high-risk areas, they are subject to theft, mugging, and other crime in the same way that any tourist would be. The risks from such crimes can be assessed in part from tourist guides and from travel advisories, such as those issued by the U.S. Department of State.

High-Risk Areas

We present detailed information on piracy and political unrest for various cruising destinations in each cruising area within the regional chapters (chapters 17, 18, and 19), under the heading Health and Safety. In addition, Piracy Updates in appendix 3, Resources, includes Web sites that can be checked for recent updates. Some warnings are very specific, and it may be possible to reduce the danger significantly by a small change in your route. For example, the IMB reported that the riskiest area for pirate attack within the Malacca Straits fell within a 25-nautical-mile radius surrounding 02° N and 102° E, where one armed gang of pirates appeared to have repeatedly mounted attacks on ships.

Hotspots for Piracy

The information we've reviewed is far from complete, but it shows that recent attacks against yachts have occurred in several different areas. Attacks against yachts seem to follow a somewhat different pattern than the more widespread attacks against ships. The following areas appear to be current hotspots and should be treated with special caution:

▶ the Gulf of Aden and waters off the coast of Somalia

- the Sibutu Passage and Balabac Strait
  (on the northeast coast of Borneo)
- the coast of Venezuela, near Trinidad

Hotspots for Political
Unrest and Related Violence

Cruisers considering heading for the following countries should obtain an update on the risk before departing:

- Colombia
- Eritrea
- Indonesia
- Solomon Islands
- Somalia
  (at this writing should be avoided at all costs)
- Sri Lanka
- Sudan

Avoiding Pirate Attack

The most obvious way of reducing the chance of attack is by not venturing into especially dangerous areas. This may not always be possible, however, or may entail too large a detour. For example, the most dangerous area for yachts at present is probably the coast of Somalia and Gulf of Aden. Yachts heading for the Red Sea must pass through these waters; the only alternative for cruisers bound for the Mediterranean is to round the Cape of Good Hope, adding many months and thousands of miles to their journey.

If you've decided on a route but are worried about the risk, try to team up with other yachts so you can sail in company. Both anecdotal evidence and common sense suggest that this reduces the risk. Set up a radio link, stay within sight of each other, and have a well-thought-out plan to follow if you are approached or attacked.

Always maintain a good visual, radar, and radio watch while you're in high-risk areas. Recent advice suggests that cruisers should not transmit via their VHF radio, which are often monitored by pirates. If you have an SSB transceiver, it is advisable to use it

to maintain radio contact. Contact any ships you see, if possible set up a schedule with shore stations, and maintain contact with yachts traveling with you or in the vicinity. By doing so you'll greatly improve your chance of getting help should you need it.

Be wary of any approaching vessels, except ships or boats whose identity is obvious. Ships' crews that have been victims of piracy report that some pirates use boats that have been disguised to resemble patrol craft. Crews have also reported that some pirate gangs were directed by individuals who spoke flawless English, and it's possible that members of the armed forces in some countries have cooperated with or directed pirate activities. Several incidents of apparent piracy in the Gulf of Aden were later discovered to have involved Yemeni coastal patrols. Patrol vessels in some countries may not be marked, and their crew may not be in uniform; what's more, some may demand cigarettes, money, or other "gifts." You might well ask how such incidents differ from "true" piracy, but it appears that in no case was violence involved. Be aware of the possibility that you may be approached by such unmarked patrols. If you're the victim of such an incident, report it to the authorities when you reach port.

Decide what action you'll take if you're approached closely by what you think are pirates. Our plan has always been to make as much noise and fuss as possible (using spotlights, setting off flares, and so on) in an effort to dissuade any potential pirates from thinking that we'd be easy pickings. What to do next (if that doesn't work) is hard to generalize about, but you should discuss the options beforehand: there won't be time in the midst of a crisis. Some cruisers are inclined to repel borders at all costs, but this strikes us as a potentially risky strategy, which could result in a more violent reaction from pirates if they do make it onboard. It could also land you in a very difficult situation with local authorities if you seriously injure or kill someone. A "shoot first, ask questions later" approach could also provoke a crisis if all the "pirates" wanted was to ask if you cared to buy

You may see and be approached by all sorts of strange boats when in remote parts of the tropics, but most will want nothing more than to sell some fish.

some fish. We've been approached in remote Indonesian waters by a variety of craft, and these always turned out to be harmless encounters.

We choose not to carry any firearms or other weapons and hope that we can either bluff or talk our way out of a crisis. This is an individual decision, however, and all cruisers should think long and hard about how they would handle an attack. If you do carry a firearm, you'll have to declare it to customs in each country you visit, and in most countries you'll have to surrender the weapon to customs, who will hold it until you clear out, bound for another country. This can present difficulties if you plan to leave the country from a different port than your entrance port, and a fee may be charged by the customs service for transporting your firearm to your exit port.

Chapter 8

Passagemaking

Passages vary in length from a few hundred miles to many thousands. There's no magic formula that determines when a "sail" becomes a passage, but passages are generally long enough that you need to stand watches, and they take you far enough offshore that help is not readily available, as it might be when coastal sailing. On a passage, you adopt a different routine than when day sailing or even making overnight hops; you'll also need to equip your boat differently and spend more time preparing your crew. One of the most important distinctions is that passages require a greater degree of self-reliance. It's probably this fact more than any other that makes many beginning cruisers pause as they prepare to head out of sight of land.

As they consider venturing offshore, many coastal cruisers think first of gear. Choosing and installing equipment is an important aspect of preparing a boat for tropical cruising, but equipment is best considered in the context of the conditions that may require it, and along with the skills that you'll also want to develop. For that reason, throughout the book we've discussed equipment, whether it be sails or drogues, at the same time we consider how and when the equipment is used. In this chapter we include a discussion of self-steering gear and the safety equipment that's advisable for passagemaking. In addition, in Equipping the Tropical Cruising Yacht we outline the equipment needed for both coastal and offshore cruising in tropical waters.

DEPARTURE

Departures are often hectic, as there's lots to do: provisioning; last-minute checks, adjustments, and repairs on the boat; monitoring the weather; saying good-bye to friends; and often dealing with customs and immigration officials. When you're rushed, stress levels go up, and you may not get enough sleep. Cruisers who haven't made many passages will often be nervous as well. People who are tired, nervous, and stressed won't be performing as well as

they should be when sailing offshore, especially at the outset of a passage. If you don't feel ready, adjust your schedule and give yourself enough time to accomplish everything at a reasonable pace.

Two major concerns are getting the right weather window and navigating safely out of port and away from land. What constitutes the right window can be a contentious issue, at times even between crew members on the same boat! You'll be

Sail changes can be a frequent event in squally weather.

looking for two things: good weather as you're leaving port and a decent long-term forecast that will see you well into your trip. The latter is the most important, and you may find that departing in stronger winds than you might ideally want makes sense if that means you'll still be sailing halfway through your trip, rather than leaving with a gentle breeze that fizzles out completely.

Navigating your way safely out of port is usually simple enough but can get complicated if there are unmarked reefs or passes that you'll need to negotiate. If that's the case, adjust your departure time so you'll be transiting those passes when the sun is overhead, and make sure that the weather is such that visibility will be good. Conditions are often rougher on the first day or two of a passage than they'll be later, due to the effects of shoaling water and land on waves and wind. Many sailors are queasy or sick for the first day or two out, and that can make even reasonable sea conditions feel miserable. And naturally there tends to be more boat and ship traffic along the coast, which means you'll need to be extra vigilant on watch. These are all good reasons to make sure you're well rested before setting out.

ON PASSAGE

When the first day or two are over, you can settle into a passagemaking routine. Then, watches set the schedule onboard, and you adjust to the rhythm of life out on the ocean. The main jobs are to keep the boat sailing well, maintain a good watch, and keep an eye on the weather. A reliable self-steering system will enormously ease the work of keeping the boat on course and sailing well—especially on short-handed boats.

Self-Steering Systems
The self-steering gear found aboard ocean cruising boats includes wind-driven equipment (primarily wind vanes) and electric (or combination electric and hydraulic) autopilots. What type you opt for will depend primarily on the kind of sailing you plan to do and on your budget, but the type of boat you sail may also have an impact on your choice. That's because even a small increase in the wind speed can cause fast boats (such as light multihulls) to speed up enough to cause a significant shift in the apparent wind. Since a wind vane steers to the apparent wind, this will cause your actual (compass) course to change. As a result, multihulls and fast monohulls are often better off using an autopilot.

An important consideration is how well your self-steering equipment will control your boat in a storm. We've used our Aries wind vane in winds up to 55 knots, and it performed faultlessly, guiding us safely down one towering wave after another. We've no reason to think it wouldn't work well in even stronger blows. If you're considering using an autopilot and are planning long passes, investigate

AUTOPILOTS AND WIND VANES EXPLAINED

Autopilots steer a boat on a constant heading, detecting course deviations using an internal compass. Course corrections are transmitted to the tiller, wheel, or quadrant via lines, belts, or mechanical linkages; a geared electric motor or hydraulic cylinder typically does the work. The cheaper above-deck models will generally perform well when motoring, or sailing in moderate conditions, and these are commonly carried aboard many coastal cruising boats, where they generally perform adequately. However, such autopilots are likely to have trouble controlling your boat properly in rough conditions. As a result, we recommend that sailors who are doing any extended blue-water voyaging and who prefer to use an autopilot invest in a robust and powerful below-deck model.

Unlike wind vanes, autopilots have the advantage that they can steer your boat even when you're motoring, and they're generally easy to install and operate. The downside is that the larger, more powerful models have substantial electrical power requirements. Because they use increasing amounts of power in rough weather, you should ensure that your charging system and batteries can meet the demand.

In contrast to autopilots, wind vane self-steering systems steer the boat at a constant angle to the wind. When the boat is on course, the vane itself (typically just a flat, narrow wood or plastic blade) will be aligned edge-on to the wind, as your sails are if you're in irons. If the boat drifts off course, one side of the blade will be exposed to the wind, causing it to pivot (or heel). With servo-pendulum wind vanes (which account for the majority on the market), a slight heeling of the blade triggers a corresponding movement by the rudderlike paddle that's in the water. The paddle is connected mechanically (usually with lines) to the helm, and the force of the water flowing past the paddle provides the power to turn your boat.

Aboard *Nomad* we use an Aries wind vane. The Aries and other servo-pendulum wind vanes have a number of advantages. They draw no power, are relatively simple to maintain and repair, and do an excellent job of steering most boats in a wide range of conditions. Their biggest drawbacks are their initial expense, and the fact that they don't steer well in very light winds, particularly when sailing downwind. However, for us the reliability of a wind vane far outweighs the cost.

All self-steering units need regular maintenance. Below-deck autopilots should require the least, but since they have both moving parts and electrical connections, it's prudent to check their condition before any passage. Many wind vanes (including the Aries) incorporate aluminum castings and are prone to corrosion wherever any stainless steel parts come into contact with the aluminum castings. Exposed bearings on any wind vane should be lubricated daily on a passage, which offers a good time to check the lines linking the servo-paddle and tiller or wheel. These are susceptible to chafe, something we've learned the hard way. We've had to replace ours several times while offshore, always on a dark and stormy night—not the best conditions for hanging over the transom with a line in your teeth!

---

how well the model you're looking at has performed for other sailors in truly rough conditions.

A wind vane's weakest point is operating in light, following winds, which, of course, is where an autopilot shines. We fit our Aries with an extra-large, light-wind blade, and it will then steer to windward reliably in winds as light as 6–8 knots. On downwind courses, however, steering becomes erratic in winds much below 10 knots. Some wind vanes, such as the Hydrovane, are designed to be used in conjunction with an autopilot; it is also possible to use a small, inexpensive tiller autopilot with a wind vane by hooking the autopilot to a modified blade. This drastically reduces the force on the autopilot to a point where even the smallest model of autopilot should be up to the task.

Although both wind vanes and autopilots can free you from the tyranny of the tiller or wheel, they won't sail your boat. Expect to do a lot of fiddling during your first season of sailing with self-steering gear. Proper boat balance is essential if any self-steering gear is to work properly, and the only way to achieve this is by choosing the proper sail combination for the given conditions. Our Aries is not very different from any other crew member, preferring a modest amount of weather helm and rounding up regularly if we delay reefing too long. But once the

Seabirds such as this red-footed booby frequently hitch a ride for a few hours, especially in stormy weather when they may get blown off course.

boat is balanced, the vane will steer through thick and thin, enduring waves, cold, and general nastiness with aplomb.

Keeping Watch

Even with a reliable self-steering system keeping your boat on course, it's imperative that you maintain a proper watch when on a passage. Keeping a proper watch is your best defense against collisions with ships or other craft. As we discuss in detail in the Safety at Sea section later in this chapter, ships won't necessarily see you, either visually or on radar, so make sure you see them. By keeping a proper watch you'll also be able to react quickly to changes in wind and weather.

Cruisers use many different watch systems, depending on the size of their crew and their preferences. With just the two of us, we usually keep watches short—about two or three hours, depending on sea conditions. Other sailors prefer longer watches of up to six hours at a stretch, which allow for longer periods of uninterrupted sleep. Use what works for you. Boats with larger crews will have greater flexibility in developing watch systems. If you have a crew of four, and all stand equal watches, a two-hour watch will be followed by six hours off. That's one of the greatest benefits of sailing with larger crews: it allows everyone to get more rest, making passages both safer and more enjoyable.

We keep a formal watch only at night, although we ensure that one of us is always alert and on deck (or takes a frequent look around) during the day. By not having strict watches during daylight hours, we find it easier to catch up on sleep, as you can take a nap when your body is ready (assuming your fellow crew member isn't already asleep). Each crew member on a short-handed boat should get a chance to sleep during the day.

Some cruisers don't keep watch at night; a number of these are single-handers, and even the most diligent will have trouble keeping a reasonable watch. That's a problem to consider before setting off alone, and one that would give either of us pause before making a single-handed passage. But we've encountered a few boats with larger crews who all take to their bunks at night. Some had radar and counted on a radar alarm to alert them of approaching ships. Others relied on their fellow mariners, suggesting that because most ships and sailboats keep watch, they didn't have to. Finally, some simply play the odds, calculating that the chance of a collision is pretty small.

Not keeping a proper watch strikes us as irresponsible and foolhardy. We've seen many ships while at sea, and we've had a number of encounters that required us to change course to avoid collision (or a near miss). In our experience, visual watch-keeping practices aboard some larger ships appear to be poor to nonexistent, and the odds of being picked up by a ship's radar are often also poor. The chances of not being seen go up during bad weather, when rain squalls and swells reduce visibility. Nonetheless, one cruiser we met—a single-hander—was hit by a ship during broad daylight in calm conditions. He was below briefly, preparing a meal; who knows where the ship's lookout was. The ship dealt his boat only a glancing blow, but it was enough to put a 90-degree bend in his steel bowsprit, batter the topsides, and demolish the spreaders. He didn't lose his boat only because it was built of steel.

Watch Routines

Keeping watch is usually uneventful, and on warm tropical nights it can be very pleasant. It's a chance to read, listen to music, learn constellations, and ponder the meaning of life. But you should take it seriously, and that means having a good look around about every 10 minutes. We use this figure because of the speed with which approaching ships can come upon you. Taking a good look around means doing a slow and deliberate scan of the entire horizon. This is pretty easy on a fairly calm, moonless night but requires much more care in rough weather, when a ship's lights may be visible only when your boat and the ship are atop a wave at the same time. Rain squalls further reduce visibility. If we're near shipping routes when the weather turns rough, we often keep a watch almost continuously because of the amount of time it takes to do a proper scan of the horizon.

You'll need to be most vigilant in coastal waters, especially in areas with heavy shipping traffic or coastal fishing fleets. Charts will generally indicate the presence of shipping lanes, if these have been officially designated, and pilots or cruising guides may give an indication that waters will be crowded. It's not uncommon, though, to encounter increasing traffic without any advance warning from such sources. We've experienced the most activity in Southeast Asia. There, the water is often aglow with bright fishing lights used by night fishermen; a good thing, because many don't use navigation lights, and the boats can be impossible to see otherwise. The area is also an extremely busy region for shipping, with hundreds of ships per day transiting major routes, such as the Malacca Straits.

There's more to watch keeping than just acting as a lookout for ships. You should also keep track of how the boat is sailing: whether it's staying on course or needs more or less sail. You should also take notice of any squalls that are approaching, because it's much easier to tuck in a reef or roll up the jib before the squall hits than after.

Ships will often approach very closely, even in midocean.

Every few hours the on-watch crew should record in the log any changes in the weather, barometer reading, sightings of ships or boats, and your position. In the days before electronic navigation, the latter would have consisted of a DR (dead reckoning) plot, but now we simply record our actual position. Many cruisers don't bother keeping such records, but a regular barometer reading is a great help in weather forecasting, while a record of your position is invaluable in determining where you are should you have problems with your GPS. Today it's possible to navigate and steer your boat entirely with electronics: punch in a waypoint at the beginning of a trip, let the GPS and autopilot steer the boat, and monitor your progress on an electronic chart. But you'll have to scramble to figure out your position should that array of black boxes fail. Take the time to record your position every few hours; we also plot it on a real (paper) chart at least once a day.

Finally, make daily rounds of the deck, examining cotter pins, clevis pins, shackles, and so on. Boats move around a lot at sea, and pieces of hardware that you swear couldn't come apart will do so. By making an inspection tour every day, you can often catch these bits in the act of wiggling loose. It's also a good time to check for chafe and to oil any moving parts that might need it, such as on your wind vane.

Comfort at Sea

How much you enjoy passages will depend a lot on how comfortable you are while at sea. You'll be

Not all vessels keep a proper lookout or show the required lights.

spending a lot of time in a small space, and little details will become surprisingly important. Ensure that you have a handy place to stow navigational books and tools and a convenient place where you can make plots on the chart, even if conditions are rough. Ensure that the galley will be easy to use even if you're well healed on either tack. Combat boredom by stocking up on good books if you enjoy reading, or tapes or CDs if your preference is music. And provide for the crew that's on watch: a few waterproof cockpit cushions, a cockpit reading light that doesn't destroy your night vision, and a thermos or two for hot drinks can go a long way toward keeping them happy during the long hours from 2 to 6 A.M.

It's also important to ensure the crew can get a good night's sleep, no matter the conditions. This requires good sea berths for the off-watch crew, with secure lee cloths. The best sea berths will be located in the middle of the boat, where motion is at a minimum; likewise, the lower down in the boat the berth is, the more comfortable it will be. Berths in the forward third of the boat will be uncomfortable except on very placid downwind runs, but even berths in an aft cabin may become uncomfortable in moderate or rough seas. Sea berths should not be overly wide, as you'll then be tossed about and will lose sleep as you tense up and fight the motion. If your boat has a double berth that you intend to use at sea, make a lee cloth that can be rigged to divide the berth in half if conditions warrant. Large pedestal or freestanding berths fitted on many modern boats can be all but impossible to convert to proper sea berths, and those crews may be better off bedding down on the cabin sole.

Crew comfort also has to do with the way in which the boat is sailed. We discuss this in chapter 6 (Sailing in the Tropics), but it bears mentioning again: in order to be comfortable, you'll want to have good control over the speed of your boat. Boats traveling at high speeds are typically noisy, because

Dolphins are frequent visitors, and many love to bowride or simply swim alongside when you're making good speed.
Tom Kieckhefer, NOAA

of water rushing past the hull, and on some courses may tend to leap off waves, or pound. Multihulls may have waves pounding on the underside of the bridge deck. None of these are conducive to a good night's sleep for the off-watch crew, or to the skipper's peace of mind. Most sailors we know regularly slow their boats to a point well below the craft's potential, primarily to make the passage more comfortable. But boats that are going too slowly can be uncomfortable as well, wallowing and rolling about so that you're thoroughly miserable. Having simple sail-handling and reefing systems can be a big help and can give you the confidence to carry an amount of sail appropriate for the conditions at hand.

Landfall

Landfall is usually exhilarating, but it can also be the most dangerous and tiring stage of a passage. You'll be leaving relatively uncrowded open waters for what's probably an unfamiliar coast. Swells and waves often increase, and wind speeds may as well.

The crew on watch will need to be especially attentive due to the likelihood that you'll encounter ships, or fishing or pleasure boats, as you close with the coast. It may be advisable to slow down while you still have good sea room, and you may have to choose or plot a route through reefs and passes. Count on spending considerable time on navigation and pilotage at the end of passages, keeping a close eye on your position and planning and timing your approach.

Because landfalls are tiring and often demanding, it helps enormously if you can ensure that the crew is well rested. This will go a long way toward preventing errors in navigation and avoiding poor decisions. This may be difficult to achieve on a short-handed boat, however, especially if one of the crew is sick and the weather is rough. If you're still a few days out and already run-down or experiencing rough conditions, consider heaving-to and resting up while still well offshore. Many boats have come to grief by heaving-to too close to land, either because they drifted in to the coast or were hit by shipping. Delaying landfall can be very frustrating to an eager (or seasick) crew, but is sometimes the best tactic.

SAFETY AT SEA

We've already talked about many aspects of boat preparation, and these will normally be done long before you embark on a passage. There's another issue that also requires advance preparation, and that's safety. Although the concerns we raise here apply to coastal cruisers as well, sailors setting off on offshore passages will want to pay particular attention.

Preparation and avoidance are the keys to sailing safely offshore. Prepare for the worst, and then do your best to avoid problems and hazards. Your concern with offshore safety should start when you buy or build a boat and as you develop your sailing skills. To set out voyaging on a boat that lacks adequate stability or is very lightly constructed is asking for trouble, and investing in the best life raft that money can buy is a poor substitute for ensuring that your boat is well-found. Likewise, we think it's vital to hone your skills and those of your crew. Although equipment is important, no flashy gear can replace a calm and well-prepared crew if and when things go wrong.

Attitude has an important effect on how likely it is that problems will develop and on how well sailors cope with crises. If you learn to sail cautiously and defensively, then you're less likely to encounter trouble. Unfortunately some accidents can't be predicted or avoided, but your attitude will still form an important aspect of your response. Many life-raft survivors ascribe their survival, in part, to their determination to survive; a similar determination to prevail will help you through less extreme situations.

Avoiding Collisions

Collisions with ships are one of the major hazards that tropical cruisers face when passagemaking. Such collisions are not common, but they do occur, and we've crossed paths with enough ships ourselves to realize that the odds of being hit are not as small as we might wish to believe. There are several

defenses that you can take to prevent a collision: maintain a proper watch at all times (as we discussed earlier in the Keeping Watch section) and make your boat as visible as possible, by always showing navigation lights and a radar reflector. Here we consider the visibility of your boat.

Navigation Lights

Showing proper lights is a basic responsibility of all mariners and an important—though far from foolproof—way of reducing the risk of collision. Yet we've met experienced cruisers who cheerfully sail without lights. They usually do so to save power, and we've heard them rationalize their action by stating that everyone else shows lights, and they'll turn theirs on if a ship or boat is sighted. It's a disaster in the making if two mariners play this game. And imagine if ships started doing this!

Cruisers who show lights typically use masthead tricolor lights. These have a low power drain (using only one bulb) and are visible over long distances, because of their height above the water. They can still be hard to see, however, and some cruisers have taken to using masthead strobe lights instead. The latter make sense for use in an emergency, or to draw the attention of a ship that's bearing down on you and doesn't see your lights. But we advocate sticking with a standard tricolor for your basic light, as only a proper navigation light will allow another boat or a ship to determine your heading. Plus, if strobes are used as a matter of routine, they'll lose their value in terms of attracting attention in true emergencies.

Radar Reflectors

Radar reflectors are another way of increasing your chance of being seen by a ship. We do advocate carrying one, but our own experience has left us wondering how effective they actually are. One night while on a passage, we were speaking with a ship's officer on VHF, having just alerted him to our presence (after it became clear that we were on a converging course). He hadn't seen us until we called him on the radio, something that took some time in itself. Once we had his attention we asked if he could see us on his radar. Although we were quite close—less than half a mile away—he couldn't detect a trace of our boat.

We carry our radar reflector high in the rigging, and independent tests have shown it to be one of the most effective on the market. We've left it up there, but have learned not to count on ships' radar actually picking it up. The reason ships often don't pick up yachts, radar reflectors notwithstanding, is that ships' crews decrease the sensitivity on their radar to filter out the "noise" generated by waves. They'll still see ships or large fishing vessels, with which a collision might be hazardous, but the tiny signal from a sailboat is filtered out.

Staying Onboard

Falling overboard while on a passage—or even when coastal sailing—is likely to be just as fatal as a midocean collision, but it's probably far more likely to occur. Don't be lulled into a false sense of security by the fact that you're a seasoned sailor. There have been enough well-publicized cases of experienced sailors who have died after going overboard in coastal waters to convince us of a simple fact: if you go overboard, you're as good as dead. Your chances of survival at night are even worse. At first glance your chances in the tropics would seem much better than your odds in temperate latitudes. Hypothermia sets in after just an hour in 50°F (10°C) water, but you can survive for many hours in warm tropical waters. The likelihood of being found and successfully brought back aboard, however, are slim, especially if you sail with a small crew; imagine going overboard early in your watch, with the self-steering gear keeping the boat on course, and the off-watch crew asleep down below.

Don't rely on lifelines to keep you onboard, unless they're truly exceptional (such as extra-high, welded stainless tubing on a steel yacht). That does not mean lifelines shouldn't be there, but most are simply not high or strong enough to prevent a person from going overboard in rough weather. You can reduce the likelihood of pitching over the lifelines by fitting temporary waist or chest lifelines. These can be of low-stretch polyester (Dacron) line; avoid using nylon due to its greater stretch. They should run from bow pulpit to shrouds and back to the stern rail, boom gallows, or other handy and strong attachment point. Even ⅜-inch (9 mm) line will be stout enough. Set these up tightly, as they will inevitably stretch if you push or fall against them. They may be just enough to keep you from testing the integrity of your harness, which is your real defense against going overboard.

Like most offshore sailors, we use chest harnesses. Although some cruisers have foul-weather jackets with built-in harnesses, ours are separate, and we'd suggest

---

MIND THOSE CONTAINERS

Ships often seem blasé about the risk of collision, perhaps because they're in no danger from us, and they're pretty sure to be seen by other ships. One night we spotted a ship but were puzzled by the lights we saw. The ship drew steadily closer, and the position of its masthead lights suggested we were on a collision course. Yet we saw only one side light, rather than both, as we should have if they were approaching us directly. We changed course, and the ship changed course, or so it seemed, and tracked steadily toward us. We made increasingly urgent calls on the radio, but to no avail. Winds were light, so we ultimately started the engine, shoved the throttle ahead, and made a more abrupt change in our heading. The radio finally crackled in response to our "all ships" call, and a very relaxed captain assured us that he could see us quite well. He was bored, he said, and had come by to have a look at us. We both slowed down, and with his container ship looming a few hundred yards away we chatted for a bit, obtained a welcome position fix (we were navigating with a sextant), and got a weather update. We then suggested he should check his navigation lights, as it was now clear to us that the starboard light wasn't working. "Hold on," he replied. Returning to the radio a moment later, he told us that his instruments indicated the light was working fine, adding "It's probably just blocked by a container."

this for tropical cruising. It's not uncommon to have rough seas but warm temperatures, and you don't want to be forced to wear a heavy foul-weather jacket when a harness is all you need. We've fitted ours with double tubular nylon tethers and locking stainless steel carabiners. Jacklines, also of tubular nylon, run from cockpit to bow. One tether is about 6 feet (1.8 m) long, and the other 3 feet (1 m), which allows us to remain clipped in—either to the jacklines, a shroud, or something else strong—at all times. Using both teth-

ers when working in one location for a while can ensure that you don't move far if the boat lurches or rolls. We use a mountain climber's water knot (see pages 347 and 348) to make loops, rather than relying on stitching. We also take the jacklines off whenever we're in port, so they don't degrade in the sun.

We wear harnesses whenever we're on deck in storms and at night in all but really calm seas. We also carry personal strobe lights that are kept with the harnesses.

ABANDONING SHIP

All sailors setting off on an ocean passage should be prepared for the possibility of abandoning ship. That said, it's a decision that should never be taken lightly, and the adage that one should *step up into the life raft from one's sinking boat* is a good one to heed. There have been many cases of sailors abandoning their apparently foundering boats in the midst of severe storms, at great risk to themselves and often to rescuers as well, only to have those same boats still afloat at the storm's end. In some cases the crew perished after taking to their life raft, and it's probable they would have survived had they stayed with their boat. But boats can and do sink, and even multihulls and other "unsinkable" craft may have to be abandoned in the event of an uncontrollable fire.

Life Rafts: The Pros and Cons

For most cruising sailors, life rafts provide the most straightforward and secure solution to the problem of abandoning ship while on an ocean passage. Life rafts are not without their drawbacks (see the accompanying Evaluating Life Rafts table), but they have several important qualities that the alternatives—primarily specially outfitted dinghies—lack. Most importantly, they are designed so that they can be deployed even in rough conditions; once in the water (if well designed and of the proper size), they will be reasonably resistant to capsizing. If you're heading offshore, and your budget allows, a life raft is the best investment you can make to ensure that

you'll have somewhere to go should you need to leave your boat.

Despite this, not all tropical cruisers carry life rafts. Their reasons for sailing without a life raft vary. Among those we've met who have made the decision not to carry a life raft are coastal cruisers, sailors on very tight budgets, cruisers with "unsinkable" boats, and others who are morally opposed to relying on rescue (in most cases a life raft cannot be propelled or steered, making outside help imperative). As an alternative, some cruisers carry an unsinkable dinghy (either an inflatable or a hard dinghy fitted with flotation), and in some instances fitted with a canopy and sail.

The viability of such an alternative varies. It strikes us as a reasonable approach for many coastal cruisers, as they're unlikely to have to endure extremely rough conditions; if they also carry an EPIRB (see discussion below) help should not be too long in arriving. Likewise, sailors with unsinkable boats—multihulls or monohulls fitted with sufficient watertight bulkheads or foam flotation to render them unsinkable—would seem to be running a reasonable risk by opting to outfit a dinghy instead of purchasing a life raft. Ocean voyagers in sinkable monohulls who opt not to carry a life raft for budgetary or philosophical reasons aren't necessarily making a foolish decision, but they do take more of a risk.

We're aware that this can be a difficult decision to make. We cruised on a very tight budget ourselves

EVALUATING LIFE RAFTS

Criteria	Life Raft*	Dinghies Adapted as Lifeboats
Deployment in rough conditions	Possible. Life rafts are designed to be placed over the lee side (with the tether secured) and *then* inflated. Canopy ensures life raft will not immediately swamp.	Extremely difficult or impossible. Both hard dinghies and partially inflated inflatables will be very unwieldy to launch and are immediately prone to capsizing and swamping.
Boarding	Variable. Many life raft tests have demonstrated that boarding can be difficult. Check for the presence of an adequate ladder, handholds, and easily accessed canopy doors.	Variable. Boarding from the deck will be very difficult in rough conditions. Boarding a hard dinghy from the water may be impossible if crew members aren't fit; even inflatables should have ladders.
Stability	Variable, but should be very good for properly sized water-ballasted rafts. Note that crew weight is important to stability; crews of 2 should use 4-person rafts, not larger 6-person models.	Poor. Prone to capsizing due to lack of ballast. May be hard to right if capsized. Risk of capsizing increases if dinghy is flooded.
Protection from the elements	Good, due to canopy. Heat is a major concern in equatorial tropics; two doors desirable for ventilation. Insulated floor desirable but not critical in tropics.	Nonexistent, unless canopy is fitted. Canopy must have support and should provide headroom.
Cost	High	Minimal extra cost, if existing dinghy is used.
Durability	Variable. Degradation from tropical heat is a major concern. Life raft should be inspected regularly and always stowed out of the sun, in a dedicated locker or below deck. Vacuum-sealed rafts are more resistant to water ingress and damage.	Variable. Most dinghies will deliver many years of service; hard dinghies and Hypalon inflatables have greatest longevity.
Reliability	Good, if inspected regularly.	Good, if well maintained.
Propulsion, steerage, self-rescue	Impossible, except for life raft – dinghy hybrids such as the Tinker. Life rafts will drift with winds and currents. Crew will reach land unaided only by chance; dependent on rescue. EPIRB advisable.	Variable. Hard dinghies with sailing rigs may sail well; inflatables will not. Potential may exist for coastal sailors to reach land unaided, but dependent on conditions. EPIRB advisable.

*Assumed to be self-inflating, with self-erecting canopy and water ballast system.

for a number of years and sailed thousands of open ocean miles without a life raft, relying instead on an inflatable dinghy we always kept partially inflated on deck. We never had to test the viability of that system but were never entirely happy with it either. We now have a valise life raft that stows in a dedicated cockpit locker when we're at sea, and that's kept below at other times. Although we don't view life rafts as a perfect solution, we do feel that by sailing with one our chances of immediate survival in an emergency situation have improved, and we consider the money well spent. If we were building a new boat, we'd outfit it with watertight bulkheads fore and aft and improve our chances of being able to stay with the boat.

Life Raft Stowage and Inspection

If you carry a life raft, find a place to store it *other than on the deck or cabin top*, even if it's in a canister. Life rafts can be swept off the deck during severe storms, despite being mounted in a through-bolted cradle. What's more, life rafts stored in an exposed spot will suffer more from heat and exposure. Canister rafts can be stored in the cockpit, reducing the volume of the cockpit in the process, so that it will hold less water if you are pooped by waves. Both canister and valise rafts can also be stored in a dedicated cockpit locker, if space allows. This is in many respects the best solution, as it protects the raft from sun and water but ensures it can be readily and quickly deployed. If a valise raft is stored below, it should be immediately inside the companionway. Wherever you stow the raft, make sure that each crew member is able to get the raft out of its storage place and over the side.

In addition to stowing your raft carefully, have it regularly inspected. Uncertainty over the condition of a life raft is the last thing you'll want on your mind if you're facing a decision about abandoning ship. Unfortunately there's no good way to test a life raft other than by pulling the cord and inflating it; although any of us can do that, seams and all gear must be carefully checked, and afterward the life raft must be repacked and the inflation system recharged. Your

best bet is to have the raft inspected by a certified inspector, on an annual or biannual basis as recommended by the manufacturer. This should be possible in most tropical areas but can be costly. Cruisers who live or cruise for extended periods in an area with no certified inspection service may face problems meeting the need for regular inspections. Life rafts usually can't be shipped by air (due to the flares and inflation systems), and sending a raft by ship will be both slow and expensive. Check with the manufacturer about the best way to handle such a situation. When you have a raft inspected, ask if you can watch while it is inflated. This will allow you to get a preview of how quickly the raft inflates, and may alert you to shortcomings in the raft's equipment.

Ditch Bags

Your biggest concern if you abandon ship in the tropics is likely to be dehydration and exposure to the sun. A proper canopy will help with the sun, but you'll still want to take precautions. We always carry a ditch bag, stowed just inside the companionway, which contains fishing gear, flashlights, compass, sunglasses and sunblock, a knife, a multitool, rain gear, sun shirts, life jackets, wet suits, and food. In addition, two 6-gallon (45 L total) water jugs are immediately accessible in a cockpit locker. Many cruisers include a hand-operated watermaker, and it may be possible to have this packed inside a life raft. The best sources of information on how to prepare for such an eventuality are the accounts of sailors who have had to abandon their boats and lived to write about it (see appendix 3, Resources).

EPIRBs

The fact that life rafts leave one at the mercy of wind and current makes it almost imperative to invest in an EPIRB (emergency position-indicating radio beacon). EPIRBs are the most effective way to summon help at sea in an emergency. There are three basic types available that are suitable for most yachts: 121.5/243 MHz EPIRBs, 406 MHz EPIRBs, and 406 MHz GPS EPIRBs.

The least expensive EPIRBs are the 121.5/243 MHz ones. They broadcast to satellites and aircraft on these frequencies, and have helped save many lives over the years. They're no longer recommended by the U.S. Coast Guard, however, due to their inherent disadvantages in comparison to 406 MHz EPIRBs. Search-and-rescue authorities in other nations also favor 406 EPIRBs over 121.5/243 MHz models. Problems with 121.5/243 MHz models include

▶ **THE SIGNAL** transmitted by a 121.5/243 MHz EPIRB isn't coded, so rescuers don't know who is in distress.

▶ **THE SATELLITE** that receives the signal must be in simultaneous contact with the EPIRB and the ground station to which the signal is broadcast. This limits offshore use, except in areas where satellite coverage is good (most North American waters are well covered).

▶ **IT IS POSSIBLE** to calculate positions only to within about 12 miles.

▶ **THE FREQUENCIES** used by these EPIRBs are highly congested, leading to a very high rate of false alarms. As a consequence, the rescue services of the U.S. Coast Guard and other nations require additional confirmation that a vessel is in distress before mounting a rescue operation.

▶ **NOAA'S ANNOUNCEMENT** that satellite processing of signals from 121.5/243 MHz EPIRBs will be discontinued after 1 February 2009 means that the usable life of these EPIRBs is limited.

Each 406 MHz EPIRB broadcasts a unique coded signal to orbiting satellites when switched on (406 MHz EPIRBs also broadcast on 121.5 MHz, but this signal is not targeted at satellites, but is intended to assist search-and-rescue aircraft to home in on your position). By registering with the Maritime Rescue Coordination Center in your home country when buying the EPIRB, the coded signal is matched to your vessel. If that signal is picked up, rescue authorities will contact the owner or next of kin; that helps them determine if the signal is false, or if the boat really is in distress. Satellites that receive 406 MHz EPIRB signals are in polar orbits, passing overhead every 100 minutes. After the signal is picked up, it's stored until the satellite is in range of a receiving station, and then it's transmitted. In equatorial latitudes, this may take up to four hours. The accuracy of the position is about 1 mile. 406 MHz EPIRBs cost about four to five times as much as 121.5/243 MHz models.

To improve both the response time and the accuracy of the position fix, a 406 MHz EPIRB that incorporates a GPS has been developed. Known as a 406 MHz GPS EPIRB, or GPIRB for short, these transmit to geostationary satellites, which are constantly in contact with receiving stations. That means there is essentially no delay between turning on the EPIRB and having the signal received. Thanks to the built-in GPS, the accuracy of the position fix is excellent, at less than 100 meters. The downside of GPIRBs is that they're even more expensive than 406 MHz EPIRBs.

EPIRBs are available in two configurations: automatically activated models that float free of the boat in case of sinking, and manually deployed and activated models. The automatically activated models are known as either class A EPIRBs (if broadcasting on 121.5/243 MHz) or category 1 EPIRBs (406 MHz types); manually deployed models are known as either class B (121.5/243 MHz EPIRBs) or category 2 (406 MHz types).

Some sailors choose not to carry an EPIRB, making the decision to be entirely self-reliant in any and all emergencies. Although we respect that approach, we carry a 406 MHz EPIRB, having decided that if we're really in distress, we want the option of calling for help. If you do decide to carry an EPIRB, consider carefully how you'll make the decision to turn it on, should an emergency arise. Flipping the switch will put into motion a complex and very costly rescue operation, one that may put rescuers at risk. Use an EPIRB only in a genuine emergency, when you've used up all your other options; don't resort to it if you're simply scared, miserable, or fed up.

EQUIPPING THE TROPICAL CRUISING YACHT

Here we present an outline of the equipment that we feel most tropical cruisers will want to have onboard their boats. This is by no means a definitive list, and some cruisers may sail without many items listed here, whereas others will want additional gear. To help sort out what you might want to carry, we've listed the gear according to three categories:

▶ *THE BASICS* (typically carried by all tropical sailors, including coastal cruisers)

▶ *EQUIPMENT FOR PASSAGEMAKERS* (additions for those who will be making offshore voyages)

▶ *EXTRAS FOR REMOTE REGIONS* (for those heading for really remote areas, where facilities, spare parts, and skilled help are hundreds or even thousands of miles away)

In some instances we've listed nonessential gear that many cruisers carry, with the notations "optional" or "desirable."

Some of the gear you'll want for tropical cruising is likely to already be aboard your boat. For example, a good steering compass, a depth sounder, a VHF radio, and a GPS receiver are all pretty standard these days. Other items—such as a proper cockpit awning or bimini and mosquito screens—are more apt to be missing on many boats outside the tropics.

For each item or category, we've indicated the section of the book where we've discussed the use or selection of that gear. We've made the following point in several of those sections, but it deserves final emphasis here: most problems or challenges won't be solved simply through a technical fix. Although GPS receivers are remarkable pieces of gear (which we wouldn't choose to sail without), they won't do all of your tropical navigation for you. Likewise, although you may want to purchase a drogue or sea anchor if heading offshore, you should also take other more difficult (and important) actions, such as devising heavy-weather strategies that are suited to your boat and developing your crew's skills for coping with such weather. The equipment on this list is not a panacea, but it will enable you to cruise the tropics more safely and comfortably.

EQUIPMENT FOR TROPICAL CRUISERS

● = Additions for tropical passagemakers   Δ = Further additions for passagemakers and cruisers bound for remote regions

Navigation

See chapter 4

Steering and hand-bearing compass

- ● Ensure that compass is easily read at night. Should carry a spare compass, unless handbearing compass can serve as a reliable steering compass.

Depth sounder

Distance log

GPS receiver

- ● Spare (handheld) GPS receiver or sextant

See appendix 1

Ratlines or mast steps

See chapters 4 and 7

Charts, pilots, and cruising guides

Weather and Communications

See chapter 3

Barometer

See appendix 2

VHF transmitter

Desirable: SSB receiver

- ● SSB receiver
- ● Optional: SSB transceiver
- ● Desirable: Weather fax receiver (can be a dedicated unit, or use an SSB receiver or transceiver and a laptop computer)

Anchors

See chapter 5

Working anchor and kedge (minimum)
- 2 working anchors and kedge

Δ 3 working anchors and kedge, OR
  2 working anchors, kedge, and
  storm anchor

Appropriate anchor rodes for the waters
  in which you cruise

Anchor snubber, buoy, and sentinel

Sails

See chapter 6

Easily handled and reefed working sails

Heavy-weather jib

Desirable: Light-air sails
- Light-air sails
- Storm sails

Spinnaker or whisker pole

Boom vang or preventer systems

Simple sail repair kit
- Extensive sail repair kit and materials

Route Planning References

See chapter 7

Pilots and cruising guides
- Pilot charts

Tourist guides and other references

Self-Steering

See chapter 8

Desirable: Autopilot capable of steering in calm
  conditions (when motoring)
- Wind vane or robust autopilot that can
  steer boat under all conditions

Safety at Sea

See chapter 8

Standard USCG-required safety equipment
  such as life jackets and flares

Lifelines, harnesses, and jacklines

Desirable: Coastal EPIRB (121.5/243 MHz)
- Desirable: Satellite EPIRB (406 MHz)

Dinghy equipped with flotation and stowed so
  as to be readily and quickly launched
- Life raft (or dinghy specially equipped to serve
  as a lifeboat)

Ditch bag

Coping with Heavy Weather

See chapter 9
- Desirable: Drogue, parachute anchor,
  or other drag devices

Living Aboard

See chapter 10

Cockpit awning or bimini for use when underway,
  and deck awning for use in port

Combination of hatches, vents, ports, and scoops
  to provide good ventilation

Adequate water storage
- Water purification and catchment system

Proper food storage

Mosquito screens

Dinghy

Proper engine fuel filtration systems and air vents

Health

See chapters 12 and 13

Basic first-aid kit
- More complete first-aid kit

Δ Comprehensive first-aid supplies sufficient to
  deal with most medical emergencies

Tools and Spares

See chapter 14

Basic spares and related tools, including pump
  impellers, engine filters, and lubricating fluids
- Comprehensive tool and spares assortment,
  including pump seals; additional engine filters and fluids; wire and fittings for rigging
  repair; and materials for wiring and basic
  electronic repair.

Δ Extra spares in all categories, including engine cooling pumps and
  injectors; bilge pump and spare
  hoses; rigging wire and fittings;
  anchor chain and line. Include
  materials for hull and deck repair.
  Ensure you have adequate tools and
  ensure you can repair and maintain
  all vital systems.

Chapter 9

Heavy Weather in the Tropics

You're more likely to run into heavy weather on a passage than when coastal sailing, because with a good forecast you can time your coastal hops to avoid lousy conditions. And the longer the passage, the less control you'll have over the weather you encounter. As a result, it's important that cruisers setting off on a passage—even one confined to the tropics—be ready to cope with heavy weather.

What constitutes heavy weather depends in part on your boat. A 24-foot (7 m) coastal cruiser will have a tough time of it in conditions that might provide an exhilarating passage for a substantial 45-foot (14 m) vessel, and round-the-world racers with big crews actively seek out weather that would see most cruisers hove-to. You are the best judge of when conditions are getting rough enough for you to start adopting heavy-weather strategies, and it matters not a whit if others are still flying spinnakers. What's important is that you remain confi-

dent and in control, which requires that you've equipped yourself with the gear and knowledge you'll need to see your boat through.

Undoubtedly the best heavy-weather tactic is avoiding rough conditions in the first place. Having access to timely, accurate weather forecasts is a key in doing this. Most tropical weather features that produce heavy-weather conditions—including convergence zones, fronts, temperate-zone lows that have strayed into the tropics, and even tropical cyclones—tend to be small enough that a 100- or 200-mile change in your position can have a dramatic impact on the severity of the weather you experience. Avoiding such features requires that you have a good idea of where they are in relation to you. Weather fax charts are the simplest way of doing this. We discuss weather fax charts and other forecasts in appendix 2, Weather Forecasts.

WAVES AND SWELLS

By itself, wind rarely poses much of a threat to a cruising boat; it's the waves that accompany strong winds that can wreak havoc. Because heavy-weather strategies are, in many respects, "big wave strategies," it's important to understand how waves develop, and why they're worse at certain times and in certain locations.

Waves form in a number of ways, but the ones of most interest to sailors are the "progressive" waves produced by the wind. Progressive waves move across the ocean in what are usually called *wave trains*. Although waves contain an enormous amount of energy, the water particles within each wave move primarily in a circular pattern (unless the wave is breaking, when water at the crest is sent shooting forward). The circular motion of the water particles means that water at the crest is moving with the wave train, while water in the trough is moving in the opposite direction. As we'll see, this has important implications for how parachute anchors and drogues should be deployed.

Wind waves vary in height with wind strength, the distance over which the wind blows (fetch), and the duration of time the wind blows. They're called *wind waves* (or seas) when they're locally generated and still under the influence of the wind that created them. Wind waves typically don't move far from where they form, unless the wind has blown for a long period, over a large fetch. When this happens, the resulting waves are called *swells*.

Potential Wave Heights

The height of wind waves increases quickly as wind speed goes up, because the force exerted by the wind is equal to the square of the wind speed. But how large wind waves get depends on the strength, duration, and fetch of the wind, as well as the depth of the water and the presence of any current. If fetch is limited, say in the lee of an island, then wave height will be limited as well. For example, in a sheltered anchorage, even a strong wind will produce only small waves. And light winds won't produce large waves no matter how far or long they blow: a gentle 12-knot trade wind, even if blowing for a week with unlimited fetch, will still generate waves of only 5 feet (1.5 m). But if the wind increases to 20 knots, the potential wave height jumps to 12 feet (3.6 m), while at 30 knots, waves can reach 25 feet (7.6 m). The accompanying table presents some potential wave heights for various wind strengths and the minimum required fetch and time.

Waves in the tropics rarely attain the outrageous heights shown toward the bottom of the table, because wind strengths aren't that high, except during tropical cyclones (hurricanes). But the steadiness of tropical winds means that wind waves that are

FULLY DEVELOPED SEAS FOR DIFFERENT WIND STRENGTHS

Beaufort Wind Force	Wind Speed	Maximum Wave Height		Wave Period	Wavelength		Minimum Fetch	Minimum Duration
	knots	ft.	m	seconds	ft.	m	nautical miles	hours
0	0	0	0	0	0	0	0	0
1	1–3	0	0	0.3	0.33	0.1	0.03	0.1
2	4–6	0.33	0.1	1.4	6.5	2	0.3	0.7
3	7–10	0.65	0.2	2.4	20	6	3.2	2.3
4	11–16	2	0.6	3.9	53	16	13	4.8
5	17–21	4.2	1.3	5.4	101	31	35	9.2
6	22–27	8.2	2.5	7	167	51	75	15
7	28–33	15	4.5	9	262	80	155	24
8	34–40	23	7	11	377	115	280	37
9	41–47	36	11	13	541	165	515	52
10	48–55	52	16	15	738	225	850	73
11	56–63	72	22	17	984	300	1,350	100
12	63+	72+	22+	17+	1,115+	340+	1,350	100+

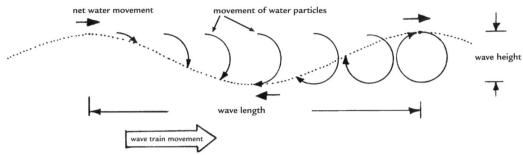

net water movement movement of water particles

wave height

wave length

wave train movement

As wave trains move through the ocean, individual water particles are displaced in a circular motion. The circular movement means that after a full wave has passed by, the water particles end up in the same position as they started. The movement of the particles is in the same direction as the wave train at the crests, but it's in the opposite direction in the wave troughs. Wave height is simply the distance from trough to crest, and wavelength is the distance from one wave crest to another.

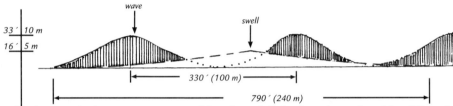

wave

swell

33' 10 m
16' 5 m

330' (100 m)

790' (240 m)

The 33-foot (10 m) waves in this drawing are representative of those that might be found in midocean after a 35- to 40-knot wind has been blowing for several days, and have a wavelength of 330 feet (100 m). The same waves will have developed into the swells shown after traveling some 1,000 nm or so from the area where they originated. The swells have only half the height but more than twice the length of the wind waves. (Vertical scale exaggerated by a factor of 2.)

present usually develop into swells. Swells may travel many hundreds and even thousands of miles from where they were formed, gradually decreasing in height but increasing in speed. Swells can be annoying when they come from a different direction than the prevailing wind waves. This can cause an uncomfortable motion, especially if both wind waves and swells are large.

Swells can also add to the apparent wave height. This happens when a swell coincides with a wind wave. The table opposite shows what to expect when the two combine.

You may often find yourself at odds with forecasters or others when it comes to wave heights, in part because waves often seem bigger than they are when you're out in a small boat, but also because wave heights vary. Forecasts are based on the *significant wave height*, which is the average of the ⅓ highest waves; maximum wave height will normally be almost twice this high. The significant wave height is used in forecasts because it corresponds most closely to the typical wave height estimate that most people make. If a sea is running with an average height of 10 feet (3 m), the significant (and forecast) wave height will be 15 feet (4.6 m), while the maximum height (about 1 in every 1,000 waves) will be 28 feet (8.5 m)! See illustration, page 138.

When Waves and Swells Get Nasty

You may have noticed while sailing that waves generated by a moderate wind often seem worse during the first day or so than they do later. That's because wind waves are steeper when they're actively growing, and they can also be chaotic: interacting,

HOW WAVE HEIGHTS GROW WHEN WAVES AND SWELLS INTERACT

Swell Wave Height		Wind Wave Height															
ft.	m	ft.	m	ft.	m	ft.	m	ft.	m	ft.	m	ft.	m	ft.	m	ft.	m
		6	1.8	8	2.4	10	3	12	3.6	14	4.3	16	4.9	18	5.5	20	6.1
6	1.8	8	2.4	10	3	12	3.6	13	4	15	4.6	17	5.2	19	5.8	21	6.4
8	2.4	10	3	11	3.4	13	4	14	4.3	16	4.9	18	5.5	20	6.1	22	6.7
10	3	12	3.6	13	4	14	4.3	16	4.9	17	5.2	19	5.8	21	6.4	22	6.7
12	3.6	13	4	14	4.3	16	4.9	17	5.2	18	5.5	20	6.1	22	6.7	23	7
14	4.3	15	4.6	16	4.9	17	5.2	18	5.5	20	6.1	21	6.4	23	7	24	7.3
16	4.9	17	5.2	18	5.5	19	5.8	20	6.1	21	6.4	23	7	24	7.3	26	7.9
18	5.5	19	5.8	20	6.1	21	6.4	22	6.7	23	7	24	7.3	25	7.6	27	8.2
20	6.1	21	6.4	22	6.7	22	6.7	23	7	24	7.3	26	7.9	27	8.2	28	8.5
22	6.7	23	7	23	7	24	7.3	25	7.6	26	7.9	27	8.2	28	8.5	30	9.1
24	7.3	25	7.6	25	7.6	26	7.9	27	8.2	28	8.5	29	8.8	30	9.1	31	9.4

Find swell height in left column and corresponding wind wave height. The intersection is the combined swell and wave height. For example, a swell of 12 feet (3.6 m) and a wind wave of 10 feet (3 m) have a combined height of 16 feet (4.9 m).

merging, and behaving randomly. They're also more prone to breaking.

Wind waves can become dramatically steeper if there is a current running, because the current serves to reduce wavelength and increase wave height. Currents are at their worst when they directly oppose the wind, but will steepen waves even if they're flowing at right angles to the waves. Short-period (wind) waves are more affected by current than are long-period swells.

Waves will also steepen as the water shallows. Waves "feel" the bottom when the depth of water is less than half the wavelength. When this happens, wavelength shortens, and wave height and steepness increase. These effects are noticeable with swells before they are with wind waves, be-

cause swells have a longer wavelength. On average, swells have wavelengths between 300 and 650 feet (100–200 m), and their height might be 6–12 feet (2–4 m). Such swells touch bottom in water 150–325 feet (50–100 m) deep. They will increase in height as the water shoals, but won't break unless depth decreases dramatically, to 80 percent of wave height.

Shoaling water (even that on continental shelves) can produce real problems for sailors if waves are especially large. Major tropical cyclones (category 3 or higher) will routinely create waves 50 feet (15 m) in height in deep water. With a wavelength of about 700 feet (215 m), these waves will feel bottom in water 350 feet (107 m) deep and then steepen as water gets shallower.

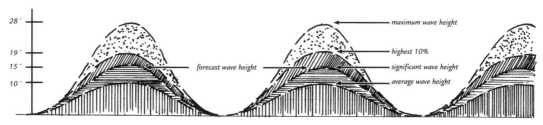

Range of Wave Heights Given a 15´ Wave Forecast (in feet)

Not all waves are created equal.

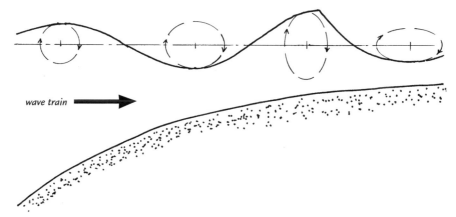

The circular pattern typical of deep-water waves becomes elliptical as the wave comes into shallow water. As a result, wave height increases and wavelength decreases.

The effect of shoaling water on waves can be especially acute if waves are at the same time funneled between islands, which also causes wave height to increase. Examples include—keep in mind that there are heaps more—the Mona Passage in the Caribbean, Penguin Bank off the island of Molokai in Hawaii, and a number of the Indonesian channels connecting the Indian Ocean and Timor Sea with the Java and Flores Seas. All these areas feature a sudden shallowing from the deep ocean, exposure to significant swell, a funneling effect between islands, and currents.

You can predict where conditions may set up steeper than normal waves by taking a close look at the bathymetry (underwater topography), studying the chart for passes that might lead to funneling, and keeping tabs on what currents, swell, and wind are doing.

Remember that although features such as bathymetry and passes don't change, currents, swell, and wind do. What was a calm passage one week might be horrible the next, if the swell is up or a current is running. Don't take conditions in potential problem areas for granted.

The effect of current, wind, and funneling on wave formation is also important at coastal inlets and passes. An ebbing tide against an onshore wind can turn an easy entrance through an otherwise benign inlet into a hazardous run through steep breaking waves. Sometimes it's worth waiting for the tide to change before attempting the inlet.

Breaking Waves

Ocean waves break in different ways. The worst type of breaking wave is probably a plunging breaker, of the sort that crashes down on a surfing beach.

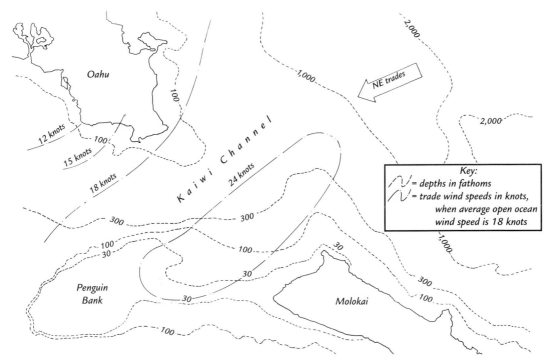

The bottom off Hawaii's Kaiwi Channel shoals from over 2,000 fathoms to less than 30 in only 40 nm. The shallowest portion of the channel, Penguin Bank, coincides with an area of extra-strong winds, which sees an average of 24 knots when surrounding waters experience only 18. To top it all off, the fetch off the northeast coasts of Molokai and Oahu is 2,200 nm, as there is no land between Hawaii and North America. The combination makes for some very steep and ugly seas within the channel.

Coastal breaking waves of this type are formed when a fast-moving ocean swell is slowed by contact with the bottom as the water shoals. Fortunately those aren't the norm at sea, but as we've discussed they can form when a big swell is running, in areas where the water has shoaled dramatically. Deep-water storm waves more typically break in the same way that a whitecap breaks in 25-knot winds, with just a small portion at the top of the wave pushed over the crest.

Deep-water storm waves that break do so because excess wind energy pushes them faster than they're able to travel. That's why breaking waves are a particular danger when the wind is increasing: waves in that condition have not yet become large enough to allow them to keep pace with the wind that is powering them. The excess energy causes these waves to increase in height more quickly than they increase in length. When the wave slope become too steep, the top portion breaks, causing white water to shoot down the wave face.

The mass of water that comes tumbling down the face of the wave moves at about the same speed as the wave itself. For a wave with a length of 300 feet (270 m; about 20 ft./6 m high), this water can strike your boat at a speed of 20 knots or more. Not surprisingly, if this catches you broadside, it can capsize your boat.

The worst storm waves probably occur when two waves, or a wave and a swell, interact. Then a much larger wave or one that's much steeper than the norm may be formed. There's no predicting when this will happen, and in our experience many of the worst waves "come out of nowhere" as waves and swell merge.

HEAVY-WEATHER HAZARDS

The primary hazard in heavy-weather situations is from breaking waves. These can act to damage and flood your boat, capsize it, or cause it to pitchpole (roll end over end).

Most well-built boats won't sustain any damage from seas that hit the hull, but cabins and hatches are susceptible to damage. The force exerted by even a small breaking wave is enormous. It can break ports, force open hatches, and stove in the companionway, forcing water below in the process and opening a route for much more water from subsequent waves. In addition, even small breaking waves can pose a serious capsize risk if your boat is not handled correctly.

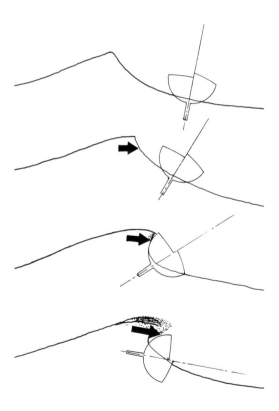

A boat caught beam-to in breaking waves can be capsized by waves that are equal in height to the beam of the boat.

Hatches and Ports

Even if no actual damage is sustained, hatches that aren't gasketed properly, don't close tightly, or don't have positive closures can put you at risk. This includes cockpit lockers in particular, and they're the easiest to overlook, as drips or leaks are not always obvious. We learned this lesson years ago when coastal sailing in Hawaii, aboard a 20-foot (6 m) fiberglass sloop. We were beating to windward in 25- to 30-knot winds and rough seas, with waves regularly sweeping the deck and filling the cockpit, but we made good progress nonetheless. When the boat began to feel sluggish we slid open the companionway and found the settee cushions and just about everything else floating about in the cabin. The cockpit lockers lacked decent seals, and in just a few hours a frightening amount of water had found its way below.

Although it's hardly necessary for everyone to have a steel boat with submarine hatches for tropical cruising, that's not a bad ideal. Inspect your hatches carefully, replace any that are suspect, and renew worn seals. Make sure they can be dogged down securely. Test them (in coastal waters) by beating to windward with a healthy sea running.

If your hatches are strong and can be well secured, the boat will likely cope well with waves that hit bow on. Waves that approach from abeam are more likely to knock in a port. Here the biggest problem is with ports that are overly large or that lack a robust frame. Acrylic or polycarbonate storm shutters—either temporary or permanent—may be the best solution and will provide the needed strength without cutting down on light.

The companionway can be the most difficult opening to seal effectively, because any door or closure has to be made in a way that still allows easy, immediate access. Old-fashioned dropboards work well but should be fitted with a latch or other closure on the top board so they can't drop out if you're knocked down or rolled. Cruisers whose boats have swinging companionway doors (which are handy in port) may be loath to give up the convenience. Consider fitting yours with take-apart hinges, so that these doors can be removed and dropboards inserted in their place if the weather deteriorates during a passage.

Capsizing and Pitchpoling

Most cruising monohulls will right themselves after capsizing, but this may take time, and serious damage is usually sustained when a boat rolls. It's not uncommon for boats to lose their rigs. If that happens, the chances of capsizing again increase dramatically. Cruisers then face having to erect some sort of jury-rig once the storm abates. Capsizing (and even being knocked down) can cause batteries to go flying or to leak acid, and may result in engines coming adrift from their mounts. Add to this the fact that on most cruising boats (our own included at the moment) many items are not stowed so that they'll stay in place in the event of capsizing, and you have all the ingredients of a disaster in the making, even if a boat rights itself without much delay. Multihulls that are rolled will stay inverted, and though they may provide shelter, their crew will be dependent on rescue.

The message is simple: do everything possible to avoid capsizing. To do that you'll want to avoid being caught beam-to in breaking waves. You won't be rolled sideways by waves that approach your boat from either bow or stern (and being pitchpoled is pretty unlikely in the tropics, except perhaps in extreme cyclone conditions). You also won't be capsized by waves that aren't breaking, even if they're big and you're caught broadside.

How big does a breaking wave have to be to be dangerous? Not very. Two rules of thumb are used. One suggests that a wave equal in height to the beam of your boat can cause you to capsize, whereas the other uses a figure equal to 55 percent of the boat's waterline length. Either figure is a simplification, and boats respond differently when caught by a breaking wave (see Resistance to Capsizing sidebar). But these figures are a handy place to start, and they indicate that most cruisers need to be on their guard when in breaking waves as small as 10–15 feet (3–4.5 m).

Keeping your boat headed into or away from the waves can be a challenge in heavy weather. Waves and swells often don't align themselves, and if you're

---

RESISTANCE TO CAPSIZING

When sailors think of stability, they usually consider how stiff their boat is under sail and how much it rolls in response to a wake or small wave. That's what's called *initial stability*, and it's measured at small angles of heel. Factors such as a wide beam, a shallow hull, and hard bilges result in high initial stability, and such boats can usually carry a lot of sail and are fast. But high initial stability doesn't make a boat resistant to capsizing, which depends instead on *ultimate stability*. In fact, a boat with high ultimate stability tends to be the opposite of one with high initial stability. High ultimate stability and good resistance to capsizing result from a narrow beam, a deep hull, and deeply placed ballast. Furthermore, some characteristics that contribute to high initial stability, such as a wide beam, may delay or even prevent a boat that has capsized from coming upright.

The best way to judge the stability of your boat is with a stability curve, which plots the righting arm (or resistance to capsizing) at all angles of heel (through 180°). The ideal in terms of ultimate stability is a boat that has a positive

righting arm even when completely inverted (a heel of 180°). Few boats achieve this, but the closer yours comes, the better. Stability curves won't have been calculated for many older designs, and it's a laborious thing to do. You can make a simple estimate, though, that will at least give an indication of your boat's relative resistance to capsizing. Here's the formula:

$$\frac{\text{beam in feet}}{(\text{displ. in lb.} \div 64)^{0.333}}$$

or in metric units:

$$\frac{\text{beam in meters}}{0.305 \times (\text{displ. in kg} \div 28)^{0.333}}$$

From a safety standpoint, the lower this number, the better; boats with values above 2 are risky to take offshore. As you can see from the formula, narrow beam and heavy displacement both result in a lower risk of capsizing.

running with the storm you may still have swells that come at you from a different direction. If one of these catches your boat and causes it to broach, you can find yourself broadside to the wind and prevailing waves and a sitting duck for a wave that could roll you over.

TACTICS FOR MODERATELY HEAVY WEATHER

Your aim in moderately heavy weather should be to maintain control and minimize risk. If you can do this while still making some progress toward your destination, or if you can at least avoid being driven far out of your way, that's a plus. There are two basic approaches: active sailing, in which you control the boat's course, and passive strategies, in which you set the boat up to cope with a storm without the need to be steered. Choose an approach that works for you, based on your boat and the size of your crew. Sailing with only the two of us, we find that hand-steering in even moderately heavy weather is too tiring to rely on as a basic strategy. Blows can last for several days and more, and hand-steering in those conditions requires both considerable strength and concentration. It is also very easy to become disoriented or distracted on a dark, stormy night, especially if you've just been slapped in the face by a wave, or if a bit of gear breaks or needs attention. All it takes is a moment's inattention, and you can end up at a bad angle to a wave.

Our approach has always been to either stop sailing and heave-to, or to keep sailing on a speed and course that allows our wind vane to maintain good control. It's probable that you'll also want to have several techniques available to you, as you may want to vary what you do depending on the severity and nature of the weather you're in.

Heaving-To

Heaving-to is a simple and time-honored technique for coping with heavy weather. Traditionally it involves sheeting the main close to the centerline while the jib is backed (i.e., sheeted on the windward side). The wheel or tiller is lashed, usually somewhat to leeward.

Start with the boat sailing upwind and with the jib and main sheeted appropriately. Tack the boat, but don't loosen the jib sheet. Once the boat has tacked and the wind has filled the main, lash the wheel or tiller to leeward, as if to tack back through the wind again. The boat should maintain a position with the bow some 50 to 60 degrees off the wind and waves; the ideal is to stop the boat almost completely and have it drift very slowly with the wind. You can heave-to in winds of various strengths, carrying an amount of sail that's appro-

---

STABILITY CHARACTERISTICS OF DIFFERENT HULL FORMS

Type 1. Boats with the features shown in type 1 (narrow beam, slack bilges, and a heavy, deep wineglass hull) were more typical 50 years ago than they are today, but they haven't been improved upon when it comes to ultimate stability. Such boats have stability curves that are positive throughout the range of heel, meaning that if they are ever rolled, they will right themselves immediately.

Type 2. This type is characteristic of more modern cruising designs but still shows substantial displacement and a moderately vee'd hull form. Boats of this type, with their larger beam and freeboard, will have greater initial stability than type 1; here the righting arm drops below that of type 1 only when heeled to more than 110°. The negative area of the stability curve is small and usually limited to the zone between about 135° or 140° and 180°. Boats of this type will typically right themselves quickly, though some may require minor assistance from a passing wave.

Type 3. This type is typical of many racing designs and increasingly of coastal cruising boats as well. The wide beam makes for good initial stability, and the light displacement and flat bottom ensure good speed off the wind. Stability suffers, however, with the righting arm dropping below that of type 1 at some 65° and never equaling that achieved by type 2. The righting arm becomes negative at just 110°, and boats of this type may be stable inverted and not able to right themselves unless rolled partially upright by another large wave.

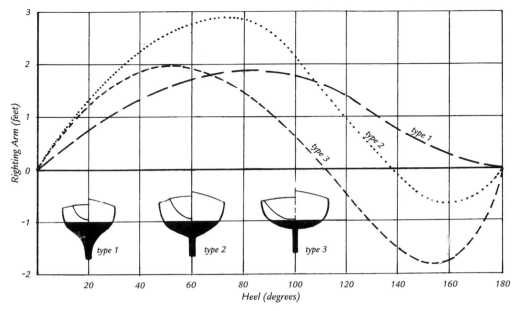

Stability curves for three hull types; see also the sidebar opposite.

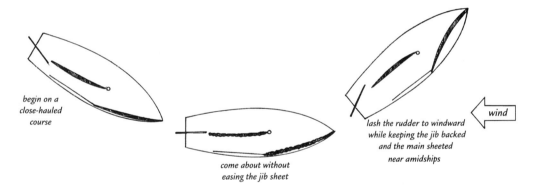

Heaving-to is a vital skill that a surprising number of cruising sailors lack.

priate for the wind strength, be that reefed main and working jib or trysail and storm jib.

In practice, heaving-to appears to work best with long-keel boats that have a fairly deep forefoot. Our own boat, which has a short full keel sharply cut away forward, does not stop as completely as we'd like, but sails slowly along at about a knot, on a close reaching course. Some sailors with fin-keel boats have reported that their boats are not stable when hove-to, with the bow pivoting aft about the small fin keel and ending up broadside to the waves. Such boats may be better if hove-to under just a main; this may be especially true for fin-keel designs that are equipped with roller furling. Experiment with heaving-to in a variety of wind strengths and see what works for your boat. *Do this before you set out on a passage.*

DON'T SAIL TOO SLOWLY

If there are any breaking waves, be wary of slowing your boat too drastically, as you may then become a sitting duck. We sustained the only real damage we've ever suffered in heavy weather when running before a storm between Samoa and Tonga. We were heavily reefed and averaging between 5 and 6 knots in steep 20-foot (6 m) seas, carrying only a small heavy-weather jib. One wave larger than the rest, with a heavily breaking crest, caught us as we slowed in a trough, and swept aboard from the stern. It bent the stern rail severely, ripped several stanchions out of the deck and bent others over at 45 degrees, and wreaked havoc with our dodger. Earlier we'd been sailing under double-reefed main alone and averaging 7–8+ knots, and if we'd kept up that pace we probably wouldn't have been nailed by that wave.

Heaving-to has a number of pluses. It requires no extra equipment and can be done in less time than it takes to describe. It provides instant, remarkable relief from motion and makes it possible to perform tasks that would be very difficult when actively sailing. It can be used to wait out a storm, rest, cook, effect repairs, or simply wait for daylight before entering a pass or harbor. Heaving-to is a fundamental technique that we've used in everything from average trade winds to 50-knot blows, and every cruiser should be familiar with it.

Running Before a Storm

Although heaving-to is very useful, there are times when you'll want or may need to do something different. If you're able to run with a storm and stay more or less on course (and can do so safely), then you may choose that option rather than waiting out a blow. How risky running with a storm is depends on many factors, such as:

➤ the buoyancy of the bow

➤ how vulnerable your boat is to being pooped

➤ whether or not your boat can surf

➤ how well it steers in large following seas

Sailors will have to decide for themselves when running becomes too dangerous to continue.

Going too fast when running with a storm can cause your boat to bury its bow in a trough or go out of control when surfing down a wave. If speed is a problem, and you already have minimal (or no) sail up, then you can slow the boat by dragging something behind you. Warps, often in combination with weights, anchors, tires, and other gear have been used for many years, and today there are also a number of specially designed drogues available, such as the Galerider. One of the biggest problems for many sailors is in deploying and retrieving such gear, and this is something that should be practiced in moderate weather.

We've never felt the need to slow our own boat more than we could by simply reefing down to our storm sails, but we do carry warps that can be trailed from the stern. Most cruisers will also have a stash of spare anchor line aboard. Two long warps can easily be shackled to either end of a length of anchor chain. Ease the chain over the stern, and lead each warp to a winch. The weight of the chain will keep the warps well submerged, and the amount of drag can be controlled to a degree by easing out more line; retrieval is simple if one line is cast off, as the drag is then sharply reduced. Towing a bight in this way will help control your boat's speed in moderately heavy weather and may help reduce yawing as it sails down waves.

Forereaching

Forereaching is another technique that many boats use to cope with heavy-weather conditions. The boat is heavily reefed so that speeds are kept moderate, and it's sailed on a close reaching course, angling across the waves. This technique requires that the boat be actively steered, but it should be possible for a good wind vane or autopilot to do this. How long such a tactic can be employed will vary from boat to boat, but some have used it successfully even in hurricane-strength winds.

TACTICS FOR EXTREME CONDITIONS

Techniques such as heaving-to and running with the storm have seen us through all the storms we've experienced in the tropics, but we've never been confronted by winds of more than Force 9–10. Stronger winds are unlikely in the tropics, but they can occur, either in a tropical cyclone or from a deep, temperate-zone low. The biggest danger comes when the wind builds suddenly, quickly increasing the size and steepness of the seas. If conditions are rough (but not dangerous) to start, the increased wind can rapidly create a very chaotic sea, with breaking waves that could threaten your boat. In such situations it's imperative that you have a reliable means of keeping your boat properly oriented, either into or away from the wind and seas.

Our standard approach of heaving-to becomes problematic because of the possibility of being caught broadside to a wave. With the boat sitting at some 50 degrees to the wind, a first breaking sea may catch the bow and turn the boat so that it's sitting broadside. If that breaking sea is followed by a second, you may face a real risk of capsizing.

Parachute Anchors and Drogues

Many sailors rely on drag devices—parachute anchors or drogues—to help control their boats in extreme conditions. Parachute anchors (sea anchors large enough to all but stop a boat's motion through the water) are deployed from the bow with a long rode. If they work as intended, parachute anchors can dramatically lower the risk of capsizing. There are some potential problems with them, however, that deserve mention:

▶ **IN A SEVERE STORM**, loads from a sea anchor are extremely high and are likely to far exceed the working load of your nylon anchor rode (which many cruisers plan on using with a storm anchor). Nylon rodes are also susceptible to weakening when repeatedly loaded to close to their maximum strength, especially when wet. This means it may be necessary to carry a dedicated parachute anchor rode, preferably of polyester. The diameter should be at least equal to what's needed to hold your boat on a mooring in hurricane-force winds. For our 35-foot, 15,000-pound (10.6 m, 6,800 kg) boat, a rode of 1⅛ in. (28 mm) diameter is required.

▶ **THE PARACHUTE ANCHOR** needs to be placed two wavelengths away from your boat. In moderate winds, where wavelengths may be 200 to 300 feet (60–90 m), that means using a 400- to 600-foot (120–80 m) rode. But it suggests you'll need a much longer rode in hurricane conditions, where wavelengths may be 500 feet (150 m) or more.

▶ **BOATS** (such as our own) that are prone to sailing about when anchored normally will do the same when riding to a parachute, and as a boat sheers back and forth, loads are increased, and the likelihood of getting nailed by a breaking wave goes up.

▶ **PARACHUTE ANCHORS** can be very hard to deploy and retrieve in rough conditions.

A second option is to trail a drogue from the stern. Two of the best-known modern options are the Galerider and the Jordan series drogue; both are designed to slow the boat sufficiently to prevent wild surfing under extreme conditions. The Jordan series drogue incorporates a series of small cones as drag devices on a long line, rather than the more typical approach of using a single drag device at the end of a long line. Both types will help keep your boat in line with the wind and seas. Because of its many small cones, the Jordan series drogue loads up very quickly, and it should be unnecessary for the crew to steer or otherwise control the boat. When using any drogue, make sure that the stern of the boat is capable of withstanding repeated wave impacts. This includes not just the hull and transom but also the cockpit, companionway, and steering gear.

Practice Before Departing

Books have been written about the techniques to use when confronted with really severe storms, and anyone going offshore would do well to read up on the subject before determining what ap-

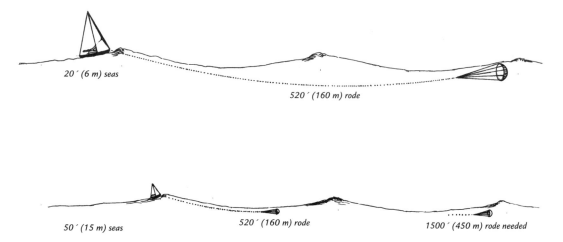

A parachute anchor should be set two wavelengths away from the boat, which may be impossible in severe storm conditions. The 40-foot (12 m) boat in the upper drawing is sitting to a parachute anchor in 20-foot (6 m) seas, where the wavelength is some 270 feet (80 m). These are typical of what may be found in open ocean after a 35-knot wind has been blowing for some 36 hours. The rode is 520 feet (160 m) long, placing the anchor the recommended two wavelengths from the boat. The lower drawing depicts the same boat in 50-foot (15 m) seas, where the wavelength is 750 feet (230 m). These will likely develop when 50-knot winds have been blowing for two to three days or more. The rode used in 20-foot (6 m) seas is clearly too short, and the ideal 1,500-foot (460 m) rode is far too long to be practically stowed aboard most cruising boats. A compromise may be to set the anchor one wavelength from the boat, but this still requires a 750-foot (230 m) rode and begs the question of what to do if the wind increases and the seas grow still more in height and length.

proach to adopt (see Heavy Weather section in appendix 3, Resources). But in addition to reading about the experiences of others, and possibly investing in some type of drag device, cruisers should practice aboard their own boat before setting sail. Deploying warps, a sea anchor, or a drogue in 25-knot winds will be far simpler than doing so in 50 knots, but the experience will be invaluable nevertheless. You'll learn what works and what doesn't, and you'll know what hurdles you're likely to face if you ever have to use this equipment in a real blow.

CYCLONE STRATEGIES

Cyclones are without a doubt the worst weather phenomenon the tropical sailor can encounter. As we've outlined in chapter 7 (Route Planning), you should do all you can to reduce the risk of encountering a cyclone. However, if one threatens, you'll have to ride it out, either in port or at sea. Which option is preferable will depend on your circumstances. If a good cyclone hole is available, it will logically be your first choice. In many areas there may be no cyclone holes, however. Likewise, if a cyclone catches you in the midst of a passage, the storm must be weathered at sea.

Cyclone Holes

Any cruiser who decides to sail in a cyclone-prone area during the summer season should have a secure anchorage picked out for use should a cyclone strike. Good cyclone holes can be natural inlets or man-made harbors. The primary consideration is protection from swell and surge; the anchorage must not be directly open to the sea. You might be adequately protected in a bay that is partially open to the sea, depending on the path a cyclone takes. But cyclone tracks are notoriously hard to predict, and in such a situation even a small shift in the cy-

This is why we do all we can to avoid bad weather.
Marine Prediction Center, NOAA

clone's movement could turn your haven into a hell. Therefore, any cyclone hole should offer swell protection from all directions. Reefs often provide reasonable swell protection in normal conditions, but large storm waves will readily cross a reef, sometimes with surprisingly little reduction in their height and power. You are best off relying on islands and other landforms (which, unlike reefs, extend well above sea level) for swell protection. It is also important to limit the fetch (in which wind waves will develop) as much as possible, and from this standpoint the smaller a cyclone hole, the better.

Protection from wind is a third criterion but is hard to ensure, as strong winds may form gusts and "bullets" as they cross hills. Land that is well vegetated, with substantial trees and shrubs, will provide more wind protection than bare ground or grassy slopes. A truly severe storm presents additional worries, in that trees and large branches can become airborne. Severe cyclones that hit developed areas typically result in all sorts of flying debris (including potentially lethal objects such as metal roofing). Keep such hazards in mind when selecting a cyclone anchorage.

Cyclone holes are found in many, but not all, areas; make sure to investigate them before you decide to stay in an area during the dangerous summer months. Keep in mind that refuges may fill up quickly when a cyclone threatens, and that other boats that are not properly secured may pose a real threat to your own boat in a crowded anchorage.

How to secure your boat depends on the nature of the cyclone hole and the gear you have available. We offer several alternatives for setting multiple anchors in chapter 5, Tropical Anchoring, and these can be put to good use in securing your boat in a way that it can cope with wind from changing directions, as will happen in a cyclone. Many cyclone holes are lined by mangroves, and you may be able to secure long lines to these or other trees ashore. The storm surge (the rise in sea level that accompanies an intense low-pressure cell) can be 10 to 20 feet (3–6 m). In addition, flooding on land is often severe and can wash an amazing amount of debris downstream. The best cyclone hole is therefore not within a creek or river, but in a well-protected inlet that isn't threatened by upstream flooding.

Weathering a Cyclone at Sea

If you're forced to cope with a cyclone at sea, then the need to keep tabs on where the storm is and where it's likely to go become even more imperative. This requires ready access to weather forecasts, via voice broadcast, fax, or the Internet. (We look in some detail at various forecast types and sources for obtaining forecasts in appendix 2.)

Predicting Cyclone Movement

Although weather faxes will give you the best idea of where cyclones are and how they're moving, all you'll ever know for sure is where the storm was when the last observations were made. What's more, the movements of severe storms such as tropical cyclones can't be precisely forecast, and the U.S. Navy suggests a fudge factor of 120 nautical miles be incorporated when plotting a 24-hour forecast position; this figure should be doubled for a 48-hour forecast position. That means that today's cyclone with storm force winds that cover an area 350 nm in diameter could affect waters within a circle 590 nm in diameter tomorrow, and even more if the storm is expanding. The accompanying diagram illustrates how this works in practice.

Intricate winding channels such as this one can make excellent cyclone holes.

Even moderate cyclones will generate large waves, which can cause problems even if you are well outside the area of gale-force winds. The size of the waves varies with wind strength and your distance from the storm's center. The graph on page 150 illustrates this relationship.

If you're caught in the path of a cyclone, the forecast positions (and the fudge factor) should be plotted and a rough estimate made of the area that will be affected by sizable waves using the information in the graph on page 150 (unless wave information is included in the forecast). Such plots should be up-

dated frequently. As the plot on page 151 shows, a fast-moving cyclone can rapidly overtake the average cruising boat, and the inherent uncertainty in position forecasting makes dodging a cyclone a dangerous game.

Cyclone forecasts will be more accurate in some areas than in others, and it may at times be possible to more accurately define the danger zone. For example, the Tropical Prediction Center, which is part of the National Weather Service (NWS), has developed a "1-2-3" rule for use in the North Atlantic, in which 100 nautical miles is added to the forecast radius of

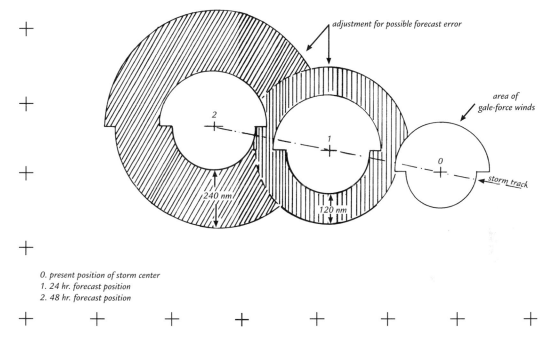

0. present position of storm center
1. 24 hr. forecast position
2. 48 hr. forecast position

The uncertainty in predicting cyclone movements means that it's necessary to enlarge the potential danger zone when plotting forecast positions. After plotting the forecast centers, the zone of forecast gale-force winds is drawn and then the area of uncertainty added; the latter is 120 nm for the 24-hour forecast and 240 nm for the 48-hour forecast.

34-knot winds for a one-day (24-hour) forecast, 200 miles is added on day two (48-hour forecast), and 300 nautical miles is added on day 3. Unfortunately the 34-knot wind radius isn't given for forecasts more than 36 hours into the future, requiring that the 50-knot wind radius and some simple calculations be used when plotting possible two- and three-day positions. The procedure is clearly explained in the excellent NWS publication, *Mariner's Guide for Hurricane Awareness in the North Atlantic Basin*. It's a valuable guide to have onboard even if you're sailing in other areas; see Hurricanes, Cyclones and Typhoons section in appendix 3, Resources.

Even if you can't avoid a cyclone completely, you should do all you can to stay clear of the storm's center, where wind strengths are highest.

Cyclone Semicircles

Cyclones are traditionally divided into two halves, or semicircles: the dangerous semicircle and the navigable semicircle. Although no part of a severe tropical cyclone should be thought of as navigable by any yacht, there are differences in what would be experienced. In the navigable semicircle the storm is headed in a direction opposite to that from which the wind is blowing, so the storm's speed is subtracted from the wind speed. Maximum wind strengths are also generally lower. In the dangerous semicircle, winds are stronger, and in addition the wind you'd experience is equal to the actual wind strength plus the speed of the storm (see illustration, page 152).

If these distinctions don't sound important, think again. Take a cyclone with winds of 80 knots (a strong category 1 storm) moving at 10 knots (the

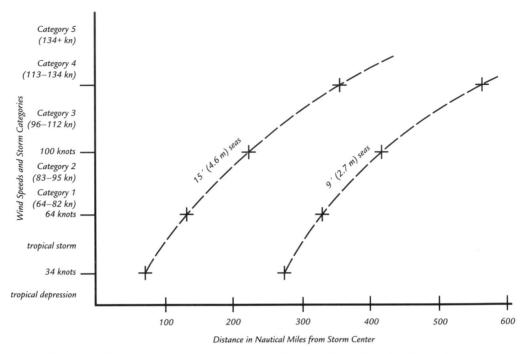

Wave size will increase rapidly as one approaches the center of a cyclone. The curves of wave heights shown here are based on actual storm data from the western Pacific.

mean speed for cyclones, though some travel much faster). In the dangerous semicircle, the wind you feel is 90 knots, and it exerts *twice* the force of the 70-knot winds you'd have in the navigable semicircle.

The recommended strategy for coping with a cyclone varies depending on which semicircle you're in, and this needs to be determined first.

▶ **THE DANGEROUS SEMICIRCLE** lies to the left (if you're facing an approaching storm) in the Northern Hemisphere and to the right in the Southern

▶ **THE NAVIGABLE SEMICIRCLE** is to the right in the Northern Hemisphere and to the left in the Southern

Note that the position of the semicircle in each hemisphere is different if the cyclone is moving in an easterly direction than if it's moving toward the west. Dangerous and navigable semicircles for each situation are shown on pages 153 and 154.

Cyclone Paths

A cyclone that is headed west one day may be going east the next. Changes in direction may be temporary or can be caused by a cyclone "re-curving." Most cyclones travel in a westerly direction (SW in the Southern Hemisphere and NW in the Northern), until reaching 20 or 25° latitude, when they may re-curve and head SE in the Southern Hemisphere and NE in the Northern. No two cyclones follow the same path, however, and some make amazing twists and turns.

If a voice or fax forecast is available, plot the storm's position and direction of movement versus your own and determine which semicircle you're in. In the absence of a reliable forecast position, base your estimate of where the storm is relative to you on what the wind and pressure are doing. It's easy to get confused when doing this, so draw yourself a picture (see illustration opposite, bottom).

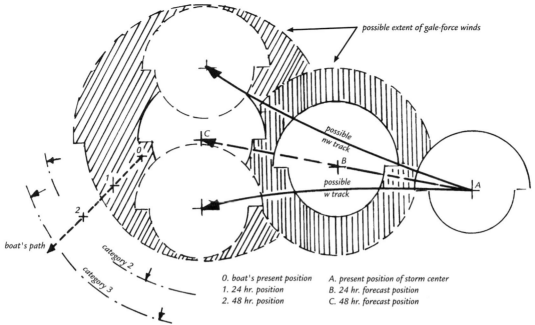

possible extent of gale-force winds

possible nw track

possible w track

C

0

1

2

B

A

boat's path

category 2

category 3

0. boat's present position
1. 24 hr. position
2. 48 hr. position

A. present position of storm center
B. 24 hr. forecast position
C. 48 hr. forecast position

Curves for 15-foot (4.5 m) wave heights have been added to our cyclone plot, with the extent of the zone of 15-foot (4.5 m) waves varying according to cyclone strength. You wouldn't want to join the crew of the vessel plotted in the left center of the drawing. On day 0 they are a comfortable 1,150 nm from the approaching storm. How they fare after that depends on the cyclone's movements. If it veers northwest, then on day 2 they will find themselves 700 nm from the center, still well out of the area of gale-force winds. If the storm moves due west instead, they will finish day 2 only 400 nm from the cyclone's eye and directly in its path.

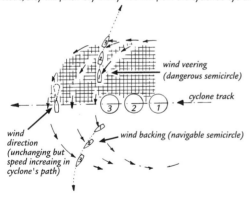

wind veering
(dangerous semicircle)

cyclone track

3   2   1

wind direction
(unchanging but
speed increaing in
cyclone's path)

wind backing (navigable semicircle)

Determining cyclone semicircle by wind direction in the Northern Hemisphere.

NORTHERN HEMISPHERE

▶ **WIND GRADUALLY BACKS** (changes counterclockwise): you're in the navigable semicircle.

▶ **WIND GRADUALLY VEERS** (changes clockwise): you're in the dangerous semicircle.

SOUTHERN HEMISPHERE

▶ **WIND GRADUALLY BACKS** (changes counterclockwise): you're in the dangerous semicircle.

▶ **WIND GRADUALLY VEERS** (changes clockwise): you're in the navigable semicircle.

BOTH HEMISPHERES

▶ **WIND REMAINS STEADY** in direction but builds in speed while the barometer drops. You're in or near the path of the cyclone, and it's approaching.

▶ **WIND REMAINS STEADY** in direction but decreases in speed, while pressure rises. You're in the cyclone's path, but in a safe position behind the center, and it's moving away.

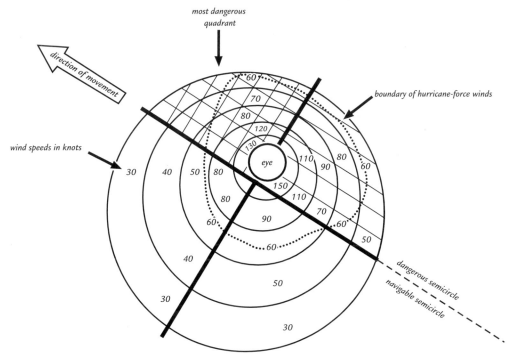

How wind strengths vary within a cyclone (Northern Hemisphere example).

Cyclone Sailing

At a minimum, your goal should be to stay out of the area where winds are above 34 knots. Most advice given in books is targeted at ships, which may be able to make some distance to windward against even considerable wind and swell. Most yachts can forget about making much progress to windward in winds over 30 knots, particularly with rough seas and swells. This makes it especially important to *take action early, before the wind and sea conditions make sailing on anything except a largely downwind course impossible.*

We'll address the simpler situation first. If caught in the navigable semicircle, maintain a course on the port tack in the Southern Hemisphere and on the starboard tack in the Northern Hemisphere. Keep the wind on or aft of the beam. The most important things are to keep boat speed up and to put as much distance as possible between you and the storm's

center. If the storm hasn't re-curved, you'll be heading for the equator, which helps minimize the chances of being caught by a storm after it does re-curve, as cyclones rarely head back in that direction.

Vessels directly in the storm's path should broad-reach away from the storm center making all possible speed; again, stay on a port tack in the Southern Hemisphere and a starboard tack in the Northern.

If you're in the dangerous quadrant, you'll be forced toward the storm's center by both wind and waves. The best option is to beat to windward, again on a port tack in the Southern Hemisphere and a starboard tack in the Northern. Keep this up for as long as you can, motor sailing if possible or necessary to make progress. If progress to windward is impossible, the only other option for small craft in the dangerous quadrant is likely to be heaving-to or riding to a sea anchor (such as a parachute), in an attempt to prevent being blown farther toward

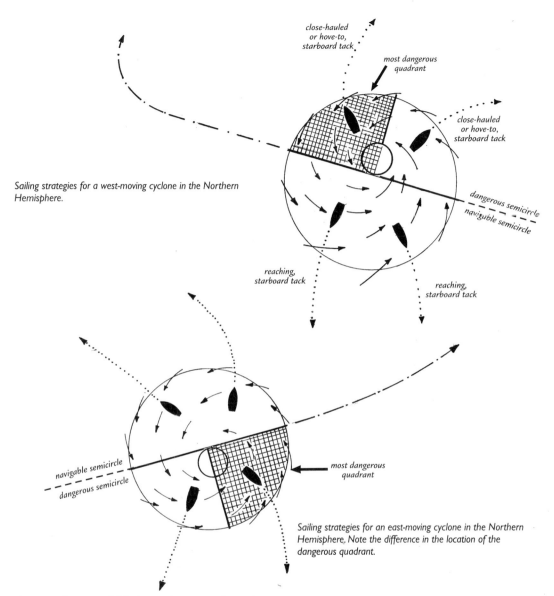

close-hauled or hove-to, starboard tack

most dangerous quadrant

close-hauled or hove-to, starboard tack

Sailing strategies for a west-moving cyclone in the Northern Hemisphere.

dangerous semicircle

navigable semicircle

reaching, starboard tack

reaching, starboard tack

navigable semicircle

dangerous semicircle

most dangerous quadrant

Sailing strategies for an east-moving cyclone in the Northern Hemisphere. Note the difference in the location of the dangerous quadrant.

the storm's center. This is one instance where the ability to beat to windward (which we discuss at length in chapter 6, Sailing in the Tropics) could save your boat, and you as well.

The figures above and on page 154 illustrate avoidance techniques for east- and west-moving cyclones in both hemispheres.

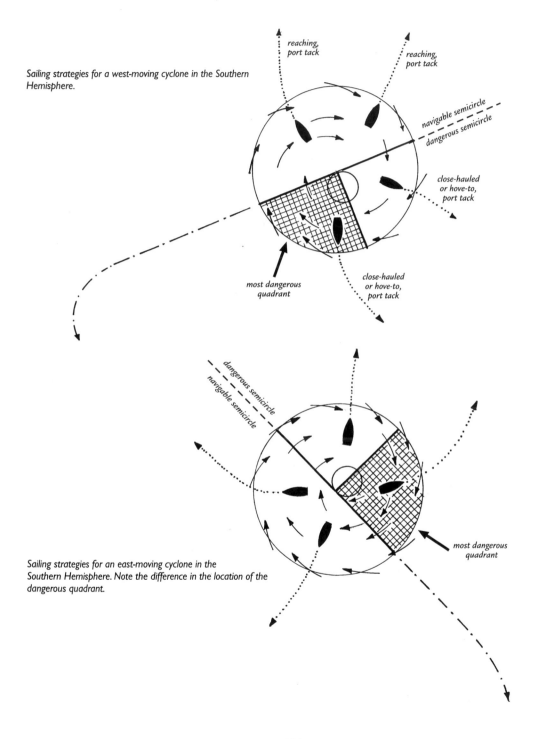

Sailing strategies for a west-moving cyclone in the Southern Hemisphere.

reaching, port tack

reaching, port tack

navigable semicircle

dangerous semicircle

close-hauled or hove-to, port tack

most dangerous quadrant

close-hauled or hove-to, port tack

dangerous semicircle

navigable semicircle

most dangerous quadrant

Sailing strategies for an east-moving cyclone in the Southern Hemisphere. Note the difference in the location of the dangerous quadrant.

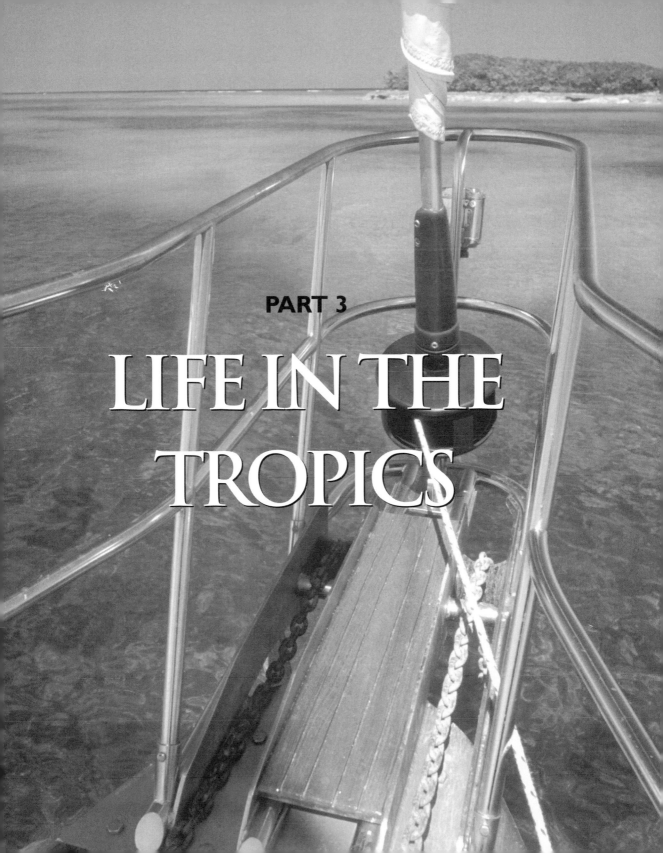

PART 3

LIFE IN THE TROPICS

Chapter 10

Life Aboard

As important as it is to hone your skills as a tropical sailor and navigator, you shouldn't overlook the need to ensure that your boat will be a comfortable home afloat. And although comfort at sea is part of this, in actual fact, most of the time you'll be in port, doing a little swimming, exploring an island or town, reading a book, catching up on a bit of maintenance, and simply living the good life. In most respects a boat that's proven comfortable to live on in temperate latitudes will work out well in the tropics. There's immense variety among the layouts and comfort level of the many cruising boats sailing in tropical waters, and naturally what works for some people won't work for others. But there are some challenges shared by all tropical sailors, no matter what size and shape their boat is:

- staying cool and comfortable on board
- obtaining and storing pure fresh water
- provisioning
- keeping tropical pests at bay
- keeping engines and other mechanical systems working
- avoiding getting ripped off

SHADE

First on your list of necessities to make life comfortable on board should be proper shade from the tropical sun. You'll need this when sailing and also in port. The requirements for the two are different. A cockpit awning or bimini for use when sailing needs to be robust, not interfere with sailing gear, present minimum windage, and able to be taken down very quickly if a severe storm threatens. An awning for use in port should be big, shading as much of the deck as possible, and should be rigged high enough so that you can comfortably walk around on deck.

Cockpit Awnings and Biminis

The details of how cockpit awnings and biminis are made and fitted vary widely, but there are some shared basic requirements. First, they need some type of support. This can be in the form of a separate framework, or the awning can be supported by attaching it to a dodger, the rigging, or anything else that's handy. Ketches and yawls may be able to use the mizzen mast or shrouds to help support an awning, and a properly placed boom gallows can work as well.

If a separate framework is used (and this is how

A simple type of cockpit awning that uses the back of a dodger for support. Here full side panels provide good shade but may cut down on the breeze.

most biminis are rigged), it should be strong. Small-diameter, thin-walled aluminum tubing common on many small coastal cruising boats won't cut it. We've seen many materials used successfully, including stainless and bronze tubing and solid aluminum rod.

All cockpit awnings should be made so that the fabric is very well tensioned when the awning is in use, as otherwise the fabric will flap and flutter when the wind blows, which is annoying and hard on the awning as well. If the awning is big, it may help to include a few battens and to place these under a bit of tension.

Resist the temptation to rig a cockpit awning or bimini too high. Although it's nice to have heaps of headroom underneath, you'll pay in terms of increased windage and less shade when the sun is anything but directly overhead. Some type of side curtains are a real help in shading the cockpit in the early morning and late afternoon.

Awnings for Use in Port

Although they needn't be as tightly rigged as cockpit awnings, awnings for use in port should also be well tensioned so they can be left up in stiff trade winds without flogging or flapping and should be fairly simple to rig and take down. Given these requirements, most cruisers opt for one of two types: a roped awning, which incorporates sewn-in ropes that run fore and aft, or a battened awning with battens in pockets that run athwartships.

Both systems work, but in our experience roped awnings have the edge and provide several extra benefits: they take less space to stow (having no long battens), they generally provide better shade in early morning and late afternoon, and they're more effective water catchers (we discuss rain catching below). Our own awning has three ropes: one along the centerline and another along each side to form a kind of roof. For sloop and cutter rigged boats we suggest an awning that stretches from the mast to the stern; boats with good biminis or cockpit awnings may choose to stop the awning short of the bimini. The center rope ties to mast and backstay, while the side ropes tie to shrouds and to a spreader pole mounted behind the backstay. Boats with split rigs will tie the center rope to main and mizzen masts, while side ropes go from main shrouds to mizzen shrouds. Split-rigged boats may need an extra cover over the cockpit if the latter is aft.

Side curtains that tie to lifeline or rail are a good addition to any awning. These provide extra shade, give some privacy while in port, and help keep rain out of the hatches. You'll want to be able to keep hatches open during rainy weather, especially if you plan on cruising in equatorial waters where squalls and storms are frequent. On our sloop we have an additional awning—also roped—that covers the foredeck, allowing us to keep the forward hatch open even during heavy downpours. Another option is to make small covers that can be rigged over individual hatches. These are also handy if you're anchored for a short time and don't want to go the trouble of rigging your main awning, or if winds are too strong.

The material of choice for all tropical awnings and hatch covers is UV-resistant synthetic (acrylic) canvas. This fabric is long wearing and of medium weight, but not so heavy that it can't be sewn on a simple home sewing machine. Acrylic canvas is sus-ceptible to chafe, though, and should be protected and reinforced at any wear points with leather or vinyl patches. With care, an awning will last for years: our awning has seen about eight years of heavy use.

Appendix 1, Ropework and Sewing, includes complete instructions for making a roped awning.

VENTILATION

Air flow is next on the list of important features. You'll want considerably more fresh air moving through the cabin in the tropics than in temperate waters, both when underway and at anchor. It's important to consider how the air moves through your boat, with wind from both ahead and astern. To prevent the spread of mold and mildew, you must ensure that fresh air not only reaches you but is also drawn to the ends of the boat.

Letting Air In and Out

Any opening that lets air in or out of your boat is part of the ventilation system. The most important of these on most yachts is the companionway, especially if it is fitted with a dodger. A dodger not only provides invaluable shelter from spray and rain but also acts as a huge exhaust when the wind is from forward of the beam and as a very effective scoop if the wind is from the stern. Seriously consider mounting a cockpit dodger if your boat doesn't have one.

While the companionway usually acts to exhaust air, other hatches are most often used to take air in. They'll be most useful, though, if fitted with double hinges so that they can be opened in either direction. Most newer boats have a number of hatches, often including small ventilation hatches above galley, head, or aft cabin. Older boats more often lack these extras, and if your boat has no skylight or hatch above the main salon, it may be time to reach for the saw. Skylights are a particular asset in port but can be very useful at sea as well.

Opening ports are great, especially if you spend much time in marinas, when the breeze may often blow at right angles to the boat. If you anchor out, opening ports aren't as critical.

Ventilators are the final piece of ventilation gear. There are many different types available, but best among them are Dorade vents, which are cowls mounted atop a baffled box that keeps water out. Dorade vents (see illustration) are particularly valuable at sea, because they allow air in but keep out all but the worst seas. They should be positioned to provide airflow to those parts of the boat used most when underway: galley, head, and sea berths. Vents should be large (a 4 in./10 cm diameter deck plate is minimum) and will ideally have two deck plates, so that in mild conditions the cowl can be positioned directly above the opening to the cabin.

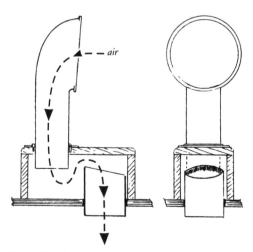

Cross section of a Dorade vent.

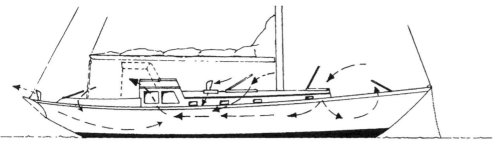

Air circulation through an anchored boat, with the wind over the bow.

Air Circulation through the Boat

Getting air in is only half the battle: it also needs to circulate before it exits. At anchor in a trade wind breeze, having the forehatch and companionway hatch open will allow a good airflow through part of the boat; if the breeze is strong enough, you may actually feel cool sitting below. But it won't ventilate the forward part of the forward cabin, or anything aft of the companionway. To solve this you need vents or hatches in the ends of the boat.

With the wind over the bow, a vent or hatch in the foredeck (as far forward as possible) should be set to exhaust air, while one at the stern acts as an intake. Air will then flow forward from the forehatch, exhausting at the bow. It will also flow aft from the forehatch, be joined by air from any vents or extra hatches, and exhaust through the companionway. Air will also enter through stern vents, and flow forward through the after part of the boat, exhausting through the companionway.

With the wind over the stern, the companionway acts as an intake, with air traveling aft from there and exiting through the stern vents; air also flows forward from the companionway, exiting through vents and other hatches. This is when reversible hatches pay off, as ideally a skylight will be set up as an intake to supplement the companionway intake, and the forehatch will be set to exhaust. A hatch or vent on the foredeck will serve as a final intake, and that air will flow aft and exit through the forehatch.

Every boat is different, and ventilation patterns will be altered on boats with center cockpits or large deckhouses. But the basic idea remains the same: you must provide a way for air to circulate through the entire boat, and it should work with wind from varying directions. Having lots of small enclosed cabins can interfere with the airflow, so make sure that each enclosed area has a hatch or vent, and that doors (including those on lockers) are fitted with openings of some sort.

Ventilation at Sea

The ultimate test of your ventilation system is whether it can provide adequate air circulation when you're at sea in the tropics, especially in rough weather. In light conditions it's often possible to keep a couple hatches partly open—facing forward if seas are really smooth, and facing aft if a bit of spray is starting to fly—and with these open, circulation is usually pretty good. When conditions deteriorate so that hatches have to be closed, then your ventilators have to provide all the incoming air (though the companionway should still be able to act as the exhaust). Most boats—including our own—get pretty stuffy in the tropics in these conditions. The answer is to provide more incoming air, by putting in extra vents. How Many Dorade Vents?, next page, gives a simple rule for gauging how many you need.

Don't make the mistake of mounting your vents farther outboard than about halfway between the centerline and the deck edge, however. Vents mounted far outboard are more prone to flooding than those toward the centerline, and this danger is more significant with larger vents.

HOW MANY DORADE VENTS?

The late Rod Stephens (originator, with his brother Olin, of the Dorade vent) devised a simple rule for calculating the number of vents a boat should have.

total intake area (for tropical sailing) = 1.5 × (beam × waterline length)

In imperial units, that's expressed as

intake area (sq. in.) = 1.5 × (beam in feet × waterline length in feet)

In metric units it becomes

intake area (sq. cm) = 105 × (beam in meters × waterline length in meters)

Using our boat as an example, this gives

1.5 × (9 ft. × 25 ft.) = 337 sq. in. of vent area
or
105 × (2.74 m × 7.6 m) = 2,185 sq. cm

Looking up the intake area of standard size vents in the accompanying table, we see that we could use

three 6-inch (15 cm) vents (area = 339 sq. in. or 2,184 sq. cm)

four 5-inch (12.5 cm) vents and 1 3-inch (7.5 cm) vent

seven 4-inch (10 cm) vents

All these combinations yield about the same area and thus pretty much the same airflow. By way of comparison, it would take twelve 3-inch (7.5 cm) vents to equal this area.

In reality we have just two 4-inch (10 cm) vents, which is less than one-third the number the rule suggests, and not surprisingly they've frequently proven inadequate. This exercise clearly shows that larger vents move proportionally more air than small ones. In fact, 3-inch (7.5 cm) vents are all but useless; 4 inches (10 cm) is a reasonable minimum size, and 5 inches (12.5 cm) is clearly far better.

Ventilation When the Boat Is Locked

Make sure your boat can be well ventilated even when securely closed up. Temperature down below can increase dramatically without reasonable air flow, and that's hard on both the boat and any fresh food. Fit your hatches with closures that allow them to be left cracked several inches while still securely locked. Some hatch closures make allowance for this, but it is simple to make your own fittings. We use a few links of heavy brass chain secured to an eyestrap inside the hatch and shackled to another eyestrap on the inside hatch frame. We once left *Nomad* for three months in warm and humid Cairns, Australia, while we flew to the United States. We left our skylight, forehatch, and anchor hatch slightly open, with awnings rigged to keep the rain out. The boat had not a trace of mold, mildew, or mustiness when we returned.

Windscoops

Even with a full array of hatches and vents you'll need to help the airflow in light-wind situations. A windscoop or wind catcher made from ripstop nylon is helpful when sitting at anchor with the wind blowing directly over the bow. A scoop positioned over the forehatch can do a lot to force air through the whole boat. There are times—such as when sitting to wind and current—when simple scoops tend to flap and collapse, requiring frequent resetting; this can be quite annoying, particularly at night. "Omnidirectional" windscoops that can cope with a breeze from any direction are the answer, but these are more costly and complex to make. We've found windscoops to be particularly important on boats with sliding—rather than hinged—skylights and forward hatches.

Fans

When the wind has died away completely and your scoop is hanging limp, it's time to turn on the electric breeze. Inexpensive 12-volt fans can be very effective, while drawing less than 0.5 amps from the ship's batteries. Fans are available from many auto supply stores and chandlers, and some even oscillate automatically. Make sure you test a fan before buying one, as some move much more air (and are much quieter) than others. Some tropical sailors we know swear by computer fans, due to their minimal power draw. These can be mounted as intake fans below your Dorade outlets, thus drawing fresh air into the boat even in a rain storm.

DRINKING WATER

Clean, high-quality drinking water is free and plentiful in some tropical areas, but costly and scarce in others. Unless you know that you will be cruising only in areas where obtaining water is simple, it pays to be as self-sufficient as possible. This means being able to either catch or make water, or both. In addition, all cruisers should have the means to ferry water from shore using the dinghy.

Water use differs a lot among cruisers. Although it's possible to establish the bare minimum a person needs to stay healthy (see How Much Water Should You Carry? section), actual usage varies widely. Some sailors get by on less than a gallon (3.75 L) per day, while others easily consume 10 gallons (3.75 L) a day or more. But all cruisers, no matter how much they use, need to have a dependable way of storing and replenishing water supplies.

Water Storage

Most cruisers carry the bulk of their water in one or more permanent tanks, with extra water carried in jerricans or other small containers. Permanent tanks can be rigid or flexible and can be made of all sorts of materials, including stainless steel, copper, neoprene, and epoxy-coated wood; what is suitable has more to do with the type of boat you have, and your budget, than anything else. If you're building or upgrading your boat and are in doubt about what to use, consult one of the sources listed under Boat Maintenance and Restoration in appendix 3, Resources. Keep in mind that tanks can spring a leak, and that the water you put in a tank may turn out to be contaminated. For that reason, it pays to have more than one tank, unless you carry a large portion of your supply in jerricans.

Some cruisers choose to forgo built-in tanks completely and have all their water in smaller containers. This is a simpler and less expensive option than using built-in tanks and has the advantage of ensuring that you have an ample supply of containers that can be easily carried in the dinghy and filled ashore.

How Much Water Should You Carry?

Start with the basic rock-bottom figure of one half-gallon (2 L) per person/day, which is how much you'll consume per day on average. This figure will increase in really hot areas, but that increase may well be balanced by consumption of other liquids. If you have two crew, this means you'll need 1 gal-

COWL INLET AREA VERSUS DECK PLATE DIAMETER

Vent Size (nominal deck plate diameter)		Inlet Area of Cowl	
in.	cm	sq. in.	sq. cm
3	7.5	28	180
4	10	50	322
5	12.5	78	500
6	15	113	728
7	18	154	995

Windscoops can be a very effective way of getting air below.

lon/day (4 L). Estimate your time spent at sea by dividing the longest passage you anticipate making by your average daily speed (see Boat Speed on Ocean Passages in chapter 7, Route Planning). If the passage is 1,500 miles, and your average speed is 125 miles/24 hours, then you'll be at sea for 12 days. In that time you can expect to use a total of 12 gallons (45 L). Now at least treble that figure as a safety margin. This means carrying at least 36 gallons (135 L) for drinking and basic cooking on a 12-day passage.

Remember that water is not necessarily available at the end of each passage you make. If that's the case, then calculate the number of days on each passage, plus any time spent in port.

We've found these minimums to be reasonably accurate, but remember that they don't include

water for bathing. We normally use seawater for this when at sea, but having a freshwater shower every day is definitely more pleasant. This can drastically increase water consumption, though, and it's not uncommon for cruisers with ample water supplies to go through 10 times as much as we do. Make sure to add in any amounts that you will be using for washing to the required minimums for drinking.

Transporting Water

Having ample capacity in jerricans or other containers is the simplest way to ensure that you can easily top off your water tanks from a shore supply. In many areas it is difficult or impossible to bring your boat alongside a wharf or dock that has a tap with drinking-quality water. Instead, you'll have to load up the dinghy with water containers and venture ashore. We've carried our jerricans up streams, loaded them in trucks as we hitched rides along dusty roads, and lugged them across mudflats. Because you'll often be forced to transport these containers a fair distance, opt for smaller, rather than larger, sizes. We use five containers that each hold 6 gallons (23 L). The total capacity of 30 gallons (115 L) is good to have. The individual 6-gallon containers, however, are definitely too large, as they weigh about 50 pounds (27 kg) each. A better choice would be ten 3-gallon (12 L) jerricans.

You should provide secure stowage for any water containers that are onboard. It's common on many cruising boats to find these lashed along the rail, and although we have occasionally carried jerricans on deck, we try very hard to avoid it. Not only do they get in the way when moving about on deck, but the added weight high on the boat does nothing for stability. What's more, the common practice of lashing these to a board that is in turn lashed or bolted to the lifeline stanchions is an invitation to wrench the latter off the deck. Water containers should be stored below, in such a way they won't move in case of bad weather. If you have to carry jerricans on deck, secure them to the shrouds, which you can be sure won't come adrift.

Catching Water

Clean drinking water can be hard to find in remote tropical areas, but downpours are often a daily occurrence. Having a good catchment system will reduce both your need to search for sources of potable water and the hassle and uncertainty of treating suspect water.

Any large horizontal surface on your boat can be used for catching water. Some cruisers have fitted their cabintop with molding and drains and use it for catching water; others plug the deck scuppers and use their entire deck. The advantage of these methods is that they can be used both while in port and underway, whereas with other rain-catching devices it's usually difficult or impossible to catch water once you leave port. It means that your deck or cabintop has to be very clean, though, and ours rarely seems to qualify.

We rely on our sun awning, which we find easier to keep clean. Roped awnings can easily be made into very effective rain catchers by the addition of two plastic through-hull fittings, one on each side of the awning just above the side ropes. A hose is then led from the through-hulls to tank fills, jugs, or buckets. We're able to replenish our water supply in the course of a good 30-minute rainstorm. (See appendix 1, Ropework and Sewing, for details on fitting an awning as a rain catcher.) Our sun awning is not suitable for use while underway, but similar options will work with the more robust cockpit awnings and biminis used while sailing.

Bleach should be added to rainwater to inhibit the growth of algae, and we make it a practice to treat all water, unless it's from a municipal supply that we know is safe. (See Disinfecting Water in chapter 12, Staying Healthy in the Tropics.)

A convenient public dock, with both a dinghy landing and a water tap.

Watermakers

An increasingly popular way of avoiding the hassles of obtaining freshwater ashore is by relying on a watermaker. They work by reverse osmosis, in which salt water is forced at high pressure through a special membrane, which excludes salt and other impurities. They're available in various sizes, from manually operated units suitable for a life raft, to large ones that produce hundreds of gallons per day.

The independence from shore supplies that watermakers provide comes at a price: they're costly to buy and need careful and frequent maintenance. They shouldn't be used if the water isn't clean, which excludes many ports and harbors. Finally, watermakers use a lot of power, most needing about 3 amp-hours of electricity to produce one gallon of water. Most cruisers who make water either run their engine or an auxiliary generator for

Laundry is a necessary chore, but one that's more pleasant when you can do it in a cool stream.
Randy Durbin

DOING LAUNDRY

Depending on where you are, doing laundry can either be a simple or onerous task. If you're in a marina or a town of some size, there's bound to be a self-service laundry nearby. But, if you're off the beaten track, the nearest washing machine may be several days' or weeks' sail away. Other factors that determine how painful this task will be are the availability of freshwater and your distance away from this source. Inquire with other cruisers (if any are around) or with the local people. There may be someone in town who is willing to do it for a fee. Alternatively, there may be a public spigot or even a stream for washing.

If there's a spigot, we find it simplest to fill jerricans and buckets and take the whole works back to the boat and do laundry by hand. We usually set several soapy buckets on deck to be heated by the sun and leave the clothes to soak. A small plunger (the same kind you use to unclog a sink) can help agitate the clothes.

Though there's always a bit of lugging of clothes and soap, doing laundry in a stream can be a treat. If locals do the same, first inquire as to where they do their washing: you don't want to pollute a source of drinking water with laundry soap. Use only a biodegradable soap (without phosphates), and use as little soap as possible in these situations.

Don't try to save on freshwater by doing a wash "cycle" with salt water and then rinsing with fresh. It takes lots of freshwater to get the salt out; if it doesn't all come out,

clothes will retain a damp and clammy feeling, as salt attracts moisture.

Once the laundry is clean, it needs to dry. We've lost so many items overboard in stiff trade winds that we have learned the hard way to string the clothesline *through* anything with an opening (such as underwear, shorts, shirts, and so on) and then tie the line in the rigging. Hung that way, clothes won't sail away no matter how hard the wind blows. Those items that can't have the line threaded through them (towels, lava lavas or sarongs, and sheets) are hung with lots of pegs and watched carefully.

Laura Durbin-Hacker has been cruising for ten years and offers these tips for doing laundry:

• If water is available on shore, at no charge, doing your own laundry is the most cost-effective method. In those places where water is available only for a fee, you'll need to assess if it will cost more to purchase the water than to send the washing out.

• Determine if it is more expensive, both in terms of money and effort, to send it out rather than use machines.

• Prolong the life of your clothing by drying it inside out and taking it in as soon as it's dry to prevent baking and fading in the sun.

• Small, dark-colored towels dry faster than larger, light-colored towels.

one or more hours every day to meet the power demands of the watermaker.

If you choose to equip your boat with a watermaker, remember that these units are not foolproof, and thus your water storage capacity should still be adequate to supply the crew's basic needs on any offshore passage. You should always check at the start of a passage that you have enough water in your tanks to see you through.

Water Conservation

The easiest way to simplify the entire business of storing, catching, and making water is by using less of it. Water conservation costs nothing and requires little more than a bit of forethought and self-discipline. Here are some simple ways to use less.

Use salt water whenever possible. We use it for both dish washing and rinsing fruit and vegetables. On most boats it's easy to tap into an existing water inlet (such as the engine-cooling water intake) and run a line to a hand or foot pump in the galley. However, we don't use salt water in busy ports or waters that might be polluted.

Don't luxuriate when taking a shower. Get used to getting wet and then shutting off the water until you're ready to rinse off. Sponge baths are also a good way to bathe without using much water.

Use a hand or foot pump instead of a pressure water system. Although there is nothing intrinsically wasteful about pressure water systems, they seem to encourage most cruisers to use water in the same way they would at home. With manual pumps you're much more aware of every drop you use.

PROVISIONING

As surprising as it may seem, food is available for purchase in the tropics. Most cruisers setting off for the topics for the first time—ourselves included—seem to overlook this fact. Granted, we were off to explore some remote uninhabited islands and didn't expect to see a store for a few months. But we stocked the boat as if we'd be out for years, including lots of fresh food (that quickly spoiled) and an assortment of canned goods. The latter included some things we don't usually eat, which were carted around until they finally got so rusty we hadn't a clue anymore what was in them and didn't dare eat it anyway. In the meantime we were busy eating lots of other more interesting food that we bought—surprise—in the tropics.

In talking about provisioning we're really dealing with several separate issues: provisioning the boat for a lengthy ocean passage, either within the tropics or to and from a tropical area; buying food on a day-to-day basis while living in a town with access to stores and markets; and provisioning for a cruise of a week or two or three that takes you to areas without stores, or where provisions are prohibitively expensive.

Provisioning for tropical passagemaking is made difficult by the fact that temperatures are warm, and produce stored without refrigeration does not keep as well as it does in temperate climates. If you're buying your passage provisions within the tropics, you'll probably find some of the convenience foods (including canned goods) that cruisers tend to rely on while at sea harder to find and more expensive than you're used to.

If you're living and cruising within the tropics for a while and visit markets often, the perishability of fresh produce won't be so much of a factor, and if you adjust your eating habits somewhat, you can avoid having to buy expensive convenience foods on a regular basis. When you stock up for a trip to a more isolated spot, you may wish to rely on some of the tricks you use when provisioning for a passage, even though you might never be sailing more than a few hours in a day.

You'll find a number of references in the following sections to how well food keeps when not refrigerated. That's in part because we don't have a fridge, but also because refrigerator space is at a premium on most boats. Keeping meat, cheese, butter, water, beer, and the like cold is a far higher priority for most people than refrigerating produce. You'll be happy to know that most foods keep just fine when not refrigerated—even those that announce in large letters that they must be kept chilled—so go ahead and stock up on the beer.

It is possible to become sick in a variety of ways from eating the wrong food and drinking the wrong water. We discuss this in chapter 12, Staying Healthy in the Tropics.

Food Storage

Basic staples that are bought in large quantities (such as pasta, rice, dried beans, flour, and sugar) are best stored in large plastic or glass containers. Yes, you can use glass onboard without trouble, as long as it is well stowed. In fact, a good glass container will last pretty much forever, whereas plastic will wear out and is also susceptible to being warped and degraded by the heat in the tropics, often refusing to make a proper seal even if it doesn't break or crack. Whatever the material, container lids should be well secured. Screw tops work well, as do lever-action gasketed lids on glass storage jars. We've learned the importance of really secure lids—by cleaning several kilograms of sugar and lentils out of the bilge. Make sure lids seal airtight. Add bay leaves to flour, pasta, and other staples prone to weevils or other vermin.

You'll also want containers for things like crackers, cereal, and cookies; in fact, anything that comes in a box. Cockroaches and other insects love hiding out in boxes, and even if they're not present, their eggs may be. The best strategy is to get rid of any and all cardboard immediately. We often do this in the cockpit, figuring we've got one more chance at catching the pests if some scamper out. If the food's in plastic within the box, leave it that way, but get the cardboard into the dinghy and back to shore as soon as possible.

Buying in bulk and disposing of the packaging while still in a larger port also reduces the amount of garbage you'll have to deal with when you're on a passage or cruising among smaller islands, where

garbage facilities are few and far between. We deal with the issue of sorting and disposing of garbage in detail in chapter 15, Green Cruising.

Place canned goods in plastic tubs (dishpans work well) before being stowed away if there is the slightest chance of their coming into contact with any moisture, including condensation from the hull. If you take this precaution they'll last for several years without getting rusty or losing their labels. Do the same with soft drink and beer cans, which will otherwise develop leaks almost immediately.

Fruits and vegetables that aren't refrigerated should be stowed in a very well ventilated locker, preferably one with slatted shelves. Plastic baskets with lots of holes work well, too. You can use crumpled newspaper to help keep produce cushioned. In the tropics it pays to keep fruits and vegetables from touching each other so they don't rot, and newspaper works here as well. We find that nets work fine for overflow when you're in port, but they're hopeless at sea, as they swing too much, bruising even the toughest produce. If you need extra storage space for fresh produce at sea, try a plastic milk crate; they offer great air circulation, can be wedged or tied into place, and are useful for all sorts of other things once you've eaten the contents. Wherever fresh food is stored, make sure you can get at it easily, because one of the secrets to making produce last is picking it over regularly and tossing out any rotting items.

Sauces and condiments like mustard, curry paste, and mayonnaise will keep fine without refrigeration as long as you *always use a clean utensil* for dipping into the jar. Products in brine such as pickles and olives will also do well, but the latter may need an extra shot of vinegar in really warm weather.

Buying Fresh Produce

Naturally, the fresher the food is when you buy it, the longer it will last. Make sure that any produce you'll be storing outside a refrigerator hasn't been previously refrigerated. That pretty well rules out almost anything from grocery stores and forces you to shop at roadside stalls and open markets, which is where you'll usually find the best prices and freshest stuff, anyway.

How well things keep depends on their freshness, the temperature, and how you treat the food once it's on board. Fruits and vegetables that keep well in the tropics include potatoes, onions, garlic, eggplant, squash, most citrus, apples (especially hard and sour varieties), tomatoes, and pineapples (if not too ripe when purchased). Bananas will ripen very quickly but do well if you can buy a few bunches at different stages. Produce that's hard to keep for more than a few days includes any kind of leafy greens, zucchini, carrots, mangoes, and papaya.

You can extend the life of most produce significantly by washing it in a bleach solution (a tablespoon of bleach per 1 gal./4 L water) as soon as it comes on board. This kills any mold or fungus that's present. We usually do this in the cockpit, where we can spread the produce out to dry on a clean cloth. Pay extra attention to bananas and pineapples, as these almost invariably have cockroaches and other insects on them. We normally dunk both bananas and pineapples in a bucket of salt water first (leave them under water awhile) before giving them the bleach treatment.

Eggs should also be purchased unrefrigerated if you'll be storing them at room temperature. Although finding unrefrigerated eggs is next to impossible in the United States, that's how they're normally sold in most tropical countries. Store them in the carton, in a reasonably cool spot. Turn

Mosquito screens are vital if you're headed for areas with diseases such as malaria, dengue fever, and yellow fever, which are transmitted by mosquito.

the carton over (180 degrees) twice a week, and they'll keep for weeks.

Bread should be purchased unsliced, and we find that brown keeps better than white. Never store it in plastic—instead use a paper bag or newspaper. Naturally, if you eat it quickly it won't get stale or moldy, but keeping bread for a two-week passage can be a challenge. The best trick we've learned is to dunk a pastry brush in undiluted vinegar (either red or white) and brush the bread with it. Let the bread dry, and then wrap it in paper. We've never had bread mold after doing this, and you can't taste the vinegar.

TROPICAL PESTS

Cockroaches, Ants, and Other Crawling Insects

We've already mentioned the importance of washing some kinds of produce and not keeping any cardboard on board. Consider what else might be home to bugs, and either ditch it or check it over carefully before bringing it aboard. Your job is vastly easier if you are anchored out, as boats in

marinas have to contend with invaders coming up the docklines as well being carried aboard.

Despite your best efforts, sooner or later bugs will get a foothold, and you'd do well to have a few tricks up your sleeve. For cockroaches our favorite is sticky traps, or "roach hotels." They're nontoxic and so can be placed anywhere, including the galley. You also know without a doubt if you're having any success. Boric acid and honey is another safe alternative. Mix the two into a paste, and place it on little "trays" of foil in various nooks and crannies. This may also work for some types of ants. Boric acid bait in tablet form is available at many supermarkets or hardware stores in the United States. We haven't tried these ourselves, but other cruisers claim they work.

Flies and Mosquitoes

Flying insects can carry serious diseases—dengue fever, yellow fever, and malaria are all transmitted by mosquitoes—so controlling them is more than a matter of comfort in some regions (see chapter 12). Flying insects are best kept out with insect screens. We have screens for the companionway, all hatches, and even the Dorade vents. Although we made these for keeping mosquitoes out when we're in areas with malaria, we've also found them invaluable where there are lots of flies.

The simplest way to put up screens is to use Velcro. Glue one side of the Velcro to the inside of hatches and glue or sew the other side onto the netting material. Such screens are easy to put up and stow, but will mar the finish on your hatches and companionway. In addition, over time the Velcro will peel off the hatches, particularly if it gets wet.

Our answer was to construct screens that are edged on all sides with fabric sleeves. Inside the sleeves are wooden dowels connected at the corners by a length of cord running through small holes. The screens fit snugly into the frames of our hatches and do not scratch the brightwork because the fabric sleeve sits between the dowels and the frame. Be aware that any screens will cut air flow in half. Therefore, you'll find that windscoops, fans, and the like become that much more important when your screens are in use.

We also make use of other bug deterrents, including mosquito coils and citronella candles. While fine on deck, these shouldn't be used below in the cabin.

KEEPING IT SIMPLE

All boats require maintenance, and most need more in the tropics than in temperate latitudes. The tropical environment will have a definite impact on your boat and its sailing gear, and we look at this question in depth in chapter 14. Ironically, though, most cruisers seem to spend most of their time working not on the boat itself but on all the extras: mechanical systems of one sort or another, including generators, watermakers, freezers, air-conditioning systems, and a host of other add-ons designed to make life more comfortable. We don't have much experience repairing any of these systems, having chosen to keep our own boat—and our lives—pretty simple, leaving more time to explore and enjoy the places we visit. We'd recommend that you do the same. We're not alone in making this suggestion, and we've found that the more experience cruisers have, the fewer complications they want.

ENGINE MAINTENANCE

You won't find engine maintenance to be any more—or less—onerous while cruising in the tropics than it is back home. The biggest differences will probably be the increased need for maintenance, because of the number of hours during which you run your engine and the variable quality of the fuel (which can create its own maintenance problems). Ensuring your engine compartment is properly ventilated is also important but liable to be overlooked by cruisers from colder climes.

Most diesel engines are remarkably trouble-free. Supply them with clean fuel, enough air, clean lubricating oil, and ensure that compression is adequate, and they've got what they need to run. By and large, they'll run for thousands of hours without needing much attention. Problems arise when engines are either not serviced regularly (leading to dirty oil and fuel) or are used in ways for which they were not designed. The latter includes the common practice of running the engine for an hour or two

LIFE BEYOND TV

Steve and Marja Vance are currently skipper and mate aboard a 92-foot (28 m) Nelson-Merek-designed performance cruiser, which they've sailed and maintained for its owners for a number years, logging thousands of miles in the process. They've also circumnavigated aboard their own boat, a Cal 2-27. Here's what Steve has to say about keeping it simple:

"For the past twenty-six years, Marja and I have been living aboard, either on our own 27-footer or someone's luxury boat as paid crew. We've made four trips into the Pacific and have circumnavigated. Over the years we've seen many changes in cruising areas, the types of boats, and certainly the numbers.

"The gear and the boats available today are definitely more 'user friendly,' and the assortment of both borders on the incredible. Cruising has become big business, with marine catalogs as big and thick as a city phone book. While this is the good news, the bad news is that we find the typical tropical cruising sailboat of today is often way too complicated. They're too expensive, and too much like a floating motor home to enable the crew to be able to enjoy what cruising is all about: sailing and being in 'paradise.'

"We do, however, enjoy meeting the increasing number of people at DHL and FedEx offices across the world. It never ceases to amaze us to see people working on their own boats as hard as we do on a large crewed boat. It's one thing to get paid for working on a boat, and something else again when it's your money!

"About a month ago we were in a cyber-café in Papeete, French Polynesia, and a cruiser was telling a couple that he had just sent off an e-mail regarding some piece of equipment for his watermaker. He told his friends that it seemed like every week was the same, and that his next boat would be a lot less complicated. The skipper of the other boat replied, 'Look, we live aboard, and we're not into camping.'

"The 'correct' viewpoint probably depends totally on the individual. However, we've sailed many miles in boats ranging from complicated and luxurious to our simple 27-footer. Our boat, on which we circumnavigated in the 1970s and into the 1980s, was equipped with nothing more in electronics than a depth sounder and a short-wave receiver. We were young and had a great time. Would we go with the same boat and equipment today? Of course not, but we would be certain that our next boat errs toward the simple rather than the complicated. *Excepting electronics, if we can't fix it, it won't be on the boat.*

"Cruising in tropical latitudes is a wonderful experience. One doesn't need to dedicate their whole life to coming up with the 'perfect boat' or duplicating one's home. There is life beyond televisions, microwaves, and air-conditioning."

---

on a daily basis to charge batteries and run a refrigeration or freezer compressor.

Diesels are designed to operate under a load, and most, when run solely to power an alternator or compressor, are doing very little work. When this is done day after day for months on end, cylinder walls become glazed, valves get clogged with carbon, and the performance of your engine suffers. What's the answer? Either find another way to supply the power you need (by using solar panels, a wind charger, a dedicated gas or diesel generator, or some combination of these), or load down the engine when you run it. The latter isn't hard to do: put your engine in gear or run a high output alternator, possibly in combination with a refrigeration compressor.

Oil Changes

Change your engine oil regularly. Follow the recommendations in your manual, or change the oil every 100 hours (more often if your engine is frequently run under light loads). Use the best oil you can buy; ensure it's intended for use in diesel engines (such oils are designated by a *C* prefix, for compression ignition), and not for gasoline engines (indicated by an *S* for spark ignition). The letter following the *C* indicates the type of additives that are in the oil. The higher the letter, the more advanced the additives, so a *CF*-rated oil is better than a *CD* oil.

Using proper oil is especially important when cruising away from developed countries. The fuel you obtain in tropical countries will often have a

The fishing fleet at Papela Bay on Roti Island. Not one of these boats has an engine!

higher sulfur content than that sold in industrialized countries. The sulfur combines with water vapor created when the engine is running to form sulfuric acid, which, as you can imagine, doesn't do the inside of your engine any good. The better the oil, the more effective it will be in neutralizing acids and protecting your costly engine bearings from wear.

Fuel Filters

Fuel filters should also be changed regularly. If your engine manual has a recommendation, follow it, but in any case the interval between changing filters will depend on the cleanliness of the fuel you put into the engine. If you use dirty fuel, you'll go through a lot of filters. You should have a primary filter (this is normally not mounted on the engine) that incorporates a water separator. Most have a plastic bowl that lets you check on the accumulation of water and gunk in the bowl, giving you a "heads-up" that the element should be replaced. This filter should be placed between the tank and the engine and is there to protect your engine's fuel system from any contamination. There will also be a filter fitted directly on most engines, just before

the fuel pump. If your primary filter is doing its job, this one should not get dirty.

It's easy to say that one should never buy dirty fuel, but sometimes that's all there is. And sometimes fuel supplies that should be clean turn out to be dirty. For that reason, all cruisers should filter the fuel they buy as they're filling the tank. A variety of filters are available, from those that exclude everything, including water, to a bit of rag or mesh stuffed in a funnel. Anything is better than nothing, but you'll save yourself the most grief by using a high-quality fine-mesh filter. Using prefilters slows the rate at which you can fill the tank, but it's a small price to pay for the added protection.

We always use a funnel with a built-in filter when fueling up, and it is sometimes surprising how much this catches even when fueling at large and apparently well-maintained fuel docks. We can tell you with confidence that it catches vastly more if you buy your fuel in a remote village in eastern Indonesia.

We've fueled up a number of times in these waters, and it's always an adventure. We once got fuel in a Bajau fishing village on the island of Roti (not far from Timor). Buying fuel in a fishing village made sense, except for the fact that the Bajau don't use engines in their boats. Still, these superbly skilled sailors found diesel for us somewhere, even delivering it to the boat in a canoe. We filtered our diesel and then motored off, jealous of the superb ghosting ability their huge rigs provided.

The fuel we bought was enough to get us to another remote village—Komodo—which is better known for its dragons than its diesel. At 9 to 10 feet (3 m) the komodo dragon is the world's largest lizard and has been known to attack and kill people, which added a little adventure to our refueling stop. We rowed ashore with the dinghy, confident of finding fuel because of the vast fleet of motorized fishing trimarans moored off the reef, but a bit leery of what might be stalking the beach. The fuel depot turned out to be a shopkeeper's stall, where a drum of diesel sat between the dried fish and quick-cooking noodles. The diesel was transferred to our jerricans with a metal scoop. A crowd of helpful onlookers offered advice, and the bill came to just 15¢ U.S./L; considering the experience, it would have been cheap at ten times the price.

Engine Ventilation and Temperature

Diesels use lots of air, which is why it's a good idea to keep clear of the air intakes when the engine is running at speed. That air has to come from somewhere, and boats with a very tight-fitting engine enclosure may not allow enough air to get to the engine. Even if enough combustion air gets in, engine-compartment air temperatures may be very high, which impairs the efficiency of your engine and accelerates the wear on gaskets, hoses, and the like. The best approach is to mount an exhaust blower and actively draw air into and through the engine compartment. That way you'll supply plenty of air for combustion and keep temperatures down at the same time. This will also help minimize the engine smell that gets into the boat.

Naval architect Dave Gerr has developed a simple

Engines do wear out, so give some thought as to how you would replace yours. Here we're preparing to hoist a rebuilt diesel off the dock and into Nomad.

formula for figuring how much vent area you need:

$$\text{vent area (sq. in.)} = \text{engine hp} \div 3.3$$
$$\text{or}$$
$$\text{vent area (sq. cm)} = \text{engine kW} \times 2.6$$

Thus if your engine puts out 40 hp, you'll need vents totaling 12 square inches (77 sq. cm) in area. But these are minimums, and we would suggest doubling these figures for tropical cruising.

Spare Parts and Repairs

What you should carry along in terms of engine spares depends a lot on the make and age of your engine, the availability of spares in various areas, and how much you'll be using it. Find a reputable mechanic before you set sail and have him or her look your engine over. The mechanic can advise you on any repairs or upgrades you should make

THEFT

Many tropical countries are poor. In some, families live for a year on less than a cruising couple might spend in a month. Although we may not be wealthy back home, compared to most of the tropics' inhabitants, even the poorest cruisers out there are rich and very fortunate to have the freedom and opportunity to travel as we do. Because we're often away from tourist areas and hotels, our lifestyle and wealth are much more visible to the inhabitants of the countries that we visit than that of most tourists. In light of all this, what's surprising to us is not that theft occurs, but that it doesn't happen more often.

The risk of theft and what it takes to protect yourself varies enormously from one country to another. In general, the risk is probably highest in urban areas, where there's a greater concentration of really desperate people, a bigger market for stolen goods, and fewer social or cultural restraints imposed by the community. In such areas you'll do well to lock your boat securely and to clear the deck of attractive and valuable items. In South America it's not uncommon for cruisers to hire local guards.

In remote regions you're much less likely to have problems. Treat both the local community and any individuals that you encounter with respect, and it's highly unlikely that you'll have to worry. If something does disappear, your chances are good of getting it back if you go to the local community leaders or police and explain what's happened.

The tough call is in all the places that are between these two, where theft isn't an obvious and immediate threat, but the community also isn't so small that a thief would be easily traced and the goods found. Our approach in these areas is to err on the side of caution until we've had a chance to talk with some locals about how safe it is. Being cautious includes locking our boat (which we normally don't do), being careful where we leave our dinghy, and once again keeping the decks pretty clear of sails, lines, and the like. This strategy has worked well, and so far we've never—knock on wood—been ripped off.

All boats should be set up so that they can be easily and *visibly* locked. In fact, in many areas the appearance of security is probably more important than how good your lock or hatch closure actually is. Unless your boat is built of steel, with steel hatches, you'll never be able to keep out a really determined thief, but a decent lock should suffice for most.

---

before setting out and on what extras you should carry along that may be peculiar to your engine. All cruisers should carry along some basics, including

> oil and fuel filters
>
> oil for engine and gearbox
>
> overhaul kits for fresh- and saltwater pumps
>
> hoses, O-rings, and belts to fit your engine

> spare injector
>
> gasket paper and sealant
>
> waterproof grease and WD-40 or equivalent
>
> spare hose clips
>
> well-stocked toolbox
>
> engine manual and a good reference on diesel engines; for the latter, see appendix 3, Resources

Chapter 11

The Business Side of Cruising

Paperwork and bureaucracy are among the things we strive to escape when we set sail, but unfortunately they're alive and well in the tropics. Sometimes formalities such as customs and immigration are handled quickly, efficiently, and even with a smile. Occasionally they can be a nightmare. Resign yourself to the fact that, someday, some official or agency or bank will make your life difficult. Fortunately the experience usually makes for a good story!

PAPERWORK

You'll need to carry along a variety of documents to keep all officials everywhere you visit happy and occupied. We first cover the paperwork that you'll need for traveling to any foreign country and that you should have on board and up-to-date at all times. Then we tackle the more difficult bits: documents for which the requirements vary from country to country, year to year, and sometimes even according to whom you talk.

Ship's Papers

Your "ship's papers" consist of the registration form that demonstrates you own (or are the managing owner and skipper of) your boat. If your boat is registered in the United States it'll be either documented with the U.S. Coast Guard or registered with an individual state; both are acceptable when cruising abroad. Cruisers from other countries should inquire about what type of registration they need to cruise in foreign waters. Whatever form of registration you carry, it's vital that the actual paper clearly states the boat's name, your name, and the fact that you own or manage and skipper the boat. That's the information most officials will be looking for. Make a copy (better yet, multiple copies) and keep it (or them) safely stowed somewhere separately from the original.

Crew's Papers

Each crew member will need a valid passport, and ideally these passports should be valid for the length of your planned cruise. If the expiry date falls somewhere in the midst of your trip, however, your passport can be renewed by contacting an embassy or consulate. Make a photocopy of your passport, as this will simplify getting it replaced should that be necessary.

A crew list is normally among the papers that are requested upon arrival in a new port. There is no standard form to use for a crew list; some countries request that you prepare the list, while others require that you use their printed form. In either case, multiple copies are the rule, sometimes as many as five. The information required usually includes the name of your vessel and any registration or documentation number; the vessel's port of registry; your home port; the name, date of birth, nationality, and passport number of the captain and each crew member; the date of arrival; the last port visited; the next port of call; estimated length of stay and places you'll be visiting in that country. Even if you don't prepare a stack of crew lists ahead of time, it's helpful to have all this information written down in one place.

Finally, although you won't need it to go through customs and immigration, whoever of your crew plans to drive while abroad will need a valid driver's license. Some countries require that you hold an international license, and these are usually available in your home country (in the United States, contact the American Automobile Association). We've been asked for an international license but have never been refused a rental car because we didn't have one.

Some countries require that you be immunized against certain diseases, most commonly yellow fever. Countries requiring this vaccination are listed in chapter 12 (Staying Healthy in the Tropics). You should carry an International Certificate of Vaccination that records your history of immunizations. These are produced by the World Health Organization and are widely available from most medical clinics.

Visas

Visa requirements vary widely, depending on your nationality and the country you're visiting. In some countries no visa is needed, in others they're granted upon arrival, and in some you'll pay a hefty fine if you dare show up without one. Be warned that visa requirements change, and what you hear from a cruiser who visited a country a few years ago may no longer be true. The best advice we can give is to check into visa requirements for the countries you'll be visiting well in advance. Do so while you still

have a chance of getting a visa for the countries in question (typically from a consulate or embassy).

When you ask about visa requirements, be sure to make it clear you'll be arriving by boat. Some countries have different requirements for sailors than other travelers, and a few require a special visa for the boat's skipper. Also ask about various types of visas and visa renewals. Holding one type of visa may prevent you from obtaining a different type, and a long-term visa obtained in advance is often much cheaper than the cost of renewing a visa when in a country. Be persistent. Many officials seem to assume we all know as much about the regulations as they do, and they don't spell out the important little details unless you ask specifically.

To get a visa you'll often need a few passport-type photos, so it pays to have a stash of these on board. You may also be asked to prove that you have adequate funds to support you while you're in the country. What constitutes such proof varies, but having recent bank statements on hand is a good idea. Some countries will accept a credit card instead of, or in addition to, a bank statement.

Entry Permits and Cruising Permits

Entry permits are usually just that: a permit that allows you to enter (but not necessarily cruise) a country's waters. These must be obtained in advance and are for the vessel rather than the crew (you'll have to meet visa requirements separately).

The term *cruising permit* means different things in different places but is generally a permit that allows you to cruise within a country's waters. Many countries don't bother with cruising permits at all, and most of those that require them issue them after you arrive. But a few require that these be obtained prior to arrival.

Ask about the need for both cruising and entry permits when you're looking into visas. And don't assume that because you don't need a visa, you won't need one of these permits. For example, Americans don't need visas to visit the Federated States of Micronesia (FSM) but do need an entry permit in hand before entering FSM's waters. Likewise, citizens of most nations can obtain two-month tourist visas for Indonesia free of charge, at their port of entry, but must already have in hand a cruising/entry permit (known as a CAIT, or Clearance Approval for Indonesian Territory). CAITs are also technically free, but it is essentially impossible to obtain one without the help of an "agent," and these naturally charge for their services.

Zarpe—Don't Leave Home without It

You've got your papers for boat and crew, and have visas and cruise permits, if required. What more could you need? A *zarpe*, or outbound customs clearance. This is the first paper customs officials will ask for when you enter a foreign port, and each customs' service will issue you a new one when you clear out of their country, bound for another. The zarpe is usually signed, stamped, embossed, and impressively official looking, and serves to reassure the customs service of the country you're clearing into that you did indeed just sail from the country that issued you the zarpe. In general, you should not try showing up somewhere without a zarpe, unless you've got a very good story to tell about why you don't have one.

Once you have your first zarpe you'll get the next one automatically, when you leave one country headed for another. But you'll have to get the first in the chain at home, before departing. In the United States a zarpe consists of Customs Form 1378: Clearance of a Vessel to a Foreign Port. Technically, there is no requirement for U.S. yachts to clear customs before departing for a foreign port. Officials in some countries recognize this and do not require a zarpe for U.S. yachts making their first landfall after leaving home. Others may, however, so it is prudent for U.S. cruisers to obtain a zarpe, especially if they are heading into the Pacific. To obtain one, simply pay a visit to the customs office at your departure port, armed with your registration and identification. Residents of other countries setting sail for the first time should contact their customs service.

Keeping Your Cool

There's one other item you'll need for clearing customs and dealing with bureaucracy, and it may be one of the most important: patience. We can't emphasize enough how critical patience, good manners, and a smile are when dealing with officials. It's not always easy, though. When you arrive in port, you're usually hot, tired, and in desperate need of a shower and a cold beer, but there's all this paperwork and running around to deal with. You need to realize that efficiency is a relative term in the tropics and may not be part of the vocabulary of the officials with whom you'll be dealing. Just plan to spend several hours or half a day clearing customs, and you'll be pleasantly surprised if it takes less time and goes without a hitch. Some cruisers argue and pound their fist on an official's desk, making all sorts of demands, only to be refused a visa extension or have their paperwork held up for an inordinate amount of time. Keeping your cool can make the difference in how long things take or how smoothly it all goes.

This not only applies to officials but to people in general. A sailing friend just relayed a story to us about how a cruiser in Vanuatu became rude with a waitress in a guest house because he'd had to ask her twice for his coffee, the water for which was being boiled over a wood fire! If you can't handle or accept that life moves at a much slower pace in these parts, then you may want to think twice about cruising the tropics.

Likewise, dressing neatly when you make the rounds goes a long way toward making a positive impression on officials. This is also important when you initially visit a village or town, or if you're invited to someone's home. It only takes a few minutes to put on a clean shirt and pair of shorts. Your dressing like a slob only confirms some of the stereotypes about cruising sailors.

It's also important to be honest. If a customs officer asks whether you're carrying firearms, or an agricultural inspector wants to know if you've brought in any fresh fruit and vegetables, don't be evasive. Little lies can get you into trouble and won't win you anyone's trust.

CUSTOMS

Making a landfall is probably one of the most exciting parts of a passage. High islands are visible for many hours as you slowly approach, while low islets and atolls generally first appear as coconut trees surrounded by water. If the wind is offshore the scent of the land will reach you as well, and in the tropics the fragrance of flowering plants is intoxicating.

Enjoy the romance of making landfall, because what comes next is less fun: paperwork. The procedure for obtaining clearance to a new country varies from wonderfully easy, with the officials meeting you on the dock, to a virtual scavenger hunt. And when you depart, or clear out, the process is reversed. In almost all cases there'll be an assortment of forms to fill out, so be sure your pen has plenty of ink.

Obtaining Clearance

In some countries it's possible to radio ahead and announce your arrival via VHF or SSB radio. In fact, some countries (such as Australia) "require" this, but if you don't know that ahead of time, don't have a working radio, or have trouble getting through, then it can be hard to comply. All the officials we've met recognize that, and the requirement for announcing your arrival seems to be more for the convenience of all concerned than anything else. Check with other cruisers or check your cruising guide, and make a few calls on the VHF as you're nearing land (try calling the port captain or harbor authority) in an attempt to contact customs.

Plan your arrival to coincide with normal business hours, and avoid holidays and weekends unless you know that clearance services are available during those times. Beware of the cost: some customs services will clear you in during their off-hours, but most charge handsomely for the privilege.

You should fly a Q signal flag (plain yellow) when coming into port, which indicates you're requesting pratique, or clearance from health officials. We'll assume you're sailing into an official port of entry, but even then it can at times be difficult to know where to go. Small ports that receive lots of visiting yachts

normally have a well-defined procedure for handling them, and it shouldn't be hard to figure out where to anchor or dock. If you get no response on the radio but see other yachts, contact them and ask. In large ports that get few yachts you'll likely be treated as larger vessels are, and you should be able to get instructions via radio on how to proceed. Small ports that get few visitors are the most challenging, as you might not have the slightest idea of where to anchor, and whether you should go ashore to clear in or wait for someone to come to you.

The practice of stopping off in a country before having checked in is illegal and not recommended. Having said that, we'll admit to making a few such stops ourselves. But we advise that you carefully consider the circumstances and the probable reaction of the country whose laws you're flouting before dropping the hook. Stopovers that are most likely to be condoned or ignored are brief visits to uninhabited offshore reefs and islands. For example, in the South Pacific, Tonga ignores visits to Minerva Reef, which lies between Tonga and New Zealand, while farther west visits to reefs and islets in the Coral Sea are tolerated by the governments of Australia and New Caledonia. But not all governments will react in the same way, and almost all will take very seriously a stop at an inhabited island or port before you've cleared in.

At such times you may be forced to simply play things by ear, selecting what appears to be a safe and out-of-the-way yet visible spot to anchor. Drop the hook, make sure your Q flag is flapping nicely, and wait. And wait, and wait. You may have to wait a few days to be cleared, if you arrive on a weekend; in some countries you'll never be able to enter officially unless you go in search of the officials yourself. Beware of doing this unless you know that's the accepted procedure; if you're unsure, stay on board with the Q flag flying until it's very obvious that no one is coming. Keep an eye out for arm waving from shore, and be ready to provide transport for the officials, to and from your boat, as they may not have any way

It can be tempting to stop before clearing customs, especially if you pass peaceful and protected anchorages.

of reaching an anchored yacht. If you do go in search of customs and immigration, only the skipper should go ashore. Make sure to take along your ships' papers, crew papers, zarpe, and some money.

Entry usually involves a number of officials or offices, including health, agriculture, immigration, and customs. At times one person may fill several roles, while at other times you'll need to deal with a few more, such as the harbormaster and the navy. The one inspection most often performed on board is that done by an agricultural officer, but even this is sometimes done ashore in an office.

Be prepared to surrender fresh foods and possibly some canned, dried, and frozen ones as well to the agricultural inspector. (We've even had a partial tin of bottom paint taken away.) The thoroughness and severity of the rules and inspections varies widely, sometimes even within the same country, but it pays to assume that fresh foods will be confiscated unless

you know otherwise. Customs officials may search your boat as well, generally on the lookout for drugs and firearms; some countries will seize handicrafts if they're made from threatened or endangered species (see chapter 15, Green Cruising).

Once you've been cleared by the agricultural and health inspectors, you can take down your Q flag and raise in its place a courtesy flag for the country you're visiting. Making these ourselves offers a fun way for us to while away a couple hours at sea. A flag of around 10 by 15 inches (4 by 6 cm) is about right for most boats.

The entrepreneurial spirit is alive and well in the tropics, and there are places where you can employ an agent to assist you in entering and clearing out. Quiz such agents carefully about the cost before employing them, and don't be bullied into accepting their services. Not surprisingly, they may attempt

CLEARING CUSTOMS

We've asked Hugh Marriott, fellow tropical cruiser and author, to share some of his experiences with the official side of cruising.

In the Caribbean, everyone who arrives by boat is traditionally welcomed by an arcane local ceremony. The details differ from country to country, but the ceremony is always full of mystery and wonder. Nobody now can remember how it started or what its real purpose is or was, but it's called Clearing Customs.

A recent cruise took us across the Mona Passage to the Dominican Republic. We were less nervous about the notoriously bumpy passage than about the reception we could expect from the customs. The standard of living in the Dominican Republic is very low, and a little graft might on the whole be excusable. But the four officials who boarded us sat meekly in the cockpit to fill in their forms, and when we asked them if they would like something to drink, they answered: "Just a glass of water, thank you, or perhaps a soft drink—no beer, no." Then they said that they ought to search the boat, so would we mind if they just had a very quick look below? They tiptoed respectfully about for three or four minutes, during the course of which the most junior stared and stared into our fruit net. "What kind of fruit is that?" "It's an apple; would you like one?" He ate it furtively and with wonder.

In the Caribbean it's important to get a proper exit document—known in the Spanish-speaking countries as a *zarpe*—when you leave. The story goes that some yachts, trying to enter the next island zarpeless, have been refused entry and told to go back and get it. Sailing back into the teeth of the trade wind is easier said than done, and our next country was to be communist Cuba, so I was more interested than usual in having the proper paperwork.

We went alongside the Customs quay, from where I was led into the navy base, up some stairs, into an office, out again, up some more, down again, and into another building. I filled in forms and signed statements and answered questions that seemed often to be of an unofficial nature ("Why aren't you staying in the Dominican Republic longer? Don't you like it here?"). Eventually I was led to a room where two of the same officials who had cleared us in were seated at desks. They sprang to their feet, and we shook hands warmly. One of them proceeded to make out the longed-for zarpe, and then the three of us proceeded in stately official style back to the waiting boat. Once aboard, they conducted another perfunctory search, and then there was more hand shaking and expressions of mutual regard and good luck, before the senior official asked if we would mind doing him a personal favor. He wanted, for his private album, a photograph of us standing on the quay beside the boat. He took more pictures as we cast off and motored out into midstream, more as we hoisted the mainsail, and he was still snapping as we wafted out of the harbor and out to sea. It wasn't until the murky water of the harbor had given way at last to deep Caribbean blue that I realized he had forgotten, in the emotion of the moment, to hand over the zarpe.

We were four days and three nights on passage to Santiago de Cuba from Santo Domingo, and we ghosted through the narrow harbor entrance at 2200, picking our way in with the intermittent help of the lighthouse beam. We played cat and mouse for a time with a Cuban patrol boat that issued unintelligible instructions and blinded us with their spotlight. To their dismay we dropped the anchor, and the barrage of Spanish continued. After awhile, struggling to be forceful though polite, I told them that I couldn't understand, that our boat was safe where she was, that we were short-handed and tired and couldn't see, so it would be dangerous for us to move, and that we were staying put. Then I said that we were going to bed. Finally I called out "Good night," went below, and turned out the cabin lights. There we crouched nervously, wondering what would happen.

Some time later, there was a crashing and a scraping and a series of thuds, and I shot out blearily into the cockpit to find six men on deck, and two gray boats made fast alongside. One of the men told me that since we had refused to go to them, they had come to us. He said they represented Customs, Immigration, Port Health, the Frontier Guard, the Department of Transport, and the Ministry of the Interior. I led them below, where they each produced a folder of official forms printed on coarse thin buff paper.

They all asked questions at the same time, so I countered with one of my own: "How are things in Cuba?" "Excellent. For the tourists." "And for you?" "Things are getting better every day," said one. The others laughed. A good joke. Then the dreaded moment arrived: "Did you get a zarpe when you left Santo Domingo?" "Yes." Long pause, then: "Well, where is it, then?" "In Santo Domingo. I left it there by mistake." An even longer pause, and a lot of eye contact between the officials sitting round our saloon table. Finally: "No problem." Phew! I poured us all a drink.

to convince you that you can't clear without their help, but we've not known this to be the case.

Cruising within a Country

Each country has its own rules about clearing in and out of ports and islands when sailing within its waters. In some you're free to sail anywhere for the period for which your visa is valid. Others will want you to carry a cruising permit that details the islands you'll be visiting, while the most stringent require you to also clear in and out of each port within the country. The latter can be quite a hassle if it involves visits to a number of offices each time, and you'll want to take this into account when planning where you'll be sailing.

Clearing Out

Clearing out is the reverse of entering, except you'll know where to go and whom to see. If they don't explain it to you when you're entering, ask the customs and other officials what you'll need to do when you leave. Normally clearing out is straightforward, but at times it involves a visit to each office you visited on arrival. Make sure you don't leave the customs office without a new zarpe in hand.

Most customs officials will ask you to state the time you plan to depart (usually within 24 hours). Some will give you much less time—just a few hours—and a few may even want to see you sail past their office or wharf on your way out of port. Inquire about what to do if your departure is delayed by weather or some other problem; you'll want to know ahead of time if they expect you to clear back in.

Greasing the Wheels

Formal clearance procedures may be time-consuming and repetitive, but they're generally straightforward. In a number of countries there are also unofficial demands and suggestions. They're not always obvious, but what is usually involved is a request for money. In some areas this is so common as to be part of the normal routine; not written down in law or regulation, perhaps, but practiced everyday nonetheless. In other places it's quite the exception and really just a wily official's way of getting something out of you.

Greasing palms goes against the grain for many of us, and not just because it increases the cost of cruising. Giving in to demands for money, from petty officials who'll do all they can to make your life miserable if you refuse, feels like just that—giving in—and can only help to perpetuate the cycle of graft. However, there may be times when you have little choice but to pay up, and it's worth querying other cruisers about whether they've met with similar requests. Demands for "a bit extra" that are made routinely and consistently will be the hardest to deny. It's good to know what you're up against. In other situations the option of greasing palms may work to your advantage, as a small payment may allow you to avoid long delays and significant hassles.

STAYING IN TOUCH

Thanks to technology, it's easier than ever to stay in touch and manage your money while cruising.

Money

Cash machines are not yet ubiquitous in the tropics, but almost all banks are equipped to issue a cash advance on a credit card, Visa being the most widely accepted. Cash advances are costly (in terms of interest), and we've found that the best approach is to use a debit card, which is accepted wherever Visa cards are. This allows direct access to your account via cash machines or bank withdrawals, with either minimal or no fees, and no interest. Exchange rates are usually good, better than those offered by banks for exchange of either cash or travelers checks. We carry a small amount of U.S. currency (in bills of $20 or less) in case we're unable to find a bank that will give us money on our debit card, but we rarely have to dig into this stash. The U.S. dollar is accepted just about anywhere in the world, and the residents of some countries we've sailed in prefer it over their own!

Mail

We know of only two practical ways for cruisers to deal with their mail. Some impose on a friend or family member to forward mail and pay bills, while others use a mail-forwarding service. The disadvantage of imposing on people you know is just that: it's an imposition. Mail-forwarding services that specifically cater to cruisers are available and are listed in the back of yachting magazines. Mail is sent via courier so you're pretty much guaranteed of getting your stuff quickly and it's traceable, but we find courier services costly. And unlike a family member or friend, a mail-forwarding service is impersonal. In the end, no solution is ideal, and you'll always receive bank statements and the like several months after they've been sent, and you'll generally chase your mail across the globe. That's why many people do as much business and correspondence as they can by e-mail.

E-Mail

This is probably the most efficient, practical, and cheapest way of staying in touch with family and friends. There are plenty of free e-mail services you can sign up with, which are easy to use. These days it seems you can find an Internet café just about anywhere. If you're one of the few who are computer illiterate, it's worth the effort to learn how to use e-mail.

Our bank is not yet able to handle transactions via the Internet, but inquire whether yours can. If you can make payments (such as for credit card bills) via the Internet, you'll be able to conduct much of your financial business very easily and inexpensively from anywhere in the world.

Chapter 12

Staying Healthy in the Tropics

I f you're like most sailors, you'll find tropical cruising to be a much healthier lifestyle than the one you've left behind. No more cities, smog, tension, or lousy winters! Instead you'll be outside a lot, breathing clean air, swimming in clear water, and enjoying a warm, benign climate. As a result, you're likely to suffer less from common illnesses such as colds and flu, or from stress-related complaints. What you need to guard against is getting sick from any number of probably unfamiliar tropical diseases and from contracting serious infections as a result of otherwise minor injuries. The risk of illness varies enormously from place to place, and where possible we discuss the distribution of specific illnesses.

Cruisers face some special problems with respect to both disease prevention and treatment. We often stay in a region for months, far longer than most tourists, and usually visit more remote areas. As a result, information and prevention strategies suggested by many authorities for other tourists may not be relevant or practical for cruisers. What's more, cruisers may be unable to summon help quickly, if at all, when sailing in a remote location, and so have to be better prepared than most travelers to deal with emergencies.

Caution: the information presented here is as up-to-date as we can make it. It comes primarily from the World Health Organization (WHO), the Centers for Disease Control and Prevention (CDC), and our own experience. But both diseases and treatment regimes are constantly evolving. Use the information to build awareness of health issues that you'll face in the tropics, but whenever possible get the most recent information you can about the relative risks of various diseases in different regions and the latest recommendations for vaccination and treatment. Both WHO and CDC have excellent Web sites with up-to-date information (see the Health section in appendix 3, Resources). Also make sure to consult with a physician before taking any medications, because many can cause serious complications in some people.

Also note that we've generally restricted the discussion of treatment to what amounts to first aid that can be administered aboard. In many instances that's all that's needed, while in more serious cases the aim is to stabilize the person until you can get professional help. Inquire about medical facilities and expertise in the areas you cruise, and give some thought to how you can get help if you need to. You may wish to consider taking out medical or travelers insurance; there are policies available that

Coastal villages are often picturesque but are usually crowded and lack health care facilities.

include remote consultation (by phone, fax, or e-mail) and evacuation, should the latter be necessary. Finally, don't forget to arm yourself with a few basic medical reference books, because you'll want to be able to self-diagnose and treat most simple and common complaints.

INFECTIOUS DISEASES

Infectious diseases can be caused by bacteria, viruses, and parasites; see the accompanying table.

To catch a disease you must somehow come into contact with the organism that causes it. This can take place through direct contact with the disease-causing organism, or through contact with a *vector*. Vectors are animals (often insects) that transmit parasitic microorganisms (and thus the diseases these cause) from person to person, or between animals and people. Examples of infection through direct contact include

▶ **AN INFECTED PERSON SNEEZES ON YOU**, transmitting a virus that gives you a cold

▶ **INGESTING AN INFECTING ORGANISM** (you drink water polluted with *Vibrio cholerae* and develop cholera)

Examples of infection via a vector include:

▶ **DIRECT TRANSMISSION BY A VECTOR** (you're bitten by an infected *Anopheles* mosquito and contract malaria)

▶ **INDIRECT TRANSMISSION BY A VECTOR** (a fly walks on your lunch after first becoming

INFECTIOUS AGENTS AND THE DISEASES THEY CAUSE

Infectious Agents	Examples of Diseases They Cause
bacteria	pneumonia bacillary dysentery cholera
viruses	common cold influenza yellow fever rabies viral pneumonia
parasites	malaria amoebic dysentery

In many poor tropical countries, toilet facilities consist of an outhouse situated close to the water.

contaminated with feces that contain *Salmonella typhi,* and you contract typhoid fever)

Disease Prevention

Avoid contact with the infectious organism, and you won't become ill. In some instances this means not coming into contact with people that are sick, or being very careful about such contacts. In other cases it means staying clear of contaminated water or food, or disease vectors, such as mosquitoes. You can also reduce your chance of getting many diseases by increasing your resistance through immunization or through the use of protective (prophylactic) drugs. Even if you're immunized, do all you can to avoid infection, and remember that for some diseases, such as dengue, this is all that can be done—there is no vaccine, prophylactic, or treatment.

Immunizations

Immunization is a simple and often effective means of preventing infection. Immunization works by triggering the body's own immune system. When foreign substances (including bacteria and viruses) enter your body, your immune system responds by forming *antibodies,* which combine with and help eliminate the foreign substance. Antibodies for specific disease-causing organisms will persist in the blood system for many years, and provide permanent immunity for some diseases.

Vaccines are composed of weakened or dead disease-causing organisms; although incapable of producing a full infection in most people, they will elicit an immune response. The antibodies thus produced provide a protection from subsequent infection by the same organism. Unfortunately, many vaccines don't produce a response as effective as that from an actual infection, and so vaccination must be repeated periodically.

Recommendations for immunizations change frequently, so get up-to-date information (see the Health section in appendix 3, Resources). Discuss your plans with a physician well before your departure date so that you can schedule immunizations, as some must be taken in stages. What immunizations you'll need depends on where you're headed— see the following detailed disease information.

Avoiding Contaminated Food and Water

The best defense against a number of tropical diseases is avoiding contaminated food and drink. Diseases that are transmitted this way include cholera, typhoid, amoebic dysentery, and hepatitis A and E. The Rule of Fs covers the problems pretty well: consider food, fingers, fluids, and feces. Many tropical nations lack modern sanitation facilities, and awareness of the need for good hygiene often isn't widespread. If you're traveling in poorer countries, be careful about what you eat and drink. Even major tourist destinations may not provide water that can be safely consumed. For example, Bali sees millions of visitors a year but has no safe drinking water supply; even the locals generally drink only bottled water.

Food in such areas is also a potential source of infection, whether bought fresh at a market or

Carefully check the freshness of any fish you buy, especially if you suspect it was not placed on ice after being caught.

Food purchased from roadside stalls is often not properly cooked or refrigerated.

purchased already cooked. Leafy vegetables are a particular risk and should be washed with water to which some bleach has been added. Fruits that you peel before eating are generally safe. Prepared food presents a problem in part because of the variety of ways it can become contaminated. You can get sick if the food isn't carefully washed or prepared, if it isn't sufficiently heated, or if the dishes and eating utensils aren't properly washed (using drinking-quality water). The risk is usually greater in small eateries such as roadside stands. Use common sense and ask other travelers if they've gotten sick from any water or food.

Freezing and refrigeration don't kill most disease-causing organisms. Ice cream should be avoided unless made with pasteurized milk, as should milk itself; the latter should be boiled before drinking if you're in doubt. Also avoid ice in drinks, unless you know it was made with pure drinking-quality water.

Disinfecting Water

The safest way to obtain water is to catch or make your own (see chapter 10, Life Aboard). If that isn't possible, buy bottled water for drinking and cooking. Failing that, water must be purified.

It's important to define at the outset the purpose of treating water. Water treatment can be used to make water more acceptable aesthetically (in terms of taste and smell) and to make it safe to drink by killing disease-causing organisms. Ideally, any water treatment method will do both, but it clearly has to do the latter.

Water can be contaminated with all sorts of harmful substances, including heavy metals and organic compounds (such as fuels, pesticides, and herbicides) but the primary problem for cruisers is with infectious organisms. Even if we're unlucky enough to encounter water with other contaminants, we probably won't drink enough for these to have a significant effect.

There are many treatment and filtration systems to choose from, all with their own advantages and problems, but many aren't practical for onboard use.

Many also don't address the problem of water that may be stored in your tanks for long periods of time, in warm conditions, which can provide an ideal setting for bacterial growth.

SUPER-CHLORINATION AND FILTRATION

Our suggestion for simple onboard water treatment is to start by using a prefilter, with a mesh size of 30–60 microns, designed to screen out sediments and larger contaminants on the way into the tank. Once the water is in the tank, it can be chemically treated using chlorine or iodine. Both will kill most organisms in the water, if used in high enough concentrations, although some parasites have managed to survive chemical treatment. We favor ordinary household bleach, as it is widely available and simple to use. The bleach normally available in the United States contains 5.25 percent sodium hypochlorite. Make sure that what you use is pure bleach and doesn't include soaps or other additives. To "super-chlorinate" your water, which will ensure that nothing grows in the tank, add 1 teaspoon bleach for every 10 gallons (5 mL in 38 L) of water. This is designed to leave a minimum chlorine residue of 3 parts per million after 5 minutes. Super-chlorination will make the water taste pretty nasty, but filtration will eliminate this; note that even water with lower chlorine concentrations, which may not taste so objectionable, should really be filtered before drinking.

Remove the chlorine by using a filter on the line that feeds the galley tap (lines that supply a shower or other water that you don't drink need not be filtered). The filter you use should take out the chlorine and also trihalomethanes (suspected carcinogens produced when chlorine comes into contact with organic compounds); it doesn't hurt if the filter is also capable of removing infectious organisms, just in case these made it past the chlorine. The simplest type is an activated carbon filter, and this will be effective in removing chlorine, trihalomethanes, and some organic chemicals. Activated charcoal filters have a few drawbacks: they're subject to contamination from bacteria, and give no ready indication when they should be replaced. Both of these drawbacks are of less concern if you super-chlorinate: it's doubtful that any organisms will survive the treatment, and with high levels of chlorine the taste of the water will act as a reliable indicator that it's time to replace the filter.

Other (generally more costly) filtration systems are also available. To discourage bacteria growth on charcoal filters, a silver coating can be incorporated. If you want to be sure of filtering out any remaining parasites or other organisms, then a filter incorporating a ceramic stage ahead of a carbon stage is needed. All these types of filters—plain activated carbon, carbon with a silver coating, and ceramic filters—are available for household use, and being small, they can be easily mounted in the galley. A typical activated charcoal filter is about 10 inches high and 3 inches in diameter (25 by 7.5 cm) and contains enough charcoal to treat about 1,000 gallons (3,750 L) of water.

In an emergency, you can ensure the safety of your water by letting it boil for at least three minutes. This is guaranteed to kill all disease-causing organisms, though it won't remove any other pollutants.

MAJOR TROPICAL DISEASES

There are hundreds of diseases that cruisers visiting the tropics could come down with, but, in fact, most never catch anything more serious than a cold. The illnesses we've chosen to discuss are ones that you're most likely to encounter, and that you should prepare for if traveling to areas where they're found. Preparation may mean nothing more than fitting your boat with mosquito screens and stocking up on repellent; for dengue there's not much more to be done. But for other diseases, you'll probably want to be vaccinated, lay in a supply of appropriate drugs for treatment, or both.

Tetanus
Although not limited to the tropics, tetanus is ubiquitous in tropical ocean waters (as well as on land), and even minor wounds can result in infections. There is no effective first-aid treatment for tetanus, which has a high mortality rate if not properly treated through hospitalization.

Avoiding Tetanus
The good news is that immunization is very effective and long lasting. If you've never been vaccinated, a series of shots is required. Others will require boosters every ten years.

Typhoid Fever
Typhoid is caused by the bacterium *Salmonella typhi*. It's contracted by drinking water or eating food that's been contaminated with *S. typhi*. Typhoid is a serious illness, with an estimated 30 million cases and 600,000 deaths annually worldwide. It's found in many tropical countries.

Symptoms
Typhoid begins with the person feeling tired and listless and having a persistent headache and poor appetite. Temperature soon begins to rise in steps, reaching a high of 102 to 104°F (39 to 40°C). It will stay elevated for about two weeks, dropping over the course of a night and then climbing again during the day to reach a similar high each evening. The pulse is usually about normal. Anyone who has a persistent temperature of this kind but a normal pulse should suspect typhoid. If untreated, the person may recover after the second week, but untreated typhoid can also result in deep coma and death.

Treatment
If you suspect typhoid, get medical help immediately. In the interim, drink plenty of fluids and control the fever. Isolate the person, as urine, feces, and vomit are all highly contagious. Eating utensils should be sterilized after use (boil for 10 minutes) and linens carefully disinfected.

Avoiding Typhoid
Typhoid immunization is only about 70 percent effective but is nevertheless recommended for travelers

going to remote areas where the disease is found. Even if vaccinated, be careful to avoid drink and food that may be contaminated.

Cholera

Spread through contaminated water and food, cholera was once widespread throughout the world, but it's now rare in areas with good sanitation and water purification. The disease is caused by bacteria, *Vibrio cholerae*, which produce a toxin that causes vomiting and profuse watery diarrhea. These symptoms occur suddenly and, if untreated, can result in rapid dehydration, cardiovascular collapse, and kidney failure. In severe, untreated cases, death can occur in a few hours.

Symptoms

The incubation period is 1 to 3 days, during which the person may notice mild diarrhea, depression, and lack of energy. The end of the incubation period brings explosive, voluminous, watery diarrhea. A person can become severely dehydrated and be in shock from fluid loss in just a few hours.

Treatment

The major danger of cholera lies in acute dehydration. Replacement of water and electrolytes by oral rehydration can prevent dehydration and shock; initially, fluids may need to be given intravenously. Antibiotics may also be required. Seek medical help immediately if you suspect cholera infection. If you're planning on traveling to a remote area where cholera is known to be a problem, but medical help won't be available, get advice beforehand from a doctor about self-treatment using an antibiotic such as doxycycline in combination with oral rehydration salts.

Avoiding Cholera

There are no reliable vaccines for cholera. All cruisers should also avoid potentially contaminated food and water.

Yellow Fever

Yellow fever is a viral disease transmitted by mosquitoes. It's endemic in equatorial regions of Africa and South and Central America, and it's found in Trinidad and Tobago. It occurs both in urban areas (where humans are the hosts) and in jungle areas, where nonhuman primates are typically the hosts. The areas where yellow fever is a risk are much larger than the officially reported infected zones. Caution is especially advised among tourists visiting rural areas. Yellow fever is a serious disease that causes death in about half the people who contract it.

Symptoms

Symptoms usually start within 3 to 6 days of being bitten. The person will alternate between feeling feverish and chilled. The fever may reach dangerous levels (105°F/40.5°C). Headache, backache, and severe nausea are all common. The person may seem to improve, with a remission of the fever for some 24 hours. The "toxic" phase follows, with the person becoming very weak and producing vomit tinged with bile and blood (termed "black vomit"). Eyes may become yellow. Watch for this or other signs of jaundice, as a mild case of yellow fever may resemble malaria or the flu, but jaundice doesn't normally occur with these diseases. If it's present, it's an important indicator that the disease may be yellow fever. Medical help should be sought immediately if yellow fever is suspected, as some 50 percent of patients don't survive the toxic phase.

Treatment

There is no specific treatment for yellow fever, but you should seek medical help nevertheless, as a doctor or clinic will be able to confirm the diagnosis and can treat potentially fatal complications.

Avoiding Yellow Fever

Anyone traveling to endemic areas should be vaccinated, which provides lifelong immunity in 95 percent of those vaccinated, but travelers are required to be revaccinated every 10 years (see Yellow Fever

YELLOW FEVER VACCINATION

Yellow fever vaccinations are recommended by the CDC for travelers going to the following countries, as yellow fever is endemic to these countries or parts of them.

Americas	Paraguay	**Central Africa**	Sudan	Guinea	**East Africa**
Argentina	Peru	Angola	Zaire	Guinea-Bissau	Burundi
Bolivia	Suriname	Cameroon	Zambia	Liberia	Eritrea
Brazil	Trinidad and	Central African	**West Africa**	Mali	Ethiopia
Colombia	Tobago	Republic	Benin	Niger	Kenya
Ecuador	Venezuela	Chad	Burkina Faso	Nigeria	Rwanda
French Guiana		Congo	Cote d'Ivoire	Senegal	Tanzania
Guyana		Equatorial Guinea	Gambia	Sierra Leone	Uganda
Panama		Gabon	Ghana	Togo	

Vaccination for anyone visiting a yellow fever endemic area is important for two reasons: vaccination can be a lifesaver, and when you travel onward to other countries, proof of vaccination is required under International Health Regulations. Proof of vaccination (i.e., a valid International Certificate of Vaccination) will be needed even if you've simply passed through endemic areas. Individual countries will also have their own requirements. The areas for which vaccination is needed are subject to change, and we recommend that you seek the latest information before leaving for any region where yellow fever is endemic.

Vaccination). In addition to vaccination you should use standard precautions against mosquitoes, such as screens, clothing, and repellents (see discussion under malaria).

Hepatitis A, B, C, and E

Hepatitis is a disease that selectively targets the liver. There are several distinct types of viral hepatitis: A, B, C, and E. Hepatitis A is caused by a virus spread through fecal contamination of food and water. Although common, it's rarely life threatening, and many people with the disease never even realize they're ill. Hepatitis B is caused by a virus spread by body fluids, usually through sexual contact. Most people with hepatitis B also don't realize they have an infection, but up to 10 percent of those infected may be ill, and a small percentage will develop chronic liver disease. Hepatitis C is spread through broken skin or mucous membranes, most often through sexual contact, contaminated needles, or exposure to blood via transfusion. It results in a high rate of chronic liver disorders. Hepatitis E is less well known than the other forms. It's spread by water contaminated by sewage and also by close personal contact with an infected person.

Symptoms

The incubation period varies from 3 weeks to 6 months. Earliest symptoms include loss of appetite, malaise, and lack of energy. Low fever, nausea, and vomiting may also occur. More serious infections may result in jaundice, which can last 3 to 6 weeks; initial symptoms may last for months.

Treatment

No specific treatment for hepatitis is available.

Avoiding Hepatitis

Protection against hepatitis A is available both as a vaccine and via gamma globulin injections; both have been shown to either prevent or reduce the severity of infection. Infection can also be prevented by avoiding contaminated food and water. Vaccines are available for hepatitis B and will afford protection for a number of years; it's also prevented by avoiding sexual contact with infected persons. No vaccines are currently available for hepatitis C or E, so avoiding contaminated blood and needles, contact with infected persons, and contaminated water in the case of hepatitis E are a must.

Dengue Fever

This is an acute viral fever, caused by any of four varieties of dengue viruses (known as DEN 1 through DEN 4), and transmitted by the mosquito *Aedes aegypti*. *Aedes aegypti* is found throughout the tropics, and increasingly in the subtropics as well; it is a highly domesticated mosquito (adapted to living close to humans in urban environments).

The "simple" form of dengue is unpleasant but rarely dangerous, but a more virulent form known as dengue hemorrhagic fever (DHF) is becoming increasingly common, especially in Southeast Asia. Tens of millions of people are believed to suffer from simple dengue each year, with an estimated 500,000 cases of DHF. See the Health section in appendix 3, Resources, for contact information for the CDC.

DHF is thought to occur primarily in people who have already suffered from simple dengue and are then infected by a different variety. The antibodies developed in fighting the first infection combine with the viruses causing the second infection, enhancing their ability to penetrate the body's defenses. While most people with DHF have already suffered from the simpler form, some develop DHF without having had dengue previously, indicating that it may also be caused by an especially nasty variety of the virus. The death rate in cases of untreated DHF is high.

Symptoms

With simple dengue the onset is sudden; symptoms are a high fever of about 104°F (40°C), severe headache, aching behind the eyes, and often intense pain in the joints and muscles. Occasionally a rash will appear on the fourth or fifth day, starting on the hands and feet and spreading to other parts of the body but remaining most dense on the limbs. The fever usually subsides within a week, but may return after a day or two.

DHF is most common in children under the age of 15, but it can occur in adults. It begins with symptoms and signs that don't differ from simple dengue, followed 2 to 5 days later by a rapid deterioration and cardiovascular collapse, sometimes with shock (known as dengue shock syndrome, or DSS), and sometimes death. The visible hemorrhagic symptoms that give DHF its name include easy bruising and the presence of purplish spots or patches on the skin. The critical phase of DHF takes place when the fever subsides, because as it drops circulatory failure may develop, in which insufficient oxygen is present in the blood. Abdominal pain is frequent.

DSS is an especially severe form of DHF. A rapid, weak pulse, cold and clammy skin, restlessness, and abnormally low blood pressure are all symptoms of DSS. Without immediate treatment, victims will frequently deteriorate rapidly and die.

Treatment

There is no treatment for simple dengue other than giving plenty of fluids and paracetamol for controlling fever and reducing pain. A careful watch should be kept to see if there is any deterioration, a change in mental status, or evidence of hemorrhagic symptoms (such as bruising), as these may indicate DHF. Seek medical help immediately if you suspect DHF or DSS. Although there is no specific treatment for DHF or DSS, a doctor or clinic can treat potentially fatal complications.

Avoiding Dengue

There is no vaccination or preventative drug for dengue, and the only sure way to avoid infection is not to be bitten by an infected mosquito. *Aedes aegypti* is a day-biting mosquito that feeds most often in the hours around sunrise and dusk. It is common in urbanized areas as well as rural village areas. Mosquito screens will help protect you when onboard, but repellent should be used when ashore or if anchored near a village.

Malaria

Malaria is a disease caused by protozoan parasites of the genus *Plasmodium*. All malarial parasites are transmitted from one person to another by female *Anopheles* mosquitoes. The parasites develop in the gut of the mosquito and are passed on through the saliva when the mosquito draws blood. Once in a human host, the parasites are carried by the blood to the liver, where they multiply. After an incubation period normally lasting 9 to 30 days the parasites return to the blood, invading and breaking down red blood cells as they continue to multiply. This causes fever and anemia in humans. In cerebral malaria, infected red blood cells block blood vessels in the brain; other vital organs can be damaged as well, sometimes resulting in death.

Four species of *Plasmodium* can cause the disease in various forms: *P. falciparum*, *P. vivax*, *P. ovale*, and *P. malariaee*. (It pays to learn these species names, because they are commonly used to distinguish the various types of malaria.) *P. falciparum* is both the most common and most dangerous; the potentially fatal complications known as cerebral malaria and blackwater fever occur with this type.

The Risk

Worldwide, malaria is a risk in 100 countries and territories, and 92 of these harbor the dangerous *P. falciparum* form. *P. falciparum is the primary malarial parasite found in tropical Africa, the Amazon, Southeast Asia, and Oceania.* There were an estimated 300 million cases of malaria in 1998 and 1.1 million deaths; 90 percent of both cases and deaths occurred in tropical Africa, where malaria is directly responsible for one in five childhood deaths.

Major urban areas in much of Asia and South America are largely free of the disease, but it's common in rural areas. It's widespread in Africa and India. Within the Pacific, malaria is present in Papua New Guinea, Vanuatu, and the Solomon Islands (all part of Melanesia). In Mexico and Central America, malaria is generally present in all rural areas, including offshore islands and resort areas (although the highlands are largely free of the disease); malaria isn't a problem in most urban areas and isn't found in Panama City or the Canal Zone. Among the Caribbean islands, malaria is found throughout Haiti and in rural areas in the Dominican Republic, especially in provinces bordering Haiti; it isn't found in the other islands.

The malaria risk is worsening in a number of countries, with treatment becoming more difficult as the resistance of *P. falciparum* to antimalarial drugs increases and spreads. Resistance of *P. vivax* to chloroquine has been reported from West Papua (Irian Jaya), Burma (Myanmar), Papua New Guinea, and Vanuatu.

Cruisers are more at risk than many travelers because they visit rural and remote areas where the disease is more likely to have a foothold. On the other hand, the risk is lowered by the fact that most anchorages have fewer mosquitoes than many towns or villages, due to the breeze that's usually present.

Symptoms

There are two general types of malaria symptoms: a fairly mild intermittent fever, where temperature rises above and falls to or below normal every 24 to 48 hours; and a severe remittent fever, where the temperature goes well above normal, drops more than 3.5°F (1.8°C)—but doesn't go back to normal—before rising again.

MILD INTERMITTENT FEVER

This pattern is seen in *P. vivax*, *P. ovale*, and *P. malariae* forms of malaria, though the length of the delay between infection and symptoms, and between attacks once they've begun, will vary with each person. Flu-like symptoms (a slight fever, headache, and generalized achiness and chilliness) may be present for several days before the start of severe fever at regular intervals. People who have not had malaria before, and who are not taking antimalarial drugs, usually experience three distinct phases.

▶ *BRIEF COLD OR SHIVERING PHASE*, lasting up to an hour. In addition to feeling cold, the person may be nauseous and aching. The skin is cold to the touch.

▶ *IN THE FEVER PHASE*, the temperature rises rapidly (up to about 104°F/40°C). Pulse is rapid and weak, the skin becomes hot and dry, and nausea and vomiting continue. The person is thirsty and has a severe headache. After two hours or more the pulse strengthens, and the breathing rate increases.

▶ *THE SWEATING PHASE* is marked by a drenching sweat. Symptoms ease, then disappear, and temperature drops to normal. The person often falls into a deep sleep and may feel quite well until the next attack. Attacks may occur once a day, or once every 2 to 3 days.

If a *P. vivax* infection goes untreated, it usually lasts for 2 to 3 months, with the frequency and intensity of attacks slowly diminishing. Half of those infected with *P. vivax* will experience a relapse anywhere between a few weeks to 5 years after the initial illness.

P. ovale infections are similar to *P. vivax* infections, although they are usually less severe. People often recover from a *P. ovale* infection without treatment.

P. malariae infections may not show symptoms for a much longer period than *P. vivax* or *P. ovale* infections. Relapse is common in those infected with *P. malariae*.

SEVERE REMITTENT FEVER

This form is caused by *P. falciparum*. The pattern is similar to the mild form, but not as well defined. There are usually no intervals in which the patient feels well. The differences in the phases are:

▶ *THE COLD PHASE MAY BE SHORT*, with little shivering, and temperature rises quickly from the outset.

▶ *THE HOT PHASE LASTS MUCH LONGER* (6–12 hours).

▶ *THERE IS NO DISTINCT SWEATING STAGE*, but the skin may be continuously moist.

In addition:

▶ *ATTACKS ARE BROKEN BY SHORT INTERVALS* (2–12 hours) and last longer (12–24 hours).

▶ *THE TEMPERATURE MAY STAY HIGH*, or if it does fall, it falls only part way before rising again.

P. falciparum malaria may develop dangerous complications at any time, including coma, altered mental status, or multiple seizures, which are collectively known as cerebral malaria. Cerebral malaria is the most common cause of death in malaria patients and is lethal if untreated. Even *with* treatment, 15 percent of children and 20 percent of adults who develop cerebral malaria die. Other complications associated with *P. falciparum* can also cause death.

Diagnosis and Treatment

Assume that any fever you get while in a malaria-prone area *may* be malaria. It's also possible, though, that it's dengue, the flu, or something else. The best course of action is to immediately consult a doctor or a clinic and have a blood test to determine if you have malaria. Self-testing for malaria is possible, but the test is not conclusive, and it can be difficult for untrained lay people to administer the test. These are called "dipstick" type tests and are available commercially; check with a doctor or clinic specializing in travel medicine.

If testing isn't possible, and cerebral malaria is present in the area, then it's safest to assume that you *do* have malaria and to self-treat with appropriate drugs. The treatment drug and regime will vary depending on where you are, and whether you have been taking antimalarial drugs as prophylactics (see Avoiding Malaria, below). Up-to-date WHO suggestions for stand-by emergency treatment, including the choice of drugs and the treatment regime, are available via the Internet; see Health section in appendix 3, Resources, for more information. *Consult with a physician who is familiar with both the side effects and contraindications of antimalarial drugs before deciding on an emergency treatment course.*

Two types of malaria (*P. vivax* and *P. ovale*) may produce a dormant form that persists in the liver of infected individuals and emerges at a later time. Therefore, these types require treatment to kill any dormant protozoan, as well as the organisms that are causing the infection at the time.

Avoiding Malaria

By far the best defense is to avoid being bitten by an *Anopheles* mosquito. There are some 60 species of *Anopheles* able to transmit malaria, and each species has its preferred breeding grounds and feeding patterns, but in general this mosquito feeds between dusk and dawn. You'll greatly reduce the chances of infection if you're protected during that time. Use mosquito netting on all hatches, ports, and vents. If screens are well designed and well made, and if they're always used, then you can largely eliminate the risk of being bitten on board. (See chapter 10, Life Aboard, for mosquito screen ideas.) Supplement screens with mosquito coils and citronella candles or oil. These are handy, for example, to have burning in the cockpit if you're venturing on deck and want to gain a bit of extra protection. They also reduce the odds of letting mosquitoes in as you slip out. If possible, you may want to screen the cockpit as well as all the hatches and vents to expand your mosquito-free living space. It will also provide an extra measure of defense if you maintain a screen over the companionway as well.

Bed nets (lightweight mosquito nets, usually treated with an insecticide) are the standard defense against mosquitoes in much of the tropics. We've never used one aboard, but this is an option for extra protection. A bed net could also be used to screen off the entrance to the cabin where you sleep. If you plan any overnight trips ashore, make sure to take and use a bed net. The insecticides used to treat bed nets (including permethrin, lambdacyhalothrin [Icon], and deltamethrin) can also be sprayed on your screens as an additional defense.

Avoid evening visits ashore if possible, and wear protective clothes and repellent when you do go. The most effective repellents contain either DEET (N,N-diethyl-meta-toluamide) or dimethyl phthalate.

The final defense against malaria involves taking an antimalarial drug to reduce the risk associated with a malarial infection. These drugs don't necessarily prevent you from contracting malaria, but they do act to keep attacks and fever from developing and should prevent any serious (or fatal) attacks. When used as a prophylactic, the drugs must be taken regularly (usually either once a day, or once a week) and without fail; some drug regimes must be started well before arriving in a malarial area. Be aware that some drugs have unpleasant and potentially serious side effects, and that malarial parasites are developing increasing resistance to antimalarial drugs (whether used as a prophylactic or for treatment).

Consult with a doctor or health service shortly before you depart to find out which drugs are currently effective in various regions; *make sure that you get information that is both up-to-date and accurate for the area in which you'll be sailing.* Information from WHO on current malaria prophylaxis recommendations for different areas is available on the Internet; see the Health section in appendix 3.

Our Experience

We've cruised for many months in malarial areas, including the Solomon Islands, Papua New Guinea, and Indonesia. We spent two wet (cyclone) seasons in these waters, a time when both rainfall and mosquitoes are plentiful. Our routine was to have all screens in place on hatches and vents before sundown, not removing them until after sunup. We did this except if anchored far (as in many miles) from any villages. (In very remote areas the risk of infection is likely to be lower; if mosquitoes don't feed on infected humans, they won't become vectors of the disease.) On breezy nights we sometimes stayed above decks after dark, but we lit mosquito coils and used insect repellent. We rarely ventured ashore after dusk, but when we did we wore long-sleeved pants and shirts, lots of insect repellent, or both.

Because we spent months at a time in malarial areas, we chose not to take any antimalarial drugs, due to their side effects. We did not contract malaria. However, not taking malaria prophylaxis was a personal decision, and not a course of action we're recommending to others. Discuss your plans with a doctor knowledgeable about tropical medicine and travel before making any decisions on this issue.

The Final Word

Malaria is a serious—and possibly fatal—disease. It's possible to cruise in malarial areas without contracting it, but only by being careful (and perhaps a bit lucky as well). Do everything you can to avoid being bitten by a mosquito, and back that up by having on board the appropriate drugs, especially drugs for treatment.

SUN- AND HEAT-RELATED INJURIES

The short-term risk from not covering up consists primarily of sunburn, but prolonged exposure to the sun can cause your skin to age prematurely and can lead to skin cancer, while excess heat or exertion can cause various heat-related injuries. The tropical sun is intense, and though a welcome antidote to temperate-zone winters, it is important to limit your exposure. The simplest and most obvious solution is to cover up, or stay out of the sun. While this is admittedly difficult when sailing on a small boat in a warm climate, the risk from skin cancer is significant, and it is especially important for high-risk individuals to be careful.

Skin Cancer

Ultraviolet (UV) radiation is a primary cause of skin cancer, and the largest amounts of UV are recorded in the tropics, where the sun's rays are closer to being directly overhead. In summer at noon, the intensity of harmful UV-B rays at the equator is two to three times that in Canada or northern Europe. As a rough guide, the skin cancer incidence doubles for every 10-degree decrease in latitude, assuming the population has the same hereditary factors. That doesn't mean that you'll be 4 or 6 times as likely to develop skin cancer if you spend a few years cruising in tropical waters as you would be if you stayed in temperate latitudes, but there's no doubt that UV exposure and sun damage to your skin will both go up.

Skin cancers are generally found in the epidermis (the top layer of skin), which contains three kinds of cells: squamous cells, basal cells, and melanocytes, which give the skin its color. The major types of skin cancer take their names from these cells. Basal cell cancer is the slowest growing, most common, and easiest to cure. Squamous cell cancer is less common and grows more quickly. Malignant melanoma is seen the least frequently, but it's most likely to spread (metastasize) and is responsible for most skin cancer deaths.

The Risk

There are about 1 million new cases of skin cancer (of all types) diagnosed annually in the United States. Skin cancer accounts for one-third of all cancer cases. The yearly death toll is about 10,000 people. Australia has the dubious honor of having the world's highest skin cancer rates. Two of every three white Australians will develop a nonmelanoma skin cancer during their lifetime; 2 in 100 will have melanoma.

Although death rates from basal cell and squamous cell carcinomas are low, these cancers can cause considerable damage and disfigurement if left untreated. However, when detected and treated early, more than 95 percent of these can be cured. Malignant melanoma, the most rapidly increasing form of cancer in the United States, can spread to other organs, most commonly the lungs and liver.

Three major factors determine a person's skin cancer risk: the amount of sun you're exposed to, your heredity, and your environment. Exposure is cumulative: both occasional sunburn and long-term (nonburning) exposure to the sun can damage the skin, leading to skin cancer. Although most nonmelanoma skin cancers appear in people over 50, the incidence of melanoma peaks at an earlier age. What's more, the sun's damaging effects begin at an early age, and evidence suggests that severe burns during childhood may be a significant cause of cancer later in life.

Skin cancer is most common in people with light-colored skin who have spent a lot of time in the sun; a history of skin cancer in your family seems to increase the risk even more. One reason Australia has the world's highest skin cancer rates is because much of the population is of English and Irish descent; they now live in an area with high levels of UV radiation, but their skin is better suited to the low UV levels found in Britain and Ireland. By contrast, skin cancer is almost unknown among indigenous Australians, whose dark skin attests to the fact that their ancestors adapted to the region's high UV levels over many millennia.

Although there may be many factors that ultimately determine whether you develop skin cancer, some indication of your relative risk is provided by your skin color and how easily you burn. The highest-risk group includes white-skinned people who always burn easily and never tan; people of Celtic descent, with blue eyes, fair or red hair, and freckly skin are in this category. White-skinned people who tan easily and fairly darkly and seldom burn have a lower but still significant risk. Those with olive skin and dark hair (such as many people of Mediterranean origin) have a risk that's only one-third as great as the highest-risk group, while risk is lowest for those with dark brown or black skin (including those of African and Aboriginal descent).

Keep in mind that although tanning may help you avoid sunburn, it doesn't protect you from skin cancer. The amount of natural melanin pigmentation in the skin (when not tanned) is what confers protection from cancer. In addition, although people who tan easily may be less likely to develop skin cancer than those who don't develop a tan, anyone who increases their exposure to the sun is increasing their risk of skin cancer.

While susceptibility to sunburn is a reasonable indicator of your chances of developing basal cell or squamous cell cancer, having a high number of brown moles on the skin is an added important factor in the development of malignant melanoma. Moles are benign (noncancerous) tumors of melanocytes, while melanomas are malignant tumors affecting the same type of cells. People with many moles have a significantly higher risk of malignant melanoma when compared to those with few moles. Although some malignant melanomas begin in preexisting moles, many appear in apparently normal skin.

Recognizing Skin Cancers

Skin cancers are hard for a layperson to identify because visible signs may vary quite a bit. A change on the skin, such as a growth or a sore that won't heal, is the most common sign. Although most changes in your skin won't be caused by cancer, you should play it safe and have any new skin lesion checked out by a doctor. An annual check up is likely to be adequate to catch basal and squamous cancers, but malignant melanoma can develop so quickly that a yearly exam may not be enough. There are some early warning signs of melanoma that you should watch for (see below). Get a checkup immediately if you recognize these.

BASAL CELL CANCER

Basal cell cancer grows slowly and may take years to develop. It occurs most commonly on areas that get the most exposure: face, nose, eyelids, ears, neck, and upper body. It often starts as a small round or flattened lump that can be red, pale, or pearly in color; it may be covered in blood vessels. Left untreated it will eat into surrounding tissue.

SQUAMOUS CELL CANCER

Squamous cell cancer can develop rapidly. It is also common on exposed areas such as face, lips, neck, legs, hands, and forearms. It starts as a red scaly area that may bleed easily, and then turns into an ulcer. It may look like a sore that doesn't heal, and is often tender to the touch. Squamous cell cancer can reach an inch (2.5 cm) or more in size if not treated, and may also spread to the lymph nodes and then to lungs, liver, and other organs.

MALIGNANT MELANOMA

Malignant melanoma appears as a new spot, freckle, or mole that changes color, size, or shape over months. It can also develop in an existing mole. It can appear *on any part of the body, even on skin that has been protected from the sun.* Carefully watch moles and freckles for changes in size, shape, or color, symptoms such as itching or bleeding, or development of a border. The ABCD warning signs of malignant melanoma are

▶ **ASYMMETRY:** a growth with unmatched halves

▶ **BORDER IRREGULARITY:** ragged or blurred edges

▶ **COLOR:** mottled appearance, with shades of tan, brown, and black, sometimes mixed with red, white, or blue

▶ **DIAMETER:** a growth more than ¼ inch (6 mm) across (about the size of a pencil eraser), or any unusual increase in size

If you see any of these, get a checkup immediately.

Avoiding Skin Cancer

Most advice on this is straightforward: stay out of the sun. But it's hard to do that and cruise the tropics at the same time! There are many simple precautions you can take that will help to keep your exposure to a reasonable level. Those with a high level of skin cancer risk should follow these most diligently, while those with a low risk may get away with being a bit less careful. But because even cumulative, nonburning exposure increases the cancer risk, it behooves everyone to make a habit of following these precautions.

▶ **TWO-THIRDS OF THE DAY'S UV RADIATION** is received between 10 A.M. and 2 P.M., so covering up—or better yet staying in the shade—during these hours is especially important.

▶ **WEAR LOOSE, LIGHTWEIGHT CLOTHING** even when under cover, if reflected light is still reaching you. That means covering up even when

under an awning. We make it a practice to wear thin long-sleeved shirts when sailing, unless there is good cloud cover. Legs are usually less exposed (as they're hidden behind coamings or in the cockpit), and so sunscreen seems to suffice there. Wear a hat (with an all-around brim) if you're in the sun.

▶ **COVER AREAS THAT ARE EXPOSED** with sunscreen. We carry several strengths, from SPF 15 for days when we're not out that long to SPF 45 for use on nose, ears, neck, and hands, which cop the worst of the sun. Reapply it every few hours, and more often if you're swimming or sweating a lot. Don't forget to protect your lips with a good sunblock, and your eyes with sunglasses that screen out *both* UV-A and UV-B.

Heavy cloud cover will filter out much of the incoming UV, but a lot will get through if clouds are thin, and thin clouds may scatter UV, increasing total exposure. UV reflection off water and grass is fairly low (less than 10 percent), but sand reflects as much as 25 percent. Even if you're sitting in the shade, shielded from direct UV, your skin may be getting significant exposure via reflection.

SUNSCREEN

The U.S. Food and Drug Administration is currently implementing new regulations to modify how sunscreens are rated. There will now be three categories of sunburn protection:

- minimum: includes sun protection factor (SPF) of 2 to 12
- moderate: SPF 12 to 30
- high: SPF of 30 or more

These ratings refer only to UV-B protection, but research indicates that UV-A also plays a role in skin cancer. Check sunscreen labels for reference to UV-A screening, often indicated by the term *broad-spectrum sunscreen.* If the ingredients include micronized zinc oxide, titanium oxide, or avobenzone (Parsol 1789), the sunscreen will protect against both UV-A and UV-B. We'd suggest not bothering with screens that give "minimum" protection; instead, always use those that offer "high" protection on frequently exposed areas.

Sunburn

We all blow it on occasion and get caught out without a hat or sunscreen. When we get burned, it's time to head for the medical kit.

Symptoms

The symptoms associated with sunburn vary, depending on the degree of the burn. First-degree burns affect only the skin's outer layer. These cause redness, mild swelling, tenderness, and pain. Second-degree burns extend into the underlying skin layer and can cause deep reddening, blisters, considerable swelling, and oozing of fluid.

Treatment

We treat mild burns with aloe vera lotion; calamine lotion or zinc ointment can also be used. Stay out of the sun, and remember the sunscreen next time! More serious burns that involve blistering should be treated like any other wound: cleaned, covered with antibacterial ointment, and bandaged. Use layered gauze as the first layer for the dressing. Leave the burn undisturbed for a while (up to a week). If well healed after that time, no further treatment should be needed. Otherwise evaluate the condition, and either dress again or seek medical help.

Heat Injuries

Different people have different tolerances for the heat, but just about everyone will feel the effects more if humidity is high. This can catch you unaware if you're not used to the high humidity of the tropics. The first reaction to too much heat and humidity is to feel uncomfortable. This is a warning sign you shouldn't ignore, as there are some serious conditions that result from too much heat. You can avoid getting heat-related conditions by minimizing severe exertion during the hottest hours, cooling off in the water or taking frequent rests in shaded or breezy areas, drinking liquids, and replacing lost salts frequently.

Prickly Heat

Prickly heat is a rash that usually affects areas where clothing rubs or is tight, but it can also be found in skin folds and joints. The rash first shows up as scattered, small red pimples that prick or sting rather than itch. In the center of the pimples tiny blisters may develop, which can become broken and infected as a result of scratching. Prickly heat can accompany one of the more serious conditions discussed below.

To treat prickly heat, avoid vigorous exercise and minimize sweating. Wear loose-fitting, lightweight clothing. Shower or sponge-bathe frequently with cool fresh water if possible, but don't use soap excessively on the affected areas. Dry by patting (not rubbing the skin), and dab with calamine lotion.

Heat Cramps

Heat cramps are caused by salt loss from profuse sweating. Drinking fluids isn't enough; lost salts must also be replaced. Severe pain and spasms of the abdominal muscles are the primary symptoms and are more severe if large amounts of fluid have been consumed without replacing the lost salt. Cramps start suddenly, usually in the muscles that bend the arms and legs, and can be severe, with the person crying out with pain. Skin may be pale and wet, and the temperature ranges between about 97 and 99°F (36.1–37.2°C). There is typically no loss of consciousness. Attacks may last for hours if untreated, but are not normally considered dangerous.

To treat heat cramps, move the person to a cool place and give water with one teaspoonful of table salt added to each glass. Start with half a glass, and repeat every 15 minutes for one hour, or until symptoms ease. Massage may help.

Heat Exhaustion (Collapse)

Heat exhaustion is caused by excessive loss of both water and salt. It occurs commonly among people who work in hot environments or are exposed to humid heat outdoors. Signs of heat exhaustion include weakness, dizziness, nausea, dim or blurred vision, mild muscle cramps, and pale and clammy skin. There is profuse sweating, a fast but weak pulse, and rapid, shallow breathing.

If fainting seems likely (or has already occurred), have the person sit with her head lowered to the

WHAT TO INCLUDE IN A FIRST-AID KIT

Bandages and Dressings

cloth (not plastic) bandages of various sizes

sterile gauze pads and dressings of various sizes
(include some nonstick pads that won't adhere to
wounds)

cotton swabs

waterproof adhesive tape

elastic bandages; include broad (6 in./15 cm) bandages
for pressure bandage, used to slow the absorption
of venom (see p. 209 for instructions on use)

Equipment

tweezers

thermometer

scissors

flashlight

hot water bottle

syringes (disposable); include a 20–50 cc syringe (with a
large-bore needle or without a needle) for irrigating
wounds

cigarette lighter (to sterilize instruments)

needles or safety pins (to remove splinters or spines)

Topical Preparations

insect repellent with DEET

Blistex or similar lip balm
(for treating chapped or blistered lips)

sunscreen for skin

sunblock for lips

vinegar (4–6% acetic acid) for box jellyfish stings

Medications

Among the medications you'll want in your medical kit are
some that are available in the U.S. only with a physician's
prescription; these include strong painkillers, most antibiotics, and disease-specific drugs, such as antimalarials.
Some physicians may be reluctant to provide prescriptions
for drugs that are to be held for future use (and will then
be self-administered), but travel and wilderness medicine
specialists are accustomed to doing so. The American Society of Tropical Medicine and Hygiene and the International Society of Travel Medicine both maintain Web sites
with directories of travel medicine clinics; see the Health
section in appendix 3.

Some people can experience serious complications from
certain medications, so be sure to discuss your personal
medical history with a physician in the course of obtaining medications for your medical kit. Inquire as well
about problems that may arise from taking two or more
medications in combination.

ANALGESICS

aspirin, acetaminophen, and/or ibuprofen

stronger pain killer per physician's recommendation

ANTIMICROBIAL PREPARATIONS

wound antiseptics
(povidone-iodine, such as Betadine)

antibiotics (specific preparations per physician's
recommendation). Include antibiotics that target
the following:

> ▶ upper and lower respiratory infections
> ▶ skin and soft tissue infections
> ▶ bacterial diarrheas

Neosporin or similar antibiotic for eye injuries

antimalarials suitable for area (for prophylaxis
and/or treatment)

GASTROINTESTINAL MEDICATIONS

antacids (such as Pepto-Bismol)

antidiarrheal (such as Imodium)

Dramamine or other treatment for motion sickness
laxative

Miscellaneous

vitamin supplements

Cavit (for emergency dental repairs)

comprehensive but understandable book
or books on first aid (see appendix 3,
Resources)

knees. When fainting no longer seems a worry, have the person recline; remove or loosen any tight clothing and sponge her with cool water. Give her sips of cool water with one teaspoonful of salt per glass, starting with half a glass and repeating every 15 minutes for an hour. Stop if the person vomits. If the condition worsens, get medical help.

Heatstroke

Heatstroke, also called *sunstroke*, takes place when the body fails to rid itself of extra heat by sweating. This is the most dangerous of the heat-related conditions and requires *immediate action*. Early symptoms such as headache, general malaise, or general heat exhaustion (see above) are sometimes present, but often the onset is abrupt, with a sudden loss of consciousness, convulsions, or delirium. There is usually no sweating. Skin will be hot, flushed, and dry; temperature is very high (over 105°F/41°C), and pulse rapid and strong. Pupils will first contract, then dilate. Muscular twitching, cramps, convulsions, and vomiting may occur, along with circulatory collapse and deep shock.

Treat heatstroke *immediately* by reducing body temperature because otherwise brain damage and death can occur. Do whatever you can to lower the person's temperature: undress him and place him in cool water; cover him with cold packs or sponge him with cold water; use fans or expose him to a breeze. Don't let his temperature drop below about 100°F (38°C) to avoid cooling too much. Massaging the skin can help stimulate blood flow and promote a rapid decrease in temperature. Get medical attention as soon as possible, because serious complications can result from heatstroke. Also, beware of a rebound in temperature, which can occur after 3 to 4 hours.

GENERAL WOUND CARE

Most sailors get a fair number of scrapes, cuts, and other minor wounds. Taken alone they're rarely that serious, but because of some unusually powerful bacteria present in tropical ocean waters, even minor wounds have a habit of quickly becoming infected if not immediately and properly treated. In our experience, the warmer the water, the greater the potential for really nasty infections that require antibiotics to clear them up. Cuts that you get in the water—from coral, barnacles, and the like—are especially prone to infection. Infections can become systemic, spreading throughout the body, and can do so very quickly. They can even be life threatening. Fortunately, you can usually keep infection at bay if you properly clean and dress any wounds as soon as you get them, and then *stay clear of salt water until they've healed*. When that's not possible—if you have cuts on your hands or feet, they'll inevitably get wet as you beach a dinghy—clean them often, at least twice a day. We start by discussing basic first aid for tropical wounds and then move on to what to do if wounds do become infected.

Wound First Aid

The first priority is to control the bleeding. Do this by applying pressure to the wound. This technique should stop even the most severe arterial bleeding (see sidebar). Once the bleeding has been controlled, inspect the wound. If it is large and deep, and you suspect serious damage (to tendons, ligaments, or blood vessels), get medical help after cleaning and dressing the injury. If the injury is complicated by other factors (a venomous sting, a blow to the head), then decide what is most serious and treat that first.

Cleaning and Bandaging

Start by cleaning the skin around the injury. Use an antibacterial agent or a povidone-iodine solution, and avoid washing dirt or other contaminants into the wound. Next, clean the wound. Start by flushing it with clean freshwater. Never use salt water, as this will simply introduce more bacteria (an exception is in the case of venomous stings, when immediate flushing to remove venom is a higher priority than preventing subsequent infection; see chapter 13, Dangerous Tropical Marine Organisms). A 20 or

CONTROLLING BLEEDING

Always use pressure bandages to control bleeding. The object is to collapse severed blood vessels, thus obstructing blood flow, and allowing clots to form. Apply pressure directly over the wound.

• If veins and capillaries are damaged, just holding a bandage in place for 2 to 5 minutes should serve to stem the bleeding.

• Arterial bleeding is much rarer and more serious. If it's occurring, the blood will be seen to be spurting from the wound with each heartbeat. It may take 20 minutes or more to get arterial wounds to stop bleeding, and they should be packed with sterile gauze and wrapped snugly with a continuous bandage.

• Bandages that surround a limb may obstruct circulation to the rest of the limb, and they should be checked carefully every few hours, especially if swelling is present. In the case of serious injuries, the limb should be immobilized.

• Do not use tourniquets except in truly exceptional cases, such as in the case of shark or crocodile attack. Apply tourniquets only as a lifesaving measure, as when a main artery has been severed, and only if pressure bandages can't be applied. The most likely scenario when a tourniquet would be needed is when the victim is still in the water and requires assistance to get to shore or in a boat, but is also bleeding so profusely that immediate action is required to stem the flow of blood. In other circumstances tourniquets are both unnecessary and unwise, as they can easily damage muscles, nerves, and blood vessels.

---

50 cc syringe without a needle works well and generates enough pressure to rinse out any bits of coral or dirt; be thorough, as anything left in the wound will lead to infection. Use forceps or tweezers to pick out any foreign matter that can't be rinsed out of the wound. (Using dirty instruments will introduce bacteria, so these should be sterile. Sterilize instruments by boiling for 15 minutes, or by washing them, dipping them in alcohol, and igniting it.) Puncture wounds should also be cleaned by flushing, though this will be very difficult if they are small.

After cleaning the wound, disinfect it using a 10 percent solution of povidone-iodine (such as Betadine), diluted with 10 to 20 times its volume of clean water. Flood the wound repeatedly with the solution.

Wounds don't need to be closed with sutures, butterfly closures, or tape. Doing so just increases the likelihood of infection by preventing wounds from draining. Use sterile dressing pads to cover wounds if necessary, held in place with waterproof tape.

Infected Wounds

Infection can show up a few hours to several days after the injury and usually appears as inflammation around the wound, with pain, redness, swelling, and heat. Pus is usually present. Serious infections can send red streaks upward along a limb, cause an elevation in body temperature (to about 100–101°F/ 38°C), and enlarge lymph nodes.

Infections are treated by draining the wound and administering antibiotics. Infected wounds may be closed by a crust of coagulated serum and pus, and this should be removed by soaking the wound in warm water to which povidone-iodine has been added. The moisture will soften the crust and permit better drainage, while the heat dilates the blood vessels and increases blood flow, which promotes healing. Do this three or four times a day for 20- or 30-minute periods. Some deeper wounds may contain pockets of pus that won't drain, and it may be necessary to gently remove these using sterile forceps, tweezers, or a needle. Pack the wound with a bit of gauze soaked in povidone-iodine solution to prevent the edges of the wound from sealing until you're certain the infection has cleared up.

Antibiotics

If an infection becomes well established and does not respond to draining and soaking, then oral antibiotics should be taken. Don't do this immediately for every minor infection, as overuse of antibiotics can lead to the development of resistant strains of bacteria that won't respond to treatment. Signs that an infection is serious and should be treated with antibiotics include fever and red streaking on the skin near the wound. You should consult with a physician prior to setting sail to determine what antibiotic you should take to treat infections resulting from wounds; make sure you keep an adequate supply (that's not out-of-date) on board at all times.

Chapter 13

Dangerous Tropical Marine Organisms

Although it may be hard for anyone who has seen the movie *Jaws* or its many takeoffs to believe, most marine life poses no threat whatsoever to humans. Just because you see an eel doesn't mean you'll be bitten; we've seen lots of sharks and are still here to write about it.

But in a few cases merely brushing against an animal (such as a box jellyfish) is enough to cause serious injury and possibly death. Tropical sailors are more at risk from marine life than most mariners, simply because we spend far more time in the water. Attractions such as coral reefs lure even otherwise reluctant swimmers into the water, and those of us who are eager explorers may spend hours in the water, day after day. That's when the chances of encountering dangerous organisms increases, and with it the

potential for injury. The risk isn't necessarily greatest from large or fearsome animals such as sharks and eels. Contact with venomous fish or jellyfish, or poisoning caused by eating toxic seafood, are more likely sources of trouble for most cruisers.

The sting or bite of most animals is usually nothing more than a defense mechanism. That's of little consolation after the fact, but it can help in avoiding injury. The simplest way to do this is by not provoking—and in a few cases actively avoiding—animals that can cause injury. For that reason all cruisers, and especially those new to the tropics, should take the time to acquaint themselves with the appearance and habits of the dangerous marine animals common in the areas they plan to cruise and to become aware of the threats these animals pose.

LARGE MARINE ANIMALS THAT BITE

This group includes those that give us nightmares: the 20-foot (6 m) sharks and crocodiles. For these predators, we humans may indeed be seen as prey. More often, though, an attack is brought on because an animal is excited by our actions (such as sharks that react to spearfishing) or is threatened by our presence (such as territorial sharks or eels that are disturbed from their hiding places).

Sharks

There are about 350 species of sharks, many of which live in tropical waters. Most sharks are very effective predators and as such can present a real—but highly unlikely—danger to sailors. Sharks range in size from 1.5 to 20 feet (0.5–6.5 m). They lack a swim bladder, an organ most fish have that allows them to maintain neutral buoyancy. If sharks stop swimming, they

A nurse shark in the western Atlantic, one of the many species found around coral reefs throughout the tropics.
National Marine Sanctuaries, NOAA

sink. They also need to keep swimming in order to keep water flowing over their gills. This helps explain why they're always swimming when you see them; they're not necessarily stalking a fish (or you).

Their sense of smell is highly developed, with 70 percent of the brain devoted to this one function. Smell is their principal means of finding prey, and sharks can detect blood present even in minute amounts (e.g., 1 part per million). Fish blood is known to attract sharks, though this hasn't been confirmed for human blood. To be on the safe side, though, it's wise to assume that blood of any type will attract sharks.

Sharks also have the ability to detect—and accurately pinpoint the source of—very low frequency sounds and vibrations and electrical fields. So even if you're not bleeding, they know you're there!

How Likely Is a Shark Attack?

In general, the odds of getting attacked by a shark are very low. In the United States, for example,

you're more likely to be struck by lightning or to be killed in a car wreck on the way to the beach, than you are to be injured by a shark. But a number of shark attacks do occur every year: estimates put the yearly number of attacks worldwide at 70 to 100, resulting in some 5 to 15 deaths.

Although many of those attacks occur outside the tropics in colder waters more commonly frequented by aggressive sharks such as the great white, shark attacks do occur in various places throughout the tropics. It's hard to provide any meaningful data on the level of risk in various areas, but it is certain that many shark species call the tropics home. Species commonly found in tropical areas include black- and white-tip reef, gray, hammerhead, tiger, lemon, and the oceanic white-tip sharks.

Types of Attack

Most attacks take place in near-shore waters. In areas with sandy beaches, sharks often feed between sandbars or inshore of a sandbar. In reef waters sharks frequently cruise the edge of a drop-off. Shark attacks on humans appear to take place for various reasons and attack patterns vary, but often a shark's behavior can serve as a warning to someone in the water that an attack is imminent.

▶ **"HIT-AND-RUN" FEEDING ATTACKS.** These account for the majority of shark attacks and occur when sharks mistake humans for prey. Surfers and swimmers may be hard for sharks to see clearly if they're in breaking surf or areas with strong currents. Sharks feeding in such an environment have to make fast decisions—and strike quickly—to capture their traditional prey. Some sources have suggested that wearing bright contrasting swimsuits and any shiny objects (such as jewelry) may attract a shark's attention and increase the chance of attack. The first bite may be "exploratory," often on the leg below the knee, and the attack is usually stopped at this point, possibly because the shark realizes that the person isn't a fish after all, or because the person is too large. These attacks are rarely fatal, and often the person in the water never sees the attacking shark.

▶ **"SNEAK" ATTACKS WITH THE VICTIM AT OR NEAR THE WATER'S SURFACE.** From below, surfers and snorkelers may look and behave much like a seal or sea lion. Sharks that hunt these animals often attack while their prey is at the surface, and do so without warning. Sharks that attack seals and sea lions are large and may well continue an attack even after discovering that a swimmer is not a seal after all. Prey may also be bitten and released. This is thought to be a tactic to avoid injury from still struggling animals. Because attacks of this type usually come without warning, the prudent strategy is to leave the water immediately if a large shark is sighted.

▶ **"CIRCLING" OR "BUMP-AND-BITE" FEEDING ATTACKS.** Sharks closing in on prey in deeper water, away from surf, typically give some warning. They first circle the prey, gradually increasing their speed and tightening and then criss-crossing the circle. They may bump or brush the prey, and their movements become jerky. When they move in to bite, they usually swim horizontally or slightly up-ward and swing their head back to project the upper teeth. (Spearfishing enthusiasts note: we've seen sharks start such circling behavior in response to blood from just a few speared fish.) Once one shark has attacked, a feeding frenzy may ensue. Sharks may attack not only the original prey or source of blood but also any other moving object. A person's size may not be a sufficient deterrent: sometimes sharks even attack each other when in the midst of a frenzy.

▶ **TERRITORIAL ATTACKS.** Many sharks are territorial and may attack if their turf is intruded upon, or if they feel threatened or frightened. The pattern of such an attack is quite different from a feeding attack. In a territorial attack the shark has an awkward motion, moving its head side to side while pointing the snout up and arching its spine. If the intruder leaves the shark's territory, the shark will usually stop its aggressive behavior and not pursue an attack.

▶ **REFLEXIVE ATTACKS.** Sharks may attack if suddenly surprised, as could happen when a person falls or jumps into the water onto or near an unsuspecting shark. Such attacks appear to be reflexive, and there is little or no warning.

Which Sharks Are Dangerous?

Some shark species have a worse track record than others in terms of attacks on humans; the great white (or white pointer), tiger shark, and bull shark being the worst. But from a practical standpoint, just about any shark as big as you are—5 to 6 feet (1.5–2 m) and more in total length—should be treated as potentially dangerous. The only sharks we tend to ignore are small (3 ft. or about 1 m) black-and white-tip reef sharks.

Avoiding a Shark Attack

We're wimps when it comes to sharks, but we enjoy swimming and snorkeling so much that we continue to get in the water. We've seen many sharks over the years, but we've only occasionally chosen to stop swimming because we didn't feel comfortable. When this happened, we've almost always been spearfishing. We follow several simple rules:

▶ *DON'T SWIM OR SNORKEL ALONE.* Two (or more people) can keep a better lookout for sharks, will greatly reduce the odds of attack, and can come to each other's aid if trouble occurs.

▶ *IF YOU GO SPEARFISHING, ALWAYS KEEP THE DINGHY NEARBY.* It's a place to put the speared fish, and it becomes a good refuge in case there's a threat from sharks. Fish should be put in the dinghy immediately after they're speared to minimize the amount of blood in the water.

▶ *KEEP A CLOSE EYE OUT FOR SHARKS AS YOU FISH OR SWIM, AND NOTE THEIR BEHAVIOR.* If they show undue interest or begin circling repeatedly, get out of the water immediately. Be especially wary of larger sharks (such as gray, tiger, and hammerhead), but we apply this rule to larger black- and white-tip reef sharks as well.

▶ *DON'T SWIM WHEN THE LIGHT OR VISIBILITY IS POOR.* This includes early morning, late afternoon, and in any murky water.

▶ *DON'T WEAR BRIGHT OR SHINY JEWELRY OR COLORS* if you're playing in the surf.

Keep in mind that not all waters are equally "sharky." This is true both regionally and locally. In some areas you may swim for weeks without sighting a single shark. In other places, small sharks (usually black-tip reef sharks) may frequent small reefs and lagoons. These are seldom any trouble and will more likely be scared of you. Areas where you're most likely to see larger sharks are deep reef passes, seaward reef edges, and reefs in areas that are seldom fished. If you're in doubt about the safety of swimming in an area, ask the locals (especially fishermen) whether sharks are a problem.

First Aid for Shark Attacks

For skin scrapes and minor wounds, see the General Wound Care section in chapter 12. If a vein or artery is severed, and the person is onshore or in a boat, immediately control the bleeding with pressure. But if you're in the water helping the person, it may be impossible to apply pressure and help them

Eels are nocturnal animals and stay mostly to themselves, hiding in the reef crevices by day. They will protect their home from intruders, but they have poor eyesight and may mistake a human hand for a fish.
Passage Productions, courtesy of National Marine Sanctuaries, NOAA

out of the water to safety at the same time. In that case you may need to apply a tourniquet to control bleeding from a massive wound—use the leash from a surfboard, the strap from a dive mask, or anything else handy—but only until you have the victim in the boat or on shore. Then apply pressure and release the tourniquet if bleeding can be controlled by pressure alone. Give first aid as detailed in General Wound Care, pages 198–99.

Eels

Although they more closely resemble snakes, eels are, in fact, fish. Some eat fin fish, and some eat crustaceans. They are found throughout the tropics. Eels can be large in size, reaching 10 feet (3 m) in length and nearly 12 inches (30 cm) in diameter. More common, though, are eels of about 3 feet (1 m) in length. Eels have a nasty reputation, backed up by an array of impressive teeth, but most are shy and try to avoid contact. An important exception are those eels that have become accustomed to being fed by divers, which may be quite bold and aggressive. You'll rarely (if ever) see an eel, except when diving or snorkeling.

Eel Attacks

The chances of being bitten by an eel are remote for most cruisers and can be further reduced by not provoking or startling them. Don't pursue or taunt an eel, and don't try to hook or spear one (they're not recommended food in any event, as they can cause ciguatera poisoning, which is described later in the chapter). Don't reach into holes or crevices, or under rocks and coral, as these are favorite resting places for eels during the day. Wear gloves when snorkeling or diving.

If you are bitten by an eel, treat the wound as described under General Wound Care in chapter 12. If there are problems in moving a finger or toe, suspect tendon damage and get medical help.

Crocodiles, Alligators, and Caiman

Crocodilians (a term that includes crocodiles and their close relatives, the alligator and caiman) are often called living dinosaurs, but in fact their ancestors were around *before* the age of dinosaurs. Today's crocodilians are little changed from those prehistoric examples, a fact that indicates they're well adapted to the environment in which they live. One or more species of these fearsome reptiles are found in many tropical areas throughout the world. The most dangerous species from the cruiser's perspective is the saltwater or estuarine crocodile (found in tropical areas in Australia, Papua New Guinea, the Solomon Islands, Vanuatu, Indonesia, Malaysia, and Thailand). Others that could pose a threat include the American crocodile, American alligator, the Nile crocodile, and the Indian mugger crocodile. True freshwater crocodiles are found only in Australia and aren't considered dangerous to humans, but be aware that other dangerous species may also inhabit freshwater lagoons and swamps.

Like many large wild animals, most crocodilians are under pressure from hunting and loss of habitat, and some are threatened with extinction. One area where they are not threatened is in Australia, where numbers are believed to approach 100,000.

Saltwater crocodiles' preferred habitat is the tidal reaches of rivers, but they can be found in salt water, in estuaries, and in freshwater (as far as 100 miles inland). Saltwater and Nile crocodiles can grow to a length of 20 feet (6 m) or more, but most adults are smaller, measuring some 12 to 13 feet (4 m). The American crocodile and alligator both top out at about 12 feet (3.5 m). Alligators are slower moving and generally less dangerous than crocodiles.

Crocodilians are intelligent creatures and are known to stalk their victims. They often rest in shallow water along the bank of a river or estuary, with just their nostrils and eyes above water. When prey comes to drink or bathe, the crocodile attacks by lunging in one swift move. They're smart enough to note a pattern in their prey's activity, and they'll lie in wait in a spot where they've observed prey on one or more occasions. They normally eat fish, snakes, crustaceans, and occasionally mammals. Large crocodiles can take down animals as massive as a water buffalo and are a definite threat to humans. One source comments that in the water, crocs can swim at speeds of up to 20 mph (32 kph); on land, they can charge short distances at 15–30 mph (24–48 kph).

Crocs in Australia are responsible for an average of about one death every year, while reports from Africa indicate a much higher death rate. We're aware of only one incident in recent years involving a cruiser. It took place in the Solomon Islands in 1998, when a Swiss sailor jumped in the water to reconnoiter before anchoring. He was attacked and killed by several crocodiles.

Avoiding Croc Attacks

Some advice on avoiding attacks can be pretty sweeping. For example, one authority recommends you shouldn't "swim, stand, or canoe in tropical waterways or estuaries." What's more, you should also

An alligator at ease on a landing along a river.
Grady Tuell, NOAA

avoid "walking along, camping, or fishing from the banks" of those same waterways and estuaries. That doesn't leave much! On the other hand, you certainly don't want to be cavalier about these animals, especially about dangerous species such as the saltwater croc. We watched a group of cruisers swimming off the back of their boat when anchored in northern Queensland, Australia, while at the same time a large crocodile basked on the mud bank a few hundred feet away.

We had our closest encounter with a croc in the Hermit Islands, a remote spot in northern Papua New Guinea. The islands are small and lie about 150 miles off the mainland coast. There's a bit of mangrove, but given the lagoon's small size and remote location, it seemed highly unlikely that crocodiles would be there. Nevertheless, we asked the chief's son if it was safe to swim. He replied that we should avoid a small patch of mangrove, as crocodiles had been spotted there on occasion, but that swimming was otherwise fine.

We did a bit of snorkeling on a nearby reef in hopes of spearing some dinner, and crocodiles were nowhere to be seen. The next day we took to our dinghy to explore a sandy beach and islet on the other side of the anchorage, quite a distance away from the mangroves that we been warned about, and we gave no thought to crocodiles. While walking the beach, we saw a path leading inland and took the chance to explore. Hearing noises from farther up the track and thinking we were about to

stumble upon someone's house or garden site, we retraced our steps. We'd no sooner reached the beach when out from the bush, not 20 feet (6 m) away, came a large adult crocodile. He paused briefly on the sand, looked our way as if to say "You're lucky I'm not hungry," and then took to the water, crossing the beach faster than we could have. A swish of the tail, and he was gone.

Were we at risk? He was certainly big enough to be a threat, but it's possible he was so well fed on the lagoon's plentiful fish that he was uninterested in us as potential prey. But we decided not to find out; we stayed out of the water (and the bush) from then on.

Cruising in Croc Country

Can you safely enjoy cruising in croc country? Yes, but accept the fact that your activities will be restricted. Start by being aware of your surroundings. Areas known to be frequented are posted in some countries (such as Australia), but don't count on this. Learn what crocodile habitat looks like. It includes estuarine areas and generally most coastal inlets with mangroves. In such places, be on your guard and follow these rules:

▸ Don't swim, wade, or snorkel.

▸ If you walk along the bank of a stream or estuary, do so a few meters back from the water's edge.

▸ Don't clean fish on a bank or beach (or in a dinghy, for that matter). Dispose of fish scraps away from where people gather.

▶ Avoid entering the water when beaching or launching your dinghy. Keep arms and legs inside the dinghy when underway. Vary your routine, and land in a different place or at a different time.

▶ If an estuary has a stream leading into it, swimming in the stream may be safe if you choose areas with shallow rapids well away from deep water. Swim in a group, not alone.

▶ Never interfere with or approach a crocodile.

Areas that don't match the description of good crocodile habitat will generally be safe. This includes offshore islets and reefs. We've done plenty of swimming in countries where crocodiles are found, and usually we haven't even been nervous. But always seek local confirmation that crocodiles aren't a threat, and even then keep your guard up.

First aid for crocodile attacks is essentially the same as first aid for shark attacks.

VENOMOUS MARINE ANIMALS WITH SPINES

Marine animals can inject venom in one of two ways: through a puncture wound or by microscopic stinging cells. Puncture wounds can result from spines or from bites.

Venomous marine animals with spines include hundreds of species of fish, sting rays, sea urchins, and cone snails (which have a venomous dart). These animals have spines for self-defense, and by and large they're not a threat unless threatened or provoked. Most injuries are the result of animals being stepped on, picked up, or brushed against.

As you'll see from the various descriptions below, the treatment for different venomous wounds varies: in some cases the venom is inactivated by heat, whereas in others it's important to keep the poison from spreading (using a pressure bandage; see sidebar, page 209). In a few instances antivenin is available. The differences in recommended treatment mean that it's important to try and identify the animal that caused the injury; even if you didn't see the animal, pay close attention to the symptoms, as these are often distinctive. Venomous wounds can be fatal, so be serious about avoiding contact with these animals and getting treatment immediately.

Venomous Fish

Many fish species have spines for protection, and most don't have venom. (But any fish spine can cause injury, so it pays to handle fish you've caught so that you avoid contact with the spines.) Spines may not be obvious: in some fish they are promi-

nent, serving as a warning to predators, but in others they're not visible unless in use.

It can be hard to identify the type of fish that injures you, however, but fish venoms are similar in the kind of symptoms they produce, although the severity can vary greatly. A person's body weight also has an impact on how severe the poisoning is.

Scorpion Fish

There are over 300 species in this family, including the most venomous, the stonefish. The term *scorpion fish* refers both to the fish and to the collective term that includes the three distinct groups of fish below. Most species of scorpion fish are very hard to spot, as they usually take on the color and even pattern of their environment. In clear tropical waters with coral reefs they are colorful—red, yellow, and blue—while in murky estuaries they'll be the color of mud. They range in size from a few inches or centimeters to about 3 feet (1 m).

A single scorpion fish can have as many as 17 spines, which stand up when the fish is wary. This can happen if a fish is touched, startled, or threatened. The spines are covered by a sheath that is pierced when the spine makes contact with a person's skin. Venom then passes along the spine and into the wound.

The scorpion fish family can be divided into three groups, listed in order of *increasing toxicity*.

▶ *LIONFISH ARE SOME OF THE MORE EX-OTIC AND SPECTACULAR-LOOKING FISH* found

Attractive and brightly colored, this lionfish is well equipped with spines. NOAA

Stingrays are bottom-dwelling fish, and their flat bodies are often hidden in the sand; only their eyes and a bit of the tail betray their presence. This ray is skimming along the bottom of a shallow lagoon.

around coral reefs. Hidden within their lacy fins are numerous spines with venom glands. Lionfish are active at night; during the day they are found near caves and crevices in the reef. Their striped coloring plus their ability to hang motionless in the water helps camouflage lionfish against the background of the reef. They're also called turkeyfish, firefish, coral cod, zebra fish, and butterfly cod. The reaction to their sting is usually mild.

▶ **SCORPION FISH USE THEIR CAMOUFLAGE** to hide among rocks, coral, or seaweed on the bottom of shallow bays and among coral reefs. The skin is usually mottled with patches of blue or red, and they resemble algae or sponges. The sting causes a moderately severe reaction.

▶ **STONEFISH ARE HIGHLY TOXIC.** They're covered with bumpy and warty skin and are, well, ugly. They grow to about 12 inches (30 cm). They partially bury themselves under sand or mud or hide among coral and rocks, and like scorpion fish, can be extremely difficult to see. They can survive many hours out of the water (such as on a drying reef) if

their skin stays wet, meaning you can stumble upon them when exploring a reef at low tide. They hunt by lying in wait for their prey (small fish); then they either suck their prey into their large mouth or catch their prey with a quick burst of speed. Their sting is severe and often fatal. Both scorpion fish and stonefish are nonaggressive, and injury is most likely caused when a person steps on them.

Fish Venom Symptoms

Symptoms start with pain near the injury that quickly builds and can become excruciating; it usually eases within a few hours. If you are stung, the puncture wound may be numb, while the surrounding area will be hypersensitive. The surrounding muscles may be temporarily paralyzed. A sting can cause severe distress in a person, and in serious cases general paralysis, with blurred vision and speech, may result. Malaise, nausea, and vomiting can also occur. After the acute phases of a serious sting, a person may

There are hundreds of different kinds of cone snails, all of which can deliver a potent sting.
Dr. James McVey, NOAA

still be anxious, weak, and depressed and have trouble concentrating. These symptoms can last for days, and even weeks. How bad the sting is depends on the species of fish, its size, and the number of spines that penetrate the skin.

Emergency Treatment

Immediately flush the wound and remove the spine(s) and any other bits (spines left in the wound will continue to release venom). Some bleeding probably helps to flush the venom. Immerse the injured area and surrounding skin in water that is as hot as you can stand it. It should not be scalding (upper limit 114°F/45° C), and you should immerse a limb that's not injured at the same time in case the area around the injury is desensitized to the heat. Use hot packs if immersion isn't possible. Hot water will improve local blood flow, which can help to disperse the venom; it may also help to par-

---

SPECIAL NOTE FOR STONEFISH STINGS

The pain from these stings is excruciating and will worsen for 10 or more minutes. It can even cause delirium or unconsciousness. A host of serious complications can ensue, including respiratory failure, cardiac failure, and cardiac arrest. Victims may require intravenous narcotic painkillers. Get medical help if at all possible, and inquire about the availability of antivenin.

---

tially inactivate the venom and/or interrupt pain pathways. If possible, elevate the injury at the same time. The hot water treatment should continue until no pain is felt. Clean and dress the wound when the heat treatment is finished, and keep the area elevated and immobilized if possible. Some sources recommend against the use of pressure pads or other means to restrict the movement of the venom.

Pain from fish stings can be very intense, but local anesthetics may provide relief. Emergency treatment is sometimes enough for mild cases, but for serious stings, you should get medical attention if at all possible. If symptoms persist even after heat treatment, then the wound may still contain a piece of the spine. X-rays will help confirm this, and surgery may be necessary to remove it. An antibiotic may be needed if infection occurs. Tetanus is a risk with any venomous spine injury, so the injured person should have a booster shot if necessary.

Avoiding Injury from Fish Stings

Get to know the more common tropical fish species, and take note of which are venomous. Learn how to handle fish that you've speared or caught (even nonvenomous fish can inflict nasty wounds with their spines). Always wear shoes or booties when wading, but remember that some spines can penetrate these with ease. We highly recommend that cruisers carry fish and other marine animal reference books on board for the areas they plan to cruise (see the Tropical Environments section in appendix 3, Resources).

Stingrays

Rays have flattened, diamond-shaped bodies, and with their winglike pectoral fins they look to be gracefully flying through the water. Some types, such as manta rays, put on wild acrobatic shows, jumping clear of the water and doing twists and loops. Mantas are the largest rays and grow to a "wingspan" of 20 feet (6 m), but sizes from several feet to 12 feet (about 1 m to 3.5 m) are more common. Although they're closely related to sharks, rays

The crown-of-thorns starfish, which have many short, sharp venomous spines, feed on coral polyps.
Dr. James McVey, NOAA

are generally harmless to humans and feed instead on plankton, small fish, crabs, or shellfish. Some rays, such as the blue-spotted ray, have venomous stingers, and these are the rays to avoid. These rays, usually grouped under the general heading *stingrays*, have between one and four venomous stingers, each 1 to 17 inches (2.5 to 43 cm) long. The stingers are imbedded in a long whiplike tail and have two rows of barbs (like a saw's teeth) and grooves on the underside, which have venom glands. The whole works is covered by a sheath with more glands and often coated with poison and mucus.

Stingrays are not aggressive, and most injuries are the result of an unwary person treading on a ray while it's resting on the bottom. The stingray typically reacts by swinging its tail up and forward, which either makes swordlike cuts or drives the spine into a person's ankle, leg, or body. In the latter case, the sheath ruptures, releasing venom and driving it, along with mucus and bacteria, deep into the wound. The spine and sheath may be left in the wound: the spine's jagged saw-like barbs often cause more damage as the spine is removed. Most stingray wounds are on the foot or ankle, but wounds in the abdomen and chest are often fatal.

PRESSURE BANDAGES TO SLOW VENOM ABSORPTION

A broad, firm bandage applied around the bitten or stung area can delay the absorption of venom and reduce its impact. Use this bandage for sea snakes, blue-ringed octopus bites, cone shell stings, and box jellyfish (after vinegar is applied). The bandage should be applied to as much of the limb as possible, using a crepe bandage or other fabric. The bandage should be wound as tightly as one would bind a sprained ankle. Once the pressure bandage has been applied, the limb should be immobilized, either by binding it to a splint or resting it in a sling.

209

Sea urchins can inflict a nasty wound if you come into contact with their long, sharp spines.
NOAA

Symptoms and Treatment

Symptoms of stingray stings are generally similar to those described for fish stings but can be more serious and longer lasting. Pain usually peaks after an hour or so, and slowly diminishes over the next 6 to 48 hours. Bleeding can be profuse. The injured area first turns a dusky blue and then bright red. Treatment is generally the same as that for fish stings, but lacerations may be larger, requiring surgery. Infection is common. There is no antivenin for stingrays.

Avoiding Stings from Rays

Rays prefer shallow coastal waters, especially sheltered bays, river mouths, and sandy lagoons. At low tide, round depressions can sometimes be seen in the sand where they've been resting on the bottom. Rays can be all but impossible to spot, even in very clear water, as their entire body, except the eyes and tail, is often buried. If you're wading in or entering and exiting the water where rays may be present, shuffle your feet to alert them and allow them to move away. Wearing shoes or reef booties may help, but the spine can penetrate most materials, and shoes are of no use if the spine ends up in your calf.

Cone Snails

Cone snails are the animals that inhabit the beautiful cone shells that are popular with beachcombers. There are hundreds of species of cone snails, a few of which are dangerous (even lethal) to humans. Most of the toxic species are found in the Indian and Pacific Oceans, while one (the textile or woven cone) is also common in the Red Sea, Florida, and the Caribbean. Cone snails live in shallow waters, reefs, tide pools, and ponds and grow to around 4 inches (10 cm) long. The snail injects its venom by means of a dart that is sharp and can penetrate gloves. The proboscis (with a kind of dart) extends out from the

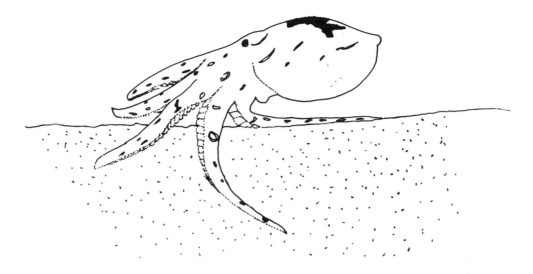

The blue-ringed octopus has a yellow-brown body, with ringed markings on the tentacles and striations on the body, which become iridescent blue when the animal is excited or disturbed.

narrow end of the shell but is capable of reaching around most of the shell; even holding a cone shell by the wide end doesn't guarantee safety.

Symptoms

The initial sting from a cone snail ranges from mild to excruciating pain. The area may become inflamed, swollen, and numb, and may even turn blue. In serious cases numbness and tingling will spread to the lips and then the entire body, usually within 10 minutes of the injury. Paralysis can spread outward from the site of injury and then affect a person's ability to speak and swallow. Vision may be blurred and double as well.

The most severe cases may cause unconsciousness, coma, respiratory paralysis, and death. Typically a person's condition will worsen for 1 to 6 hours and then slowly improve.

Emergency First Aid

You should first apply a pressure bandage over the sting (see the sidebar on page 209) to minimize the spread of venom. Some sources suggest immersing the injured part in hot water, until the pain is relieved, as this may partially inactivate the venom (see treatment for fish stings).

Watch for signs of paralysis, and be prepared to provide emergency resuscitation if necessary. Treat the wound as potentially infected, and make sure that the injured person's tetanus vaccination is up to date. Get medical help as soon as possible if the sting appears serious.

Avoiding Cone Snail Stings

Don't pick up or otherwise handle live cone snails; collect only empty shells.

Crown-of-Thorns-Starfish

The crown-of-thorns starfish is best known for its appetite for coral polyps, and some reefs have been severely impacted by infestations of this predator. The crown-of-thorns is found throughout the tropical Indian and Pacific Oceans and Red Sea and grows to 24 inches (60 cm) in diameter. Most have

13–16 arms, though some grow as many as 23. The entire body is covered by short spines (about 2 in./5 cm long). Crown-of-thorns starfish are usually found in shallow, sheltered lagoons and on leeward reefs, or the same sorts of environments that are perfect for a sheltered snorkel.

Both the spines and the arms may be of different contrasting colors but can be hard to see on the reef, and these large starfish often blend in well with their surroundings. Most injuries occur when an unsuspecting wader or diver steps on or touches a starfish; even a dead crown-of-thorns starfish washed up on the beach can cause severe pain.

Symptoms

The pain, which is usually severe, is felt immediately after a person is pricked by a spine. Spines can break off under the skin, causing inflammation and swollen lymph glands. Vomiting and retching may occur in severe cases, which can persist for days. Puncture wounds may be blue or black. Pain, swelling, and weakness can continue for weeks and even months, especially if bits of the spines are left in the wound. Severe itching can develop as other symptoms fade.

First Aid

Remove any loose spines. These must be pulled straight out; they may break off if wiggled or bent. Then immerse the affected area in hot water until pain subsides (see treatment for fish stings, page 208). Clean and dress the wound (see General Wound Care in chapter 12) and minimize movement. Painkillers and a broad-spectrum antibiotic are recommended. If you suspect that spines may have broken off in the wound, have X-rays taken. Surgery will be needed to remove any broken spines.

Sea Urchins

There are many kinds of sea urchins, and they're found in all tropical waters. The urchin's body is rounded and typically covered by sharp brittle spines. Some types have short thick spines intermixed with an array of flowerlike appendages called *pedicellariae*. The venomous effect of sea urchins varies widely, and most injuries are not overly serious. Careful attention should be given to a person's symptoms, though, as some species have been reported to deliver a potentially fatal sting. Some of the more serious problems may be caused by contact with the pedicellariae, which have hooklike jaws.

Symptoms

Pain is immediate, severe, and more than would be expected from the injury itself. Pain lasts from 30 minutes to four hours, and the area around the puncture wound(s) may become numb. Swelling and inflammation might occur, and the wound can turn black. With no complications the wound usually heals in a few weeks. If a piece of the spine stays in the wound, infection can result, with increasing inflammation, stiffness, and aching pain.

Some types of urchins cause more severe reactions, including shock, weakness, paralysis, and problems in breathing. Sea urchins can also cause severe but delayed dermatitis, which appears up to three months after contact.

First Aid

Typical cases of stings from sea urchins should be treated by very carefully removing the spines, noting if any break off in the process. If any pedicellariae are seen, remove them by gently shaving the area. Clean and dress the wound, applying local antibiotics, and give painkillers. Get medical help immediately and be ready to administer artificial respiration if the person seems to have problems breathing. Also, get medical help if milder symptoms persist, as X-rays and possibly surgery may be needed to find and remove remaining spines, and broad-spectrum antibiotics will be needed if secondary infection occurs. Finally, be on the lookout for dermatitis in the months following contact with a sea urchin.

VENOMOUS MARINE ANIMALS THAT BITE

Animals that bite and thereby inject venom are rare, and generally they're not aggressive. Take care not to startle or threaten these animals, and you should easily avoid any trouble.

Blue-Ringed Octopus

The blue-ringed octopus, also called the common ringed or spotted octopus, is found throughout the tropical Indo-Pacific, living in rock pools and shells. The name refers to the ringed markings and stripes on the brown body, which turn iridescent blue when the octopus is angry, excited, or disturbed. It's hardly a threatening animal, weighing in at just a few ounces (under 100 g), and measuring only 1 to 7 inches (2–20 cm) long with its tentacles extended. But it's by far the most dangerous of the octopi, having developed a highly toxic bite that it uses to kill the crustaceans on which it feeds. Although its bite can kill an adult, injuries have only occurred when it has been picked up or stepped on.

Symptoms

At first the bite of this octopus is almost painless and may go unnoticed. A whitened area of about one-half inch (1 cm) becomes swollen within 15 minutes, but there are few other signs on the skin. Bleeding may or may not occur. Over the course of a few hours the injured person will feel numbness around the mouth, neck, and head and will often suffer from nausea, vomiting, and disturbed vision as well. Speech, swallowing, and breathing may all become difficult, and death from the latter is the biggest threat. Complete paralysis can take place, lasting 4–12 hours; the person may be conscious (though unable to respond) throughout. Not all cases are equally severe, with some people showing only partial paralysis. Muscle spasms have been noted in milder cases.

First Aid

In the absence of paralysis, wash the toxin from the bite and apply a pressure bandage. Rest the victim on his or her side and get someone to seek medical assistance, but *don't leave the person unattended*, in case of breathing difficulties.

If paralysis is present and affects breathing, begin mouth-to-mouth resuscitation. Resuscitation may be needed for hours, until the paralysis ends as the effects of the venom wear off. There is no antivenin available.

Avoiding Octopus Bites

Avoid contact with the blue-ringed octopus, and be very careful in handling even apparently empty shells, which might contain an octopus.

Sea Snake

Sea snakes include some 50 species of air-breathing reptiles. They're found throughout the tropical Indo-Pacific, but not in the Atlantic or Caribbean. They're about 3 to 4 feet (1–1.5 m) long. There are two main types of sea snake: coastal and pelagic. Coastal snakes are restricted to relatively shallow coastal waters, lay their eggs in caves and crevices ashore, and can exist for long periods out of the water. The banded sea snake is a common example. Pelagic, or oceanic, snakes can't survive on land. They're surface feeders and can be found in packs far out to sea. In the tropics they are most often seen on the surface on cloudy or rainy days.

Sea snakes can submerge for up to two hours at a time and are good swimmers because of their flattened tail. They're inquisitive and can be aggressive if handled or stepped on. Their venom is considerably more toxic than that of a cobra, and one snake can inject enough venom to kill three people. Most don't inject a large amount when biting, however, and many sea snakes have small mouths that don't open wide enough to easily pierce wetsuits or clothing.

Sea snake venom is more than twice as potent as that of a cobra.

Symptoms

Not much pain accompanies the initial bite, and there may be a delay of 10 minutes to a few hours before symptoms develop. Then restlessness, anxiety, and euphoria may be felt, and occasionally nausea and vomiting. Paralysis is common and can result in troubled breathing due to paralysis of the diaphragm.

First Aid

All sea snake bites should be considered medical emergencies, even if there are no initial symptoms, as death occurs in up to 35 percent of cases that involve injection of venom. Slow the spread and absorption of venom through the use of a pressure bandage and by keeping both the limb and the person immobilized. Position the limb below the rest of the body. Medical assistance should be sought, and ideally the person should be brought to an intensive care unit as soon as the pressure bandage has been applied. *Under no circumstances should the person be left alone.* Mouth-to-mouth or other artificial respiration will be needed if the person has trouble breathing or stops breathing altogether.

Avoiding Sea Snake Bites

Shuffle your feet when walking on a muddy bottom. Be careful when walking along rocky shoreline areas where sea snakes may be basking, and don't handle or approach sea snakes.

MARINE ANIMALS WITH STINGING CELLS

Jellyfish, Portuguese man-of-war, sea anemones, and fire coral all look harmless, but they've developed a very efficient way of injecting venom. They use nematocysts (stinging cells) that act like tiny harpoons, shooting venom into anything with which they come into contact. Jellyfish cause by far the most serious stings and are found in all tropical oceans. Some species cause no reaction in humans when touched, but others can be fatal. Many are hard to see in the water, and so contact and injury can come without warning.

Reactions to various jellyfish species vary enormously. As a group, box jellyfish are the most venomous, but even here the reaction can range from irritating to fatal, depending on the species. But it is impractical (and, in fact, unwise) to treat every jellyfish sting as though it was caused by *Chironex fleckeri* (the most dangerous of the box jellyfish species). *If stung by a jellyfish that you can't identify, or that is of a different species than those listed here, follow the first-aid recommendations given below for the Portuguese man-of-war.* Always keep an eye out for more serious reactions, however, such as those described below for *Chironex* and other box jellyfish; be doubly on your guard if you're cruising in an area where *Chironex* is commonly found.

Portuguese Man-of-War

The Portuguese man-of-war, or bluebottle, is common throughout most tropical waters. Young man-of-wars look like patches of froth on the water. When mature, each colony of animals has a large gas-filled float, or sail, that looks like a small plastic bag. (Although it looks to be a single organism, each man-of-war is composed of four types of polyps; one forms the sail, and three other types are clustered beneath the sail, with tentacles trailing from them.)

This sail varies from 1 to 6 inches (2 to 15 cm) across in Pacific Ocean man-of-wars but can measure up to 12 inches (30 cm) in Atlantic species, which are considered more dangerous. The sail transports the animal with the prevailing wind or onto the beach with an onshore breeze. The sail and tentacles are largely blue or bluish purple. Many short frilled tentacles hang below the sail, but it's the few long tentacles (up to 30 ft./10 m in length) that are responsible for most stings. These tentacles are still venomous even if the man-of-war is washed up dead on the beach.

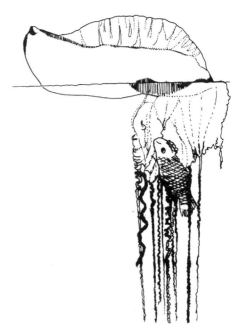

A Portuguese man-of-war colony with a fish trapped in its tentacles.

Symptoms

A sharp burning sting is felt immediately and may be aggravated by removing the tentacle, rubbing the sting, or applying freshwater. Severe pain may be felt for a few minutes or many hours. Red welts are left where the tentacles touched the skin, connected by red lines. The welts usually disappear after a few hours. More general symptoms are rare, but can include headache, nausea, and vomiting, and occasionally problems in breathing.

First Aid

Remove the tentacles using a glove, tweezers, or even a stick, but do so gently to prevent stingers from releasing more venom. Rinse the wound thoroughly with salt water, but *don't apply freshwater*, as this may cause the stingers to activate. Some sources suggest vinegar is helpful for neutralizing Atlantic Ocean Portuguese man-of-war stings, but it is usually not recommended for stings from the Pacific Ocean man-of-war. Ice may be effective for controlling pain, or a

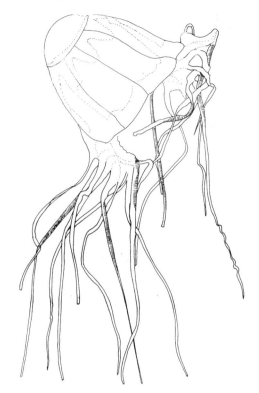

Box jellyfish (Chironex fleckeri); *the body is about 7 inches (18 cm) long.*

topical anesthetic or an anti-inflammatory (such as hydrocortisone ointment) may be applied.

If eyes are stung, flush with freshwater for at least 15 minutes. If pain continues, or vision blurs or is otherwise affected, see a doctor.

If any more general effects are noted, keep a close watch on the person, and be ready to give artificial resuscitation if needed. Get medical help.

Some lotions claim to disarm the stinging cells of jellyfish thereby protecting the skin. These lotions also act as a sunblock.

Box Jellyfish

Box jellyfish are easily recognized by their cubical shape and by the presence of one or more tentacles at each corner of the box. Sea wasp is another common name for these animals. *Chironex fleckeri* is the biggest (measuring 7–12 in./20–30 cm across the bell) and most dangerous of the box jellyfish, and one of the most venomous marine animals; it has caused a number of deaths. It occurs in tropical Australian waters and in Papua New Guinea, Indonesia, the Philippines, and Malaysia. Other box jellyfish are somewhat less dangerous than *Chironex*, but their sting is still severe and potentially fatal. One or more of the latter species of box jellyfish can be found in most tropical regions. These jellyfish are most common in shallow coastal waters, although some species have been found in offshore waters. All box jellyfish are essentially translucent in the water and can be very hard to see.

In Australia *Chironex* is not considered a threat along the Great Barrier Reef itself, but it's found along the coast (inside the reef). The threat coincides roughly with that of cyclones, affecting the same waters during the same months. The jellyfish undergoes its early development in estuaries and mangrove swamps and floods into coastal waters after rainy periods. It matures over the months of the wet season, increasing in both size and toxicity. The chances of encountering it are increased on cloudy days and following bad weather, when it moves into shallower water. Serious encounters with these jellyfish are most likely on cloudy days toward the end of the wet (cyclone) season.

Symptoms

Symptoms vary depending on the species, the size of the jellyfish, and the susceptibility of the person. The reaction to the sting of some box jellyfish species can be relatively mild, comparable to that commonly experienced with the Portuguese man-of-war, or it can be so serious that death occurs within 5 minutes. *Chironex* stings are almost invariably serious and have been responsible for a number of deaths in the Indian and Pacific Ocean region.

Pain is immediate, and often excruciating, increasing in intensity for some 15 minutes. Victims of *Chironex* stings have been known to lose consciousness before leaving the water, making drowning a real threat. The skin will be marked within seconds by red, purple, and brown lines about ¼ inch (5 mm) wide. They can develop into large welts and become ulcerated, taking weeks or even months to heal.

The most serious threat to life occurs during the first hour after the sting. Signs of a very serious sting include

- labored breathing, swallowing, or talking
- welts that cover a large area
- heart attack or other heart problems

First Aid

The first priority is to get the injured person safely ashore, where he or she can't drown or suffer additional stings. Next, douse the area with vinegar, and then remove any tentacles. Be gentle but quick (rough treatment can cause further discharge). A razor blade or credit card may help. This can be done with bare hands, as serious stings through the thick skin of the fingers are unlikely. Be ready to administer artificial resuscitation or cardiac massage if the area of the sting is extensive, and especially if the sting is thought to be caused by *Chironex*. Immobilize the affected areas, as movement can cause the venom to spread; using a pressure bandage is recommended by some sources.

If the sting is serious, get medical help, *but do not leave the person unattended.* Box jellyfish antivenin is available from medical centers in Australia and can counter both systemic effects and serious skin damage, which can be permanent. Milder stings may be treated with anesthetic sprays or ointment (see Portuguese Man-of-War).

Avoiding Man-of-War and Jellyfish Stings

Be careful in areas and seasons where jellyfish are known to be a problem (such as tropical Australian waters in the summer months). In such places, don't run or dive into the water, but walk in slowly. Don't enter the water if you see jellyfish, unless you know for certain that they are a harmless species. Be mindful of jellyfish even when walking the beach, as the tentacles of dead animals are still able to deliver venom. Wear a face-

Sea anemones have nematocysts that they use to stun prey and that can sting an unwary snorkeler, if they're touched.
Dr. James McVey, NOAA

mask and a wetsuit, Lycra suit, or similar protective clothing if you think there may be box jellyfish present.

Sea Anemones and Fire Coral

Sea anemones and fire coral spend most of their lives attached to rocks or reefs and are especially common in warm tropical waters less than 100 feet (30 m) deep. They're found in all oceans but sting only when touched by a swimmer or diver. Fire coral is not a true coral but is easily mistaken as such; it may be bright yellow, green, or brown.

Symptoms and Treatment

Burning or stinging pain begins within 5 to 30 minutes. A red rash or welts develop, and the area often itches. Rinse the affected area with seawater (avoid freshwater), and generally treat as a Portuguese man-of-war sting. In all cases the stings can be avoided if swimmers and divers don't touch or handle these animals.

POISONOUS MARINE ANIMALS

Although the vast majority of seafood that's consumed causes no problems, some marine animals can cause poisoning. Some species of fish are normally toxic (such as puffer fish) and are best avoided at all times. But most poisoning (including the most widespread, ciguatera poisoning) results from toxins that are only occasionally present.

Ciguatera

Ciguatera poisoning is the most serious and most common type of fish poisoning found throughout the tropics. Ciguatera is thought to affect 25,000 to 50,000 people per year. Most cases are not fatal, but the risk is higher in some places, especially the Indian Ocean. Ciguatera is caused by a single-celled algae, which is eaten by herbivorous reef fish. The toxin does not affect the fish themselves. These herbivorous fish are in turn eaten by carnivorous fish, which store up the toxin. Organs are especially toxic, and larger fish pose a greater threat (as they may have consumed a greater number of ciguatoxic fish). Open ocean fish (such as tuna, mahimahi, and mackerel) are rarely affected.

Some 400 species of fish may be affected by ciguatera, including red snappers, groupers, coral trout, emperors, jacks or trevallies, and barracudas, but not all species will be affected in all places. Outbreaks occur unpredictably and may spread from one area to another. The poison is not affected by cooking or freezing.

Symptoms

Symptoms are felt anywhere from 2 to 12 hours after eating the fish. Symptoms vary geographically: the nervous system is most commonly affected in the Pacific, gastronomical symptoms predominate in the Caribbean, and an entirely different type of hallucinatory symptoms are found in the Indian Ocean. The different symptoms occur because of differences in the type of toxin found in each area. The most common initial neurological symptom is tingling and numbness around the lips, mouth, and tongue. Temperature perception is often reversed, so that hot feels cold and cold feels hot. More serious neurological effects include delirium, visual disorders, convulsions, and coma. Gastronomical symptoms include nausea and diarrhea. General weakness and dull aches are also common. Hallucinatory effects include lack of coordination, loss of balance, mental depression, and nightmares. Tightness in the chest, labored breathing, and respiratory failure have also been reported.

Mild cases usually clear up within one or two days, but severe attacks may take a week or more to subside, with total recovery not occurring for weeks, months, or even years.

Treatment

Encourage vomiting if: the fish was eaten within six hours, the person hasn't vomited already, and the person is still fully conscious. Activated charcoal can help in absorbing the poison. Mix with water at a rate of ½ ounce per 1 cup (10 g/100 mL) of water, and take at a dosage of ½ teaspoon per pound (5 mL/kg) of body weight. Keep a close watch on the person, and get medical help if a severe attack is suspected.

Mannitol has been used to treat ciguatera poisoning, with mixed success. Persons with ciguatera poisoning should avoid the following foods and beverages while recovering, as these can cause symptoms to intensify:

- any fish products
- shellfish products
- alcoholic beverages
- nuts
- nut oils

Avoiding Ciguatera Poisoning

Don't eat fish implicated as affected in various regions, and always inquire with locals before you fish. Avoid eating oversized reef fish, and never eat the liver or other organs of any reef fish. A test kit has recently been developed to detect the presence of ciguatoxin in fish; we have not used this kit ourselves, or seen any independent review of its accuracy. For more information, see the Health section in appendix 3, Resources.

Scombroid Poisoning

Scombroid (or histamine) poisoning affects pelagic fish that are usually safe to eat, including bonito, all tunas, mahimahi, bluefish, sardine, amberjack, anchovy, Australian salmon, herring, mackerel, needlefish, saury, and wahoo. The poisoning is caused by eating fish containing histamines or similar compounds, and it produces symptoms not unlike those in an allergic reaction. The fish become toxic only when left at ambient temperature for some time (e.g., at a public market), giving naturally occurring bacteria a chance to produce the toxins. Once present, there is no way of removing or inactivating the toxin: cooking, refrigeration, and freezing all have no effect.

Symptoms

Symptoms begin rapidly following consumption of affected fish and are similar to those of an allergic reaction. They may include a tingling or burning sensation in the mouth, a metallic or peppery taste, flushed skin, itching, hives, abdominal pain, nausea, vomiting, diarrhea, headache, dizziness, or shortness of breath. The illness usually lasts for several hours, but recovery can take a few days.

The more affected fish that's eaten, the worse the symptoms, though the reaction between different people eating the same fish may be quite variable, as sensitivity to histamine varies.

Treatment

Get the person to vomit if he or she is awake and alert and has eaten the fish within 3 hours. Serious reactions should be treated with oral antihistamines. Hospital care is rarely needed.

Avoiding Scombroid Poisoning

Make sure the fish you buy is fresh; quickly clean and cook (or refrigerate) any fish you catch. Keep fish cool (covered with a wet cloth and kept in the shade) if there is a delay in cleaning it. If you're buying a fish, look at the eyes; these should be clear, not cloudy. The fish's flesh should be resilient and should bounce back after you apply pressure with a finger. Contaminated fish may look normal but will usually taste strong or peppery and may make your mouth tingle. If the fish tastes odd or causes any sensation of numbness or tingling, don't eat it.

Puffer Fish Poisoning

There are many species of puffer fish, whose name comes from their ability to inflate themselves by taking in large quantities of air or water. Puffers do not have typical fish scales, and some are covered by spikes. Puffer fish contain a toxin (tetrodotoxin, the same found in the blue-ringed octopus) that can cause severe poisoning and death when ingested. The flesh of puffer fish (called *fugu*) is considered a delicacy in Japan, where it's prepared by specially trained and licensed chefs; puffer fish poisoning causes a number of deaths in Japan every year.

Avoiding Puffer Fish Poisoning

Don't eat puffer fish; if in doubt about the identity of a fish, play it safe by avoiding any fish without scales.

Chapter 14

Boat Maintenance

No boat is immune from the ravages of the tropical climate, but each will be affected differently, and the work required to prepare a boat properly will vary in each case. We'll start by looking at some basics that apply to all boats and then address metal corrosion and problems that often develop with spars, hardware, and fittings. Additional sections examine the impact of the tropics on boats built of fiberglass, wood, and steel and aluminum.

TEMPERATURE, RAINFALL, AND HUMIDITY

Tropical air and water temperatures are fairly stable throughout the year, though more so near the equator than around 20° N and S. Taken alone, air temperatures aren't usually excessive; it can easily get as warm or warmer in many temperate latitudes during the summer. But combine these consistently warm temperatures with the high humidity and rainfall found in most tropical regions, and the stage is set for a significant increase in the rate of corrosion and decay. The warm, wet tropical climate makes it more important than ever to ensure your boat is both well ventilated and leakproof.

We discussed ventilation in chapter 10, but with a view to keeping the crew comfy in the heat. Ventilation is equally important for your boat, and it's not enough to rely on a propped hatch or two. Air needs to circulate throughout your boat and should be able to do so even when all hatches are closed and locked, as they will probably be when you leave the boat in port. Consider installing extra cowl or mushroom vents, or position some small ventilation hatches in spots where they can be left open regardless of rain. Solar vents (which incorporate a tiny solar panel and a rechargeable battery) are good at keeping air circulating even in still conditions. Don't forget to consider whether air can circulate to the bilge, as the humidity in such a confined area can reach saturation levels very quickly.

Keeping the water out is equally important, as leaks can lead to delamination and foam-core failures in fiberglass boats, rot in both solid wood and wood-cored decks, and rust in steel boats. Hatches and ports need to be of good design and well bedded with an appropriate sealant (see sidebar). Most hardware is bolted or screwed in place on the deck or hull, and fittings are a common source of leaks on many boats. If your boat is older, it may pay to remove, inspect, and re-bed all deck hardware before setting off on a long cruise. Keep an eye on all stainless steel hardware and fasteners while sailing in the tropics, for reasons we'll discuss below.

Many cruising boats feature teak deck overlays, with thin teak that's typically bedded in sealant and screwed down over a plywood or fiberglass sub-deck. The high temperatures and humidity in the tropics are not kind to such decks, causing the sealant to break down and the wood to warp. The first sign of trouble is usually when the plugs over the fasteners start to lift, and caulking between the planks peels up. Movement or cupping of the teak planks is next, and leaks through to the underlying deck (and on into the cabin) are inevitable. If your boat has such a teak overlay and it's more than about 10 years old, inspect it carefully, and often, and make plans for what you'll do when—and not if—problems develop.

The color of your hull and deck will help determine how hot your boat gets in the tropics. It's been said that there are only two colors to paint a boat—white and black—and that only a fool would paint their boat black. This isn't far from the truth in the tropics, where dark surfaces can heat up enough to soften both epoxy and the foam used in many cored

CHOOSING AND USING SEALANTS

Polyurethane sealants (such as 3M 5200 or Sikaflex) are the best choice for sealing just about anything more or less permanently. Use silicone or polysulfide (e.g., Life Calk or 3M 101) if removability is important. All of these sealants adhere to most materials fairly well, although oily woods (such as teak) will need to be treated with acetone or a similar solvent just prior to applying the sealant. Modern sealants are quite specialized products; check the manufacturer's recommendations if you're in doubt about the suitability of a sealant for a particular job, or about how to apply it. One common material that can be a challenge to seal properly is polycarbonate (e.g., Lexan). This is an excellent material for both ports and skylights, but most sealants will not adhere properly. Use a sealant especially formulated for polycarbonate (such as Sikaflex 295), and use the appropriate primer if the sealant will be exposed to UV.

decks and cabins; wood will dry out and may warp. Be kind to your boat and yourself and choose very light colors for both hull and deck; even cream or light gray can cause the deck to heat up dramatically compared to a true white.

KNOW YOUR BOAT

The best defense against problems, in the tropics or anywhere else, is to buy a well-designed and well-built boat to begin with, and then to make sure that the boat is well maintained. Catch problems when they first appear or, better yet, before they've developed, and you'll be well ahead. To this end, every boat owner should survey his or her own boat and carefully consider how and where trouble might develop. This needn't be done all at once and will take place to some degree just as you work on your boat. But often the most critical areas are those that are most difficult to reach, and so they don't get attention until a problem develops. Spend some time

in the bilge, under the cockpit, and peering at through-deck fasteners. Familiarize yourself with the basics of boat surveying (see the Boat Maintenance and Restoration section in appendix 3, Resources), and do your peering and prodding with a suspicious mind. If something looks amiss, it probably is. If there's wetness, discoloration, softness, movement, or corrosion, it's there for a reason. Figure out what's happening, and then take steps to fix it. Even if you choose to have your hunches checked out by a professional and to have someone else do the necessary work, you'll be much better off being involved in the process.

METALS IN THE TROPICS

Metal corrosion isn't unique to the tropics, but the warm temperatures and high humidity accelerate the

process. All boats are built using some metal fasteners and fittings, and usually metal is asked to do some of the really tough jobs onboard, such as handling heavy loads while being regularly or continuously immersed in salt water. If a metal fitting fails, be it the rudder post, a chainplate, or a seacock, the results are usually serious. For that reason all boat owners should make it their business to know something about how metals behave in tropical marine environments. We'll start by reviewing what happens when metal corrodes, and then move on to take a more detailed look at how specific metals behave and where they should and shouldn't be used.

Why Metals Corrode

Almost all metals used aboard boats are alloys: combinations of metallic elements such as iron, aluminum, tin, copper, chromium, and nickel. Alloys are used because in their pure (elemental) form most metals don't have quite the characteristics we need: they may not be sufficiently strong or corrosion resistant, or may be too costly. By combining different elements, metallurgists tailor the material's properties to better suit specific needs.

Producing a marine alloy is more difficult than simply combining two metallic elements, however, because the elements used in marine alloys are never found as the pure metal; they are always combined with other elements such as oxygen, sulfur, or carbon. In order for a pure metal (such as copper) to be produced, the metallic ore must be refined or smelted, removing the unwanted elements. This process takes lots of energy, and the resulting metals are in a high energy state. They constantly seek to escape that high energy state (and return to their original form) through reactions with oxygen, sulfur, and other substances in the surrounding environment. Corrosion is simply the term we use to describe those reactions. All common boatbuilding metals are considered reactive, which means they will readily combine with substances in the environment, and thus corrode.

Metals—and all other substances—are composed of atoms, which have a nucleus surrounded by a number of electrons; the latter are much like planets in orbit around the sun. As long as the electrons stay in their orbit around the nucleus, the metal will be in a stable condition, and won't corrode. Corrosion takes place when metals combine with other elements; in so doing, they lose electrons. Electrons don't simply drop out of orbit, but are wooed by positively charged particles in the surrounding environment (electrons themselves have a negative charge). When these positively charged particles (called *positive ions*) come calling they draw electrons away from the metal atoms. That leaves the original atom short of electrons (meaning it is now a positively charged particle). The positive metal ion that's left behind follows the electron's lead and jumps ship itself, and corrosion has begun.

Electrochemical Corrosion

The process we're describing is called *electrochemical corrosion*, as it involves both chemical and electrical reactions. Electrochemical corrosion is a fact of life with just about all metals, but they don't all corrode at the same rate. Metals that corrode slowly—such as silicon bronze and stainless steel—protect themselves from the relentless loss of electrons by forming a protective coating. This coating, called an *oxide film*, is a combination of an element within the metal (the positive metal ion we described above) and an oxygen ion from either the air or water. Metals that corrode quickly, such as mild steel and iron, also produce an oxide coating, but it's the brown, scaly stuff we call *rust*. With these metals, the oxide coating is permeable to both oxygen and water, so corrosion continues. Metals with more protective oxide films still corrode, but the process may take many decades rather than days or months.

In order for electrochemical corrosion to occur, metals must be in the presence of an electrolyte, a fluid that enables the transfer of ions between the metal and the corrosive agents, such as oxygen, salt, or acid. The most prevalent electrolyte for the tropical sailor is seawater, which contains an abundance of dissolved salts and thus is loaded with positive ions looking for an electron.

GALVANIC SERIES

Metals and Alloys Corrosion Potential (volts)

Least Noble (Anodic)	Voltage Range	
magnesium and magnesium alloys	-61	-1.63
zinc	-0.98	-1.03
aluminum alloys	-0.76	-1
cadmium	-0.7	-0.73
mild steel	-0.6	-0.71
wrought iron	-0.6	-0.71
cast iron	-0.6	-0.71
stainless steel, type 410 (active in still water)	-0.46	-0.58
stainless steel, type 304 (active in still water)	-0.46	-0.58
stainless steel, type 316 (active in still water)	-0.43	-0.54
aluminum bronze (92% Cu, 8% Al)	-0.31	-0.42
naval brass (60% Cu, 39% Zn)	-0.3	-0.4
yellow brass (65% Cu, 35% Zn)	-0.3	-0.4
red brass (85% Cu, 15% Zn)	-0.3	-0.4
muntz metal (60% Cu, 40% Zn)	-0.3	-0.4
tin	-0.31	-0.33
copper	-0.3	-0.57
solder (50% Pb, 50% Sn)	-0.28	-0.37
admiralty brass (71% Cu, 28% Zn, 1% Sn)	-0.28	-0.36
aluminum brass (76% Cu, 22% Zn, 2% Al)	-0.28	-0.36
manganese bronze (58.5% Cu, 39% Zn, 1% Sn, 11% Fe, 0.3% Mn)	-0.27	-0.34
silicon bronze (96% Cu max, 0.80% Fe, 1.50% Zn, 2.00% Si, 0.75% Mn, 1.60% Sn)	-0.26	-0.29
stainless steel, type 401 (passive)	-0.26	-0.35
copper nickel (90% Cu, 10% Ni)	-0.21	-0.28
75% Cu, 20% Ni, 5% Zn	-0.19	-0.25
lead	-0.19	-0.25
70% Cu, 30% Ni	-0.18	-0.23
nickel 200	-0.1	-0.2
stainless steel, type 304 (passive)	-0.05	-0.1
Monel (70% Ni, 30% Cu)	-0.04	-0.14
stainless steel, type 316 (passive)	0	-0.1
titanium	-0.05	0.06
platinum	0.19	0.25
graphite	0.2	0.3

Most Noble (Cathodic)

However, metals don't have to be immersed in water to corrode. All metals are affected to some degree by atmospheric corrosion. Atmospheric corrosion also relies on an electrolyte, but it's a very thin, almost imperceptible film of water that forms on metallic surfaces once a critical level of relative humidity is reached. Exactly what constitutes a critical level varies with the metal and the amount of atmospheric pollution. In the absence of pollution, atmospheric corrosion of iron begins when relative humidity reaches about 60 percent. If there are large amounts of salt or pollutants present, atmospheric corrosion can be more rapid and more severe.

Controlling corrosion in a single metal (whether in air or water) is primarily a matter of slowing or eliminating these reactions. This can be achieved with protective coatings (such as zinc or paint on steel), by alloying various elements to form a stronger natural oxide layer (combining iron and chromium in stainless steel), or by reducing contact with the agents that steal electrons (that's what we do when hosing the salt from metal fittings after a sail).

Galvanic Corrosion

Galvanic corrosion is a specific type of electrochemical corrosion that occurs primarily between two different metals. When immersed in seawater, every metal shows a different level of stability, or tendency to lose electrons and so corrode. This can be measured as an electrical current, which is just a flow of electrons. The galvanic series lists many common metals and alloys in order of their corrosion potential when immersed in seawater (see the accompanying table).

Generally speaking, the more "noble" a metal is (i.e., the lower in the table), the more slowly it will corrode. But more important from the perspective of galvanic corrosion, metals that are close together in the series will produce less of a reaction than those that are far apart. When galvanic corrosion occurs, the more noble metal corrodes at a slower rate than it normally would, while the metal that is less noble corrodes more rapidly.

Galvanic corrosion won't take place unless the two metals are in direct electrical contact (as they would be if they're bolted together), and are immersed in an electrolyte, such as seawater. Galvanic corrosion will attack metals that are very resistant to single-metal electrochemical corrosion. A piece of 6061 aluminum fastened with a bronze bolt will quickly corrode, although either metal would be considered corrosion resistant by itself.

It's possible to take advantage of galvanic corrosion to protect metals. That's what we do when we attach zincs, or sacrificial anodes, to the bottom of the hull or to the prop shaft during a haul-out. Zinc is a highly reactive metal, meaning it will corrode more readily than the other metals below it. Place the zinc in direct contact with the metal you want to protect (by bolting it to the prop shaft, for example), and the process of galvanic corrosion will take care of the rest: the zinc will corrode but in so doing will protect the prop shaft from corrosion.

Galvanic corrosion can take place in just one type of metal if there's a difference in the corrosion potential in two different places on a single fitting. Such differences can arise in various ways, including simply from imperfections in the metal itself. This is a common cause of problems with stainless steel. If one area of a fitting is protected by an oxide film it will be "passive," with a low corrosion potential (note passive stainless is one of the most noble metals). Another area of the same fitting that lacks an oxide coating will have a much higher corrosion potential (the metal here is "active," and among the least noble). Being part of the same fitting, the two areas are linked electrically; when immersed in salt water, the area that's passive will be protected, but at the expense of rapid corrosion of the active area.

Problems can also arise with some alloys if one of the constituents is attacked, but the other is not. This happens with brass, which is made from zinc and copper. When used underwater (such as on a rudder fitting or a fastener), the brass will "dezincify": the zinc corrodes out of the fitting, leaving behind the corrosion-resistant but much weaker copper.

STAINLESS STEEL

The term stainless steel is applied to many steel alloys, only a few of which are intended or suitable for marine use. In addition to iron, marine-grade stainless steel alloys include varying amounts of chromium and nickel, depending on the type. The chromium in marine-grade stainless steel reacts with oxygen to form an oxide film that is tough and protects the underlying metal from corrosion. If enough chromium is used (12% or more) then corrosion resistance will be quite good.

Problems with stainless steel arise primarily when the oxide film is either worn away or prevented from forming. This exposes the metal to any corrosive elements in the environment. Unfortunately for us, the chloride found in salt water is one of the worst around. What kind of corrosion takes place depends on the type of stainless and how it's used.

Types of Stainless Steels

In the United States, stainless steel is commonly graded according to an American Iron and Steel Institute (AISI) system whereby each type is given a number, and we'll use these designations in this book; other organizations and countries use different designations (see the Stainless Steel Alloy Equivalents table for equivalents). Common marine grades occur within the AISI 300 series. They can be distinguished from nonmarine grades because marine grades are not normally magnetic, although fittings made from 304 will often show a slight degree of magnetism. But it's very hard to tell if a fitting is made with 304 or 316, and the difference is important.

▶ **TYPE 302:** Also called 18-8 because it's made with 18 percent chromium and 8 percent nickel. Many fasteners are made from this alloy, but it's not suitable for marine use, except perhaps in the interior. It's often used for the manufacture of rigging wire.

▶ **TYPE 304:** The most common marine grade, and the minimum that should be used in the tropical marine environment. 304 is suitable for noncritical deck and interior fittings. It is also commonly used for rigging wire.

▶ **TYPE 316:** Contains 2 to 3 percent molybdenum for higher corrosion resistance than 304. It won't readily develop a rust film and is very resistant to pitting in salt air. It's the material of choice for any important stainless steel deck and rigging fittings.

▶ **TYPE 304-L AND 316-L:** Extra-low-carbon versions used for welded fabrications to prevent problems with "weld-decay" that can lead to sudden and catastrophic failure in welded fittings. 304-L and 316-L should be used for any welded parts, even if these are to be used below decks.

▶ **TYPE 318:** A "duplex" stainless steel, 318 has significantly better corrosion resistance and higher strength than 316. It's expensive and often difficult to obtain.

Types 316 and 316-L offer much better resistance to corrosion than 304 and 304-L and should be used in their place whenever possible. But even 316 is not suitable for use as a fastener in any situation where water may be present, but oxygen isn't readily available (see discussion below on crevice corrosion). Type 316 is sometimes used for seacocks in aluminum hulls, but they must be well insulated from the hull. Type 316 is also used for propeller shafts, but it must be protected with zinc anodes, and problems with pitting corrosion may still occur; Aquamet or similar alloys may be a better bet.

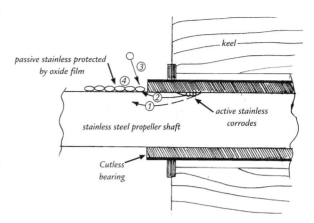

In this cross section of a stainless steel propeller shaft, the shaft that is exposed to seawater is "passive," while the shaft that's encased in the Cutless bearing is "active." Because of the lack of oxygen in the water within the Cutless bearing, the shaft there cannot form a protective oxide coating. Corrosion takes place, and a current is set up that flows from the active part of the shaft to the passive area (1). Metal ions are released as corrosion occurs (2), and these combine with oxygen available outside the bearing (3) to form a protective coating on the shaft (4). Because the active and passive areas are electrically connected, the corrosion in the active area is enhanced, while the metal in the passive area corrodes even more slowly than it otherwise would.

General Corrosion of Stainless

Widespread corrosion takes place when there's an overall breakdown of the passive film that usually forms. This causes the entire surface to have a sponge-like appearance. The rate of attack varies, but goes up dramatically as temperature increases. Some sources indicate a doubling in basic corrosion with an 18°F (10°C) rise in temperature of either the corrosive agent (in our case, seawater) or the metal part. This doesn't bode well for boats in the tropics and helps explain the high rate of corrosion often experienced with stainless steel exhaust manifolds. In general, though, fittings made from marine grades of stainless steel won't suffer from rapid general corrosion.

Pitting

Pitting takes place when the oxide film is broken only in a few places, instead of over the entire sur-

STAINLESS STEEL ALLOY EQUIVALENTS

AISI (American Iron and Steel Institute)	British Standard (new)	ISO (International Standards Organization)	UNS (Unified Numbering System)
302	302S25	G83/XIII Type 12	S30200
304	304S50	G83/XIII Type 11	S30400
304L	304S14	G83/XIII Type 10	S30403
316	316S16	G83/XIII Type 20	S31600
316L	316S24	G83/XIII Type 19	S31603

Equivalent designations for 318 have not yet been developed.

face, and is a simple example of galvanic corrosion. Because passive stainless is far more noble than active stainless, the areas without a protective film are attacked (functioning as a anode, in the same way that an underwater zinc does), while the rest of the material is protected. The area of protected (passive) stainless is much larger than the area of active (corroding) stainless, speeding the corrosion and causing the pits to grow. Pitting is common on poorly finished hardware, which may have impurities left on the surface that make for a less-than-perfect protective oxide film. It also takes place under O-rings and seals or in the way of stern bearings, because these can all act to wear away the protective film.

Tests show that 304 stainless steel is relatively unaffected by pitting corrosion in marine environments if temperatures are about 68°F (20°C) or below; 316 will be relatively immune up to about 86°F (30°C), while 318 shows good resistance up to 150°F (65°C). That indicates that 304 is really unsuited for use in tropical environments, and that even 316 is likely to experience some pitting.

Weld Decay

When a common marine stainless steel is welded, carbon moves out of the immediate area of the weld while the metal is molten, and combines with chrome in the adjoining areas to form chromium carbide. This in turn starves these areas of the chrome they need for corrosion protection. Put the welded part in or near seawater, and the result is galvanic action, with the chrome-rich areas protected, while the chrome-poor areas are attacked. There is normally no sign of trouble (perhaps only a bit of light brown staining), but weakness develops along the weld, which can lead to sudden failure. The best way to combat weld decay is by using a low-carbon stainless steel (such as 304L or 316L) for any welded fittings.

Crevice Corrosion

Crevice corrosion can take place whenever oxygen doesn't reach the surface of the stainless steel. It's especially common in the presence of salt water, because chlorides are ready and waiting to attack the surface of the stainless steel as soon as the protective layer is disturbed. Once that happens, pits form, and the lack of oxygen prevents a protective layer from reforming. Under the right (or rather, the wrong) conditions crevice corrosion can destroy metal very quickly, and it does so in places that can't be seen without taking fittings apart or removing fasteners. Examples of where crevice corrosion is likely to occur include wet wood (both above and below the waterline), wet fiberglass, and any underwater fittings, such as fastenings for seacocks, struts, and shaft logs.

Crevice corrosion in seawater starts at temperatures around 20–30°F (10–15°C) below those at which pitting occurs. That rules out the use of 304 below the water in all marine environments and makes 316 an unwise choice except in very cold waters. Type 318 should be free of problems below about 120°F (50°C).

Stress Corrosion

Stainless steel that's under tensile stress (which includes any fitting that's under tension, such as chainplates and rigging tangs) is especially susceptible to pitting and stress cracking. The biggest contributor to these types of stress-induced corrosion is again the presence of chloride.

Passivated and Polished Stainless

The passive, protective surface layer on stainless steel is never static (or permanent). The layer is affected by the environment and slowly erodes. That's not a problem if there's oxygen present allowing it to reform, but if there isn't, one of the various types of corrosion we've discussed will likely result. You may hear of companies offering "passivated" stainless, and that would seem a good solution, but unfortunately such coatings are likewise not permanent. Stainless is made passive by immersing it in an acid bath, which removes the oxide film and provides an ideal surface for a new layer to form; this happens as soon as the stainless steel is exposed to oxygen. Although it was once thought that the acid treatment acted to thicken the subsequent passive film (making the steel more corrosion resistant), it's now known it has little long-term effect, and that the film will form at the same thickness when exposed to the environment without being treated. The acid can act to remove small bits of iron and other impurities on the surface of the stainless steel, though, and the metal will certainly look better initially. Another technique that improves the appearance of stainless is polishing. In contrast to passiva-

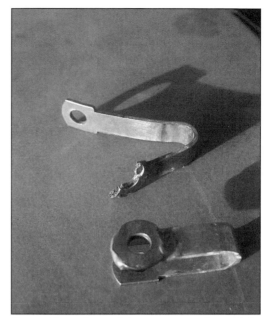

These stainless steel rigging fittings incorporate washers welded to the tang in an effort to increase the bearing surface. The result was weld decay; the fitting that broke was on the headstay and let go during a rough offshore passage to windward. If not for an inner forestay, we would have lost the rig.

tion, polishing can help reduce the chance of future corrosion; it eliminates roughness that might otherwise lead to pitting or crevice corrosion.

Preventing Problems with Stainless Steels

Duplex stainless steels such as 318 appear to be largely free of many corrosion problems that plague 304 and to a lesser degree 316. They are very expensive, however, and not easily distinguished except by the manufacturer; you're also unlikely to find any fittings made from duplex stainless, except possibly for propeller shafts. Practically speaking, you're limited to using 304 and 316 for most applications. With these alloys, the following rules apply:

▶ **DON'T USE STAINLESS STEEL IN ANY LOCATION WHERE** it will be constantly in contact with salt water, especially in areas where water is trapped or not moving (and may become oxygen starved). This means stainless steel shouldn't be used for underwater fastenings or fittings, exhaust manifolds, and structural items (such as frames, floors, and the like).

▶ *AVOID USING STAINLESS WHERE* it will be in contact with substances such as wood that might be saturated with salt water.

▶ *DON'T USE STAINLESS FOR HIGHLY STRESSED FITTINGS*, especially if these are often immersed (e.g., a bobstay fitting at the waterline).

▶ *USE STAINLESS STEEL FOR RIGGING FITTINGS*, rails and stanchions, winches, and shackles. Even then, be sure to buy 316, and keep a close eye on the fitting.

▶ *MAKE SURE THAT ANY STAINLESS FITTING IS WELL POLISHED*, as this may help prevent corrosion. There's no need for a mirror finish, but it should be smooth and even.

ALUMINUM

Aluminum alloys for use on boats are generally limited to the 5000 and 6000 series. The former contain aluminum and magnesium and are used for plating on aluminum hulls, whereas the latter add silicon as well and are used for extruded shapes (such as masts and other spars). Both types of alloys form a tough oxide film on the surface, which is light gray in color. Thanks to that film they're sufficiently corrosion resistant that they need not be painted, and aluminum boats with unpainted hulls and even decks are becoming increasingly common, while unpainted aluminum spars have been around for years. But much as with stainless steel, these aluminum alloys can suffer from several kinds of corrosion if the naturally occurring oxide film is broken or prevented from forming. They're also quite vulnerable to galvanic corrosion.

Pitting Corrosion

Pitting corrosion is the most common type of corrosion seen with aluminum and shows up frequently on spars. It first forms at a weak point in the oxide film, after which chemical reactions within the pit will increase the chloride concentration and sustain the reaction. It shows itself as a white or gray powdery deposit, which blotches the surface. Clean the deposit away, and small pits or holes will be seen.

Pitting in aluminum exposed to salt water can be fast at first—with the pits reaching a depth as much as $\frac{3}{64}$ inch (1 mm) in the first 2 years—but it typi-

cally slows after that, taking 20 years to reach $\frac{3}{32}$ inch (2 mm). Given that many masts are quite thin ($\frac{5}{32}$–$\frac{3}{16}$ inch/4–5 mm), pitting can be a very real and serious concern.

Stress Corrosion

The corrosion rate varies depending on the situation, but it can increase if the aluminum parts are under stress. Corrosion fatigue can be caused by a combination of stress and ongoing corrosion and can cause a metal part to fracture long before it "should," given the strength if corrosion wasn't present. The degree of visible, external corrosion isn't a good indicator of relative corrosion fatigue, and the only defense is to choose the right materials for any parts subject to alternating stresses.

Galvanic Corrosion

Aluminum is among the least noble marine metals, meaning it'll lose out to almost any other metal with which it's in contact. It must be electrically isolated from other metals, if the two are in the presence of an electrolyte. Failure to do this will result in the aluminum corroding, often at a very rapid rate.

Crevice Corrosion

Crevice corrosion takes place in narrow areas where pieces of aluminum are joined or where aluminum joins another material. Different mechanisms can work to start crevice corrosion in aluminum, but it generally progresses due to galvanic

A lifeline secured with a Nicopress fitting and a lashing.

STAINLESS STEEL RIGGING AND LIFELINES

The vast majority of cruising boats use 1 x 19 stainless steel wire for standing rigging, and we'll restrict our comments to this type of rigging. Of course it's also possible to use other materials, including galvanized or stainless wire of 7 x 7, 7 x 19, or 1 x 7 (Dyform) construction; see Boat Maintenance and Restoration in appendix 3, Resources, for sources that discuss rigging in detail.

Corrosion and wire fatigue are the primary problems with stainless steel rigging wire. Although inevitable, both can be delayed: corrosion can be slowed by using the best quality stainless wire you can buy, and by careful choice and installation of terminals. Keeping the rig properly tuned and ensuring that toggles are used on both ends of all shrouds and stays can reduce fatigue. Using good-quality wire is very important, as even small imperfections can lead to greatly accelerated corrosion. Quality control is uneven in wire manufacturing, and you should only purchase wire from reputable manufacturers. Finally, you can slow corrosion by buying a superior grade of stainless: 1 x 19 wire is available in both 304 and 316 grades; 316 is more corrosion resistant but is typically weaker for the same diameter. Make sure to check the breaking strength of any wire you use.

Rigging wire rarely fails in the middle of a shroud or stay but instead at (or even in) an end fitting such as a swage or other terminal. Swaged fittings are especially prone to crevice and stress corrosion, and our advice is not to use them. Compression fittings (such as Sta-Lok and Norseman) have a number of advantages:

▶ they can be taken apart at any time to check on the condition of the fitting and the wire

▶ they can be reused even if the wire requires replacing

▶ they're much less prone to crevice corrosion because they're filled with sealant when assembled

▶ they're easy to assemble, so you can do the work yourself, saving money and ensuring the job is done correctly

Standing rigging should be replaced immediately if there are any signs of pitting or broken strands. Even wire that's in good condition should be renewed every 5 to 6 years in the tropics, although this might be extended somewhat if the wire is 316.

If stainless steel is used for running rigging it should be 7 x 19 construction, which is more flexible than the 1 x 19 used for standing rigging. This wire is also suitable for lifelines. The latter should never be plastic coated, as this will encourage (and hide) corrosion. If your boat has plastic-coated lifelines, replace them with bare wire, and increase the size so that the outer diameter of the solid wire equals the outer diameter of the plastic-coated wire. They'll be stronger and will last longer. Ends should be fashioned with a thimble and Nicopress sleeve and a lashing used to secure and tension the lifeline. Replace running rigging and lifelines whenever you replace standing rigging.

An example of severe pitting that took place beneath a halyard winch.

The bubbling paint is a telltale sign that pitting corrosion is taking place around this cleat. The cleat is bronze but is isolated from the spar with rubber gaskets; the problem is likely to be the stainless steel machine bolts.

The stainless steel gooseneck fitting is isolated from the aluminum mast using a Tufnol spacer, and no corrosion is evident..

action once two areas on the same surface have become passive and active.

Preventing Corrosion

Because it will corrode whenever the oxide film is prevented from forming, aluminum should always be separated from other materials, even other pieces of aluminum. This can be done in various ways: by using an adhesive waterproof paint such as epoxy, with spacers and gaskets made of plastic or a nonconductive material, through application of a waterproof bedding compound, or with a protective agent such as a zinc chromate paste. (A zinc chromate paste marketed as Duralac is widely available

These bilge pumps have aluminum bodies, and galvanic corrosion around the small stainless bolts holding the check valves in place was so rapid that both ceased to function, despite having been serviced only a few months before.

in New Zealand, Australia, and the United Kingdom; check with your marine supplier to see if they can import this, or if a similar product is available in the United States.) The best protection will be achieved by using a combination of these techniques. Make sure that whatever you use doesn't create additional problems. For example, avoid using silicone caulk on aluminum unless it's "neutral cure," as acidic-cure silicone (which smells like vinegar) will produce corrosion.

Anodizing is a process whereby an especially tough oxide film is created on the surface of the metal. Anodized spars look good when new, and anodizing will slow pitting corrosion. However, it won't prevent pitting corrosion, and it's no defense against either crevice or galvanic corrosion.

COPPER ALLOYS: BRASSES AND BRONZES

Copper has been in use longer than any of the other metals typically used onboard—about 6,000 years. In its pure form copper is quite soft, but it has excellent resistance to corrosion and conducts electricity very well. True copper doesn't see much use, except in wiring and as wooden boat sheathing, but copper alloys constitute some of the best metals available for the marine environment.

Brass

Brasses are copper alloys that include zinc, with the percentage of the latter varying from about 10 to 40 percent. Brasses are the least useful of the copper alloys for marine applications because their zinc content makes them prone to general corrosion, and dezincification when immersed in seawater. Dezincification takes place when galvanic

ALUMINUM SPARS

Alloy spars require much less in the way of regular maintenance than do wooden ones (discussed below under Wooden Boats). Coatings are essentially optional: although most masts are either anodized or painted, they can be left bare with no harmful effects. Problems with aluminum masts crop up where they're welded, where fittings and hardware made from other materials are attached, and at cutouts or openings.

Aluminum and plastic (or other electrically and chemically inert) fittings can be mounted directly on a mast or boom using alloy rivets. Galvanic action won't be a problem, but it's advisable to apply some zinc chromate paste (such as Duralac) before installation. Apply it to the fitting if it's aluminum, and on the rivets in all cases, to forestall any problems with pitting corrosion.

Stainless and bronze fittings—including sail tracks—must be electrically isolated from the spar, or pitting and galvanic corrosion will result. They should be mounted using stainless machine screws or Monel rivets, as galvanic action between the fittings and fasteners will cause alloy rivets to corrode rapidly. Isolate the fittings using a durable plastic spacer, and liberally apply zinc chromate to the fasteners. These fittings should be removed and re-bedded every year or two in the tropics.

Aluminum masts are susceptible to cracking in the vicinity of any welds, and these are most common near spreader sockets. Check welds frequently for signs of cracking or corrosion. Cracks may also develop around any openings, such as exit points for internal halyards. All openings should have rounded (rather than square) corners. If internal halyards are fitted, ensure that there's a hole at the base that will allow the mast to drain, as a surprising amount of water will find its way in and can produce serious corrosion at the base of the mast.

Aluminum alloys used in making castings, such as spinnaker and whisker pole ends, are not as corrosion resistant as the marine-grade alloys used for the poles themselves. Serious galvanic corrosion between the pole and the casting can result and may cause the pole to split. The only solution is to disassemble the pole periodically and apply liberal amounts of zinc chromate or other anticorrosion compound.

This spinnaker pole is splitting around the stainless machine screw that holds the end fitting to the pole.

corrosion attacks a brass fitting; the zinc (the less noble metal) is eaten away, leaving just the soft copper. Brass is suitable for interior fittings but should not be used for any underwater fittings or fasteners. Much confusion results from the fact that some brasses are incorrectly called "bronzes"; these include commercial, manganese, and tobin bronze. If in doubt, check the composition, and avoid using any "bronze" that contains zinc below the waterline.

Bronze

True bronzes are alloys that include varying amounts of silicon, aluminum, and tin. Common types include silicon bronze, aluminum bronze, and phosphor bronze. Bronzes are protected by a very tough oxide film, which gives them their characteristic green color when exposed to seawater or marine air. Although they do corrode, they do so very slowly and uniformly, and they're not subject to problems such as pitting, crevice, weld, or stress corrosion. Silicon bronze can be easily welded, with no loss in strength, meaning that it can be used to fabricate a wide range of fittings that are more commonly made of stainless. An increase in temperature (within the range found in the tropics) causes the oxide film on bronze to form more quickly, but it doesn't otherwise enhance the corrosion rate.

Bronzes are the metals of choice for use underwater, except on aluminum boats, where they can cause serious galvanic corrosion. Otherwise, use bronze for through-hull fittings, hardware, fasteners, propellers and shafts. Silicon bronze is a good all-around choice for most applications.

FIBERGLASS BOATS

The biggest problem facing fiberglass boat owners heading for the tropics is blistering (also commonly called osmosis, or "boat pox"). High water and air temperatures make blistering more likely to occur than in cooler climes, and it's common to hear accounts of boats that had been blister-free for years in temperate waters but developed a bad case after a season or two in tropical latitudes. To understand why this is so, let's first review how and why boats develop blisters.

Permeable Gelcoat

Polyester gelcoat isn't impervious to water but acts like a semipermeable membrane. In a perfect hull this water might find itself with nowhere to go, but to a water molecule no hull is perfect. Even the best layup will have tiny cavities, caused either by the bundled structure of fiberglass roving or by small air bubbles trapped within the laminate during the molding process. These cavities often contain small amounts of unreacted resin curing agents and the water-soluble binding material used to hold glass fibers together in mat form. Water molecules passing through the gelcoat can form droplets within the cavities, and these droplets combine with and dissolve whatever material is there, creating a concentrated, acidic solution. Once such a solution is present, the stage is set for both blistering and osmosis to begin.

Osmosis simply refers to a fluid of lower density (in this case seawater) being drawn through a porous membrane (the gelcoat) into a fluid of higher density (the liquid in the voids). Osmosis is not the cause of blistering but simply acts to draw water through the gelcoat at a faster rate than would otherwise be the case.

Blistering

Osmosis helps to increase the pressure within fluid-filled voids in the boat's hull. If there's enough pressure, a blister will form. What happens next depends on many factors. In the worst case the blister might crack the gelcoat, but it's more common for pressure to equalize, with the blister stabilizing. It's even possible for the blister to drain if the boat is hauled.

Blisters are typically round, from $\frac{1}{16}$ inch (1.5 mm) to several inches (50 mm) in diameter. Although they can appear anywhere—within laminates, between laminates and the gelcoat, and even between gelcoat layers—the most common site is in, or just under, the gelcoat. Gelcoat blisters are usually small (less than $\frac{1}{4}$ inch/6 mm in diameter), and appear as a rash. While they alone have little impact on the boat's structure, they can hasten the onset of a truly serious case of boat pox.

Blister formation can also be caused and enhanced by wicking. This usually occurs in hulls laid up with chopped strand mat. Even if mat is not a major element in the layup, many hulls include a layer of mat just below the gelcoat, to prevent "print-through" of the underlying roving to the topsides. Moisture permeates the gelcoat, but instead of collecting in a void it's drawn down the length of individual glass fibers in the mat as a result of capillary action. This causes elongated, random blisters or ridges to form on the surface, often mimicking the appearance of chopped strand mat. If left untreated this can cause serious delamination, weakening the hull to a depth of $\frac{1}{4}$ inch (6 mm) or even $\frac{1}{2}$ inch (12 mm).

Blisters don't often form in the structural laminates because the heavy fibers these incorporate are generally too strong; gelcoats and barrier coats

These silicon bronze rudder fittings (fastened with bronze bolts) will likely last for the life of the boat. The bottom is sheathed with copper for worm protection.

aren't fiber reinforced and are far more prone to surface deformation.

Who's at Risk?

By now you'll be asking which hulls are susceptible to blistering. No polyester gelcoat is 100 percent waterproof, meaning that all that's needed is for the underlying glass fibers to be imperfectly wetted out (leaving behind voids), or for small cavities to be present. Unfortunately this puts most boats at risk: experienced surveyors have suggested that 50 percent or more of older boats (10 years of age and older) show signs of blistering. The risk is probably greatest for boats built between about 1970 and sometime in the mid-1990s.

Now the really bad news: warm water enhances the rate of water penetration through gelcoat, dou-bling it for every 18°F (10°C) increase. Warm conditions also accelerate any chemical reaction that may be taking place. If your home waters average 50°F (10°C), but you're headed for the tropics, where water temperatures often climb to 85°F (30°C) or more, the rate of water penetration may well be four times as rapid. This explains why so many boats develop blisters after sailing to the tropics.

There are some builders with a terrible history of blistered hulls, and others that have almost never experienced a problem. That's because although every boat is theoretically susceptible to blisters, the use of good materials and workmanship will make it less likely for blisters to develop. Many of these qualities are hard to judge after the boat is built, but here are some of the factors that make a boat less likely to develop blisters:

- ► use of high-quality resins

- ► proper, complete wetting out of all laminates and a suitable glass/resin ratio

- ► construction techniques that ensure a chemical (and not simply mechanical) bond was achieved between all layers of the laminate

If you're buying a new or used fiberglass boat, do some serious checking on the reputation of the builders, the materials used in construction, and any history of blister problems with other boats of the same class. Try to get information on boats built at about the same time, because building practices often change over time, and this may influence the likelihood of blister development. A marine surveyor experienced in surveying cruising sailboats will often have this kind of information.

Guarding against Blisters

The best strategy for avoiding blisters is to protect your hull while it's still blister-free. Both new and older boats can benefit from protective coatings. The simplest is a solvent-free epoxy resin paint. To supply good protection the coating should be $^{20}/_{1,000}$ to $^{25}/_{1,000}$ inch thick (0.65 mm), or about the thickness of most gelcoats. This means three coats of

BOAT GEAR: RIGGING FITTINGS AND DECK GEAR

Turnbuckles are frequently doused with salt water from waves and are susceptible to stress, crevice, and pitting corrosion if made from stainless steel. This is especially true of closed-body turnbuckles used in the tropics, as they're impossible to flush with freshwater and are perfect sites for corrosion. All-stainless turnbuckles are also prone to thread damage if not adequately lubricated, which can weaken the turnbuckle. All of these problems can be avoided by using open-body silicon bronze turnbuckles; at the very least ensure that the turnbuckle bodies are bronze. All turnbuckles should be checked for wear and regreased annually.

Chainplates on steel and aluminum boats usually form an integral part of the boat's structure and rarely develop problems. On wood and fiberglass boats they're typically mounted on the outside of the hull, or somewhat inboard, piercing the deck or cabintop. In either case they'll be metal (usually stainless steel or bronze) and fastened with bolts. Bronze chainplates shouldn't suffer from corrosion, but chainplates made from stainless steel are prone to both stress and crevice corrosion.

Outboard mounted chainplates of stainless will develop problems where they're bedded against the hull and where they're pierced by bolts; the bolts that secure them to the hull are also very susceptible to crevice corrosion if made from stainless. Sealing inboard mounted chainplates completely against leaks is very difficult, and there's usually corrosion where chainplates come through the deck. With both types, problems are likely to be hidden from view and will be found only by completely removing the chainplate and pulling all the bolts. Even if they look to be in good condition, stainless steel chainplates should be replaced every 10 years or so in the tropics. Use silicon bronze chainplates and bolts whenever possible if replacing these fittings, as the bronze ones will last for the life of the boat.

Mast tangs are typically made of stainless and are subject to weld decay and to stress corrosion at any bends. Carefully inspect these fittings for cracks, and replace them immediately if any are found. Problems can be avoided if bronze is used to fashion replacements, but you should be very careful to isolate these completely from an aluminum mast.

Blocks are often made with a combination of aluminum and stainless steel parts, and these will corrode after a number seasons in the tropics. There's little to be done, except rinse them frequently with freshwater, disassemble them if possible and apply zinc chromate paste, or replace them, preferably with blocks made from a single type of metal.

Winches, roller-furling gears, and windlasses are all susceptible to much more severe corrosion when cruising in the tropics than will be experienced during occasional weekend use. Don't believe any manufacturer that claims a unit is equipped with sealed bearings that will deliver a "lifetime" of service. We've seen examples of serious corrosion problems with all of these types of equipment; all were produced by major, reputable manufacturers. If you're thinking about purchasing equipment, keep the principles of metal corrosion in mind, and try to buy gear that has the least potential for corrosion, especially for galvanic action. For example, "old-fashioned" anchor windlasses made of bronze (with perhaps some stainless gear shafts) are far less likely to develop trouble than models that combine aluminum and stainless. The same holds true for winches: don't buy winches with alloy drums, although they're cheaper and lighter; look instead for models with bronze or type 316 stainless drums and gears.

There's no magic formula for maintaining equipment, other than to strip it down frequently and to always use good-quality lubricants.

Open-body bronze turnbuckles are the least likely type to give trouble in the tropics; here cotter pins are covered by rigging tape.

about $8/1,000$ inch (0.21 mm) each are required. Solvent-free paints are suggested, as solvent paints lose half their thickness in drying.

If you're buying a new boat, consider one built using epoxy resins, which form a better water barrier than do polyester; using them throughout the construction is perhaps the best blister insurance. There are also differences among polyester resins, and use of isophthalic resins in place of orthophthalic resins is recommended. The use of these products should extend to laminating resins as well as gelcoat. Care should also be taken to use chopped strand mat with a polyester powder binder instead of a polyvinyl-acetate emulsion binder.

Treating Blisters

If your boat already has blisters, then some sort of treatment is advisable, especially if you plan on spending considerable time in warm, tropical waters, which will only worsen a case of boat pox. Detecting blisters can be difficult, especially on older boats with a few seasons worth of bottom paint buildup. To check for blisters, carefully remove some small areas of antifouling (patches of 2 by 2 in./50 by 50 mm). Blisters may show up only as wet patches in these areas, or you may see actual raised blisters. If blisters appear to be present, remove the rest of the bottom paint and do a complete survey of the boat's bottom.

If blisters are less than ¼ inch (6 mm) in diameter, then chances are they're confined to the gelcoat. If they aren't too extensive, the best remedy may be to open and drain each one individually and to fill them with epoxy filler once they've dried. If blisters are widespread, then individual treatment is no longer practical. At this point the gelcoat, and perhaps even the adjacent layer of mat, should be removed below the waterline. With extensive deep blisters it's a good idea to steam clean the hull to fully remove acids and contaminants. Serious blister problems are not simply treated, and you'd do well to hire (or at least consult) a professional.

Even if you're simply treating blisters individually, drying the hull is a vital process that can take many weeks, depending on the temperature and humidity. Dehumidifiers and heaters can help, and good interior ventilation is also important. Make sure the bilge is dry, and get the boat as dry as you can make it. Professionals with moisture meters can help here, but the bottom line is the drier, the better. While the hull is dry, take the opportunity to clean the bilge and then paint any sections that come into contact with bilge water using epoxy paint. Water in the interior of a hull can cause blistering just as surely as water on the outside; the only difference is that it'll take longer. Boats that are poorly ventilated and kept in warm climates are especially at risk.

WOODEN BOATS

Wooden boats are constructed in many different ways. Traditionally built boats typically rely on metal fasteners to hold them together and on oil-based coatings to protect the wood. These will usually have the highest maintenance requirements. At the other extreme are wood-epoxy craft, which may in essence be fiber-reinforced epoxy boats with wood cores. Their maintenance requirements will be among the lowest of all boats, including fiberglass and aluminum craft. Our comments here are directed toward the traditional end of the spectrum.

Owners of traditional wooden boats traveling to the tropics should get ready for an increase in all basic maintenance. Wood will tend to move more than in a stable temperate climate, while bedding compounds won't stand up as well in the heat and humidity, resulting in the opening of plank seams and other joints that may have formerly been tight. Paint and varnish won't hold up as well, calling for more frequent renewal. Tropical conditions are also perfect for the development of rot, the scourge of all wooden boats. None of this means that wooden boats aren't suited for tropical cruising. Our own boat is built of wood and has spent the better part of 37 years in the tropics. What's required is some fore-

Replacing soft planks in Nomad's *bow. One advantage of wooden boats is that the tools and techniques used in repair are usually simple and familiar.*

thought and preparation and a willingness to stay ahead of the inevitable upkeep.

Regular maintenance using good-quality materials is the only way of ensuring a wooden boat survives. All protective coatings such as paint and varnish will break down faster, so be prepared to renew them more frequently. We use simple polyurethane enamel paint on the topsides and a good-quality marine varnish with a high level of UV inhibitors on the brightwork. We repaint the topsides once a year and apply a couple of coats of varnish every three months or so. Polyurethane enamels on fiberglass surfaces such as the deck lasts two to three years. Bottom paint on any wooden boat in the tropics should be renewed about once a year. If bottom paint flakes or chips off between haul-outs, it's possible to cover the bare timber with a small piece of copper sheathing. We've also had good success

with underwater epoxy putty, but adhesion of epoxy to wet timber is not always good.

Longer-lasting coatings, such as two-part polyurethanes, can be used on some wooden boats. They resist chalking and peeling better than one-part polyurethane enamels and in theory will have a much longer life. They're less flexible, though, and so will tend to crack if there is significant movement in plank seams or other joints. For that reason we suggest using two-part paints only on very stable surfaces, such as glued masts and sheathed plywood decks, and on hulls that have been built using epoxy. For traditional carvel-planked boats even the single-part polyurethane enamel we use on our strip-planked hull can prove too inflexible. We've met very experienced professional boat painters who opted for top-quality enamel house paint for traditionally built boats. They chose such paint not for the price, but because the house paint contains more oils and, as a result, is more flexible and easier to apply than polyurethane paint.

If you slip up on regular maintenance, the initial result will be chipped and peeling paint, and then weathered and possibly degraded wood. How quickly timber degrades varies widely. Some woods (such as teak) can be left completely bare without damage, whereas others (such as spruce) will quickly deteriorate. The timber used in the construction of your boat will determine the penalty you'll pay for less than perfect maintenance. A fine boat can be built completely of softwoods (such as Douglas fir), but it won't withstand the neglect that a vessel built of teak can sustain.

Types of Wood

How well wood holds up depends on a number of factors. The species of wood determines the basic rot resistance and how much oil is naturally present. Both are important (but so is the quality of an individual piece of timber). Species that hold up best include many tropical timbers (such as teak), most cedars, and a number of eucalyptus species. Woods that fare the worst include spruce, pine, and ash.

Owners of wooden boats face a dilemma when buying wood to repair their boats. The best woods are becoming increasingly scarce (and expensive), because the rate at which they've been logged has vastly outstripped the rate at which they're planted or regenerate naturally. What's more, logging is often carried out in a way that has disastrous environmental consequences. It's possible to buy plantation-grown timber—much of the standard construction-grade softwood in the United States is grown on plantations—but the quality is a far cry from what's needed for boats, especially boats that spend a lot of time in the tropics. Although there is no ideal solution, there are a few alternatives to contributing to yet more clear-cutting of old-growth forests, in either temperate or tropical areas:

▶ *USE RECYCLED WOOD*, which may be salvaged from demolished houses, factories, or even boats. The quality is often better (and the price

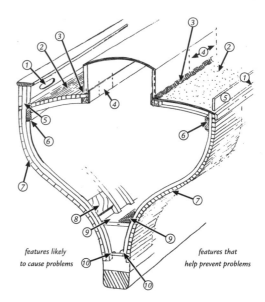

Features likely to cause problems in tropical climates compared with those more likely to be trouble free. (Keyed to table opposite.)

features likely to cause problems

features that help prevent problems

lower) than what you pay for new timber, as the use of beautiful vertical grain wood for all construction was common 50 and more years ago. You can begin by saving every scrap of sound wood you might remove from your boat in the course of even small interior remodeling jobs.

▶ *BUY "CERTIFIED" WOOD PRODUCTS.* A complex system for certification of sustainably produced woods has been developed, overseen by the Forest Stewardship Council, an international organization that includes environmental and industry groups. They can provide you with local sources for certified wood products. Fortunately, an increasing number of suppliers in the U.S. are offering certified products.

Wood Decay

If you neglect maintenance long enough, the result will likely be rot, which is the problem most feared by wooden boat owners; the very word is defined as decay. Rot can afflict newly built boats as well as

FEATURES LIKELY TO CAUSE OR PREVENT PROBLEMS
IN WOODEN BOATS IN THE TROPICS
(NUMBERS KEYED TO ILLUSTRATION)

No.	Feature	Trouble Prone	Trouble Free
1	scuppers	small, raised scuppers trap water on deck	raised bulwark provides drainage along entire length
2	decks	laid decks prone to leaking	plywood decks sheathed with epoxy and cloth don't leak
3	deck-cabin joint	caulked joint without sill opens and leaks as wood flexes or shrinks	joint sealed with fiberglass tape and epoxy doesn't open
4	trunk cabin fasteners	screws into cabin side are weak, don't prevent plank cabin sides from splitting	bolts through cabin side create a strong joint and help prevent splitting
5	bulwark stanchions	bulwarks supported by frame ends or separate wood stanchions are hard to seal and apt to rot	plank bulwarks can use metal bulwark brackets that bolt through the deck
6	clamp position	clamp fitted tight against underside of deck traps air behind it	clamp fitted below deck beams allows air to circulate
7	planking	carvel planking is very dependent on frame strength and is prone to drying and leaking	strip planking is stronger with the same framing, moves and leaks less
8	longitudinals	butt block tight to frame traps water on upper side	clearance should be left between butt block and frame
9	bilge ventilation	cabin sole fit tightly to frames prevents ventilation	grating provides good ventilation
10	limbers	small limbers in frames or floors clog easily, prevent drainage, and promote rot	large limbers stay clear

old and is caused by fungi that feed on the cellulose in cured lumber. Rot won't take hold in dry timber, and because it needs oxygen to survive, it is typically absent from water-saturated timbers as well. Salt inhibits the growth of these fungi to some degree, which is why rot occurs less often in wood below the waterline than it does in decks and cabin structures. The ideal environment for rot is one with warm temperatures, some freshwater, and poor ventilation. These are precisely the conditions that can be found in the tropics aboard a poorly ventilated wooden boat with leaky decks.

Keeping a boat free of rot isn't hard, at least in concept: eliminate deck leaks; provide good drainage (via limber holes in the bilge) to avoid standing water from any leaks that might develop despite your efforts; and make sure below-decks ventilation is good. If you're successful, you shouldn't have any trouble. What you should do if rot gets a foothold is more complicated and depends in many respects on how the boat is built. The best approach is to keep rot from occurring in the first place.

Deck Leaks

The ideal deck from the standpoint of leaks would be a one-piece structure with no joints or openings. Not very practical, but the closer you can come to this the better. Unfortunately, unless you're building a new boat or completely refitting an older one, you'll have to cope with whatever your boat has in the way of deck seams and hardware. But keep this in mind as you work on your boat; every hard-to-seal deck opening you eliminate will reduce the chances of rot.

Regrettably (because they do look great), laid decks are much harder to keep tight than a deck made of plywood covered by epoxy and synthetic cloth. If your boat has laid decks, they should be kept properly caulked and should be wetted down every morning and evening with salt water, which will help keep the wood from drying out. Awnings will also help in this regard. The latter are absolutely critical if you leave a boat with caulked decks unattended for any length of time in the tropics, as then you won't be able to keep the wood swollen with daily dousings. Unless it's bedded in epoxy, thin teak laid over plywood is a construction that invites rot.

Deck hardware that's bolted through the deck is the simplest type to seal. Small pad eyes and similar fittings will stay free of leaks for years, if a good grade of caulk is used. Deck hardware subjected to higher loads will be much harder to keep from leaking. Lifeline stanchions are a particular problem because of the stanchion's long lever arm. Apply a moderate amount of force at the top of the stanchion—as you do when grabbing the lifelines to board the boat—and a very high force is placed on the base. We've found we need to re-bed these every few years.

Vertical wooden or metal members that pierce the deck are notorious trouble spots, especially if they are ever subject to significant side loads. The latter include vertical inboard chainplates, frame ends that pierce the deck and serve as bulwark stanchions, or separate wooden stanchions that do the same and are bolted to the frames below decks. These are all potential trouble spots, and should be checked very carefully for leaks. There is no magic solution to curing such leaks other than to make sure there is no rot, to dry and degrease the wood completely before sealing it, and to use an appropriate sealant.

The deck-to-cabin joint is another common source of trouble. If your boat has laid decks, then this joint must be caulked with a flexible compound. If decks are plywood, however, this joint can often be made leak-proof by sealing it with several layers of fiberglass cloth tape set in epoxy resin. For such a fix to work, there must be no movement between cabin and deck and good adhesion between the fiberglass tape and both the cabin and deck.

Drainage

Despite your best efforts, some water is likely to find its way below, and it should have a clear and easy path to the low point of the bilge. You'll know if water is collecting somewhere within the boat (other than in the bilge); if it is, don't just fix the leak, but improve the drainage so that water won't sit in puddles. This involves ensuring that all limber holes in frames and floors stay clear, and that water doesn't collect against longitudinal members such as stringers or butt blocks. Keeping the bilge of the boat clean can also help in promoting good drainage and preventing rot.

Ventilation

We've said it already, but with wooden boats it's so vital we'll repeat ourselves: if you're going to win the battle against rot, you must have good ventilation. Consider how air will circulate even when the boat is closed and unattended; pay particular atten-

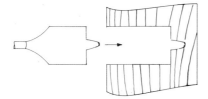

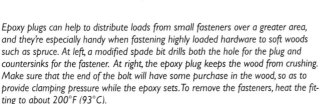

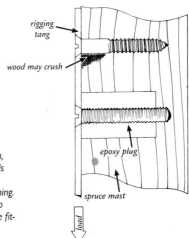

rigging tang

wood may crush

epoxy plug

spruce mast

load

Epoxy plugs can help to distribute loads from small fasteners over a greater area, and they're especially handy when fastening highly loaded hardware to soft woods such as spruce. At left, a modified spade bit drills both the hole for the plug and countersinks for the fastener. At right, the epoxy plug keeps the wood from crushing. Make sure that the end of the bolt will have some purchase in the wood, so as to provide clamping pressure while the epoxy sets. To remove the fasteners, heat the fitting to about 200°F (93°C).

tion to the ends of the vessel, as the small enclosed spaces of forepeak and lazarette are ideal breeding places for rot. A cowl or mushroom vent fitted forward and aft, in addition to several Dorade vents amidships, will help to keep air circulating, but only if it can find a clear path. Ventilating the bilge is especially important; do not fit a tight cabin sole right across the hull without providing some other means of air circulation.

Wooden Spars

Wooden spars are rarely fitted aboard new boats these days but are still found on many older ones. They're perfectly suitable for extending voyaging, but they'll take a beating in the tropical environment. Wooden spars have a reputation for developing rot, in part because they're usually made from a rot-prone softwood, such as spruce. Most are also hollow, and the interior of a mast or boom is a perfect site for rot to develop undetected. It's important to stay ahead of the inevitable maintenance in order to prevent problems.

Wooden spars can be painted or varnished, and there are good arguments for both. Masts are constantly exposed to the sun, and even a good grade of UV-resistant varnish will have to be replenished with an additional couple of coats every three to four

months. Paint will survive much longer, and it should be possible to get several years from a good two-part polyurethane. But paint hides any problems that do develop, which would otherwise be immediately visible beneath the varnish. Other options include coating a mast with epoxy prior to painting or varnishing, and using a clear two-part polyurethane. Whatever coating system you use, it should be kept in good condition if it's to prevent water damage and rot.

All fasteners and hardware that are mounted on the mast must be properly bedded to keep water out. Highly loaded fasteners may crush the relatively soft wood fibers. If this happens, either use additional fasteners, or set them in epoxy plugs, which will serve to distribute the loads and prevent crushing.

Carefully and frequently check all areas where water may find a way in. This includes around sheaves and other openings in the mast and at spreader sockets and ends. Also keep a close eye on the mast heel and on the condition of the mast where it passes through the deck or cabintop, if keel stepped.

Wooden bowsprits are also common sources of problems. Bowsprits should never be mounted flat on deck, as this is asking for rot to develop between the sprit and the deck. If yours is mounted in this way, remove and inspect it, and then remount it so it clears the deck by at least an inch. Bowsprits also develop trouble under hardware and where they pass through bulwarks. Inspect them often, and re-bed hardware at least every few years.

METAL BOATS

There are many corrosion-related issues that metal boat owners should be aware of, and a comprehensive discussion of these is beyond the scope of this book. Instead we'll review those areas that should be given extra attention, as these are where accelerated corrosion rates are most likely to give problems.

Areas especially prone to corrosion include any that are chronically wet or have standing water. In the interior this may be around the stuffing box or shaft seal, in a bilge sump, and on the lower ends of floor or frames if there is ever water in the bilge. On deck, water tends to be trapped under any wood trim or decking, even if it's been bedded with sealant. Problems also develop adjacent to drains or scuppers if these do not drain away moisture completely and at the junction between deck or cabintop and vertical members such as coamings, bulwarks, and deck boxes. Finally, on steel boats corrosion is inevitable anywhere that chafe occurs. The deck or rail adjacent to cleats, anchor chain, and the like are common problem areas.

Although this aluminum boat is only a few years old, all the hardware and fittings had to be removed and re-bedded, and painted areas sanded, re-primed, and repainted, all because proper care had not been taken when it was originally fitted out.

How these problems are best dealt with depends in part on the specific boat, but in general steel boats will require careful attention to the condition of the paint and other protective coatings, and owners of aluminum boats will have to be very careful to isolate aluminum from other metals. Serious recurring problems—such as might be caused by a wooden deck that isn't bedded properly—may be difficult to solve with either type of material and are likely to require a major refit.

Coating systems are critical on steel boats, as these are relied upon to provide a protective film to stop rusting. New systems are constantly being developed, but at this point flame-sprayed zinc and epoxies seem to do the best job. The tropics provide a good test of the effectiveness of any coating system, and in many cases the most serious problems develop on the interior of a boat rather than on the exterior. That's because surface preparation is the key to getting any coating to adhere properly, and grit blasting is the only truly effective way to prepare the surface of steel. The exterior of a steel hull can be grit blasted at any time, if old paint and rust need to be removed, but it's impossible to do on the interior, unless the boat has been specially built with all interior joinerwork removable. If that hasn't been done, any measures taken to stop rusting on the interior will be less than ideal. That's why steel boats are said to rust from the inside out.

Marine aluminum alloys needn't be painted, but freedom from painting doesn't equal freedom from corrosion; the key to the latter lies in isolating the aluminum from other materials and in eliminating sites where pitting and crevice corrosion can get started.

Although galvanic corrosion below the waterline is unlikely to accelerate dramatically in the tropics, it's such a menace to metal hulls that it deserves mention. Zincs should always be used on metal boats, and naturally these should never be painted.

PART 4

CRUISING LIGHTLY

Chapter 15

Green Cruising

Imagine arriving in a picturesque, remote tropical anchorage only to find the beach littered with plastic. We've had that happen all too often, and almost always the trash wasn't deposited by the area's few inhabitants, but instead resulted from years of ocean dumping by ships and boats. It's equally disturbing to contemplate a morning swim in the anchorage's calm waters, only to decide against it because of the raw sewage being pumped out by the other boats at anchor.

On a global scale the dumping of oil, garbage, and other waste is increasingly being addressed by treaties, laws, and regulations that specify what can and can't be released into the ocean. There's not a lot we can do about pollution from ships except support such efforts at regulation. It's possible, however, to do something about the waste we generate ourselves, and we feel that blue-water sailors should go the extra mile, not merely doing what may be required by law in any particular place. As cruisers, we need to develop a "green code" by which to sail, one that truly minimizes the impact on the waters in which we sail and the places we visit. This isn't an easy task—and we're far from perfect aboard *Nomad*—but it's something we should all strive toward if we want others to also be able to enjoy the places we're fortunate enough to have visited.

GARBAGE

What constitutes garbage depends on your perspective, but in this context we're referring to anything you throw away. Historically, mariners have simply heaved their garbage over the side. For some types of garbage, that is still acceptable—readily biodegradable food scraps can be chucked overboard when you're out at sea. But some types of garbage, especially plastics, should never be thrown overboard.

Legal Considerations

Through international agreement (see The International Legal Framework, below), the dumping of plastics is prohibited *anywhere* in the ocean, and the disposal of other types of garbage is restricted. U.S. law on the issue is perhaps typical, dictating that all plastics shall remain aboard for disposal ashore, but allowing for the disposal of some types of garbage in offshore waters, depending on the distance from shore and how finely the garbage is ground up. All garbage, including food scraps, must remain on board when sailing on lakes, rivers, bays, and sounds and within 3 nautical miles of the shore. The apple core you chucked over the side when sailing in the bay last weekend should've stayed on board!

Although having an international treaty addressing the disposal of garbage at sea—and rigorous national legislation to enforce it—certainly helps, anyone who has cruised either coastal waters or offshore will be aware that the problem has not been solved. To get a handle on how much garbage is out there, and what sort of impact it's having, let's look at what is easily the worst type: plastic.

The Impact of Plastic Garbage

Plastics are lightweight, strong, extremely durable, and long-lasting. These characteristics, which make plastics so useful, also make them an environmental nightmare. Plastics can be carried for many hundreds and even thousands of miles by ocean currents and winds. Sadly, no place, no matter how remote, appears to be free of plastic trash and debris. We've seen piles of plastic trash and other garbage on far-flung, uninhabited Pacific atolls. Plastics are a primary component of beach litter even in the remote Aleutian Islands and along the shorelines of Antarctica. And studies over the last 20 years have shown that an overwhelming majority of trash floating in the oceans is composed of plastic.

The problem is not merely aesthetic. Since the early 1980s, some 50,000 North Pacific fur seals have died due to entanglement with plastic, and sea lion and monk seal populations have also been affected. Sea turtles, dugongs, seabirds, and fish are all susceptible to entanglement in plastic debris and face a host of problems from ingesting small pieces and fragments of plastic. Plastic particles are often eaten inadvertently by seabirds.

Plastic does degrade slowly, as anyone who has carried plastic fuel or water jugs on deck will know. But it can take many years. Polystyrene cups and pellets (used as packing material) have a projected lifespan of 500 years; until recently, six-pack rings were made from plastics that didn't biodegrade for some 450 years. Now, some are made from photodegradable materials, although many still are not.

Human demand for plastic products is huge, running into the many billions of pounds in the United States alone. Much of it is not disposed of properly: more than 100 million pounds (45 million kg) of garbage (much of it consisting of plastic) is tossed into U.S. coastal waters by boaters and fishermen each year. In the late 1980s, some 450,000 plastic containers were dumped into the ocean *every day* by the world's fleet of merchant vessels, and most of those items are still floating around.

Given that plastic should never be disposed of at sea, and that it's unlikely to be recycled at most cruising destinations, it may be worthwhile asking if it belongs onboard at all. Our answer is, not if it's designed

---

THE INTERNATIONAL LEGAL FRAMEWORK

The International Convention for the Prevention of Pollution from Ships (also known as the MARPOL Protocol) was negotiated among the international community in 1973 and 1978, and today the International Maritime Organization (an agency of the United Nations) is responsible for MARPOL's enforcement. MARPOL includes five annexes that deal with different types of waste. Annexes 1 and 2 (dealing with pollution from oil and bulk liquids) are mandatory and must be enforced by MARPOL signatories, whereas annexes 3 (packaged hazardous materials), 4 (sewage), and 5 (garbage) are optional. The United States is a signatory to annexes 3 and 5.

Unfortunately, the ideal of effective international regulation of high seas pollution can get bogged down by the reality of life on small islands. For instance, the Wider Caribbean Region was designated as a "special area" under the provisions of annex 5 of MARPOL. This means that ships of any size are prohibited from discharging any waste material (except food waste, which in the Wider Caribbean may be discharged when ships are more than 3 miles from land). However, in order for the special area designation to become effective, facilities to receive wastes must be established in the ports of the region—and this has not yet happened in much of the Caribbean. Thus, many small Caribbean nations are ineligible to sign the MARPOL Treaty, and as a result there are no special rules protecting Caribbean waters.

The laws of individual nations often serve to enforce the provisions of MARPOL and other treaties. In some instances national laws go much further, as with laws regulating sewage discharge in U.S. waters.

Sea turtles can become entangled in and ingest plastic debris.
National Estuarine Research Reserve Collection, NOAA

for one-time use. Limit your purchase of plastic goods to products designed to last, avoiding items such as plastic plates, cutlery, and foam cups. Plastic products that make sense are sturdy plastic containers, which we use to stow foodstuffs, tools, cameras, water, fuel, and fishing gear. But even then, aim for those containers that will last; cheap, clear plastic jugs disintegrate after only a season's use. Heavier-gauge, colored plastic containers are generally resistant to UV and will last for years. Shampoo and similar products are rarely available in anything but plastic bottles these days; buy the biggest container you can, decanting it into smaller containers. When the big bottle is empty, use it to store used engine oil.

Garbage Onboard

The simplest way of dealing with garbage is to reduce the amount you produce. To do that, buy in bulk whenever possible, and transfer foodstuffs into your own containers before leaving port, while you can easily dispose of any packaging ashore. You can also reduce the amount of garbage by reusing as many items as possible. Aboard *Nomad*, empty plastic bottles—from cooking oil, bleach, or liquid soap—get used for everything from containing old engine oil to dinghy bailers. Tin cans are good for painting and varnishing projects, and islanders in remote areas are often on the lookout for glass bottles. Small glass jars and plastic containers can be reused for spices, leftovers, screws and washers, and spare parts. Finding a new use for whatever's in the garbage means you'll still have to pack it away, but at least you're dealing with stowing something useful.

What do you do with the stuff that's left? First, keep various types of trash separate; by no means mix food scraps with anything else. By separating trash you'll make it easier to recycle or dispose of later, as well as easier to stow. Make sure to give everything a good rinse (use your dirty dishwater), as things can get pretty smelly otherwise after a few weeks in the tropics. Finally, reduce the volume of your garbage as much as possible by removing the ends of tins and flattening them and by folding paper or cardboard.

Can you throw anything overboard? On *Nomad*, all nonfood waste gets saved for disposal ashore. We dispose of all food scraps over the side starting about one day (or 100 miles) into a passage. If we're island hopping nothing goes over, unless it's something that occurs naturally in the tropics, such as coconut husks or banana peels. Use your judgment on this, but remember that some biodegradables (such as orange peels) can take many months to break down.

Don't forget to look through your trash to make sure there's nothing there that will cause future grief for wildlife; even garbage you dispose of "properly" ashore isn't always dealt with the way it should be. For example, the plastic yokes that hold bottles, tins, and aluminum cans together should be *cut up with scissors immediately*. Seabirds and marine animals can end up with the plastic rings around their necks and slowly strangle to death as a result; this can happen to land birds that frequent a landfill, as well.

SEWAGE

Sewage impacts the marine environment in more than one way. When sewage is released it serves to "fertilize" the water body by inputting nutrients. The presence of these nutrients can cause explosions in the algae population (blooms), which in turn decrease the amount of available oxygen and diminish the amount of light penetrating the water column. In some cases the environmental impacts can be extreme. Sewage discharge also introduces viral and bacterial pathogens into the water, which can cause a variety of infectious diseases. Waters need not be choked with sewage to present a health risk. Research has shown that pollution with human fecal waste can result in a significant health risk, even in waters that appear perfectly clean to the eye. A group of boats that congregate in a harbor or inlet and dump toilet waste can pose a serious risk to nearby swimmers, contaminate shellfish and bottom feeders, and cause significant concentrations of fecal coliform bacteria in the water (fecal coliform is the standard indicator for the presence of disease-causing organisms in marine and fresh waters).

U.S. and Other Laws
Governing the Discharge of Sewage

The discharge of sewage generated aboard ships and boats is not regulated by international treaty at the present time, but many individual nations have passed laws that deal with the issue. We'll look briefly at U.S. law, as the equipment most American readers have aboard will likely have been designed to cope with U.S. requirements.

The U.S. Clean Water Act essentially mandates that all vessels equipped with a marine toilet also be capable of treating or holding the waste by means of a marine sanitation device, or MSD. The MSD is not the toilet itself, but the device into which a marine toilet flushes. The U.S. Coast Guard groups MSDs into three types and certifies them for marine use. Type 1 MSDs are equipped with macerators to liquefy any solids and use chemical treatment to reduce the coliform bacteria count to less than 1,000

per 100 milliliters. Type 2 MSDs are similar but have more stringent standards for discharge, both in terms of bacteria and particulate matter. A type 3 MSD is a holding tank, which includes anything from a portable toilet to an installed tank. Most cruising boats are equipped with a type 1 or 3 MSD. Type 2 MSDs are large, power-hungry, and costly, and they're found more commonly aboard very large boats.

No discharge is allowed within 3 miles of shore anywhere within U.S. waters. Many states have established even more restrictive no-discharge zones covering whole stretches of coastline, entire bays and harbors, lakes and tributaries, and other waterways; the Great Lakes are but one example. The increasing prevalence of no-discharge zones helps to explain the popularity of type 3 MSDs, which are the only type that can be used legally in these areas.

Note that the law does not require vessels to be equipped with a marine toilet. If you use a bucket, rather than an installed toilet, then you're not in violation, except that you will violate water-quality standards if you're caught in the act of dumping the bucket's contents overboard!

Many other countries have also enacted laws governing sewage discharge from vessels in their waters. Such laws are not always obeyed or effective, however. For example, Australian regulations are similar to those in the United States, prohibiting direct discharge into most enclosed bays, lakes, and rivers. Regulations are increasingly requiring new vessels to be fitted with holding tanks, but the problem of where to empty the tank remains. A recent survey of 36 Queensland marinas found that only 5 were equipped with pump-out stations.

Sewage Onboard

We'll take the easy cases first. When offshore—and by this we mean at least the U.S. legal minimum of 3 miles—sewage should be pumped overboard, preferably without any chemical treatment. The environmental and health impacts can safely be considered negligible, and it's the only practical approach. When you're in a marina or otherwise tied up to shore, use facilities ashore. This avoids any problems with local authorities and means you don't have to worry about your holding tank filling up, or your type 1 or 2 MSD discharging chemicals into shoreside waters.

The tough choices come whenever you're anchored out or moored alongshore in areas without shore facilities. Most U.S. cruising boats are equipped with holding tanks, but pump-out stations are few and far between in the tropics (or anywhere outside North America, for that matter). If you use your holding tank in areas without pump-out stations, you should wait until you're offshore to empty the tank; this strategy is fine if that's your plan anyway, but rather absurd if it forces you to sail offshore just to pump the tank. But to empty a holding tank inshore, especially in restricted waters, can cause significant environmental impacts. According to the U.S. Environmental Protection Agency, dumping a 20-gallon (5 L) untreated holding tank has the same impact as discharging several thousand gallons of sewage from an efficiently run sewage treatment plant.

A type 1 MSD is about the only other option for most cruising boats. The Raritan Lectra/San, one of the most common, uses an electrical current to make hypochlorous acid (chlorine), which chemically treats the sewage. Designed for use in salt water, it can also function in brackish and freshwater by adding salt to the salt feed tank that is included with each unit. The power draw is considerable—45 amps for three minutes after each flush—and the system has no holding capacity. It's also not legal in zero-discharge areas.

We're in a quandary on this issue ourselves. Our boat, built in 1964, has no holding tank, and all waste is simply discharged straight overboard. We haven't encountered a single pump-out station since we were last in Hawaii, six years ago. There have been only a few instances—such as when we knew we would be heading offshore soon—in which we would have used a holding tank if we'd had one aboard. Many of the remote islands we've visited in the past few years lack sewage facilities of any kind ashore, and the bay in which one is anchored is often the depository for a village's waste. That doesn't mean we're helping the situation by adding our waste, but it does help to put the issue in perspective.

The Caribbean sees many more tourists and boats than the Pacific, but the sewage situation isn't much better. Studies estimate that only about 10 percent of the sewage that's produced in the Caribbean is treated properly; on land, pit latrines are still the most common form of waste disposal system. In that context, it's not so surprising that pump-out stations are few and far between.

We've always wondered why so many boats are fitted with more than one head, when space on most vessels is at a premium, but in fact there may be a good argument for it. The best way to comply with both U.S. law and the practicalities of tropical cruising might be to have two heads. One would be a Lectra/San type 1, allowing for guilt-free (and legal) discharge in most coastal waters. The other would be a dead-simple vacuum-flushing Lavac, connected to a holding tank and also plumbed for direct discharge. This would be the head to use when offshore (pumping straight overboard) and would allow you to be legal when sailing in a zero-discharge area (by using the holding tank).

ANTIFOULING PAINTS

The rate at which barnacles, algae, sponges, and soft corals grow on the bottom of boat hulls in warm tropical waters is astounding, and translates into more frequent haul-outs than in temperate waters. For this reason, some tropical cruisers use antifouling paints containing tributyltin (TBT), a highly potent ingredient but one with detrimental impacts on the marine environment.

Antifouling paints negatively impact the environment when they're applied, when they're removed

248

(through scrubbing in the water or sanding and scraping when on land), and through leaching, as they act to prevent bottom growth. The significance of the impacts depends in part on the active ingredients in the paint, but all metal-based paints will have some negative effects. We take a look at the issues, consider what makes sense for the blue-water cruiser, and review the legal considerations.

TBT Paints

Tributyltin has been used as a component in antifouling paints for many years, and even now TBT paints remain the antifouling paint of choice for 70 percent of the world's deep-water shipping fleet. Restrictions on the use of TBT, particularly for small craft, were implemented after research traced die-offs in a range of marine life to the use TBT bottom paints. Impacts included the near collapse of oyster farming in France, declines in dog whelk populations in British waters, and negative effects on sea otters, dolphins, whales, seabirds, fish, and shellfish. TBT has been shown to be toxic to marine species at concentrations down to a few parts per trillion, while at the same time concentrations of over 100 parts per trillion have often been measured in British ports with high densities of small craft. TBT does naturally degrade over time, but the input rate has greatly exceeded the rate of degradation.

So TBT is bad news. Given the fact that it's not legal in the United States and Europe, why worry about it? Because it's still readily—and legally—available in many other countries, and, in fact, it's sought after by many cruising sailors. Even in countries where use is restricted, we've encountered companies quite happy to break the law and supply (and apply) the paint, and plenty of eager customers. In the same vein, even in environmentally aware countries it's not hard to find a boatyard that will look the other way as you grind bottom paint, sending the dust flying in the wind and disposing of the remnants as ordinary waste.

Facilities such as this where you can scrub and paint your boat between tides are rapidly disappearing throughout the tropics, because of concerns over the impact of bottom paints on the environment.

Many boaters and boatyards view the increasing restrictions surrounding antifouling paints as a pain in the neck—and they can be—but underlying even the stiffest regulations is the fact that the poisons we apply to our boats pose a very real threat to ourselves and the larger environment. By being careless about choosing, applying, and later removing these paints, we help to degrade the very environments we're setting out to see.

Antifouling and the Tropical Cruiser

New paint technology is rapidly evolving. At this time, the best option still seems to be copper-based paint, although there are various alternatives being developed that incorporate naturally occurring toxins, and that may prove more effective and less harmful. Resist the temptation to use anything more toxic than copper paints, and explain to other cruisers why they should not use TBT paints even if these paints are available. If possible, seek out alternatives that are even less toxic than standard copper paints. For fiberglass or wood/epoxy boats, a coating of epoxy mixed with copper dust may prove an effective bottom-paint alternative, while for traditional wood craft the old-fashioned approach of covering the bottom with a suit of copper sheeting is still hard to beat. Either of these choices will get around the need for an annual antifouling session in the boatyard, saving you money and reducing your exposure to the toxins.

Choosing which product to apply is a tough call, and we've found that there's generally a direct link between effectiveness, copper content, and price. In the tropics you'll need the highest copper content you can find. We've used both ablative and hard paints, and generally prefer the latter, as they're not as easily worn off by a dinghy kept alongside the boat, and they don't rub off nearly as quickly if growth necessitates removing bottom growth while the boat is in the water. Minimize the loss of paint by using a smooth dish scrubber (or a piece of AstroTurf) for the slime and a plastic scraper for any barnacles.

In the boatyard, we've taken to using wet-dry sandpaper, water, and elbow grease instead of an electric sander or grinder on a dry hull. This minimizes the airborne bottom paint dust. Another option is to use air tools (which won't give you a shock if used with water), but that's only practical if you have a compressor on board. If the paint is in decent shape, it should need little more than a quick roughening up before a new coat is applied, though you should always check the directions that accompany the paint you're applying. If you need to remove a large buildup of bottom paint, you may be forced to resort to a grinder, but do all you can to contain the resulting dust and debris and to dispose of it properly—like you would any other hazardous waste. Dust screens are the norm in many boatyards. Make sure you protect your skin with proper clothing, your lungs with a respirator, and your eyes with safety glasses.

Legal Considerations

Although no international agreements presently govern antifouling practices, an agreement banning the application of TBT-based antifoulants is expected to be in place by 2003. In the meantime, some countries have banned the use of TBT paints outright; these include the United States and New Zealand, and the bans include use by each country's naval fleet. In many other countries the use of TBT paints is restricted, and in both Australia and Britain TBT paints are legal only for vessels over 25 meters in length. Although the use of copper paints remains legal, the ways in which they are applied, removed, and disposed of are being increasingly regulated, both in the United States and abroad.

We urge you to obey U.S. law on the use of antifouling paints, even when you are far from home.

THE DISCHARGE OF OIL

Coastal, reef, and estuarine environments are far more sensitive to oil pollution than the open ocean. These areas are habitat for a great number and diversity of near-shore marine organisms as well as many oceanic species during their juvenile stage.

Seabirds are greatly affected by an oil spill, as demonstrated by the Exxon Valdez spill, which killed hundreds of thousands. Oil causes birds' feathers to be matted, allowing water to penetrate to the body, which then results in hypothermia and loss of buoyancy. To counteract these effects, birds will attempt to rid themselves of oil by preening, but the ingestion of oil causes damage to liver, kidneys, and intestinal tracts. Diving birds such as boobies, shearwaters, and tropic birds (all common in the tropics) are at the greatest risk. Other marine animals are affected by an oil spill as well, including seals, sea otters, and sea turtles, for whom ingestion of oil and tar balls and the inhalation of hydrocarbon vapors can be deadly.

Dealing with Oil Onboard

If you do nothing else, fit an oil pan under the engine. Even with one in place, however, leaks into the bilge will occur. Many engine fuel systems are impossible to bleed without spilling some diesel fuel, and even the best-maintained engine is likely to develop small leaks as it ages. So in addition to an oil pan, oil absorbing pads that line the bilge near the engine are a must. If you do end up with oil in the bilge, don't make the mistake of using detergent or other dispersants to break down the oil, as this will only cause it to sink (when the bilge is pumped), where it will do significant harm to whatever lives on the bottom. Instead, use absorbent material to mop up the oil. Once you've gotten all you can, add a small amount of water and some detergent, and then mop up and save all of that. Keep at it until you really consider the bilge clean. It's a major hassle, one we've faced a number of times. It may mean turning a spare fuel container into an oily water and waste jug, but it's the only environmentally safe and responsible way to go. We've sailed many hundreds of miles with two former fuel jugs and a plastic tub full of the remnants of our bilge-cleaning adventures, waiting until we reached a port with proper facilities where we could dispose of the waste.

Legal Considerations

International agreement restricts discharges of oil and oily mixtures to effluent containing no more than 15 parts per million of oil. How much is that? Practically speaking, almost none. The U.S. standard, part of the Clean Water Act, is easier to gauge. It prohibits the discharge of oil or oily waste into U.S. waters if the discharge "causes a film or sheen upon, or discoloration of, the surface of the water, or causes a sludge or emulsion beneath the surface." Many other countries have similar regulations. The bottom line is that *no oil should go overboard*.

CORAL REEFS

As we saw in chapter 2, Tropical Environments, coral reefs are home to more than 25 percent of all marine life and are one of the world's most fragile and endangered ecosystems. Among the threats facing reefs are sedimentation (from coastal construction, mining, agriculture, and logging), fishing with explosives and cyanide, runoff from the land, dredging (coral is often used for construction), global warming, and careless recreation. While there's not a lot that individuals can do to combat most of these threats effectively, there are some things that every cruiser can do about the last impact: careless recreation.

Destruction and Protection of Coral Reefs

The most obvious and dramatic recreational impacts involve preventable actions such as anchor damage and oil spills. We've addressed these in more detail elsewhere, but keep the following basics in mind when cruising in reef areas:

▶ **NAVIGATE CAREFULLY** so your boat's keel doesn't scrape or gouge coral heads.

▶ **USE A MOORING BUOY** whenever possible.

▶ **IF YOU ANCHOR IN AREAS WITH CORAL**, find sand patches, and never drop your anchor onto live coral.

▶ **KEEP YOUR ENGINE AND OUTBOARD WELL TUNED**, and avoid oil and gas leaks and spills.

▶ **IF POSSIBLE, USE PUMP-OUT STATIONS** to keep sewage out of the water and off the reefs.

▶ **DON'T DUMP ANY TRASH OVERBOARD** in coastal or protected waters (e.g., inside a reef).

Once you've got yourself and your boat into an idyllic anchorage, you'll no doubt want to go for a swim, dive, or snorkel. The physical damage from a diver, though less than from a boat or anchor, still has an impact.

Adopt a "look-but-don't-touch" approach when you're in the water.

▶ **DON'T TOUCH**, stand on, break off, or collect coral.

▶ **LIKEWISE, MAINTAIN CONTROL** of your fins, dive gauges, underwater camera equipment, and other gear so they don't touch or break off coral branches.

Legal Considerations

Despite their importance for the tropical marine environment, most coral reefs are not effectively protected. This is partly because threats to coral reefs are complex and varied—including contentious issues such as global warming—with the result that there are no simple ways to comprehensively protect reefs. But the track record for protection is poor even for simpler, well-defined threats (see Living Reefs for Living Rooms sidebar, page 255).

As cruisers, we're fortunate to be able to directly enjoy and benefit from the world's reefs, and we're also in a unique position to be able to contribute to their protection.

FISHING AND SHELL COLLECTING

Legal Considerations

Restrictions on fishing are nothing new; they've been used by coastal and island inhabitants for centuries. In traditional societies there were many variations in how restrictions were applied. Sometimes special foods were set aside exclusively for chiefs or nobility, while in other instances some species of fish or mollusk were off-limits to everyone at certain times of the year. A common restriction limited access to fishing grounds to people who lived adjacent to the reef. But whatever form they took, in most cases the effect of fishing regulations was to limit pressure on the resource. Generations ago, most island inhabitants realized that marine resources were limited, and that there needed to be controls on how much was taken.

Fishing regulations are still with us, and although you're generally free to catch what you want while trolling in offshore waters, most countries have enacted fishing regulations for inshore and reef areas. These vary enormously from outright bans on fishing in selected areas to restrictions on the use of gear such as spear guns and/or size and seasonal limits. It's your responsibility to know what the regulations are in the places you visit, so inquire locally before you fish.

Fish and shellfish are not the only resources that can become depleted. Ornamental shells, such as cowries, conch, cone shells, and others all serve as wonderful souvenirs of your travels, but overcollec-tion has meant they're becoming increasingly scarce and subject to regulation in a number of areas.

There's a financial as well as a moral incentive to obey regulations, as fines for violators can be severe. For example, collecting on Australia's Great Barrier Reef is strictly controlled. There, it's forbidden to collect giant clams, helmet shells, and triton shells. Fishing illegally within marine park zones of the Great Barrier Reef can incur penalties of up to $10,000 and confiscation of gear and vessel.

Overfishing

Overfishing and excessive harvesting of marine resources is a problem in many parts of the world. In some instances declines in fish catch may be worsened by the destruction of spawning habitat or pollution, but in many cases the cause of a "crash" in a fishery is simple: greed. The restraint traditionally practiced by some island residents has never been the norm in larger, western societies, where the links between one person's action and the depletion of a resource are harder to see. But as with every environmental issue we've discussed, a solution will come only when we all act responsibly as individuals, and do so willingly, not because we're forced to by law or regulation.

Cruisers are in an unusual position when it comes to fishing because we have access to remote areas that are often hard for others to reach, where highly prized resources such as lobsters or conch may still be found. For most of us, lobsters are a real treat; we've been known to get pretty excited when we've collected a couple for dinner. But it's important to know when to stop. If cruisers stuff their freezers with a dozen lobsters and then pass the good news on, before you know it there'll be 20 boats in the anchorage filling *their* own freezers. Soon no large lobsters are left, and small ones are caught instead. The much-sought-after spiny lobsters take several years to reach sexual maturity and can live for many years. Catching small ones that haven't yet reproduced puts enormous pressure on the local lobster population and may even wipe it out altogether. Resist the temptation to take undersized fish as well. The purpose of a size limit is so that juveniles can reach sexual maturity, spawn, and produce more fish.

Although most people understand the need for limits on how much fish, lobster, and other edible resources they catch, few seem to extend this to animals they collect for their shells. We've had cruising sailors tell us about collecting shells with the snail still inside and boiling them alive to remove the organism. "I know I shouldn't, but the shell was too gorgeous to pass up" or, "I don't care; I won't be passing through again, and it's a nice memento" are commonly heard statements made by people who can't resist. Mollusks may be valuable to us for their pretty shells, but they're also an important part of the reef communities in which they're found. If one cruiser takes a few live mollusks, the impact is negligible; if hundreds do it, mollusk populations will certainly decline, altering a reef's ecological balance, as well as depriving

Anchors act like picks, tearing coral off the bottom. It can take a reef many years to recover from such damage.

future visitors of the joys of finding shells. What's the answer? Never take live mollusks; collect only empty shells.

ENDANGERED SPECIES

International Law

Species become threatened with extinction in many different ways, but a few stand out. Overfishing, overhunting, or collecting for many years is a frequent cause, imperiling many species of whales and other marine mammals. Another is loss of habitat, which today has large animals such as the mountain gorilla and the Florida panther on the verge of extinction. Eradication programs, which have sought to eliminate "nuisance" animals, have contributed as well, as in the extinction of the Tasmanian tiger, or thylacine. In most instances the problem is a combination of multiple factors, a fact that makes protecting species difficult. That's espe-

All these lovely shells were empty when we found them, either on isolated beaches or in shallow water. Included here are cowries, nautilus, conch, and a bailer.

cially true if the animals are highly mobile, as most marine species are.

Legal protection for endangered species usually addresses one of these basic issues. At the national level, preserves or conservation areas serve to protect nesting and breeding habitat, while laws prohibit the killing of animals considered endangered. Protecting endangered wildlife from exploitation through international trade is harder. To address that issue, an international treaty titled the Convention on International Trade in Endangered Species of Wild Fauna and Flora (or CITES) was passed in 1975 to regulate trade in species deemed to be threatened with extinction; 145 countries are signatories to the convention. Under the CITES treaty, all international commercial trade is prohibited in species considered

under threat of extinction or products made from them. The treaty also regulates trade in species classified as under pressure but not threatened with extinction, with the goal of preventing further decline.

Tropical marine species listed under CITES as threatened with extinction and protected from all international trade include all species of marine turtle, many species of whales and dolphins, estuarine crocodiles (outside of Australia, Indonesia, and Papua New Guinea), the Amazonian and Caribbean manatee, and a number of seabirds. In addition, giant clams and many species of corals are classified under CITES as being under pressure, and trade in them is regulated to prevent their further decline.

Unfortunately, international recognition that a species is threatened with extinction, and even list-

Turtle tracks leading to a nest site. These are a dead giveaway for poachers seeking turtle eggs.

Although turtles are protected by international treaties, in most parts of the tropics locals hunt turtles for their meat. The eggs are considered a delicacy, and the shells of hawksbills have been used for jewelry for centuries.

ing by CITES, doesn't result in real protection. For example, despite the fact that all sea turtles are considered endangered, marine turtles continue to be hunted and traded. Some countries haven't outlawed the taking of these species: in the Caribbean and nearby North Atlantic, the Bahamas, British Virgin Islands, Cuba, and Haiti allow the taking of sea turtles, and the latter three countries allow the taking of hawksbills, a critically endangered species of sea turtle. The sale of eggs and turtle meat is not uncommon, and shell jewelry, curios, and stuffed shells are actively sold in the Bahamas, Dominican Republic, Haiti, Jamaica, and Mexico. The situation is much the same across the tropics and may be at its worst in Southeast Asia, where there is a flourishing trade in endangered species.

Practically speaking, the trade won't end unless individuals stop buying products made from these animals. There are some good reasons—beyond any ethical arguments—to do just that. Most

LIVING REEFS FOR LIVING ROOMS

One example of a threat to reefs that's easy to identify (and should be controllable) is the harvest of and trade in coral for use as curios and in aquariums. It's a big and growing business, but one that can decimate the reefs where the corals are harvested. This has been recognized for years: a complete ban on both collection and export of corals instituted by the Philippine government in 1977, has remained in place since then except for brief periods. However, this law has been consistently and flagrantly violated; in just one year, the United States imported some 600,000 pieces of coral, imports that were illegal under both Philippine and U.S. law. Why? The demand (and profits) are both high. This emphasizes the role that consumers play in reef destruction. Almost all the coral that's harvested for use in aquariums ends up in wealthy western countries, with an estimated 90 percent going to the United States. There's little doubt that the trade would dry up, and the coral would not be harvested, if there was no demand.

A FISHING AND COLLECTING CODE OF ETHICS

Fortunately, the "get while the gettin' is good" mentality is the exception rather than the rule among cruisers, but with more and more people setting forth each year, even those of us with the best of intentions can have a serious collective impact on the places we visit. Stop to consider the effect of your actions on the island, reef, and culture you're visiting. Find out about local regulations—and in traditional societies ask permission—*before* you fish or take shellfish or shells. Take only what you need, and always remember to leave some for others.

Fish: catch only what you and your crew can realistically eat that day. Pay attention to the fine print of the regulations (if there are any), which may specify size, species, and seasonal restrictions, but which may also outline the gear you can or can't use and the time of the day when you can fish. In New Caledonia, for instance, the use of scuba gear for catching fish or other organisms is prohibited, and you may not dive for fish between sunset and sunrise. In some Caribbean marine parks, spearguns are prohibited, even if they're not being used.

Lobsters: as with fish, take only what you can eat that day. Check on size and number limits as well, and *never* take a female lobster with eggs. In some places, a minimum head size of 7.5 centimeters is the size limit. The use of scuba gear for taking lobsters is widely prohibited throughout the tropics. In many marine protected areas, the taking of lobsters is prohibited. *Don't* fill your freezer—leave some for others.

Mangrove Crabs: a common regulation requires that mangrove crabs (also called mud crabs) measure at least 15 centimeters across the shell to be legal. As with lobsters, do not take female crabs with eggs.

Clams and Mollusks: the taking of clams and mollusks is often regulated both by seasonal closures and daily limits. In Queensland, Australia, a limit of 50 of any species of clams or mollusks (excluding oysters) can be taken at any one time, while oysters must be eaten at the spot they are collected, rather than taken back to the boat. In many parts of the Caribbean, the taking of queen conch is strictly regulated.

Buying Fish and Shellfish: if the fishing isn't good and you head for the market instead, think about the source of the seafood you choose to eat. You'll want seafood that's fresh and hasn't been caught at too high a cost. For example, prawn farms are a booming business in many tropical Asian nations, but they can lead to the destruction of mangroves. Shrimp caught in the wild would seem an answer, but these are often collected by dragging nets that end up killing all marine life in their path. About 10 pounds of fish are usually wasted for each pound of shrimp gathered.

Ornamental Shells: take only shells that are "uninhabited," even if the original occupant has left and a hermit crab has taken its place. If you pick up a shell and find an animal inside, enjoy looking at it and then place it back on the reef or beach the way you found it. With a keen eye and a little patience you'll find gorgeous shells that have been recently abandoned and are waiting to be discovered. Giant clams, triton shells, and helmet shells shouldn't be collected, as they are endangered in many places.

This turtle shell and the stuffed juvenile turtle and crocodile were all seized by the Australian Customs Service.

Manatees (and their close relative, the dugong) are endangered species and are under threat from pollution and poaching.
National Estuarine Research Reserve Collection, NOAA

countries that are signatories to CITES have laws that make it illegal to possess handicrafts or other articles made from endangered species. Countries such as the United States, Australia, New Zealand, and most European nations take these laws seriously and can impose heavy fines on violators, in addition to confiscating the illegal items. Ignorance is no excuse: it's your responsibility to determine if the wildlife product you purchased was made from a protected species.

There've been a number of instances when local people have tried to sell us handicrafts made from endangered species, and we've seen impressive collections of such handicrafts on friends' boats. These items have a real appeal: beautiful necklaces, rings, earrings, and combs made from hawksbill turtle shell; armbands

from the vertebrate of dugong; and many types of jewelry from black coral. Many cruisers seem not to realize that in most countries possession of rare, threatened, or endangered species—or anything made from them—is illegal. No one may bat an eye in remote areas, but if you're caught with these items aboard in most Western countries, they'll be confiscated and a hefty fine will be levied. More importantly, buying them encourages tropical peoples to continue exploiting these species and encourages further extinctions.

The best way to avoid problems is by educating yourself and asking sellers the origins of the handicrafts they're selling. If you decide not to buy, tell them why. It remains legal in some countries for islanders to hunt and use endangered species for subsistence purposes. Those purposes, however,

THINK BEFORE YOU HIDE IT
We were surprised when one European cruiser showed us several complete hawksbill turtle shells he'd bought to round out his collection of carvings. He was headed for Australia, so we warned him that possession of sea turtle products was illegal in Australia. We don't know what he ended up doing, but when we returned again to Australia we queried a customs officer about their procedures. He indicated that while they had the option of imposing fines, they didn't usually do so if people voluntarily gave up any illegal items. If customs discovered these items during a search, however, he said they were liable to throw the book at the offender.

don't include trade; and although it may be legal for locals to hunt and eat a turtle, it's illegal for we cruisers to possess the meat, shell, or items made from the shell. Islanders are not likely to know that, though, and so may innocently offer them for sale or trade.

Some species that are not officially protected may be scarce locally; by buying them you'll hasten their decline. It isn't forbidden to own a handcrafted ebony bowl inlaid with nautilus shell, but Solomon Islanders have told us that they've been

forced farther and farther afield to find ebony trees of a size suitable for large carvings. Other woods are equally beautiful—and usually much less expensive—and by choosing them you can lessen the impact on the local environment. Inform yourself before you buy, and don't encourage the harvest and trade in threatened species by buying products made from them. Here are some of the more common tropical species that we make sure to avoid:

▶ **BLACK CORAL, TURTLE SHELL, WHALEBONE, OR DUGONG** are often made into jewelry. Don't buy items made from these.

▶ **MEDICINES ARE MADE FROM RHINOCEROS, SEAHORSES AND TIGER.** Do not buy items made from them.

▶ **ALLIGATORS, CROCODILES, AND TURTLES ARE MADE INTO LEATHER PRODUCTS** in some tropical countries. Avoid leather products made from these animals or products originating from areas where they're threatened.

▶ **TURTLE EGGS, SOUP, OR MEAT** are still found on the menu in many tropical countries. Don't order them.

Chapter 16

The Quest for Paradise

In *A Voyage Round the World*, Georg Forster wrote, "It is much to be lamented that the voyages of Europeans cannot be performed without being fatal to the nations whom they visit."

Paradise. It's a notion that's captivated westerners for centuries. Explorers searched for it and at various times declared it to be found. The church railed against it, while sailors reveled in its pleasures. Paradise has appeared across the globe, but for the last 200 years it's been found more often than not on tropical islands, with their benign climate, apparently plentiful resources, and attractive inhabitants. Yet paradise was never purely physical, and tropical island life has also represented innocence and simplicity, an escape from the complexities and evils of the world at large. English explorer Captain James Cook summed it up when he described Tahiti as "a golden isle of blessed beautiful people, their wants supplied by a bountiful nature and mercifully ignorant of the burden of civilization." His French counterpart, Louis Antoine de Bougainville, concurred: "As we walked over the grass, dotted here and there with fruit trees and intersected by little streams, I thought I had been transported to paradise. Everywhere we went, we found hospitality, peace, innocent joy and every appearance of happiness."

An elder welcomes us to his island.

In some respects our world has changed dramatically in the last few hundred years, with jets whisking travelers to the far corners of "paradise" in just a few hours. But while technology has changed enormously, our thinking has not: for many, Cook's vision still dances in their heads. Few will have read his account, but countless books, magazines, and movies continue to portray islanders as attractive bronze-skinned natives, their volcanic island homes draped in lush tropical vegetation and ringed by sugary white beaches. The image speaks of carefree days, with work consisting of a few hours of fishing in a turquoise lagoon.

The notion of paradise in the tropics is tailor-made for the tourism industry and easy to exploit. Ads suggest that clothing is all but optional, while architecture is usually simple and "traditional." Photographs feature colorful dress and dances; natives, lit by a setting sun, gaze out to sea as if awaiting an incoming canoe. The "noble savage" is alive and well, and welcomes us to his world.

Or does he? Paul Theroux spent months paddling his folding kayak among many Pacific Islands. He chronicled his adventures in *The Happy Isles of Oceania: Paddling the Pacific*, a litany of unhappy experiences and unfulfilled expectations. Theroux is not alone: during our years of sailing we've met cruisers for whom the reality of the tropics is but a pale reflection of their paradisiacal dreams. And consider the following statement by Haunani Trask, a native Hawaiian and professor at the University of Hawaii: "If you are thinking of visiting my homeland, please don't. We don't want or need any more tourists, and we certainly don't like them. If you want to help our cause, pass this message on to your friends."

TODAY'S REALITY

As Theroux discovered, the reality is rather different than the dream. Living standards across the tropics vary enormously: contrast desperately poor nations such as Haiti or Kiribati with the wealth of tiny Brunei or Singapore. Or compare the poverty of the indigenous populations of countries such as New Caledonia with the wealth of the European residents. Traditional architecture is still found in some areas, but so are modern glass towers; even in small villages, cement, corrugated iron, and plywood are far more common than thatched houses. Western dress, meanwhile, is all but universal. Dances and ceremonies still take place, but today it's usually the church or the tourism industry that provides the focus. None of this should come as a surprise: all tropical islands and countries have dynamic, evolving cultures, and all have been increasingly influenced by the larger world, through colonialism, development, and tourism.

In many regions, the changes that followed upon the heels of contact with Europeans were both sudden and devastating. Islands were depopulated due to disease and slavery. In some cases entire populations were wiped out, and slaves, convicts, and settlers took their place. When native peoples survived, their way of life was changed forever as a result of new religions, cash economies, and new laws and regulations.

Traditional dress, beliefs, knowledge, practices, and language—all fundamental elements of a culture—were banned or discouraged in many societies, often by the missionaries that came to "save" the pagan souls.

Although most islands are today politically independent, the pattern of cultural and economic domination by outside forces, often with the help of an island elite, continues. Between nuclear testing, strategic interests, mass tourism, commercial fisheries, and the mining of precious metals, larger nations have found many reasons to maintain a quasi-colonial role in the tropics. When economic dependence is combined with the pervasive impact of western media, there seems to be little room for any independent culture, even in the remote and isolated islands of the Pacific.

Boatbuilders in Indonesia shaping a plank for a traditional prahu.

PERSISTENT TRADITIONS

Yet despite the odds, different ways of living and thinking persist. We've met islanders who are experts in the medicinal properties and uses of plants. Some can treat serious ailments such as diabetes and malaria as well as commonplace skin infections. We've learned from fishermen and -women whose understanding of the marine environment in which they live is enormous, to the point that they may know more about the habits of tropical marine organisms than a professional fisheries biologist. We've also marveled at islanders' skills in boatbuilding and sailing. We've met canoe builders whose tools were simply modern steel versions of the traditional stone ax and adze, but with which they fashioned beautiful oceangoing prahus 35 feet in length.

Without exception, the island residents we've encountered acquired their "traditional" skills the old-fashioned way: by word of mouth, often from a parent or grandparent. All were religious adherents to a major world faith, who nonetheless found it important to practice a traditional ritual, build a fishing shrine, or carve a totem in the prow of their canoe to ensure safe passage over the waters. And each participated in the cash economy as well as practicing their traditional skills. The need for money—to pay children's school fees, to travel, and to buy tools, food, and clothes—is universal, and so when the opportunity arises, islanders make carvings, fashion jewelry, work for the nearby mission, or collect *beche-de-mer* for export.

In a way that few of us can truly appreciate, many tropical peoples are straddling two cultures, working to maintain their traditions while also feeding, clothing, and educating their families. Their

261

position is not an easy one, and it becomes increasingly difficult as population and resource pressures increase, and as external, global cultures penetrate ever farther.

SHOWING RESPECT

Regrettably, we cruisers don't always make it any easier for them. Consider a simple thing, such as how we dress when we visit. Westerners think nothing of skimpy bathing suits, and for many Europeans nudity is commonplace on the beach. This was once true in many parts of the tropics; even today, Gauguin's Tahitian maidens remain a powerful image. But today's reality is different in most areas. Many local people consider it offensive if a woman walks through the village in a swimsuit or short shorts, exposing her thighs; in some areas men are expected to wear fairly long shorts, unless in the water or on the beach. Unfortunately some cruisers continue to dress and behave as if they were at home. We were joined on a walk in Fiji, on a Sunday no less, by a group of men and women sailors from Europe and the United States. None wore more than thong bikini bottoms. While that would have been commonplace in Rio, even modest bikinis would have been out of place in Fiji. When we tried to suggest that the locals might find their dress inappropriate, they retorted that they were simply dressing the way islanders formerly did. Such an attitude indicates no understanding of the last few hundred years of Pacific Island history and a complete lack of respect for the Fijians whose beach we were on.

Shell jewelry being made in the same way that it has been for generations.

It's not just our bodies that are on display, but our way of life as well. The impact will vary enormously from one tropical region to another. Yachts are commonplace in most Caribbean anchorages and have long lost their novelty value. But that's not the case in many of the more remote tropical areas, be they in South America, Southeast Asia, or the Pacific. From the moment one drops the anchor anywhere near a rarely visited village, a yacht and its crew are on parade. Stay for more than a day or two, and you have joined, albeit peripherally, the local community; as a result, you'll be scrutinized and will often receive loads of visitors. Some want to talk, others just to look, but all will be curious. How we respond to them and their curiosity is important. It's important in an immediate sense, as the "manners" and friendship we show will help determine the quality of our visit. But our response has a deeper meaning as well, one that says a lot about why we are traveling and the value we place on different cultures.

Although apparently living in utter isolation, this family keeps up on world news via shortwave radio.

RECEIVING VISITORS

It's not uncommon for visitors to arrive as the anchor hits the bottom. We've found this to be especially true in the Pacific, where men will typically make the first contact, paddling out to welcome you, inquiring where you're from and how long you'll be staying. In Indonesia, many also come to barter. We usually welcome their arrival, although there have been times when we've entered a bay at dusk after a long sail, tired, hot, and looking forward to peace and quiet, not to receiving and entertaining a multitude of visitors. When that happens we take five minutes to exchange a few pleasant words and then explain that we're very tired and have traveled a long way. We then ask them to come for a visit the next day, after we've had a chance to rest up. Most people we've come across are gracious and understanding.

The arrival of visitors is oftentimes announced by a bump and scrape: that of a dugout canoe, fiberglass skiff, or other craft against our topsides. There's no wish to make us angry, but most people simply don't share our concern for cosmetics. We've learned to set out plenty of fenders and keep extra painters at the ready, as many islanders don't use them. This way, local craft can trail well behind the boat, and we're able to enjoy our visitors much more.

In many island societies the water and the beach are generally public spaces, and boats are practical things used for fishing and transport. To us, of course, the boat is much more. As well as being our home, it serves as a retreat, a sanctuary that we carry along as we travel. As a result, it can be upsetting when people come alongside in their boats and peer through the ports. Some of the bolder folks have gone one fur-

Traditional sailing craft are still used daily in some places.

ther, climbing on deck and looking around without an invitation. Our reaction is to be friendly but firm when incidents like this take place, explaining why we object and relating that climbing on board or star-ing in the ports is the equivalent of us going through their village and peering or walking into their houses. Our visitors have always understood, and we've usually gone on to develop a fine rapport.

MAKING VISITS

Although we've occasionally felt guilty about not welcoming visitors at all times, we've come to realize that our reaction to uninvited guests has been quite mild. We've seen boats with signs reading "taboo" and sailors who loudly warn off any small craft that approach closely. Such a response shows no awareness of the fact that it is *we* who are in fact the visitors—and uninvited ones at that—having dropped our anchors in *their* front yard. We try to carry that awareness one step further by inquiring if islanders have any objections to our stopping and visiting their bay or village. The best way to do this is by going ashore to meet the village chief or a village elder. We make it a practice to ask about the bay or village we're anchored off and include a direct query: "Is it OK to anchor here?" We've never been refused, and usually we've been given a grand tour of the village.

Visiting the chief, headman, or elder is not only polite, but also good politics. It's one's entree into the community, and it typically ensures that you and your boat will be well treated. If something should go missing, the chief will make it his responsibility to get your property back. If you talk to the chief or an elder, ask about where it's permissible to walk or swim. Even where land is owned communally, it's not always open to all; for example, some villages in the Pacific still have areas that are taboo or sacred, and you won't want to offend your hosts by being somewhere that you shouldn't be.

When you're on a walk, don't assume that the bananas growing alongside the trail are free for the taking. In most island cultures, every bush and tree, and nearly every strip of land or beach, is owned or used by someone. What to a Westerner might appear to be a hillside of wild growing shrubs and greenery is often a family garden. Islanders generally don't plant their "crops" in neat rows but instead integrate their gardens with a variety of tubers (sweet potatoes or taro), fruits (bananas, papaya, pineapple), and medicinal plants. Land ownership on many islands is complex, and we've seen instances where a family's garden plot was located deep in the bush; in another situation, where arable land was scarce, gardens were located on another island altogether. The message is simple: ask before you pick. If you do, you'll generally be given more fresh fruit and vegetables than you can hope to eat.

TRADING

In many places, it's common for local people to offer fruits, vegetables, handicrafts, fish, or lobsters to cruisers, either for cash or in exchange for something they need. In the western Pacific in particular, cash is still rarely requested. Instead, islanders ask for practical trade goods, such as fishing gear, fabric, batteries, soap, reading material, seeds, and clothes. Kids will sometimes come out and ask for "lollies" or some sort of sugar treat. We don't like to hand out candy, so instead we offer up balloons, colored pencils, or writing pads. Men will sometimes ask for tobacco or alcohol, but we've made it a practice not to trade these and have always found a substitute.

If you're trading, it's important to be fair. Being too stingy is insulting and certainly won't win you any friends, whereas being overly generous may lead to problems for future visitors, who will be trading in a climate of vastly raised expectations. Most importantly, be honest and don't misrepresent the goods you're offering. We've known more than one cruiser who knowingly traded damaged electrical tools, radios, and tape players for beautiful handicrafts that undoubtedly took time and care to make. Needless to say, the people who received the goods were less than pleased.

INTEREST AND SENSITIVITY

Much of the pleasure we've derived from visiting remote islands has come from developing an understanding of how islanders live. We read about places before we arrive in an attempt to get a broader, historical perspective. More importantly, though, we ask our hosts to talk about themselves, to explain how and why they do things, and to share with us what they know.

We have a small boat, and not a lot of fancy gear, but our radio, GPS, and even our charts are very foreign and modern to many local people. While we're happy to show visitors our boat and explain how it is we sail across the ocean, we try to do so without showing off. While there's no question that we've got some nifty toys, it's also become clear to us that many island inhabitants have been more successful than Westerners at retaining a cohesive and supportive family life and a culture that values quality of life over quantity of goods. So after they've shaken their heads at all our neat "stuff," we try to steer the conversation to what they have that our society lacks. These are messages that they won't receive through the little Western media to which they're exposed, but that can be very important in determining how they'll think back on us and the culture we represent when our visit is over.

Our responsibility to be sensitive doesn't end when we sail away. During our travels we've met cruisers who consider themselves "cultural connoisseurs," swapping experiences and stories with one another in the yacht club or over the radio. We've listened as cultures are ranked and graded, with scores compared to see who had the more "traditional" experience with the natives, who received the most fruit and vegetables or handicrafts, and who could count the most friends. The number of smiling faces and proffered banana stalks seem to tip the balance for any given culture, and more likely than not the "winner" will have sent another fleet of yachts scurrying off to that favorite island.

How can we best avoid the disillusionment we spoke of at the outset? At the risk of suggesting we all learned it in kindergarten, it's by showing interest in, respect for, and understanding of the people and places we visit. Captain Cook's world is gone forever, but not everyone has joined our virtual version. Set sail ready to accept people for who they are, rather than what you want them to be, and seek to understand and appreciate their uniqueness. Both you and the people you visit stand to benefit.

PART 5

TROPICAL CRUISING DESTINATIONS

Chapter 17 provides an overview of the major tropical cruising areas in the Atlantic Ocean; chapters 18 and 19 cover the Pacific and Indian Oceans. We don't cover all potential cruising areas but instead focus on those most frequently visited in a particular region. The information we include is necessarily limited and isn't intended to take the place of what is typically found in a cruising guide. Our aim is to provide information that's useful in planning a cruise; we also try to give sailors a "heads up" regarding the need for advance visas or the availability of facilities. Much of the information here isn't time sensitive and thus won't become rapidly dated, but some aspects—especially the health and safety situation—are subject to change. Try to obtain updated information before actually setting sail, especially if you're headed for an area where we've noted significant health and safety risks.

In the weather sections, seasons are discussed relative to each hemisphere. For example, when we review South Atlantic weather in summer, we mean the southern summer (December to March).

The major ocean currents we discuss are shown on the global maps on the inside front and back covers.

Chapter 17

Tropical Atlantic Ocean

The Caribbean region is the primary cruising area within the tropical North Atlantic, and commonly visited areas include the West Indies and the Caribbean coasts of Central and South America. Other destinations include the Cape Verde Islands, coastal nations in Africa, and Suriname, Guyana, and French Guiana in South America. Most visits to these latter regions occur in the course of a longer voyage, however, and few sailors make these areas the focus of a cruise. Thus our focus remains on the greater Caribbean region. We also provide an overview of the Cape Verde Islands but don't consider the other destinations here.

In the South Atlantic, Brazil is the primary cruising destination. The Atlantic Ocean has very few islands compared to the Pacific and Indian Oceans, but the island of St. Helena is a popular stopover point for boats sailing north from Cape Town, and we provide a brief overview of what this island offers. Most of West Africa is off the usual cruising itinerary due to safety concerns, so we do not cover it here.

◄ *North Atlantic Ocean* ►

North Atlantic Weather

The northeast trade winds extend to 25° N in winter and 30° N in summer. Strength is highest (20 to 25 knots) in winter, but averages 10 to 15 knots. The location of the Bermuda–Azores High means that the trades are northeasterly in the eastern Atlantic, becoming more easterly (and even southeasterly at times) in the western Atlantic and Caribbean.

The southern boundary of the trade winds is set by the position of the Intertropical Convergence Zone (ITCZ), which is generally found north of the equator, especially during summer months. The width of the zone averages 200 to 300 miles, and within it winds are generally light; squalls and thunderstorms are frequent. Winds between the ITCZ and the equator tend to be from the east or southeast in the western Atlantic but may become southwesterly in the east, where a monsoon effect develops as a result of low pressure over Africa.

Although hurricanes (tropical cyclones) can occur at any time, they're most common between May and December; September has the highest frequency. Most hurricanes spawn in the ITCZ west of the Cape Verde Islands and then track west toward the Caribbean. A secondary spawning area lies in the western Caribbean, where storms are more likely to begin early or late in the season.

North Atlantic Currents

A major west-setting flow of water in the North Atlantic is made up of two parallel currents: the west-setting North Equatorial Current (10 to 20° N) flows from the Cape Verde Islands to the Caribbean at an average rate of ½ knot, while the weaker North Subtropical Current (20 to 30° N) flows from the Canaries to North America. Part of the North Equatorial Current continues on into the Caribbean, while another portion branches off and flows north along the eastern side of the Lesser Antilles (the Antilles Current). This current continues north and west along the Greater Antilles, joining with the Florida Current and becoming the Gulf Stream. Gulf Stream velocities are highest in the southern portion, where they may reach averages of 3 knots. The Gulf Stream heads north along the East Coast of North America until it's deflected to the east by the south-setting Labrador Current.

Sailors heading for the Caribbean from the U.S. East Coast should familiarize themselves with the characteristics of the Gulf Stream and review their route options carefully (see the Gulf Stream sidebar and Coping with Currents, in chapter 7, Route Planning).

South of 10° N is found the east-setting Equatorial Counter Current, which originates at 45° W in summer and about 20° W in winter. In summer it is narrower in the west (flowing between 5 and 10° N) and expands as it nears the African coast (0 to 10° N), while in winter the current is restricted to about 2 to 6° N latitudes. When this current reaches Africa it becomes the Guinea Current, which flows east and southeast along the coast at rates up to 1¾ knots.

The South Equatorial Current is a west-setting current found south of the Equatorial Counter Current; it moves farther north in winter and in the west merges with the North Equatorial Current. The current is diverted to the northwest upon reaching South America and may reach 2 knots as it flows along the Brazilian coast near the equator.

WEST INDIES

When people speak of cruising the Caribbean, they are usually thinking of the islands of the West Indies, which include both the Bahamas and the Greater and Lesser Antilles. The West Indies include 23 separate countries and other political entities, and thousands of islands. This area forms the most popular tropical cruising area worldwide and is home to a large and expanding charter fleet as well as being visited by many cruising yachts. Perhaps because they are part of the West Indies, many people associate the Bahamas with the Caribbean, although they are not within the Caribbean Sea, and experience somewhat different weather systems. The Bahamas are closely linked to the Caribbean through both history and culture, however, and for convenience we treat them together.

Many factors contribute to the West Indies' popularity, including practical issues such as proximity to North America and Europe, easy access to goods and services, and consistently pleasant weather. But these islands are popular as well for their diverse cultures, which are a mixture of indigenous, European, African, and Asian influences.

Although most cruising sailors view the Caribbean as a distinct and coherent region, many of the region's inhabitants do not. Contacts between the residents of the various nations are often surprisingly limited, due to differing languages and cultures. But these islands do have much in common. Europe has played a major role throughout the region for the last 500 years, starting the establishment of a Spanish settlement on Hispaniola in 1496, just 4 years after Columbus's arrival in 1492. That marked the beginning of a long period of colonialism, in which sugar plantations, slavery, and battles between the Spanish, French, British, and Dutch featured heavily. The European presence is still strongly felt, and a number of islands remain

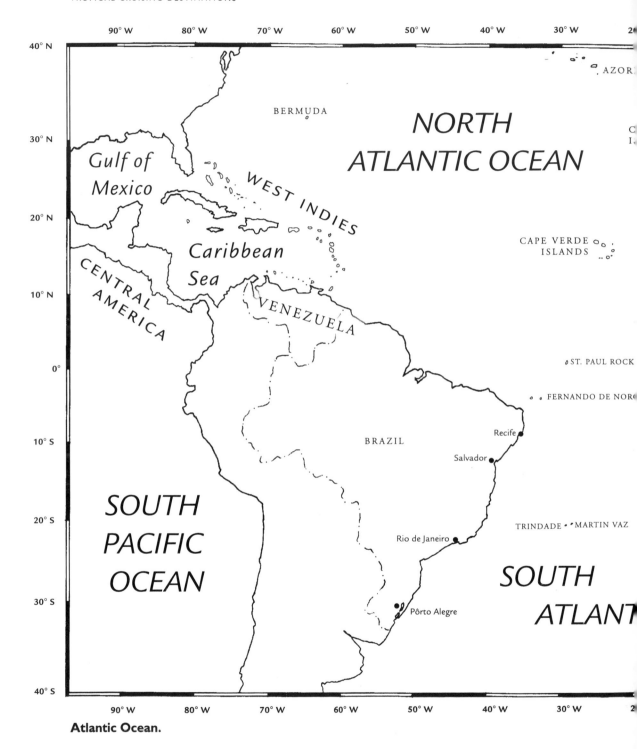

Atlantic Ocean.

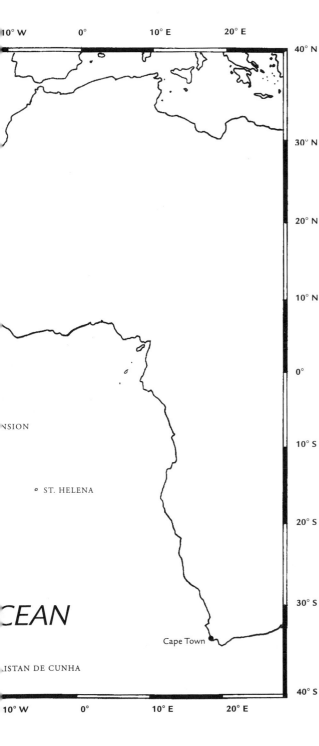

10° W   0°   10° E   20° E

40° N

30° N

20° N

10° N

0°

10° S

NSION

ST. HELENA

20° S

30° S

CEAN

Cape Town

ISTAN DE CUNHA

40° S

10° W   0°   10° E   20° E

politically tied to France, Britain, and the Netherlands; all rely heavily on economic links with the United States or Europe.

Currents in the Caribbean Sea

The North Equatorial Current flows northwest through the Caribbean until reaching the Yucatán Channel between Cuba and Mexico, when it veers north. A portion of this current proceeds east through the Florida Straits to become the Florida Current, which achieves average velocities of 3 knots. The Florida Current merges with the North Equatorial Current off the Florida coast and becomes the Gulf Stream. An eddy flows counterclockwise along the Central American coast, south of about 12° S.

West Indian Winter Weather

The West Indies are influenced by easterly quadrant trade winds throughout the year. These winds are strongest in the winter season, when they blow predominantly from the northeast to east-northeast, typically between 15 to 20 knots, though occasionally reaching 25 to 30 knots and more. During the winter season the trade winds regularly veer from northeast/east-northeast to east or even east-southeast as high-pressure cells move east across North America and into the Atlantic. With the formation of a new high, winds revert to northeast/east-northeast, in a cycle that typically lasts 3 to 5 days.

These wind changes can be more dramatic if a temperate-zone cold front moves through the area. Most midlatitude highs are interspersed by low-pressure cells that trail cold fronts behind them. These cold fronts frequently affect the northern islands, including the northern Bahamas and Cuba. On occasion a strong cold front will penetrate farther, even reaching well into the Lesser Antilles. Cold fronts cause the wind to veer, first to the east/southeast, then south and southwest. When the front passes, the wind typically veers northwest and builds, often to 20 to 30 knots. Squalls and thunderstorms may precede a cold front.

West Indies.

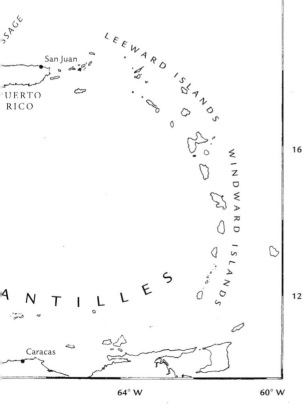

64° W 60° W

NORTH ATLANTIC OCEAN

24° N

20° N

16° N

12° N

PASSAGE

San Juan

PUERTO RICO

LEEWARD ISLANDS

WINDWARD ISLANDS

ANTILLES

Caracas

64° W 60° W

Trade wind patterns can also be interrupted by "northers," which are cold north or northwest winds caused by a larger-than-normal high-pressure area over North America. Once again, the northern islands (the Bahamas, Turks and Caicos, and the Greater Antilles) are most frequently affected. Northers are often dry but can also bring squalls and rain.

Tropical lows can develop in winter over South America, and if they become cyclonic they may affect the Dutch West Indies and Venezuelan Islands with southerly winds. Even noncyclonic South American lows can create a greater pressure gradient (and thus stronger winds) in the southwestern Caribbean.

West Indian Summer Weather

Winds in the summer are generally lighter than in winter and usually blow from the east/southeast. The shift in both wind strength and direction occurs because of a seasonal shift in the location of North Atlantic high-pressure systems, which move farther north during summer. This makes temperate-zone cold fronts less of a factor in Caribbean summer weather, but easterly waves arrive from Africa to take their place. Easterly waves are troughs embedded in the trade wind flow, and move in a generally westerly direction with the trade winds. They form every 3 to 4 days; some will affect all of the Lesser Antilles and Virgin Islands. The wind backs with the approach of a wave, generally into the northeast. Rain squalls and gusty winds to 45 knots are common. As the waves move on the wind veers back to east/southeast and slowly drops back to normal levels.

Hurricanes often begin as depressions within easterly waves. Spawning areas for hurricanes include the western Caribbean, especially for early (June) and late (October to November) season hurricanes. Midseason hurricanes usually begin in the southern North Atlantic, west of the Cape Verde Islands, but they've been known to originate just east of the Lesser Antilles. The latter are especially dangerous because there may be little warning that they are forming.

Hurricane tracks vary widely, but areas most frequently affected are the northern Lesser Antilles, Virgin Islands, Greater Antilles, Bahamas, and Florida. Note that hurricane frequency is directly related to ENSO (see chapter 7, Route Planning).

Navigation

All countries in the West Indies use the IALA (International Association of Lighthouse Authorities) maritime buoyage system for region B ("red right returning"). Markers and lights are generally reliable, but some problems have been reported in the Dominican Republic, Haiti, and the Turks and Caicos Islands. Remote reefs and shoals in many areas may not be marked. There are many cruising guides and charts available for these waters, more than for any other tropical region. Most good marine bookstores and chart agents will have a wide selection.

Bahamas Archipelago

Geography

The Bahamas archipelago is outside the Caribbean Sea, in the western North Atlantic, and much of it lies north of the tropics, including Nassau, the capital of the Commonwealth of the Bahamas. The Bahamas archipelago includes the British Crown Colony of the Turks and Caicos Islands at their southern end, in addition to the Commonwealth of the Bahamas. There are over 3,000 islands, islets, cays, and rocks in the archipelago, which stretches almost 600 miles from Walker Cay in the north (lying only 75 miles from Palm Beach, Florida) to the Turks Islands in the south. The highest point on these islands is about 250 feet (75 m) above sea level, and most islands are just a few feet above the water.

Culture

Arawak peoples originally populated the Bahamas, but they were quickly slaughtered after the arrival of the Spanish—either killed directly or felled by introduced diseases. English settlers moved into the area in the 17th century; their efforts at agriculture proved unrewarding, and piracy became a way of life for many. The islands were a popular retreat for British loyalists who fled the U.S. after the American Revolution, many of whom brought slaves. A majority of the people in both the Commonwealth of the Bahamas and the Turks and Caicos Islands today are of African origin, with the balance primarily of European ancestry. Tourism and offshore financial services are big income earners in both island groups. English is the principal language.

Coral Reefs

There are thousands of reefs in the Bahamas. Most are small patch reefs, but there are also a number of narrow fringing reefs and even a few that resemble atolls. Reef development is limited in some places due to hurricane impacts, while cold winter temperatures in the northern islands place limits on reef growth. Many reefs are in good condition, although fishing pressure is heavy in some areas. There are a number of parks and reserves, and mooring buoys are provided at many dive sites. Direct human impacts are low in the remote parts of these islands, and that's where you'll find the best reefs.

Formalities and Facilities

BAHAMAS

The primary attractions of the Bahamas are the countless islands and reefs to explore. Their proximity to the United States makes these islands an easy place to visit, but it's still possible to leave the crowds behind when cruising away from the main islands. There are a number of clearance ports in the Bahamas. Visas are not needed for citizens of most countries, and U.S. and Canadian citizens on short visits require only proof of identity (passports are needed for longer stays). Officials will come to the yacht for clearance in the larger ports, but in small ports the captain may have to go ashore. A cruising permit will be issued on arrival. Boats entering the Bahamas are currently required to purchase a cruising permit, for a substantial fee. There are restrictions in place to protect the marine environment, both within the national parks and generally, and some fees are charged. Marinas, repairs, chandleries, and provisions are all available in Nassau and Freeport. Provisioning and facilities are more limited in other areas.

TURKS AND CAICOS ISLANDS

These islands are less frequently visited than the Bahamas, and a number are uninhabited. There is excellent snorkeling and diving. There are three ports of entry: Cockburn Town on Grand Turk, Providenciales, and Cockburn Harbour on South Caicos. Arriving yachts should contact the customs service for directions on VHF channel 16. Citizens of most countries do not need visas. Cruising permits are required and are issued on arrival. There are marinas and repair facilities on Providenciales, while yachting facilities on the other islands are fairly limited. Fuel, water, and provisions are available on the principal inhabited islands.

Health and Safety

There are no serious concerns in these islands, although dengue fever and hepatitis A both occur. Health-care facilities are best in Nassau, and there is also a good hospital on Grand Turk in the Turks and Caicos Islands. There are medical clinics on most of the inhabited islands in both countries.

Greater Antilles

The Greater Antilles are the large islands of the Caribbean and include Cuba, Jamaica, Hispaniola (divided into the nations of Haiti and the Dominican Republic), and Puerto Rico; we also include the Cayman Islands here.

Geography

The Greater Antilles are made up of the remnants of an ancient chain of mountains that once extended from Central America through the Caribbean. Mountainous terrain still exists on many of the islands: for example, the Blue Mountains in Jamaica,

El Morro is at the entrance of Havana's harbor.

the Sierra de los Órganos and the Sierra Maestra in Cuba, and Duarte Peak in the Dominican Republic, the highest peak in the Caribbean at 10,400 feet (3,170 m). The Greater Antilles are large enough to create substantial rain shadows in their lee, and the southern coasts are arid.

Culture

Life for the indigenous population of these islands took a dramatic turn for the worse when Columbus established a settlement on Hispaniola in 1496, and most of the indigenous peoples were killed in the years that followed. The Spanish then brought African slaves to the islands to provide labor. That history is reflected in the present population, which primarily has mixed Spanish and African ancestry.

The primary language in the Greater Antilles is Spanish, which is spoken in Cuba, the Dominican Republic, and Puerto Rico (though in the latter English is also common). French and Creole are spoken in Haiti, while English is the language in the Cayman Islands. The population of the Greater Antilles dwarfs that of the remainder of the West Indies, and these islands have large cities: Havana (Cuba) and Santo Domingo (Dominican Republic) are cities of more than 2 million and 1.8 million, respectively. San Juan (Puerto Rico) and Port-au-Prince (Haiti) have more than 400,000 inhabitants each.

Coral Reefs

Cuba is home to the best and most extensive reefs in the Greater Antilles, with fringing and barrier reefs bordering much of the coast. Some nearshore reefs have been impacted by industrial and urban development, but away from population centers the reefs are generally in good condition. The island of Hispaniola has far more limited reef development, and those that do exist have been very heavily impacted by human activities. Jamaica's reefs have also been severely degraded over the last 20 years. The condition of most Cayman reefs is relatively good, but veteran divers say these are deteriorating; a number of controls are now in place to protect these reefs.

Formalities and Facilities

CUBA

By far the largest of the Caribbean islands, Cuba offers fantastic cruising grounds. There are a number of ports of entry; in all cases port authorities or the coast guard should be contacted immediately upon entering Cuban coastal waters. Follow directions regarding mooring, and await the arrival of officials. Visas are not normally required, but visitors should obtain a tourist card in advance. A cruising permit is required for cruising the coast. A number of restrictions apply to yachts while in Cuban waters.

U.S. citizens should note that although travel to Cuba is not restricted by the U.S. government, the Cuban Assets Control Regulations of the U.S. Treasury Department require that persons subject to U.S. jurisdiction have a license to engage in any transactions related to travel to, from, and within Cuba. Such licenses are not issued to typical tourists, so the net effect is to bar spending by U.S. citizens in Cuba. In addition, boaters are required by law to report their Cuban travel plans to the U.S. Coast Guard. Some returning boaters have been required to prove (by the U.S. Office of Foreign Assets Control) that they have not spent any money while in Cuba; potential penalties include large fines and jail terms. Thousands of Americans have visited Cuba by boat in recent years, so don't be put off by the regulations, but we would advise getting an update on the situation before departing. At this writing U.S. citizens typically receive a warm welcome from both Cuban officials and average citizens.

CAYMAN ISLANDS

Although not routinely grouped with the Greater Antilles, the Cayman Islands are located just 75 miles south of Cuba. These tiny islands are a British Crown Colony. There are two ports of entry for the three islands: Georgetown on Grand Cayman and Creek on Cayman Brac. Arriving yachts should contact Port Security on VHF channel 16. Advance visas are not required. There are a marina and repair facilities on Grand Cayman, and fuel, water, and provisions are available. Facilities are much more limited on the other two islands. The Cayman Islands have grown phenomenally in the last 30 years, from an undeveloped country to a thriving financial center and popular tourist destination. The resident population has grown from 8,500 to 30,000, but 600,000 people a year visit on cruise ships, and another 280,000 tourists, including many divers, come each year. Seafood is very popular, and there are considerable pressures on stocks of conch, lobster, and fish. A number of regulations have been imposed to protect marine life on Grand Cayman.

JAMAICA

Although Jamaica is a beautiful island with many natural harbors, it receives comparatively few cruising yachts. Ports of entry include Kingston, Montego Bay, Ocho Rios, and Port Antonio; the first two have the simplest entry procedures. Visas are not required for U.S. citizens and citizens of most European and British Commonwealth nations. A cruising permit is required but can be obtained on arrival. There are several marinas in Kingston, and some repair facilities are available. Fuel, water, and provisions are all available, but the selection of imported goods may be limited.

HAITI

This poor nation occupies the western third of the island of Hispaniola. There are a number of ports of entry. Advance visas are not required for citizens of most countries, and cruising permits can be issued by the port captain. There are marinas in Port-au-Prince and Port Morgan, but facilities are generally very limited. Fuel, water, and very basic provisions are available, but any luxuries or necessary spares should be carried onboard.

DOMINICAN REPUBLIC

There are a number of ports of entry. In all cases yachts should anchor, raise the Q flag, and wait for customs and immigration officials to arrive. Tourist cards, if required, can be obtained for a fee upon arrival. Yachts must clear between each port. There are a number of marinas and some repair facilities, and provisions, fuel, and water are widely available.

PUERTO RICO

A self-governing commonwealth in union with the U.S., Puerto Rico includes the islands of Mona, Vieques, and Culebra. There are a number of ports of entry for Puerto Rico. The captain should go ashore and visit the customs office, or place a call to customs by phone. All non-U.S. citizens must obtain an advance visa. Make sure you obtain a multiple-entry visa if also visiting the U.S. mainland or U.S. Virgin Islands. Cruising permits are required and should be obtained in advance if coming from the Virgin Islands. Yachts must check in at each new port or anchorage. There are many marinas and repair facilities; the best are in and around San Juan. Chandleries are well stocked, and spares can be shipped in from the United States by air in a few days. Provisioning is good in all major ports.

Health and Safety

The primary safety risk to travelers in the region occurs in Haiti. Travel to Haiti is currently not advised by either the U.S. Department of State or the Canadian Department of Foreign Affairs. Criminal activity is increasing throughout Haiti, especially in urban areas; downtown Port-au-Prince is considered extremely dangerous, and armed gangs are common. Crime is present in other islands and nations in the Greater Antilles, and cruisers should be prudent, but violence isn't common.

Malaria is present in all areas of Haiti and in rural areas of the Dominican Republic, especially those bordering Haiti. Dengue fever occurs on all the islands, as does hepatitis A. Typhoid fever is present in all countries except Jamaica, tuberculosis occurs in Cuba and the Dominican Republic, and schistosomiasis is present in Puerto Rico and the Dominican Republic. Medical facilities are available in the larger centers throughout the region.

Lesser Antilles

The Lesser Antilles include the Virgin Islands, the Leeward Islands (from Anguilla to Dominica) and the Windward Islands (from Martinique to Grenada), as well as Barbados. Here we also discuss the Netherlands Antilles.

Geography

The Lesser Antilles include a mixture of island types. The eastern island arc, from Anguilla to Barbados, is composed of coral islands; white sand beaches, low hills, and scrubby vegetation predominate. The western islands, from Saba to Grenada, are mountainous volcanic islands, cloaked in rainforest and bordered by black sand beaches. Trinidad and Tobago, which lie just north of Venezuela, were once connected to the South American mainland but have now become separated from the rest of the continent. Trinidad's Northern Range is a continuation of the Andean system, as are the islands north of Venezuela, but the southern plains of Trinidad were deposited by the Orinoco River in Venezuela.

The native flora and fauna of the Lesser Antilles islands is related to that found in South America. The greatest variety is found on Trinidad and Tobago, as these islands are closest to South America. Introduced species, especially goats and rats, have wreaked havoc with the natural vegetation throughout the Lesser

Lesser Antilles.

Antilles. Today plantations have replaced native forests in many areas; sugar cane is an important part of the economy and landscape in Barbados and St. Kitts, while in Dominica, St. Vincent, and St. Lucia it's bananas. In Trinidad oil is a major resource.

Culture

First settled around 4000 B.C., the Lesser Antilles were home to several different cultures prior to the arrival of Europeans in the late 15th century. The vast majority of the indigenous inhabitants were killed not long after (only tiny remnant populations of Carib islanders survive today on Dominica, St.

Vincent, and Trinidad). The islands were colonized by the British, French, and Dutch in the 17th century, and African slaves and indentured servants from India were brought by the Europeans to provide labor for agricultural plantations. A number of nations became independent in the 20th century, but many islands have either remained as colonies or have become more fully integrated with their former colonial power. Agriculture and tourism now dominate the island economies.

The present population is primarily of African descent, with minority populations of European, East Indian, Middle Eastern, Asian, and American

278

origin. A wide range of religions are practiced. English is the primary language, except on the French islands of Guadeloupe, St. Barts, Martinique, and the French side of St. Martin. Dutch is the official language of Saba, St. Eustatius (Sint Eustatius), and the Dutch part of St. Martin (Sint Maarten), but English is very common. Carnival is a major festival throughout the eastern Caribbean, with calypso singers and steel bands, street dancing, parades, and costume competitions.

Coral Reefs

There are some excellent reefs in the Lesser Antilles, but both natural impacts such as hurricanes and increasing human impacts are taking their toll. There are a growing number of marine parks and protected areas, but some attract so many visitors (one million people visit the Virgin Islands National Park annually) that the condition of reefs continues to decline despite protection. Not all reefs are well surveyed, but on two islands—the French islands of Guadeloupe and Martinique—scientists report that 80 percent of reef ecosystems are degraded. The best reefs are found away from areas of intensive tourism development. Some good examples include offshore reefs in Anguilla, and reefs around Saba and the islands of St. Kitts and Nevis (all in the Leeward Islands), and reefs around the Grenadines (in the Windward Islands). In addition, Bonaire in the Netherlands Antilles is well known for its reefs.

On some islands the surrounding shelf is very narrow, making it hard for reefs to develop but still allowing coral growth along rocks, steep slopes, and walls. Dominica in particular is known for such corals.

Formalities and Facilities

Hundreds of charter and cruising boats ply the waters of the eastern Caribbean every year. This can make it difficult to find solitude at times, but it also means that officials are accustomed to dealing with yachts, and that yachting facilities are never far away. There are more than 20 distinct island groups in the eastern Caribbean, and new facilities are currently being built on many islands. Get updates on procedures and available facilities before setting sail.

The close proximity of these islands means you'll be clearing customs (and exchanging currency) frequently if cruising rapidly through the chain. A number of different currencies are used. Other currencies include the Caribbean dollar, French franc, Netherlands Antilles guilder, Barbados dollar, and Trinidad and Tobago dollar. If you carry just one, the U.S. greenback is your best bet.

Health and Safety

There are no major health and safety issues for cruisers heading for the Lesser Antilles. Theft and petty crime can be a concern on some islands. Yellow fever occurs in Trinidad and Tobago, outside rural areas, and dengue occurs on all islands. Medical services are available on the more developed islands.

VIRGIN ISLANDS

This island group is situated between Puerto Rico and the Leeward Islands; the western half is U.S. territory, and the eastern half is British. Geographically the islands offer superb cruising, but they are crowded: the British Virgin Islands (BVI) are home to the world's largest bareboat charter fleet.

Ports of entry for the U.S. Virgin Islands include Charlotte Amalie on St. Thomas, Christiansted on St. Croix, and Cruz Bay on St. John. Customs offices are on the waterfront on all islands, and the captain should go ashore for clearance. Non-U.S. citizens must obtain an advance visa; make sure you obtain a multiple-entry visa if visiting both the U.S. mainland and the U.S. Virgin Islands. Most of the 65 islands are uninhabited. St. John offers the most isolation of the inhabited islands, while St. Thomas has the most facilities. Provisioning is very good in St. Thomas and St. Croix.

Ports of entry for the British Virgin Islands include Road Harbour and Sopers Hole on Tortola, Great Harbour on Jost van Dyke, and Virgin Gorda Yacht Harbour on Virgin Gorda. Customs offices are near the waterfront in all harbors; the captain should go ashore for clearance. (Note that you must go through entry procedures if coming from the U.S. Virgin Islands to BVI.) Visas are not needed for stays of six months or less for citizens of the United States, British Commonwealth countries, and most of the European Union (E.U.) countries; some other nationalities need advance visas. Most repair facilities are concentrated on Tortola, and a marina and boatyard are also located on Virgin Gorda. Provisioning is good in the larger population centers.

ANGUILLA

This is the most northern of the Leeward Islands and relatively undeveloped. The primary port of entry for yachts is Road Bay. The immigration office is found at the police station near the dinghy dock and can direct cruisers to customs. Visas are not required for citizens of E.U. countries, the U.S., or British Commonwealth countries; most others need visas. All Anguillan waters are incorporated into a national park with strict regulations to protect reefs and the marine environment.

NETHERLANDS ANTILLES

This is a self-governing part of the Netherlands and includes St. Maarten, Saba, and St. Eustatius (Statia) in the northern Leeward Antilles, and Bonaire and Curaçao off the coast of Venezuela (discussed below under the ABC islands). Nationals of most countries do not need visas for stays of less than three months in any of the Netherlands Antilles.

ST. MAARTEN

This is the Dutch half of the island of St. Martin (as the French call their half; information for St. Martin is listed under Guadeloupe). The sole port of entry for St. Maarten is Philipsburg, where clearance can be obtained at Bobby's Marina or the commercial pier at Pointe Blanche. There are marinas, full repair facilities, and excellent provisioning. Note that boats must go through immigration procedures when sailing between the French and Dutch halves of the islands.

SABA

This volcanic island lies southwest of St. Maarten. The port of entry is Fort Bay; clear customs ashore after anchoring. Basic provisions and fuel are available. There are no beaches, but the snorkeling is very good. All the waters are a marine park, and regulations and fees apply.

ST. EUSTATIUS

St. Eustatius, or Statia, lies between Saba and St. Kitts. The port of entry is Oranjestad, and clearance is available ashore at the head of the pier. Fuel, water, and basic provisions are available.

ANTIGUA AND BARBUDA

Formerly a British possession, these islands now form an independent nation. English Harbor was a major English naval base for centuries and retains its historic flavor.

Ports of entry for Antigua are English Harbour, Falmouth Harbour, Jolly Harbour, and Crabbs Marina. In all cases the captain should go ashore to complete clearance formalities. Visas are not required for citizens of E.U. and British Commonwealth countries, and the U.S.; citizens of other countries may need to obtain advance visas. Port entry, cruising permit, and mooring fees apply. There are excellent repair facilities and chandleries.

Customs and immigration for Barbuda are at the boat harbor near Codrington, the island's only town. There are no facilities and only basic provisioning.

ST. KITTS–NEVIS

This independent nation is composed of the two islands of St. Christopher (or St. Kitts) and Nevis, which are separated by a narrow pass. There are two ports of entry: Charlestown on Nevis and Basseterre on St. Kitts. In both places the captain should go ashore for entry procedures. No visas are needed for citizens of British Commonwealth and most E.U. nations for visits up to one month; U.S. and Canadian citizens can stay up to six months without a visa. Cruising permits are needed to visit outlying areas on both islands, and yachts must clear when sailing from one island to the other.

MONTSERRAT

This British Crown Colony is volcanically active and has a mountainous lush interior. The sole port of entry is Plymouth; customs are near the main dock. No visas are needed for citizens of British Commonwealth and E.U. nations, and U.S. citizens. Cruising permits are needed for anchoring outside Plymouth. Facilities are minimal, but provisions and water are available.

GUADELOUPE

This island, the largest of the Leewards, is administered by France as an overseas department. Included in this designation are the nearby islands of La Desirade, Les Saintes, and Marie-Galante, as well as St. Martin and its neighbor, St. Barts (located about 100 miles to the north).

Ports of entry for Guadeloupe include Pointe-à-Pitre, Basse Terre, and St. François; the captain should go ashore for entry. Nationals of most countries do not need visas for visits of less than three months. Yachting facilities in Guadeloupe are very good, with marinas, boatyards and chandleries. Provisioning is also good.

Ports of entry for St. Martin are Marigot Bay and Anse Marcel. The captain should go ashore for entry. Nationals of most countries do not need visas for stays of less than 3 months. There are marinas, repair facilities, and good provisioning.

The port of entry for St. Barts is Gustavia; the captain should go ashore after anchoring. St. Barts is a duty-free port. Port dues are charged. Fuel, water, and provisions are available.

DOMINICA

This rugged island was a British possession until 1978, when it became independent. There are few beaches, but the interior offers good hiking in a lush environment. Ports of entry are Roseau and Portsmouth; the captain should go ashore to obtain clearance. Permits for 3-week stays are granted on arrival. Facilities are basic; water, fuel, and provisions are available.

MARTINIQUE

This still-active volcanic island is a French department and is administered separately from Guadeloupe. Ports of entry include Fort-de-France, Marin, and St. Pierre. The captain should go ashore for customs clearance. Citizens of non-E.U. countries staying for more than 3 months need visas. Marinas, repair facilities, and chandleries are excellent, and there is good provisioning.

ST. LUCIA

This beautiful island is a former British Crown Colony but has a strong French influence. Ports of entry are Vieux Fort, Marigot Bay, Castries, and Rodney Bay. The captain should go ashore for clearance upon arrival. Visas are not needed for E.U., British Commonwealth, and U.S. citizens. A cruising permit should be obtained at entry. There are marina and repair facilities; fuel, water, and provisions are available.

ST. VINCENT

This independent nation includes the island of St. Vincent and more than 30 small islands in the Grenadines. Ports of entry include Kingstown, Wallilabou Bay, and Young Island Cut on St. Vincent; Port Elizabeth on Bequia; Grand Bay on Mustique; and Clifton on Union Island. The captain should go ashore to complete customs and immigration formalities. Visas are not required prior to arrival. The most complete facilities are in Kingstown, where repairs of all sorts are possible. Kingstown also offers the best provisioning. On the outlying Grenadines facilities range from basic to nonexistent.

BARBADOS

This island is not nearly as scenic as the islands to the west and offers limited cruising opportunities. Bridgetown is the sole port of entry; arrival should be announced via VHF. Most European, British Commonwealth, and U.S. citizens don't need visas. Repair facilities and chandleries are available, as are most provisions.

GRENADA

This country includes the main island of Grenada and the smaller islands of Carriacou and Petit Martinique to the north. Ports of entry include St. George's, Prickly Bay, Grenville, and Secret Harbour on Grenada, and Hillsborough on Carriacou. Visas are not needed by most European and British Commonwealth citizens, or citizens of the U.S. Cruising permits are needed and can be obtained on arrival. There are restrictions on anchoring in certain areas. Marinas and repair facilities are available on Grenada, and provisioning in St. George's is very good.

TRINIDAD AND TOBAGO

These islands, lying outside the hurricane belt, have become a very popular cruising destination. A former British Crown Colony, they became independent in 1962. Ports of entry are Port of Spain and Chaguaramas on Trinidad and Scarborough on Tobago. Yachts should announce their arrival to the coast guard on VHF channel 16. Entry permits for visits of 3 months are given on arrival. There are excellent facilities for repair and storage on Trinidad; facilities are basic on Tobago.

THE ABCS

Aruba, Bonaire, and Curaçao make up what is informally known as the ABC islands. All are part of the Kingdom of the Netherlands; Bonaire and Curaçao are part of the Netherlands Antilles, but Aruba is autonomous. Ports of entry are Oranjestad on Aruba, Willemstad and Spanish Water on Curaçao, and Kralendijk and Bonaire Marina on Bonaire. Visas are not needed for nationals of most countries if staying less than 3 months. There are marinas and good provisioning on all the islands; good repair facilities are located on Curaçao. Bonaire has become a popular diving destination, and strict regulations have been adopted to protect its superb reef environment.

CENTRAL AMERICA

Most of the countries of Central America have both Atlantic and Pacific coasts (Belize and El Salvador are the exceptions, bordering on just the Caribbean and Pacific, respectively). Generally speaking, the cruising is better on the Caribbean coast, though that's not the case in Costa Rica. Here we present weather and cruising information for both coasts; sailors planning a trip on the Pacific side will also want to refer to the weather and current information for the greater Pacific.

Weather

On the east coast, winds in winter are generally dominated by northeast trades, which may tend almost northerly. Trade winds are periodically interrupted by northers and cold fronts (see West Indian Winter Weather, page 271). Both are less common south of Honduras. Sea and land breezes are common. In summer the area is still subject to northeast trades, but daily winds are often dominated by alternating land and sea breezes. Hurricanes are relatively rare but do strike this coast.

The Pacific coast of Central America has less consistent trade winds than the Caribbean coast, due to the blocking effect of the Sierra Madre range and the seasonal movement of the ITCZ, which causes a monsoonal wind pattern in these waters. To the north (off the coast of Mexico), winds tend to parallel the coast, but land and sea breezes dominate along many areas with high mountains. Northeast winds predominate off the coast in winter as far south as 4° or 5° N. Late fall and early winter bring both northers and west or southwest fronts. Late winter months bring the most settled weather. Summer winds are more likely to be west or southwest, due to the movement of the ITCZ to the north, which allows the Southern Hemisphere's southeast trades to extend farther north. The southeast trade winds curve to the right after crossing the equator, becoming southwesterlies. They are typically moist and warm, having traversed equatorial latitudes, and can bring heavy rains to this coast. Hurricane season is June to September.

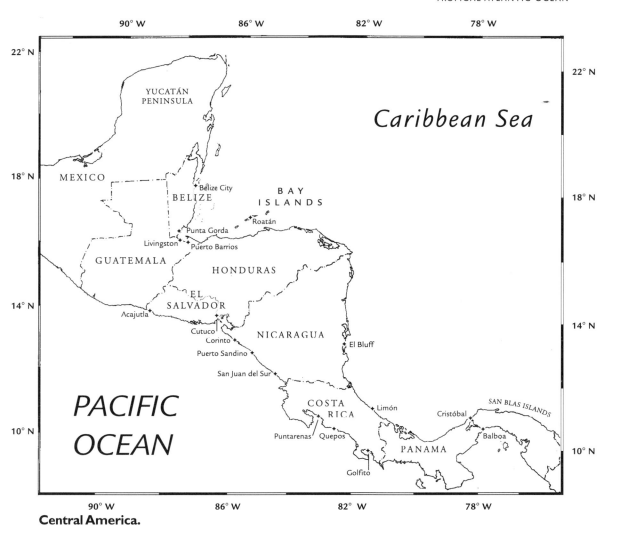

Central America.

Geography

Four different tectonic plates meet in this small area, causing frequent earthquakes (severe earthquakes in early 2001 caused extensive damage in El Salvador). There are over 40 volcanoes between Guatemala and Costa Rica, another sign that the area is geologically active. The highest reaches almost 14,000 feet (4,270 m), and many are still active. Most of the land is mountainous; a narrow coastal plain is found on the Pacific side, with a larger area of flat land along the Caribbean coast. The dramatic topography means there are many different climatic zones, and the proximity to both North and South America has resulted in a rich and varied flora and fauna.

Culture

The countries of Central America have a very long and complex history, but two themes stand out:

domination by the Spanish between the 15th and 18th centuries and frequent civil wars and fighting thereafter, with the instability often exacerbated by frequent U.S. intervention in the region. There is considerable wealth, but much of the population in most of these countries remains very poor. The indigenous ("Indian") peoples have been all but wiped out in some countries (such as Costa Rica) and are most numerous in Guatemala, where Indians account for more than half the population. British influence is notable in a number of areas popular with cruising sailors, including Belize (a British Crown Colony until 1981), the Bay Islands of Honduras (ceded to Honduras by Britain in the 19th century), and the Caribbean (Miskito) coast of Nicaragua, a British protectorate until the end of the 19th century. English is widely spoken in all these areas (and is the official language in Belize); Spanish is the official language in the rest of Central America. Most people live in the highlands between 3,000 and 8,000 feet (900–2,400 m). The Caribbean coast is, for the most part, sparsely populated and remains mostly forested.

Coral Reefs

The reefs of the Pacific and Caribbean coasts of Central America are very different. Reefs on the Pacific side are some of the poorest in the region, as the natural conditions don't favor corals, and the reefs that are present have come under heavy pressure from both natural events and human activities in recent decades. The best remaining reefs on this coast are in Panama and Costa Rica.

In contrast, reefs on the Caribbean side of Central America include the area's finest. Belize has reefs of all sorts, including the Caribbean's longest barrier reef, shallow platform reefs, and even a series of oceanic atolls. Many reefs have been damaged in recent years by storms and bleaching from El Niño events, but human pressure from fishing is fairly low in comparison to other parts of the Caribbean. What's more, most of Belize's tropical and mangrove forests are still intact, greatly reduc-

ing the amount of sediment that ends up on the reef. The net result is that Belize is home to the Caribbean's best reefs.

Heading southeast, most of the reefs in Honduras are fringing reefs, either along the shore or around the offshore islands such as the Bay Islands (Islas de la Bahia). The reefs in this area have been stressed by natural events in recent years, including bleaching in the 1998 El Niño and Hurricane Mitch, which struck in 1998. A marine reserve is planned for the Bay Islands.

Panama has relatively few reefs, and these have been heavily degraded in recent years from a variety of impacts including overfishing, oil spills, and development. The San Blas Islands include some of the most extensive reef areas in Panama and are a popular cruising destination. Sadly, much of the coral in the San Blas Islands has been destroyed or seriously impacted over the last 20 years. The damage is most acute on the inhabited islands.

Navigation

All countries in Central America use the IALA B buoyage system and markers and lights are typically well maintained, though problems have been reported in Belize, where a number have been out of service. Many remote reefs and shoals are not marked. Charts of the area are generally good, and a number of cruising guides are available.

Formalities and Facilities

BELIZE

The primary attraction from the perspective of the cruising sailor is the barrier reef and the hundreds of islands within it. Official ports of entry in Belize include Belize City and Punta Gorda in the south. Formalities are simplest in Punta Gorda; Belize City is a major commercial port, and it is best to contact the port captain on VHF channel 16 for entry procedures. Advance visas are not required for most E.U., British Commonwealth, and U.S. citizens. Yachting facilities in Belize are minimal. There is a marina at Moho Cay, north of

Belize City, where basic repair facilities, water, fuel, and provisions are available; boats can be left here for trips inland. Provisioning is also good at Ambergris Cay. Equipment repair can be undertaken in Belize City, but there are no yachting facilities or chandleries.

GUATEMALA

The biggest attractions for cruisers are the rivers on the Caribbean coast, such as the Rio Dulce, which can be navigated upstream to Lake Izbal. There are several ports of entry on the Pacific and Caribbean coasts. Livingston and Puerto Barrios on the Caribbean coast are both accustomed to providing clearance for yachts. Visas and tourist cards are required but are issued upon arrival. Yachts staying more than one month need a cruising permit. There are marinas on the Caribbean coast at Livingston and El Golfete, and boats can be hauled out and basic repairs made.

EL SALVADOR

This small country facing the Pacific is quite industrialized in comparison with its neighbors. There are two ports of entry: Acajutla and Cutuco (near La Unión). All yachts should contact the navy on VHF channel 16 to inquire about procedures for clearance. Visas or tourist cards are required for citizens of most countries. There are no yachting facilities, but engine and machinery repairs can be arranged.

HONDURAS

The most popular cruising area in Honduras is the Bay Islands in the Gulf of Honduras on the Caribbean side. There are a number of ports of entry on the Pacific and Caribbean coasts and in the Bay Islands. The main entry port for the latter is Roatán. Yachts in this port should anchor and await the arrival of a customs official; in many ports it's necessary to go ashore and seek entry. It is necessary to clear with the port captain in each port when cruising through Honduran waters. Citizens of the E.U., U.S., Canada, Australia, and New Zealand don't need visas; others should inquire

ahead. There are slipways and repair facilities in the Bay Islands, and provisions, water, and fuel are all readily available.

NICARAGUA

The Miskito coast on the Caribbean side of the country offers many anchorages, but care must be taken when navigating these reef-strewn waters. Ports of entry include Corinto, Puerto Sandino, and San Juan del Sur on the Pacific coast and El Bluff on the Caribbean side. U.S. and some European citizens do not need advance visas for stays of up to 90 days, but nationals of many countries will need advance visas. Permits (available in the capital city of Managua) are required to visit some offshore islands. Simple repairs are possible, but there are no yachting facilities, and provisions are limited in many areas.

COSTA RICA

The wealthiest nation in Central America, Costa Rica offers some of the most accessible wildlife. Ports of entry include Playa del Coco, Golfito, Puntarenas, and Quepos on the Pacific side and Puerto Limón on the Caribbean side. Arriving yachts should contact the port captain on VHF channel 16. Citizens of most countries do not require advance visas. A temporary importation certificate must be obtained at the first port of entry. Permits are needed to visit the marine parks of Isla del Coco and Isla del Caño. Various repair facilities are available in Puntarenas; provisioning is good there and at Golfito.

PANAMA

In addition to being home to the Panama Canal, Panama offers good cruising in the offshore islands on both coasts. Ports of entry are Cristóbal, Balboa, Porvenir, and Rio Diabolo (the two latter ports are in the San Blas Islands). For Cristóbal and Balboa, arrival should be announced on VHF channel 16; in the San Blas Islands the captain should go ashore for entry. Tourist cards are required for citizens of most counties and are issued on arrival. Many also need advance visas. Cruising permits are required and will be issued on arrival for a fee. Fees for transiting the Panama Canal are high. Facilities are good in both Colón and Panama City, and there is excellent provisioning.

Health and Safety

Crime is a problem throughout Central America and is increasing. Petty theft and other common "urban" crimes are a problem in all urban areas, but violent crime, including rape, muggings, and kidnappings, is a significant problem in some areas. The safest countries currently are probably Belize and Panama, though southern areas of Panama near the Colombian border are considered very dangerous. El Salvador is probably the most dangerous, with a significant risk of armed robbery, rape, and kidnapping, but serious ongoing problems are also reported in Guatemala, Honduras, Costa Rica, and Nicaragua. The good news here is that coastal areas have traditionally been relatively safe. There have been a number of incidents over the years involving cruisers, however, including the murder of a sailor in Honduras in 2000. The situation with respect to safety can change quickly, and we advise all cruisers to get updated information. See the Government Travel Advisories and Information for Cruisers sections in appendix 3, Resources.

Tropical diseases are widespread in Central America. Malaria, hepatitis A, dengue fever, cholera, and typhoid occur throughout the region. Panama also has a risk of yellow fever in some areas; tuberculosis occurs in Nicaragua, Guatemala, and Honduras. These diseases are not found uniformly throughout each country, so obtain detailed information before traveling to better define the risk in various areas. In addition, epidemics of some diseases may occur periodically, greatly increasing the risk in some places. For example, in late 2000 a dengue epidemic resulted in thousands of cases and a number of deaths; El Salvador declared a national dengue emergency and Honduras a national alert.

CARIBBEAN SOUTH AMERICA

Because of the increasing risk of travel throughout Colombia (see below), Venezuela is the only Caribbean South American country that can be considered a safe cruising destination at present and thus the only one discussed here in detail.

Venezuela

Geography and Culture

Venezuela is a large country with much to attract the cruising sailor. The interior of the country is dominated by the Andes in the west, which attain a height of over 16,000 feet (5,000 m); remnants of the mountain range continue east through Barcelona, all the way to Trinidad. In the very south there is rainforest at the headwaters of the Rio Negro, which flows into the Amazon at Manaus (Manáos) in Brazil. Extensive grasslands and a high plateau comprise the east, which has the world's highest waterfall. The Caribbean coastline extends for over 1,500 miles, and there are more than 70 offshore islands. In the east, south of Trinidad, is the Orinoco River delta, which is navigable by keel boats.

The Spanish colonized the country in the 18th century and mixed with both the indigenous population and African slaves brought to work on sugar plantations. The present population of some 21 million is primarily of mixed descent; about one-fifth of the people are of European (mostly Spanish) origin. Spanish is the primary language. Agriculture and oil are the big industries in the country.

Coral Reefs

Reef development is limited because of freshwater and sediment runoff and extensive development. Better reefs are found around the offshore oceanic islands, which include the archipelago Los Roques, but there is intensive fishing at Los Roques (for lobster, conch, and fish). The island reefs are less exploited

Local craft off Margarita Island, Venezuela.

than mainland reefs for tourism; large-scale bleaching of corals occurred in the 1980s and 1990s.

Navigation

The IALA B buoyage system is used, and navigational aids are reliable. Venezuela is covered by various Caribbean cruising guides.

Formalities and Facilities

There are a number of clearance ports in Venezuela. It is generally necessary to go ashore to obtain clearance. All visitors need advance visas, available from Venezuelan consulates (there are a number in the Lesser Antilles). Yachts must clear customs to enter and exit each state as they cruise through Venezuelan waters. There are fees for both entry and departure. There are extensive facilities for yachts, and repairs of all sorts are possible; many cruisers leave their boats here for extended periods. There is excellent provisioning in most larger towns.

Health and Safety

There have been increasing problems with crime in recent years. Violent crime is on the increase, and there have been reports of attacks on cruising sailors; cruisers were victims of two violent pirate attacks in early 2001. In one incident a cruiser was shot and

seriously wounded while underway between Isla Margarita and Trinidad. On land, problems have occurred both on the mainland and in the islands; the border area with Colombia in particular is not considered safe. Cholera, dengue fever, hepatitis A, tuberculosis, and typhoid fever occur in Venezuela, and malaria and yellow fever are a problem in some parts of the country. Good health-care facilities are available in private clinics in larger cities.

Colombia

We can't recommend Colombia as a cruising destination at present. The U.S. Department of State warns Americans not to travel to Colombia because of the security risk. There have been bombings, kidnappings, and murders in all parts of the country, and the risk has been increasing. The U.S. has greatly increased the amount of military aid to Colombia as part of Plan Colombia, and this is likely to worsen an already dangerous situation.

Nonetheless, some cruisers continue to visit select coastal ports; the historic city of Cartagena is the most popular landfall. Visas are not required for visitors from most countries, but all yachts must use an agent when clearing in and out of the country. Repair facilities and good provisioning are available in Cartagena.

CAPE VERDE ISLANDS

The Cape Verde islands, located in the eastern North Atlantic near the west coast of Africa, are a common stopover point for boats making their way from the Canaries to either the Caribbean or Brazil. The islands are volcanic; nine are inhabited. The highest volcano, Cano (at 9,300 ft./2,830 m) is located on Fogo and is still active. The Cape Verde Islands are at the northern edge of the area affected by the African coastal monsoon, which supplies almost all the rainfall. In years when the monsoon does not come sufficiently far north, severe droughts result. Droughts were responsible for many deaths in the 18th and 19th centuries and have continued in recent years. Primary winds are from the northeast.

The islands were discovered by the Portuguese in the mid-15th century and were at that time uninhabited and cloaked in vegetation (hence the name). Plantations were established a few years later, and African slaves were brought in to work them, along with goats, which devastated the vegetation. The islands had exclusive trading rights with Portugal and West Africa and became central to the slave trade. The islands became independent from Portugal in 1975, following years of warfare. Today about half the population lives overseas, and the country is heavily dependent on aid. The official language is Portuguese.

Navigation

The IALA A buoyage system is used. There may be problems with the accuracy of charts.

Formalities and Facilities

There are three ports of entry: Mindelo, Praia, and Sal. Visas are not required for short stays, but those wishing to spend any time cruising in these islands are advised to obtain a visa in advance. Fees are charged for visas and for clearance. Facilities are basic in the Cape Verde Islands, but there is a small yacht club in Mindelo (located in Porto Grande Bay) that welcomes visitors. Basic repairs can be made by some workshops; provisions are available, but most food is imported and, therefore, expensive. There are fresh produce markets in Mindelo and Praia.

Health and Safety

The Cape Verde Islands are generally safe, though some problems with theft have been reported. Cholera, hepatitis A, malaria, tuberculosis, and typhoid fever all occur in the islands. Medical facilities are poor. Basic medical procedures are available in Praia, but cases requiring specialized care may need to be evacuated. Tap water is not safe to drink, and even bottled water may be unsafe; all water should be treated, or mineral water purchased.

◄ *South Atlantic Ocean* ►

South Atlantic Weather

Southeast trade winds dominate the wind regime in the South Atlantic, generally blowing between about 25° S and the equator. They extend farthest north (at times to about 10° N) in the northern summer. Wind strengths average about 10 to 15 knots and tend to be from the southeast or south-southeast in the eastern South Atlantic and from the east in the western South Atlantic. The tropical South Atlantic has a reputation for having the best weather of any ocean, in part because it's free from tropical cyclones and because the ITCZ generally stays north of the equator.

South Atlantic Currents

The west-setting South Equatorial Current extends well south of the equator and reaches a maximum of 1 knot at about 6° S latitude, while a weaker westerly flow called the South Subtropical Current extends to about 20° S latitude. When the South Equatorial Current reaches the Brazilian coast, most of it is diverted north, but a portion, along with the

South Subtropical current is deflected southwest and becomes the Brazil Current. The Brazil Current flows south parallel to the coast until reaching about 25 degrees, when a portion turns southeast and east. Along the African coast the Benguela Current sets northwest year-round. It extends as far as the equator between February and April.

Brazil

Geography and Culture

By far the largest and most populous nation in South America, Brazil is a place of great contrast and vitality. The tropical east coast has an extensive coastal mountain range with just a narrow band of lowland along the coast. Inland of these mountains—and south of the Amazon—lies a large high plain, the Planalto de Mato Grosso. The Amazon basin dominates the north of the country from the coast to the western borders with Peru, Colombia, and Venezuela. Almost 4,000 miles (6,400 km) long, the Amazon is the world's longest river, and despite the vast areas that have been cleared, the Amazon rainforest still accounts for a large portion of the world's total forested area. With its many different ecological zones, Brazil has an extraordinarily rich flora and fauna, but many species are under threat from logging, poaching, and growth.

The indigenous population of Brazil before European contact is thought to have numbered in the millions. The Portuguese arrived in 1500 and wasted no time in settling the country, establishing sugar plantations, and enslaving the indigenous population; only about 200,000 native peoples survive today. In the 17th century African slaves were brought to work the plantations, and then the mines, after gold was discovered in the 1690s. Brazil became independent of Portugal in 1822 when the Brazilian Empire was established. It lasted until the late 19th century, and there have been a number of coups since then. The distribution of wealth remains extremely unequal in Brazil, even when compared with its South American neighbors. Portuguese is the official language, and most people are Catholic. The present population numbers over 170 million.

Brazil extends north of the Equator, and the northern coast is influenced by the northeast trades (strongest in the southern summer). The east coast (south of the equator) experiences southeast trades (strongest in the southern winter). Primary cruising areas are the east coast between Salvador and Rio de Janeiro and the Amazon River delta.

Navigation

The IALA B buoyage system is used.

Formalities and Facilities

There are many ports of entry in Brazil. The normal procedure in most ports is for the skipper to go ashore, see the port captain, and then clear customs. A clearance is needed each time one enters another port, and a cruising permit must be carried; these can be obtained upon arrival in Brazil. Visas should be obtained before arrival. There are yacht clubs in a number of ports, and they typically welcome foreign visitors. There are haul-out and repair facilities in many larger centers, catering mostly to local pleasure craft. Provisioning is typically good, though some imported goods may be hard to find.

Health and Safety

Crime is high in large cities, including Rio de Janeiro, São Paulo, Recife, and Salvador, and you should inquire locally before leaving your boat unguarded; this can be arranged through a yacht club. Crime is less of a problem in outlying areas and smaller cities. Cholera, dengue fever, hepatitis A, malaria, schistosomiasis, tuberculosis, typhoid fever, and yellow fever occur in Brazil. The risk for most diseases is higher in rural areas, and many are not a problem in urban centers. Good health-care facilities are available.

St. Helena

First discovered by the Portuguese in the early 16th century, this mid-Atlantic island was used as a regular port of call for the next 150 years. The island was then controlled by the English East India Company, until it became a British colony in 1833. It was long a popular stopping point for ships, but today the island is visited primarily by yachts. Ascension and Tristan da Cunha are both dependencies of St. Helena.

Jamestown is the port of entry in St. Helena and the site of the only anchorage. Yachts should anchor or use a mooring if one is available. Officials come to the yacht for clearance. No visas are required for any visitors. Modest immigration, harbor, and other fees are charged. There are no yachting facilities, but showers are available, and simple repairs can be made. Fresh produce and various tinned provisions are available, as are water and fuel.

Chapter 18

Tropical Pacific Ocean

The primary cruising destination in the tropical Pacific is the region often termed Oceania, made up of the many thousands of islands that constitute Micronesia, Polynesia, and Melanesia. This is a vast area, stretching for thousands of miles. It includes both long-time favorite destinations such as Tahiti and many remote and rarely visited islands. Australia is another popular cruising area. Most boats visit the east coast, which includes the Great Barrier Reef. In the eastern Pacific, the Galápagos Islands are an intriguing and popular destination.

◄ *North Pacific Ocean* ►

Weather

Most of the North Pacific is subject to northeast trade winds throughout the year. There is considerable variation in the direction and strength of the trades across the Pacific and a seasonal variation as well.

In winter, northeast trades combine with the northeast monsoon winds in the far west to allow northeast winds to prevail across virtually the entire tropical Pacific. The exception is a narrow band east of the dateline where the ITCZ is found north of the equator, allowing southeast winds to cross the equator. Trades are generally strongest in winter, and generally blow hardest in the mid-Pacific, including around Hawaii, where winds of 25 knots and more are not uncommon. Winter is the season for south and southwest storms in the mid-Pacific (including Hawaii, where they are known as kona storms). They generally bring rain and gusty winds. Farther west, in the Caroline Islands, winter is the dry season, as it is in the Philippines. Winter is the "safe" season for cyclones, except in the western Pacific, where they can (and do) strike all year.

In summer the East Pacific High is stronger and farther north than it is in winter, and as a result the trades extend farther north (to about 32° N). Summer also sees the trades replaced by the southwest monsoon west of about 150° E and also east of about 120° W, between the ITCZ and the equator. Trade winds are generally more easterly in summer and may tend southeast in the western Pacific before the onset of the southwest monsoon, in June to July. The southwest monsoon is generally less steady than the northeast trades and is more frequently interrupted by variables or even easterly

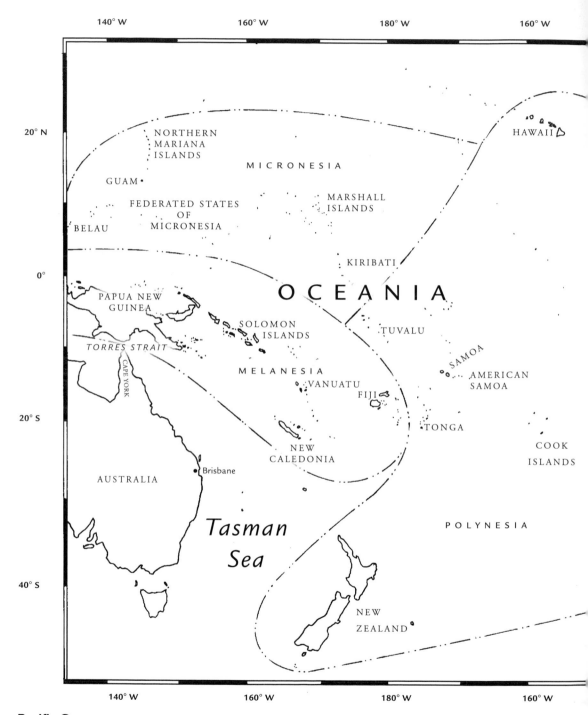

Pacific Ocean.

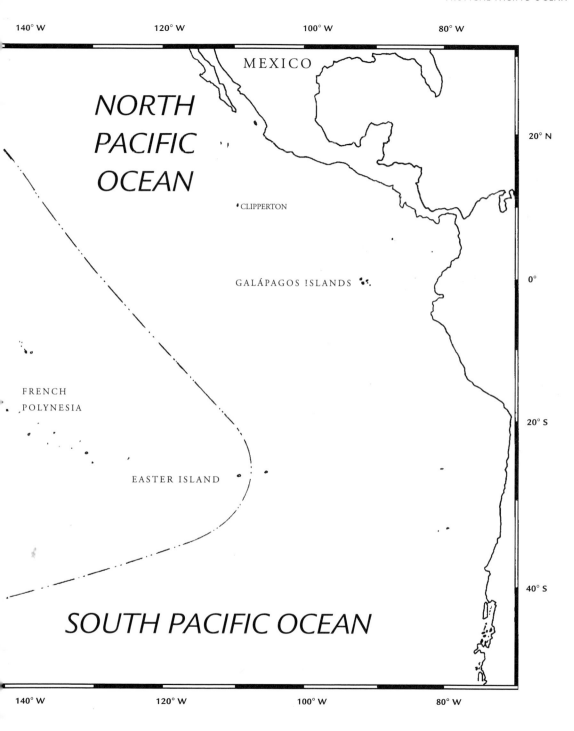

140° W   120° W   100° W   80° W

MEXICO

NORTH
PACIFIC
OCEAN

20° N

• CLIPPERTON

0°

GALÁPAGOS ISLANDS

FRENCH
POLYNESIA

20° S

EASTER ISLAND

40° S

SOUTH PACIFIC OCEAN

140° W   120° W   100° W   80° W

Na Pali coast, Kauai, Hawaii.

winds, except in the South China Sea, where it averages Force 3 to 4. Hurricanes and typhoons are most likely to occur in summer (June to November). There are two major spawning areas for tropical cyclones in the North Pacific, one off the coast of Mexico, where the ITCZ curves well north of the equator, and the other in the Caroline Islands.

Currents

The west-setting North Equatorial Current is strongest in its southern reaches (around 10 to 12° N) and slowly decreases in strength as you move north. The opposing east-setting Equatorial Counter Current flows in a band about 4 degrees wide, roughly between 2 and 6° N in winter. It shifts north in the summer months, especially in the

east Pacific, when it flows between 6 and 10° N. The Equatorial Counter Current is strongest in the west, between 130 and 145° E. Immediately south of the Equatorial Counter Current, and moving north and south in tandem with it, is the west-setting South Equatorial Current, with its northern extent between 1 and about 5° N.

Upon reaching the Philippines, the North Equatorial Current splits, with part flowing north along Taiwan to form the Kuro Shio Current. A smaller portion flows south, into the Celebes Sea, and then through Makassar Strait.

Currents are more variable in the eastern Pacific, off the coast of Central and South America. The main flow of the Equatorial Counter Current is usually at about 6° N; it branches north and northwest as it nears the coast. Part of the current branches south along the Colombian coast early in the year.

In a La Niña year, the west-setting North Equatorial and South Equatorial Currents flow more strongly, while the east-setting Equatorial Counter Current is weak and narrow. In an El Niño year, all currents are weaker, especially the west-setting South Equatorial Current. This is because the southeast trade winds have slackened.

North Pacific Islands

The islands of the tropical North Pacific include the Hawaiian Islands and most of Micronesia. We discuss generally the islands of the Pacific within the traditional ethnogeographic categories of Micronesia, Polynesia, and Melanesia, but we'll diverge from that at the outset by taking a separate look at Hawaii. Although Hawaii is part of Polynesia and Hawaiian culture and language are closely related to other Polynesian cultures such as those in Samoa, Tonga, Tahiti, and New Zealand, Hawaii doesn't fit when lumped in with the other islands of Polynesia for at least two reasons. First, Hawaii is in the North Pacific, where the weather patterns are different. More importantly, perhaps, the fact that Hawaii is part of the United States affects all aspects

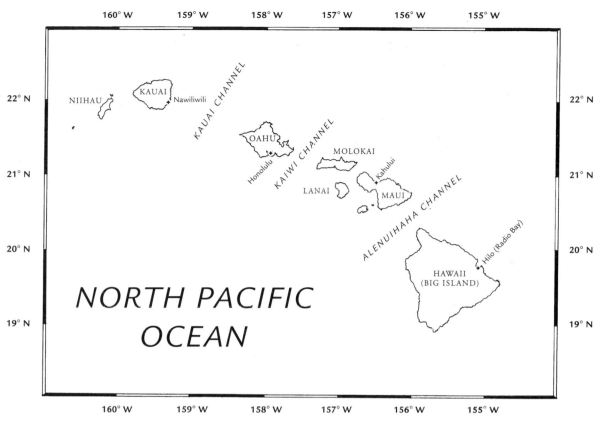

Hawaiian Islands.

of life. The present culture, standard of living, and system of government are more akin to other parts of the United States than to the rest of Polynesia. In many ways Hawaii straddles two worlds, combining a Pacific Island climate and history with all the trappings of the modern world.

Hawaiian Islands

Geography

Hawaii consists of a chain of 7 major inhabited islands and some 124 small islands and reefs. All of the main islands are located within the tropics, but the smaller islets and atolls, which make up the Northwestern Hawaiian Islands, stretch north as

far as 28° N latitude. Hawaii's main islands are volcanic, formed by a midoceanic hotspot that's now located beneath the southernmost island of Hawaii (the Big Island), the youngest in the chain. The age of the islands increases as one travels north, and in the Northwestern Islands the volcanic core of the islands has subsided and eroded to a point that all that remains visible above the surface are coral reefs. The difference in age is immediately apparent in the main islands, with active eruptions and fresh lava flows visible on the Big Island, while the island of Kauai is heavily eroded, with steep, knife-edged cliffs and hanging valleys. The relative age of the islands is also reflected in their elevation above sea level. The Big Island is the highest in the Pacific outside of New Guinea at 13,600 feet (4,179 m), and heights decrease to just above sea level among the islets of the Northwestern Islands.

Culture

Hawaii was one of the last areas of the Pacific to be settled by Polynesians who arrived from the Marquesas and Society Islands around 500 A.D. The earliest confirmed contact with Europeans occurred in 1778–79 during Captain James Cook's third and last voyage. In the 1,300 years between settlement and European contact, Hawaii had developed a complex society, with a population numbering in the hundreds of thousands spread across all the main islands. The native population declined rapidly after European contact, primarily as a result of diseases. Hawaii became a popular port of call for whalers and traders and attracted significant American investment. American business interests were instrumental in overthrowing Hawaii's monarchy in 1893; the big losers were native Hawaiians, who to this day remain economically disadvantaged in their own islands.

Today, agriculture, the U.S. military, and tourism dominate Hawaii's economy and society. Hawaii's population is now a diverse mix of Asian, European, and Pacific Island ancestry, all of whom contribute to the unique culture of modern Hawaii.

Coral Reefs

All of the main islands are too young to have well-developed barrier reefs, although one small barrier reef does enclose Oahu's Kaneohe Bay. Most of Hawaii's reef systems are fringing reefs, which provide no protection for the sailor. This, combined with the lack of major river systems in the islands, results in there being few protected anchorages. Unfortunately for cruisers, what is probably the best natural harbor in the tropical Pacific—Pearl Harbor—is off limits to sailors, because it's home to the U.S. Navy's Pacific fleet.

Many of the reefs around the main Hawaiian Islands have been heavily impacted by agricultural and urban runoff and by construction projects (the main runway for the Honolulu International Airport is built atop a reef). Reefs in the Northwestern Islands are in far better condition and have recently been incorporated into the Northwestern Hawaiian Islands Coral Reef Reserve, by far the largest of its type in the United States. It's too soon to know what this will mean in terms of actual protection, but it bodes well for these reefs, which include critically important habitat for seabirds, monk seals, sea turtles and other marine life.

Navigation

Hawaii uses the IALA B buoyage system. NOAA charts cover the Hawaiian Islands, and their accuracy is excellent. Navigational aids are reliable. Several cruising guides to the Hawaiian Islands are available.

Formalities and Facilities

Ports of entry include Hilo (Hawaii), Kahului (Maui), Honolulu (Oahu), and Nawiliwili (Kauai). The port captain or customs office should be notified on arrival; the captain can go ashore to do this, or contact can be made via VHF or cell phone. In Hilo, yachts should call in at Radio Bay; at Kahului and Nawiliwili, proceed to the commercial wharf; in Honolulu, proceed to the Ala Wai yacht harbor and tie up at the customs office dock, located near the harbormaster's office. U.S. vessels do not need to clear with customs or immigration if arriving directly from a U.S. mainland port, but they will need to obtain clearance from State of Hawaii agricultural inspectors. U.S. yachts arriving from any port other than the U.S. mainland (including U.S. possessions and territories) must clear with customs on arrival, as must all foreign flag yachts. The latter need a cruising permit (issued on arrival); citizens of some countries are not eligible for cruising permits, in which case they need clearance from customs when cruising between the islands. Citizens of all foreign countries other than Canada are required to obtain visas in advance. There are strict quarantine regulations in Hawaii for all animals.

The State of Hawaii has passed restrictions on anchoring in Hawaiian waters, and a permit is required for boats anchoring for more than 72 hours; the rule is not widely enforced. There are also restrictions on fishing and anchoring in marine protected areas, of which there are a number around the state.

Hawaii offers access to the same range of goods and services available in the U.S. mainland, albeit often at a higher cost. The majority of marinas are state owned, and moorage is at a premium. It's generally possible for visiting yachts to find space in Honolulu's Ala Wai marina, but for a limited time only. The Hawaii Yacht Club (located in Ala Wai Harbor) will generally accommodate visiting yachts for two weeks. Honolulu offers the greatest selection of marine services, including a number of boatyards and chandleries, and has the state's largest marinas. Haul-out fees are high, but any repairs can be made.

Health and Safety

Health-care facilities are excellent, and communicable tropical diseases are not found in Hawaii. The U.S. Coast Guard provides rescue services. Normal precautions against theft are advisable in urban areas.

Micronesia

Weather

The islands of Micronesia cover an immense swath of the central and western Pacific, and weather conditions can vary considerably between islands and nations. Islands to the east of about 160° E experience primarily easterly quadrant winds, and these tend to be more northeasterly in the Marshall Islands, and easterly or east-southeasterly in Kiribati. Farther west some of the islands come under the influence of the southwest monsoon during the height of the summer, but northeast trades still predominate in winter.

The Mariana Islands have the distinction of being located in a very active area for tropical cyclones (called *typhoons* in this region). They can occur at any time of the year in the waters near Guam and the other Mariana Islands, but they're most frequent in the summer months, peaking in August. The Caroline Islands serve as the spawning ground for these typhoons, but both the Carolines and Belau have been hit on occasion. Weather forecasting is very good, and the U.S. Navy's Joint Typhoon Warning Center (based in Hawaii) tracks typhoons in this area.

Geography

The islands of Micronesia lie scattered in a broad band west of the dateline, between about 12° S and N. The easternmost nation in Micronesia is Kiribati, which includes some 33 islands in the North and South Pacific. Kiribati includes much of the Line Island chain, the Phoenix Islands, and the Gilbert Islands. All are low islands. West and north of Kiribati are the Marshall Islands, consisting of 29 coral atolls with over 1,000 islands and islets. All are low-lying and small, and the total land area is just 70 square miles. The Caroline Islands—over 600 in all—stretch west from the Marshalls toward the Philippines. The Carolines include both high islands (such as Kosrae and Pohnpei) and many atolls. A string of raised islands, Marianas, stretches north of Guam and arcs toward Japan.

Culture

Western Micronesia (as far east as Yap) was settled by migrations from Indonesia and the Philippines, starting at least 4,000 years ago. Eastern Micronesia was settled somewhat later by migrations from northeastern Melanesia (Vanuatu or the Santa Cruz Islands). There was considerable travel throughout Micronesia during this period, with communication between islands and also with Asia. Complex societies developed, which built the extensive stone cities of Nan Madol (on Pohnpei) and Lelu (on Kosrae), unique in the Pacific.

Magellan arrived in Micronesia in 1521, and the Spanish quickly established a presence in the Mariana Islands, which they used as a stopover on trips to the Philippines. The remainder of Micronesia largely escaped European colonial influences until the late 18th century, but since then the

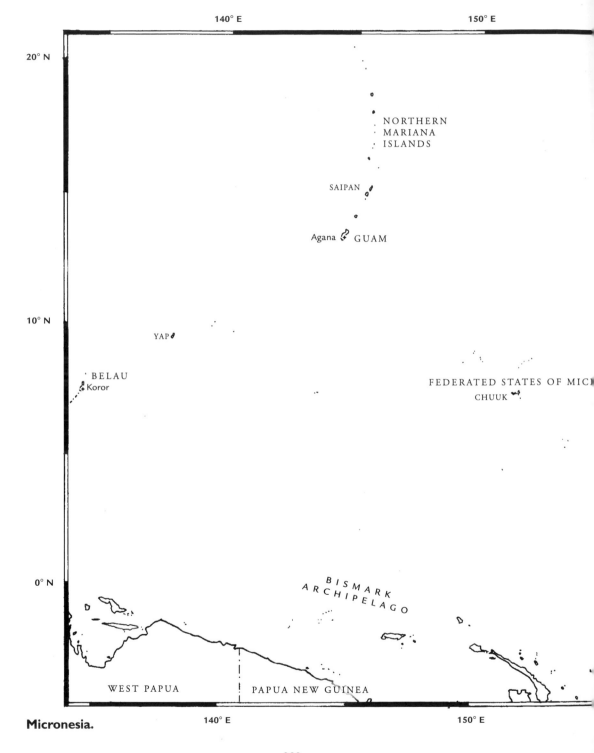

Micronesia.

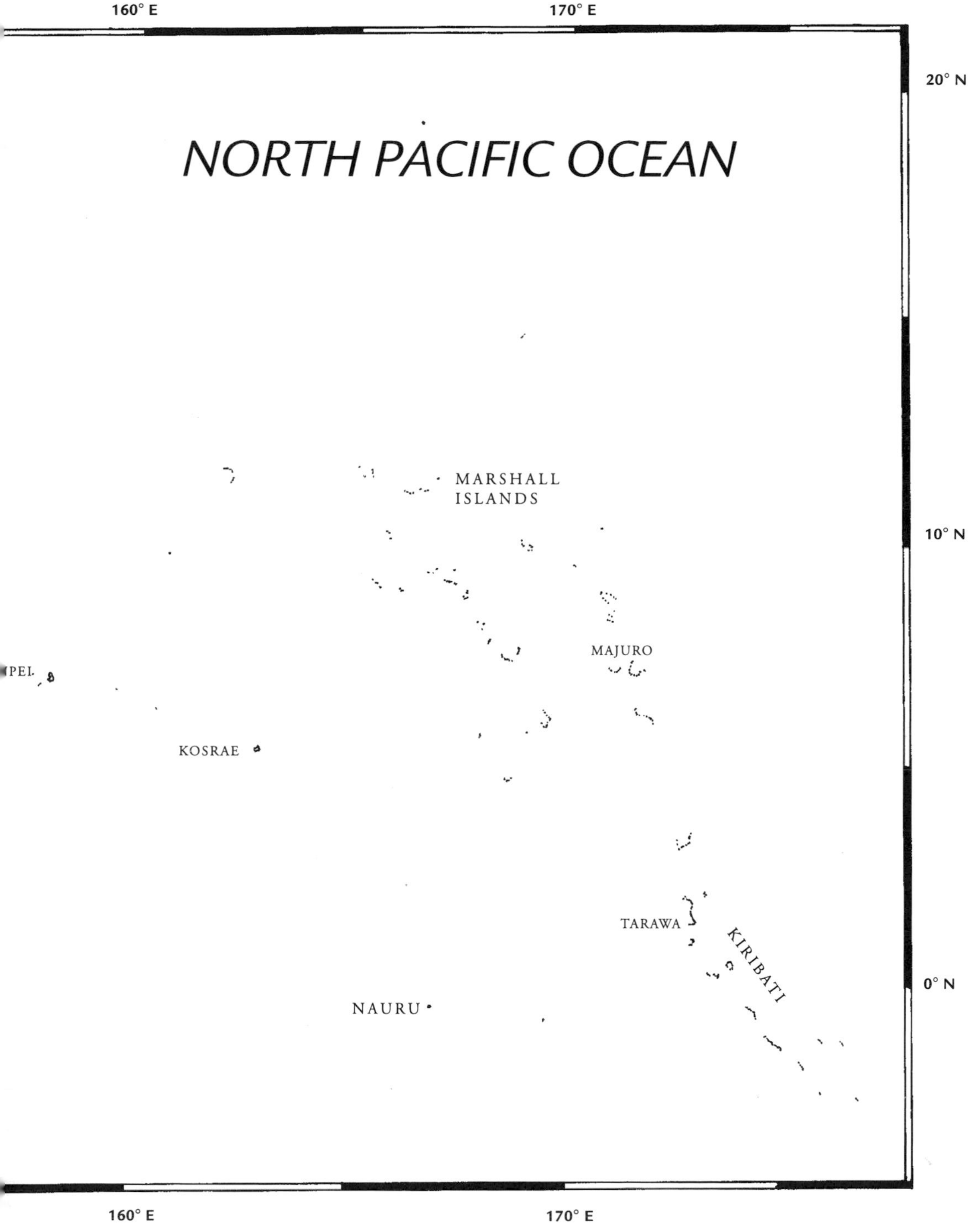

160° E   170° E

20° N

NORTH PACIFIC OCEAN

MARSHALL
ISLANDS

10° N

PEI.

MAJURO

KOSRAE

TARAWA

KIRIBATI

0° N

NAURU

160° E   170° E

British, Germans, Japanese, and Americans have all been involved. In recent years most of the islands of Micronesia have been closely associated with the United States; Kiribati, the exception, was formerly part of the British colony of the Gilbert and Ellice Islands. Guam is an unincorporated U.S. territory, and the neighboring Northern Mariana Islands are a U.S. commonwealth. The Marshall Islands form a republic; the Caroline Islands are divided into two nations: the Federated States of Micronesia and the Republic of Belau (formerly Palau). All three are signatories to a Compact of Free Association with the United States, under which islands receive aid and technical assistance, and the United States gains military access. Kiribati is an independent nation and a member of the British Commonwealth. English is the official language (used by governments and many businesses) across Micronesia and is spoken by many residents.

Coral Reefs

Micronesia features a wide range of reef types, with more than 82 atolls, barrier reefs in Chuuk (formerly Truk), Belau, and Pohnpei, and fringing reefs around a number of the region's volcanic islands. Reefs in Kiribati receive few natural stresses (being largely outside the area affected by tropical cyclones), and those away from urbanized areas, such as Tarawa, are generally in excellent condition. Likewise, reefs in most of the Caroline Islands are in good condition, especially in remote areas. The most diverse and spectacular reefs in the Carolines (and probably in all of Micronesia) are in Belau, a popular dive destination. A number of the Marshall Islands (which are all either atolls or coral islets) have been heavily impacted by human activities such as military occupation, major World War II battles, and nuclear testing. Urban crowding on Majuro and Kwajalein atolls (the latter a U.S. military base) continues to have serious impacts. The reefs of Guam and the other Mariana Islands have all suffered heavily from widespread development and are generally in the poorest condition of any in the region.

Navigation

Charts of Micronesia are generally good, and U.S. (NIMA) charts are likely to be the best for the entire region. The IALA A buoyage system is used. Markers and lights in major ports are generally working, but this should not be relied on in remote areas. Most reefs and shoals are not marked.

Formalities and Facilities

Much of the tropical Pacific is without yachting facilities. There are essentially no facilities catering to yachts in the North Pacific other than in Hawaii and Guam, while south of the equator yachting facilities are concentrated in the Society Islands, Fiji, and New Caledonia and aren't found north of about 15° S. That doesn't mean that repairs can't be made, but you must be prepared (and able) to make use of facilities that are not intended for yachts. It also means that almost all of your time must be spent at anchor, and water and fuel must often be brought aboard with jerricans.

KIRIBATI

There are ports of entry in each of the three major island chains in Kiribati, including: Fanning (Tabuaerean) and Christmas (Kiritimati) in the eastern Line Island chain; Betio Islet on Tarawa Atoll in the Gilbert Islands (capital of Kiribati), and Canton in the Phoenix Islands. In addition, Banaba (Ocean Island) is also a port of entry, but there is no sheltered harbor or anchorage on this raised coral island. Yachts arriving at Tarawa should call the Marine Guard in advance on SSB (2182) or VHF channel 16. Formalities are completed at the small craft harbor.

Boats arriving at Fanning should anchor inside the pass (on the southern side), while boats arriving at Christmas should anchor outside the lagoon, to the west of the settlement of London. On Fanning, officials generally come to the yacht for clearance; if they don't, the captain should go ashore to seek clearance, which is the norm on Christmas. There are conflicting reports on how long yachts are allowed to stay at Canton, and it would pay to make inquiries in advance.

Sailors wishing to cruise the Gilbert Islands should obtain a cruising permit when clearing customs at Tarawa. Advance visas are officially required for citizens of a number of countries (including the United States), but this has not been enforced in the past in the Line Islands (Fanning and Christmas). Inquiries about the current situation can be made with Kiribati honorary consuls (in Hawaii, the U.S. mainland, Australia, and New Zealand) or with the Principal Immigration Office on Tarawa. There are a slipway and a number of workshops on Tarawa, and some very simple repairs may be possible at Christmas. Some provisions are normally available at Tarawa and Christmas, but facilities and provisions on other islands are very basic or nonexistent.

MARSHALL ISLANDS

There are two ports of entry into this country of more than a thousand islands: at Uliga on Dalap Island on Majuro Atoll and at Ebeye Island on Kwajalein Atoll. The latter is a U.S. Army installation, and clearance at Majuro is recommended. In both ports, arriving boats should attempt to contact Port Control via VHF channel 16; if no reply is received, anchor your boat, and the skipper alone should go ashore to the government offices to clear. Immigration permits are required for visits over 30 days, and these should be obtained in advance from the chief of immigration or from the consulate in Honolulu. Permits are required to visit the outer islands, and these must be obtained from the Ministry of Interior and Outer Islands Affairs. There is a fee levied when visiting the outer islands. There are no yachting facilities and only a limited selection of spares. Provisions are available, as is fuel. Water should be considered contaminated unless from a catchment source.

FEDERATED STATES OF MICRONESIA

Ports of entry for the Federated States of Micronesia (FSM) include Lelu and Okat Harbors on Kosrae Island (for Kosrae State), Kolonia Harbor on Pohnpei Island (Pohnpei State), Weno Island in Chuuk Lagoon (for Chuuk State), and Tomil Harbor on Yap Island and Ulithi Atoll (both in Yap State). Arriving yachts must clear customs at one of these ports of entry before stopping at any other islands. Arrival should be announced via VHF to Port Control (when arriving in Pohnpei) and Marine Resources (in Kosrae). Boats calling in at Tomil Harbor should anchor or come along the dock in the small boat harbor; at Ulithi Atoll there's a government wharf. The port of entry at Weno Island is near the airport. It is necessary to clear with customs and immigration when arriving initially and when sailing between the various states.

Arriving yachts are issued renewable 30-day immigration permits (with a new permit granted on arrival in each state); stays of more than 90 days in any one state require a visa. A cruising permit (valid for all of FSM) must be obtained from the chief of immigration in Pohnpei prior to arrival. There's no charge for the permit, which is valid for one year.

Yachting facilities are very limited in FSM, and there are no marinas or boatyards catering to pleasure boats. It may be possible to effect repairs on hull or machinery at one of the main ports, but facilities are very limited. Cruising boats should carry all essential spares and cruisers should plan to do routine maintenance that requires a boatyard elsewhere.

Provisioning is reasonably good in the main ports, but very limited in the outer islands. Water supplies in FSM should be considered suspect, unless they are fed by catchment.

GUAM

The sole port of entry into Guam is Apra Harbor. Contact the harbormaster on VHF channel 16 on arrival; yachts can generally clear customs at the Marianas Yacht Club. All arriving yachts must clear customs, except U.S. yachts arriving directly from another U.S. port. U.S. immigration requirements apply, and foreign citizens will need advance visas. There are limited yachting facilities in Guam, but most repairs can be made. Apra Harbor provides sheltered anchorage except during typhoons (tropical cyclones); limited space is available in a cyclone hole in the harbor. There is good provisioning in Guam, and spares and supplies are readily flown in from the U.S. mainland if not available locally.

COMMONWEALTH OF
THE NORTHERN MARIANA ISLANDS (CNMI)

The 14 islands that make up the Commonwealth of the Northern Mariana Islands (CNMI) are a U.S. Commonwealth. The sole port of entry is Tanapag Harbor in Saipan; the port superintendent should be notified prior to arrival. Visas are not required for stays of up to 30 days. A cruising permit must be obtained in advance from the chief of immigration on Saipan or the CNMI representative in Guam or Honolulu. There are restrictions in place regarding visits to some of the outer islands, a number of which are wildlife refuges. Entry, docking, and immigration fees apply. There is a marina on Saipan, and basic repair facilities are available. Provisions, fuel, and water are available.

BELAU (FORMERLY PALAU)

The sole port of entry for Belau is the commercial port at Malakal Harbor on Koror. Sailors should attempt to announce their arrival to port authorities in advance. Advance visas are not required, and a 30-day immigration permit is issued on arrival. A maximum of two extensions of this permit are granted (thus allowing a 90-day visit); extensions are costly. An entry permit must be obtained prior to arrival from the chief of immigration. A hefty fee is charged for the permit, with the fee escalating if the permit is not obtained in advance. Permits are valid for 30 days; 30-day extensions cost as much as the original. In addition to the entry permit, a harbor fee and a Rock Island fee are both charged. Boats staying more than 30 days are charged an assortment of other fees for each additional 30-day period. Boats are not allowed to stay more than a total of 90 days, and the fee schedule encourages brief visits. A 30-day visit currently costs about $300 U.S.; if a yacht with two crew stayed for 90 days, the total would come to about $1,300 U.S. Yachting facilities in Belau are minimal, but some repairs can be made. Provisions, water, and fuel are available.

Health and Safety

Micronesia is free of most serious tropical diseases, although there was an outbreak of cholera in Pohnpei in 2000 that claimed at least 15 lives. Health care is most advanced in Guam; health-care facilities across the remainder of Micronesia are generally in poor condition, and only the most basic services are available outside the urban centers. Water quality should be considered suspect in all parts of Micronesia except Guam and CNMI.

◀ South Pacific Ocean ▶

Weather

The trade winds in the South Pacific generally vary between southeast and easterly, blowing in a band between about 5° and 25° S; they're most consistent in the winter months. Winds generally average 15 to 20 knots but can climb to as much as 30 knots in the western Pacific (or Coral Sea), if a large high is present to the south in the Tasman Sea. The ITCZ is typically found north of the equator, but will dip into the Southern Hemisphere during the southern summer, in an area near the dateline. The South Pacific Convergence Zone (SPCZ) forms and reforms periodically, and migrates seasonally. It generally stretches from the Solomon Islands in the west to the Cook Islands and French Polynesia in the east; in the summer months it joins the monsoon trough that develops over northern Australia. Winds are often light northeasterlies between the SPCZ and the equator.

The western Pacific (within 10 to 12 degrees of the equator and west of about 180 degrees) is subject to northwest winds during the summer months, as a result of the southward movement of the SPCZ. These winds are generally light.

Tropical cyclones occur in the South Pacific between November and April; January to March are the months with the highest cyclone frequency. Major spawning areas include the waters to the south of the Solomon Islands, and central Pacific. Cyclones are more frequent in the eastern Pacific during El Niño years and more frequent in the Western Pacific and Coral Sea during La Niña years.

Currents

The west-setting South Equatorial Current is strongest near the equator and weakens as one moves south. Between 6° and 20° S the movement of water is still to the west but more variable, and the current is called the South Subtropical Current.

In the eastern Pacific there is a counterclockwise circulation in the vicinity of the East Pacific High. On the eastern edge the cold northerly flow along the coast of South America is called the Peru Current (formerly the Humboldt Current), which is at its strongest along the coast. This current brings fog to the tropical waters off the Peruvian Coast and lowers temperatures on land. A branch of the Equatorial Counter Current flows south along the coast of Colombia and northern Ecuador in the early months of the year, reaching to about the equator. This is the infamous El Niño current, which, under certain conditions, penetrates much farther south, to the vicinity of Lima, replacing the cold waters of the Peru Current with warm tropical water.

Current patterns in the western South Pacific change seasonally, under the influence of the southeast trades and northwest monsoon. In the southern winter (between about April and September) the South Equatorial Current splits upon encountering the Solomon Islands, with part of the flow continuing northwest along the coast of New Guinea, and another portion tending slightly southwest and into the Torres Strait. The currents in this area are generally less than one knot, but they may be considerably stronger in places, including within Torres Strait and off the north coast of New Guinea at about 140° E. In the southern summer the flow along both New Guinea and through Torres Strait is reversed, flowing to the east or southeast. There are considerable eddies and variations in the northern Coral Sea and Solomon Sea, where this east-setting flow meets the west-setting South Equatorial Current.

South Pacific Islands

The islands of the South Pacific include the Galápagos Islands off the coast of Ecuador, most of Polynesia, and all of Melanesia. These islands and waters have lured sailors for generations, and not without reason.

Galápagos Islands (Archipélago de Colón)

There are 13 major islands and a number of minor islands within the Galápagos archipelago, which straddles the equator about 600 miles off the South American coast. The islands are a province of Ecuador. All are volcanic, and the lowlands are typically stark. The islands are most famous for their wildlife (which includes giant tortoises, iguanas, and a variety of bird life) and for the role they played in the development of the theory of evolution. Today a number of areas have been set aside as a wildlife sanctuary, and together they form the Galápagos National Park.

Unfortunately, it has become very costly for yachts to cruise these islands, if they intend to visit areas within the national park. Brief stops are still allowed for boats in transit. There are two ports of entry: Puerto Baquerizo Moreno, Wreck Bay (on San Cristóbal), and Puerto Ayora, Academy Bay (on Santa Cruz). The captain should go ashore upon arrival and seek clearance from the port captain and immigration office. Advance visas aren't required. Cruisers who don't intend to visit areas within the Galápagos National Park typically receive clearance from the port captain to remain in the islands for a minimum of 3 days, with longer stays possible at the discretion of the port captain. Crews of transiting yachts can visit national park areas only as part of an organized tour, leaving their boat moored in one of the clearance ports.

Those wishing to visit national park areas with their own boat must secure a permit and must be accompanied by a guide. Permits are not easy to get, and fees are high, possibly amounting to many hundreds of U.S. dollars per day. There are very minimal repair facilities available in the islands.

Fuel and water are not always available, and provisions are expensive.

Polynesia

The fact that many Polynesian islands are accustomed to tourists and have been visited by yachts for many years helps make Polynesia an easy region to visit. There are also more services catering to yachts in Polynesia than elsewhere in tropical Oceania. Outside of Hawaii, the Society Islands are the best place to buy spares and organize boat repairs, but the cost is high. Limited services are also available in Tonga. Bareboat charters can be arranged in both the Society Islands and Tonga.

Geography

Almost all the islands of Polynesia are volcanic in origin, and active volcanism continues in Hawaii. Because of coral growth and island subsidence, Polynesia includes diverse island types: high volcanic islands such as the Society Islands (including Tahiti and Bora Bora), limestone islands in Tonga, and coral atolls such as the Tuamotus and Tuvalu. The age of an island and the amount of reef growth are both important in determining what kind of cruising it offers. The Marquesas (which are young, high volcanic islands) lack extensive reefs, making for rather exposed, roily anchorages. The Society Islands are also volcanic, but have much more extensive reef development, opening up a greater range of sheltered harbors and sailing. The Vavau group in Tonga is composed of raised limestone, and the highly indented coast and many small islands, all surrounded by reef, make for excellent sheltered-water cruising. Finally, coral atolls, 78 of which are found in the Tuamotus alone, offer a very different sailing

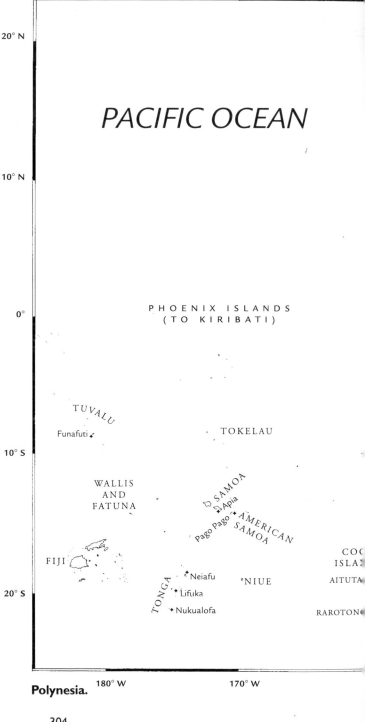

Polynesia.

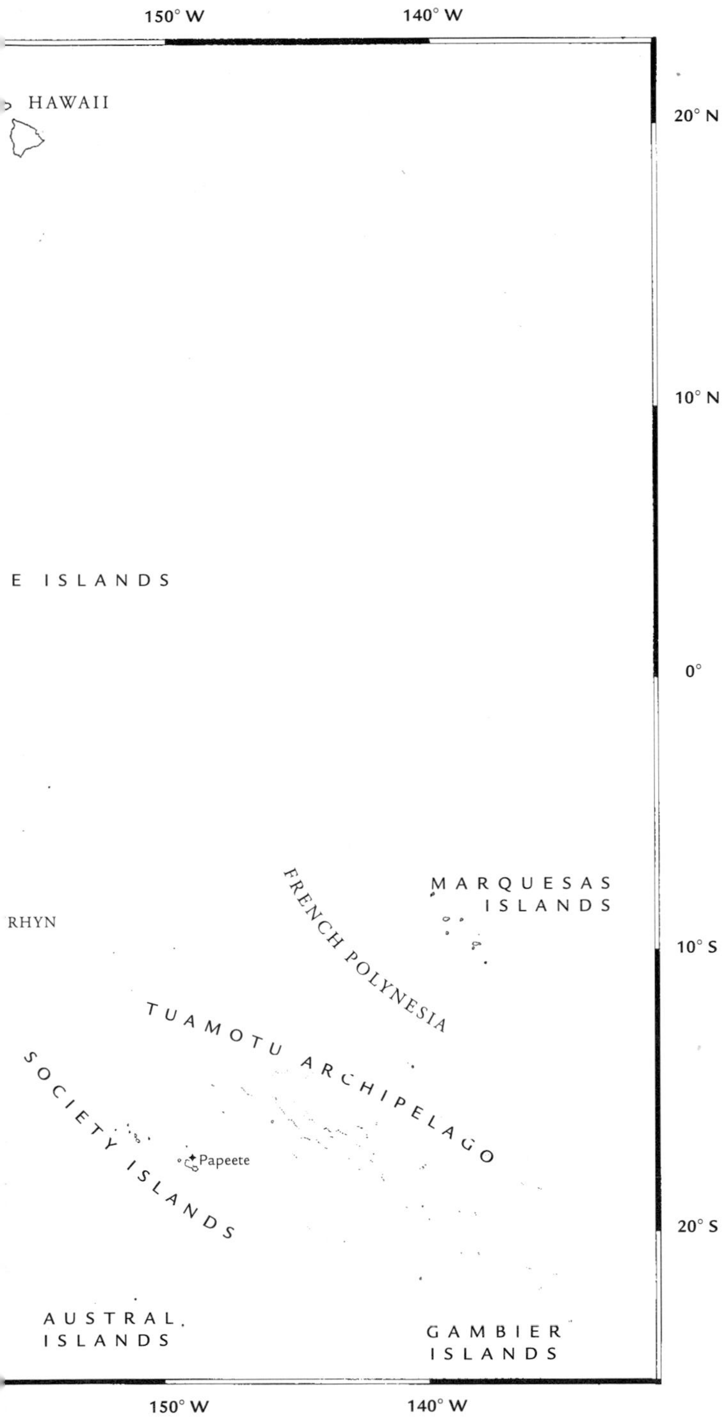

150° W 140° W

HAWAII

20° N

E ISLANDS

10° N

0°

FRENCH POLYNESIA

MARQUESAS
ISLANDS

RHYN

10° S

TUAMOTU ARCHIPELAGO

SOCIETY ISLANDS

Papeete

20° S

AUSTRAL
ISLANDS

GAMBIER
ISLANDS

150° W 140° W

experience to the cruiser willing to sail among reefs.

Culture

The settlement of Polynesia began with Samoa and Tonga, about 3,000 years ago. Islanders reached the Marquesas some 1,000 years later and from there went on to colonize the remainder of Polynesia, reaching New Zealand by about 750 A.D. The islands of Polynesia are more closely related in terms of language and culture than are Micronesia and Melanesia, in part because Polynesia was settled much more recently. Significant contact with Europeans didn't take place for 1,000 years after all the island groups were settled. Although there were occasional visits to Polynesian islands by European explorers in the 16th and 17th centuries, it wasn't until the late 18th century, following the voyages of Captain James Cook, that the way of life in Polynesia began to change rapidly.

Polynesia, more than any other region, gave birth to the romantic idea of the South Seas. You can blame this on the accounts of European explorers such as Bougainville and Cook, who visited Tahiti and experienced a vastly different approach to life and love than they knew back home; it could also be ascribed to the works of authors and artists such as Robert Louis Stevenson and Paul Gauguin, who in the late 19th century found and lived their dreams. Whatever the case, the allure is alive and well, causing tourists and cruisers to flock to these islands.

English is spoken throughout much of the region, although a knowledge of French is very useful in French Polynesia, especially on outlying islands.

Coral Reefs

The majority of the islands in Polynesia (in particular, the many atolls) have extensive reef systems, and the majority of reefs remain in good condition. Exceptions include those areas—including the Marquesas and the Galápagos—which have poorly developed reefs due to adverse natural conditions, such as relatively low seawater temperatures, rapid sinking of the islands, and heavy wave action. Reefs in parts of the Society Islands have been impacted by rapidly growing populations, and coral bleaching has also taken its toll.

Navigation

The IALA A bouyage system is used. Charts of the region are generally accurate, and most major ports are well marked with navigational aids. Cruising guides are available that give general coverage for the entire region, and detailed guides cover French Polynesia.

Formalities and Facilities

FRENCH POLYNESIA

French Polynesia includes five major island groups (the Marquesas, Tuamotus, Society, Austral and Gambier Islands) that are all combined into a single French overseas territory. The sole official port of entry for the islands is Papeete on Tahiti in the Society Islands. Yachts arriving in Papeete should contact the port captain on VHF channel 16, and anchor or moor as directed.

It's possible to clear customs temporarily at one of the other islands and then complete the entrance formalities in Tahiti. Yachts arriving at an outer island should report to the local police (gendarmerie); if the island is very small, report to the island chief. A 6-month cruising permit is normally issued, which must then be stamped by the chief or police at any other islands that are visited; extensions are available only in Papeete. Yachts from the European Union and some other countries are generally allowed to stay for 90 days without advance visas, whereas yachts from the United States and Canada are granted 30 days. Yachts must arrive in Papeete before the visa-free period elapses, at which time a 60-day visa extension can be requested. It is possible to extend for a further 3 months, but this requires permission from the high commissioner in Papeete. Yachts can cruise in the islands for 6 months without paying duty.

Citizens of E.U. countries arriving by yacht are no longer required to post a bond, but all non-E.U. citizens must deposit a sum equal to a one-way air ticket back to their home country. If cruisers arrive in the Marquesas, the bond must be posted there, but for those cruisers arriving at a small island with no banking facilities, it's possible to delay depositing the bond until arrival in Papeete. The bond requirement is normally waived for those staying less than 30 days, and it can also be satisfied by holding an actual airline ticket. It's reportedly possible to pay the bond via credit card. Fees are charged for visas, and there are port duties.

Yachting facilities in French Polynesia are concentrated in the Society Islands. The best facilities are on Tahiti and Raiatea. Papeete has no marina, but there are a number of Mediterranean-style moorings, which have both electricity and water available. Elsewhere on Tahiti there are two marinas where it may be possible to arrange moorage. There's a charter base on Raiatea, and it's possible to leave your boat there either in or out of the water. Haul-out facilities are available on both islands. Tahiti offers the best provisioning in all of French Polynesia. There is a reasonable selection of goods on most of the other Society Islands, but provisioning in the other islands is very limited, aside from canned goods and local produce.

COOK ISLANDS AND NIUE

Two Polynesian countries are internally self-governing states in free association with New Zealand: the Cook Islands (a group of 15 islands), and Niue (a single uplifted coral island). Both Cook Islanders and Niueans are citizens of New Zealand.

The Cook Islands are divided into a southern and northern group; the northern group is composed of atolls, and the volcanic southern islands are a continuation of the Austral Islands of French Polynesia. There are three full-time clearance ports in the Cook Islands: Omaka on Penrhyn Atoll in the far north, Arutanga on Aitutaki, and Avarua on Rarotonga. Contact the harbormaster on VHF channel 16 before entering the harbor on Rarotonga; on the other islands the captain should go ashore for entry. It may be possible to clear customs at Atiu and Pukapuka for a fee (to pay transport costs for customs agents). A 30-day permit is issued on arrival and can be extended up to a maximum of 90 days; extensions must be obtained in Rarotonga. Those wishing to stay longer than 90 days should obtain a visa in advance from a New Zealand or British consulate. Boats are allowed to make brief stops at Suwarrow, where there is a permanent administrator. Yachts are not allowed to remain in the islands during cyclone season. There are various harbor and immigration fees. There are no facilities catering to yachts. Provisions, fuel, and water are available on Rarotonga and some of the other islands, but provisioning is limited.

Niue is a single raised coral island lying south of Samoa, between the Cook Islands and Tonga. Alofi is the sole port of entry. Arriving yachts should contact Niue radio (monitored 24 hours) on VHF channel 16 to arrange clearance, which must be completed before landing. Entry permits are issued on arrival. Moorings are available for use by visiting yachts (installed by the Niue yacht club), and these should be used if possible to prevent coral damage. The harbor is an open roadstead and is untenable in westerly winds. There are no haul-out facilities, but some provisions, fuel and water are available.

WALLIS AND FUTUNA

These islands, the smallest of France's three Pacific overseas territories, are administered from New Caledonia. The indigenous inhabitants of Wallis were originally from Tonga, and Futuna was settled by Samoans. There are two ports of entry: Mata Utu on Wallis and Sigave on Futuna. In both ports the captain should go ashore for clearance. Citizens of the European Union, the United States,

Canada, and some other countries don't need visas. Wallis has a lagoon with a protected anchorage, but there is no lagoon around Futuna. Provisions, water, and fuel are best obtained on Wallis; there are no yachting facilities on either island. French is the official language.

SAMOA

The islands of Samoa are divided into two political entities: American Samoa consists of five high islands and two atolls and is an unincorporated U.S. territory; Samoa (formerly Western Samoa), is an independent nation consisting of two high islands.

Pago Pago is the sole port of entry for American Samoa. Arriving yachts should contact Harbor Control on VHF channel 16, or berth at the customs wharf on the south side of the harbor. U.S. citizens need passports, and citizens of other nations are issued 30-day permits on arrival, which can be extended up to 90 days. There's no limit to how long U.S. citizens can stay. Note that all arriving yachts must have a customs clearance (zarpe) from their previous port; this applies even to U.S. yachts arriving directly from another U.S. port (such as Hawaii). Clearance and moorage fees are charged.

In addition to normal clearance procedures, it is necessary to arrange a mooring or anchorage area with the harbormaster; a careful check is kept on where boats are anchored at all times in this crowded port. It is advisable to make use of a mooring if at possible, as the holding in the harbor is very poor, and many yachts routinely drag anchor.

There are no haul-out facilities for yachts, but mechanical repairs can be arranged. There are some marine supplies available. U.S. postal rates (with very fast service) apply, and phone rates are also very low compared with other South Pacific countries. Provisioning is the best in Polynesia outside of Hawaii, and fuel and water are readily available.

When approaching Samoa (formerly Western Samoa), an estimated time of arrival should be announced (via Apia Radio) 24 hours in advance if possible; otherwise contact Harbor Control via VHF channel 16 well in advance of entering port. Yachts

Pirogue sailing on Baie d'Upi, New Caledonia.

should not come alongside the main wharf until permission is granted. Cruisers are required to use the services of an agent. No immigration permits or visas are required for stays of less than 30 days, but a visa is needed for longer stays. This can be obtained in advance (from Samoan, New Zealand, or British consulates) or from the immigration office in Apia. A cruising permit will be required for visiting areas outside of Apia. There are no yachting facilities in Samoa, and only simple repairs are likely to be possible. A reasonable range of provisions is available in Apia (though much less than in neighboring American Samoa); selection is very limited in other areas. Fuel and water are both available.

TONGA

Tonga is an independent kingdom and a member of the Commonwealth. Ports of entry are the capital Nukualofa (on Tongatapu in the south), Li-

fuka (in the Haapai Islands), Neiafu (in the Vavau group), and Niuatoputapu Island and Niuafoou Island (both in the Niua group in the far north). Advance visas are not required. In general, yachts should anchor and fly the Q flag; the skipper should proceed ashore to request clearance. In Nukualofa, contact the Port Control on VHF channel 16 and request instructions; clearance is usually handled near the commercial wharf. A coastal clearance will be needed when cruising between clearance ports. There are repair facilities in Nukualofa and Neiafu, and reasonable provisioning in both. Water in all of Tonga may be suspect; inquire locally. Fuel is available in Neiafu, Nukualofa, and the Haapai group.

TUVALU

The country of Tuvalu (formerly the Ellice Islands) consists of nine atolls; it is an independent nation, with a language closely related to Samoan. The sole port of entry is Funafuti. Arriving yachts should anchor and fly a Q flag; officials will come to the yacht for clearance. Advance visas are not required. Permission is needed to visit any other islands. There are no repair facilities, and only basic provisions are available. Water is not generally available, although fuel is.

Health and Safety

There are no significant safety concerns in Polynesia, though precautions against theft should be taken, especially in urban centers. There is no malaria in Polynesia, but outbreaks of dengue fever do occur on some islands in French Polynesia and Tonga. Medical facilities vary considerably across Polynesia, with the best level of care (outside of Hawaii) available in the Society Islands of French Polynesia. Most countries and territories have adequate facilities in the major population centers.

Melanesia

The nations of Melanesia offer the greatest contrast and adventure of any in the Pacific. Sophisticated centers such as Noumea and Port Vila are juxtaposed with islands where traditional ways of life are still commonly practiced. The region has Oceania's best reefs and highest mountains. It also has more political unrest than other parts of the Pacific, but, to date, it remains a relatively safe region in which to cruise.

Geography

Melanesia (meaning black islands, so named because of the inhabitants' very dark skin color) has the Pacific's largest and most varied islands. Melanesia is composed of just five countries: Papua New Guinea (PNG), Solomon Islands, Vanuatu, New Caledonia, and Fiji. PNG is by the far the largest nation in Melanesia and in the Pacific; it occupies roughly half of the island of New Guinea, the western half being the Indonesian province of West Papua (Irian Jaya). PNG's environment is remarkably diverse, ranging from atolls to glaciers. The remoteness of PNG's mountainous interior kept the population of some 1 million Highlanders isolated from the rest of the world until the 1930s, and helped spawn its hundreds of different languages. New Guinea was connected with Australia by a land bridge across Torres Strait until some 8,000 years ago; as a result, PNG has a unique fauna related to that in Australia.

Located east of New Guinea, the Solomon Islands form Oceania's second-largest nation and include hundreds of islands, six of them very large and densely forested. The western Solomons feature some superb cruising in a number of extensive protected lagoons, while remote islands such as Choiseul and Isabel are still rarely visited by outsiders.

Vanuatu is southeast of the Solomons, and incorporates some 80 islands spread out over about 500 miles. There is a mixture of coral and volcanic islands and some of the latter are still active.

Slightly south and west of Vanuatu, New Caledonia is dominated by the large island of Grand Terre and includes a number of smaller islands as well as the Loyalty Islands to the east. Fiji, located well to the east of the other Melanesian islands, is about midway between Samoa and New Caledonia. Fiji includes hundreds of islands, the larger of which are remnants of a submerged mountain chain.

Culture

The island of New Guinea was settled long before the remainder of the Pacific, about 40,000 years ago, by people known today as Papuan. The languages of many Highland New Guinea societies, native Australians, and of a few island peoples are classified as Papuan. A much later migration of Austronesians took place from Southeast Asia some 6,000 years ago, and the Austronesians went on to settle the remainder of Melanesia (reaching Fiji about 3,500 years ago) and from there the islands of Polynesia.

A number of European nations established colonies and territories in Melanesia, including Britain, Australia, Germany, and France; New Caledonia is today a French overseas territory, but the other island groups are independent nations.

A majority of the inhabitants of PNG, Solomon Islands, and Vanuatu continue to live in small villages and practice subsistence agriculture. Many Fijians on the larger islands now work in agriculture, tourism, or industry; Noumea is a rapidly growing urban center, but much of the population in the remainder of New Caledonia still lives in small villages.

Coral Reefs

Within the five countries of Melanesia there are some 36 barrier reef systems, including the world's second largest (surrounding Grande Terre in New Caledonia). There are also many fringing reefs and atolls. The diversity of reef species is higher here than elsewhere in the Pacific. Vanuatu has the least reef development in Melanesia (because the islands are fairly young); reefs in Fiji, New Caledonia, Papua New Guinea, and Solomon Islands are all extensive and generally in good to excellent condition. They can also be a serious hazard to navigation in some areas, as many remote reefs in Papua New Guinea and the Solomons are not well charted. Reefs in the Solomon Islands are considered to be the least disturbed in the Pacific, and reefs throughout the region are generally in good to excellent condition.

Navigation

The IALA A buoyage system is used. Markers and lights in New Caledonia are well maintained. Those in the other countries of the region are generally reliable in major ports but may be out of commission in more remote areas. Many reefs and shoals are not marked. Charts are of variable quality, and remote areas have often never been completely surveyed. Some islands may be incorrectly

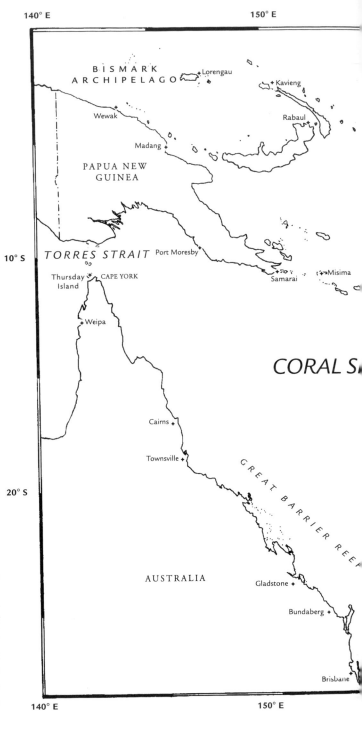

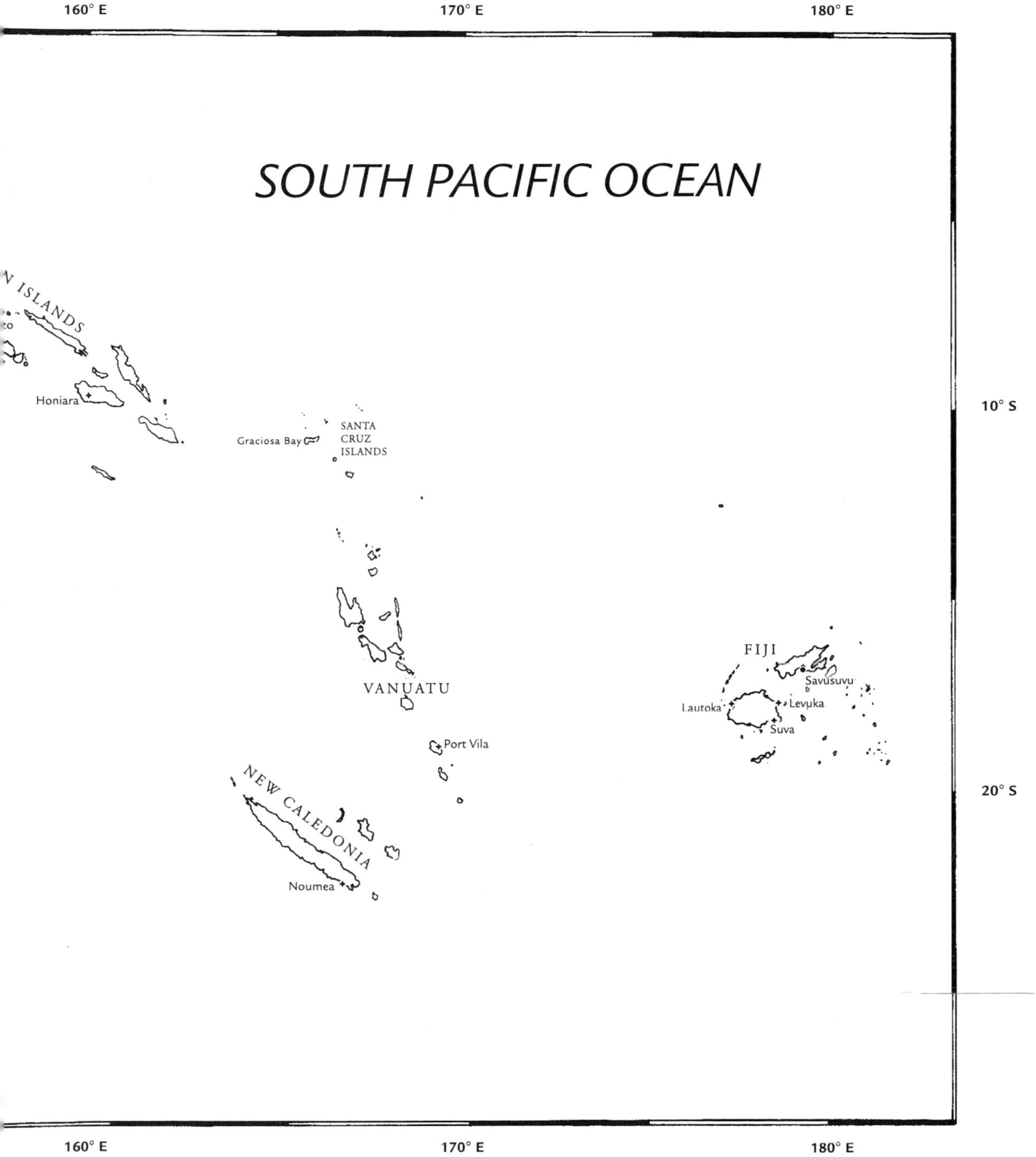

160° E   170° E   180° E

SOUTH PACIFIC OCEAN

N ISLANDS

Honiara

SANTA
CRUZ
ISLANDS

Graciosa Bay

10° S

VANUATU

FIJI

Savusuvu

Lautoka   Levuka

Suva

Port Vila

NEW CALEDONIA

20° S

Noumea

160° E   170° E   180° E

Melanesia.

positioned, even on recent charts, if they are based on older surveys.

Formalities and Facilities

FIJI

The easternmost of the Melanesian countries, Fiji is composed of some 322 islands, most of which are remnants of a former continental mountain range; there are also coral islands and atolls. There are only four ports of entry for this large archipelago: Savusavu on the island of Vanua Levu in the north; Levuka on Ovalau island to the east of Viti Levu; and Suva and Lautoka on the main island of Viti Levu. Yachts must clear customs at a port of entry before stopping elsewhere. Upon arrival, cruisers should contact Port Control on VHF channel 16 for instructions about where to anchor or moor for clearance. No visas are required for stays of up to 4 months (with extensions possible to 6 months) for citizens of most countries. A cruising permit is required for visiting ports other than the four ports of entry. These can be obtained in any of the ports of entry. A special permit is required to visit the Lau Islands in eastern Fiji, and this must be obtained from the President's Office in Suva. These permits are, however, not generally granted.

The Royal Suva Yacht Club, the most popular anchorage in Suva, makes their facilities available for a small fee. There's a small marina. Other marinas are located at Savusavu, Lautoka, and Musket Cove on Malololailai Island in the Mamanutha Islands (in the far west). Reasonable repair facilities are available in Suva, Lautoka, and Musket Cove. A limited selection of marine supplies is available; provisioning is best in Suva and Lautoka, but water and fuel are widely available.

NEW CALEDONIA

New Caledonia enjoys a much higher standard of living than the rest of Melanesia, and the capital, Noumea, is very much the Paris of the Pacific; access to foods and most other goods and services is unmatched elsewhere in the South Pacific. The sole port of entry is Noumea; yachts must receive clearance in Noumea before visiting other islands or ports. Cruisers should call Noumea Radio on VHF channel 16 or SSB, or Port Moselle on VHF channel 16 and announce their arrival. Clearance takes place at the visitor's dock at Port Moselle marina; the marina staff will inform customs of your arrival. Advance visas are not required for citizens of the European Union, the United States, and Canada; others should inquire at a French consulate. U.S. and Canadian citizens need to renew visas after 30 days and, if staying longer, may prefer to obtain visas in advance. There are two marinas in Noumea where visiting yachts can stay if space is available; all yachts are granted one night's berthing at Port Moselle free of charge. There are two boatyards with travel lifts and a number of chandleries. There's a daily produce and fish market adjacent to Port Moselle.

VANUATU

There are over 80 islands in Vanuatu, made up of a group of 13 large and some 70 smaller islets. There are only two ports of entry: Port Vila (on Efate) and Luganville on Espíritu Santo. Tanna may become an additional port of entry in the future. It may be possible to stop at some islands after receiving clearance at a port of entry. Contact Port Control or customs on VHF channel 16 on arrival, or anchor, fly a Q flag, and await clearance. No visas are required for citizens of the Commonwealth, European Union, United States, and some other countries, who will be given renewable 30-day permits. Others will need advance visas. Obtain a cruising permit in Port Vila if you intend to cruise between different islands. Repairs can be made in Port Vila and Luganville, but little in the way of yachting facilities or equipment is available. Provisioning is best in Port Vila, but basics are available on many islands.

SOLOMON ISLANDS

This island group includes some 900 islands, dominated by a number of large, high continental islands that are part of a submerged mountain range that once reached from New Guinea to New Zealand. Ports of entry include Korovou in the

Shortland Islands (in the far north), Gizo in the New Georgia Group (in the west), Honiara on Guadalcanal Island, and Graciosa Bay on Ndeni Island (in the Santa Cruz Islands). Yachts should anchor, with the captain going ashore to seek clearance. Advance visas are not needed for citizens of most countries. The best repair facilities are on Tulagi Island, some 20 miles north of Honiara. There are no marinas, chandleries, or other yachting facilities in the Solomons, but there are a number of small slipways where repairs could be made in a pinch. Provisioning is best in Honiara; Gizo also offers a reasonable selection of canned goods and produce. All water should be treated unless it is from a catchment system; fuel is readily available.

PAPUA NEW GUINEA

There are a number of ports of entry in this large country. Those of most interest to cruising sailors include Port Moresby, Samarai (on the eastern tip of the mainland), Misima (in the Louisiade Archipelago), Rabaul (on New Britain), Madang and Wewak (on the mainland north coast), Kavieng (on New Ireland) and Lorengau (on Manus in the Admiralty Islands). It is advisable to obtain a visa in advance; make sure to specify that you'll be arriving by yacht, as the captain's visa includes an endorsement for the yacht. Visa extensions require that passports be sent to Port Moresby. The best repair facilities are in Port Moresby, where there are several slipways. Provisioning is reasonably good in most large towns. Fuel and water are widely available, but water may need treatment; inquire locally.

Health and Safety

Melanesia has experienced a number of political upheavals in recent years, with coups in Fiji in the late 1980s and again in 2000, and armed uprisings in the Solomon Islands in 2000 and PNG's Bougainville Island in the 1990s. Travel to Fiji is currently safe. Cruisers should inquire with a PNG embassy or consulate before planning a trip to Bougainville; other parts of PNG have not been affected. Cruisers headed for the Solomon Islands should also seek advance information. At present it is advisable not to visit the capital (Honiara).

Violence or theft is generally rare in Melanesia except in mainland PNG, where "rascals" are responsible for continuing violence against visitors and PNG residents alike. The problem is worse in mainland urban centers and should not be underestimated; conversely, the yacht club in Port Moresby continues to welcome cruisers and is reportedly a safe location to be based in while visiting the city. The offshore islands are largely free from problems, and we've visited a number of the latter without experiencing any trouble. Overall the people of PNG are among the most friendly and welcoming of any in the Pacific.

Dengue fever is present across Melanesia, and malaria is present in PNG, the Solomons, and Vanuatu. Health services vary, being very good in Noumea and reasonable in Port Moresby, Suva, and Port Vila. Access to health care is very limited in remote areas, especially in PNG and Solomon Islands.

Australia

The only country that is also a continent, Australia is roughly as large as the continental United States and includes a very lengthy tropical coastline. A number of visiting yachts cruise in Australian waters every year, and there are many local cruising yachts. The country offers the most extensive yachting facilities of any tropical Pacific nation.

Weather

The east coast experiences southeast to east trade winds throughout the year, which average Force 4. The months of October and November see the highest percentage of northerly winds, and this is the time when most boats head south along the tropical coast.

The northern coast experiences southeast trade winds during the winter months (May to October) and is influenced by the northwest monsoon during the winter (December to February), when west to northwest winds predominate. March and November are often transitional months, with light winds. Both trade and monsoonal winds average Force 3 to 4.

The northwest coast experiences variable winds in March and April, predominantly southeast winds in midwinter (May to August), and southwest to west winds in September to February. Wind strengths again average Force 3 to 4.

The entire tropical region is subject to tropical cyclones between November and May. Cyclone risk is highest in northwest Australia, but a significant risk exists along the east and north coasts as well. Cyclones that threaten Australian waters generally spawn in the waters off northern Australia. The east coast has a number of good cyclone holes.

Weather forecasting in Australia is generally excellent, with a well-developed warning system for tropical cyclones and other dangerous weather.

Currents

The East Australian Current sets south off the country's east coast, south of about 15° S, and is fed by the South Equatorial Current. The East Australian Current can reach 4 knots at times. Large counterclockwise eddies are set in motion in the southern Coral Sea, which may also have speeds of 3 knots. They can persist for many months, which makes accurate current predictions in these waters difficult. Currents along the immediate coast (within the Great Barrier Reef) are variable, influenced by tide and wind.

Currents along the north Australian coast vary with the monsoon (see Currents, page 303, under South Pacific Ocean).

Geography

The Australian continent is an old and stable landmass, which accounts for the lack of dramatic topography. The continent has been isolated from other land areas (except New Guinea) for 100 million years, in which time a unique flora and fauna has developed. The Australian tropics consist of three fairly distinct regions. The most popular region is the tropical east coast, extending from about Gladstone to the tip of Cape York and including the

islets and countless individual reefs that make up the Great Barrier Reef. The northern coast stretches west from Cape York to Darwin and is rarely cruised as such, but it's transited by almost all yachts heading from the Pacific to the Indian Ocean. The tropical west coast, from Darwin south to North West Cape, offers some spectacular cruising but is a remote and rugged area that's visited primarily by Australian cruisers. There are also a number of offshore islands in the Coral Sea, and these can be briefly visited by yachts on a passage prior to clearing with customs; note that this does not apply to reefs or islands within the Great Barrier reef.

Culture

Australia is home to the world's oldest culture, as the Aboriginal inhabitants have lived here continuously for about 70,000 years. The northern coast was visited periodically by fishermen and traders from Southeast Asia, but otherwise, Aboriginal peoples were isolated from outside contact. European explorers sighted and occasionally landed on the shores of Australia in the 17th and early 18th centuries, but it wasn't until Captain James Cook's visit in 1770 that serious interest was shown in the continent. Cook took possession of Australia for England, and by 1788 the English had established a penal colony. Settlement expanded rapidly, and within 100 years the indigenous population was vastly reduced and largely confined to marginal areas in central and northern Australia.

The present population of about 18 million is primarily of British and Irish descent but includes many people of Southern and Central European and Asian ancestry, as well as the indigenous Aboriginal population.

Coral Reefs

Australia has a greater area of coral reefs than any other country, and many of these reefs form part of the Great Barrier Reef (GBR). The entire GBR is now incorporated into the Great Barrier Reef Marine Park, which extends along the country's east coast for some 1,200 miles. The park has been zoned for different uses, and maps are available showing what activities are allowed in various zones.

Reefs extend north through the Torres Strait almost to New Guinea, and a series of reefs is found scattered across the Coral Sea as well. The north tropical coast has few reefs, while a limited number of reefs are present along the western tropical coast, both along the shore and around offshore islands.

Most of Australia's reefs are in good to excellent condition, and there are virtually unlimited opportunities for snorkeling and diving. Access to the reefs is not always simple, however, as much of the GBR lies well offshore (as much as 60 miles in the south). Because of Australia's low population density, most of the impacts to reefs are natural, with the exception of inshore areas that are impacted by runoff, sedimentation, and tourism. Natural impacts, which include bleaching and severe crown-of-thorns starfish outbreaks, have caused temporary problems in some areas, but recovery is generally good due to a lack of other stresses.

Navigation

The IALA A buoyage system is used. Charts and surveys are of high quality, but not all waters in remote areas (including portions of the Great Barrier Reef) have been surveyed. Agreement between GPS positions and recent charts is excellent. Major routes are well buoyed, and navigational markers are well maintained.

Formalities and Facilities

There are many ports of entry in Australian waters. East coast ports of entry include Brisbane (yachts clear at Scarborough), Bundaberg, Gladstone, Bowen, Townsville, Cairns, and Thursday Island (in Torres Strait). Ports of entry in northern Australia include Gove and Darwin. Broome is a principal port of entry in the northwest. Customs officials request that arriving yachts give 48 hours advance notice of arrival by calling Townsville or Darwin Radio on SSB (2182, 4125, or 6215 kHz). Yachts that lack an SSB should place a call on VHF channel 16; there are VHF repeaters on many coastal and

reef islands, so range is generally good. These services will provide instructions from customs officials regarding where to anchor or moor your boat for clearance in each port.

Cruisers of all nationalities (with the exception of New Zealanders) must have a visa before entering the country. Large fines are charged for cruisers entering without visas. Three-month multiple-entry visas, valid for up to one year, are available free of charge from any embassy or consulate outside Australia. Three-month visas are renewable when in Australia, but such renewals are costly. Cruisers staying for periods longer than three months will save by obtaining long-stay multiple-entry visas prior to arrival. Strict quarantine regulations apply, and there's a fee for inspection. Yachts require a cruising permit to cruise in Australian waters, but the formerly strict regulations have been eased significantly in the last few years. Permits can be obtained from customs after arrival.

The standard of living in Australia is quite high, and access to all services and goods is excellent in all relatively populated areas. The east coast is the most developed and sees by far the most cruising yachts, with most international yachts making a stopover in these waters as part of a Pacific or global circumnavigation. There are numerous slipways, boatyards, and marinas along the east coast between Brisbane and Port Douglas (north of Cairns) capable of handling any repair work. Good chandleries are located in Brisbane, Bundaberg, Townsville, and Cairns.

Along the north coast the only city with comprehensive facilities, including slipways and marinas, is Darwin; provisions and some yacht services are available in the ports of Thursday Island, Gove, Weipa, and Broome. Most of the north and tropical west coast is remote, with few towns of any size. Facilities may be available in some areas, but cruisers exploring these waters should inquire carefully before sailing to ascertain what is available.

Health and Safety

The level of health care in Australia is generally excellent, although no medical facilities of any kind exist in large parts of northern Australia. The Royal Flying Doctor Service, established in 1933, has long provided remote areas of Australia with medical services and might prove an option in case of an emergency.

Australia's tropical environment is endowed with more than its fair share of health hazards, including saltwater crocodiles, deadly stinging jellyfish and oc-topuses, as well as more common hazards such as sharks. See chapter 13, Dangerous Tropical Marine Organisms, for details. Australia is free of most common tropical diseases, but beware of dengue fever and Ross River fever, or epidemic polyarthritis. These are transmitted by mosquitoes, and the risk is highest along the east coast in the middle of the wet season (January and February).

Chapter 19

Tropical Indian Ocean

Traditionally the geographic boundary between the Indian Ocean and the Pacific has been drawn along the Indonesian islands of Sumatra, Java, and the Lesser Sundas, placing all of Indonesia within the Pacific. But we'll ignore that and place the boundary where it more naturally falls for the cruising sailor: at Torres Strait, separating Australia from Papua New Guinea. The thousands of islands of Southeast Asia are an increasingly popular cruising destination, although piracy and unrest in Indonesia have kept many boats from doing much more than sailing quickly through Indonesian waters in the last few years. Sri Lanka is also suffering from significant violence, but India has become a popular stopping point for boats cruising the North Indian Ocean. The many islands of the South Indian Ocean are generally free from major troubles and offer a surprising mix of cultures and attractions. Tensions have been high in the Comoros in the past but appear to be easing. The Red Sea and Gulf of Aden are both attractive destinations and important transit routes. Unfortunately piracy against yachts has been ongoing in the Gulf of Aden. Yachts are still sailing these waters, but extreme caution is advised.

North Indian Ocean

Weather

The weather pattern in the Indian Ocean is monsoonal. The winter monsoon corresponds in season and direction to the northeast trades in the Pacific and Atlantic, blowing from the northeast at 10 to 15 knots during the winter months (roughly November to March). The ITCZ moves well south of the equator during these months, allowing the southeast winds to be drawn south of the equator. April to May are transition months during which the ITCZ shifts just south of the equator across most of the Indian Ocean. Winds are light and variable.

The southwest monsoon blows from June to September in response to the heating of Asia and India during the northern summer. Winds average 20 knots in strength but can be considerably stronger in the waters off Suqutrā Island (Socotra) in the western Indian Ocean, due to the development of a deep-heat low north of the Persian Gulf. Because the southwest monsoon winds are blowing *from* the equator, the air is moist, and rainfall is frequent.

October and November are once again a transition period between monsoons, marked by light winds and a shift in the position of the ITCZ.

Tropical cyclones occur in both the Arabian Sea and Bay of Bengal. The North Indian Ocean is unusual in that there are two distinct cyclone seasons: in the two transition periods between monsoons. October has the highest cyclone frequency.

Currents

North Indian Ocean currents are caused by the monsoon, with the sole exception of the Equatorial Counter Current, which sets east at or south of the equator.

November to March: this is the time of the northeast monsoon, and currents generally set west, turning southwest along the African coast. A counterclockwise circulation sets up in the Arabian Sea between February and April, producing southerly currents along the Indian coast.

May to September: during the southwest monsoon currents across the central Indian Ocean and in the Arabian Sea set east. The circulation is fed by the Somali Current, which flows northeast along the coast of Somalia and south of Suqutrā. Gale-force winds are not uncommon in this area and push the average speeds of the Somali Current to 3 knots.

April and October are generally transition months, with current patterns across the central ocean less well defined.

Currents in Indonesian and Northern Australian Waters

The currents in these waters alternate with the monsoons. In the northern summer (May to September), currents in the South China Sea set largely northeast, pushed by this southwest monsoon. Currents in Indonesian waters and northern Australian waters (including the Arafura, Banda, and Java Seas) set west, pushed by the southeast trade winds. These patterns alter in the southern summer (December to March), when currents in the South China

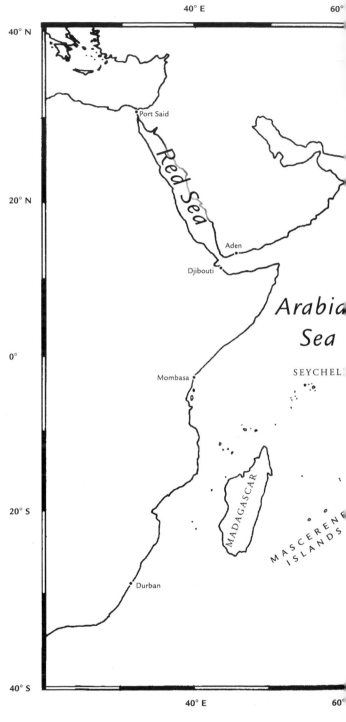

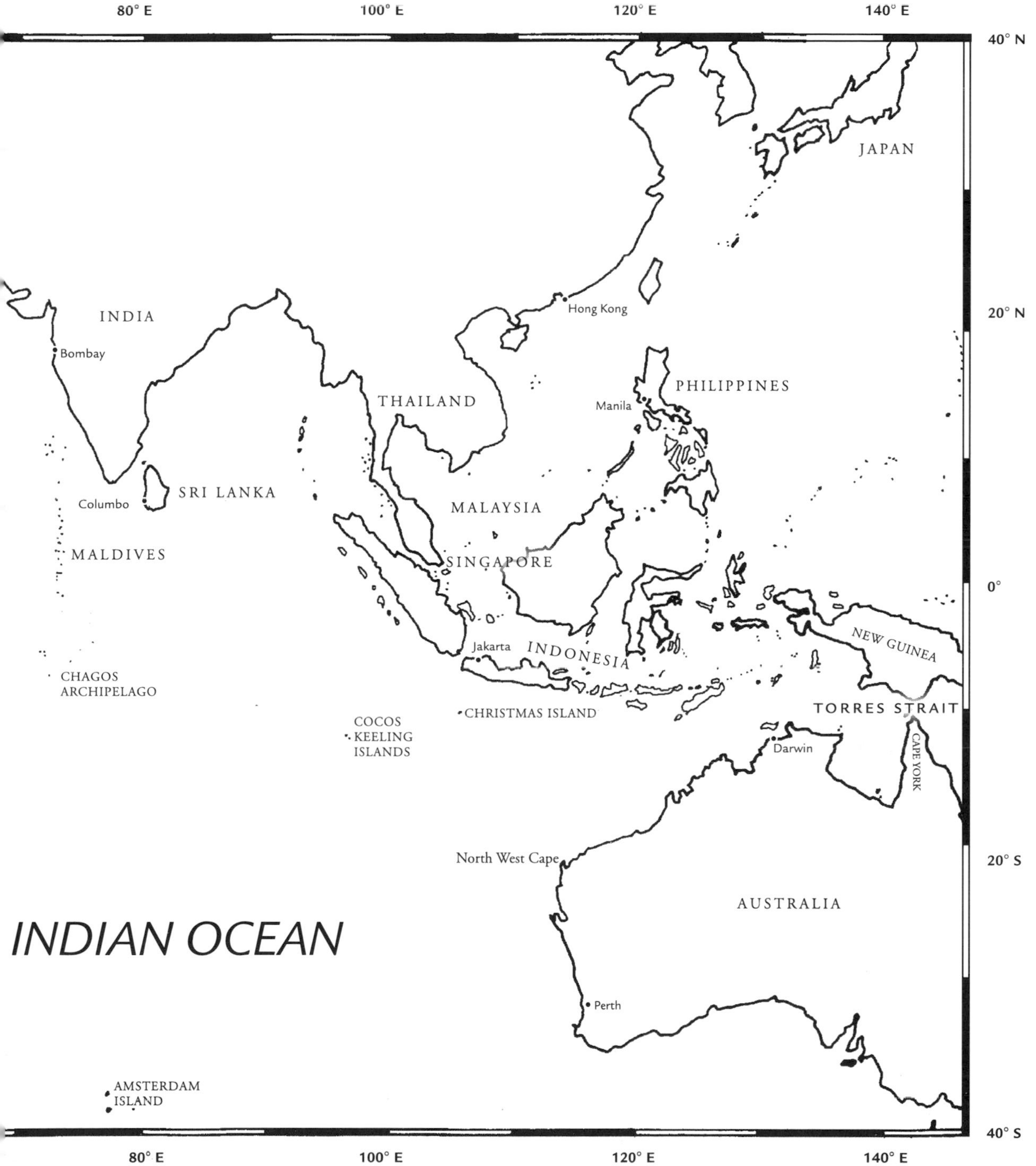

80° E 100° E 120° E 140° E

40° N

JAPAN

20° N

INDIA

Bombay

Hong Kong

PHILIPPINES

THAILAND

Manila

SRI LANKA

Columbo

MALAYSIA

MALDIVES

SINGAPORE

0°

NEW GUINEA

Jakarta INDONESIA

CHAGOS
ARCHIPELAGO

TORRES STRAIT

COCOS
KEELING
ISLANDS

CHRISTMAS ISLAND

Darwin

CAPE YORK

North West Cape

20° S

INDIAN OCEAN

AUSTRALIA

Perth

AMSTERDAM
ISLAND

40° S

80° E 100° E 120° E 140° E

Indian Ocean.

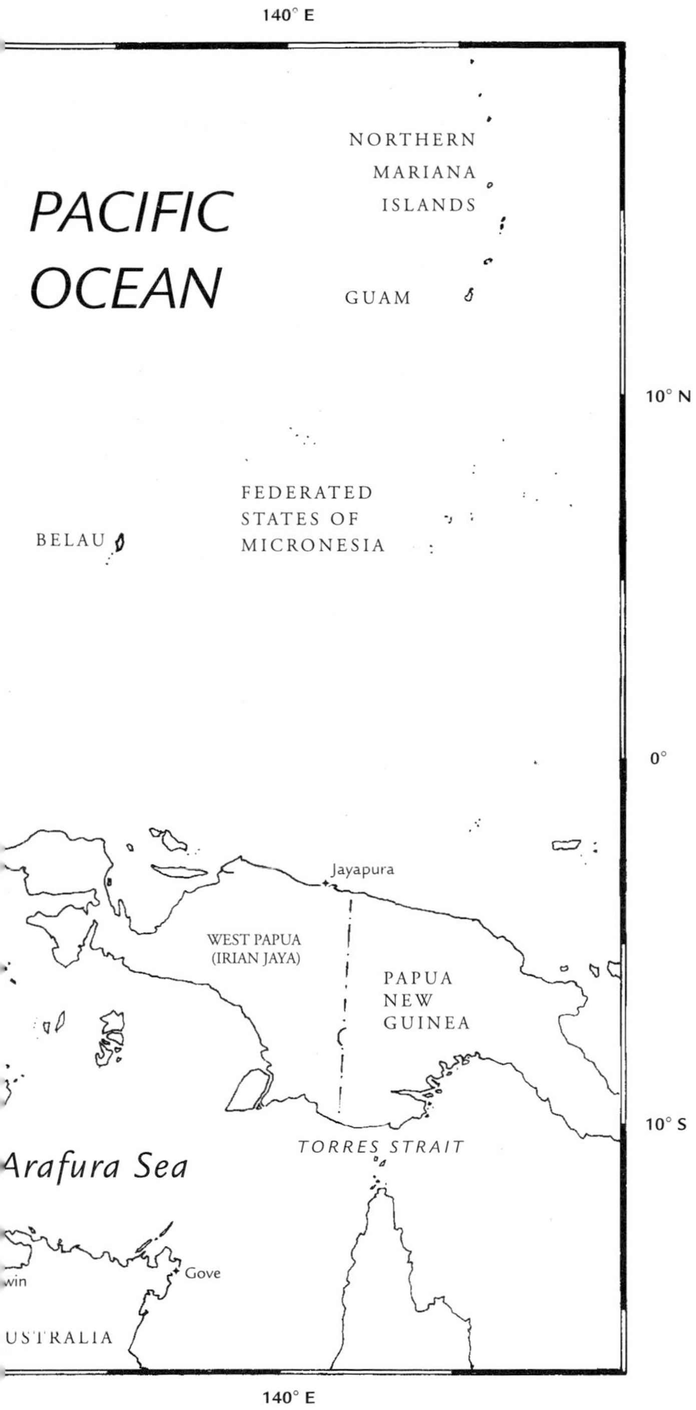

Map labels

140° E

PACIFIC OCEAN

NORTHERN MARIANA ISLANDS

GUAM

10° N

BELAU

FEDERATED STATES OF MICRONESIA

Jayapura

0°

WEST PAPUA (IRIAN JAYA)

PAPUA NEW GUINEA

10° S

TORRES STRAIT

Arafura Sea

Gove

AUSTRALIA

...win

140° E

Southeast Asia.

Sea set southwest, while currents in the Arafura, Banda, and Java Seas set east. Currents are often 1 knot or more in strength. The months of April, October, and November are transitional, and currents may be found flowing in either direction.

Southeast Asia

The countries of Indonesia, Malaysia, and Thailand are far and away the most popular cruising grounds in the North Indian Ocean, with Singapore as a stopover port en route to western Malaysia and Thailand.

Geography

Indonesia is composed of over 13,000 islands, spread over thousands of miles of ocean. Many of the islands are volcanic, and there is still active volcanism in parts of the archipelago. Indonesia's islands are continental; the volcanism is caused by the collision of the Indian and Eurasian tectonic plates. The flora and fauna of eastern and western Indonesia are very different. Species on islands to the west have much in common with those found in other parts of Southeast Asia, whereas islands to the east are home to birds, reptiles, and marsupials that evolved together with those in New Guinea and Australia. Many of the islands are mountainous and rugged, in particular in West Papua, where peaks are over 16,000 feet (5,000 m) high. There are countless protected bays and anchorages; the seasonal change in prevailing winds and currents makes it possible to make a large circuit of the country, though this may be hampered by immigration restrictions (see below under Formalities and Facilities).

Malaysia is composed of two distinct parts: Peninsular Malaysia, which is bordered by Thailand on the north and Singapore on the south, and the provinces of

Prahus on Roti Island, Indonesia.

Sabah and Sarawak, which share the island of Borneo with the Indonesian province of Kalimantan and the independent state of Brunei. Some 400 miles of the South China Sea separate these parts of Malaysia. Most of the country's 22 million people live in Peninsular Malaysia. Much of Sabah and Sarawak is covered by dense rainforest and large river systems; a popular attraction in Sabah is Mt. Kinabalu, with a peak over 13,000 feet (4,000 m) high. The most popular cruising area in Malaysia is on the west coast of Peninsular Malaysia, especially the area around Langkawi, near the border with Thailand. Anchorages in this area are sheltered during the northeast monsoon (November to March). Cruisers sailing in Malaysia in the southwest monsoon will find better shelter in anchorages on the peninsula's less frequently visited western side.

Thailand shares borders with Malaysia, Burma (Myanmar), Laos, and Cambodia. Most cruising boats visit the west coast of the peninsular region (just north of Peninsular Malaysia), which is low-lying and has a number of offshore islands. The best shelter is again during the northeast monsoon season.

Culture

All of Southeast Asia has a long history of human habitation, which led to the development of many distinct cultures and languages. This is especially true in Indonesia, where the isolation provided by the many islands has allowed different cultures to persist. Before European contact a number of Buddhist, Hindu, and Muslim empires and kingdoms struggled for supremacy, but the Portuguese and then the Dutch moved into the Indonesian islands to gain a monopoly on the lucrative trade in spices. They eventually ruled all of what is now Indonesia. In the 52 years since Indonesia became independent from the Dutch, the Indonesian government has tried to subdue tensions between the many ethnic, religious, and cultural groups. The present population of 225 million people speaks over 350 different languages and dialects, but Bahasa Indonesia (similar to Malay) is the national language; English is frequently spoken in tourist areas. The policy of forced assimilation has failed, and there has been widespread fighting and protest in various parts of Indonesia, at times between ethnic groups but more often targeted at the government (most military and security forces are Javanese). The best-known struggle is that of the East Timorese (formerly a Portuguese colony). East Timor won its independence from Indonesia in 1999, but only after a bloody struggle in which thousands died. Other ongoing independence struggles are at Aceh (on Sumatra) and in West Papua (Irian Jaya). Religious fighting has been intense in Kalimantan and eastern Indonesia (especially in Ambon).

Malaysia is also a multicultural society. Here the main groups are Malays, Chinese, and Indians, of which Malays are the most numerous. The languages and religions of these groups are very different: Malays are Muslims and speak Bahasa Melayu; Chinese are primarily Buddhists and Taoists, speaking Cantonese, Hokkein, and Hakka; and the Indians are primarily Hindus who speak Hindi and Tamil. English is often used by these groups as a common language. A small percentage of the population is made up of Eurasians and indigenous tribes (principally the Iban and Bidayuh of Sarawak). The Portuguese were the first European power in what is now Malaysia in the 16th century, and they were followed by the Dutch and then the British. Malaysia became independent in 1957. Today the population is about 20 million.

Thailand is a predominantly Buddhist country, with a unique language and alphabet. It has never been under colonial rule and is a constitutional monarchy. The population is about 55 million.

Coral Reefs

Though it occupies just 2.5 percent of the world's ocean area, Southeast Asia has 30 percent of the coral reefs. This region includes over 25,000 islands and has the highest diversity of coral and reef fish species worldwide; traditionally it has been unequalled for its fantastic underwater scenery. All reef types are common, including oceanic atolls, barrier reefs, and platform reefs, and many of the islands have fringing reefs. All of the physical requirements for coral reef growth are met here, combined with a general absence of tropical storms.

Tragically, the reefs in this area have been hard hit, and the most severe impacts have been from people. The region's population currently stands at about 450 million and is projected to reach more than 700 million by 2025. Pollution, overfishing, the harvesting of coral for souvenirs and building materials, and destructive fishing practices have all combined to wreak havoc on coral reefs in the region and will likely continue to do so. There has also been extensive coral bleaching in recent years, with losses in many areas of 30 to 60 percent of corals; there have even been localized extinctions of prominent corals.

The best coral reefs in the region are generally found away from population centers, though even then there may be severe impacts, either from roving cyanide and dynamite fishermen or from sedimentation caused by logging and land clearing. Overall, surveys suggest that Thailand's reefs are in the best condition, with some 17 percent ranked as being in excellent condition (as compared to 2.6 percent for Indonesia). Practically speaking, cruisers are apt to find the best snorkeling and diving in eastern Indonesia, Sabah in Malaysia, and the Andaman Sea coast of Thailand.

Navigation

The IALA A buoyage system is used. Markers in Indonesia may be in poor repair and should not be relied upon. Markers in the other countries are generally reliable and well maintained. Charts of this region are generally accurate, but reefs and islands in remote areas may not always be correctly charted.

Formalities and Facilities

INDONESIA

There are a number of ports of entry for Indonesia. Arriving vessels should anchor and display the Q flag; the captain should then go ashore to complete entrance formalities. Nationals of most countries are issued a 60-day visitor's permit on arrival. Those wishing to stay longer must obtain a visa in advance, as the 60-day permits are not renewable. All yachts must also carry a cruising permit (officially a Clearance Approval for Indonesian Territory, or CAIT). The CAIT must be applied for well in advance, and it's best to have it in hand when you arrive. If the latter proves impossible, and you're planning to obtain clearance at Bali, you can request that the CAIT be forwarded on to the marina there. Similar arrangements may be possible at other clearance ports.

The CAIT includes basic details about your boat, names and passport numbers for all crew members and any passengers, a list of all the places you plan to visit while you are in Indonesia, and the date of your intended arrival. It will also carry approvals from the Departments of Foreign Affairs and Defense and Security as well as the Directorate General of Sea Communications. Although the basic cruising permit requirement is simple, the Indonesians are quite particular about the details and will hold you to them. For example, your CAIT, which is valid for three months, begins on the arrival date that you submit with your application. Arrive a month later, and you'll be left with a permit valid for only two months; carefully plan your sailing schedule so that you arrive close to the date shown on your CAIT.

Bali is the most popular cruising destination; there is a small marina that offers services such as Internet access and mail forwarding; water, fuel, and a variety of mechanical repairs are available nearby.

There are no haul-out facilities for yachts at present. Provisioning is good on Bali.

MALAYSIA

There are a number of ports of entry in both Peninsular and East Malaysia. In general, the captain must go ashore to obtain clearance. Visas are not generally required for nationals of the United States and the European Union, though those wishing to stay longer than one month should inquire in advance about requirements. Visitor passes are issued upon arrival and may be difficult to extend. Light dues and harbor fees are charged. The best facilities are in the Port Klang area, including the Royal Selangor Yacht Club. Boats can be left here for trips inland. There are marinas and haul-out facilities at Pangkor, Penang, and Langkawi; the provisioning is good in most areas.

THAILAND

Ports of entry in Thailand include Bangkok, Phuket, and Krabi. Upon arrival, fly a Q flag and then go ashore to seek clearance. Thirty-day visas are issued on arrival, but those wishing to make a longer visit should obtain visas in advance. (Inquire about the difference in visas for "crew" and "passengers.") A bond may need to be posted if the captain and the boat are to stay more than 30 days; there are a variety of fees charged by customs and immigration. Most of Thailand's waters have been designated as national parks, and various fees apply for anchoring and park visitation. The best repair facilities are in Phuket, which also has several marinas. Provisioning here is very good. Tap water should generally be treated.

SINGAPORE

Yachts arriving in Singapore should anchor (the favored site is in the northeast near the Changi sailing club, where facilities can be used for a fee) or, if preferred, find a slip at Raffles Marina. The captain should report within 24 hours to immigration and customs. Yachts are not normally boarded. U.S., Canadian, and most E.U. citizens do not need visas. Renewable 2-week passes are issued by immigration upon arrival. There is no time limit for how long yachts can remain in Singapore. Repairs of all kinds can be done in Singapore. Provisioning is excellent.

Health and Safety

Problems with piracy and political unrest have worsened in these waters over the last few years. We provide a detailed review of the situation for each country below, but cruisers heading for Southeast Asia should make inquiries before departing. In general, any yachts heading into Southeast Asian waters should take the following precautions:

▶ *AVOID VISITING AREAS WHERE TROUBLE IS LIKELY.* At this writing those areas traditionally frequented by cruisers remain safe. These include the Indonesian islands between Timor and Java (such as Flores, Sumbawa, Lombok, Bali, and the many smaller islands around them), the popular cruising areas in western Malaysia, and the islands near Phuket in Thailand.

▶ *BE ON YOUR GUARD AGAINST PIRACY.* The most risky area for yachts is currently likely to be in the northern Celebes Sea and southern Sulu Sea, between northern Borneo and the Philippines. We were warned about these waters several years ago by Indonesian mariners, and the risk has increased since then. We suggest avoiding these areas. Traveling in company with another yacht may be a good way to avoid problems in other potential trouble spots that can't easily be avoided, such as the Straits of Malacca.

▶ *KEEP A CLOSE EAR ON THE NEWS WHEN CRUISING,* and consider registering with your country's embassy before departure. Talk to locals, cruisers, and any expatriates you meet. News of violence and potential trouble usually spreads like wildfire.

INDONESIA

There are two primary safety concerns for cruisers heading to Indonesia: piracy and violence from religious and ethnic struggles. The International Maritime Bureau's Piracy Reporting Centre reported 158 acts of piracy in Southeast Asia in 1999, most of which took place in Indonesian waters. Problems are ongoing, and almost every weekly bulletin brings news of several new attacks in Indonesian ports or waters. The Piracy Reporting Centre advises mariners to exercise extra caution in all Indonesian ports and in most coastal waters and passes (such as the Malacca Straits). The only good news in all of this is that attacks against yachts appear to be very rare, with almost all pirates targeting ships. But piracy is definitely a problem to be aware of.

Political and religious tensions are also ongoing. A bombing campaign targeted at churches throughout Indonesia on Christmas Eve in 2000 killed a number of people. Some political protestors were killed in the provinces of Aceh and West Papua in late 2000 and early 2001. Americans have been the target of "sweeps" by protestors in various cities, who have attempted to identify U.S. citizens and force them to leave the country. Consequently, the U.S. Embassy in Jakarta suggests deferring all nonessential travel to Indonesia and states that all travel by U.S. and other foreign government officials to Aceh, Papua, and the Moluccas (provinces of North Maluku and Maluku) has been restricted by the Indonesian government because of security concerns. The embassy suggests that private American citizens should adhere to these same restrictions. As we write this, the Australian Embassy in Jakarta is advising Australian citizens not to travel to the Wamena region of West Papua, West Timor, or the provinces of Aceh, Maluku, or North Maluku; the Canadian Department of Foreign Affairs extends the same advice about travel to central Sulawesi and central Kalimantan.

Based on these reports, it might seem crazy to head for Indonesia on a cruising boat. But about 100 yachts did just that during the 2000 cruising season, according to the manager of the Bali Marina. He does recommend staying away from the "hot spots," which he defines as all of Timor, Maluku, Aceh, and Jakarta. Otherwise, he told us that, "Arriving cruisers are reporting friendly treat-

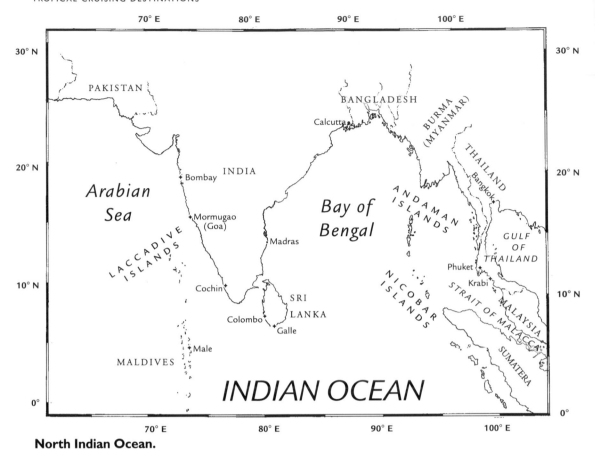

North Indian Ocean.

ment along the way from Darwin. Even the Komodo dragons have been friendly to the tourists. No one has been eaten or hassled in any way, and the pirates are going for bigger stuff."

Diseases found in Indonesia include cholera, dengue fever, hepatitis, Japanese encephalitis, malaria, typhoid, rabies, and tuberculosis. Good health facilities are available only in larger population centers.

MALAYSIA

At present there is a serious risk from piracy and kidnapping in the coastal waters of Sabah in eastern Malaysia. In April 2000, twenty-one people, including a number of foreign tourists, were kidnapped from a dive resort in Sipadan; in September three Malaysian nationals were kidnapped from a dive resort in Pandanan. In both cases the victims were held hostage in the southern Philippines. Malaysian authorities have increased security as a result, but further kidnapping attempts involving foreigners may occur. There is also a serious risk of piracy in the Malacca Straits, where many ships have been targeted. We are not aware of problems in the popular cruising areas to the north. Theft and assault are rare in most of Malaysia, but the country has one of the highest rates of credit card fraud in the world. Safeguard credit cards at all times, and be careful when using them. The magnetic strips of cards have been duplicated even in international hotels.

Malaria, cholera, dengue fever, hepatitis A, Japanese B encephalitis, and typhoid fever can occur in various parts of Malaysia. Medical care and facilities are good in larger population centers.

THAILAND

Political tensions between Burma (Myanmar) and Thailand are high, and there have been shelling and gunfire along the border, with civilian casualties. There is also tension along the border with Cambodia. In addition, there have been problems with robbery and assault in remote areas. Diseases present in various parts of Thailand include dengue fever, Japanese B encephalitis, hepatitis A, malaria, tuberculosis, and typhoid fever. Medical facilities are available in tourist areas.

SINGAPORE

There are ongoing problems with piracy in waters near Singapore, as already discussed. Theft and other crimes are uncommon in Singapore, and there are no problems with tropical diseases. Health care is excellent and widely available.

Sri Lanka, India, and the Maldives

Sri Lanka, India, and the Maldives are three popular stopping points for boats traversing the North Indian Ocean. Both India and Sri Lanka have long and complex histories. As the world's seventh largest and second most populous nation (with over a billion people), India in particular offers a wealth of attractions to the traveler. English is widely spoken in both India and Sri Lanka. The Maldives are less well known and consist of an archipelago of coral atolls southwest of India. There are about 1,300 islands and sand banks (some 200 of which are inhabited by the country's 270,000 people); none of the islets rise to more than a few feet above sea level. The country is very poor, with most people dependent on fishing and farming for a subsistence lifestyle. There are hotels on Male and several resort islands. Divehi is the official language, and Arabic, Hindi, and English are also used.

Despite their interesting cultural traditions and natural features, the cruising potential in all of these countries is currently limited by geography, safety, and regulations. As a result, we include only a summary of basic information of most use to cruisers in transit for these countries.

Coral Reefs

Reef growth along the Indian mainland is severely limited by freshwater and sedimentation from the many rivers, and what reefs exist are heavily impacted by a host of human activities. India's best reefs are located on the offshore islands, including the Andaman and Nicobar Islands to the east and the Laccadive (Lakshadweep) Islands to India's southwest. Reefs in the former groups are primarily fringing and extend up to 1 kilometer wide in the Nicobar Islands. Most are still in excellent condition, but there are increasing problems from sedimentation, overfishing, and pollution. The Nicobar Islands provide habitat for dugong and turtles, including the best nesting sites for leatherback turtles in the Indian Ocean.

The Laccadive Islands, a northern extension of the Maldives, include 36 islands and lagoons. Coral growth is the best to be found in India, and giant clams and turtles are present.

Only a small fraction of the Sri Lankan coastline is covered by reef, and nearshore reefs are generally heavily impacted by both human activities and natural events, with extensive coral death due to coral bleaching in 1998. The Maldives are the southern part of the Chagos-Laccadive Ridge and include 22 atolls, with over 800 small vegetated coral islands and many sand cays. All are low, with a maximum elevation of only 15 feet (5 m). The condition and abundance of coral was excellent until major coral-bleaching events in the 1980s and 1990s killed many corals, with up to 80 percent wiped out in many areas. There are also increasing human impacts on these reefs, both from coral mining (coral is the primary building material) and tourism (there are some 75 resorts on the central islands).

Navigation

The IALA A buoyage system is used.

Formalities and Facilities

SRI LANKA

Colombo and Galle are Sri Lanka's two ports of entry. Colombo is not recommended as it is a commercial port and has no facilities or provisions for yachts; furthermore, it is currently in a state of emergency due to the fighting. Yachts calling at Galle should announce their arrival to the harbormaster, who will arrange clearance procedures. Yachts are currently being required to employ an agent for clearance purposes. Fees for port dues, customs, and the agent are not insignificant, amounting to approximately $200 U.S./month. Anchorage anywhere in Sri Lanka other than within designated areas in the clearance ports of Galle and Colombo is prohibited. One-month extendable visas are granted to crews of all nationalities upon arrival. Basic repairs may be possible in Galle, but no marine supplies are available. There are very limited provisions available, although there's a good fresh produce market. Both fuel and water are available.

INDIA

Bombay, Cochin, and Marmagao (Goa) are the ports of entry in India recommended for cruising yachts. Yachts clearing into Cochin should anchor off the north tip of Willingdon Island, fly a Q flag, and await the arrival of customs officials who will come out by launch. Yachts arriving in Bombay or Goa should contact the port control on VHF channel 16. All visitors must have a tourist visa in hand when arriving. Visas valid for 6 months from date of issue are available from Indian embassies or consulates. Landing passes are issued to crew members allowing restricted travel ashore, but those wishing to explore inland should obtain permission. Special permits are also needed to visit Amindivi and Laccadive (Lakshadweep) Islands in the Arabian Sea and the Nicobar and Andaman Islands in the Bay of Bengal. Yachts visiting the Andaman Islands should check in at Port Blair (South Andaman) and call authorities on VHF channel 16 for instructions on where to anchor.

Bombay is presently recommended as the best location to leave a yacht for an extended trip inland. Arrangements can be made with the Royal Bombay Yacht Club to watch your boat; they will also assist with clearance formalities. A variety of repair facilities are available.

MALDIVES

Male is the sole clearance port in the Maldives. Officially all yachts arriving in the Maldives must first proceed to Male, though brief stops at Uligamu in Haa Alifu Atoll and Gan in Addu Atoll (in the far south) may be allowed if a yacht is stopping only briefly and does not cruise farther in the islands. Yachts arriving at Male should contact the coast guard on VHF channel 16 (monitored 24 hours); it is expected that all yachts will use an agent, whose services should be arranged in advance. Agents are reported to be charging approximately $150 U.S. for their services; fees for anchoring and for permits to visit outlying atolls are also levied. Visitors are normally issued 30-day permits by immigration on arrival, which can be extended, for a fee.

Fuel and water are available only on Male. Most provisions are flown in by air from Sri Lanka and are costly, but local fresh produce and fish are available. Health facilities are available on all the inhabited atolls; Male has an international airport and some repair facilities.

Anchorages throughout the Maldives are generally deep and not well protected. There is a small area at Male about 50 feet in depth, but vessels are often forced to anchor in depths of 150 feet. Thulusdhoo and Himmafushi are exceptions, and both are popular destinations for yachts due to their shallow, protected anchorages.

Health and Safety

SRI LANKA

Sri Lanka has suffered from recurring clashes between Tamil separatists and government forces over the last 20 years. Travel to the east and north of the country is not safe at present, due to continued fighting between the Tamil Tigers and the government;

the southwestern third of the island is open to travelers. There were numerous terrorist attacks, including suicide bombings, in 2000. Many of the attacks occurred in Colombo, but no part of the country can be considered free of risk. There have also been a number of attacks on ships in the last few years. The northern, eastern, and southeastern coastlines have been declared restricted zones by Sri Lankan authorities and should be avoided. The Sri Lankan navy has fired upon unauthorized ships in these areas. Tropical diseases present in Sri Lanka include cholera, dengue fever, hepatitis A, Japanese B encephalitis, malaria, tuberculosis, and typhoid fever; get additional up-to-date information about the risk in the areas you may visit. Medical help is available.

INDIA

Travel in some parts of India (such as in the state of Kashmir) is not advised due to safety concerns, but we're not aware of any special problems along the coast at present. Much of the population is poor, and reasonable precautions against theft should be taken. Most tropical diseases occur somewhere in India, including cholera, dengue fever, hepatitis A, Japanese B encephalitis, malaria, schistosomiasis, tuberculosis, and typhoid fever. In such a large country the risk will vary enormously from place to place; seek detailed information and advice before traveling. Health-care facilities are widely available.

MALDIVES

There are no serious safety concerns for cruisers visiting the Maldives. Tropical diseases include dengue fever, hepatitis A, and typhoid fever. Medical help is available on Male and on many outlying islands as well.

◀ *South Indian Ocean* ▶

Weather

The southeast trade winds predominate year-round in the Indian Ocean south of about 12° S and extend as far as 25° S in the southern winter and 30°S in summer. Wind strengths average 10 to 20 knots and are stronger in winter than summer; the direction is typically southeast or east-southeast. During the southern winter the ITCZ extends well south of the equator, allowing the northeast monsoon of the North Indian Ocean to be drawn south; the Coriolis force bends these winds so that they are from the northwest. Note that these northwest monsoon winds affect only the area between the equator and about 12° S. In the southern winter the ITCZ moves close to the equator, and winds are from the southeast across the entire South Indian Ocean.

The cyclone season in the South Indian Ocean corresponds to that found in the South Pacific. It extends from November to May, with the greatest frequency of storms in January.

Currents

The South Equatorial Current sets west throughout the year, and its northerly limit is between 6 and 10° S. It is less well defined in the eastern Indian Ocean, especially in the southern summer, when flows in the Arafura Sea, along the southern coast of Java and the eastern Indonesian Islands, and the northwestern coast of Australia are all to the east. On its western end the South Equatorial Current splits when it reaches Madagascar, with a portion being deflected south along the coast. The latter, the Madagascar Current, is strongest close inshore, with averages of 1 to 2 knots. North of Madagascar the South Equatorial Current flows west until reaching the African coast, where it divides into two branches. The southerly current is called the Mozambique (which becomes the powerful Agulhas Current farther south). The northerly branch flows along the Tanzanian and Kenyan coasts and becomes the Somali Current in the North Indian Ocean.

Islands of the Eastern and Central South Indian Ocean

There are only three widely separated island groups in the eastern and central Indian Ocean: Christmas Island, the Cocos (Keeling) Islands, and the Chagos Archipelago. These islands are typically visited by yachts transiting the Indian Ocean, either en route to the Red Sea or South Africa. Both Christmas and Cocos Islands are Australian territories, while the Chagos Archipelago is a British possession.

Geography

All of the islands are volcanic in origin, but they've evolved rather differently. Coral growth is very limited at Christmas Island, which has steep cliffs in many areas, and reaches a height of about 1,200 feet (360 m). Anchorage is in an open roadstead, protected from the prevailing southeast winds and seas but affected by swell. The Cocos Islands are composed of two atolls (North and South Keeling), which include a total of 27 flat coral islets within them. North Keeling is accessible only to dinghies (and has been protected as a national park). Good shelter is available within the lagoon at South Keeling. The Chagos Archipelago is a varied collection of reefs, banks, and low coral islets that includes the Salomon Islands; Peros Banhos Islands; Three Brothers, Eagle, and Danger Islands; the Egmont Islands; and Diego Garcia atoll, the largest in the group. Diego Garcia offers the best shelter, but is a U.S. military base and off-limits to visitors. Of the remaining islands, the Salomons offer the best shelter.

Culture

None of these islands were inhabited prior to European colonization; both Christmas and Cocos became British possessions in the second half of the 19th century and were transferred to Australia in the 1950s. Chagos was discovered by the Portuguese in the early 16th century and was for centuries a dependency of Mauritius. In 1965 it was separated from Mauritius as part of the newly created British Indian Ocean Territory.

Christmas Island had extensive phosphate deposits, but these have been largely exhausted by mining during the last 100 years. Most of the present population of less than 2,000 are descended from Chinese and Malay laborers brought in from Malaysia, Singapore, and the Cocos Islands to work in the phosphate industry. The island has become increasingly popular as an eco-tourism destination, and most of the island and surrounding reefs have been designated as a national park. The inhabitants of the Cocos Islands are primarily descendants of original coconut plantation workers and their dependents, brought to the islands in the early 19th century from Malaysia. Copra is still the primary industry.

The islands of the Chagos Archipelago are today uninhabited, except for the Diego Garcia base, where some 3,000 British and American military personnel are stationed. The islands were previously inhabited by the Ilois, descendants of African and Indian plantation workers who had lived there for a number of generations. The Ilois were evicted by the British between 1967 and 1973 and resettled on Mauritius, itself a British colony until 1968. The Ilois have been fighting their eviction in court and apparently achieved victory in late 2000, when the British High Court ruled that they had been illegally evicted from their islands. The United States has a 50-year lease on Diego Garcia, however, a base that is viewed as highly strategic. As we write this, it's not clear what the outcome of this battle will be.

Coral Reefs

Reefs at both Christmas and Cocos (Keeling) Islands are in excellent condition, thanks to small human populations in both areas. There are restrictions in force to protect reefs in both areas. The Chagos Archipelago includes what is probably the largest area of relatively undisturbed reef in the Indian Ocean, and some of the best, though there are reports of severe widespread coral bleaching in the last few years. There is fishing pressure from boats that are catching sharks for shark fin and sea cucumbers, and there's a growing concern that cyanide fishing boats are targeting the area. The entire Chagos Archipelago has been designated a marine reserve, and all flora and fauna (including corals and shells) are protected. Spearfishing is prohibited.

Navigation

The IALA A buoyage system is used. All of these islands are well charted, and navigational aids are in good condition at Cocos and Christmas Island.

Formalities and Facilities

CHRISTMAS ISLAND

Cruisers arriving at Christmas Island should contact the harbormaster on VHF channel 16; clearance is conducted at Flying Fish Cove, the island's only anchorage. The same immigration and quarantine regulations and fees that apply in mainland Australia apply here, and all visitors (except New Zealand passport holders) must obtain visas in advance. Eggs, fresh meat, and most fresh produce are likely to be confiscated. An anchorage fee is charged, as is a departure tax. The anchorage is unprotected and can be roily. Fuel, provisions, and basic spares are available; prices are reasonable, considering the island's isolation. Communication links are good, and there are regular flights to Australia.

COCOS ISLANDS

Visitors to Cocos Islands should announce their arrival via VHF channel 20, or should anchor adjacent to the quarantine buoys at Direction Island and await clearance. Australian immigration and quarantine regulations apply (see above). Anchorage is restricted to Direction Island. A limited amount of expensive provisions is available; it may be possible to obtain help with engine repairs, and spares could be sent from Australia. There is telephone service, and twice-weekly flights to Australia.

CHAGOS ARCHIPELAGO

There are no procedures for clearance in the Chagos Archipelago, but this is British territory, and patrols are made on occasion from the base at Diego Garcia. Sailors may be asked to show papers and pass-

ports. Cruisers are expected to spend no more than one month in the islands, and regulations prohibit spending the night ashore. There are also regulations that prohibit anchorage in some areas of the archipelago; reportedly an anchorage fee of $55 U.S. is now being charged, though it's not clear where or how that fee is collected. No provisions or other facilities of any kind are available to sailors in the islands.

Health and Safety

All three island areas are free from most tropical diseases. Medical assistance is available on both Christmas and Cocos Islands. The sole medical facilities at Chagos are on Diego Garcia, where excellent care is no doubt available to military personnel, but don't count on obtaining help; you *may* be able to obtain assistance in a genuine emergency.

Islands of the Western South Indian Ocean

Island groups in the western part of the South Indian Ocean include the Seychelles, the Mascarene Islands of Réunion, Mauritius, and Rodrigues, the Comoros Archipelago, and Madagascar.

Geography

These islands are a mixture of continental and volcanic types. Many unique plant and animal species have developed on the continental islands as a result of millions of years of isolation; the flora and fauna on the volcanic islands is generally much more limited.

The Seychelles include about 115 islands that collectively form the independent Republic of the Seychelles. They consist of both granitic islands (separated from India some 65 million years ago) and a number of coral atolls, including Aldabra Atoll, one of the world's largest and a world heritage site (for which permission to visit must be obtained in advance on Mahé). The environment in the Seychelles has been less disturbed than on other island groups in the Indian Ocean, and regulations concerning environmental protection are more strict, which bodes well for the survival of some of

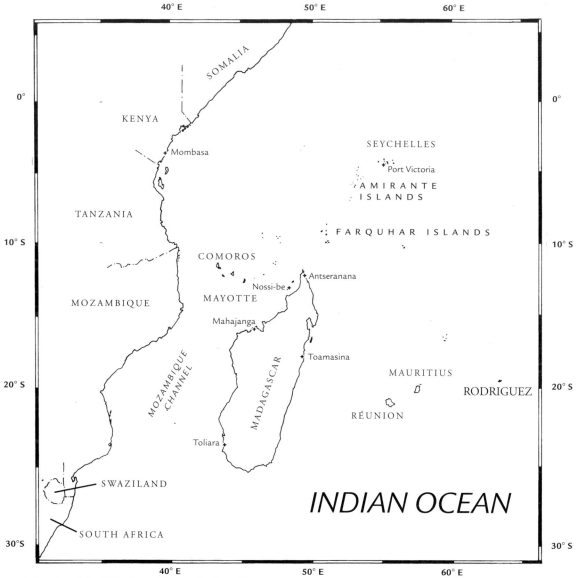

Islands of the Western South Indian Ocean.

the unique flora and fauna. There are a number of marine national parks, and some islands have been set aside as bird sanctuaries. The giant tortoise is still found on several islands, as is the giant coco de mer (which lives to be many hundreds of years old).

South of the Seychelles the volcanic Mascarene Islands stretch from the southwest to northeast. Réunion, the youngest and southernmost of these islands, is a still-active volcano, with impressive, rugged peaks rising to over 10,000 feet (3,000 m).

It's a French "collective territory" and offers superb hiking in the mountainous interior. Réunion includes within its jurisdiction several uninhabited atolls and coral islands spread over a wide area of the Indian Ocean and Mozambique Channel: Tromelin (north of Réunion), the atolls Europa and Bassas de India in the Mozambique Channel, and Juan de Nova and the Îles Gloricuses off the coast of Madagascar. All are claimed by Mauritius as well.

The independent Republic of Mauritius includes the now extinct volcanic island of that name as well as the smaller island of Rodrigues, Cargados Carajos and Agalega Atolls, and various smaller islands. The environment on Mauritius has been hard hit by the expanding population, but less so on Rodrigues.

An independent republic, Madagascar (Madagasikara) is the world's fourth-largest island. Madagascar was originally part of the African continent but split off some 165 million years ago. Its long period of isolation led to the evolution of many unique forms of plants and animals, but with just 15 percent of the original forest cover remaining, many are now threatened with extinction. Most of the rainforest is found on a narrow strip along the east coast; the central island forms a high plateau (cool enough to have an occasional snowfall in winter), dropping to plains on the western side.

The Comoros are a chain of small volcanic islands lying between Madagascar and the African coast. Mayotte (Mahore), the easternmost and oldest island, is a French territory. The three remaining islands of Anjouan (Nzwani), Moheli (Mwali), and Grande Comore (Ngazidja) make up the Federal Islamic Republic of the Comoros. Grand Comore is the youngest in the archipelago and is still volcanically active.

Culture

Most of the islands of the southwestern Indian Ocean were uninhabited prior to European voyages of exploration. The primary exceptions were Madagascar and the Comoros, which were settled by voyagers from Indonesia and Africa.

The Seychelles were undoubtedly known to Arab navigators and later to European sailors, but significant settlement didn't take place until 1770, after the island was claimed by France. French ruled until 1814, when the islands were ceded to the British, but French culture and language remained in widespread use. The Seychelles became independent in 1976. Culturally, people of the Seychelles are a mixture of European, African, and Malagasy influences. The official languages are English and French, and both are widely used, but a Seychelles Creole (similar to what is spoken in Mauritius and Martinique) is the most common everyday language. The present population is about 80,000.

Réunion was first settled by the French in the 17th century, when it was used as a base by the French East India Company. The island was slowly developed for plantation agriculture, using African slave labor. The present culture reflects the mixture of African and French origins; French is the official language, but Réunion Creole is the most widely spoken. Few people speak English. The present population is over 700,000 and growing rapidly, and there is high unemployment. Tourism and agriculture are the primary industries.

Mauritius was known to Arab navigators from at least the 10th century, but no attempts were made to settle the island until the Dutch arrived in 1598. They abandoned the island in 1710, and the French took possession in 1721. The British captured the island in 1810, and it remained under British rule until independence in 1968. The present population is made up of descendants of African slaves (first brought by the Dutch), French settlers, and Indian and Chinese brought to the island as indentured agricultural workers. Many languages are used by the various ethnic groups, but English is the official language, and Creole is the most commonly spoken language. The population density in Mauritius is one of the highest in the world. The population grew rapidly after malaria was eradicated in the 1960s, and today, almost one-third of the country's population of about 1.2 million is under 15 years of age.

Madagascar was first settled some 2,000 years ago by people of Indonesian origin. Arabs and Africans also settled in Madagascar, especially along the coast, beginning 1,000 years ago. Various ethnic groupings developed, and about 20 are recognized today. All share the same language (Malagasy). French is also officially recognized. Madagascar has been independent for most of its history, except for a period from the late 19th century to 1958 when it was a French colony. Many of the cultural traditions can still be clearly traced back to their Indonesian roots. Traditional belief systems are still practiced by a sizable portion of the country's 15 million people. The rapidly growing population has had significant impacts on the natural environment.

Like Madagascar, the Comoros Archipelago was populated by people of Indonesian descent some 1,500 to 2,000 years ago. Later migrations brought people from Africa, Madagascar, and Arabia, and many of the inhabitants converted to Islam. Significant European influence did not occur until the mid-19th century, when France took possession of Mayotte; it later took the other islands in the group under its "protection" as well. The islands became a French overseas territory in 1947. The islands of Anjouan, Moheli, and Grande Comore declared independence in 1975, but residents of Mayotte voted to remain associated with France. Mayotte is still claimed by the Comoros Republic, which has been beset by a series of coups and secessionist attempts over the last 25 years. The economy in all the Comoros Islands is based on subsistence agriculture. The Comoros Republic is one of the world's poorest countries, with a rapidly growing population that is expected to reach almost 800,000 by 2010. Mayotte's population is about 80,000 and is likewise growing rapidly. The official languages in the islands are French and Arabic in the Comoros Republic, and French in Mayotte, although most of the inhabitants speak Comorian (a Bantu language related to Swahili).

Coral Reefs

Reef development in the islands of the southwestern Indian Ocean varies considerably depending on the age of the islands. The diversity of species is not as high here as in the eastern Indian Ocean and western Pacific. Reefs of all types are found here, from narrow fringing reefs to atolls, and like most areas, reefs that are remote and protected from human impacts are typically in the best condition. Natural impacts have also been severe, however, with many reefs north of about 15 degrees severely affected by coral bleaching in recent years.

In the Seychelles fringing reefs occur around the main granitic islands, while there are numerous patch reefs and coral islands on the outer banks. There are also atolls with well-developed coral reefs, Aldabra Atoll (a world heritage site) being the best known. In general, human impacts on the reefs in the Seychelles are minimal, though fishing pressure is increasing in response to increasing population and tourism; other impacts include the coral bleaching event of 1998, which was severe, killing many shallow corals. Spearfishing is prohibited in the Seychelles, and there are a number of marine protected areas, with strict controls to protect the reef ecosystems. There is an active dive-tourism industry.

Because it is quite young, Réunion has only limited fringing reefs. The Mascarene Islands of Mauritius and Rodrigues are older and have well-developed reefs. Mauritius is nearly surrounded by reefs, with fringing reefs bordering channels and protected bays, and with patch reefs in the lagoon. Rodrigues is older and has well-developed coral reefs. The Cargados Carajos Shoals (north of Mauritius) include a large area of reefs as well. Reefs around Mauritius and Rodrigues have, for the most part, escaped the coral bleaching that occurred farther north, but the reefs of Mauritius have been damaged by overfishing, tourism and development activities, and a lack of management. Runoff from sugarcane farming is a major problem for reefs in the lagoon.

Madagascar has numerous coastal reefs, which are most extensive in the northwest and southwest, and which have suffered damage from runoff due to forest clearing and slash-and-burn agriculture. In addition, fishing pressure is intense on many reefs. There are only two protected areas in the country at present.

Fringing reefs are found around Grand Comore, Anjouan, and Moheli in the Comoro Islands, and the south side of the latter is a popular snorkeling destination for cruisers. Mayotte has an extensive barrier reef that offers excellent diving. There are no marine protected areas in the Comoros and only one fishing reserve in Mayotte lagoon. Coral bleaching in the Comoros was severe in 1998.

Navigation

The IALA A buoyage system is used. Markers may not be in good repair in the Comoros and Madagascar. British and French charts are generally the best for the western Indian Ocean waters, due to their colonial history in the area. Care should be exercised when sailing among remote reefs and uninhabited islands, which are typically unmarked. In addition, charts may not be updated to conform to the WGS 84 or other GPS-compatible standard.

Formalities and Facilities

SEYCHELLES

Port Victoria on the island of Mahé is the only clearance port. Port officials can be reached on VHF channel 16 (monitored 24 hours). Two-week immigration permits are granted on arrival, with the possibility of extension (up to 3 months). A clearance for visiting other islands in the group must be obtained. Restrictions regarding anchoring are in force in a number of areas, either because an island is privately owned, or because it is within a protected area. Harbor dues of about $10–15 U.S./day are charged for vessels below 20 tons (more for larger vessels). Landing fees are charged on many islands, and parks levy fees for both day visits and overnight anchoring. No marinas exist in the Seychelles at present, but

yachts are welcome to use the facilities of the Seychelles Yacht Club in Port Victoria's inner harbor, which offers protected anchorage as well as fuel and laundry facilities. Port Victoria has several boatyards but minimal marine supplies; provisions are available at supermarkets and a daily produce market.

RÉUNION

Pointe de Galets (west of the capital) is the clearance port, and the port captain can be reached on VHF channel 16. French immigration regulations apply, and no visas are needed for 3-month visits for citizens of the U.S. and E.U. countries. There is a marina at Pointe de Galets and also at St. Pierre (on the southwest coast). The latter has a travel lift. Marine supplies are expensive and limited. Most foodstuffs are imported and expensive, but locally grown produce is available.

MAURITIUS

Port Louis is the sole clearance port, although separate clearance for Rodrigues can be obtained at Port Mathurin on that island. The port authority at Port Louis maintains a 24-hour watch on VHF channel 16. Visitors from most countries are eligible to stay for 3 months without an advance visa. A marina at Port Mathurin supplies electricity and water to the dock. Provisioning on Mauritius is excellent; provisions are also available at Port Mathurin on Rodrigues, but water should be treated.

MADAGASCAR

There are five ports of entry for Madagascar, well distributed around the island: Toamasina (on the central east coast), Antseranana at the northern tip, Nossi Be (Hell-Ville) and Mahajanga on the northwest coast, and Toliara in the southwest. Arriving yachts should contact the harbormaster on VHF if possible; otherwise, anchor or moor, fly a Q flag, and await the arrival of officials. Advance visas are required, and nearby consulates are located on Mauritius, Réunion, and Tanzania. The maximum stay (with extensions) is generally 30 days. There are no yachting facilities, although there are slipways for fishing craft in Toamasina and Mahajanga. Local produce is widely available, but imported provisions are very expensive and scarce. All water should be treated.

COMOROS

Mutsamudu (on Anjouan) and Moroni (on Grande Comore) are clearance ports. Instructions should be obtained from the port captain on VHF channel 16. Visas valid for 3 months can be obtained on arrival. There is a small boatyard at the commercial port at Mutsamudu, and basic provisions are available.

MAYOTTE

Dzaoudzi is the clearance port, and the Commandant du Port should be contacted on VHF 16 for clearance. French immigration regulations apply. The main harbor at Dzaoudzi is well protected, and has some basic repair facilities. Provisioning is better than in the neighboring Comoros.

Health and Safety

The risk of theft or violence in the Seychelles is low, and normal precautions should suffice. Diseases present in the islands include dengue fever, hepatitis A, and typhoid fever. There is no malaria. Health care is available on the main islands but is very expensive; many smaller islands have no medical facilities.

There have been reports of speedboats injuring swimmers in Mauritius, so care should be taken when swimming or snorkeling. Dengue fever, hepatitis A, schistosomiasis, and typhoid can occur in Mauritius; malaria *(P. vivax)* is present in northern rural areas. Malaria is not present on Rodrigues.

Robberies and break-ins (often involving the use of weapons and violence) are reported to be increasing in Madagascar, especially in and around the capital. Muggings, purse snatching, and pickpocketing are common in all urban areas. It's recommended that visitors not walk in urban areas after dusk, and that caution should be used when visiting beaches or other isolated areas. Major illnesses in Madagascar include malaria (choloroquine-resistant *P. falciparum*), cholera, typhoid fever, various parasitic diseases, and tuberculosis. Health care is available, especially in larger cities.

Petty crime (such as pickpocketing, purse snatching, and scams) is common in crowded market areas in the Comoros Islands, on beaches, and in parks. The Comoros are an Islamic country, and conservative dress is recommended, especially for women. Shorts and revealing clothing are not appropriate. As of early 2001, travel to the island of Anjouan (which declared itself independent from the Comoros in 1997) is not recommended. Since late 1998 fighting has occurred between various armed groups resulting in a number of injuries and deaths. An Organization of African Unity embargo on travel and some goods was recently lifted, but access to the island of Anjouan still requires prior permission from authorities there. Cholera, hepatitis A, malaria, and typhoid fever can occur in the Comoros. Medical facilities are available in Grande Comoroe and Mayotte. All water should be regarded as potentially contaminated.

◄ *Red Sea and Gulf of Aden* ►

The Red Sea and Gulf of Aden region comprises both an important transit route for many cruising sailors and a unique cruising destination in its own right. Regrettably there have been a number of incidents of piracy against yachts in these waters in recent years, some of which have resulted in injury and loss of yacht. The problem may not be as widespread as has been reported or is generally assumed: at this writing

over 500 yachts have passed through the Red Sea in the last 3½ years, with only 5 or 6 confirmed cases of piracy during that time. Several incidents reported as piracy (none of which apparently resulted in injuries or theft) appear to have been caused by demands for baksheesh ("gift") by crews of Yemeni patrol craft. Authorities in Yemen appear to be working to address the situation, and responsible crews have been

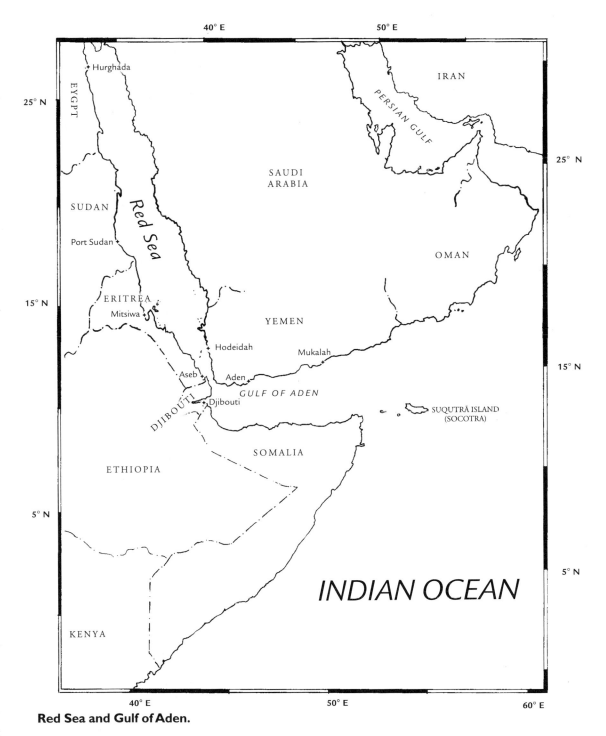

Red Sea and Gulf of Aden.

Pharaoh Island, Gulf of Aqaba, Egypt.

punished by Yemeni authorities in several instances. The risk of true piracy in these waters is very real, however, with the data suggesting about 1 act of piracy for every 100 boats that pass through the area. Sailors heading through these waters should be sure to obtain updates on the situation *before* committing themselves to this route and should take adequate precautions if they do sail.

Red Sea Winds

Winds in the Red Sea tend to blow from either the northwest or southeast. Northwest winds predominate in the summer months, while winter sees southwest winds in the southern Red Sea (south of about 18° N), with northwest winds to the north. There are no tropical cyclones in the Red Sea.

Red Sea Currents

Current patterns change seasonally in these waters. In the Gulf of Aden, currents generally follow the pattern for the Indian Ocean, setting west in winter and east in summer. Summer currents are generally stronger (over 1 knot) than the winter currents, which average ½ knot. Countercurrents and eddies are common close to the shore of Somalia and may run as fast as 2 knots in summer.

Currents in the Red Sea flow north in winter, except for a weak clockwise circulation in the far north. May is a transitional month, and then currents flow south during the summer (June to September). October is a transitional month.

Geography and Culture

The entire Red Sea region is generally hot and dry, although temperatures can become quite cool in the north during the winter, dropping as low as 55°F (13°C) at night. Summer temperatures of about 110°F (43°C) in the south are not unusual. Fortunately humidity is typically fairly low.

This region has been inhabited for thousands of years, and Egyptian civilization in particular has a long and complex history. The British (and to a lesser degree the French) have been heavily involved in the region in recent times, and many countries that border on the Red Sea have gained their independence only relatively recently, which probably helps account for some of the continuing border disputes. Although visits are not without risk (see Health and Safety below), the following countries are visited by cruising yachts:

▶ **YEMEN**, which was occupied by the British until 1967 and then divided into North and South Yemen; the two were reunited in 1994.

▶ **DJIBOUTI**, which was annexed by France in 1862 and gained independence in 1977; French troops are still stationed here.

▶ **ERITREA**, which was formerly an Italian colony and then occupied by the British; it became part of Ethiopia in 1962, but following decades of civil war it became independent in 1993.

▶ **SUDAN**, which is a legacy of British colonial rule and contains a number of different cultures; the country gained independence in 1956, and there have been a number of coups and civil wars since then.

▶ **EGYPT**, which was occupied by the French and the British, and then became a British protectorate; the country became independent in 1922, but British forces remained until 1956.

Somalia should be avoided by all yachts due to the risk of piracy and violence, and Saudi Arabia is not open to tourists (though yachts with true emergencies have been allowed to stop and effect repairs).

Coral Reefs

The waters of the Red Sea are largely protected from destructive wave action, and there is very little sediment in the water, due to a lack of runoff in this very arid climate. These factors have resulted in widespread reef growth, most of it in the form of fringing reefs. The waters off the coasts of Egypt, Saudi Arabia, Sudan, and Somalia all feature extensive reefs, many in good to excellent condition. The dive-tourism industry in Egypt has been expanding rapidly in recent years, though, with severe impacts on the reef as a result of destructive anchoring practices. Moorings have been installed at a number of popular dive spots, and these should be used if possible.

Some of the Red Sea's best anchorages will be found in small breaks and openings within the fringing reefs along the shores. These have names and characteristics that are unique to the region.

sharm: narrow, deep, and winding passages that penetrate as much as a mile or more through the fringing reef

marsa: natural bays that are lined and sometimes interspersed with coral; such bays often form at creeks (where freshwater inhibits coral growth) or around headlands

wadi: the valley of a stream, which may flow only occasionally

khor: harbor that is located within a *wadi*

ras: a vestigial *marsa*

Navigation

The IALA A buoyage system is used. Lights and markers in the Red Sea should not be relied upon, and this is especially true of minor markers. Admiralty charts provide the most comprehensive and detailed coverage, but NIMA charts also cover the Red Sea, and agreement between the charts and GPS positions may be better with the latter. On the other hand, French charts may show reefs much more clearly. We advise you to make comparisons, if possible, before deciding on your source.

Formalities and Facilities

YEMEN

Ports of entry include Aden and Mukallah on the Gulf of Aden and Hodeidah in the southern Red Sea. Yachts are able to call in at ports of entry without advance visas, but visas are required for inland travel (those without visas are issued shore passes that restrict movement to the port area only). Yachts arriving at all ports should contact the port authority on VHF channel 16, and it is advisable to establish a contact schedule and itinerary with Yemeni authorities if traveling between Mukallah and Aden (see Health and Safety, below). A coastal cruising permit may be required if cruising (and stopping) in coastal waters. Fuel, water and provisions are all available.

DJIBOUTI

Djibouti is the port of entry. Yachts normally anchor near the yacht club, which can be contacted on VHF channel 16, after which the port captain should be contacted on VHF channel 12. Clearance procedures are handled in the commercial harbor. Visas are not required for short visits; advance visas for longer stays can be obtained from French embassies. Some port dues and fees are charged. Fuel, water, and good provisioning are available, and repairs can be arranged. There is a French naval base in the port.

ERITREA

There are two ports of entry, Mitsiwa (Massawa) in the north and Aseb (Assab) in the south. Port authorities should be contacted via VHF prior to arrival. Advance visas are not required. Provisions, water, and fuel are available in both ports.

SUDAN

Port Sudan is the sole port of entry, but yachts can also stop at Sawakin (Suakin), just to the south.

Formalities at the latter appear to be simpler and less costly, and Port Sudan is easily visited overland. Arriving yachts should contact port control on VHF channel 14. Advance visas are not required, and some agent and port fees are charged. Water, fuel, and provisions are available.

EGYPT

Ports of entry in the Red Sea include Safaga, Hurghada, Sharm el Sheikh, and Port Said. Visas are not required for yachts simply transiting the Suez Canal. It's possible to anchor at night while sailing along the Egyptian coast, despite not having first obtained clearance. Crew must not go ashore in this instance, however, and it's likely that you will be watched and visited by Egyptian Coast Guard vessels that are stationed in most ports. Crews desiring to explore inland should get clearance at one of the ports of entry. Visas are required (they are available in Djibouti), and these are less costly if obtained in advance. A monthly fee, currently set at $300 U.S./month, is now levied on all yachts given clearance in Egypt. The fee is reportedly not charged in all ports, with Safaga possibly the safest bet for avoiding this fee. A receipt should be obtained if the fee is paid, which can be shown to officials at subsequent ports. Fuel, water, and provisions are available in a number of ports along the coast.

Health and Safety

The biggest hazard in these waters is from piracy, particularly off the coast of Somalia. There have also been several incidents off the coast of Yemen (between Mukallah and Aden) that reportedly involved fishermen or Somali refugees. In general, the safest waters in the Gulf of Aden extend south from the Yemeni coast about one-quarter of the way to the Somali coast (note that yachts have been attacked even when in the middle of the gulf). According to the French Navy, the piracy hotspots include a 100-nautical-mile radius around Suqutrā, the southern two-thirds of the Gulf of Aden along the northeast coast of Somalia, and the southern three-fourths of the gulf from the northwest coast of Somalia. Yachts transiting the Gulf of Aden should approach the Yemeni coast near the border with Oman and then make their way west. Those approaching Djibouti should not close with the Somali coast but should instead make their approach from the northeast. To avoid problems along the coast of Yemen, it is advised that yachts keep at least 5 miles off the coast in the center of the region between Mukallah and Aden. Authorities in Mukallah can provide updated information on the risk in this area; Yemeni coastal waters to the west of Mukallah are presently reported to be safe. Checking in at Salalah (Oman) or Mukallah may be advisable if only to enable you to inquire about the current situation and to ensure that authorities are advised about your travel plans and estimated time of arrival. You should endeavor to maintain contact with authorities ashore (via radio or phone) whenever possible.

Cruising in these waters also presents a risk due to the frequent civil wars within nations and border fighting between them. Areas currently deemed hazardous include the following:

▶ **ERITREA.** A peace agreement was signed between Eritrea and Ethiopia in December 2000, but the Eritrean coast south of Massawa and near the border with Sudan remains dangerous.

▶ **SUDAN.** There is a state of emergency in Sudan due to the ongoing civil war. The coastal area is not directly affected by the fighting, but Sudanese land borders are closed, and yachts should not approach the coast in border areas (both in the north and south). The U.S. Department of State currently advises Americans not to travel to Sudan.

▶ **YEMEN.** There have been a number of kidnappings of Westerners in Yemen recently, as well as a terrorist attack on a U.S. Navy ship in Aden in October 2000. U.S. officials currently advise Americans to defer travel to Yemen.

Major tropical diseases in the region include hepatitis A, malaria, cholera, typhoid fever, and yellow fever (in parts of Sudan and Eritrea). Medical facilities are generally poor, except in Egypt.

APPENDICES

Ropework and Sewing

Below we describe three projects mentioned in the text. Rope ratlines are a tried-and-true means of getting aloft, which is critical for visual piloting in coral waters. A rope-to-chain splice is the best way to connect the anchor rode and chain. A roped awning will protect you and your boat from the intense tropical sun while in port.

ROPE RATLINES

Rope ratlines are probably the oldest method of getting aloft, and also one of the best. They are inexpensive, easy to make, and secure to use. And unlike wood ratlines or mast steps, rope ratlines can be fashioned or repaired anywhere using materials and tools that are probably already on board.

The first consideration in making rope ratlines is the type and size of the line. Three-strand Dacron is the optimum line because it's easy to splice, low in stretch, and UV resistant. If you don't have access to three-strand Dacron, nylon anchor rode can also be used. The line should be ⅜–½ inch (10–12 mm) in diameter; ¼ inch (6 mm) may be strong enough to support most people's weight but would be uncomfortable to stand on for any length of time, whereas line over ½ inch (12 mm) is awkward to splice in the short lengths that the ratlines require.

Spend time on aligning the lowest rung, as all the rungs above will be based on it. To begin, determine how high you want the lowest rung to be—ours start 30 inches (75 cm) above the deck. Mark the aft lower shroud at this point (a permanent felt-tip marker works well). Next, using the horizon as your level, sight over to the forward lower shroud and mark it at the same height. Don't follow the line of the sheer, or your ratlines will slope uphill.

The next step—applying service to the shrouds—is a vital one if your ratlines are to stay in place. Our simplified approach to "serving" involves wrapping the shroud tightly with a waxed twine, in this case to provide a nonslip surface for securing your ratlines. This is especially important with stainless-steel rigging. The service should extend for about 3 inches (7.5 cm), centered at the spot you've marked for the ratline. Traditionally, service is applied after the wire has first been parceled: wrapped with a waterproof covering to keep moisture out of the wire's interior. Because we are serving only short sections of wire, it seems doubtful that the parceling would be effective; and it may increase the risk of corrosion. We suggest simply serving over the bare wire.

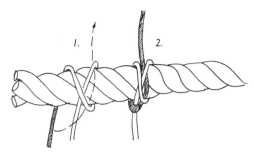

Tying a constrictor knot to a piece of three-strand line. 1. Begin by placing the line atop the twine. Take the right-hand portion of the twine and loop it twice around the line, tucking the right-hand end under the previous loop. 2. Next, pass the left-hand end of the twine over the right-hand end and under the bottom and top of the right-hand loop. Grasp right- and left-hand ends and pull tight.

Detail of a spliced eye lashed to a serviced shroud.

The service is applied from the top down using waxed sail thread. Take about 3 feet (1 m) of thread, and tie it to the shroud using a constrictor knot (see illustration). Apply firm, even pressure on the sail thread as you make your turns, ensuring that there are no gaps between them. When you reach the bottom of the section to be served, make three or four loose wraps. Draw the remaining line up through the loose wraps and tighten, being careful not to overlap the wraps. Trim any loose ends and then repeat the process for the other shroud. You may wish to apply a second layer of sail twine service over the first to ensure a good gripping surface on which to lash the rungs (see photo); we experienced a small amount of slippage on ratlines lashed to single-layer service, whereas those lashed to twice-served shrouds have not budged.

You're now ready to splice the first rung (see drawing next page). To start the splice, take a piece of ½-inch (12 mm) line and, using waxed sail thread, tie a constrictor knot around the line about 5 inches (12.5 cm) from the end. Bend the end over to form a small eye about 1 inch (2.5 cm) in diameter with the constrictor knot at the throat of the eye. Unlay the 5 inches (12.5 cm) of line so that you end up with three individual strands (step 1 in drawing). Apply tape to the ends of each strand to keep them from unlaying;

using different colors is handy to differentiate strands as you splice, and melting the ends wrapped by the tape will help keep them together. The first tuck is the most critical. The left-most strand (A) should be tucked under, over, and under against the lay of the line. From this point on the splice proceeds by just tucking the strands under the appropriate standing strand. First tuck B (2) and C (3) under, and then make 4 more complete series of tucks, always starting with strand A. Turn your work over, and tuck the third strand (C) under the remaining standing strand (3). Once the splice has been completed (4), cut off the remaining ends with a sharp knife and melt with a lighter. Ideally, you should whip the end of the splice to ensure it does not come undone, but ours are doing fine without this extra step. Before you splice the other end, hold the spliced eye against the shrouds as if it were already lashed to the rigging, and mark the line where the center of the other eye should be. The two eyes should just touch the rigging. (Once it's lashed and stood on a few times by the heaviest crew member, it will take on a bit of a bend.)

With eyes spliced at both ends you're ready to lash your first ratline to the shrouds. We used small, braided Dacron twine—beware of using nylon, as it will degrade quickly. Begin by tying a length of the twine through the eye of the ratline, and then make a series of square turns by passing the twine around the shroud (step 5 in drawing page 345) and back through the same side of the eye. Repeat this square turn, pulling the lashing tight each time, until the lashing covers about 1 inch (2.5 cm) of the shroud

(7). To really snug things up, finish off with several frapping turns around the lashing at the tip of the eye (6), using a marlinspike hitch (8–9) if necessary to apply tension. Finish the lashing with several half-hitches. Repeat the process for the other side of the ratline. The photo show the final product. Now it's time to test the results—some vigorous jumping on the rung should do it.

Repeat this procedure for the remainder of the ratlines, and you'll have a dandy ladder ready to take you aloft at any time. The procedures for the upper ratlines vary only in that you'll need a bosun's chair to properly measure the length of the upper rungs, as you'll draw the shrouds together if you measure while standing on the lower ones. You may also find it easier to serve and lash from the bosun's chair, as that way both hands are free for the work. Finally, although a set of ratlines on one side of your rig is far better than none, we strongly suggest that you have ratlines on both port and starboard, as it's impossible to see through the headsail when your ratlines end up on the lee side.

ROPE-TO-CHAIN SPLICE

A rope-to-chain splice is the best way to permanently join rode and chain (see drawing page 346). The splice is no larger than the chain itself, and so it passes easily through hawse pipes, over anchor rollers, and the like. Although such a splice would appear to be at risk from chafe where the line passes through the chain, we've experienced no problems with any splices after years of constant use. In fact, it's been our experience that the splice will long outlast the galvanizing on your chain. The splice works best if rode and chain are roughly matched in terms of strength. (If the rode is far oversize, the strands will not pass cleanly through the chain.) We use ⅝-inch (14 mm) line with ⁵⁄₁₆-inch (8 mm) BBB chain without difficulty.

Begin by unlaying the strands about 30 inches (75 cm) and tucking two of the strands through the last link in your chain (strands B and C in step 1 in drawing). Snug the chain up against the third

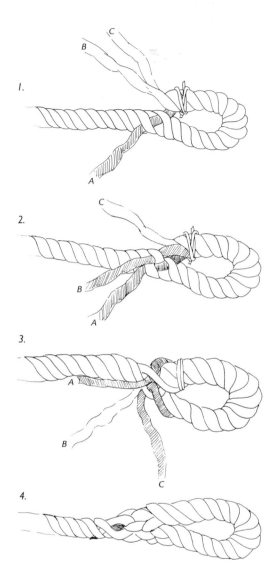

Splicing an eye in 3-strand line. **1.** Form a small eye about 1 inch (2.5 cm) in diameter with the constrictor knot at the throat of the eye. Unlay 5 inches (12.5 cm) of line so that you end up with three individual strands. Tuck the left-most strand (A) under, over, and under against the lay of the line. **2.** Now take the middle strand (B) and tuck it under where the first strand (A) went over. **3.** Turn your work over and tuck the third strand (C) under the remaining standing strand. Next, make four more series of tucks, beginning each time with strand A. Note: after the initial tuck, strand A is passed under only one standing strand, in the same manner as strands B and C. Roll your work between your hands after each series to settle out the tucks. **4.** Completed splice.

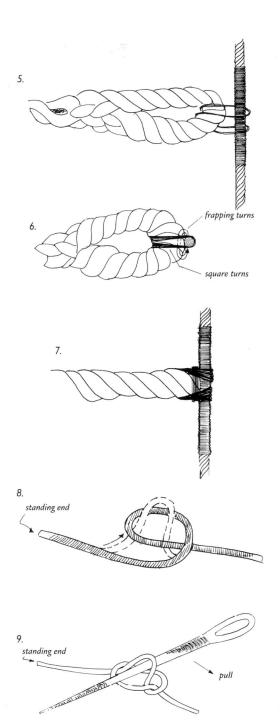

5.

6.

frapping turns

square turns

7.

8.

standing end

9.

standing end

pull

Finished ratlines.

Lashing the rung to the shroud. 5. To lash the rung to the shroud, begin by tying a length of the twine through the eye of the rung. Pass the twine around the shroud and back through the same side of the eye; pull tight. **6.** Repeat this square turn—coming out of the eye, around the served shroud, and back through the same side of the eye—until the lashing covers about 1 inch of the shroud. **7.** Now take about six frapping turns around the lashing at the tip of the eye, using a marlinspike hitch (8–9) if necessary to apply tension. Finish the lashing with several half-hitches.

Marlinspike hitch. 8. Begin by forming a loop in the twine with the standing part lying on top. Now draw a bight of the standing part through the loop, and insert the marlinspike (or fid) in the bight. **9.** Pull on the spike, exerting tension on the standing part, and the hitch will tighten.

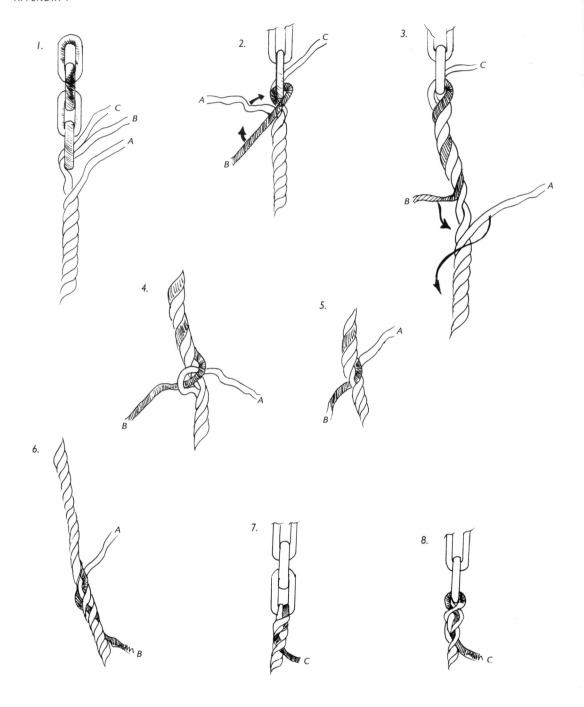

Rope-to-chain splice.

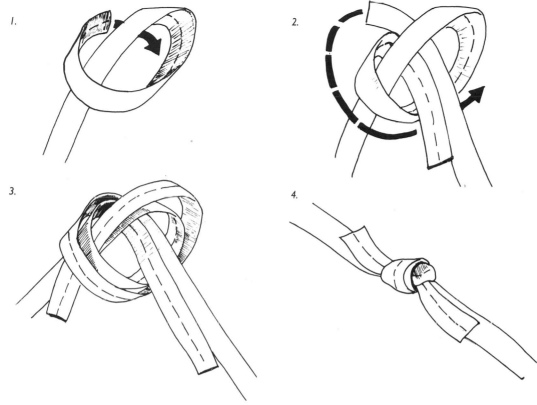

Mountain climber's water knot. **1.** *Begin by making a loose overhand (granny) knot.* **2.** *Starting where the working end of the granny knot comes out, follow it backwards with the other end of the webbing (or with the second piece, if you're joining two separate pieces). Lay the second piece of webbing flat atop the first.* **3.** *When you've followed the first knot around completely with the webbing, begin tightening both knots. You should leave about 3 inches (8 cm) of tail on each.* **4.** *The finished knot. Check it periodically for loosening.*

untucked strand (A in step 1), and then hold the chain in this position while unlaying the untucked strand a short distance. Take one of the two strands you tucked through the chain (B in step 2), and lay it into the spiraling groove that you opened up by unlaying strand A. Continue unlaying A and laying B in its place for about 24 inches (60 cm), or until 6 inches (15 cm) of B remain (3).

Next tie strands A and B together using an overhand knot (4). No gaps should be left; the knot should just fill the space between the two strands, and the transition should be barely visible (5). Then tuck the ends of both strands in, working them over and under against the lay (6). Note that strands are tucked in opposite directions; A is tucked toward the chain, while B is tucked away from it. Tuck each end a half-dozen times, and then cut off the ends, rolling the splice between your hands afterward to fair things up.

Now return to the chain, and taking the third strand (C), proceed to tuck it under itself. Snug this first tuck up, and then follow it with another half-dozen tucks, against the lay (7, 8). Cut off the excess and roll the splice as before.

The finishing touch is provided by three sets of seizings, one placed over each tucked strand, and each covering about an inch of rode. Use waxed sail twine for the seizing. You're now ready to anchor!

Nomad's *roped awning.*

Measuring for an Awning

A = centerline   1–5 = width measure-
B and D = "roof" lines   ments from lifelines
C = side lines   over roof and back
                    down to opposite
                    lifelines

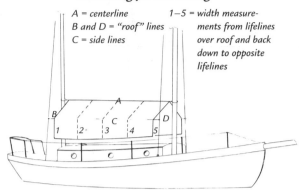

Determining the dimensions of your awning. The height at which the centerline is tied determines the amount of headroom you will have underneath your awning. Standing headroom is nice, but remember, the higher the awning, the more windage it creates. Taller awnings also use more fabric and are, thus, more costly.

MOUNTAIN CLIMBER'S WATER KNOT

The water knot is used for tying knots in webbing. Use it if you want to join two pieces of webbing, make a single piece into a sling (or continuous loop), or want to tie a loop in the end of a longer piece. We use this knot for our harness tethers, and also for jacklines. See drawing previous page.

ROPED AWNING

The benefits of awnings are not limited to keeping your boat cool: in addition, they protect brightwork from sun damage, provide a sheltered place to hang laundry, expand your private living space, and can serve as excellent rain catchers (see photo). Making an awning is surprisingly easy. You'll need a simple home sewing machine and a grommet set, but no other special tools or skills are needed, and you can easily save hundreds of dollars.

Roped awnings look a bit like a tent. A single center rope stretching from mast to backstay (or mizzenmast) forms the peak, and two side ropes, running from mast shrouds to a spreader pole at the backstay (or to the mizzen shrouds), form the roof's eaves. The side walls or curtains tie to rail or lifelines.

Awnings are best made from acrylic canvas, the same fabric commonly used for sail covers, weather cloths, and dodgers. This fabric is expensive, but it'll long outlast cotton canvas. Sources for acrylic canvas include canvas shops, sailmakers, and large chandlers.

Measuring Your Boat

To determine your awning's dimensions, tie a line from the mast to the backstay (or mizzenmast). Next, tie lines from the mast to the outermost shrouds so that they make a slight angle with the centerline. These lines represent the roof of your awning. Tie lines from the same point on the outermost shrouds to a spreader pole placed on the aft side of the backstay (or to the mizzen shrouds). Use any convenient stick for now, lashing it to the backstay at the same height at which the sidelines are tied to the main shrouds. Finally, tie lines from the aft ends of the sidelines to the aft end of the centerline (see drawing).

Now stand back and eyeball things; make sure that the sidelines and centerline are parallel, both to each other and to the water.

348

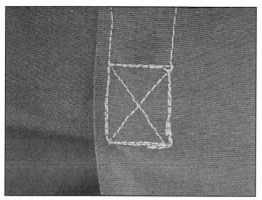

Reinforcement patch, or X, at the upper end of the side curtains. Also note use of simple overlapping seam above the X.

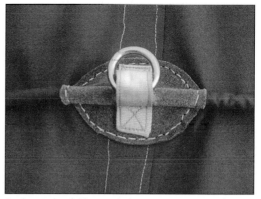

Leather patch with lifting eye for longer awnings. You can also use suede patches to help prevent chafe.

Measure the distance along the centerline between the mainmast and the backstay (or mizzenmast). This figure is the total unhemmed length of your awning. The width of the roof is determined by measuring from the centerline to the sideline. Decide now how long you want your side curtains to be, and add this measurement to the roof measurement. We suggest making side curtains that stop at least 3 inches (8 cm) above the lifelines to avoid chafe on stanchions and lifelines. Take several width measurements along the length of the awning, to allow for taper and differing side curtain lengths that vary with the boat's sheerline. If your boat narrows sharply, or if you have a double-ender, you may want to consider tapering your awning to match the varying width of your boat.

Panels

Divide the centerline length by the width of your fabric to determine the number of fabric panels your awning will need; allow for a 1-inch (2.5 cm) seam allowance. The panels run athwartships and are continuous, stretching from the bottom of one side curtain, up and over the roof to the bottom of the other side curtain. Add 6 inches (15 cm) to your width measurements to allow for 3-inch (7.5 cm) hems on both sides, and then cut your panels accordingly. The centerline length measurement you

made includes a 4-inch (10 cm) hem allowance at the fore and aft ends; the finished awning should be 6 to 8 inches (15–20 cm) shorter than the original centerline length in order that it can be rigged as tightly as possible.

Before you begin sewing the panels together, mark where the side curtains begin. Sew the panels together by simply overlapping the panels a couple of centimeters. Sew two lines of stitching for extra strength, and make sure you stop at the marks you made for the side curtains. Reinforce this point with an X (see photo). Then hem the forward and aft ends of the awning.

If your awning is more than about 15 feet (4.5 m) in length, you should add a lifting eye along the roof to limit sag. Cut a circle of suede or vinyl about 5 inches (12.5 cm) in diameter and a piece of 1-inch nylon webbing about 12 inches (30 cm) long. You'll also need a stainless-steel D-ring. Center the circular patch on the roof and sew around the edge. The nylon webbing runs athwartships; double it over and sew one end to the patch using a reinforcement X. Then slip the D-ring over the webbing and stitch down the other end (see photo).

Ropes and Side Curtains

The ropes are next. The length of the centerline rope should be your original measurement plus an

On our awning we sewed two rows of stitching next to the ropes to provide additional strength. We also hand-stitched the ropes to the fabric for the first 3 inches (7.5 cm) at both the forward and aft ends because these areas take a lot of stress.

additional meter at either end that will be used to tie the awning to the mast and backstay. If you have a mizzenmast, do the same for the sidelines. If your boat is a sloop or cutter, the aft sidelines should extend beyond the awning's aft hem an amount equal to the length of the spreader pole.

Place the centerline rope in the middle of the awning and then fold the awning in half. Stitch as closely to the rope as possible. Then sew the side ropes in place in the same way (see photo).

If you plan to have short side curtains, go ahead and hem them now. But if your curtains come down close to the lifelines, we suggest you rig the awning on your boat before you hem. Many boats have quite a curve at the sheer, and you'll want your side curtains to follow this line (it's not so noticeable when your curtains are short and sit well above the sheer). Use tailor's chalk to mark the finished length on your curtains.

To finish the curtains, set a grommet in each lower corner plus an additional two toward the top. Use small line (about 3/16 in./5 mm in diameter) for tying the side curtains to the lifelines or rail. Tie about 24 inches (60 cm) of line through each upper grommet, as you would a reefing line on a sail (see photo) so that you can roll your curtains up. The basic awning is now complete.

Check the Fit

Before you add any finishing touches, rig the awning and leave it up for a couple of days in light winds to make sure it sits the way you want it to. When you go to rig the awning, start with the centerline. Use a trucker's hitch when you tie this, and tension for all you're worth. Rig the sidelines in the same way, using a bit less effort (see photo). If you're using a spreader pole, run the sidelines through the blocks at the ends of the pole (see photo), and then tie them off on the backstay. (If you keep the aft side curtains rolled up, you may find it necessary to rig short lines from the pole ends to the lifeline or rail, in order to keep the pole from tilting.)

Once you're happy with the set of your awning, look to see if the awning will chafe anywhere and mark these spots with chalk. We sewed patches of suede or soft leather on these areas. If you want your awning to catch rainwater, mark the roof where you want the through-hull fittings to be (see photo).

Side curtains are rolled up using reefing lines tied through upper grommets.

Secure side (and center) ropes using a trucker's hitch.

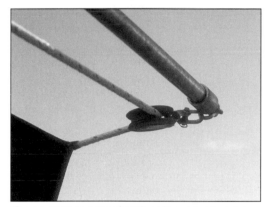

If your awning uses a spreader pole, make sure that the pole is of heavy wall stainless steel—small diameter aluminum poles are not up to the job. Our first pole was of ¾-inch-diameter (19 mm) stainless but proved too weak, and we have since replaced it with heavy wall ⅞-inch (22 mm) tubing. End fittings, to which small blocks are shackled, complete the spreader pole.

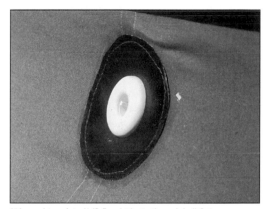

We used two 1-inch (2.5 cm) plastic through-hull fittings, one on each side of the awning. Use a 5-inch (12.5 cm) diameter piece of vinyl (such as Herculite) as a reinforcement patch at each through-hull fitting. Sew these patches in place and then cut a hole through both patch and awning fabric to accommodate the fitting. A bit of rubber cement or other sealant on the stitching of the patch will help stem any leaks.

When it looks like it's going to rain, we attach sections of hose to the fittings and run one of these directly into our water tank and the other into a bucket or jug. We can catch up to eight liters per minute during a heavy downpour.

Take care with your awning by replacing worn stitching, patching holes as soon as they appear, and making certain it is dry and clean before stowing it. If you follow these simple precautions, you'll get years of shade and freshwater from your awning.

Materials List

Sunbrella or other acrylic fabric

heavy bonded polyester thread

⅜-inch (10 mm) diameter line

2-inch (5 cm) brass grommets

small ⅛- to ¼-inch (3 to 6 mm) line, about 16 feet (5 m) for each panel

1-inch (2.5 cm) nylon webbing, about 12 inches (30 cm)

one stainless-steel D-ring

soft leather or suede

⅞-inch (22 mm) diameter stainless-steel pole, with end fitting and blocks for ⅜-inch (10 mm) diameter line (for sloop and cutter rigs only)

two 1-inch (2.5 cm) diameter through-hull fittings, 1-inch (2.5 cm) hose, and a scrap of vinyl fabric (for raincatcher awnings only)

Weather Forecasts

SOURCES OF WEATHER INFORMATION

There are many sources of weather information from which today's cruisers may choose, including voice forecasts from weather bureaus, informal radio weather nets and relays, weather fax broadcasts, direct satellite broadcasts, and a host of weather sources on the Internet. In addition, there is a very valuable (but often overlooked) source, which is your own weather observations and analysis. In general, more information is better than less. We always try to get forecasts from more than one source—and of more than one type, if possible.

Voice Forecasts

A number of different types of voice forecasts are broadcast in various parts of the tropics. Voice forecasts issued by government weather services typically are split into local (or coastal) and offshore forecasts. For example, in the United States, *coastal forecasts* cover waters out to 25 miles and are broadcast via dedicated VHF transmitters; these forecasts can be heard at any time. *Offshore marine forecasts* cover areas from 25 miles offshore out to the edge of the continental shelf. *Offshore waters forecasts* address waters seaward of the continental shelf. Offshore waters forecasts are broadcast on marine single-sideband (SSB) frequencies. These different forecasts are

developed by various branches of the National Weather Service (NWS) and are broadcast by the U.S. Coast Guard.

It's still possible to voyage quite safely using just voice weather broadcasts, which is what we've relied on for many thousands of miles of tropical sailing. The quality of these forecasts does, of course, vary, and even the best forecasters sometimes get it wrong, but we've found that they're usually quite accurate. These days, professional forecasters employ a variety of computer models to predict what's going to happen. They supply the models with a host of data, most of it from satellites, but often some from ships, buoys, and weather balloons as well. The predictions from various models are then compared, modified on the basis of the forecaster's experience, and developed into an official forecast.

The biggest drawback with voice forecasts is often what they don't tell you—the weather you'll be getting in 2 or 3 days' time, and which you could avoid if you knew it was coming. Short-term, 24- to 36-hour predictions are common, and you can bet that every forecaster who makes such a prediction also has some hunches about what will happen after that. Those hunches won't always be right, but making decisions out at sea is simplified if you have access to them. This is one reason for always visiting the local forecasting office before leaving on a passage. Forecasters are usually happy to talk with sailors and to share their insights as to what is or is not brewing. This is also a good reason for receiving weather faxes (see below), as these contain lots of information that is not delivered in a voice broadcast and that you can use to make some informed guesses about what's in store.

The World Meteorological Organization (WMO) has divided the oceans into a number of geographic regions, with responsibility for forecasting in different areas handled by the various WMO members. Some will give forecasts that overlap area boundaries, but many don't, and it can make life difficult for the sailor who is near such a boundary. When you can, it pays to compare several different forecasts, as they often give slightly (and sometimes wildly) different interpretations and predictions.

Forecasts are often read very quickly, and with pronunciations that may be different than you're used to. You'll find it handy to develop your own shorthand and to have a cassette recorder with which you can record broadcasts and then play them back a few times if needed. A good single-sideband receiver (it's important for it to have digital tuning) and antenna are vital if you're cruising offshore; the receiver should allow you to tune in any frequency.

Text Forecasts

Text forecasts are the next step up from voice broadcasts and are available via weather fax, HF Radio, or the Internet. These typically contain a good deal more information than is broadcast in voice forecasts, and they may be much easier to understand than a quickly read voice broadcast. They also don't require the interpretive and forecasting skills that a weather fax chart viewed in isolation requires. Text forecasts are best understood when viewed in combination with a fax chart, but even by themselves can provide a wealth of information.

Weather Faxes, Satellite Images, and Model Output

A wide range of fax and Internet products round out the forecast options; this group includes everything from pretty basic surface maps of wind strength and direction and wave height to real-time satellite data, with a bewildering array of model-generated output in between. If you have a fast Internet connection, have a look at what's out there (see appendix 3, Resources, for sources); there's a wealth of valuable material. Unfortunately, many of the complex Internet products aren't really viable seagoing forecast options for most cruisers at this time, due to the high cost of most satellite connections. But using the Internet is a very good way to become familiar with what's available and to practice your interpretive skills; all NWS fax products are also available on the Net.

At sea, most cruisers opt to receive weather faxes using a SSB receiver together with a computer and special software and modem. Dedicated fax receivers (and various satellite options) are also available. The dedicated fax receiver is the simplest approach, but sailors are increasingly opting to use a computer and SSB, as both can be used for other things as well. Most fax software also allows the user to clean up a received image onscreen, something that's not possible with a dedicated receiver.

There are many different types of weather faxes available, and with all types of fax charts it will take study and practice to understand what you're looking at and to be able to reliably predict what kind of weather is on the way. For the sailor who's willing to work at it, these fax charts (used in conjunction with your own observations and, if possible, some text broadcasts) are probably your best chance of getting advance warning of what the weather is up to.

Weather Nets and Routing

Weather forecasting and interpretation is a very specialized skill, one that can be complex and time consuming. Fortunately, modern communications technology makes it possible to get help interpreting the weather even if you're offshore. This is done informally by many amateur forecasters on ham and SSB nets; the frequencies and schedules used by these nets change frequently, but you can quickly find out what they are by asking other cruisers in the area.

It's also possible to get help interpreting the weather from professional weather routers, typically via radio or e-mail. We've benefited from such a service only once, on a passage from New Caledonia to Australia. We'd been waiting to leave port for a week or so but were hesitant to go because of a persistent low to the north, between the Solomons and Vanuatu. Such lows are common in the Southern Hemisphere summer and frequently develop into cyclones. This was mid-November, within the cyclone season but still early by most local sailors' reckoning. We met daily with other cruisers to discuss forecasts, pour over weather faxes, and debate. Finally, one cruiser tired of the analysis and enlisted the services of a well-known American weather router. He shared the prediction with us, which called for light but consistent southeast to east winds over the course of the next week. We left port the next day and had a perfect passage, flying a spinnaker for several days in winds of 10 to 12 knots. The forecast was so accurate that we could almost have trimmed the sails according to the router's predictions. But what the forecast didn't predict—and what the forecaster made clear he couldn't effectively anticipate—was the emergence of a tropical cyclone out of the monsoon low to the north. Two days after we left port, a cyclone was headed south toward Noumea. It didn't affect us, as we had a good head start and were quickly moving south into cooler waters. But the cruisers who had delayed, including the fellow who had paid for the router's advice, were sent scurrying for the nearest cyclone hole.

Keeping Track of Local Weather Conditions

One of the difficulties that even professional forecasters face when forecasting for tropical ocean areas is that accurate surface data is scarce, especially in remote regions with little shipping. When this happens, forecasters are forced to rely heavily on what their models tell them, as they lack real on-the-ground information to confirm the model's prediction. That's why keeping tabs on the prevailing conditions yourself is important. If you see a trend developing, based on changes in the barometric pressure, clouds, wind, swell, and so on, you may be able to anticipate developments that a forecaster wouldn't know about. This is especially true in the tropics, as some of the forecaster's favorite tools (such as 500 mb charts) aren't of much use. To keep track of weather trends yourself, you need little more than a barometer and a few extra columns in your logbook. Note what the barometric pressure, wind, swell pattern, and clouds are doing every hour or two. Then when conditions begin to change, you'll have an idea of what the trends in all of these are, and you'll be able to add that knowledge to any voice or fax forecasts you receive.

Where to Get Forecasts

Forecasts and warnings are available from many sources and in many forms; it can get confusing. For example, forecast products of various types providing weather information and hurricane warnings for the North Atlantic and Caribbean are available in the following forms—and this is just what's put out by the NWS and U.S. Coast Guard (USCG):

- High Frequency (HF) Fax
- WWV HF Voice
  (at 8 and 9 minutes past the hour)
- USCG HF Voice
- USCG Medium Frequency Voice
- USCG VHF Voice
- NOAA Weather Radio
- NAVTEX broadcast
- INMARSAT-C-SafetyNET
- Internet
- E-mail (FTP mail)

Cruisers in the Caribbean will do well to obtain a copy of the *Mariner's Guide for Hurricane Aware-*

ness in the North Atlantic Basin, which outlines the various weather products that are available for the North Atlantic region from the sources listed above. This volume also provides detailed information on broadcast frequencies and times for this region (see Weather section in appendix 3, Resources).

Cruisers with weather fax capability should obtain a copy of the Worldwide Marine Radiofacsimile Broadcast Schedules, compiled by the NWS (available in PDF format on the Internet; see Broad-cast Schedules for Forecasts and Faxes section in appendix 3, Resources). This publication is worth having even if you don't have fax capability onboard, because it contains listings of Internet links, which can be checked whenever you're in port. There is also a section on obtaining forecasts via e-mail.

A comprehensive listing of foreign voice forecast sources is contained in the Admiralty's List of Radio Signals, available from most marine bookstores.

UNDERSTANDING WEATHER FORECASTS

All weather forecasts, no matter if they take the form of voice broadcasts, text, or fax charts, use specific terms and concepts to explain and predict the weather. Many are familiar enough—a forecast might state that winds are expected to reach 20–25 knots—but the precise meaning may be different than might be assumed by a casual listener. On weather faxes, symbols rather than words are used to convey most of the information, but concepts such as wind strengths are defined in the same way.

Forecast Concepts and Terminology

Wind

The wind is rarely steady. Turbulence results from instability in the atmosphere, which can be caused by heating of the land, cool water, or the passage of a cold front. But wind observations and forecasts are typically given for a single figure or a small range, such as 11–16 knots. This figure represents the mean anticipated wind speed, measured at 30 feet (10 m) above the ground or sea and averaged for 10 minutes. Now here's the rub: *it's standard practice to issue forecasts for which the peak gusts may be up to 40 percent higher*, meaning 15 knots can become 21 knots. Of course, the 40 percent figure is simply the anticipated maximum, and in actual fact peak gusts may be higher or lower. But this is a reasonable figure to use when interpreting forecasts. Because wind pressure varies with the square of the wind speed, the force on your sails from gusts 40 percent higher than the average will have double the force.

It's not uncommon for sailors to forget to take into account the inherent spread in forecast wind speeds when making decisions on the basis of a forecast. A notable instance of this occurred during the 1998 Sydney–Hobart Race, in which 6 lives and 5 yachts were lost. There has been a lot of debate about whether the Australian Bureau of Meteorology accurately forecast maximum wind strengths, but there's no doubt that few of the crews properly interpreted the forecast that *was* issued. The storm warning that was issued (calling for winds of 45–55 knots) should have been interpreted by the racers to mean that hurricane force gusts of 63–77 knots could be expected. Apparently few did so.

Squalls

It's common to use the term *squall* rather loosely to mean a small passing disturbance, one that often contains some rain. In forecasting terms, squall has a more precise and somewhat more serious definition, though, referring to a *sudden increase in wind speed by at least 16 knots*, resulting in the speed rising to at least 22 knots and lasting for at least one minute. For average wind strengths, a forecast calling for squalls is predicting a more serious disturbance than one mentioning gusty winds. In the wind strengths common in the tropics—say 20 knots—a squall forecast anticipates winds of at least 36 knots in the squalls; a forecast for gusty 20-knot winds anticipates winds of only 28 knots.

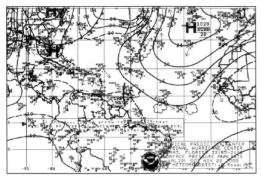

Atlantic Surface Analysis for 6 November 2000 from the NWS Tropical Prediction Center. An easterly wave is approaching the Caribbean, and a tropical cyclone is off the Pacific coast of Mexico.

Beaufort Wind Scale

The Beaufort wind scale seems at first an anachronism, given that it was developed almost 200 years ago as a guide for how much sail square-rigged ships could carry in various wind strengths. But the scale still has relevance in that official wind warning categories still correspond with divisions within the Beaufort scale. In it's modern form, it is also a handy way to correlate wind strength with the expected sea.

Wave Heights

We look at waves in detail in chapter 9 (Heavy Weather in the Tropics), so here we'll just reiterate our remarks on forecast wave heights. The wave-height figure used in forecasts is for *significant wave height*, which is the average of the one-third highest waves. Maximum wave height will normally be almost twice this high. The significant wave height is used in forecasts because it corresponds most closely to the typical wave height estimate that most people make. If a sea is running with an average height of 10 feet, the significant (and forecast wave height) will be 15 feet, while the maximum height (about 1 in every 1,000 waves) will be 29 feet.

Weather Charts

Weather charts (and thus weather faxes, which are simply facsimiles—or copies—of original charts) take many forms.

Surface Synoptic Analysis

One of the most basic and familiar weather charts is the Surface Synoptic Analysis, which presents a summary of features at the surface (either at ground or sea level). The term *synoptic* indicates this is a summary or compilation of various features, while the term analysis indicates that the chart represents an interpretation of an existing situation (rather than a forecast of what's to come). In some cases these charts go by slightly different names; our example is termed a surface pressure analysis, for example.

Not all weather services will include the same features on their surface analyses, but these are among the common elements:

ATMOSPHERIC PRESSURE

Pressure will be indicated by isobars, or lines of equal pressure. These are typically spaced at 4 hPa (or mb) intervals, though spacing can vary; here it drops to 2 hPa in the tropics. You'll see closed isobars circles at high- and low-pressure cells; the center is sometimes marked by an X, and the pressure reading noted. Most services annotate high-pressure cells with an H, but some use an A (for anticyclone); lows are either shown with an L, or a D (for depression).

WIND STRENGTH AND DIRECTION

Surface charts often include some wind barbs. The feathers and pennants on the tail indicate the direction from which the wind is blowing, and their length and number vary with the wind strength. In temperate latitudes wind strength and direction can also be interpreted from isobar spacing.

FRONTS, TROUGHS, AND RIDGES

The position of weather fronts will be shown on most charts, and the type of symbol used indi-

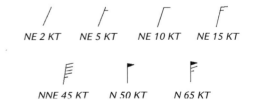

Symbols showing wind speed and direction.

BEAUFORT SCALE

Common Forecast Term	Beaufort Number	Wind Speed (knots)		Sea State	Probable Wave Heights (average/ maximum)		Weather Warning Categories
		Mean	Gusts		feet	meters	
Calm	0–calm	< 1	< 1	calm, like a mirror	none	none	none
Light winds	1–light air	1–3	1.4–4.2	ripples with the appearance of scales; no foam crests	0.3/0.3	0.1/0.1	none
	2–light breeze	4–6	5.6–8.4	small wavelets, short but pronounced; glassy crests do not break	0.6/1	0.2/.03	none
	3–gentle breeze	7–10	10–14	large wavelets with some breaking crests; glassy foam and possibly scattered whitecaps	1/3.25	0.6/1	none
Moderate winds	4–moderate breeze	11–16	15–22	small waves becoming longer with more frequent whitecaps	3.25/5	1/1.5	none
Fresh winds	5–fresh breeze	17–21	24–29	moderate waves with more pronounced form; many whitecaps and possibly spray	6.5/8	2/2.5	none
Strong winds	6–strong breeze	22–27	31–38	large waves begin to form; extensive white crests and probable spray	10/13	3/4	No international warning: issued only for coastal waters. Names vary: strong wind warning/small boat alert/coastal wind warning
	7–near gale	28–33	39–46	sea heaps up; some white foam blowing in streaks	13/18	4/5.5	
Gale-force winds	8–gale	34–40	48–56	moderately high waves with edges that break into spindrift; well-marked streaks	20/25	6/7.5	gale warning
	9–strong gale	41–47	57–66	high waves; dense foam streaks; wave crests tumble and topple	23/33	7/10	
Storm-force winds	10–storm	48–55	67–77	very high waves with long overhanging crests; large patches of foam blown in dense white streaks; sea surface looks white; tumbling of sea heavy and shock-like; visibility affected	30/41	9/12.5	Storm Warning: highest warning for nontropical areas, where it can cover winds of unlimited maximum strength
	11–violent storm	56–63	78–88	EXCEPTIONALLY high waves (small- and medium-sized ships may disappear behind waves); sea completely covered with long white foam patches; all edges blown into froth; visibility impaired	38/53	11.5/16	
Hurricane-force winds	12–hurricane	64+	89+	air is filled with foam and spray; sea completely white; visibility seriously impaired	46/53+	14/16+	Hurricane warning: used to describe winds of 64+ knots in all tropical areas, even if storms that cause them are termed cyclones or typhoons

Symbols for various tropical systems.

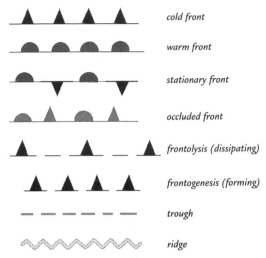

Symbols showing various types of fronts.

cates the type of front (warm, cold, occluded, or stationary).

TROPICAL CYCLONES

Standard international symbols (see above) depict tropical cyclones.

Understanding Surface Charts

In looking at the isobars you'll commonly see that they are more closely spaced at higher latitudes than they are near the equator. The spacing of the isobars indicates the steepness of the pressure gradient, and pressure differences are normally larger in high latitudes than they are in the tropics.

Wind strength is directly related to the pressure gradient: in general, the more closely spaced the isobars, the stronger the wind. But wind strength also varies with latitude. The closer you are to the equator, the more wind you'll have for a given isobar spacing.

Sailors in temperate latitudes may be accustomed to using a geostrophic wind diagram, which indicates wind speed in knots for various isobar spacing at different latitudes. These are of little value in the tropics, however, and in fact the standard isobaric chart is of little use. Looking at a surface weather chart for the tropics, sailors from higher latitudes are often struck by how little is there. Cold fronts are usually absent, and isobars are widely spaced. This is one of the first rules to remember in tropical weather forecasting: small pressure differences lead to much greater wind strengths than would be the case in temperate latitudes.

In fact, although standard surface charts are helpful at the edges of the tropics—north and south of about 20° latitude—closer to the equator they are of limited value. The relative absence of frontal systems and sharply contrasting air masses in tropical waters (and the fact that the typical 4 hPa isobar spacing is in many respects very crude for wind predictions relating to fronts that do appear in these areas) has led to the development of "streamline" charts. Streamline charts depict wind direction and speed directly with continuous lines. Some fax charts use standard isobars in temperate latitudes, switching to streamlines in tropical areas; this can be seen in the NWS Pacific Ocean Fax chart, where streamlines are used south of about 20° N (see art page 360). Surface charts will typically show the presence of significant frontal systems and will depict tropical features such as easterly waves and tropical cyclones.

Surface Prognoses

In addition to the surface analysis, most forecast offices also prepare surface 24- and 48-hour prognoses; some go even further into the future. While the surface analysis is a picture of the current situation at the surface, the latter gives you an idea of what the forecaster thinks will develop in 24 or 48 hours. It's unlikely to be very different from the out-

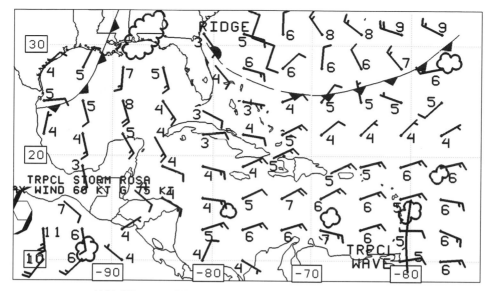

VALID: 12Z NOV 07 2000 - FCSTR: RM

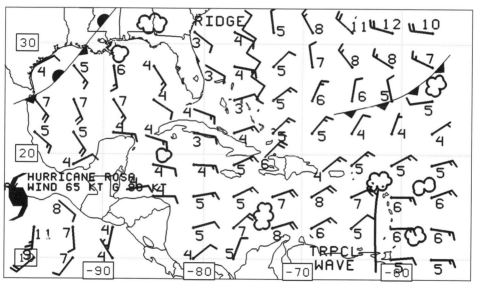

VALID: 00Z NOV 08 2000 - FCSTR: RM

WIND (KT) & SEAS (FT)
24-HR FORECAST (TOP)
36-HR FORECAST (BOTTOM)
THUNDERSTORMS...SCALLOP LINES

TROPICAL PREDICTION CENTER
MIAMI, FL 33165-2149
U.S.C.G. NEW ORLEANS, LA

Wind and Sea "nowcast" (showing current conditions) and 12-hour forecast for 12Z 7 November and 00Z on 8 November 2000. Wind strengths (in knots) are designated by the barbs, or feathers, on the wind.

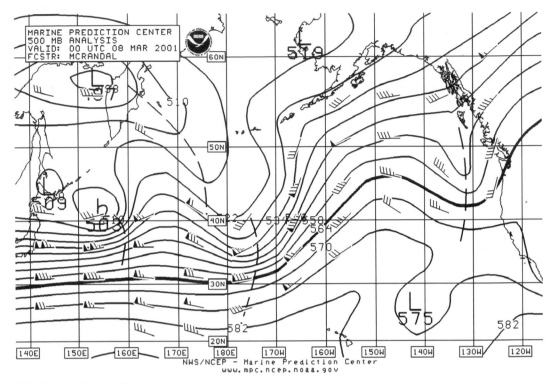

500 mb analysis for the Pacific.

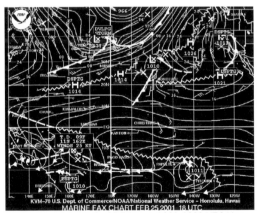

Pacific surface analysis for 25 February 2001, 1800 UTC. Here streamlines replace isobars in the tropics. Note the tropical depression in the South Pacific.

look you might obtain in a voice forecast, which typically extends for 24 hours, but it contains lots of other information that you can use to formulate your own plan of action. The appearance of the prognosis charts is generally very similar to that of the surface synoptic analysis.

Wind and Sea Forecasts

A type of chart that's very easy to is the wind and sea analysis or forecast. This is usually just what you'd think: an analysis or forecast of the surface wind and sea state. The charts on page 359 are for 7–8 November 2000, one day after the sea surface pressure analysis shown on page 356 and provide a far better summary of the wind and sea state in the Caribbean. The fronts to the north of the tropics are shown, as is the easterly wave making its way west into the Caribbean.

Upper-Level Charts

Various charts of the conditions aloft are available. Five-hundred-millibar charts are a primary forecasting tool in temperate latitudes, where they're used to get a handle on what's happening within the jet stream, which acts to "steer" temperate-zone lows. Like standard isobaric surface charts, they're of limited value in predicting weather in latitudes lower than about 20 degrees. The contours on 500 mb charts don't show pressure, but instead show the height above the surface at which the pressure is 500 mb. Add an extra 0 to the contour labels to get the height in meters; the 575 just east of Hawaii indicates 5,750 m. For more on 500 mb and other charts, see the Marine Prediction Center's Radiofacsimile Charts User's Guide, a publication of NWS. This publication is available on the Internet (see the Weather Fax and Forecast Interpretation section of appendix 3, Resources).

In general, 500 mb charts give the tropical sailor advance warning of extratropical lows that threaten to move into the tropics. They're also valuable if you're sailing to or from the tropics from temperate latitudes. Five-hundred-millibar charts are also commonly available in the form of an analysis of current conditions, and as a 24-, 36-, 48-, and 96-hour prognosis.

Resources

PART I. TROPICAL ENVIRONMENTS

Flora and Fauna

Coral Reefs

Allen, Gerald, and Roger Steene. *Indo-Pacific Coral Reef Field Guide.* Singapore: Tropical Reef Research, 1999.

Kaplan, Eugene, and Susan Kaplan. *A Field Guide to Coral Reefs of the Caribbean and Florida: A Guide to the Common Invertebrates and Fishes of Bermuda, the Bahamas, Southern Florida, the West Indies, and the Caribbean Coast of Central and South America (Peterson Field Guides).* Boston: Houghton Mifflin, 1982.

Status of Coral Reefs Worldwide

Global Coral Reef Monitoring Network, www.aims.gov.au/news/pages/global-efforts-to-conserve-coral-reefs.html.

Reef Conservation

CITES and the International Coral Trade (National Oceanic and Atmospheric Administration), www.publicaffairs.noaa.gov/iyorwk22.html.

Coral Reef Alliance, www.coral.org/.

International Trade in Coral and Coral Reef Species (U.S. Coral Reef Task Force), http://coralreef.gov/trade.html.

Maintenance of Biological Diversity (U.N. Environment Program: Caribbean Regional Co-Ordinating Unit), www.cep.unep.org/issues/biodiversity.html.

Reefs at Risk (World Resources Institute), www.igc.org/wri/indictrs/reefrisk.htm.

UNEP World Conservation Monitoring Centre, www.unep-wcmc.org/.

Fish

Lieske, Ewald, and Robert Myers. *Coral Reef Fishes: Indo-Pacific and Caribbean.* Rev. ed. Princeton: Princeton University Press, 2002.

Myers, Robert F. *Micronesian Reef Fishes: A Comprehensive Guide to the Coral Reef Fishes of Micronesia.* 3rd ed., rev. and exp. Barrigada, Guam: Coral Graphics, 1999.

Randall, John E., Gerald Allen, and Roger Steene. *Fishes of the Great Barrier Reef and Coral Sea.* 2nd ed. Honolulu: University of Hawaii Press, 1997.

Shells

Abbott, R. Tucker, and S. Peter Dance. *Compendium of Seashells: A Color Guide to More than 4,200 of the World's Marine Shells.* New York: E. P. Dutton, 1982.

Invertebrates

Colin, Patrick, and Charles Arneson. *Tropical Pacific Invertebrates: A Field Guide to the Marine Invertebrates Occurring on Tropical Pacific Coral Reefs, Seagrass Beds and Mangroves.* Beverly Hills: Coral Reef Press, 1995.

Seabirds

Harrison, Craig S. *Seabirds of Hawaii: Natural History and Conservation.* Ithaca: Comstock, 1990.

Harrison, Peter. *Seabirds of the World: A Photographic Guide.* Princeton: Princeton University Press, 1996.

Cetaceans

Carwardine, Mark. *Whales, Dolphins and Porpoises.* New York: Dorling Kindersley, 1998.

Weather

General Marine and Tropical Weather

Dashew, Steve, and Linda Dashew. *Mariner's Weather Handbook: A Guide to Forecasting and Tactics.* Tucson: Beowolf, 1998.

Jones, David. *The Concise Guide to Caribbean Weather.* Road Town Tortola, British Virgin Islands: Nautorama, 1996.

Kotsch, William J. *Weather for the Mariner.* 3rd ed. Annapolis: Naval Institute Press, 1983.

Laughlin, Gregory. *The User's Guide to the Australian Coast.* Frenchs Forest NSW, Australia: New Holland, 1997.

Mariners Weather Log, www.nws.noaa.gov/om/mwl/mwl.htm.

McGregor, Glenn R., and S. Nieuwolt. *Tropical Climatology: An Introduction to the Climates of the Low Latitudes.* 2nd ed. New York: Wiley, 1998.

ENSO

CDC's El Niño/Southern Oscillation (ENSO) Information (NOAA-CIRES Climate Diagnostics Center), www.cdc.noaa.gov/ENSO/.

El Niño-Southern Oscillation (ENSO) home page (NOAA), www.ogp.noaa.gov/enso.

NOAA El Niño home page, www.elnino.noaa.gov/.

Hurricanes, Cyclones, and Typhoons

Global Guide to Tropical Cyclone Forecasting (Bureau of Meteorology Research Centre), www.BoM.GOV.AU/bmrc/pubs/tcguide/globa_guide_intro.htm.

Mariner's Guide for Hurricane Awareness in the North Atlantic Basin, www.nhc.noaa.gov/marinersguide.pdf.

Tropical Cyclone Forecaster's Reference Guide (Naval Research Laboratory), www.nrlmry.navy.mil/~chu/tropcycl.htm.

Tropical Cyclone Related Links and Websites, www.nrlmry.navy.mil/~chu/tclinks.htm.

PART 2. TROPICAL SEAMANSHIP

Navigation and Seamanship

General Sources

Bowditch, Nathaniel. *The American Practical Navigator: An Epitome of Navigation.* Pub. no. 9. Bethesda: National Imagery and Mapping Agency, 1995. (Available online as a PDF file, http://pollux.nss.nima.mil/pubs/pubs_j_apn_sections.html?rid=100.

Cunliffe, Tom. *The Complete Yachtmaster: Sailing, Seamanship, and Navigation for the Modern Yacht Skipper.* 3rd ed. London: Adlard Coles Nautical, 1999.

NIMA Digital Navigation Publications, http://164.214.12.145/pubs/.

Rousmaniere, John, and Mark Smith. *The Annapolis Book of Seamanship.* 3rd ed. New York: Simon & Schuster, 1999.

SailNet, Web site with many useful cruising-related articles, www.sailnet.com/index.cfm.

SetSail.com, Web site by Steve Dashew, www.setsail.com/index.html.

Van Dorn, William, and Richard Van Dorn. *Oceanography and Seamanship.* 2nd ed. Centreville MD: Cornell Maritime Press, 1993.

Route Planning

Cornell, Jimmy. *World Cruising Routes.* 4th ed. Camden ME: International Marine, 1998.

U.K. Hydrographic Office (Admiralty), Admiralty Charts and Publications, www.hydro.gov.uk/paper_publications.html.

U.K. Hydrographic Office (Admiralty), *Admiralty Sailing Directions.* Multiple volumes with worldwide coverage, www.hydro.gov.uk/sailing_directions.html.

U.K. Hydrographic Office (Admiralty), *List of Signals.* 8 vols.

U.K. Hydrographic Office (Admiralty), *Ocean Passages for the World*, www.hydro.gov.uk/additional_publications.html.

U.S. Government National Oceanic and Atmospheric Administration (NOAA) charts and *Coast Pilots*, http://chartmaker.ncd.noaa.gov/.

U.S. Government National Imagery and Mapping Agency (NIMA), NIMA Maritime Safety Information Center, including NIMA navigation and hydrographic products, http://pollux.nss.nima.mil/index/.

U.S. NIMA, *Pilot Chart Atlas.* 5 vols., http://205.156.54.206/om/marine/pub.htm.

U.S. NIMA, *U.S. Sailing Directions*, multiple volumes with worldwide coverage, http://pollux.nss.nima.mil/index/uncon/pub_avail/# SAILING DIRECTIONS-ENROUTE.

Cyclone Holes and Tracks

Hurricane Havens Handbook for the North Atlantic Ocean, https://www.cnmoc.navy.mil/nmosw/tr8203nc/0start.htm.

Tropical Storms, Worldwide, www.solar.ifa.hawaii.edu/Tropical/tropical.html.

Typhoon Havens Handbook for the West Pacific and Indian Oceans, https://www.cnmoc.navy.mil/nmosw/thh_nc/0start.htm.

Seasonal Updates on ENSO, Tropical Cyclones, and Monsoons

ENSO Forecasts

El Niño Forecasts (NOAA-CIRES Climate Diagnostics Center), www.cdc.noaa.gov/ENSO/enso.forecast.html.

Forecast ENSO Conditions (Bureau of Meteorology Australia),www.bom.gov.au/climate/ahead/ENSO-summary.shtml.

Pacific ENSO Update, http://lumahai.soest.hawaii.edu/Enso/subdir/update.dir/update.html.

Seasonal ENSO Outlook (Climate Prediction Center), www.cpc.ncep.noaa.gov/products/analysis_monitoring/lanina/ensoforecast.html.

Southern Oscillation Index graph, frequent updates, www.bom.gov.au/climate/current/soi2.shtml.

Tropical Pacific SST Predictions with a Coupled GCM (Institute of Global Environment and Society), www.iges.org/nino/.

El Niño and Cyclone Frequency

Hurricane, Typhoon, and Cyclone Strike Probabilities, www.solar.ifa.hawaii.edu/Tropical/StrikeProb.html.

Seasonal (Cyclone) Forecasting, www.BoM.GOV.AU/bmrc/pubs/tcguide/ch5/ch5_1.htm.

Atlantic Cyclone Outlook

NOAA: 2001 Atlantic Hurricane Outlook, www.cpc.ncep.noaa.gov/products/outlooks/hurricane.html.

Southwest Pacific Cyclone Outlook

The 2000/2001 Tropical cyclone and wet season outlook for North West Australia (Perth Tropical Cyclone Warning Centre), www.bom.gov.au/climate/current/trop_cyclone.shtml.

Weekly Tropical Climate Note, covers the SW Pacific and eastern Indian Oceans, www.bom.gov.au/climate/tropnote/tropnote.shtml.

Indian Monsoon Outlook

(India) Centre for Atmospheric and Oceanic Sciences, http://cas.iisc.ernet.in/.

Indian Monsoon, www.ara.polytechnique.fr/india.html.

Monsoon On Line: Weather and Climate Monitoring, www.met.rdg.ac.uk/cag/MOL/Monitor/frameindex.html.

Piracy Updates

International Maritime Bureau Weekly Piracy Report (International Chamber of Commerce), www.iccwbo.org/ccs/imb_piracy/weekly_piracy_report.asp.

International Vessel Casualties & Pirates database, www.cargolaw.com/presentations_casualties.html.

Maritime Security Research Center, worldwide maritime piracy report, frequent updates, www.maritimesecurity.com/research_center.htm.

NIMA Anti-Shipping Activity Messages, http://pollux.nss.nima.mil/asam/asam_j_query.html.

Piracy update from Jimmy Cornell, www.noonsite.com/News?news_topic=piracy.

Seven Seas Cruising Association "news flash," www.ssca.org/newsflsh.htm.

U.S. Office of Naval Intelligence. Worldwide Threat to Shipping, weekly updates, http://164.214.12.145/onit/onit_j_main.html.

Survival at Sea

Callahan, Steven. *Adrift: Seventy-Six Days Lost at Sea.* North Salem NY: Adventure Library, 1999.

International Maritime Organization Safety and Distress Information, www.imo.org.

Robertson, Dougal. *Survive the Savage Sea.* Dobbs Ferry NY: Sheridan House, 1994.

Heavy Weather

Bruce, Peter. *Adlard Coles' Heavy Weather Sailing.* 30th ann. ed. Camden ME: International Marine, 1999.

Dashew, Steve, and Linda Dashew. *Surviving the Storm: Coastal and Offshore Tactics.* Tucson: Beowolf, 1999.

Drag Device Data Base homepage (see "News"), www.dddb.com/index.html.

Gutelle, Pierre. *The Design of Sailing Yachts.* Camden ME: International Marine, 1984.

Marchaj, Czeslaw A. *Seaworthiness: The Forgotten Factor.* Camden ME: International Marine, 1986.

Pardey, Lin, and Larry Pardey. *Storm Tactics Handbook: Modern Methods of Heaving-to for Survival in Extreme Conditions.* Vista CA: Pardey Books, 1995.

Rousmaniere, John, ed. *Desirable and Undesirable Characteristics of Offshore Yachts.* New York: W. W. Norton, 1987.

USCG Drogue Information: Investigation of the Use of Drogues to Improve the Safety of Sailing Yachts, www.multihullboatbuilder.com/droguereport/.

PART 3. LIFE IN THE TROPICS

Health

General Sources

Chin, James E., ed. *Control of Communicable Diseases Manual.* 17th ed. Washington DC: American Public Health Association, 1999.

eMedicine World Medical Library, updated daily, www.emedicine.com/ (accessed 15 July 2001).

Skin Cancer (see links page), www.cancerindex.org/skin/.

Wilkerson, James A., ed. *Medicine for Mountaineering and Other Wilderness Activities.* 5th ed. Seattle: Mountaineers, 2001.

Travel Medicine Updates and Information

American Society of Tropical Medicine and Hygiene, includes travel clinic directory, www.astmh.org/.

Comprehensive List of Vaccinations (WHO), www.who.int/ith/english/table6.htm.

International Society of Travel Medicine includes travel clinic directory, www.istm.org/.

International Travel and Health (World Health Organization), www.who.int/ith/english/index.htm.

Travelers' Health (Centers for Disease Control), www.cdc.gov/travel/.

Travel Medicine Program (Health Canada), www.hc-sc.gc.ca/hpb/lcdc/osh/tmp_e.html.

Disease-Specific Sources

Dengue in the Americas, www.cdc.gov/ncidod/dvbid/dengue/map-ae-aegypti-distribution.htm.

World Distribution of Dengue, www.cdc.gov/ncidod/dvbid/dengue/map-distribution-2000.htm.

Malaria

Choice of Stand-by Treatment According to Chemoprophylactic Regimen, www.who.int/ith/english/table4.htm.

Recommendations for Malaria Drug Prophylaxis by Area (WHO), www.who.int/ith/english/map3.htm.

Dangerous Marine Organisms

Cigua-Check (Ciguatoxin test), www.cigua.com/.

Edmonds, Carl. *Dangerous Marine Creatures.* Frenchs Forest NSW, Australia: Reed, 1989.

Halstead, Bruce. *Dangerous Marine Animals: That Bite, Sting, Shock or Are Non-Edible.* 3rd ed. Centreville MD: Cornell Maritime Press, 1995.

Boat Maintenance and Restoration

General Sources

Calder, Nigel. *Boatowner's Mechanical and Electrical Manual: How to Maintain, Repair, and Improve Your Boat's Essential Systems.* 2nd ed. Camden ME: International Marine, 1996.

Casey, Don. *This Old Boat.* Camden ME: International Marine, 1991.

Collier, Everett. *The Boatowner's Guide to Corrosion: A Complete Reference for Boatowners and Marine Professionals.* Camden ME: International Marine, 2001.

Good Old Boat magazine, 763-420-8923, www.goodoldboat.com.

Gougeon, Meade, Joe Gougeon, and Jan Gougeon. *The Gougeon Brothers on Boat Construction: Wood and West System Materials.* 4th ed. Bay City MI: Gougeon Brothers, 1985.

Spurr, Daniel. *Spurr's Boatbook: Upgrading the Cruising Sailboat.* 2nd ed. Camden ME: International Marine, 1993.

Vaitses, Allan. *The Fiberglass Boat Repair Manual.* Camden ME: International Marine, 1988.

Warren, Nigel. *Metal Corrosion in Boats: The Prevention of Metal Corrosion in Hulls, Engines, Rigging, and Fittings.* 2nd ed. Dobbs Ferry NY: Sheridan House, 1998.

WoodenBoat magazine, 207-359-4651, www.woodenboat.com.

Boat Surveying

Marine Survey Online, http://marinesurvey.com (accessed 15 July 2001).

Nicolson, Ian. *Surveying Small Craft.* 3rd ed. Dobbs Ferry NY: Sheridan House, 1994.

Yacht Survey Online, http://yachtsurvey.com (accessed 15 July 2001).

Rigging and Sail Repair

Marino, Emiliano, and Christine Erikson. *The Sailmaker's Apprentice.* Camden ME: International Marine, 2001.

Toss, Brion. *The Complete Rigger's Apprentice: Tools and Techniques for Modern and Traditional Rigging.* Camden ME: International Marine, 1998.

PART 4. CRUISING LIGHTLY

Green Cruising

University of California, Sea Grant Extension Service, http://commserv.ucdavis.edu/cesandiego/seagrant/guide.htm.

Endangered Species and Trade

Bryant, Peter J. *Biodiversity and Conservation.* Hypertext book, http://darwin.bio.uci.edu/~sustain/bio65/Titlpage.htm#Table of contents.

U.S. Fish and Wildlife Service. The Endangered Species
Program, http://endangered.fws.gov/.
U.S. Fish and Wildlife Service. International Affairs,

http://international.fws.gov/index.html.
WWF Global Network, www.panda.org/home.cfm.

PART 5. TROPICAL CRUISING DESTINATIONS

Government Travel Advisories
Travel Reports (Canada Department of Foreign Affairs
and International Trade), http://voyage.dfait-
maeci.gc.ca/destinations/menu_e.htm.
Travel Warnings and Consular Information Sheets (U.S.
Department of State), www.travel.state.gov/
travel_warnings.html.

Information for Cruisers
Cornell, Jimmy. *World Cruising Handbook.* 3rd ed.
Camden ME: International Marine, 2001.
Noonsite, updates from *World Cruising Handbook* and
World Cruising Routes, www.noonsite.com/.

Cultural and Country Information
Anthro.Net, anthropology information and links,
www.anthro.net/index.html.
Library of Congress Country Studies,
http://lcweb2.loc.gov/frd/cs/cshome.html.
Resources for Indigenous Cultures Around the World,
www.nativeweb.org/resources.php?type=2.
Visa Requirements Worldwide, www.embassyworld.
com/Visa_Search/Visa_Search.html.
WWW Virtual Library, www.vlib.org/.

APPENDIX 2. WEATHER FORECASTS

Weather Fax and Forecast Interpretation
Bermuda Race Gulfstream, analysis tips, www.
bermudarace.com/~bermuda/bohlen_mnu.html.
Carr, Michael. *International Marine's Weather Predicting
Simplified: How to Read Weather Charts and Satellite
Images.* Camden ME: International Marine, 1999.
Fleet Numerical Meteorology and Oceanography Center
Satellite Tutorial, http://152.80.49.204/PUBLIC/
SATELLITE/TUTORIAL/.
Marine Prediction Center's Radiofacsimile Users Guide,
www.mpc.ncep.noaa.gov/UGbegin.html.
U.S. Coast Guard Auxiliary, www.cgaux.org/.

Broadcast Schedules for Forecasts and Faxes
Marine Text Products, NWS Marine Product Dissemination Information, www.nws.noaa.gov/om/
marine/forecast.htm.
NWS Marine Charts on the NET, marine radiofax
products, http://weather.noaa.gov/fax/marine.shtml.
NWS Marine Product Dissemination Information,
www.nws.noaa.gov/om/marine/home.htm.
NWS Marine Weather Program,
http://205.156.54.206/om/marine.shtml.
Worldwide Marine Radiofacsimile Broadcast Schedules,
available online as a PDF file, www.nws.noaa.gov/
om/marine/home.htm.

Weather Analyses and Forecasts

All Regions
Current Analyses (National Centers for Environmental
Prediction), www.iges.org/pix/analyses.html.

Internet links for foreign meteorological services (World
Meteorological Organization), www.wmo.ch/web-en/
member.html.
Weather Forecasts (National Centers for Environmental
Prediction), www.iges.org/pix/wx.html.

North Atlantic (Southwest), Caribbean Sea, and Gulf of Mexico
Caribbean weather, www.caribwx.com/.
Tropical Analysis and Forecast Branch Forecast Products
(NHC Tropical Prediction Center), www.nhc.noaa.
gov/forecast.html.

Northeast Pacific
Tropical Analysis and Forecast Branch Marine Forecasts
(NHC Tropical Prediction Center), www.nhc.noaa.
gov/text/MIAHSFEP2.html.

Central Pacific
NWS Guam, www.nws.noaa.gov/pr/guam.
NWS Honolulu, Hawaii, includes forecasts for both
North and South Pacific, www.nws.noaa.gov/pr/hnl/
pages/marine.html.

Southwest Pacific and Coral Sea
Australian Bureau of Meteorology,
www.bom.gov.au/marine/.
Fiji Meteorological Service, www.met.gov.fj/.
New Caledonia marine forecast, in French,
www.meteo.nc/temps/previson/Bulletins/
sous_panneaux_public.html.

South China Sea and Southeast Asia

China, Hong Kong: Northeast, East, and Southeast Asia Weather Charts, www.underground.org.hk/wxmap.html.

Malaysian Meteorological Service Weather Forecasts and Warnings, www.kjc.gov.my/wxwarn.htm.

Indian Ocean

Australian Bureau of Meteorology, www.bom.gov.au/marine/.

Indian Ocean Satellite Derived Winds and Analyses (Cooperative Institute for Meteorological Satellite Studies), http://cimss.ssec.wisc.edu/tropic/real-time/indian/winds/winds.html.

Meteorological Analyses Over Africa (National Centers for Environmental Prediction), http://grads.iges.org/pix/af.00hr.html.

MTOTEC. Cyclone Basin of the South-West Indian Ocean, in English and French, www.mtotec.com/.

Seychelles Meteorological Services, www.pps.gov.sc/meteo/.

Wave Forecasts

Current Marine Data and Observations (Oceanweather Inc.), www.oceanweather.com/data/index.html.

NOAA Wavewatch III, wave models and predictions, http://polar.wwb.noaa.gov/waves/Welcome.html.

Wind/Wave Forecasts (Tropical Analysis and Forecast Branch: Tropical Prediction Center), www.nhc.noaa.gov/forecast.html#windwave.

Extended Forecasts

Australian 7-day forecasts, www.bom.gov.au/bmrc/medr/mslpTH8.html.

European Center for Medium-Range Weather Forecasts, www.ecmwf.int/.

Weather Maps (Fleet Numerical Meteorology and Oceanography Center), http://152.80.49.210/PUBLIC/WXMAP/GLOBAL/.

Gulf Stream Observations

Oceanographic Products, Gulf Stream and ocean fronts analysis, http://192.207.216.107/newpage/oceans/.

U.S. Navy sites: http://www4.nlmoc.navy.mil/data/oceans/gulfstream.html and http://128.160.23.54/products/OFA/gsncofa.gif.

Tropical Cyclone Observations and Forecasts

All Regions

Tropical Cyclones (University of Hawaii), http://lumahai.soest.hawaii.edu/Tropical_Weather/.

Tropical Cyclones (University of Wisconsin), http://cimss.ssec.wisc.edu/tropic/tropic.html.

Atlantic

Gulf Coast Hurricane Page, hurricane strike probabilities, www.sam.usace.army.mil/op/opr/hurr.htm.

NWS National Hurricane Center, www.nhc.noaa.gov/text/MIATWOAT.html.

East Pacific

Mexico: México SMN (Servicio Meteorológico Nacional, in Spanish), http://smn.cna.gob.mx/SMN.html.

NWS National Hurricane Center, www.nhc.noaa.gov/text/MIATWOEP.html.

Central Pacific

NWS Central Pacific Hurricane Center, http://205.156.54.206/pr/hnl/cphc/pages/cphc.shtml.

Western and South Pacific

Joint Typhoon Warning Center, www.npmoc.navy.mil/jtwc.html.

Southwest Pacific

Fiji Meteorological Service: RSMC-Nadi Tropical Cyclone Center, www.met.gov.fj/.

Australia

Brisbane Tropical Cyclone Warning Centre, also links for Northern and Western Australia, www.bom.gov.au/weather/qld/cyclone/.

Southeast Asia

Hong Kong Observatory, www.info.gov.hk/hko/informtc/informtc.htm.

Weather Underground of Hong Kong, Hong Kong cyclones, www.weather.org.hk/tc.html and www.typhoon.org.hk/.

Indian Ocean

Joint Typhoon Warning Center, www.npmoc.navy.mil/jtwc.html.

Index

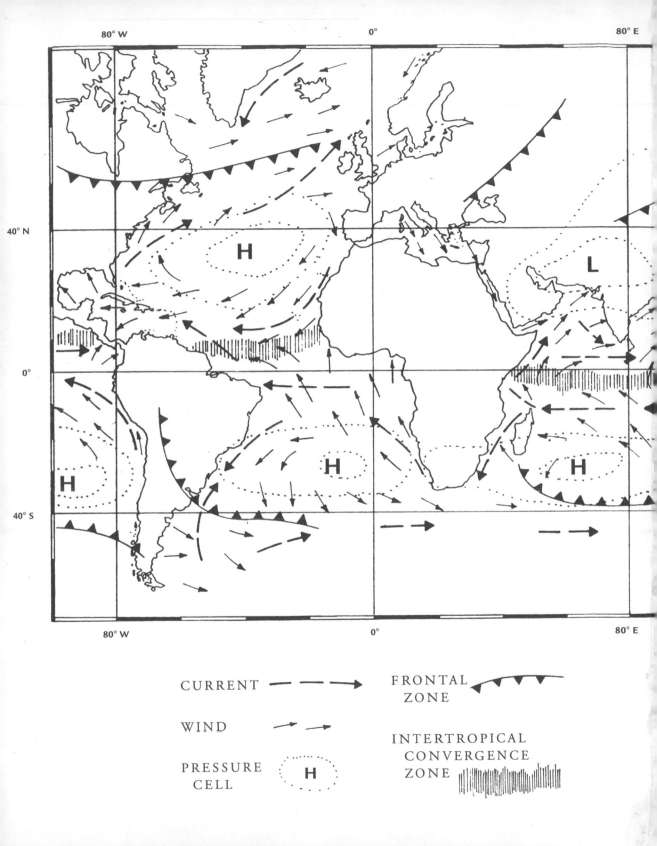

| 80° W | 0° | 80° E |

40° N

H

L

0°

H

H

H

40° S

CURRENT ⟶   FRONTAL ZONE ◣◣◣

WIND ⟶

PRESSURE CELL ⬭ H

INTERTROPICAL CONVERGENCE ZONE